Hear Then the Parable

Hear Then the Parable

A Commentary on the Parables of Jesus

Bernard Brandon Scott

FORTRESS PRESS   MINNEAPOLIS

COPYRIGHT © 1989 BY AUGSBURG FORTRESS

Library of Congress Cataloging-in-Publication Data

Scott, Bernard Brandon, 1941–
  Hear then the parable.

  Bibliography: p.
  1. Jesus Christ—Parables. I. Title.
BT375.S348   1989   266'.806   88-45248
ISBN 0–8006–0897–6

3469G88   Printed in the United States of America   1–897

For Mariah and Jonathan,

treasure not hidden in a field

Contents

Part Two.   *Family, Village, City, and Beyond*

Part Three.   *Masters and Servants*

Part Four.   Home and Farm

Preface

Writing an exposition of all Jesus' parables is a daunting task. Solutions to many of the methodological problems involved are highly debated, and even though Adolf Jülicher initiated a dominant tradition in parable criticism, there has been substantial dissent, some well taken. Some critics doubt the whole project, rejecting as too methodologically tenuous the effort to reconstruct the parables of the historical Jesus. An even greater number of studies in orality question exactly what it is we seek.

Even if we can weave our way through these problems, a graver issue faces us. To undertake an exposition of parables runs counter to the very nature of parable. Exposition seeks to explain, to contain, and in that effort risks substituting what is not parable for parable. Not only can a parable's richness not be exhausted but its form is such that it subverts the effort at control. If at times my expositions seem elliptical or laconic, I hope that that is due to the respect I pay to the openness of the parables and not to the fragility of the exegesis. Others will object that my expositions are overly subtle, that Jesus' parables are simple stories for simple people. Such is the arrogance of us moderns that we fail to recognize true complexity when it appears in unfamiliar forms. As Kafka ironically remarks, "All these parables really set out to say merely that the incomprehensible is incomprehensible, and we know that already."

I owe many people thanks for supporting this project over the years. Several scholars have read parts and made helpful suggestions—in particular, Jack Kingsbury, Ron Cameron, and Charles Hedrick. The project began when I was a member of the Parables Seminar of the Society of Biblical Literature, and the inspiration of those scholars—especially Robert Funk, Dan Via, Dominic Crossan, and in memory, Norman Perrin—has continued to support me. For the past several years I have been a participant in the Social World Task Force of the Catholic Biblical Association. From the other participants, I have learned much, and I hope their footprints are evident in this work—and also that they will not protest too much. Members of the National Seminar on the Sayings of Jesus, organized by the Westar Institute, have wrestled with some results of this work, and their debate and conversation have helped me sharpen the issues. The administration of St. Meinrad School of Theology has arranged my schedule so that I might have time for writing, and Leander Keck, Dean of the Yale Divinity School, provided me with a visiting professorship at the time when the final draft was completed. Many students in several seminars have contributed immeasurably to the project. Their patience, hard work, and stimulating ideas frequently helped me move forward when no path appeared. Special acknowledgment is due several of these students, although I run the risk of leaving out others who deserve to be noticed. My thanks must go to Ruth Brooks, Chester Corina, Greg Corrigan, Guerric DeBona, Justin Dzikowicz, James Hunt, Don Lauderdale, Michael McKinley, Joel Macul, Roy Marien, Trudy Markos, Jennifer Meyers, Dagmar Rosenberg, Micah Schonberger, Chris Vasko, and Terry Wiegand. Professor David Buttrick, of Vanderbilt, has continued to encourage me and stimulate my thought. My colleagues at St. Meinard, especially Gene Hensell, Harry Hagan, Colman Grabert, and Ephrem Carr, have let me pick their brains time and again. I will miss them. A very special thanks to Damian Dietlein, who has been my close friend for these many years and who took time from a sabbatical to go through the manuscript in great detail. He is better than any computer spelling program. Father Damasus, Interlibrary Loan Librarian at St. Meinrad, found everything I sought and then regaled me with stories of his Holmesian solutions. John Hollar, as usual, has been an editor and friend who nourishes scholarship. Finally, my wife has put up with this now for way too many years.

1

Prolegomena

*I*ntroduction

In novels of an earlier century the author often began with an address to the reader. This conceit unfortunately has fallen out of favor in modern times, under the pretense of objectivity and distance. But I have resurrected its spirit for the introduction to the Prolegomena in order to offer the reader some advice in approaching what follows.

Since the analysis of the parables was written before the Prolegomena, I already know how things turn out, how I have interpreted the parables. My interpretations often digress from traditional ones, and some of my arguments may at the present stage be less than convincing, because the evidence supporting them is found in the detailed analyses of the parables which are to follow. A modest circularity is consequently inevitable. One may want to refer ahead to relevant sections as evidence and questions mount.

The book has been designed in a way that should make it easy to use. The Prolegomena addresses those matters that require a decision before approaching the parables. Principally, this involves a definition of parable. In the body of the book each major parable receives an independent study, so that one can consult the analysis of any parable without undue reference to other parts of the book. The aim is to protect the autonomy of each parable at the same time that the book is made easy to use. This arrangement means that one will not end up reading a whole chapter only to find the parable of interest to have been subordinated to the chapter's theme. The parables have been divided into three major groups based on the social dynamics of first-century peasant culture. Some minor parables are used in the introduction to each division as examples. One should read the appropriate introductory section before reading the extended analysis of a parable.

Throughout the book the translations from the New Testament are my own unless I specify otherwise. Since translations are interpretations, I have tried to present translations that would exhibit the character of the Greek text under discussion. This sometimes leads to rather wooden and seemingly ungrammatical translations. Old Testament translations, unless otherwise noted, are from the Revised Standard Version.

Titling the parables creates a predicament. The parables originally had no titles, and the traditional titles frequently embed summaries of inherited meanings. To refer to the parable at Luke 15:11–32 as the parable of the prodigal son not only ignores the elder son of the parable's second part but also summarizes and evaluates the younger son's behavior. The title unconsciously and unknowingly provides the reader with a definite perspective on the parable. In weighing the advantages and disadvantages of traditional titles, I have chosen to retitle all the parables. My proposed titles are neutral since they are derived from the parables' first words. For example, the parable of the prodigal son is retitled A Man Had Two Sons. The table of contents lists all the parables, and in the Appendix I have provided a listing of the traditional titles along with the new titles.

Sexist language is an important issue to deal with. It is not simply that it offends others but also that it betrays, sometimes without intent, a point of view that distorts. No language is innocent, whatever the protestations. A special problem is presented in the phrase *basileia tou theou*. Should it be translated "kingdom of God," "reign of God," or "ruling activity of God"? The first is a literal translation of the Greek; all three are possible translations of the Aramaic. Some object to "kingdom" because of its male associations. After due consideration, I have chosen to retain "kingdom" as a translation because of an important semiotic phenomenon in the parables. Maleness is a component in the signified of "kingdom"; it belongs to the metaphorical structure of power and strength associated with "kingdom." Yet the subversion of this male notion of power and strength is a consistent feature of Jesus' parables. Therefore, to translate *basileia tou theou* neutrally with regard to sex would eliminate an important dynamic in the interaction and tension of parables with the symbol of the kingdom of God.

Source criticism is an unresolved dilemma of recent New Testament scholarship on the Synoptic Gospels. Charles Talbert has referred to it as shifting sands.[1] Neutrality is not really possible, since to be neutral can imply that there is no literary dependence, which obviously is not the case. I have judged each case on its own merits instead of opting for a single solution, either the two-source theory or that of the priority of Matthew. This is possible and preferable in the study of parables because the parables are products of oral tradition and continued to circulate orally even after being written down. Since I accent the performance character of parables, each extant version of a parable, even if literarily dependent on another version, is a new performance. But in the end, after working through the entire corpus of parables, I find that the two-source theory, with Mark and Q as sources for Matthew and Luke, best accounts for the data. I also accept as a hypothesis that the *Gospel of Thomas* represents an independent source.[2]

1. Talbert, "Shifting Sands," 393–94.
2. The best formal argument for *Thomas*'s independence is that from order. See Solages, "L'évangile de Thomas."

Naming the Parable

Parable scholarship exposes an intricate web of issues that affect directly how we understand the parables of Jesus. Rather than write a history of scholarship, which has been done several times,[1] I will here outline my definition of parable. This will allow me to note the important moments in the history of scholarship as well as to focus attention on how parables fit into their cultural-historical matrix.

To name a thing is to know a thing, or so it seems. Yet we name many things we cannot precisely define. Such is the case with parable both now and in ancient times. The English word "parable" is a transliteration of the Greek *parabolē*, which in turn translates the Hebrew *mashal*. In neither Greek nor Hebrew do the respective words signify a specific literary genre. Rather they have a broad signification that is applied to a variety of forms and genres. Proverbs, riddles, and sentences of the wise are all called *mashal*.[2] Although both the Jesus tradition and the rabbinic tradition contain *meshalim* like those in the Hebrew Bible, yet in both appears a new group—what we call parables—a genre not found in the Hebrew Bible. What is most striking and similar about the Jesus and rabbinic *meshalim* is that they are short narrative fictions.

Thus we must recognize three things in defining the parables of Jesus: (1) They belong to a literary type the Hebrews called *mashal* that involve

1. For a recent thorough survey and bibliography, see Kissinger, *Parables*, 1–230.
2. Jeremias (*Parables*, 20) notes the wide variety of forms, concluding that the form-critical classification is fruitless.

distinct yet related genres. (2) Jesus and the rabbis developed and employed a genre of *mashal* not evidenced in the Hebrew Bible. (3) We designate and distinguish this type in ways the ancients did not.[3] Even though we use "parable" to translate *mashal, mashal* designates more than "parable" does. *Mashal* is perhaps best viewed as a continuum along which a variety of genres are situated.

What then is a parable? I propose as a definition that a parable is a *mashal* that employs a short narrative fiction to reference a symbol. This definition attempts to account for one type of *mashal* represented in both the Jesus and rabbinic traditions. It is not a definition of simply the Jesus parables, as though they were something unique.

The definition has four components: (1) A parable is a *mashal; mashal* defines the genus of which parable is one species. Because the concept of *mashal* comprises a continuum or spectrum, at its edges one genre or form blends into the next and there a classification or taxonomy will break down. Though we can agree on what a *mashal* is and for the most part intuitively recognize a parable, some *meshalim* will be parables whereas others will not. (2) A parable is a short, narrative fiction. This initially differentiates parables from other *meshalim* like proverbs, riddles, sentences of the wise, and so forth. (3) What a parable does is reference. I have deliberately chosen a neutral verb to deal with the transference involved in parable, for this raises the issue of whether a parable is metaphor or allegory. Given the corpus of Jesus and rabbinic parables, this issue is impossible to predetermine. Nor is the answer univocal. (4) What a parable references is a symbol. In Jesus' parables the symbol is the kingdom of God; in rabbinic parables it is the Torah. Symbol defines parable's hermeneutical horizon.

This definition has emerged from an analysis of Jesus' parables, rabbinic parables, and the history of scholarship on parables. In expounding this definition, I will indicate what type of methodological positions are most appropriate for understanding parables and what format is best suited for analyzing each parable.

Mashal

A parable is a **mashal** that employs a short narrative fiction to reference a transcendent symbol.

---

3. This giving of a definition to a form not so specifically recognized by the ancients is a common problem with *mashal*. McKane (*Proverbs*, 24) admits that he must define *mashal* as proverb in a narrower sense than that intended by the Hebrews. Pautrel ("Les canons," 6) claims that one only need call *mashal* what the rabbis did, but as Johnston (*Parabolic Traditions*, 340) points out, that is simply too broad to be useful.

Now we will investigate the history of *mashal* and *parabolē* so that we can situate the parables of Jesus in their proper historical, linguistic context.

Mashal in the Hebrew Bible

The Hebrew root *m-sh-l* means "to be like."[4] The verb form occurs infrequently in the Hebrew Bible. A typical occurrence is in Ps. 143:7:

> Make haste to answer me, O Lord!
>> My Spirit fails!
> Hide not thy face from me,
>> lest I be like [*m-sh-l*] those who go down to the Pit.[5]

More frequently it occurs as a noun. The apparently earliest recorded usage in the Hebrew Bible is in 1 Sam. 10:12, where the story of Saul's association with a band of prophets provides a teleological explanation of the proverb *mashal* "Is Saul also among the prophets?"[6] This is a proverb because Saul's behavior "has such potential that it has become a comment on incongruous behavior in anyone, at anytime and in any place."[7] A proverb is popular, concrete, open to interpretation, and representative. This meaning of *mashal* as proverb persists throughout the Hebrew Bible and subsequent Hebrew literature and is the archetype for *mashal*.

Rooted in popular wisdom, the proverb is a very common genre of traditional wisdom in all cultures.[8] The common, popular origin of the *mashal* determines other usages of the term *mashal*,[9] and Jesus' parables belong to this common strand. Yet at the same time, *mashal* undergoes a literary development in the schools, as can be seen in the wisdom literature of the Hebrew Bible. The Hebrew word used for the title of the Book of Proverbs is *mashal*: "The Proverbs [*meshlê*] of Solomon, Son of David, King of Israel." Further, the two collections of proverbs in the book (Prov. 10:1—22:16; 25:1—29:27) are introduced by the formula

4. BDB, 695; A. R. Johnson, "*Mashal*," 162. See also Hauck, "*parabolē*," 747; George, "Parabole," 1149. The verb does not occur in the Qal. Some have speculated that the meaning "to rule" is the more primary root of *m-sh-l* so that *mashal* is word of power. McKane (*Proverbs*, 24–26) reviews the evidence and rejects such an argument.

5. This phrase occurs also in Ps. 28:1.

6. See McKane, *Proverbs*, 26. This proverb is also used as the conclusion to a derogatory story about Saul (1 Sam. 19:18–24). See also 1 Sam. 24:13 (MT, 14): "As the proverb of the ancient says, 'Out of the wicked comes forth wickedness.'"

7. McKane, *Proverbs*, 27.

8. Dundes, "On the Structure," 103–18; Kirshenblatt-Gimblett, "Towards a Theory," 821–27.

9. Eissfeldt, *Der Mashal*, 26.

"Proverbs of Solomon." So by extension, *mashal* is applied to the collection as well as to individual proverbs.

The teacher's prologue to the work occurs in Prov. 1:6. The wise one is "to understand *mashal* [proverb] and *meliyṣah* [figure, parable] *dibre* [words] of the wise and their *ḥidotham* [riddles]."[10] *Mashal, meliyṣah, dabar,* and *ḥidoth* are not clearly delineated genres but parallel and overlapping genres in the wide spectrum of gnomic wisdom tradition.[11] In this context *mashal* clearly means proverbs, the one-line, sentence sayings that encapsulate wisdom. *Mashal* is the paradigm of hidden or allusive truth[12] that demands the skill of the wise to interpret. The verse ends with *ḥidoth,* "riddle," which indicates a specific genre not common in the Book of Proverbs. A riddle plays upon language's ambiguity.[13] "Words [*dabar*] of the wise" may refer to the admonitions and precepts in Prov. 22:17—24:22 and 24:23–34.[14] Because *meliyṣah* is a rare word, it is more difficult to define. The root *lyṣ* means "scorn" (Qal). The noun occurs in the Hebrew Bible only at Hab. 2:6, in combination with *mashal.* "Shall not all these take up a taunt-song [*mashal*] against him, and a sharp satire [*meliyṣah*] against him" (Chicago Bible). Scott suggests that the meaning of *meliyṣah* in Proverbs is "warning speech" and that the word may there refer to the ten discourses in chapters 1—7.[15]

The opening verse of Proverbs underlines not only that the primary sense of *mashal* in the Hebrew Bible is "proverb" but also that the word combines with other terms to indicate a broader spectrum of wisdom language. The wise one needs the skill to understand, to interpret, and to ponder meanings that are hidden.[16] The *mashal* belongs to the connotative aspect of language; it employs nonliteral language, speaking by indirection and suggestion. It demands interpretation precisely because it is about something else. The model in figure 1 diagrams the problem.

10. The four terms are variously translated in English:

KJ	proverb - parable	- words of the wise	- dark sayings
RSV	proverb - figure	- words of the wise	- riddles
NEB	proverb - parable	- sayings of wise men	- riddles
NAB	proverb - parables	- words of the wise	- riddles
Chicago	proverb - parable	- words of the wise	- epigrams
Jerusalem	proverb - obscure sayings	- sayings of sages	- riddles

11. For an informative comment on this verse, see R. B. Y. Scott, *Way of Wisdom,* 53–54.

12. McKane, *Proverbs,* 26.

13. Crenshaw, *Samson,* 99.

14. So R. B. Y. Scott, *Way of Wisdom,* 55.

15. Ibid., 54.

16. Williams, *Those Who Ponder Proverbs,* 17–34; McKane, *Proverbs,* 267.

Figure 1

content	expression

expression	content

In denotative language the expression is directly related to the content. Such is ordinary language. For example in the command "Go home" the expression, the words, are directly related to the demanded activity. In connotative language the expression and content themselves stand for an *unnamed* content, and for this very reason such language is suggestive, in need of interpretation.[17] From the proverb or riddle's primary language the interpreter draws a signification not directly implied. For example, in the proverb "Spare the rod and spoil the child" the hearer draws signification for dealing with a particular child in a particular situation. The proverb is not interpreted literally; one does not have to use a rod to carry out punishment or even be dealing with a child. *Mashal* is inherently connotative language, and that aspect ties together proverbs, riddles, taunts, and words of the wise. Connotative language sets a premium on the activity of the interpreter: one must learn to understand, to interpret *meshalim*. In connotative language something hidden always needs interpretation.

Throughout the Hebrew Bible *mashal* is associated with taunt and riddle. In Psalm 49, it is used with "riddle":

My mouth shall speak wisdom;
  The meditation of my heart shall be understanding.
I will incline my ear to a proverb [*mashal*];
  I will solve my riddle [*ḥidoth*] to the music of the lyre.
(Ps. 49:3–4)

And again in Psalm 78, *mashal* and *ḥidoth* are combined:

Give ear, O my people, to my teaching;
  incline your ears to the words of my mouth!
I will open my mouth in a parable [*mashal*];
  I will utter dark sayings [*ḥidoth*] from of old,

17. For a theoretic discussion of the semiotics of denotative and connotative language, see Eco, *Theory of Semiotics*, 55.

things that we have heard and known,
   that our fathers have told us.

                (Ps. 78:1–3)

It is possible that the association with riddle allows *mashal* to take on the extended meaning of taunt:

In that day they shall take up a taunt
   song [*mashal*] against you,
   and wail with bitter lamentation,
and say, "We are utterly ruined."
                (Micah 2:4)[18]

Because of this association with taunt, *mashal* by extension means proverbial suffering:[19]

Thou has made us the taunt [*mashal*] of our neighbors,
   the derision and scorn of those about us.
                (Ps. 44:13, MT, 14)[20]

The use of *mashal* to designate both the genre of proverb and, at other times, that of taunt and riddle leads to its application to larger compositions that have the characteristics of connotative language. The oracles of Balaam in Numbers 23—24 are introduced by the formula "he said his *mashal*" (Num. 23:7, 18; 24:3, 15, 20, 21, 23). These are extended oracles that need interpretation.

Ezekiel uses *mashal* to refer to a *narrative* unit. The story of the great eagle (Ezek. 17:3–10) is introduced with the formula "This is the word [*dabar*] of the Lord which came to me: Son of man, riddle a riddle and *mashal* a *mashal* to the sons of Israel." Riddle and *mashal* are aligned as equivalent. The redundancy of "riddle a riddle" and "*mashal* a *mashal*" accentuates the interpretive skill needed, and so the Lord provides an interpretation (allegory) of the story of the eagle (17:11–24).[21] On two other occasions this doubling of *mashal* occurs in Ezekiel. In the prophecy of the burning forest of Negeb (20:45–49; MT, 21:1–5) the prophet's concluding remarks are "Lord God, they are saying about me, 'Is he not *mashal*ing a *mashal*?'"[22] The actual prophecy, one of doom much like

18. See also Isa. 14:4; Hab. 2:6.
19. So A. R. Johnson, "*Mashal*," 166.
20. See also Ps. 69:11 (MT, 12); Ezek. 14:8.
21. Immediately after this passage *mashal* is used in the traditional sense of "proverb" (Ezek. 18:2–3).
22. RSV: "Is he not a maker of allegories?"

those of Balaam, is not a narrative, and no interpretation is given. Thus *mashal* is here used more in the sense of taunt. Likewise in Ezekiel 24 the prophet *mashal*s a *mashal* to a rebellious house (24:3). The *mashal* concerns a boiling pot and is applied by the Lord to Babylon laying siege to Jerusalem. This *mashal* is not a narrative but has an authoritative interpretation. Here the redundant use of *mashal*, especially in combination with "riddle," indicates that an extended sense of *mashal* is being employed. These are *meshalim* because they are representative and paradigmatic and need interpretation.

Hebrew Bible usage of *mashal* provides a background against which to understand the usage in the New Testament and by Jesus. Several conclusions emerge:

1. Proverb is the archetypical *mashal*; its characteristics allow other connotative language to be called *mashal* by extension. Appropriately the Hebrew Bible employs a *mashal* sense for what a *mashal* is. Whatever is proverblike is a *mashal*.

2. As a result, *mashal* refers also to genres to be distinguished from proverbs (e.g., the genres of riddles, words of the wise, oracles, prophecies of doom, and allegories).[23] Thus, *mashal* is a genus, and the genus is defined by an archetype species, that of proverbs.

3. All the various items that are referred to as *mashal* involve connotative language. Inference and interpretation are of the essence of *mashal*. In semiotic terms, *mashal* is the expression for a suppressed content.

4. The language of *mashal* is intensive, or in terms of an oral culture, memorable.[24] Since proverbs constitute a primary way for oral cultures to remember their wisdom, proverbs must be memorable. Hence they use metaphors and vivid images and favor concrete and not abstract language.

5. *Mashal* is not context-specific but representative, typical. Since proverbs are representative, they are applied or employed in a variety of contexts.

6. Finally, no *mashal* in the Hebrew Bible directly parallels parable as a short narrative. We begin to see the development toward parable in the Ezekiel tale of the eagle and perhaps in Nathan's allegorical warning to David, but parable has not yet emerged as a genre in the Hebrew Bible.

Mashal in Rabbinic Literature

The rabbinic *mashal* continues to exhibit the same characteristics as the Hebrew Bible *mashal*, with one important difference: in rabbinic liter-

---

23. Besides the case of the allegory of the eagle in Ezekiel, there is also Nathan's allegory for David, which is *not* called a *mashal*.

24. Ong, *Orality and Literacy*, 33–36.

ature there appear "parables" in great numbers. *Mashal* still refers to proverbs, similes, allegories, and other figurative sayings,[25] but a new use takes center stage. The rabbinic parable has long been the chief exhibit for those who wish to overturn Adolf Jülicher's legacy.

What sets these *meshalim* apart is that they are narratives, usually told in the third person, that focus on the action of a main character and describe a general situation and not a specific past event. They are fictions.[26] Frequently a direct inference is drawn from the parable to an interpretation of Scripture.

A major problem confronting the use of rabbinic parables as a model for Jesus' parables is the time gap between the first century and the collections of materials making up the corpus of rabbinic literature. Within that literature the genre has obviously undergone development. This time span of two hundred to four hundred years requires that the evidence be used with care and consideration for its own integrity. The recommendation of caution is not meant as derogatory toward rabbinic parables, for they obviously belong to the same genre as Jesus' parables. Even more, I certainly would want to distance myself from the position represented, for example, by Wilhelm Bousset: "There [in rabbinic literature] the parables are designed to illustrate the distorted ideas of a dead learning, and therefore often—though by no means always—themselves become distorted and artificial. Here [in the Gospels] the parable was handled by one whose whole soul was set, clearly and simply with nothing to impede its vision, upon the real."[27] Even Joachim Jeremias's argument that Jesus' parables are unique is too strong.[28] We can speak of distinctiveness but not uniqueness.

A survey of the rabbinic materials turns up a curious anomaly. In those layers of the tradition that can be isolated as belonging to the Pharisees there are no parables. Jacob Neusner in his survey of Pharisaic traditions concludes that there are wisdom sentences, which he does not see as developing on the patterns found in Proverbs. "As to other sorts of Wisdom literature, such as riddles, parables, fables of animals or trees, and allegories, we find nothing comparable in the materials before us."[29] He argues that Rudolf Bultmann's use of rabbinic materials in *The History of the Synoptic Tradition* relies on evidence from post-70 C.E. masters.[30] He concludes not only that there is no equivalent to similitudes or

25. Jastrow (*Dictionary* 2:855) offers a representative sampling of usage.
26. See Gereboff, *Early Rabbinic Storytelling*, 817. Gereboff has made relevant parts of his manuscript available to me.
27. Bousset, *Jesus*, 44.
28. Jeremias, *Parables*, 12.
29. Neusner, "Types and Forms," 360. The textual evidence and analysis for Pharisaic material is contained in Neusner's *Rabbinic Traditions*.
30. Neusner, "Types and Forms," 376.

similar forms but that "paradox is not a dominant characteristic. . . . Hyperbole and metaphors are not common. . . . As to such similitudes as *master/servant, tower/war, lost sheep/lost coin,* the thief, faithful servant, children at play, leaven, seed growing of itself, treasure in the field, pearl of great price, fish net, house builder, fig tree, returning householder, prodigal son, unjust steward, two sons, and the like—we have nothing of the sort."[31] The absence of this type of material is all the more striking given Neusner's conclusion that both Jewish and Christian traditions around the time of the destruction of the temple "exhibit much the same literary and formal tendencies."[32]

Conclusions dependent on arguments from silence are notoriously treacherous. It is perhaps too much to say with John Dominic Crossan that this indicates Jesus' "even more fundamental linguistic originality and generic creativity."[33] And yet the absence of parables attributable to the Pharisees should stand as an initial warning to those who would equate Jesus' parables with the later rabbinic parables. Ignoring this lack of contemporary evidence is a primary problem with those who would overturn Jülicher.[34] We should be aware of the lack of contemporaneous evidence, of dissimilarity at this point between the *preserved* Jesus traditions and those of the Pharisees, despite general similarity.

The Mishnah contains only one parable, and it concerns whether one may empty the rain from out of a tent at the feast of tabernacles: "They propound a parable: To what can it be compared?—to a slave who came to fill the cup of his master and he poured the pitcher over his face."[35] The comparison to the legal situation is not obvious. In his notes, Herbert Danby argues that rain at the feast of tabernacles was a sign of God's anger and so "the slave (Israel) would perform his duties . . . but his master (God) only shows his displeasure."[36] But the parable does not easily elucidate the case, as Danby's note strikingly illustrates. Given the Mishnah's time (200 C.E.),[37] it is striking that only one parable occurs in the collection. Again, though an argument from silence, this should

31. Ibid. Jeremias (*Parables,* 12) notes this but then goes on to remark on the uniqueness of Jesus' parables.

32. Neusner, "Types and Forms," 390.

33. Crossan, *Cliffs of Fall,* 18.

34. Ziegler (*Die Königsgleichnisse,* xxii) remarks that parable making "was being practiced and cultivated in all of the alleys and in all the synagogues." Petuchowski ("Theological Significance," 78) quotes Ziegler with approval. Johnston ("Parabolic Traditions," 116–17) knows Neusner's work but ignores any possible implications. He argues (p. 195), quoting 2 Esd. 8:1–3, that "first century Palestine was the time and place of the rebirth of parabolic teaching of the *mashal*-form used by Jesus and the rabbis."

35. *m. Sukk.* 2.9 (Danby, 175).

36. Danby, 175.

37. On dating the Mishnah and the following works, see Schürer, *History of the Jewish People* 1:76.

caution us about just how prevalent *mashal* as parable was in first-century Judaism.

In Tosephta[38] and in the Palestinian (400 C.E.) and Babylonian (6th cent.) Talmuds, the presence of parables is more extensive.[39] Beginning tentatively with the Tannaim (70–200 C.E.) but especially with the Amoraim (3d to 6th cents. C.E.), the genre of parable is regularized both by means of a specific literary contextualization and by means of stereotyped plots and characters.

Parable emerges as a common exegetical device in rabbinic midrash.[40] This context is important not only for the resulting formal characteristics of the parable but also because of the way parable references its symbol, Torah (see below, "Symbol"). The parable's context is exegesis, not narrative as in the Synoptics. Robert Johnston has isolated five elements that recur in the patterning of the midrashic context.[41] His proposal has drawn widespread support.[42] Here I will give Johnston's headings and follow each with an example given by M. Stern (Midr. Lam. 4:11).[43]

1. Illustrand (the point illustrated)

   "And He hath kindled a fire in Zion, which had devoured the foundations thereof" (Lam. 4:11). It is written, "A song of Asaph, O God, the heathens are come into thine inheritance" (Ps. 79:1). A song! it should have said, "A weeping." R. Eleazar said:

2. Introductory formula

   It is like [*mashal le*] . . .[44]

3. Parable proper

   . . . a king who made a bridal-chamber for his son. He fixed the house, plastered, cemented and decorated it. One time his son angered him, and the king destroyed the bridal-chamber. The pedagogue sat down and began to sing. [A person] said to him, "The king has destroyed his house, and you sit and sing!" He said to him, "For this reason I sing: because he poured out his anger upon his son's bridal-chamber, and not upon his son."

---

38. Probably slightly later than the Mishnah. It uses traditions contemporaneous with those of the Mishnah. See Schürer, *History of the Jewish People* 1:78.

39. Comparatively speaking, parables are rare in Tosephta. Gereboff (*Early Rabbinic Storytelling,* 809) lists only twelve parables in Tosephta.

40. Stern, "Rhetoric and Midrash," 263.

41. Johnston, "Parabolic Traditions," 164–66; idem, "Study of Rabbinic Parables," 342.

42. Crossan, *Cliffs of Fall,* 18; Stern, "Rhetoric and Midrash," 278; Gereboff, *Early Rabbinic Storytelling,* 810–11.

43. Stern, "Rhetoric and Midrash," 278–81.

44. Johnston ("Study of Rabbinic Parables," 341), Feldmann (*Parables and Similes,* 15), and Guttmann (*Das Mahsal-Gleichnis,* 3–6) provide lists of formula openings. Johnston is quite correct that the variations make no substantial difference.

4. Application

Similarly [*kakk*],[45] people said to Asaph, "the Holy One, blessed be He, has destroyed His temple, and you sit and sing!" He said to them, "For this reason I sing: because the Holy One, blessed be He, poured out His anger upon trees and stones, and not upon Israel."

5. Scriptural quotation

That is what is written. "And He hath kindled a fire in Zion, which hath devoured the foundations thereof."

The model, which becomes clear in the later traditions of the parables, does not require the presence of all five elements; often one or more elements are missing.[46] The only essential or indispensable element is the third, the parable proper.[47] In the material surveyed by Johnston, the fourth and fifth elements are frequently omitted.[48]

This model cannot simply be applied to the Jesus parables, because as a rhetorical device for exegesis it reflects the regularization that took place after 70 c.e. and reached its climax in the period of Ammoraic rabbis (3d to 6th cent. c.e.).[49] In Jesus' parables the first three elements are frequently present. The illustrand is sometimes the kingdom of God, and various introductory formulas are employed. The application introduced by "similarly" or "it is like," *kakk*, does not occur, nor does the reference to Scripture. What applications do occur are the result of the early church and not Jesus. Jülicher's enduring legacy is his rejection of the application as representing the *Sitz im Leben* of the church.

A second element of regularization concerns the development of stereotyped plots and characterizations. This regularization is most visible in the dominance of the king parable.[50] Of the 324 Tannaim parables collected by Johnston,[51] 180 (55 percent) concern a king; 49, "one"; and 40, "a man."[52] In the Ammoraic period, the percentages are even higher.[53]

But regularization goes beyond the stereotyped character of the king and involves also the stereotyping of plot, phraseology, and the use of

---

45. This is the standard introduction for the application (Johnston, "Study of Rabbinic Parables," 342; idem, "Parabolic Traditions, 165).

46. Gereboff (*Early Rabbinic Storytelling*, 814) remarks that none of the parables in Tosephta contain all five elements of the form.

47. Johnston, "Parabolic Traditions," 165.

48. Johnston, "Study of Rabbinic Parables," 342.

49. Stern, "Rhetoric and Midrash," 267–68. Crossan (*Cliffs of Fall*, 18) correctly warns against a diachronic or genetic use of rabbinic parables to understand the Jesus parables.

50. Ziegler has collected 937 king parables in *Die Königsgleichnisse*.

51. Johnston, "Parabolic Traditions," 352.

52. Gereboff (*Early Rabbinic Storytelling*, 815) notes that the percentages are about the same for the twelve parables in Tosephta.

53. Stern, "Rhetoric and Midrash," 267.

formulas. Stern suggests that the parablist "was able to draw upon a kind of ideal thesaurus of stereotyped, traditional elements" so as to be able to improvise a parable for the illustrand under spontaneous conditions.[54] Thus the parablist operated like the singers studied by Albert Lord and Milman Parry or the tellers of Russian fairy tales analyzed by Vladimir Propp. This explains the extraordinary accounts of a parablist telling three hundred parables in a day.[55]

The suggestion of a thesaurus is important for understanding the development and transmission of the Jesus parables. The period of regularization reached its climax much later than Jesus, but even so Jesus employed stereotyped plots and characters. His parables should be viewed not as carefully composed and written in the modern sense but as composed out of the elements of a traditional thesaurus. His characters and plots are well known and probably well worn. The thrill is in the arrangement of the elements and its relation to the illustrand, which is where the interpretive act takes place. Because of the use of an ideal thesaurus, we can view the parable proper as a structure, with the extant version being a performance of that structure. Thus we will be seeking not the original words of the parable (*ipsissima verba*)[56] but the structure (*ipsissima structura*)[57]—how the stereotyped elements of the thesaurus are conjoined in narrative to create a parable.

This shift from *verba* to *structura* also affects the model for the transmission of parables. Jakob Petuchowski notes an interesting example of this problem in dealing with a parable ascribed to Yohanan ben Zakkai, one version of which occurs in Tosephta and the other in *Midrash Debharim Rabba* (9th cent.). The parable in Tosephta is so laconic that it defies interpretation, whereas the latter version is full of detail. Petuchowski concludes that ben Zakkai's parable was surely fuller than that preserved in Tosephta and shorter than that of the Midrash.[58] As this example points out, extant versions of a parable are performances of a parable's structure. It is futile to seek the original words of a parable. The efforts of those who preserved the parables should not be viewed as the efforts of librarians, archivists, or scribes preserving the past, but of storytellers performing a parable's structure. We must distinguish be-

---

54. Stern ("Rhetoric and Midrash," 268), Ziegler (*Die Königsgleichnisse*, xxii), Fiebig (*Altjüdische Gleichnisse*, 25) and Abrahams (*Studies* 1:90–91) also argue that Jesus draws upon a common stock of parables. Their suggestion does not have the sophistication of Stern's, however.

55. Three hundred is a traditional number. For an extensive listing of the three hundred, see Stern, "Rhetoric and Midrash," 286 n. 39; Johnston, "Parabolic Traditions," 174.

56. Contra Jeremias, *Parables*.

57. With Crossan (*Cliffs of Fall*, 27).

58. Petuchowski, "Theological Significance," 79.

tween performance, which exists at the level of *parole*, actual spoken or written language, and structure, which exists at the level of *langue*, an abstract theoretical construction. Practically, this means that we must reconstruct the originating structure. Even though this is a hypothetical enterprise, that does not mean it is unreal, as is sometimes suggested. Hypothetical thinking is characteristic of modern thought. Our task is like that of restoring paintings that over the ages have darkened and lost their original luster and coloration. Just as the restoration of Michelangelo's Sistine Chapel has generated controversy in the art world between those who see the project as restoring the painting's authenticity, its original colors, and those who see it as a travesty, so the restoration of the parables generates controversy. The removal of patina may reveal contours and shapes we are unaccustomed to seeing in our favorite images.

Parabolē in Greek

Does *parabolē* in the New Testament represent the Hebrew heritage of *mashal*, which we have just examined, or Hellenistic rhetoric, where *parabolē* has its own history of usage? To advance the discussion of this question, we will first probe secular Greek usage, then that of the Septuagint (LXX), and finally that of the Synoptic Gospels.

Parabolē means literally "to set beside," "to throw beside," and so functions as a comparative term, indicating similarity or parallelism. The notion of being thrown beside or of parallelism in the signified of *parabolē* makes it an appropriate translation for *mashal*, which also implies a comparative notion in the sense of parallel.[59]

Greek does not develop an extensive use of parable in the sense of either the Hebrew Bible or the New Testament and rabbinic literature,[60] nor does "parable" become a rhetorical term until Aristotle. Before him, *parabolē*, *homoiōsis*, and *eikōn* are used synonymously,[61] and even afterward the usage and definition of *parabolē* are uneven. For example, Demetrius's *On Style*, written in the first century B.C.E., uses *parabolē* to mean poetic image.[62]

Aristotle's influence was decisive, as it usually was in matters of Greek rhetoric. In *Rhetoric*, 20.2, he deals with the general means of persuasion. He distinguishes two types: *paradeigma* (example) and *enthymemē* (a "rhetorical syllogism and drawn from probable premises").[63] For Aris-

---

59. See the suggestive remarks of Miller in "Parable and Performative," 58.
60. Hauck, "*parabolē*," 747.
61. See McCall, *Ancient Rhetorical Theories*, 6–7, 18.
62. Ibid., 147–48. McCall's index provides a guide to a thorough summary of the issues.
63. LSJ, 567; Conley, "Enthymeme," 168–87.

totle, the latter is the stronger and preferred form of argument. "Examples" are of two types, those based on historical or actual incidents and the "invention of facts by the speaker," that is, fiction. Fiction itself subdivides into two types, parable (*parabolē*) and fable.[64] He defines parable as follows:

> The *parabolē* is the sort of argument Socrates used: e.g., "Public officials ought not to be selected by lot. That is like using the lot to select athletes, instead of choosing those who are fit for the contest; or using the lot to select a steersman from among a ship's crew, as if we ought to take the man on whom the lot falls, and not the man who knows most about it."[65]

Although there is an apparent similarity to the rabbinic model, the parallel turns out to be less than imagined, for *parabolē* designates not a genre but an illustrative parallel.[66] In closely analyzing Aristotle's definition, M. McCall gives two reasons for rejecting *parabolē* as marking a genre in Greek literature. First, there is no formal difference in Aristotle's definition between the historical example, the fable, and the parable. So parable is not a distinctive genre. Second, there is the careless phrasing of Aristotle's illustration of parable. "Translated literally, the illustration of *parabolē* would begin: 'Those selected by lot must not rule, for this is like just as if . . .' A series of comparative words . . . is used making the illustration in form partly a simile and partly conditional." [67] The genre is that of example (*paradeigma*), of which parable is one type.

Although the LXX was a conduit for the usage of the Hebrew Bible to Hellenistic Christianity,[68] it neither moves beyond the Hebrew Bible nor introduces a singularly Greek notion of *parabolē*. In all but one case *parabolē* in the LXX renders *mashal*. In the Hebrew text of Eccles. 1:17 there is a doublet "to know wisdom and to know madness and folly." The LXX reads the second part of the doublet not negatively but positively: "to know parables and knowledge." In a number of instances, however, *mashal* is not translated by *parabolē*. Since five of these cases involve *mashal* in the negative sense of proverbial taunt,[69] the LXX clearly prefers not to use *parabolē* in a negative sense. In five other cases a word other than *parabolē* translates *mashal*, usually because a more specific Greek term is used to specify the sense of *mashal*. The opening

---

64. The rabbinic parable *mashal* clearly includes both short narrative fictions about people and fables.

65. Aristotle, *Rhetorica*, 2.20.1393b4–8. (*Works of Aristotle Translated into English* 11:36).

66. McCall, *Ancient Rhetorical Theories*, 27.

67. Ibid.

68. Hauck, "*parabolē*," 749.

69. E.g., *thryllma* (Job 17:6), *threnos* (Isa. 14:4; Micah 2:4), *eis aphanismon* (1 Kings 9:7; Ezek. 14:8).

of the Book of Proverbs uses *paroimai,* "proverbs" or "maxims," although in the triad in v. 6 (see above) *mashal* is translated by *parabolē.* Again, *paideia,* "learning," occurs in the title to the collection beginning in Prov. 25:1. In the introduction to two of Job's speeches, where the Hebrew reads *mashal* the LXX reads *prooimios,* probably in the sense of "exordium." Finally, in Num. 21:27 the Hebrew uses *meshalim* to designate "singers" or "performers of *meshalim*" and the LXX translates *antigmatistai,* "propounders of riddles." Overall, the LXX breaks no new ground in its use of *parabolē* and actually restricts the meaning somewhat, especially as regards the negative sense. The LXX accents the notion of comparison in translating *mashal* by *parabolē.*[70] .

Parabolē in the Synoptics

Where do the evangelists fit? Does their usage correspond to or modify the Hebrew and LXX usage? Given the undoubted fact that Jesus was a teacher in the wisdom tradition,[71] that he worked in a form of *mashal* we call parable which is unattested in the Hebrew Bible, how do the evangelists reconcile their heritage with the Hellenistic situation? How do they translate this Jewish genre not only into a new cultural context but also into the narrative context of the Gospels?

Parabolē occurs fifty times in the New Testament, all but two in the Synoptics.[72] For the most part the Synoptic usage corresponds to the Hebrew usage although without its range[73] and with the important distinguishing feature that *parabolē* is frequently used in an introductory formula to introduce a short narrative fiction like those in rabbinic literature.

Parable in Mark. Mark normally uses the plural "parables" in reference to short narrative fictions. The occurrences cluster around Mark 4, a collection of parables. The chapter is introduced by "he taught them many things in parables" (4:2), and after A Sower Went Out, the Twelve ask about "the parables" (4:10), to which Jesus responds that to those outside, all is "in parables" (4:11). "Do you not understand this parable? How then will you understand all the parables?" (4:13). Finally the

---

70. So also Sider, "Meaning of *Parabolē,*" 458.

71. Bultmann, in introducing the section "Similitudes and Similar Forms" in *History of the Synoptic Tradition* states, "We have only to compare our material with what we know of the hortatory and edificatory literature of Hellenistic Judaism, or with the letters of Paul and other Christian Hellenists, to realize most clearly how unhellenistic, seen as a whole, is the Synoptic tradition of the saying of Jesus" (p. 166).

72. In Heb. 9:9, *parabolē* means "symbol"; in Heb. 11:19, it is used in a prepositional phrase to mean "figuratively."

73. With Sider ("Meaning of *Parabolē,* 454–55) and against the common consensus (e.g., Jeremias, *Parables,* 20).

parable discourse closes, "With many such parables he spoke the word . . .; he did not speak to them without a parable" (4:33–34). Only the introduction of A Grain of Mustard Seed deviates from this usage: "With what can we compare the kingdom of God or what parable shall we use for it?"[74] So striking is this in comparison with Mark's other usage that it must be taken as traditional and not redactional.

Outside Mark 4, only one other narrative parable occurs in the Gospel: A Man Planted a Vineyard (12:1–12). Introduced with the standard formula "he began to speak to them in parables," it concludes not with the disciples' lack of understanding but with the understanding of the "builders" that the parable was told against them, so that they, the religious leaders, tried to go out and arrest him.

Mark's three other uses of *parabolē* vary somewhat from his customary practice. The first appearance of *parabolē* in the Gospel (3:23) betrays the distinctive plural formula "in parables" but introduces a proverb that has the character of a warning taunt: "How can Satan cast out Satan?"[75] In Mark 7:14–23, Jesus announces the riddle that it is not what goes in but what comes out that defiles a person, and the disciples inquire about the riddle *parabolē*. After reproaching the disciples' lack of understanding, Jesus explains the riddle. The scene's structure clearly harks back to Mark 4, where too the disciples are in a house, ask about the parables, are chided for lack of comprehension, and then have the parable explained. Mark's final usage (13:28) again deviates from his usual pattern; here, in "From the fig tree learn its parable," the *parabolē* is an object lesson.

Mark concentrates his parables in chapter 4, where the so-called hardening theory appears. The crux of the problem turns around 4:11–12:

> And he said to them:
> "To you has been given the mystery of the kingdom of God,
> but to those outside everything comes in parables;
> so that [76]
> seeing they may see but not perceive,
> and hearing they may hear but not understand;
> lest they should turn back and be forgiven."

Many suppose that this understanding of parable as dark mystery contradicts the purpose of Jesus' open, simple stories. F. Grant, who argues

---

74. See the similar introduction to From the Fig Tree (Mark 13:28).
75. In the parallel passage in both Matthew and Luke, "in parables" is missing.
76. Chilton (*Galilean Rabbi*, 94–95) convincingly argues that this is result and not purpose even in Mark.

that Jesus' parables "were a device to aid his hearers' understanding, not prevent it," refers to Mark's theory as "perverse."[77]

Many and varied efforts have crashed on the shoals trying to explain away or avoid the implications of Mark's hardening theory. Jeremias offers a reconstructed Aramaic *Vortext* based on the Targum of Isa. 6:9. First he notes that *parabolē* in this passage means "riddle."[78] Then he argues that *mēpote*, "lest," represents an Aramaic idiom that means both "lest" and "unless"; the latter of course is what it means here, so that the offensive Scripture quotation should read, ". . . unless they turn and God will forgive them."[79] Thus, for Jeremias, because the saying deals with riddles, it has nothing to do with parables and therefore cannot guide exegesis. Furthermore, as employed by Jesus, the saying was hopeful, since it held out the hope that if those outside repented, God would forgive them.[80]

Among the more severe problems afflicting Jeremias's reconstruction is the difficulty of sustaining an argument for the passage's authenticity. The theme of inside and outside is definitely Markan, and even though it may well be that Mark inherited the quotation from Isaiah based on the *Targum of Isaiah*,[81] as the text reads in Greek, *mēpote* can have the meaning only of "lest" and not of "unless." Jeremias intends to protect Jesus from contamination by the Markan hardening theory, which "led to the predominance of the allegorical method of interpretation."[82] What is helpful about Jeremias's argument is the recognition that *parabolē* here has the sense of "riddle" and that the quotation from Isaiah is a piece of traditional material.

Still others argue that Mark was such a slave to tradition that he preserved this piece even though it did not agree with his own position, which is more clearly presented in 4:21–23: "For there is nothing hidden except that it may be made evident."[83] The problem with this approach is the evident redactional character of vv. 10–13. Jan Lambrecht in a careful redactional analysis of Mark 4 has maintained convincingly that Mark inserted these verses into an original source in which the interpre-

---

77. F. Grant, "Mark," 699.

78. Many commentators have seen this point, beginning with Jülicher (*Die Gleichnisreden* 1:40).

79. Jeremias, *Parables*, 17. See also Gnilka, *Die Verstockung Israels*. Even Jeremias admits that the Targum was not intended in this benevolent sense.

80. Jeremias, *Parables*, 18. One of the many holes in Jeremias's logic is that Mark's usage suggests the sense of riddle.

81. Chilton (*Galilean Rabbi*, 90–98) argues that v. 12 may be an authentic Jesus saying that "rebuked his hearers for a dull wittedness akin to that described in the Targum" (p. 98).

82. Jeremias, *Parables*, 13.

83. E.g., Anderson, *Gospel of Mark*, 130–32.

tation of the sower followed on the people's request for an interpretation. For him vv. 10 and 13 are redactional.[84] Verse 10 shows heavy Markan editing in the mention of the Twelve,[85] the use of the plural "parables," and the motif of being alone.[86] Verse 13 is a Markan composition. Lambrecht notes the frequent use of *pōs*, "how," and the double question,[87] which is frequently associated with the theme of the disciples' blindness (7:18; 8:17).

Verses 11–12, frequently seen as traditional,[88] likewise exhibit Markan redaction. In v. 11, the following items are telling: "those outside," "everything in parables," and "kingdom of God."[89] Lambrecht's proposal that the quotation from Isa. 6:9 is Mark's free working of the text seems, however, less than convincing. Its closeness to the Targum and the use of this quotation from Isaiah in Acts 28:26–27 and John 12:40 suggest that it may have been an early Christian proof text.[90]

Since Mark is clearly responsible for his parable theory and did not inherit it or misunderstand an Aramaic *Vortext*, what then do we make of it? First, Mark's parable theory is not as outrageously outside the bounds of *mashal* as F. Grant, among others, has supposed. He does accent the notion of riddle and mystery, both integral to *mashal*. That parables are simple, clearly understandable stories is not supported by the evidence of *mashal*. Since Mark most probably inherited an interpretation of the parable of the sower, he knew that the parables were not easily understood. Interpretation is an inherent aspect of *mashal*, and because it is connotative language, misunderstanding is an inevitable risk. Finally, the interaction of Mark's apocalyptic ideology with Christian reflection on the obduracy of the Jews probably accounts for his parable theory.[91]

Not only is Mark not outside the bounds of parabolic intention, but Werner Kelber has argued that Mark understands his whole Gospel as parable.[92] More specifically, Kelber sees Mark following out the logic of the hermeneutics of parables. Parable determines those inside and out-

84. To be exact, v. 10 was reworked by Mark; originally it was a request for understanding. For a reconstruction of Mark's editing process for 4:3–20, see Lambrecht, "Redaction and Theology in Mk. 4," 279.

85. Esp. Kertelge, "Die Funktion der 'Zwölft,'" 193–206.

86. Lambrecht ("Redaction and Theology") notes 13:3–4; 5:37, 40; 6:14–15, 17–23; 9:14–27, 28–29; 10:1–9, 10–12. See also 3:31–35, in which there is a strong linguistic similarity with the section under discussion.

87. Neirynck, *Duality in Mark*, 56, 125–26; Snoy, "La redaction marcienne," 465–68.

88. For a list of various positions, see Snoy, "La rédaction marcienne," 465 n. 285.

89. Lambrecht, "Redaction and Theology," 282–83.

90. So Haufe, "Erwähungen," 418.

91. Lambrecht (*Once More Astonished,* 94) takes a similar line of argument.

92. Kelber (*The Oral and the Written Gospel,* 120–21) offers a summary of those who have proposed that Mark's Gospel genre is related to parable. As suggestive as Kelber's argument is, it relies on a romantic reading of Jesus' parables.

side: those who can interpret are on the inside; but for those outside all things are insolvable riddles. Even the disciples' blindness is part of the parable thematic, for if Mark is to be faithful to parable as genre he cannot allow the disciples a privileged position. So although they are on the inside, their misunderstanding puts them on the outside. "If Mark is as rigorous a parabolic thinker as we claim, he cannot narrate the insider-outsider dichotomy, we noted, as a constitutive feature of parabolic language. But a genuinely parabolic story aims at defying the structure of expectancy, even the expected structure of a parable."[93]

This riddling of the disciples, shifting them from the inside to the outside, is at play for Mark's reader. When Jesus proclaims, "To you has been given the mystery of the kingdom of God" (4:11), the reader expects a mystery to be revealed, but none is.[94] The problem for the reader is to find out what the mystery is, to be on the inside. The misunderstanding of the disciples is both encouragement and problem. Where is the inside? Where is the outside? Mark has achieved a genuinely parabolic reading and presentation of his parables.

Parable in Matthew. Only twice does Matthew use *parabolē* in reference to something other than a short narrative. There are no examples of Matthew's using *parabolē* in the sense of proverb independently of a parallel in Mark. In the parable/lesson From the Fig Tree (Matt. 24:32), Matthew's reading is identical to that of Mark (13:28). In addition, in the riddle concerning defilement (Matt. 15:10–20), Matthew's structure is similar to that of Mark but with a slight twist. After the riddle's announcement, the disciples remark at the Pharisees' offense and Jesus responds, "Every plant which my heavenly Father has not planted will be rooted up" (Matt. 15:13). Just as the Markan pericope refers to Mark 4, so Matthew clearly echoes the parable The Wheat and Tares by referring to planting and rooting up. Peter then asks for an explanation of the parable/riddle, and the structure again parallels Mark.

The structure of Matthew 13 parallels closely that of Mark 4, and the usage of *parabolē* varies little.[95] Differences are due to the exigencies of Matthew's performance. For example, he develops the parable intro-

---

93. Ibid., 125.
94. Kea, "Perceiving the Mystery," 190.
95. Even though we have chosen to take a neutral position with regard to Synoptic source criticism, it is clear that Matthew is following the outline present in Mark's Gospel. He even repeats the Markan conclusion (Matt. 13:24–25//Mark 4:33–34) but then goes ahead with the parable The Wheat and Tares and ends with his own positive evaluation of the disciples' understanding (Matt. 13:51–52). In A Grain of Mustard Seed, Matthew's subordinative constructions appear to be a literate version of Mark's more oral paratactic style and, furthermore, the Matthean parable is a conflation of Mark's and Luke's versions (see chap. 19 below).

duction "Another parable he put before them" (Matt. 13:24, 31; and the variation in v. 22)[96] and twice employs the imperative "Hear the parable" (Matt. 13:18, introducing the interpretation of A Sower Went Out; 21:33, introducing A Man Planted a Vineyard). Only the parable A Man Gave a Banquet (Matt. 22:1) has an introduction that identifies the narrative as a parable.

On the whole, Matthew's use of *parabolē* is conservative and narrow, staying well within the range occupied by Mark; nor does it betray the extended plasticity of *mashal* in the Hebrew Bible. Of course, this is extremely strange, since Matthew is supposed to be the most Jewish of the Gospels.

If Matthew generally follows the structure of Mark's usage, he still has put his own stamp on it. He so subordinates parable to kingdom that critics frequently doubt his ascription of the introductory kingdom formula, for example, in A King Wished to Settle Accounts (Matt. 18:23). In chapter 13, all the parables have explicit references to the kingdom in their introductions except A Sower Went Out. Yet even in that parable's interpretation, Matthew identifies the seed with the word of the kingdom (13:19). The other parables that occur in Matthew either have an explicit kingdom introductory formula or appear in a context of a kingdom discussion—for example, A Man with a Hundred Sheep, A Man Had Two Children, and The Faithful and Wise Servant. A Man Planted a Vineyard has a kingdom reference in its application (21:43). For Matthew, the kingdom of heaven is God's kingly rule manifested now eschatologically through Jesus as Lord in his church, and in the future at the Parousia before the whole human race.[97]

Matthew has no interest in Mark's hardening aspect of parable; throughout the discourse in chapter 13, his accent is on hearing, understanding, and kingdom.[98] He contrasts those who know the secrets of the kingdom (v. 11) and those who do not. Since "the knowledge of the secrets is knowledge of the impending judgment,"[99] the parables selected accent this notion of eschatological judgment. The three parables that receive an extended interpretation all deal with judgment and producing fruit. So the scribe trained for the kingdom (Matt. 13:52) is one who knows how to understand the kingdom's secret.

The judgment theme provides the focusing ideology for Matthew's performance of the other parables. In the Ecclesiastical Discourse (18:1–35), the parable A Man with a Hundred Sheep warns church leaders not

96. Kingsbury (*Parables of Jesus*) shows this to be redactional.
97. Ibid., 21.
98. Cope, *Matthew*, 19–20.
99. Ibid., 17.

to despise the little ones (18:10) and, more to the point, that "it is not the will of my father who is in heaven that one of these little ones should perish" (18:14). A King Wished to Settle Accounts concludes the discourse with a warning that if one does not forgive from the heart, the heavenly Father will do as the king did to his servant (18:35).

Around Jesus' approach to Jerusalem and the climactic final discourse of judgment, Matthew clusters sets of parables. Again these parables accent kingdom as judgment. When Jesus first enters Judea, the disciples quarrel among themselves as to who is the greatest, and A Householder Went Out Early warns that "the last shall be first and the first last" (20:16). For the debate in the temple precincts, Matthew arranges three parables: A Man Had Two Children, A Man Planted a Vineyard, and A Man Gave a Banquet. All three exemplify that "many are called but few are chosen." True Israel is the church, and the parables stand in judgment on Israel. Immediately prior to the final discourse, which climaxes with Matthew's famous last-judgment scene separating the sheep and goats, are three more parables: The Faithful and Wise Servant, Ten Virgins, and A Man Entrusts Property. These three parables contrast good and faithful service (25:21) with service that produces no works, and so warn the reader and Christian community about the impending judgment. In the parables the master is the returning *kyrios* (master/lord) who will judge the world as promised in the parable The Wheat and Tares (Matt. 13:24–30).

Parable in Luke. Among the Synoptics, only Luke employs a range of usage that begins to correspond to that of *mashal.* He diverges from the other Synoptics in having no long parable chapter (see Luke 8:4–18), and in contrast to Mark, who had a propensity for "parables," he normally prefers the singular (e.g., 8:4, 9; 20:9, 19).

Luke uses *parabolē* in the sense of "proverb" several times. He designates as *parabolē* the proverb of physician heal yourself (4:23), as well as the proverbs of the blind leading the blind (6:13)[100] and patching an old garment with new cloth (Luke 5:36).[101] Even a negative sense is present. The pericope concerning watching for the day of the Son of man begins with a proverbial statement about how a householder would be prepared if only he knew when the thief was coming. Peter responds, "Lord, are you telling this *parabolē* for us or for all?" (12:41). Here *parabolē* equals *mashal* proverb in the sense of warning.

By far Luke's most important use of *parabolē* is in the introductory

---

100. This proverb occurs in Matt. 15:14 but without designation as a *parabolē.*
101. This proverb appears in Mark 2:21 and Matt. 9:16, likewise without reference to *parabolē.*

phrases by which he creates interpretive contexts for his readers. He does this in two distinct but related ways. In four cases he introduces a parable with its implied point, parallel to but not identical with the illustrand in the rabbinic parable.

- Introduction to A Man Entrusts Property:
  He proceeded to tell them a parable, because he was near to Jerusalem and because they supposed that the reign of God was to appear immediately. (Luke 19:11)
- Introduction to Two Men Went Up to the Temple:
  He also told this parable to some who trusted in themselves that they were righteous and despised others. (Luke 18:9)
- Introduction to In a City There Was a Judge:
  He told them a parable to the effect that they ought always to pray and not lose heart. (Luke 18:1)
- Introduction to A Man Gave a Banquet:
  He told a parable to those who were invited, noting how they chose the places of honor. (Luke 14:7)

Luke moves beyond Matthew and Mark by developing his own format for presenting parables. He anticipates his readers by providing an explicit reading before they read the parables, thus robbing *mashal* of one of its chief characteristics, the need for interpretation. Luke uses parables as examples for his preestablished meanings.

Three times he uses the formula "he told them a parable" to introduce a parable that exemplifies a saying, similar to the illustrand in the rabbinic model.

1. "Take heed of all covetousness; for a man's life does not consist in the abundance of his possessions. And he told them a parable, saying . . ."
   There follows the parable The Land of a Rich Man.
2. ". . . unless you repent you will all likewise perish. And he told them this parable . . ."
   There follows the parable A Man Had a Fig Tree.
3. "This man receives sinners and eats with them. He told them this parable, saying . . ."
   There follow the parables A Man Had a Hundred Sheep, A Woman with Ten Drachmas, and A Man Had Two Sons.

Luke has no parable theory parallel to Mark's; his version of the parable discourse is greatly abbreviated without elaborate discourse. Unlike Matthew, he has no single hermeneutical principle like the kingdom of heaven to interpret the parables. His formulas of introduction and conclusion achieve a remarkable integration of parable into narrative discourse. So clever is this integration that Luke has convinced many critics since Jülicher of the existence of a type of parable that they call example story (*Beispielerzählung*).[102] An example story has no figurative element but offers an example of correct behavior or of negative behavior to avoid. Since the story is literal, the behavior exhibited in it is the vehicle for inference.

Usually four Lukan parables are classified as example stories: From Jerusalem to Jericho (10:29), The Land of a Rich Man (12:16), A Rich Man Clothed in Purple (16:19), and Two Men Went Up to the Temple (18:10). That all four occur *only* in Luke should arouse suspicions about the proposed genre. No serious challenge has been laid to the authenticity of three of the four stories, but the criterion of multiple attestation raises questions about whether the genre of example story belongs among those genres used by Jesus. This criterion maintains that genuine genres will be found among the several Gospels and traditions that have preserved the sayings of Jesus.[103]

When Robert Funk asked about the significance of the Samaritan in the parable From Jerusalem to Jericho, that was an important moment in the history of parable criticism. He argued that the Samaritan could not be simply an example of neighborliness; otherwise why choose such an unacceptable example for a Jew?[104] As he has argued later, only a *goy* would see a Samaritan as good.[105] The historical, literal sense of the parable creates its shock. Thus the Samaritan cannot be an example.[106] The critic and audience must ask what the character's significance is. Paradoxically, the literalness of the Samaritan turns the story into a metaphor. These parables are examples for Luke, but do they formally demand such a reading? Funk's observations argue no.

These four parables exhibit metonymic characters. Although recent parable research has identified the figurative element with metaphor, metaphor is only one pole of figurative possibility. The other pole is metonymy, which "may be defined as a linguistic substitution in which a thing is named not directly but by way of something adjacent to it either temporally or spatially."[107] Metonymy implies or suggests that a real relationship exists between the thing and that which is adjacent to it.

---

102. Jülicher, *Die Gleichnisreden* 1:112–15; Bultmann, *History of the Synoptic Tradition*, 177–79. Even when working with an explicit structuralist model, Magass ("Zur Semiotik," 2) assumes that the parable is an example story.

103. Perrin, *Rediscovering the Teaching*, 45–47.

104. Funk, *Language*, 213.

105. Funk, *Parables and Presence*, 33.

106. Funk, "Good Samaritan," 74–81 (in *Parables and Presence*, 29–34); Crossan, "Good Samaritan," 82–112. Crossan ("Parable and Example," 63–104) supports Funk; Via ("Parable and Example Story," 105–33) argues against.

107. Miller, "Fiction of Realism," 9. The classic essay on the distinction between metaphor and metonymy is Jakobson's "Aphasia," 55–82.

The basic difference between metonymic and metaphoric parables is that the former use real "parts-of-the world" for their figure whereas the latter create "mini-worlds."[108] An alternative to Jülicher's example story may be formulated: the issue of transference revolves not around behavior to be imitated or avoided (example story) but around the question of what part of the real world something is adjacent to.

The Gospel of Thomas

In 1945, thirteen codices of a gnostic monastic library were discovered buried near Nag Hammadi, Egypt.[109] Among the documents was a Gospel ascribed to Didymos Judas Thomas. The document is in Coptic but is obviously a translation from a Greek Gospel, fragments of which had been found at Oxyrhynchus and published by Arthur Hunt and Bernard Grenfeld in 1903.[110] Publication of the Coptic text was slow and at first overshadowed by the discovery of the Dead Sea Scrolls, yet by the 1960s scholars were recognizing the importance of the parables in this Gospel for an understanding of Jesus' parables.

Realizing the importance of *Thomas*, Jeremias first treated its parables as independent witnesses to the Jesus tradition.[111] Perhaps even more astonishing was the awareness that the version of A Man Planted a Vineyard found in the *Gospel of Thomas* agrees almost word for word with Dodd's reconstruction proposed long before the discovery of the *Gospel of Thomas*.[112]

What impressed scholars about the parables in *Thomas* was that they lacked allegories and, for the most part, applications. The three parables in the Synoptics with extended allegories appear in *Thomas* without any (i.e., A Sower Went Out, The Wheat and Tares, and A Man Planted a Vineyard). This was even more astounding because *Thomas* was then considered to be a later gnostic document. Why were the parables without allegory? Had *Thomas* for some reason preserved the tradition of the parables in a superior form?

We must be careful. The nonallegorized parables confirmed scholarly opinions and conclusions that originally Jesus' parables were without extended allegory, but that did not guarantee the authenticity or originality of the *Thomas* parables. Had the allegories been stripped away for some reason? William Schoedel, for example, examining The Net,

---

108. Crossan, *Raid on the Articulate*, 108.
109. For further details and references, see *Nag Hammadi Library*, ed. Robinson, 1–25.
110. See Quispel, "*Gospel of Thomas* Revisited," 218–19; Ménard, *L'évangile selon Thomas*, 1–4.
111. Jeremias, *Parables*, 24; the 6th Germ. ed. (1962) took cognizance of *Thomas*.
112. Wilson ("'Thomas' and the Growth," 239) first called attention to this striking fact. Wilson was a student of Dodd's.

The Wheat and Tares, A Man with a Hundred Sheep, and The Leaven, argued that all these were secondary as compared with the Synoptics and had been reworked to fit gnostic exegesis.[113] The author of *Thomas* had deliberately eliminated the allegories of these parables because of a gnostic rejection "of the ecclesiastical explanations and allegories which begin to appear already in the New Testament."[114]

Whether gnostic ideology governs *Thomas* will determine how we interpret it. The debate concerning the gospel's religious environment continues unresolved. Because the *Gospel of Thomas* was found among a collection of books belonging to a gnostic group, many scholars assumed that it was a gnostic Gospel and so interpreted it.[115] A case in point is the *Thomas* parables, where the introductory formula tends to be "The kingdom of the father is like a person who," whereas in the Synoptics the tendency is for the object to be first. In The Leaven, *Thomas* begins, "The kingdom of the Father is like a certain woman" (*Gos. Thom.* 96). In the Synoptics, The Leaven begins, "The kingdom of heaven is like leaven which a woman took" (Matt. 13:33). W. Schrage argues that putting the person first is conditioned by gnostic thought: the kingdom is realized in the Gnostic.[116] But it is not clear that this is the necessary response. Many of Jesus' own parables begin with "a man who,"[117] and so we may be dealing with a more original way of introducing the parables, or it may simply be a matter of *Thomas's* style. But it does not demand a gnostic understanding.

There are two negative reasons for challenging the assumption that the *Gospel of Thomas* is gnostic. First, it lacks the typical speculation about gnostic mythology so commonly found in other gnostic texts. Being found among gnostic texts indicates only that it can be interpreted gnostically, not that it is gnostic. The canonical Gospels and Plato, among other writings, are also found in gnostic collections, and that does not make them gnostic. Second, the *Gospel of Thomas* lacks specific gnostic vocabulary. Its vocabulary appears within the range of normal usage in the ancient world.

Stevan Davies has mounted a strong and perhaps one-sided argument that *Thomas* is a primitive example of Jewish Christian wisdom. Simply put, he argues that the vocabulary and constructions of *Thomas*

---

113. Schoedel, "Parables."

114. Ibid., 560. The gnostic character of the parables has continued to be asserted. See Lindemann, "Zur Gleichnisinterpretation." See also the rejection by Koester in "Three Thomas Parables," 195–96.

115. Ménard's *L'évangile selon Thomas* is a classic example.

116. Schrage, *Das Verhältnis*, 37–39. Similarly, Ménard, *L'évangile selon Thomas*, 89.

117. Breech, (*Silence of Jesus*, 74–75) argues that the Jesus parables normally began in such a way.

make sense in the world of Jewish Christian wisdom. The Gospel represents an early form of Christology (or better, Jesusology) in which Jesus
is identified with wisdom and the kingdom is God's wisdom to be
found.[118] The kingdom, wisdom, is within and without, spread upon the
earth.

While Davies's argument is important in indicating that the gnostic
interpretation of *Thomas* is not mandatory, at present no consensus
exists on exactly where in the history of religions the Gospel fits. Giles
Quispel in a recent survey of studies of the *Gospel of Thomas* still insists
on an Encratite background because of the use of *monachos* to mean
"bachelor" (*Gos. Thom.* 75). According to Quispel, *Thomas* rejected
women, wine, and meat, and taught that only bachelors would go to
heaven.[119] For our purposes, it seems safe to assume that *Thomas* is not
gnostic and should be interpreted neutrally within the pluralist traditions of early Christianity and Hellenistic religions.

The Gospel's dating depends principally on one's view of its background. Hunt and Grenfeld dated around 200 c.e. the Greek fragments
of what we now know to be the *Gospel of Thomas*, so the composition of
the Gospel must predate those manuscript fragments. Yet Boudewijn
Dehandshutter, who sees the gospel as gnostic, dates it at the end of the
second century.[120] Quispel maintains the traditional date of around 140,
but Davies, arguing that the Gospel belongs to Jewish Christian wisdom,
dates it around 50–55.[121] It is perhaps best to assume that the *Gospel of
Thomas* is contemporaneous with the later Synoptic Gospels and represents another independent form of the tradition contained in them.

A consensus seems to be emerging that *Thomas* is not dependent on
the Synoptic Gospels.[122] Two arguments are in my judgment decisive.
First, there is no way to account for the order and arrangement of the
parables in *Thomas* by appealing to the order in the Synoptics.[123] To
illustrate, *Thomas* has both The Leaven and A Grain of Mustard Seed,
yet its order is different from that of the Synoptics. Mark has only one of
the parables, A Grain of Mustard Seed, located in his parable chapter;
Matthew and Luke twin the two parables; *Thomas* has them in separate
places. A Grain of Mustard Seed appears early in *Thomas* (*Gos. Thom.*
20), whereas The Leaven (*Gos. Thom.* 96) is grouped with The Empty Jar
(*Gos. Thom.* 97) and The Powerful Man (*Gos. Thom.* 98).

118. Davies, *Gospel of Thomas*, chaps. 3 and 5.
119. Quispel, "*Gospel of Thomas* Revisited," 236.
120. Dehandshutter, "Gospel of Thomas," 157–60.
121. Quispel, "*Gospel of Thomas* Revisited," 237; Davies, *Gospel of Thomas*, 3.
122. Recent exceptions are Gundry (*Matthew*) and Lindemann ("Zur Gleichnisinterpretation").
123. The most convincing argument is by Solages in "L'évangile de Thomas," 102–8.

Second, although *Thomas* contains parables that appear in all three Synoptics, in Q, as well as two unique parables, the *Thomas* parables exhibit none of the redactional features characteristic of the Synoptic authors. Is it conceivable that if the author of *Thomas* knew the Synoptics, he could have eliminated so cleverly those features that later scholars would identify as redactional even before *Thomas* was discovered? I think not. Therefore, he did not know the Synoptic Gospels.

While awaiting a scholarly consensus to emerge on the religious background and structure of *Thomas*, we will move forward in as neutral a position as possible. We will confine our observations to those aspects of the text that can be verified in the text itself. We assume that the parables of *Thomas* represent traditions independent from the written Synoptic Gospels. The quality of the performance they represent will be determined on a case-by-case basis, just as it will be in the Synoptics.

How many parables *Thomas* contains again depends somewhat on what the interpreter considers a parable. I count thirteen, Ron Cameron fourteen, and Crossan fifteen.[124] Since *Thomas* does not have a special word for "parable," it is impossible to know what its author's count was. Table 1 indicates the Synoptic relations.

Table 1
Parables in the Gospels

Thomas	Mark	Matthew	Luke
The Net (8)		X	
A Sower Went Out (9)	X	X	X
A Grain of Mustard Seed (20)	X	X	X
The Wheat and Tares (57)		X	
The Land of a Rich Man (63)			X
A Man Gave a Banquet (64)		X	X
A Man Planted a Vineyard (65)	X	X	X
The Merchant (76)		X	
The Leaven (96)		X	X
The Empty Jar (97)			
The Powerful Man (98)			
A Man with a Hundred Sheep (107)		X	X
Treasure (109)		X	

A distinguishing characteristic of the *Thomas* parables is a lack of alle-

124. Cameron, "Parable and Interpretation," 3; *Sayings Parallels*, ed. Crossan. Crossan includes Harvest Time (*Gos. Thom.* 21) and Children in a Field (*Gos. Thom.* 31); Cameron includes Children in a Field.

gorical interpretation, especially in the case of the three parables with extended allegories in the Synoptics. Even more, only two parables have explicit applications. A Man Gave a Banquet (*Gos. Thom.* 64) concludes with the warning "Businessmen and merchants will not enter the Places of My Father," and The Merchant (*Gos. Thom.* 76) concludes, "You too, seek his unfailing and enduring treasure where no moth comes near to devour and no worm destroys."[125]

Eight of the parables in *Thomas* are explicit kingdom parables, usually introduced by a phrase dealing with the kingdom of the Father. Five of these are also kingdom parables in the Synoptics: A Grain of Mustard Seed, The Wheat and Tares, The Merchant, The Leaven, and Treasure. A Man with a Hundred Sheep is a kingdom parable in *Thomas* but not in the Synoptics; The Net is a kingdom parable in the Synoptics but not in *Thomas*. Finally, there are two kingdom parables in *Thomas* that do not occur in the Synoptics: The Empty Jar and The Powerful Man.

Except for A Grain of Mustard Seed, all the parables in *Thomas* begin with an initial nominal: "a man who," "a certain man," "a certain woman," etc. In four of the Synoptic parallels, the initial is an object: The Net, The Land of a Rich Man, The Leaven, and Treasure. In four other cases the Synoptics and *Thomas* agree with the initial being a nominal: The Wheat and Tares; A Man Gave a Banquet; A Man Planted a Vineyard; and A Man with a Hundred Sheep.

A number of *Thomas* parables deal with the theme of the "largest" or with a contrast between small and large. In A Man with a Hundred Sheep, the shepherd goes after the largest one, who went astray; in The Land of a Rich Man, the man specifically has "much money," whereas in Luke the land brings forth by implication superabundant crops. In The Net, the large fish is contrasted with the little fish; the great mustard plant is contrasted with the smallest of all seeds; and the great loaves are contrasted with the little leaven. This contrast is part of the contrast pattern of wisdom which is found in the kingdom.

Finally, there are some patterns to be observed in the arrangement of the parables in *Thomas*. There are two groupings of three that probably are meant to interpret each other. *Gospel of Thomas* 63–65 consists of The Land of a Rich Man, A Man Gave a Banquet, and A Man Planted a Vineyard. These three are probably connected by a pattern of loss: a man lost much money, a man lost a party, a man lost a vineyard and a son. *Gospel of Thomas* 96–98 likewise forms another group of three: The Leaven, The Empty Jar, and The Powerful Man. The pattern is that of

125. Four parables—The Net (*Gos. Thom.* 8), The Land of a Rich Man (*Gos. Thom.* 63), A Man Planted a Vineyard (*Gos. Thom.* 65), and The Leaven (*Gos. Thom.* 96)—have the conclusion "Whoever has ears . . ."

contrasts: little leaven and large loaves; full jar and empty jar; powerful man and weak man. This type of patterning is typical of the additive connections of oral performance.

Short Narrative Fiction

A parable is a *mashal* that employs a **short narrative fiction** to reference a symbol.

If *mashal* defines the semantic field to which parable belongs, then to call a parable a short narrative fiction allows us to distinguish it from other types of *meshalim* like proverbs, riddles, words of the wise, and so forth. Even more it indicates the method we should follow in understanding parable.

"Short" is not a precise term. When does a story become so long that it is no longer a parable? My answer is that A Man Had Two Sons is about as long as a parable can be. That parable is extremely complex, with two scenes tied together by the interaction of a father and his younger and elder sons. How short can a parable be? As short as a sentence, like The Leaven or From the Fig Tree. "Short" hints at the primarily oral character of parables.[126] The parables are among the smallest complete narrative units of oral tradition. Short is what one can hold in the ear, much like a joke. Long elaborate jokes are too long to remember, too long to perform easily. Smaller units would be themes or formulas that would belong to the thesaurus.

The parables of the Jesus tradition display the characteristics of orality.[127] As Walter Ong remarks, the great tragedy in an oral culture is forgetting, so it is important to think memorable thoughts.[128] At the surface level—at the level of the way the words are arranged—we notice those items that make it easy to remember the parable. The vividness and outlandishness of many of the parables are part of this aspect. So are the mnemonic devices of repetition, formulas, and the law of threes. In the parable A Man Entrusts Property, the scenes of the first two servants are identical; in A King Wished to Settle Accounts, the forgiven servant repeats the master's scene with his fellow servant. Formulas are frequent: "Take your ease, eat, drink, and be merry" (Luke 12:19); "a judge who neither feared God nor regarded man" (Luke 18:2). The law of threes underlies many of the parables. Even though in A Householder Went Out Early the master's trips to the marketplace are patterned

126. Crossan (*Cliffs of Fall*, 3–5) deals with the "brevity" of the form, but he derives his theory from written exemplars.
127. Ong (*Orality and Literacy*, 16–30) summarizes modern studies on orality.
128. Ibid., 34.

around the hours of the day to make them memorable, the story really deals with three characters—the master, the first-hired, and the last-hired. The others drop out of view.

Because parables are oral and short, their language and structure are intense and tensive. They appear scrubbed clean, with few if any useless details. Three of the four parables that deal with seeds do not specify the kind of seed; it apparently makes no difference. But in A Grain of Mustard Seed the fact that it is a mustard seed is critical because of the characteristics of this particular seed. In A Man Had Two Children the children are only "child one" and "child two," whereas in A Man Had Two Sons they are younger and elder sons. Again these details are not irrelevant but hark back to a major story tradition in Israel of elder and younger sons.

As these two examples indicate, parables draw on the conventions of Israel's heritage. This is part of the ideal thesaurus or repertoire of the narrative.[129] The characters are stock characters, the plots are stock plots. This may seem only to take notice of what other critics have referred to as the everydayness of the parables. But it does more. Everydayness is part of the conventional character of parables. We are given no insight into a character's psychological motives. Why in From Jerusalem to Jericho was the man on a dangerous road by himself? Why did the priest and Levite pass by and the Samaritan stop? No answers are provided. Apparently only in A Man Had Two Sons do characters move beyond the one-dimensionality of stock characters, yet even there the move is an illusion. The younger son's conversion, his coming to himself and returning to his father, is motivated by an empty stomach, not self-knowledge. The elder son is a stock melodramatic villain. The cry of the third servant against his master in A Man Entrusts Property is the complaint of every peasant against the upper classes: "Sir, I knew you to be a hard man, reaping where you did not sow, and gathering where you did not winnow" (Matt. 25:24). The plot of A Rich Man Had a Steward is a traditional trickster plot in which, to use the marvelous phrase of Dan Via, the hearer is encouraged to go on a moral holiday.

Oral stories operate on additive rather than subordinative principles. Causation is rare. Events are laid one after another. In A Householder Went Out Early, the master returns to the marketplace time after time throughout the day to hire more laborers without any reason being specified. In A Man Casts Seed the seed is sown, the sower sleeps, the seed grows, and the sickle is put in. A hearer must work out the connections; the narrator refuses to provide the missing links. A classic example

129. Iser, *Implied Reader*, 288; idem, *Act of Reading*, chap. 3.

of this is The Leaven, in which a hearer must combine and juxtapose a series of conflicting signifieds: leaven, woman, hide, three measures, till all is leaven. The first three are such strong negative symbols that it is hard to understand how they can relate to the kingdom.

That parables are hard to understand raises what is for us literates an exceptionally difficult problem. Parables are examples of concrete thought, not abstract thought. Nor are parables substitutes for or even illustrations of abstract thought. Oral peoples think concretely. "The kingdom of heaven is like . . ." is not a simple way of talking to simple people, but it is the way an oral culture thinks.[130] Our attempts to translate parables into abstractions, into parables of grace, advent, and so forth, are just that—translations into our way of thinking. The illustrative *mashal* character of parables should not deceive us; parables are not illustrations of abstract concepts. Even rabbinic parables that appear as illustrations of Scripture verses are, as Stern has pointed out, a way of doing exegesis. It is not simply that an oral culture has a fondness for formulas and concrete language, for stories and tales; rather, such are their vehicles for thinking.

The difference between the way we literates think and the way an oral culture thinks raises forcefully the question of how myth relates to parable. To answer that question we must probe what is meant by mythical thinking, and to do that we will engage Claude Lévi-Strauss in dialogue.

For Lévi-Strauss, myth is founded on a demand, even a passion, for order. It is a science of the concrete, ordering in story discrete, concrete reality. In myth a thing is sacred because it is in its proper place, and if taken out of its place "even in thought, the entire order of the universe would be destroyed." [131]

The myth maker is a *bricoleur* (a possible English equivalent is "jack-of-all-trades"). Myth is created from whatever is at hand, because it has nothing else at its disposal. The debris of human life is woven together to create stories. Like a junkman who tinkers with things, putting together things that did not originally belong together, the myth maker uses mythemes (bundles or sets). A myth teller operates with a repertoire of mythemes. Mythemes are part of what we have identified as the thesaurus or repertoire of the parables. The identification of the mythemes employed in a parable is among the most important operations

---

130. I made a similar point in my *Jesus, Symbol-Maker*, 11–17; there I employed a method of insight to deal with the problem. Via's critique of this position (*Ethics of Mark's Gospel*, 8) seems overdrawn. I find myself in substantial agreement with Via's position.

131. Lévi-Strauss, *Savage Mind*, 10.

in interpretation. I will distinguish for convenience between mythemes, by which I mean traditional elements of the thesaurus or repertoire that have a definite story or narrative form, and the metaphoral network, which indicates the interconnections and implications of a metaphorical system.

The structure of mythical thinking is invariable.[132] "Mythical thought always progresses from the awareness of oppositions toward their resolution. . . . Two opposite terms with no intermediary always tend to be replaced by two equivalent terms which admit of a third one as mediator; then one of the polar terms and the mediator become replaced by a new triad, and so on."[133] One step in this model is illustrated in figure 2.

Figure 2

$$
\left.\begin{array}{l}
\text{item A} \;\rightarrow\; \text{item A}' \\[1em]
\text{item B} \;\rightarrow\; \text{item B}'
\end{array}\right\} \quad \text{item C}'
$$

In this representation, items A and B are oppositions that of themselves have no mediation. Items A' and B' are equivalent to A and B, but they have a mediator, item C'.

An example may make this abstract model clearer. American society poses a fundamental opposition between our belief that all are created equal and the evident fact that all are not equal. The Horatio Alger cycle of stories resolves this opposition. The Alger hero, by honesty, cheerful perseverance, and hard work, achieves a just reward. The hero's poor state at the beginning of the story is equivalent to the inequality in society; his final wealth is equivalent to our all being created equal. His hard work is the narrative bridge by which he moves from lack of wealth to wealth. Thus the opposition between reality and belief is resolved by a narrative that has a mediator, the Alger hero's hard work. Inequality in society is due to some fundamental error not in the belief system but in the individual who fails to work.[134] As Lévi-Strauss's model makes clear, "the purpose of myth is to provide a logical model

132. Lévi-Strauss's baffling algebraic-like formula for explaining the structure of myth is highly debated, and I side with those who believe it should not be taken too seriously. For the formula, see "Structural Study of Myth," 228. For astute comments about the formula's significance, see Sperber, "Claude Lévi-Strauss," 20–21.

133. Lévi-Strauss, "Structural Study of Myth," 224.

134. An ironic aside to this whole discussion: The giving of this example to make clear an abstract model indicates the perseverance of orality's concreteness even in a literate form like the "scholarly introduction."

capable of overcoming contradiction (an impossible achievement if, as it happens, the contradiction is real)."[135]

For Lévi-Strauss, it is not so much that the untamed thinker thinks in myths as that "myths operate in men's minds without their being aware of the fact."[136] Both the myth-making culture and the myths of a given culture order a person, defining who that person is. Consequently, myths are anonymous, existing only as elements embodied in a tradition; "they are messages coming from nowhere."[137] There is no individual; the hearer is made aware of a group instinct, of being rooted in society.[138] Just as the oral singer believes he or she is not creative and is only repeating what has been heard before, so a mythic culture discovers uniqueness in the group, not in individuality as we literates do. This explains why myth, unlike poetry, can be preserved in the worst translations, and why even without a great knowledge of a particular culture or society we recognize myth so easily. "Its substance does not lie in its style, its original music or its syntax, but in the story which it tells."[139] It is the triumph of the group over the individual; it demands an empathic and participatory stance, not objectivity. Myth classifies, orders.

The Jesus parables are not myth; they are antimyth.[140] Because they disorder the mythical world, they are world-shattering. But their relation to mythemes is important to observe, for parables take up mythical elements and usually block their mediating function. Yet because myth belongs to the conservative, homeostatic character of culture, myth frequently manages to reclaim the parable. In A Grain of Mustard Seed, the original version of the parable subverts the great cedar of Lebanon as mytheme for the kingdom by insisting on the mustard shrub as metaphor for the kingdom. Yet the myth reasserts itself in the oral tradition by changing the mustard plant into a tree, thus reinstituting the mythical order. Sometimes myth's triumph happens outside the text. To compare the kingdom to leaven attacks the identification of the holy with unleavened and ignores the constant association of corruption with leaven. Yet in traditional interpretations the obvious sense of leaven is ignored in favor of making it holy (i.e., unleaven). This interaction of parable and myth is an important element in the interpretation of the

---

135. Lévi-Strauss, "Structural Study of Myth," 229.
136. Lévi-Strauss, *The Raw and the Cooked*, 12.
137. Ibid., 18.
138. Ibid., 28.
139. Lévi-Strauss, "Structural Study of Myth," 210.
140. Crossan, *Raid on the Articulate*, 98–99.

Jesus parables. Only later when we deal with the interrelation of kingdom and parable will we see why this subversion of myth takes place.

The parables' orality makes our quest of the parables of Jesus problematic. An older methodology, as exemplified by the work of Jeremias, sought to reconstruct the very words of Jesus. Such a method presupposes literacy and imagines that people memorized words.[141] Memorization of words is only possible when a written archetype exists against which to compare memory. Because the parable was oral, it passed out of existence as soon as it was spoken. There is no possibility of "having" or possessing an original parable. In oral cultures what is remembered is the structure or outline.[142] Neusner, in the preface to his new translation of the Babylonian Talmud, comments concerning the text of the Talmud,

> If I had to make a guess as to what we have, I should imagine we deal with nothing more than brief notes, notations really, out of which a whole and complete discourse is supposed to be reconstructed by those essentially familiar with the (original) discourse. The Babylonian Talmud is a kind of abbreviated script, a set of cue cards drastically cut down to a minimum of words.[143]

What Neusner is describing is structure, and the Talmud is meant to be performed by others. Likewise, differences between various versions of a Jesus parable result from different performances of the structure.

We seek the structure of Jesus' parables, not the words. The structure that undergirds the extant performances exists at the level of *langue* as an abstract construct. We have no parable of Jesus as he performed it. All extant parables ascribed to Jesus show the traces of performances by others. Because Jesus' parables were oral, as *parole*, actual performance, they passed out of existence as soon as they were spoken. What remained, what was repeated, what was remembered was structure even if, as was most probable, the parables were often repeated by Jesus. Those parabolic structures were performed by others in the oral tradition and by Gospel writers including Thomas. Traditional storytellers, preachers, teachers, and evangelists were not simply passive memory receptacles but performers, shaping and adapting the structure in a concrete performance. The performances reflect their peculiar situations. Because there exists no performance, no concrete version of a

---

141. Lord, *Singer of Tales*, 13–29. Ong (*Orality and Literacy*, 57–68) provides a convenient summary of studies of "oral memorization."

142. This is another reason, besides the existence of the thesaurus or repertoire, for seeking *structura* and not *verba*. See p. 18 above.

143. *Talmud of Babylonia, Tractate Berakhot*, ed. Neusner, 7.

parabolic structure that goes back to Jesus, the structure has to be reconstructed from the extant versions.

Besides being short, the parables are also narrative fictions. Narrative fiction is something we easily recognize but find hard to define. Shlomith Rimmon-Kenan's minimal definition will suffice: "By 'narrative fiction' I mean the narration of a succession of fictional events."[144] Sometimes the fictional character of the parables is laid aside as when Jeremias or others argue that a parable is based on an actual event. That is beside the point and mistakes verisimilitude for reality.[145] Parables have high verisimilitude, as attested by their use of everydayness, but everydayness has been fictionalized by being taken up into story.

Traditional categories of parables distinguish between similitudes, many of which are grammatically similes, and parables proper. Jülicher has sharply contrasted similitude (*Gleichnis*) and parable, which he sometimes terms fable. The similitude calls upon what is universally valid (*Allgemeingiltiges*), the parable upon a one-time event (*einmal Vorgekommenes*).[146] Although there is some validity to this distinction, it should not be overdrawn. Similitudes are still narrative even though the narrative is extremely condensed and the situation described is not generally one of human interaction but of nature and household artifacts. The parable of The Leaven is more than a picture. It has a true succession of events: the woman hides, then the leaven works its way through all. Part of the problem results from the nature of *mashal*. If we imagine *mashal* as a continuum, similitudes are on the border between parable and proverb,[147] and it is better to treat them with parable than proverb.[148]

Via, by describing parables as aesthetic objects,[149] has drawn attention to the narrativity and fictionality of parables. Because parables are aesthetic objects, narrative fictions, they have a freedom or independence vis-à-vis their contextualization.[150] As narrative fictions they have a priority over their context.[151] To put it another way, they interpret the

144. Rimmon-Kenan, *Narrative Fiction*, 3.

145. Culler, *Structuralist Poetics*, 131–45.

146. Jülicher, *Die Gleichnisreden* 1:97. For Jülicher, the parable is a higher form because it is more subtle.

147. See my *Jesus, Symbol-Maker*, 65–67.

148. Bultmann (*History of the Synoptic Tradition*, 174–75), in defending Jülicher's distinction, nevertheless remarks, "But no intelligent person would expect any particular instance to give pure expression to any particular form. This means that there is no point in much debate over any particular example."

149. Via, *Parables*, 70–71.

150. See Bauman, *Verbal Art*, 7–14.

151. This is true of all narratives. Among many literary theorists, see Rimmon-Kenan (*Narrative Fiction*, 6–8) and Iser (*Act of Reading*, chap. 1).

context, not the other way around. Thus Jeremias's obsessive search for a parable's *Sitz im Leben* is misdirected, for a parable can have more than one *Sitz im Leben*, just as the same rabbinic parable can illustrate more than one Scripture verse or the evangelists can situate the same parable in different situations or even no situation. There is no reason to assume that Jesus used a parable only once. That is highly unlikely. Storytellers develop a corpus of stories that they employ in a variety of situations.

This independence of parable from an immediate contextualization does not make the parable ahistorical, because the cultural context of the parables is first-century Judaism. Futhermore, that cultural context is critical for the parables' interpretation. What I reject is that a specific situation in the ministry of Jesus accounts for a parable. It seems especially untrue that that situation is Jesus' controversy with the Pharisees.

Because parables are narrative fictions, we will need to employ literary criticism to analyze them. I have chosen to use a methodology that accents the interaction between text, narrative, and hearer/reader.[152] Such a method has the advantage of uncovering the structural dynamics that allow a text to communicate and structure its perception in a variety of situations.

Referencing

A parable is a *mashal* that employs a short narrative fiction **to reference** a transcendent symbol.

"Referencing" denotes an essential characteristic of parable because the "laying-beside" of narrative and referent creates the parabolic process, or what Paul Ricoeur calls the metaphorical process.[153] But referencing or transference raises an issue that has plagued parable criticism since Jülicher's foundational work: Are parables allegories? To deal adequately with the issue of metaphor and allegory, whether in parable studies or secular literary criticism and linguistics, is a daunting task. My tactic is to probe four moments in parable criticism (Jülicher, C. H. Dodd, Funk, and Crossan) and four recent theorists of metaphor (Umberto Eco, George Lakoff and Mark Johnson, and Ricoeur).

Jülicher initiated modern parable criticism with his monumental *Die Gleichnisreden Jesu*.[154] His achievement was to attack and destroy the

---

152. I am greatly influenced by the method of Iser in *Act of Reading* and *Implied Reader*.

153. Ricoeur, "Biblical Hermeneutics," 75–106.

154. Vol. 1 was published in 1886, and vol. 2 in 1899. Slight revisions appeared in 1910.

allegorical interpretation of parables that had reigned until his time.[155] Despite continued attacks, Jülicher's position, although greatly modified, remains the critical position.

The abiding significance of Jülicher's attack is his rejection of the existing allegories of Jesus' parables as products of the early church,[156] and his arguments remain the rock that breaks those who would counterattack in favor of allegory. His strategy for blocking allegorical interpretation is to reject its multiple points in favor of a "single point" methodology. The parable consists of two parts, *Sache* (the reality being represented) and *Bild* (the figure representing the reality). The *tertium comparationis* (the third item of comparison) bridges these two and constitutes a parable's point.[157] Allegory for Jülicher is an extended set of metaphors wherein each item in a story is a separate metaphor. Over against allegory's multiple metaphors is the parable's "single point."

Jülicher's *strategy* for blocking allegory differs from his primary reason for rejecting allegory, the manifestly later nature of the Synoptic allegories. We may reject Jülicher's strategy but still face his conclusions.

For Jülicher, a parable's point refers to the widest possible moral generality.[158] Both Dodd and Jeremias have adopted the "single point" methodology but have shifted the point to Jesus' eschatology. Dodd in examining the parables of the kingdom has advanced a realized eschatology; Jeremias has advocated an eschatology of yet and not-yet. Even more, Jeremias has tied the parable to a specific context in Jesus' ministry, so that Jeremias employs not only a "single point" but also a "single situation" methodology.

The tradition of interpretation from Jülicher forward has not been without those who demur. Fiebig, whose first substantial rebuttal of Jülicher appeared in 1904, can stand for those who come after him.[159] He protested that Jülicher's rejection of allegory was without basis. Fiebig based his opposition on rabbinic parables. He rejects Jülicher's sharp distinction between parable and allegory, arguing that many rabbinic parables are a mixture of simile (metaphor, in the terms of the current

155. Kissinger's *Parables* has an excellent survey of parable interpretation; for the pre-Jülicher period, see pp. 1–71. For a summary and critique of Jülicher and his tradition, see also Johnston, "Parabolic Traditions," 1–122. For a recent German response to Jülicher, see Klauck, *Allegorie und Allegorese*, 4–20.

156. See Jülicher, *Die Gleichnisreden*, esp. 1:39–42, 52–68, 148–53.

157. Ibid., 52.

158. Jeremias (*Parables*, 19) provides a convenient sampler of Jülicher's generalizing points.

159. Snodgrass (*Wicked Tenants*, 13–26) provides a very recent survey of those rejecting Jülicher.

debate) and allegory.[160] Especially prevalent are the conventional metaphors of God as king, Israel as sons, and Israel's enemies as wolves or robbers.[161]

The nagging protest against Jülicher's rejection of allegory revolves around two issues: that many rabbinic parables are allegorized (or more accurately mixed metaphors and allegories), and that the Synoptic Gospels and the early church understood Jesus' parables as allegories. Curiously, the *Gospel of Thomas* has been left aside in recent discussions.[162] Although many rabbinic parables are allegories, not all are. Many are also metaphorical. Nor were all rabbinic parables created for the sake of their interpretation: since some parables are used to interpret several different scriptural verses, these clearly exist separately from their *nimshal* (application). Thus the correct conclusion is that *the parable as genre is neither by necessity allegorical nor by necessity metaphorical*. The importance of this conclusion needs to be insisted upon: Jülicher's categorical rejection of the possibility of allegory in Jesus' parables is unwarranted. The genre parable can be allegorical, metaphorical, or mixed.

Even though the Synoptic Gospels and the *Gospel of Thomas* read many of the parables as allegories, distinctions must be made because allegorization occurs in a variety of ways. There is the explicit allegorical interpretation of A Sower Went Out, The Wheat and Tares, and A Man Planted a Vineyard. Yet all three parables occur in *Thomas* without explicit allegory, so it is clear that the allegory is independent of the parable. Furthermore, the abiding significance of Jülicher's work is the demonstration that these allegories represent the situation (*Sitz im Leben*) of the early church and not that of Jesus.[163] The problem with allegory in the parables is not allegory per se, but the ideological[164] reading of the parables with an ideology that is manifestly later. For example, the allegory of A Man Planted a Vineyard demands salvation history as its ideological structure. If the son is Jesus, no one in the contemporary audience would have recognized it as a reference to Jesus.

While most parables in the Jesus tradition do not have an explicit allegory, many have generalizing conclusions that point toward an

160. Fiebig, *Altjüdische Gleichnisse*, 25–73.

161. Ibid., 99–100.

162. Snodgrass (*Wicked Tenants*, 52) argues that *Thomas* is dependent on the Synoptics but has omitted the allegory.

163. The refusal to deal with this issue undermines most attempts to refute Jülicher. E.g., Boucher (*Mysterious Parable*, 45–53) seems to accept the interpretation of A Sower Went Out as Markan, at the same time maintaining that it could represent Jesus' authentic interpretation.

164. "Ideological" is here used in the technical sense of Uspensky in *Poetics of Composition*, 8. The ideological or evaluative point of view is a "general system of viewing the world conceptually and is the most basic point of view."

implicit allegory. In A King Wished to Settle Accounts, the generalizing conclusion; "So also my heavenly Father will do to every one of you, if you do not forgive your brother from your heart" (Matt. 18:35), identifies the king with God, a standard move in rabbinic parables. Or again at the conclusion of A Rich Man Had A Steward there are a series of conclusions (Luke 7:8b-13) that, as Dodd has noted, appear to be notes for a sermon. But again the generalizing conclusions are either manifestly later, as in the first example, or they reverse the relation between parable and illustrand so that they are efforts to say what the parable means— that is, they are illustrations of the parable, as in the latter case. Thus even though parables were sometimes performed by the Synoptics and *Thomas* as allegories, those allegories illustrate the ideology of the evangelists and the early church and not the situation of Jesus' preaching. Therefore, even if we reject Jülicher's strategy of the "single point," his conclusion of the secondary nature of the Synoptic allegories stands.

Although Jülicher's "single point" methodology and Jeremias's corollary "single situation" were powerful strategies for combating an allegorical interpretation, they fatally fall victim to what I. A. Richards has termed "the proper meaning superstition." Such a method assumes that a word or narrative has only one proper meaning. As Richards remarks, the method assumes "that water, for all its virtues, in canals, baths and turbines, were really a weak form of ice."[165] Words and, even more, connotative narratives naturally move toward polyvalency. It is a manipulation of reality to select only one out of a number of possibilities suggested by a narrative.[166] A methodology that seizes on the one point of likeness as a parable's meaning destroys the parable. Allegory's openness to the multiple points of contact is more in line with polyvalency.

Ironically, Funk, who joins Jülicher in rejecting allegory and sees himself explicitly in the tradition of Jülicher, develops a program of parable as metaphor that is an implicit attack on Jülicher. When Dodd began his famous definition with "The parable is a metaphor or simile,"[167] he had only wanted to designate it as a trope. But Funk escalates Dodd's observation by bringing to bear the modern tradition since Coleridge that has privileged metaphor and symbol as authentic and minimized allegory as inauthentic.[168] For Funk, trope is secondary. On the one hand, he distinguishes between simile and metaphor, arguing that simile is illustrative and metaphor "creative of meaning," yet again

165. Richards, *Philosophy of Rhetoric*, 48.
166. Eco, *Semiotics and the Philosophy of Language*, 103.
167. Dodd, *Parables*, 5.
168. Jülicher (*Die Gleichnisreden* 1:171-73) used the language of "authentic" and "inauthentic" in reference to Jesus' parables and the rabbis, without the ontological tinge.

he argues that the grammatical difference is irrelevant.[169] What is critical for Funk is that metaphor involves language different from that of the everyday. "To say *A is B* is a metaphor, which, because of the juxtaposition of two discrete and not entirely comparable entities, produces an impact upon the imagination and induces a vision of that which cannot be conveyed by prosaic or discursive speech."[170] Thus parables are not simple didactic stories illustrating a single point, whether moral or eschatological, but are privileged speech bearing an ontological reality. "It is not too much to say that true metaphor reveals a mystery: the mystery of kaleidoscopic reality directly apprehended."[171]

The key to a new methodological proposal is its ability to produce a new insight into familiar material. Jülicher, Dodd, and Jeremias did this with their progressive refinements of the "single point" strategy. Funk's use of metaphor is likewise insightful when he turns his attention to the parable From Jerusalem to Jericho. Why, he asks, if the parable is to be an example of neighborliness, did the storyteller choose a Samaritan, since such a figure would be an obvious scandal to a Jewish audience and not a likely example of "goodness." "The Samaritan is he whom the victim does not, could not expect would help, indeed does not want help from. The literal, i.e., historical significance of the Samaritan is what gives the parable its edge."[172] The literal significance makes the parable a metaphor, but then it is no longer an example for neighborliness. Funk's argument that parable is metaphor subverts the "single point" methodology and prepares the way for Crossan's accent upon the paradoxical and polyvalent character of parables.[173]

Funk's program of parable as metaphor imported into biblical studies the Romantic tradition of understanding metaphor. That tradition set off symbol/metaphor against allegory in a paradigm in which symbol/metaphor was privileged ontologically. Metaphor exposed the real, "was organic, non-intellectual, pointing to some mystical connection between the mind of the poet"[174] and the real world obscured by everydayness. Allegory was used in a pejorative sense, identified with the didactic, rational, descriptive, and artificial, whereas metaphor was creative of meaning. This privileging of metaphor, as Paul de Man has argued, is an act of ontological bad faith,[175] drawing a distinction where none is

---

169. Funk, *Language*, 136, 137.
170. Ibid., 136.
171. Ibid., 140.
172. Ibid., 213.
173. See esp. Crossan, *Cliffs of Fall*; idem, *Finding*; idem, *Raid on the Articulate*.
174. Scholes and Kellogg, *Nature of Narrative*, 106.
175. Man, "Rhetoric of Temporality," 173–91; Kermode, *Genesis of Secrecy*, 28–34, 41–45.

possible.[176] Allegory and metaphor are not juxtaposed but are part of the same continuum.

Romanticism's privileging of metaphor may be naive, especially in its claim of a direct apprehension of reality and its overly sharp distinction between metaphor and allegory; nevertheless its perception of the centrality of the metaphorical process to language is critical. As Eco has argued, theories about metaphor face a radical choice:

> Either (a) language is by nature and originally, metaphorical, and the mechanism of metaphor establishes linguistic activity, every rule or convention arising thereafter in order to discipline, to reduce (and impoverish) the metaphorizing potential that defines man as a symbolic animal; or (b) language (and every other semiotic system) is a rule governed mechanism, a predictive machine . . . with regard to which metaphor constitutes a break down, a malfunction, an unaccountable outcome.[177]

Eco lays bare the choice the Romantics have bequeathed us: that either all language is inherently metaphorical or metaphor is a breakdown of language. Jülicher and Jeremias, with their "single point" and then "single situation" method (rules) have attempted to control the unruly parable, because for them without rules parable becomes allegory. For Funk and the early Crossan, parable rescued from rules opens out onto reality itself.

Romanticism's sharp distinction between allegory and metaphor forces on parable an unreal either-or. The real issue, however, is the direction of transference. Does the transference go from parable to referent or the other way? Does the referent determine the understanding of the parable? To put it even more boldly, is the parable a true illustration or is it dictated by what it illustrates? Even more, is parable an ornament or does it have cognitive value? What Eco says about metaphor is true likewise about parable. "As an ornament, the metaphor is of no interest to us because, if it says more pleasantly that which can be said otherwise, then it could be explained wholly within the scope of a semantics of denotation. We are interested in the metaphor as an additive, not substitutive, an instrument of knowledge."[178] This issue can be approached from two directions. First, there is the nature of the parable as narrative, and second, the function of parable in rabbinic literature.

As a *mashal*, parable is connotative; its literal level is supposed to lead

176. Crossan (*Raid on the Articulate*, 115) has acknowledged his own shift from a Romanticist view supporting his *In Parables* to a "structuralist" view for his later work. My *Jesus, Symbol-Maker* is likewise supported by a Romantic hermeneutics.

177. Eco, *Semiotics and the Philosophy of Language*, 88.

178. Ibid., 89.

to nonliteral interpretation, a metaphorical interpretation. There is
always a tension between the literal and the nonliteral level. Ricoeur
distinguishes in narrative two levels of reference, a literal reference and
a second-level reference when the literal level is suspended. At this
second level, narrative is a model for redescribing reality. The mimesis of
fiction is not a copy of reality but its redescription.[179] As fictional redescriptions, parables demand that the primary direction of transference be
from parable to referent, because the redescription exposes something
new, not simply copying the already known.

Rabbinic parables exhibit a similar phenomenon. Since with regularization, rabbinic parables illustrate and justify the interpretation of Scripture, it would seem that the direction of transference is from referent to
parable. But this turns out not to be so, for the interpretation is frequently novel, a modification of traditional interpretation or even an
invention of new interpretation. The parable is made to seem as though
it produces the exegesis, and once the text is reinterpreted, it then
authenticates the parable. Thus the procedure is circular. The parable is
not primarily didactic but is primarily hermeneutical, explaining how
one is to interpret. It accomplishes this by a sleight of hand. The parable
is authenticated by the reinterpreted verse of Scripture, while actually
the parable makes evident this reinterpretation. So then, as Stern remarks, parable has a cognitive value independent of its rhetorical function, "telling us something in its own right."[180] In the rabbinic parables
quoted below (see "Symbol") the rabbis assume that the parable is a
window onto Torah, that is, a metaphorical opening, and that without
parables Torah is unknowable (cf. Mark 4).

Jesus' parables lack a direct referent to Scripture, and in many cases a
referent is left unspecified. Yet the assumption is that the parables at a
second level of reference are about the kingdom of God, or in Ricoeur's
terms, are fictional redescription of the kingdom. The vagueness of the
referent has created problems in the history of interpretation. In *From
Jerusalem to Jericho*, Luke assumes that the parable is about "neighborliness." For Augustine of Hippo, it is about the salvation of the soul, and
for Jeremias, it is about boundless love.[181] All three interpreters have
bypassed the literal level for a secondary level and, even more, have
employed their understanding of the referent to determine what the
parable is about. For them the direction of transference is from referent
to parable. An even more subtle example occurs in the interpretation of
The Leaven, when interpreters consistently argue that even though

179. Ricoeur, *Rule of Metaphor*, 244–45.
180. Stern, "Rhetoric and Midrash," 275.
181. Augustine, *Quaestiones Evanqeliorum*, 2.19 (quoted in Dodd's *Parables*, 1–2);
Jeremias, *Parables*, 202.

leaven in all known examples from the ancient world stands for moral corruption, in this parable it cannot signify that because this is a parable about the kingdom (i.e., something good). The parable is stripped of its cognitive value and becomes a mere ornament, an illustration of an already-known-about referent. It is altogether illegitimate to deny the literal level because it conflicts with the supposed second level of reference.

The parables' verisimilitude and their highly disjunctive features challenge this reversal of transference. Careful attention must be given the literal level, for it is the vehicle for the nonliteral level, the tenor. The almost total absence of king parables in the Jesus tradition is conspicuous in light of their domination in rabbinic parables. The anonymous man, the standard character in Jesus' parables, corresponds very much to the everyday world, to verisimilitude, but is metaphorically disjunctive to the referent of God as a king. The king in Jesus' single king parable, A King Wished to Settle Accounts, turns out to be even more disjunctive, since he is a tyrant who goes back on his word. The verisimilitude of the king parables in rabbinic literature is with the Roman court.[182] They are metaphorically more congruent for their referent, God's activity toward this people as revealed in Torah.

Even though strong verisimilitude to the everyday blocks an easy transference from referent to parable, dogmatic assertions about the allegorical status of characters, images, or themes in parables should be avoided. The stock, stereotyped characters, themes, and plots employed by parables function as conventional metaphors. Fathers, sons, slaves, vineyards, fig trees, leaven, and so forth, play conventional roles in Israel's religious and linguistic repertoire. How those conventional roles fit into the narrative often provides important clues as to how to move to the second-level reference.

How does a parable reference its symbol? The common notion underlying both *mashal* and *parabolē* is helpful. Literally, a parable is something "laid beside," "parallel," so that the narrative is laid beside its referent. It provides no explicit instructions for its hearer/reader to employ in relating narrative to referent—that is the task of interpretation. Yet there are implicit rules or instructions. Indeed, we have been attempting to discover the rudimentary rules—genre, narrative structure, and now, the direction of transference.

Why is metaphor such a suggestive model[183] for a parable's functioning? According to Lakoff and M. Johnson, "The essence of metaphor

---

182. The burden of Ziegler's *Die Konigsgleichnisse* is to show that the rabbinic parables accurately reflect Roman custom.

183. Tolbert (*Perspectives*, 43–44) correctly notes that a parable is not technically a metaphor but that at the semantic level a parable functions in the way a metaphor does.

is understanding and experiencing one kind of thing in terms of another."[184] This definition underscores the parallel, laid-beside notion so prominent in parable. Even more it blocks the *tertium comparationis*. Funk's and Crossan's insistence that the whole parable is the comparative activity makes the same point. To select only one out of all the possibilities suggested by the metaphor/parable is manipulative of reality, ideology in its negative sense.

Understanding one thing in terms of another involves employing a metaphorical network to which item A belongs to understand item B. Aristotle understood metaphor as relating a single aspect of A to a similar aspect of B. In his famous example, "Hercules is a lion," courage is the similar element, *tertium comparationis*, in the signified of both Hercules and the lion. Lakoff and Johnson argue that A is understood in terms of B, and B is not a single word or term but a network or structure of possibilities.[185] They point out that in English we use "war" as a metaphorical network to understand "argument."

Your claims are *indefensible*.
He *attacked every weak point* in my argument.
His criticisms were *right on target*.
I *demolished* his argument.
I've never *won* an argument with him.
You disagree? Okay, *shoot?*
If you use that *strategy*, he'll *wipe you out*.
He *shot down* all of my arguments.[186]

A metaphorical network undergirds a systematic understanding of the other thing. Even more than just understanding (a cognitive activity), the metaphorical network affects experience and behavior, so that, for example, in English when we *engage* in arguments, we behave as though we were at war and get angry. Lakoff and Johnson even go so far as to argue that an abstract phenomenon like love receives whatever structure it has from the metaphors used for it.[187] The metaphorical network structures the experience, behavior, and understanding of that other reality it stands for.

Because parabolic narrative is a way of understanding one thing in terms of another, the metaphorical network exposes both similarities and differences. Dissimilarities are not only instructive, they may be critical. Richards once remarked that "the mind is a connecting organ, it works only by connecting and it can connect any two things in an

184. Lakoff and Johnson, *Metaphors We Live By*, 5.
185. Ibid., 112.
186. Ibid., 4.
187. Ibid., 110.

indefinitely large number of different ways."[188] Parable calls on the connecting capacity and even demands connections where none were previously seen. In commenting upon this, Ricoeur notes that Richards's theory gives equal status to both dissimilarity and resemblance. "Perhaps," he says, "the modifications imparted by the vehicle to the tenor is even greater because of their dissimilarity than because of their resemblance."[189] In narratives where there is strong dissimilarity to the expected values of the referent, as there frequently is in Jesus' parables, dissimiliarity may well be a way of redefining and subverting a hearer's vision of the referent so as to redescribe reality.

Because metaphor understands one thing in terms of another and employs a network consistently and systematically to structure both understanding and experience of the referent, the B item may tyrannize that for which it stands. Metaphor only understands A in terms of B; some uses of metaphor forget that A and B are not identical. A metaphorical network highlights (reveals) aspects of the referent, but at the same time it *hides* other aspects. Thus its structuring power is only partial, not exhaustive. Nevertheless, the hiding aspect of metaphor is frequently forgotten both in the power of the structuring and in the forgetfulness of everyday language. Similarity can block remembrance of what metaphor hides; dissimilarity highlights what previously was hidden.

Symbol

> A parable is a *mashal* that employs a short narrative fiction to reference a **symbol.**

Parables in the technical sense in which we have been speaking of them belong to religious discourse. Their secularity and everydayness are at the service of a religious meaning. What separates them from modern parables, for example, those of Kafka or Borges, is not so much genre[190] as the religious dimension that is distinctive and explicit in these parables, perhaps hidden and implicit in the latter.

Parable and Torah

As part of the regularization of parable in rabbinic literature, the context for the use of parable became exclusively the exegesis of the Torah. But the import of this is even greater than simply context. As Stern remarks, the "greater significance" of the *nimshal* (application) emerges "if it is

188. Richards, *Philosophy of Rhetoric,* 125.
189. Ricoeur, *Rule of Metaphor,* 82.
190. As Crossan (*Raid on the Articulate,* 99–114) makes clear in the case of Borges.

borne in mind that an over-all tendency of midrashic literature in general is always to subordinate every context—narrative, historical, sociological—to the all-encompassing context of the Torah, literally to make the words of the Torah embrace everything in the universe."[191] Stern points towards the Torah as the hermeneutical horizon in which the rabbinic parable exists. The *nimshal* exists to draw the reader's attention to the relations between parable as elusive tale and the Scripture under discussion.

Parable in rabbinic literature is the gate to the Torah. *Midrash Rabbah* on the Song of Songs, in discussing the verse "Besides being wise, the Preacher also taught the people knowledge, weighing and studying and arranging proverbs [*meshalim*] with great care" (Eccles. 12:9), comments at great length on the use of parables. For the rabbis, Solomon, the preacher, created *meshalim*, which they read as parables, not proverbs.

> Let not the parable be lightly esteemed in your eyes, since by means of the parable a man can master the words of the Torah. If a king loses gold from his house or a precious pearl, does he not find it by means of a wick worth a farthing? So the parable should not be lightly esteemed in your eyes, since by means of the parable a man arrives at the true meaning of the words of the Torah.[192]

The rabbis were aware of the parable's trivial appearance, and it is a common assumption even today that parables are simple, clear stories.[193] Yet this is an illusion, for parable can open up the whole of the law to understanding. Earlier in the same passage the Midrash comments that until Solomon no one could properly understand the words of the Torah but because Solomon was wise and set out many parables all could understand the Torah:

> [Solomon] pondered the words of the Torah and investigated [the meaning of] the words of Torah. He made handles to the Torah. You find that till Solomon came there was no parable. R. Nahman gave two illustrations. Said R. Nahman: Imagine a large palace with many doors, so that whoever entered could not find his way back to the door, till one clever person came and took a coil of string and hung it up on the way to the door, so that all went in and out by means of the coil. So till Solomon arose no one was able to understand properly the words of the Torah, but as soon as Solomon arose all began to comprehend the Torah. R. Nahman gave another illustration, from a thicket of reeds which no one could penetrate, till one

---

191. Stern, "Rhetoric and Midrash," 266. Fiebig (*Altjüdische Gleichnisse*, 105) and Klausner (*Jesus of Nazareth*, 264) also note the almost exclusive use of parable in connection with Scripture.

192. *Midrash Rabbah* on the Song of Songs 1.1.8 (Freedman 3:10).

193. E.g., Meagher, *Clumsy Construction*, 86.

clever man came and took a scythe and cut some down, and then all began to enter through the cutting. So did Solomon. R. Jose said: Imagine a big basket full of produce without any handle, so that it could not be lifted, till one clever man came and made handles to it, and then it began to be carried by the handles. So till Solomon arose no one could properly understand the words of the Torah, but when Solomon arose, all began to comprehend the Torah. R. Shila said: Imagine a big jug full of hot water with no handle by which it could be carried, until someone came and made it a handle, so that it began to be carried by its handle. R. Haniana said: Imagine a deep well full of water, cold, sweet, and wholesome water, but no one was able to get a drink of it, until one man came and joining rope to rope and cord to cord, drew from it and drank, and then all began to draw and drink. So proceeding from one thing to another, from one parable to another, Solomon penetrated to the innermost meaning of the Torah.[194]

This text is based on a set of simple yet elaborate plays. Two scriptural allusions start the train of thought. In 1 Kings 4:32 (MT, 5:12) it is said of Solomon, "He also uttered three thousand proverbs [*meshalim*]; and his songs were a thousand five." This text, combined with that of Eccles. 12:9, quoted above, is interpreted by the rabbis to mean that Solomon invented the parable. There is yet another wordplay involved in the Ecclesiastes text, where the RSV translates, "The Preacher also taught the people knowledge, *weighing* . . ." A more literal rendering of "weighing" would be "to listen," "to give ear." *A-z-n* means an ear, and ears are the handles of the head, so the noun by extension means "handle." The Talmud commenting on the same Ecclesiastes verse notes, "'Yes, he pondered [*a-z-n*], and sought out, and set in order many proverbs.' [This alludes to the fact], said 'Ulla in the name of R. Eleazar, that the Torah was at first like a basket which had no handles, and when Solomon came he affixed handles [*a-z-n*] to it."[195] In the Talmud, the wordplay ear/handle is so abbreviated that it almost seems to assume the parable of R. Jose quoted in the *Midrash Rabbah*.

Besides the supporting wordplay, the text's oral patterning stands out. There are five parables, four of which begin with "imagine." The first, second, and fifth parables are versions of the labyrinth; the third and fourth directly relate to the metaphor of the handles. All but the second parable conclude with a note about Solomon. The parables are parables about parables, entrances into a mystery, the mystery of the Torah, but they are the entrances left for others to follow. Not only is their meaning not exhausted in a single point but their point though obvious is difficult

194. *Midrash Rabbah* on the Song of Songs 1.1.8 (Freedman 3:9–10).
195. *m. Erub.* 21b (Soncino 3:151). In the same passage the text for 1 Kings is also commented on, so the combination is traditional.

to specify exactly. Maurice Simon in his notes to the Soncino translation of *Midrash Rabbah* remarks, "Apparently R. Nahman means that by means of parables Solomon enabled students of the Pentateuch to understand the connection between the different parts."[196] But each parable shifts the focus on the framing Torah. Each parable has in its way a scandalous image for the Torah. A palace with so many doors one gets lost: does that mean that the Torah lacks order? A thicket in which some must first be cut down: must some of the Torah be eliminated? The Torah, like a basket, is incomplete without its parable handles. And one could continue in a like vein. These parables are not simple allegories, as Jülicher would have it. They are complex metaphors, hermeneutical efforts to affix handles, parables, on the Torah. Nor were these parables created for just this midrashic occasion. The first two, for example, occur in *Midrash Rabbah* on Genesis to indicate how impenetrable is the king of kings,[197] and in the *Midrash Rabbah* on Ecclesiastes they demonstrate how impossible it is to understand the foundation of the universe.[198]

The parable is not completely exhausted in its application, because it can have multiple applications and can exist independently of the application. The application is the immediate referent, which can shift and change. The hermeneutical horizon is the mediate referent, which determines or organizes the parable's narrative and symbolic structure. These parables were created under the horizon of the Torah as a symbol of God's dealing with his people.[199]

Parable and Gospel

The most obvious difference between rabbinic parables and Jesus' is the lack of the exegesis of the Torah as either a context or a hermeneutical horizon of Jesus' parables. In the Synoptic Gospels, the context is the gospel narrative. We will return later to the significance of this. A number of parables maintain a relation to Scripture, although there is no consistent pattern. A Grain of Mustard Seed and A Man Casts Seed both end with allusive quotes from Scripture, but the parables are not illustrations of these quotes. From Jerusalem to Jericho is set in the context of a debate in which Scripture is quoted, but this context is clearly secondary. Between A Sower Went Out and its interpretation occurs a targumic-like quote from Isaiah, but again the quotation does not relate to the parable. Finally, early in the oral tradition the reference to the

196. *Midrash Rabbah* on the Song of Songs 9 (Freedman 7:11).
197. *Midrash Rabbah* on Genesis 12.1 (Freedman 1:87).
198. *Midrash Rabbah* on Ecclesiastes 1.9.1 (Freedman 8:61–62).
199. M. Fishbane ("Torah and Tradition," 275–300) has some very interesting things to say about this development in midrashic exegesis.

proof text of the cornerstone was added to A Man Planted a Vineyard so that the resurrection, demanded by the ideology of salvation history, could be accomplished outside the parable's narrative time. Thus in only two parables, A Grain of Mustard Seed and A Man Casts Seed, is there an integral relation to Scripture, and there the relationship is quite other than in the rabbinic form.

A number of parables have as their explicit, immediate referent the kingdom of God. Dodd, in his important book *The Parables of the Kingdom*, studied these parables as a group. The tradition as it developed probably had a tendency to make explicit the kingdom as referent. Moreover, Mark, Matthew, *Thomas,* and to a certain extent Luke place the parables in the context of the kingdom. Mark sets the interpretation of A Sower Went Out in a context in which Jesus promises the disciples, "To you has been given the secret of the kingdom of God but for those outside everything is in parables" (Mark 4:11; see Matt. 13:11; Luke 8:10). The parable for Mark is a secret bearer of the kingdom, and his Gospel's narrative is a hermeneutical context for the parables. Mark's Gospel not only proclaims the kingdom of God but is also like parable a bearer of the kingdom.[200] The narrative context functions as a fictional redescription of the kingdom. By setting the parable within the narrative context of his Gospel, Mark makes the kingdom the hermeneutical horizon of parable. Matthew does a quite similar thing, but since a primary concern of his understanding of the kingdom is the theme of Jesus as Lord of the kingdom, he situates many of the parables in the context of judgment (e.g., Matthew 25). Luke, on the other hand, has a much less prominent role for the kingdom in his Gospel and stresses Jesus as preacher of the kingdom, so that many of the parables become example stories of the kingdom's ethics. *Thomas* frequently sets the parables in a context in which the kingdom is the wisdom to be found in parable.

The effect of the Gospel context establishes an inevitable dialectic and paradox between parable and its context. Ricoeur states the problem nicely:

> The insertion of the parable into the Gospel-form is both a part of its meaning for us who have received the text from the church, *and* the beginning of its misunderstanding. This is why we have to interpret the parables both *with the help of and against the distortions* provided by the ultimate context.[201]

The Gospels, as fictional redescriptions of the kingdom, are faithful to the parables' original hermeneutical horizon, and thus it is proper to

---

200. See, among many others, Kelber, *The Oral and the Written Gospel,* 123.
201. Ricoeur, "Biblical Hermeneutics," 106.

state paradoxically that the parables generate the Gospels—they generate their own context. Or more correctly, the kingdom generates parable, which in turn generates Gospel. Yet in the performance of those parables by the evangelists there is what Ricoeur calls "distortion," which is inevitable since every narrative exists only as performance yet no performance exhausts the narrative's potential. Narrative structure has precedence over the context in which it is employed. This is true even of the rabbinic parables: their allusiveness is not exhausted by a single situation, nor is the application always most appropriate.

Parable and Kingdom

To focus the issue of parable and kingdom, I will take as my point of departure the work of Norman Perrin, since in this context his understanding of the kingdom inaugurates a decisive moment in this history of scholarship.[202]

Although the centrality of the kingdom of God in the language, message, and teaching of Jesus is a commonplace in contemporary scholarship,[203] a debate has raged around the semantic status of the kingdom of God.[204] Historians have sought in the main to secure the status of the kingdom of God as a concept identical to apocalyptic's expectation of the new age. Early in his career (1963), Perrin argued strongly for this position.[205] The chief characteristic of apocalyptic is an "eschatological dualism, the sharp distinction between the present age and the age to come."[206] In this way Perrin, like most scholars since Johannes Weiss and Albert Schweitzer, made time the paramount issue and fused the concept of the kingdom with the event of the coming new age.[207]

In a later work (1976), Perrin has still maintained that the background for Jesus' preaching of the kingdom is apocalyptic, but major shifts in his position have occurred. He questions "whether it is legitimate to think of Jesus' use of Kingdom of God in terms of 'present' and 'future' at all."[208] But more decisively he rejects the kingdom of God as concept in favor of the kingdom of God as symbol. Symbol places the kingdom in a different semantic field than does concept. Concept grasps cognitive expe-

---

202. See Duling's excellent survey in "Norman Perrin and the Kingdom of God," 484–500.

203. E.g., Conzelmann, *Jesus*, 51; and the anthology of essays *The Kingdom of God*, ed. Chilton.

204. See my *Jesus, Symbol-Maker*, chap. 1.

205. Perrin, *Kingdom of God*, 158–59.

206. Ibid., 164.

207. See also Perrin, *Rediscovering the Teaching*, 59 n. 7.

208. Perrin, *Jesus and the Language*, 40.

rience and can be translated and stated in discursive speech. Symbols are perceptive, experiential, but even more, stand "for some larger meaning or set of meanings which cannot be given, or not fully given, in perceptual experience itself."[209] If the kingdom is a concept, its referent can be fully specified in denotative, discursive language; if it is a symbol, it is connotative language, pointing to a second-level reference.

Perrin borrowed from Philip Wheelwright the distinction between tensive and steno symbols. A steno symbol has a one-to-one relation to what it describes. Wheelwright has used the mathematical symbol *pi* as an example. A tensive symbol cannot be expressed by any one referent or can express one whose referent itself is symbolic or not capable of complete capture. For Perrin, the kingdom of God was an apocalyptic steno symbol in Judaism and a tensive symbol in the language of Jesus. Crossan has assessed and rephrased Perrin's argument in a suggestive fashion: "All signs/symbols are intrinsically tensive, open-ended, and polyvalent; and all interpretations are intrinsically steno and univalent."[210] Interpretations are steno, whereas symbols are tensive.

Crossan's critique of Perrin underscores an important problem in both their positions: a lack of a clear understanding of what constitutes a symbol. Perrin has the virtue of borrowing an established definition from Wheelwright, but Crossan confuses symbol and sign and bestows on all signs/symbols a playful polyvalency. The problem arises in Perrin's argument that the apocalyptic use of the kingdom of God is a steno symbol.[211] Wheelwright's example of *pi* indicates that he understands steno symbols to be of the precise kind where a "sign" can stand for an exactly coded signified. The important distinction is "coded." Such symbols "are based on precisely coded transformational and projective rules."[212] *Pi* is shorthand for a complex mathematical operation. The kingdom of God cannot be such a symbol, because there is no precise coding of its referent.

A tensive symbol, for Wheelwright, signals that the referent is open, allusive—uncoded. Funk expresses a similar notion by locating the difference between a symbol and a metaphor in the suppression of the primary term.[213] The shorthand for metaphor is "A is B" (A is understood in terms of B), whereas in symbol the A term is left unstated. Symbols operate by indirection. Eco explores this in more subtle detail. "The symbol displays a certain disproportion, a tension, an ambiguity, an

209. Wheelwright, *Metaphor and Reality,* 130.
210. Crossan, "Literary Criticism," 78.
211. I appraised this from a different point of view in *Jesus, Symbol-Maker,* 11–12. See the remarks of Duling in "Norman Perrin and the Kingdom of God," 479–80.
212. Eco, *Semiotics and the Philosophy of Language,* 138.
213. Funk, *Language,* 137.

analogical precariousness. In 'genuine symbolism,' the forms do not
signify themselves; rather, they 'allude to,' hint at a wider meaning. Any
symbol is an enigma, and 'the Sphinx stands as a symbol for symbolism
itself.'"[214] For Eco, a symbol is an expression correlated to a *content
nebula*, that is, indistinct, unformed content.[215] A symbol is full and
empty of meaning at one and the same time. A symbol employs a
specific semiotic strategy in which it violates rhetorical maxims in such a
way that the interpretant is to be found outside the normal textual
implications. Eco uses the example of the Zen master who when asked
about the meaning of life merely raises his hand. One is forced to look
outside the rhetorical significance to find the implication. "The appearance of the symbolic mode depends on the presentation of a sentence, of
a word, of an object, of an action that, according to the precoded narrative or discourse frames, to the acknowledged rhetorical rules, to the
most common linguistic usages, *should not* have the relevance it acquires
within that context."[216] Within Eco's understanding, allegory is overcoding of a symbolic text to establish authority over the text so that its
content will not be nebula but known.[217]

Eco's discussion is helpful in sorting out the issues involved.[218] In the
sentence "God is King," "King" is a metaphor; it stands for God, and the
structural network of kingship is used to understand God so that he
rules, conquers, redeems, and so forth. Stories told about God as King
form the mythemes or mythological background that can be woven into
the network.[219] "Kingdom of God" is a symbol because its content is
nebula, cannot be coded with specificity. Recent scholarship has tried
without noticeable success to code the symbol by historical background-
ing in order to control its meaning.[220] That it is "preached," "announced,"
and "revealed," and that it "comes," indicate that its structural network is
discongruent with kingship, since these are not terms identified with
kings. When we consider the rhetoric of the usage of the symbol, it
appears like the Zen master's symbol. That much of this language rheto-
rically is no longer dissonant to us only shows how we have domesticated it or overcoded it, as when we identify it with church or some
other activity.

---

214. Eco, *Semiotics and the Philosophy of Language*, 144. Eco is quoting Hegel's
Ästhetik.
215. Eco, *Semiotics and the Philosophy of Language*, 144.
216. Ibid., 185.
217. Ibid., 144–56.
218. See the critical questions raised by Via in "Kingdom and Parable," 181–83.
219. Perrin (*Jesus and the Language*, 16–32) sketches out the elements of these
mythemes.
220. See my *Jesus, Symbol-Maker*, chap. 1; Chilton, *God Is Strength*, 277–78 n. 2.

"Kingdom of God" as a phrase appears infrequently in extant Jewish literature—except in rabbinic literature, where it appears frequently. "The kingdom of the heavens" refers to the divine authority, the yoke of the law, that one takes on by obedience.[221] Typical is a comment from *Sifra* on Leviticus:

> "Speak to the children of Israel and say to them: I am Jehovah your God. After the manner of the land of Egypt . . . ye shall not do." R. Simeon b. Yohai (c. a.d. 150) said: In another place (Ex. xx. 2) it says, "I am Jehovah thy God". I am Jehovah and you took my Kingdom upon you in Egypt (referring to Ex. xv. 2, 18). They said to him: Yes, Yes. [God answered:] If you have taken my Kingdom upon you, take also my Commandments: 'Thou shalt have not other God but me" (Ex. xx. 3). Here (Lev. xviii. 2) it says, "I am Jehovah your God". I am he whose Kingdom you took upon yourselves at Sinai. They said to him: Yes, Yes. [God answered:] If you have taken my Kingdom upon you, take also my Commandments: "After the manner of the land of Egypt . . . ye shall not do."[222]

While an abstraction, a cipher for obedience to the law, the kingdom yet maintains a symbolic potential since it is more than the commandments. What this example indicates is how a textual reference can restore the symbolic character, fight off the overcoding of seeing the kingdom simply as an abstraction for observing the law.[223]

Perrin isolates seven times in which the kingdom of God occurs in apocalyptic literature.[224] One example can stand for the group.

> But we hope in God, our Saviour
> For the might of our God is forever with mercy,
> And the Kingdom of our God is forever
> over the nations in judgement.[225]

Perrin concludes that in apocalyptic literature, the kingdom of God is "used to express the expectation of God's decisive, eschatological intervention in history and human experience."[226] Even in his last work on the kingdom, Perrin notes that "in ancient Jewish apocalyptic Kingdom of God was predominantly understood as a steno-symbol."[227] This is not an adequate description, for what actually occurs is the overcoding of

---

221. Glasson, "The Kingdom," 187–88.
222. *Sifra* on Leviticus 18.1; quoted in Manson's *Teaching*, 131.
223. Perrin (*Kingdom of God*, 95, 24–27) reads the rabbinic evidence too narrowly.
224. Ibid., 168–81. The examples are *Ps. Sol.* 5.18, 17.3; *Sib. Or.* 3.46, 767; *As. Mos.* 10.1; 1QM 6.6, 12.7; and posssibly, 1QSb 3.5, 4.26.
225. *Ps. Sol.* 17.3 (Charlesworth 2:665).
226. Perrin, *Kingdom of God*, 170.
227. Perrin, *Jesus and the Language*, 32.

the symbol so that it is allegorically interpreted as a literal kingdom. The rhetorical dissonance has been muted.

Outside apocalyptic and still contemporaneous with the language of Jesus, the kaddish exhibits kingdom language similar to Jesus' usage:

> Magnified and sanctified be his great name in the world that he has created according to his will.
> May he establish his kingdom in your lifetime and in your days and in the lifetime of all the house of Israel, even speedily and at a near time.[228]

Here the kingdom is a symbol, since the referent is left to the hearer, yet "to establish a kingdom" is certainly within normal usage and so may be only a metaphor for God as King.

Beyond the references in rabbinic literature and those noted by Perrin from apocalyptic literature, Bruce Chilton has called attention to targumic usage of "kingdom of God" that is strikingly similar to Synoptic usage. Although again the usage is infrequent, it is distinctive. He quotes six examples that he considers to be from the first century (dismissing two as much later). A phrase from the *Targum of Isaiah* is typical:

> . . . because the kingdom of the LORD of hosts will be revealed on Mount Zion [MT: because the LORD of hosts reigns on Mount Zion].[229]

For the kingdom "to be revealed" is familiar from rabbinic literature,[230] and the Targumim may bridge the first-century usage and that of the rabbis. But here the kingdom is not a cipher for observing the law. In agreement with normal Synoptic usage, the Targumim employ "kingdom of God." Thus the phrases "kingdom of God," "kingdom of the heavens," and "kingdom of the Lord of hosts" have currency in the first century, and their referent is not at all precise but *content nebula*, indicating a plastic symbolic character.

The stereotyped form of the targumic quotations suggests that they are plays on a common confession of which Tg. Isa. 40:9 and 52:7 may be the model. "The kingdom of your God is revealed" (MT: "Behold your God" [Isa. 40:9]; "Your God reigns" [Isa. 52:7]). The kingdom is both present and future; it awaits only to be revealed. As Chilton concludes,

> The kingdom here is not . . . simply a periphrasis for the verb *mlk* [to rule]; it is neither an autonomous regime nor does it merely refer to the LORD's assertion of sovereignty. . . . the evidence of the Tg Isaiah shows that all the

228. Quoted in ibid., 28.
229. *Tg. Isa.* 24:23; quoted in Chilton's "Regnum Dei Deus Est," 265–67.
230. As Chilton ("Regnum Dei Deus Est," 265) notes, quoting Dalman (*Words of Jesus*, 97) and Moore (*Judaism* 2:374).

time we have been talking about aspects of God's activity, which cannot be limited by time.[231]

In searching diligently for the background against which to decipher Jesus' use of "kingdom," modern scholarship has tended to opt for apocalyptic. But this has overcoded the symbol of the kingdom of God, thus misconstruing it as an apocalyptic concept for the end time. It is not as though the kingdom of God as symbol cannot be used in an apocalyptic system; it can, and Perrin has indicated the evidence. Yet as a symbol it opens onto a much wider spectrum. It varies from the kaddish and the Targumim, especially that of Isaiah, where it is used as a confession, to the later rabbinic coding of it for the yoke of the law. All this merely points out that as a symbol it is polyvalent. Its textual implication indicates how the symbol functions, effects meaning. Symbol functions within a discourse, not abstracted from that discourse.

In Jesus' language the primary discourse for the kingdom's implication is the parables, which set the context for discovering or interpreting the symbol. Precisely the kingdom's symbolic character demands that the transference be from parable (discourse) to kingdom (symbol). But the issue is more complex because kingdom as symbol is not vacuous. As image it conjures up the metaphor "God is a king," the history and mythology of Israel as God's kingdom, and the notions of power and strength associated with kings and kingdoms. These associations are part of the signified, the structural network, implied in the symbol. When the symbol is encompassed in a discourse, the discourse can either exploit these notions (epiphor) or turn against the associations (diaphor). Most common metaphors are epiphoric: the associations are bearers of the implied symbolic meaning. But in the Jesus tradition, the relation is frequently diaphoric: Jesus' discourse changes or challenges the implied structural network of associations. To situate "kingdom" in a discourse that begins with a woman taking leaven and hiding it violates the primary associations of male power and moral goodness, driving a hearer into symbolic disjunction. It is at this point that parabolic discourse can be described as paradoxical.[232]

How then are we to view the parable? The quotation from *Midrash Rabbah* on the Song of Songs provides the most helpful metaphor I know: Solomon put handles on the Torah. In the Jesus tradition, parables are handles on the symbol of the kingdom of God; they enfold and

231. Chilton, "Regnum Dei Deus Est," 268.
232. Against Crossan (*Cliffs of Fall*, 2), who locates paradox in the essence of parable.

encompass the symbol. By means of parable one penetrates to the mystery of the kingdom—but only in parable. Mark's promise to deliver the secret of the kingdom outside the parable is as illusory now as it was in his own story.

Perhaps a way to speak about this in nonparabolic language is as Ricoeur does when he says that the kingdom of God qualifies[233] the parables. At first glance, this would seem to argue for a direction of transference contrary to what I have maintained. But such is not the case, since the symbol of the kingdom of God gives a parable its specific religious content. By means of this qualification, symbol and discourse "converge upon an extreme point which becomes their point of encounter with the infinite."[234] Or as Eco remarks, a symbol is both full and empty—full with a hearer's expectation and empty awaiting discourse to give it specification. Thus the mediate referent of a parable is the kingdom of God, but the ultimate referent is human existence qualified by what Ricoeur calls the limit-experiences.[235] Narrative becomes parable when it enters into the kingdom's field of reference. A hearer confronts simultaneously story and the expectations implied in the kingdom of God, expectations drawn from the religious heritage's repertoire. Just as a hearer must make sense of the story, so also he or she must make sense of the relation between story (discourse) and the kingdom.

The hearing and grasping of a parable is a process leading a hearer through a series of stages. We expect it as a *mashal* to be laid beside something; we know that its literal first level is for the sake of an unexpressed something else, that it is the expression for an unknown content. But just understanding the narrative is not sufficient, for it is laid beside or is handles for the symbol of the kingdom of God. It is in laying a narrative beside a symbol that parable occurs, for symbol is implicated in the parable's discourse. The kingdom makes narrative religious; the narrative discloses the kingdom; together they create parable.

233. Ricoeur, "Biblical Hermeneutics," esp. 119ff.
234. Ibid., 109.
235. Ibid., 34, 122–28.

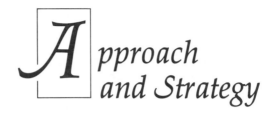

*A*pproach
and Strategy

Corpus of Parables

We do not approach the parables with a *tabula rasa*. We carry with us a history of scholarship and, more importantly, traditions of interpretation. Both the method and format for dealing with parables should respect the parable, the tradition that follows in its wake, and the history of scholarship that has sought to illuminate it.

Having decided what a parable is, we must sort through the Jesus material and identify those parables which will make up the corpus. Although the history of scholarship provides ready-made lists, they must be approached with care because too often they make assumptions no longer valid. Besides the issue of what constitutes the list of parables, we must decide the question of authenticity. Which structure of which parables has the highest claim to derive from Jesus?

Even though Perrin's dictum states that the burden of proof falls on the one who would claim the authenticity of a saying,[1] the case with the parables is otherwise. Here the burden of proof should fall on the one who would claim that the originating structure of a parable is not from Jesus. My reasons for reversing the burden of proof are threefold:

1. The parable genre does not appear in the Hebrew Bible nor in Hellenistic literature. There are short, narrative fictions, but they do not

1. Perrin, *Rediscovering the Teaching*, 39.

63

use the distinctive formula "it is like." The ingredients for the genre are present, but the particular configuration does not occur.

2. Although parables are frequent in the rabbinic tradition after the Mishnah, they are strikingly lacking in the preserved traditions of the Pharisees from before 70 C.E. When later parables do occur, they appear in the regularized context of exegesis. The lack of parables in Neusner's survey is all the more striking given his general conclusion that both Jewish and Christian traditions around the time of the destruction of the temple "exhibit much the same literary and formal tendencies." We should not push this evidence too far. It does not indicate the uniqueness of Jesus' parables, because it is an argument from silence based on preserved traditions. But it does block those who argue that parable telling was widespread (e.g., Ignace Zeigler, among many others) and shifts the burden of proof to those who would argue against the authenticity of a parable.[2]

3. The absence of parables in the Hebrew Bible and in the traditions of the Pharisees is even more striking when it is taken together with the relative paucity of parables in the early Christian traditions. Only the Synoptic Gospels, Q, the *Gospel of Thomas*, and the *Apocryphon of James*[3] contain parables. Outside these texts no parables occur.[4] The tradition was not as creative in regard to parables as it was with other elements of the Jesus tradition.

These three observations do not prove the authenticity of Jesus' parables—that all the parables go back to Jesus. Rather, they shift the burden of proof to those who would argue that a parable or its originating structure is not from Jesus.

The lack of evidence does not allow us to argue that Jesus as parable teller was unique, that the genre was sui generis. Others were creating parables, were performing the traditional thesaurus or repertoire, as the stock character of Jesus' own parables evidences. But the scarcity of parables in the preserved tradition indicates that creativity was not widespread. Those who preserved Jesus' parables were not passing on memorized texts but were themselves performing the originating structure, tailoring the performance to fit the situation. Just as we pass on a joke without memorizing it but by performing it anew in different situations, so we should imagine the tradition in its constant reperformance of the inherited Jesus structures. Those performances were creative, and we must reckon with the possibility that the performers created new parables or imitated existing patterns. In the case of the latter it may

2. The evidence for the first two points is given on pp. 13–19 above.
3. Hedrick, "Kingdom Sayings."
4. See Stroker, *Extra-Canonical Sayings*.

indeed be difficult to determine if a parable is from Jesus or created in imitation of his parables. For example The Merchant (Matt. 13:45–46) has probably been conformed to The Treasure in the actual performance of Matthew's Gospel.

Assuming the integrity of the parable tradition is not the same as assuming that all the parables come directly from Jesus. As we have just indicated, the tradition was creative, not passive. The extensive scholarship on the parables since Jülicher alerts us to where problems exist. We must pay attention to serious challenges to the authenticity of a parable, and objections must be answered. It is not enough to fall back on the assumed integrity of the tradition. For example, since Jülicher serious challenges have been mounted to the authenticity of A Man Planted a Vineyard (Mark 12:1–12) because of the reference to the "son." If the son is Jesus, it is impossible to understand how the parable can go back to Jesus. Who, after all, in the original audience would have understood the allusion?

How, then, do we assess the issues of authenticity? How can we detect whether a parabolic structure derives from Jesus? How do we sort out those parables whose claim to belong to the corpus is suspect? First, those parables that reflect common wisdom are not verifiable: they may be from Jesus but they may not. This is, of course, a restatement of the negative criterion, and by excluding common wisdom we risk presenting an eccentric portrait of the Jesus material.[5] But since the parables belong to the wisdom tradition and that tradition tends toward commonality, the presence of common wisdom adds nothing.

To state the issue positively, I am looking for the "voice" of the parables. By "voice," I mean those distinct elements in the style of the language. The argument involves an unavoidable circularity. To determine what the distinctive elements of the voice are we must rely initially on scholarship's identification of a core of parables as authentic. The circularity is broken somewhat by the rarity of the parable genre at the time of Jesus and in the later Christian tradition.

The notion of voice implies a distinctive, creative presence. Yet this is not the historical Jesus in the sense of Jesus as author of the parables. Rather, it is a reconstruction of the implied speaker/author of the corpus of parables. If those parables exhibit a consistency (and to show that they do was the burden of my earlier work, *Jesus, Symbol-Maker for the Kingdom*), then we can reconstruct the implied author. The implied author is not to be identified with the real author. They are distinct. According to Seymour Chatman, the implied author "instructs us

5. Keck, (*Future*, 33–34) warns against the distorting effect of the negative criterion.

silently, through the design of the whole, with all the voices, by all the means it has chosen to let us learn."[6] Thus, when we speak of the Jesus of the parables, we are dealing with the implied author, the implied speaker, of those parables, who is a construct, a projection, of the parables.

This distinction parallels one James Williams has drawn between proverb and aphorism. What is decisive "is the difference in principle between a *collective* voice and an *individual* voice."[7] The construct of the implied author of the parables represents a distinctive, individual voice whose patterns, accents, styles, themes, and even ideology are recognizable. This is to be distinguished from other parables whose implied author is "anonymous," the projection of common wisdom.

The most important characteristic of this distinctive voice is to borrow a musical metaphor, a tendency to play in minor keys. Employing traditional stories and plots and stereotyped characterizations, the parables invoke not the major themes of the tradition but its minor ones. The most obvious example of a minor key, although not usually noticed as one, is found in the fact that the presiding symbol of Jesus' language is the kingdom of God, a relatively infrequent term in the first century. The more dominant themes such as those of the day of the Lord, or of God as king, or even of the Torah, are virtually suppressed in the Jesus parables.

This preference for the minor key looms even in the parables themselves. The Land of a Rich Man draws on a common mytheme that pertains to greed, a major problem in a limited-goods society like first-century Palestine. Since wealth is finite, what the rich man possesses is not available for distribution. Greed, then, is a denial of community. The *Thomas* version of this parable represents this major theme: the rich man of that parable seeks to use his money to make more money. Since *Thomas* takes a negative view of merchants, this is not surprising. The voice of the *Thomas* parable is common wisdom. But the Lukan version differs. There the problem is not the accumulation of wealth (greed) but its disposal, or rather the lack of disposal. This represents a very minor theme in the tradition and discloses a distinctive voice.

In A Man Had Two Sons, there is the traditional mytheme of two sons, one elder and the other younger, in which the sons play stereotyped roles. The elder son, usually loyal and upright, is rejected in favor of the younger son, usually in the role of a rogue. This mytheme was used by Israel as part of its own self-identification. At the conclusion of the Jesus parable, when an audience expects the father to reject the elder son for his protest at the younger son's reception, the father instead

6. Chatman, *Story and Discourse*, 148.
7. Williams, *Those Who Ponder Proverbs*, 80.

responds, "Child, you are always with me and all that is mine is yours"—a profound shock to the audience's expectations.

Even in the use of stereotypes the parables play against expectation. A Grain of Mustard Seed employs a common metaphor that suggests that the parable will develop a theme of smallness, since the mustard seed is proverbially small. Instead, at the parable's conclusion the incongruous theme of the great cedar of Lebanon is introduced. The third servant in A Man Entrusts Property charges the master with an accusation that represents the peasant's classic stereotype of a master: "I know that you are a hard man, reaping where you did not sow, gathering when you did not scatter." Yet the master had behaved in no such way toward the first two servants. The hearer is left in a quandary over whether to trust common wisdom or how the master has behaved toward the first two servants.

Playing in a minor key correlates with what others have noticed as the world-shattering or unexpected character of the parables. World-shattering as it is, the language of apocalyptic and existentialism may be too dramatic. As a metaphor, however, it indicates the effect of language that works against the hearer's expectation.

In each of these parables which play against the expectations of common wisdom, a distinctive voice speaks, and from the characteristics of that voice we can reconstruct the implied speaker/author. But that voice is in jeopardy because, even though these parables come out of and play against common wisdom, in the end common wisdom frequently wins. Each of these parables has been reclaimed by common wisdom, either in the performance of the structure, as in the case of *Thomas*'s version of The Land of a Rich Man, or outside the performance, in the parable's interpretation. The common wisdom of interpretation has often removed the parable's fangs. In each of the above parables the expected mytheme has overwhelmed the parable so that most people think that the elder brother is punished, the mustard seed grows into a great tree, or the master is cruel. This contest between the distinctive voice and common wisdom is a central problem in the parables' interpretation.

The contest between common wisdom and distinctive voice furnishes a two-edged criterion. On the one hand, it says that those parables which exhibit only common wisdom do not belong to the Jesus corpus. On the other hand, it says that those which exhibit the minor key, the contest with common wisdom, do belong to the corpus. But the problem is not quite that simple, for the issue often involves the ability of an interpreter to reconstruct the common wisdom of the period, to be sensitive to the clues contained in the parable's narrative when it invokes that wisdom tradition. Even more, we must imagine how a parable would function in the matrix of Jesus' language. The issue is not *Sitz im Leben* as conceived by Jeremias but reconstructing the linguistic, mythical, and wisdom traditions in which the parables operate as a semantic phenomenon.

Imagination is an important reconstructive tool, and its failure can prematurely cut off avenues. For example, coherence between a parable and the themes of an evangelist is a priori evidence not of evangelical composition but only of performance. If a parable did not cohere with the themes, it would not be preserved and performed. More often, the issue is imagining the parable outside the Gospel narrator's point of view, imagining the parable not as imagined by the Gospel narrator but with the parable's implied speaker as narrator.

The classic example of this use of imagination has already been mentioned in Funk's analysis of From Jerusalem to Jericho. The narration of Luke's Gospel had determined the story as an example story, an example of being a good neighbor. Funk challenged this by questioning the Lukan point of view as arbiter of meaning and by imagining the parable as metaphor within the language of Jesus. The result was a quite different reading of the parable. Yet the parable still exhibits themes (Samaritan, care of neighbor) that are typical of Luke. Likewise in A Rich Man Clothed in Purple, many themes from Luke are on display: the contrast between wealth and poverty, the use of father Abraham, and the failure of belief in the resurrection. But only this last theme is suspect, for it betrays the concerns of the early community and not those of a Jewish Jesus.

This example brings into view a major criterion for excluding parables from the Jesus corpus: they are to be excluded when they reflect exclusively the concerns of the early Christian community. Yet even this requires caution, for surely the concerns of Jesus and those of the early communities overlap. But where the parables seem more concerned with community maintenance, we will be safe in locating their own creation. Two parables, The Wheat and Tares and Ten Virgins, appear to be excluded on the basis of this criterion. A careful examination of each parable will illustrate the criterion.

Excursus: The Case against Two Parables

The Wheat and Tares. Anyone defending the authenticity of The Wheat and Tares (Matt. 13:24–30; *Gos. Thom.* 20) faces a thicket of problems not easily penetrated. Since Jülicher argued that Matthew created the parable, he has not lacked for supporters.[8] Some have seen the parable as created

8. For a summary of positions, see Kingsbury, *Parables of Jesus*, 65. Kingsbury's observations on the parable and its interpretation are still extremely acute.

out the fragments of Mark's parable A Man Casts Seed or as a creation of Matthew to fit his allegory. What challenges these interpretations is the existence of another version of the parable in the *Gospel of Thomas*, because if Matthew created the parable, how do we explain *Thomas*'s version, granted this Gospel's independence from a written Synoptic Gospel?[9] Therefore we must work with the presupposition that both Matthew and *Thomas* are performances of an inherited structure. Complicating the matter is the observation that the *Thomas* text is so elliptical that it seems to demand a Synoptic-like version to understand it. The collapsing and expanding of parables is common in rabbinic literature. Jacob Petuchowski quotes an example of a parable of Yohanan ben Zakkai that in Tosephta is so elliptical as to be unintelligible but in *Midrash Debharim Rabba* (10th cent. C.E.) is very long. Most probably neither version is what ben Zakkai literally spoke.[10] So also Matthew may be too detailed and *Thomas* not detailed enough.[11]

Assuming, then, that Matthew and *Thomas* are extant versions of the same originating structure, we will examine the similarities and differences line by line.

Matthew: the kingdom of heaven may be compared

Thomas: the kingdom of the Father is like

Both begin with a comparison to the kingdom, so that is probably part of the originating structure.[12] The next three phrases are also similar. Matthew is more specific in each phrase:

Matthew: a man who sowed good seed in his field

Thomas: a man who had [good] seed

Matthew: but while men were sleeping, his enemy came

Thomas: his enemy came at night

Matthew: and sowed weeds among this wheat and went away

Thomas: and sowed weeds among the good seed

At this point Matthew continues the narrative with no parallel in *Thomas:*

Matthew: so when the plants came up and bore grain, then the weeds appeared also and the servants of the householder came and said to him, "Sir, did you not sow good seed in your field? How then has it weeds?" He said to them, "An enemy has done this."

The continuation of the plot requires the appearance of the grain and weeds together, and the absence of this in *Thomas* makes that performance difficult to understand. The dialogue reproduces the narrator's comment, a

---

9. See pp. 32–33 above. Gundry (*Matthew*, 265), aware of this problem, argues that Matthew's creation of the parable rules out extracanonical derivation for *Thomas*. That is why it is important to base the independence of *Thomas* on formal grounds, as Solages does in "L'évangile de Thomas."

10. Petuchowski, "Theological Significance," 79.

11. See, among many, Ménard, *L'évangile selon Thomas*, 159. For references to early literature on *Thomas*, see Kingsbury, *Parables of Jesus*, 152 n. 135.

12. Kingsbury, (*Parables of Jesus*, 65) argues that it was Matthean, but even though it is a favorite of Matthew's, that seems unlikely here. *Thomas* uses the phrase "kingdom of the Father" frequently; see, e.g., *Gos. Thom.* 3.

literary device of which Matthew is fond.[13] Since the accent on the mixed nature of the harvest tallies with Matthew's ecclesiological interest, his expansion at this point is not surprising:

Matthew: the servants said to him, "Then do you want us to go and gather them?" But he said, "No . . ."

Thomas: the man did not allow them to pull up the weeds

Matthew continues in dialogue but the underlying structure is the same:

Matthew: lest in gathering the weeds you root up the wheat along with them

Thomas: he said to them, "I am afraid that you will go intending to pull up the weeds and pull up the wheat along with them"

Matthew: let both grow together until the harvest; and at harvest time I will tell the reapers, "Gather the weeds first and bind them in bundles to be burned, but gather the wheat into my barn"

Thomas: for on the day of the harvest the weeds will be plainly visible, and they will be pulled up and burned

Even though Matthew's theological interests are plainly at stake here,[14] one would have to say that both Matthew and *Thomas* are performing an originating structure that is compatible with their hermeneutical performance. And that is the problem. For although one can isolate the underlying structure, that structure easily fits the needs of the primitive church to explain "whether it should expel from its ranks those whose lives are in some way evil."[15] Setting up boundaries is part of community building; attacking them appears to represent Jesus' position (e.g., From Jerusalem to Jericho; Two Men Went Up to the Temple). Lacking any compelling argument for the parable's coherence with Jesus' preaching of the kingdom, one must assume that such preaching derives from the early Christian community.

Ten Virgins. The parable Ten Virgins is another whose authenticity has been strongly contested. Jülicher, Dodd, and Jeremias have defended its authenticity;[16] Bultmann, Günther Bornkamm, and Erich Grässer have rejected it as a Matthean allegory.[17] Recently the debate has been rejoined with Karl Donfried arguing for Matthean creation and Armand Tarrech making a case for its authenticity.[18] Since Tarrech's analysis is the most thorough, I shall use it as the point of departure.

Tarrech summarizes the positions of those who argue against the par-

---

13. Kingsbury, *Parables of Jesus,* 65; for references, see p. 152 n. 137.
14. So ibid., among many others.
15. Beare, *Gospel according to Matthew,* 305.
16. Jülicher, *Die Gleichnisreden* 2:457; Dodd, *Parables,* 136–39; Jeremias, *Parables,* 51-53.
17. Bultmann, *History of the Synoptic Tradition,* 119; Bornkamm, "Die Verzögerung Parusie," 46–55; Grässer, *Das Problem,* 125–27.
18. Donfried, "Allegory," 415–28; Tarrech, *La parabole des dix vierges.*

able's authenticity.[19] The late arrival of the bridegroom is unexplained, and there is no mention of a bride. The late hour of the night does not correspond to the marriage customs of the day,[20] and finally, the delay of the Parousia explains the story's various elements.[21] Donfried goes further and shows that the allegory both makes the story incoherent and fits so well with Matthew's themes and redaction that it must be considered his creation. The fifth discourse in which this parable occurs revolves around practicing (*poieō*) and keeping (*tereō*) what Jesus has commanded, and is dominated by stories of contrast: two men, one taken and one left, and two women, one taken and one left, then an admonition to watch for the day of the Lord (24:40–42); the faithful and unfaithful servants whose master comes at an unknown hour and punishes the faithless servant (24:45–51); the five foolish and five wise maidens waiting for a delayed bridegroom (25:1–13); and the five- and two-talent men who enter into the joy of their master and the one-talent man cast into the outer darkness (25:14–30). The coming of the master and eschatological judgment dominate the discourse. Thus Matthew deals with the delay of the Parousia with a double strategy. The church is both to watch and to be prepared.[22]

In response to this argument, Tarrech has pointed to two overlooked issues. Few commentators notice in the dialogue of the maidens the scandalous way in which the wise ones treat the foolish and, even more important, the redactional nature of vv. 5–7a and 10c–12 which transforms the story into a concentrated résumé of Matthean theology (ideology).[23] The key to Tarrech's argument lies in his accepting an analysis much like Donfried's of Matthew's redactional intention but then using that to understand how Matthew might have performed and transformed the parable. Matthew's concerns are watching, waiting, being prepared, and judgment. These concerns are most evident in vv. 10c–13: the door is shut and judgment takes place. This leads him to argue that v. 5—"as the bridegroom was delayed, they all slumbered and slept"—reflects the delay of the Parousia. Moreover, this was a major element in the parable that Bornkamm had found incompatible with Palestinian marriage customs. If v. 5 is redactional, then so is v. 7a, the rising of the maidens from slumber, and v. 1c, "went to meet the bridegroom," may also be due to attraction to v. 5.[24] Tarrech argues that v. 6a, "at midnight," was added in the oral tradition and suggested to Matthew the slumber motif. It seems more likely that it is part of Matthew's allegorical performance. Tarrech is unsure whether v. 2 is part of the originating structure, but it is redundant, since the foolishness

19. Tarrech, *La parabole des dix vierges*, 125–29.
20. Bornkamm stresses this point in "Die Verzögerung Parusie."
21. So Grässer, *Das Problem*, 121.
22. Donfried, "Allegory," 420–21.
23. Tarrech, *La parabole des dix vierges*, 139.
24. Tarrech (ibid., 143–79) mounts an elaborate "lexicale, lexico-syntatique et syntactico-stylistique" analysis of the parable to back up his arguments. These are interesting but at times seem to me to be overkill.

and wisdom of the maidens is something the hearer would soon discover, and so it is the kind of formula that would be added in repeated perform-ances.[25]

Tarrech's reconstruction reads,

> Then the kingdom of heaven shall be compared to ten maidens who took their lamps and went to meet the bridegroom. Five of them were foolish, and five were wise. For when the foolish took their lamps, they took no oil with their lamps; but the wise took flasks of oil with their lamps and trimmed them. And the foolish said to the wise, "Give us some of your oil, for our lamps are going out." But the wise replied, "Perhaps there will not be enough for us and for you; go rather to the dealers and buy for yourselves." And while they went to buy, the bridegroom came, and those who were ready went in with him to the marriage feast.

Though Tarrech's reconstruction is interesting and plausible, it fails to convince, because there is no imaginative reconstruction of how this par-able would fit into the language of Jesus, how as parable it references the kingdom, or how it coheres with the distinctive voice of the parable teller. Further, the reconstructed parable still revolves around who is in and who is out, concerns of community building and maintenance. On the evidence of the other parables, Jesus is concerned more about eliminating bound-aries than about creating them (e.g., From Jerusalem to Jericho). And fin-ally, the parable is dominated by common wisdom. The roles of its char-acters are predictable; it does not play against expectations and so does not exhibit a distinctive voice.

Strategy

After a review of the problems in assessing a corpus of parables, it is time to turn attention to the parables' arrangement, for every ordering prejudices the answer. Ideally the arrangement should be dictated by the data themselves.

Jülicher divided his famous commentary into two massive parts. Part 1, "The Parables of Jesus in General," ran to 322 pages of text. In five chapters he dealt with the genuineness and the nature, purpose, worth, and design of the parables. In a final chapter, which constitutes a third of volume 1, he surveyed the history of interpretation. Volume 2 consti-tuted his exegesis of the parables. Each parable was dealt with sepa-rately under the headings of the appropriate forms: *Die Gleichnisse* (Similes), *Die Parabeln* (Parables), and *Die Beispielerzählungen* (Example stories). The advantage of Jülicher's format is that each parable is dealt with individually; the disadvantage is that he has classified the parables

---

25. Tarrech (ibid., 181) exhibits in diagram from his reconstruction.

under form-critical categories that do not adequately account for the material.

Most subsequent parable commentators have not chosen to emulate Jülicher. Dodd has organized the parables of the kingdom under three headings: "The Setting in Life," "Parables of Crisis," and "Parables of Growth." Jeremias encapsulated the parables under the general heading of "The Message of the Parables of Jesus," but this message looks conspicuously like an outline of the history of salvation: now is the day, mercy for sinners, great assurance, imminence of catastrophe, may be too late, challenge, discipleship, *via dolorosa*, and exaltation of the Son of man, the consummation. Crossan follows Heidegger's categories of time: parables of advent, reversal, and action. Many other examples could be elaborated.

These various organizational plans, by subordinating the parable to some scheme outside the parable, view the individual parable from the perspective of the scheme. Jülicher's instinct to treat the parables individually was correct, since such a method allows for a parable to develop its own polysemy without reference to an overall scheme.

And yet an interpreter's mind recoils at a purely random arrangement of the parables. Is there no scheme or pattern that would at least help to organize them? Following up on the common observation that the parables draw on everydayness, I have employed three of the elementary aspects of Mediterranean social life and culture as basic categories for the parables. Society in the ancient Mediterranean basin was divided along two axes. The horizontal axis reached out from the family to organize the social exchange of the society; the vertical axis centered on client-patron relations to organize society's power exchange. Finally, the artifacts of daily life were often used to symbolize the larger transcendent values of life.

The horizontal axis, the axis of social exchange, has as its archetype the family. In Mediterranean societies, social organization moves out in concentric circles from the family, the central social unit. Family defines what is "inside"; away from the family is "outside." Farthest away from family is the foreigner, one completely outside. Where one fits within the circles defines who one is and how others behave toward one. If one moves far enough outside, one is a foreigner. A group of parables I have entitled "Family, Village, City, and Beyond" exploit this concentric organization of society. They fall into three groups, family parables, village parables, and parables about the city and beyond, a beyond that runs even to a Samaritan, who is definitely outside.

A second group of parables, "Master and Servants," embodies the model of client and patron. Since the vertical axis is primarily a way of organizing power exchanges, these parables normally involve a test between master and servant. There are two groups of these parables. In one the departure and return of the master provides an occasion for a test; in the second group an accounting scene serves the same function.

The third and final group of parables invest the artifacts of daily life with metaphorical and symbolic significance. Almost like magic, like talismans, things receive value as a way of locating and dividing the world into symbolic portions. These parables, which I have entitled "Home and Farm," play with the predilection to code everyday things with symbolic power. The Contents lists the parables that belong to each of these three major groups.

Mediterranean and Jewish culture employed these three elements, the horizontal and vertical organization of society as well as its everyday artifacts, to represent symbolically the organization of the sacred. Thus God was the ultimate patron for Israel, and Israel the ultimate family of God, and various objects, like unleavened bread, took the place of, were metaphors for, the sacred. The Jesus parables take these structures and patterns up into their repertoire and most often play against them so that the patron is a fool, the Samaritan is savior, and the kingdom is like leaven. Because of the importance of this social-world perspective, I begin each section with an introduction into the social dynamic involved and buttress that with a few examples selected from the parables.

With a macro classification in place to arrange the parables, there is still the question of the method for considering each individual parable. The parable itself, its history of interpretation, and the interpreter's insight set the direction. Yet a consistent strategy can be anticipated. Because parables are first of all fictions, the primary method will be literary. Even though I value the social-world studies, the social context is part of the parable's repertoire and is subsumed into the literary, fictional world of the parable.

The analysis of each parable will be divided into three major parts: they have to do with redaction, with a reading, and with the kingdom of God. Because the parables in their extant versions are performances of individual, anonymous authors (the evangelists), the first part will deal with the function of the parable in its present context(s), both the Synoptics and *Thomas*. The second part, a reading, analyzes how the originating structure effects meaning, paying attention to imaginative reconstruction of the parable in the language of Jesus. Finally, the third part will draw out the narrative's juxtaposition to the kingdom, from which emerges the parabolic effect.

Forming a bridge from the evangelists's performance to the originating structure is the parable's surface structure. The surface structure can be spotted in the mnemonic features of oral language, the use of formulas, chiasmus, wordplays, and so forth. By paying careful attention to these features, we can sketch out how the originating structure takes on form, how it oscillates between *langue* (structure) and *parole* (actual speech). One needs to be aware of these mnemonic features because they are intrinsic to the meaning effect of oral language. They are not simply ornaments or aids for memory.

The second major part in the analysis of the parable will involve a reading, an effort to construct the dynamic whereby the text as narrative seeks to structure its own perception and in turn is structured by the receiver's (hearer/reader's) response. By stressing the text as dynamic process, our literary method belongs to reception-theory analysis.[26] To aid analysis, the parable will be divided into lines so as to observe the interaction between text and receiver.

The fictive, narrative quality of parable bestows on it an independence of its immediate *Sitz im Leben*: as narrative with open meaning, parable can be used in a variety of situations. Thus we can distinguish two levels of meanings. Situational meaning is the particular meaning that a given real hearer or reader imparts to the text depending on his or her situation and context. But a second level, the literary level, concerns textual structuring, a semantics which is self-referential. To switch metaphors, this second level supports and is the condition for the first, for it provides the possibility of both multiple and specific application in the situation of Jesus and the narrative of the Gospels and in subsequent readings. This respects the autonomy of the text, the world created by the text.

The difference between the first level of situation meaning and the second level of literary meaning is highlighted by the distinction between implied reader and real reader. The implied reader is not a real reader. A real reader, active at the first level of meaning, brings the pragmatics of a specific situation to bear in the production of meaning. When Jeremias seeks the specific situation (*Sitz im Leben*) of a parable, he creates, unbeknown to himself, a fictive audience, usually the Pharisees, as the context for his "real" reading of the parable. The implied reader, however, is a textual strategy that represents the predispositions necessary for a literary work to exercise its magic. "Texts must already contain certain conditions for actualization that will allow their meaning to be assembled in the responsive mind of the recipient. . . . The implied reader designates a network of response-inviting structures, which impel the reader to grasp the text."[27]

Why should we engage in a reading or reconstruction of an implied

26. See esp. Iser, *Act of Reading;* idem, *Implied Reader.* See also *Reader-Response Criticism,* ed. Tompkins. For a broader picture, see McKnight, *The Bible and the Reader,* 58– 82.

27. Iser, *Act of Reading,* 34.

reader when parables were first performed orally? The objection has the validity of reminding us not to assume an identity between orality and literacy, something too often done in the history of scholarship. Yet at the level of narrative structure there is a relative continuity between oral and written literature.[28] What we are reconstructing is the implied receiver, whether a hearer or a reader.

Despite our agnosticism about discovering a single actual, real situation of the parable, our reading is not ahistorical. The text belongs to a specific world, a phenomenological world. Such a world refers "to the fundamental horizon or referential nexus in which consciousness apprehends and things are apprehended."[29] That world is first-century Palestine, and it forms part of the nexus in which the narrative operates and which is taken up into the text and transformed into the narrative. It informs the repertoire, the conventions, world view, ideologies, and stereotypes active in a text.

We seek to understand how a text structures meaning and the conditions it sets for its own performance. We are not looking for a single meaning hidden in or behind the text. Rather, meaning is here understood as a performative act. "The meaning of a literary text is not a definable entity but, if anything, a dynamic happening."[30]

In the final major part of each parable analysis we will explore the relation between the story and the kingdom. This adds an important dimension, because a purely literary analysis of a parable reduces its genre to simply being a narrative. More is needed because a parable is "laid beside," "parallel," and what it is laid beside is the kingdom of God. How, then, do narrative and the kingdom interact to create parable? The theoretics of this we have already discussed in dealing with referencing in the definition of parable. In this part of the analysis of each parable we will search out the interaction and intersection of narrative and the kingdom.

In each analysis of a parable, therefore, the reader can expect a progression from extant versions to narrative structure to parabolic effect. It will, of course, become obvious that the depth of any powerful narrative can never be fathomed. But I hope that the reader will discover in the parables the freedom to follow Kafka's advice: "If you only followed the parables you yourselves would become parables and with that rid of all your daily cares."[31]

28. Lord, *Singer of Tales*, 130; Scholes and Kellogg, *Nature of Narrative*, 12–17.
29. Funk, *Jesus as Precursor*, 66.
30. Iser, *Act of Reading*, 22.
31. Kafka, "On Parables," in *Parables and Paradoxes*, 11.

2

Family,
Village, City,
& Beyond

I dentity

In the ancient Mediterranean world everyone had a social map that defined the individual's place in the world. It told people who they were, who they were related to, how to react, and how to behave.[1] At the center of that map was the family, especially the father; then came the village; finally came the city and beyond, to the ends of the world. This social map furnishes a metaphorical system for the kingdom of God.

The world of Jesus' parables is the Galilean village. The parables draw their repertoire from peasant experience.[2] Only a few draw outside those narrow bounds. The parable Two Men Went Up to the Temple is alone set explicitly in a large urban setting. Some imply urban characters—for example, absentee landlords or the priest and Levite in the parable of the Good Samaritan. When urban characters do appear, they normally play negative roles, as is fitting for parables told from a peasant's point of view.

Family

In a peasant society the family rotates around the father. He and the mother form the basic biological dyad and, by virtue of interrelations

1. The map analogy was suggested by Jerome Neyrey in an unpublished paper, "The Idea of Purity in Mark's Gospel."
2. According to Dodd (*Parables*, 10), the parables are a reliable index to peasant life in the ancient world.

with children and siblings, generate the other fundamental dyads of society.[3] A peasant's economic goal is to maintain the family,[4] not to build a surplus for investment. The father represents the family, and the family's maintenance is his chief concern. Correspondingly, peasant families favor socialization techniques that make the child dependent on the family, so as to maintain it. This, of course, creates tension when new roles for family members emerge, as for example at times of inheritance or death.[5]

Two of Jesus' parables embody the family situation, and both revolve around a father and two sons at times of stress. In A Man Had Two Children (Matt. 21:28–31a) the family's support is at issue; A Man Had Two Sons (Luke 15:11–32; see chap. 2 below) is an elaborate narrative of dangers provoked by inheritance and a consequent new role for the younger son.

A Man Had Two Children

A man had two children. And coming to the first one he said, "Child, go today and work in the vineyard." And he answered and said, "I don't want to." Afterwards he regretted and went. Coming to the other he said the same. And he answered and said, "I will, sir." And he didn't go. (Matt. 21:28–30)

The text critical problems in A Man Had Two Children are more likely problems of parabolic performance than has commonly been suspected. In the textual tradition there are three versions, which are schematized in table 2.

Table 2

Three Versions

	I	II	III
First son	no/goes	yes/does not	no/goes
Second son	yes/does not	no/goes	yes/does not
Answer	first	second	last
		(last)	

In version I, the first son says that he will not go, then changes his mind and goes, while the second son says yes he will go but then does not. In reply to which son does the father's will, the audience replies that it is the first. If version I is original, then version II is a simple scribal reversal,

---

3. Wolf, *Peasants*, 61–62.
4. Diaz, "Economic Relations," 51.
5. Wolf, *Peasants*, 73.

and vice versa if version II is original. The narrative remains the same with the order reversed.

Version III moves in a surprisingly different direction, for the audience responds that the son who says that, yes, he will go, but does not, is the one who does his father's will. Some text critics have favored version III because it is the more difficult reading;[6] others have called version III nonsensical[7] because it violates the sense of the Matthean context. But does it violate the parable itself? We thus begin with the Matthean context and ask about the underlying parabolic structure.

The parable is the first of three that challenge the legitimacy of the Jewish leadership. They all expose Matthew's ideology[8] of the true Israel, demonstrating the claims of the Pharisees to be false and those of the church true.[9] The parables of the two sons, the wicked tenants, and the king who gave a marriage feast exhibit a progression from John the Baptist to the rejection of Jesus and punishment of those who rejected him through the final judgment, when those without a wedding garment will be cast out.

In comparison with Mark, Matthew unfolds this scene of debate in the temple with three initial parables. Only the parable of the wicked tenants is parallel to Mark. When the Jewish leaders challenge Jesus' authority, he responds with a question about John's baptism: "Whence was it? From heaven or from men?" (21:25). This provides the occasion for the first parable of the two sons, which he applies to John the Baptist: John came to the Jewish leaders and they did not believe, but the tax collectors and harlots did (v. 32). Since John and Jesus are strongly aligned in Matthew's Gospel,[10] the same pattern by implication applies to Jesus and to the church. The parable parallels the question that provokes the three parables, and Matthew's design emerges, at least in outline. In the first confrontation the Jewish leaders are on the offensive, but Jesus' question about John leaves them unable to answer. The question is a conundrum, so the debate is unresolved. The parable carries forward the debate with the question "What do you think?"; and its concluding question, "Which of the two did the will of his father?" forces the Jewish leaders to answer, thus convicting themselves when Jesus

6. E.g., Lachmann, Merx, Wellhausen, Hirsch; see also Metzger, *Textual Commentary*, 55. Michaels ("Parable," 15–26) offers a suggestive reconstruction of the history of the textual tradition. Unfortunately his solution requires an untenable reconstruction of the original text. He correctly accents the influence of the oral tradition. Cadoux (*Parables*, 117–18) accepts this version as more in accord with oriental custom.

7. E.g., the editors of Metzger's *Textual Commentary*; see pp. 55–56.

8. Uspensky, *Poetics of Composition*, 8–16.

9. See chap. 10 below, as well as chap. 5.

10. Wink, *John the Baptist*, 33–39.

applies the parable to their response to John. The unresolved first confrontation finds resolution in the second.

The structure of the first confrontation is clear:

Question/counterquestion (vv. 23–25a)
Logic of conundrum (vv. 25b-26)
Response/counterresponse (v. 27)

The implied reader knows that Jesus has convicted his challengers, but the fictional audience does not—for in fiction the controversy leads to a draw. The parable reopens the controversy, forcing the leaders to answer. Here is the structure:

Question/parable (vv. 28–30)
Question/answer (v. 31a)
Conviction (v. 31b)
Application (v. 32)

In this structure the leaders' answer and the application, which exposes the logic, are public. The conviction "Truly, I say to you, the tax collectors and the harlots go into the kingdom of God before you" precedes the parable's application that makes this conviction evident. By drawing the argument into the open, Matthew cements a reader with the narrator's ideology. The reader is convinced of Israel's false character, while by implication the church is the true Israel.

At a macro level, we can observe Matthew's careful weaving of the parable into the narrative context. The question "What do you think?" which is surely Matthean,[11] draws attention not to the parable but to the question it provokes. The parable exemplifies one of Matthew's chief accusations against the Pharisees, that they say but do not do the right thing.[12] The parable and its application band together with a clever word-recall scheme that contrasts the positive son's plot with that of Jewish leaders.

"I do not wish," and *afterwards regretting* he went (v. 29)
"and you seeing *did not regret afterwards* so as to believe" (v. 32).

The phrase "afterwards regretting" is repeated in the last line but in reverse order with the participle becoming the main verb. There is an ironic twist even at the level of grammar, for the son's regretting pro-

---

11. So Grundmann, *Das Evangelium nach Lukas*, 457; *Matthew*, 422, 355–56. The question occurs six times in Matthew, never in the other Synoptics, and once in John (11:56). Twice there is no Synoptic parallel: in A Man Had Two Sons, and in 17:25, about the payment of the temple tax. In the other four cases there are parallel Synoptic passages but without the question (18:12; 22:17; 22:42; 26:66).

12. Trilling, *Das Wahre Israel*, 189. The key texts are 7:21; 23:2.

vokes the action to go into the vineyard but the "not regretting"[13] of the Jewish leaders becomes the description of what they did, the main action that prevents them from taking the real action, to believe.

Matthean redaction demands that one son regret his action so as to parallel the action of the tax collectors and harlots while the other say the right thing but do the wrong to parallel the response of the Jewish leaders. Thus as regards the textual question, either version I or II makes good sense within the Matthean context. The son who says no but does go to the vineyard could come first in sequence because the tax collectors and harlots are mentioned first (v. 31b), but he could just as easily come second to match the order of Jews first and then the Gentiles.[14] But this in no way explains the existence of the nonsensical version III.

Matthew's ideology demands that the son who says no but regrets must be the approved one. Therefore the answer to the question "Which one did the will of his father?" is part of the Matthean performance and not part of the original parabolic structure.[15] The parable does provoke a question, but that it demands this answer is not obvious. Answer and application are part of Matthew's performance.

Where then does version III come from? How did it happen that a minority within the textual tradition has preserved a version in which the audience responds that the one who says yes but does not go to the vineyard does did the will of his father? This version, which has good but not overwhelming support[16] and was known by Jerome in the fourth century C.E., who said it exhibited the perversity of Jesus' enemies, springs from the oral tradition and represents another performance of the parable. An examination of the parable's relation to family structure will bear this out.

A rabbinic parable with a similar theme but from the master-servant axis illustrates the problem:

> When God was about to give the Torah, no other nation but Israel would accept it. It can be compared to a man who had a field which he wished to entrust to metayers [tenant farmers]. Calling the first of these, he enquired: "Will you take over this field?" He replied: "I have no strength; the work is too hard for me." In the same way the second, third, and fourth declined to undertake the work. He called the fifth and asked him: "Will you take over this field?" He replied, "Yes." "On the condition that you will till it?" The reply was again, "Yes." But as soon as he took possession of it, he let it lie

13. Michel (*"metamēlomai"*) shows the difference between *metamēlomai* and *metanoein*.

14. So Metzger, *Textual Commentary*, 56.

15. Against Jülicher, *Die Gleichnisreden* 2:370; Bultmann, *History of the Synoptic Tradition*, 177; Jeremias, *Parables*, 80.

16. See Metzger, *Textual Commentary*, 55.

fallow. With whom is the king angry? With those who declared: "We cannot undertake it," or with him who did undertake it, but no sooner undertook it than he left it lying fallow? Surely, with him who undertook it.[17]

In this rabbinic parable all five characters offend the king, the first four by refusing his offer of a field, but even more the fifth by accepting the field and then doing nothing. The king is angry because he has been made to look foolish, to lose face. Israel concludes that even though God is angry with the nations who did not accept the Torah, he will be even more angry with those who accept the Torah but let it lie fallow, because they will embarrass his honor.

The parable of the two sons is a variation on this theme. It does not deal with the theme of "how much more angry" but exploits a fundamental problem within the peasant family system: a conflict between the demands of family and those of honor. When the parable hearer is asked to choose between the two sons, a dilemma arises. Both sons have insulted the father, one by saying no, the other by saying yes but doing nothing. But one comes to the family's aid by going into the vineyard and upholding family solidarity, while the other maintains the family's good name by appearing on the surface to be a good son. Would the father choose to be publicly honored and privately shamed, or publicly shamed and privately honored? In the first century c.e. that is not much of a choice. The real question is with which one he would be more angry. But in being forced to choose, he must choose between the apparent and the real, between one who appears to be inside the family and one who appears to be outside.

The metaphorical network invoked by the parable states that the kingdom is a family, and a father is a normal metaphor for God. In the kingdom all will be united as in a perfect family. But the father faces a problem. Which son did right? Does one choose the kingdom with public honor and no deeds or the public shame and private deeds? The parable ironically employs the metaphor of the kingdom as a family because this family is not perfect but ordinary, rife with the tensions of normal families.

The family system provides a metaphorical system for distinguishing those inside and those outside the kingdom. The social map explains who I am, where I am, and by inference who is not with me. This social structure as a metaphor for the kingdom replicates those inside and outside the kingdom. In the parable of the two sons, the audience and

---

17. *Midrash Rabbah* on Exodus 27 (Freedman 3:329); Str-B 2:865. The application is then to Israel at Sinai.

the father must choose, and there is no obvious logic for the decision. Both sons have brought shame and honor on the family. The textual tradition preserves both answers. Obviously Matthew's ideology would prefer the case of the son who says no but regretfully goes. Yet the oral tradition preserves another answer, and in time it creeps into the textual tradition. Choosing between two sons recurs in the parable A Man Had Two Sons, where father and audience will again be asked to choose between an elder and younger son, and in the end the audience will choose but the father will not.

Village

Between the family and the outside world stands the village. It plays such a key role in peasant life that primary identification is with the village,[18] as is evidenced by the use of the village name for personal identification (e.g., Jesus of Nazareth). Because of the primary role of village life, it is not surprising that a large group of Jesus' parables draw on the conventions of village life for their repertoire. The dynamic of village life furnishes another metaphorical model for envisioning the kingdom of God. There are four parables in this group: Who Has a Friend? The Land of a Rich Man (chap. 3), A Rich Man Clothed in Purple (chap. 4), and A Man Gave a Banquet (chap. 5).

Peasant communities are basically conservative and traditional in their organization and structure. In communities of long standing, people are sorted into different kinds, classes, and interrelations.[19] The duration of peasant communities leads not only to conservatism but also to external and internal pressures. There are basically three pressure points.[20] First, there is the ecosystem with its drought, famine, floods, overgrazing, and so forth. The land itself is hard put to support adequate life, and in Palestine existence was subsistent.[21] Second, the local village social system generates its own stress. Households and families are required to maintain themselves in the face of individual needs and dissatisfactions. The flight of the younger son from the family farm as in A Man Had Two Sons is not unique in a peasant world. Overpopulation and scarce land place limits on development. There is competition from competing forms of industry, plantations, and the cities. In Galilee, the high number of absentee landlords placed great pressure on peasant solidarity, as in the parables A Man Entrusts Property and A Rich Man

18. Diaz and Potter, "Social Life," 161.
19. Redfield, *Little Community*, 33.
20. Wolf, *Peasants*, 77.
21. Applebaum, "Economic Life in Palestine," *JPFC* 2:631– 700.

Had a Steward. Third and finally, the outside world pressures the village. The power of the world beyond the village puts the peasant at a great disadvantage. There are taxes, wars, harassment from the cities, and in the case of Galilee, foreign conquerors. Galilee was an oppressed, conquered land, and it generated its own guerrilla movements to respond.[22]

Pressured on all sides, peasant societies develop systems that relieve the pressure as much as possible, that spread the risk as widely as possible. So the family is never isolated. Its problems become those of every family in the village. The proverb "There but for the grace of God . . ." illustrates the common wisdom of village life. "This insight is based much less on accessions of Christian charity than on the hard-hearted realization that some aid to one's neighbor may simply be a form of insurance against the rainy day."[23] Because of outside and uncontrollable pressures, peasants are suspicious and hostile toward city elites and the state.[24] They prefer to settle disputes within the village, where all members are known as full human beings, belonging to families, work groups, and so forth.[25] But this reliance on village solidarity is based not on a romantic impulse or friendship but on the harshness of peasant life. Gossip and criticism, rampant in the village, keep others from taking advantage of one's weaknesses. Villagers cooperate on the basis of formally defined ways such as work exchange.[26] The village defends a peasant from the pressures of the outside. "Within the village the effort is to restore the torn fabric of the society,"[27] and this healing, restoring dimension most naturally furnishes a metaphorical model for the kingdom of God.

Who Has a Friend

Which one of you has a friend and goes to him at midnight and would say to him, "Friend, lend me three loaves, since my friend has come to me from off the road and I do not have anything to set before him." And that one answering from inside will say, "Do not make trouble for me; already the door is shut and my children are with me in bed. I am not able to help you." I tell you, even if he does not give to him and get up because he is his friend, yet because of

22. Rhoads, *Israel in Revolution,* 47–60.
23. Wolf, *Peasants,* 80.
24. See Applebaum, "Economic Life in Palestine," *JPFC* 2:663. Applebaum remarks that the antagonism between town and country was especially strong in Palestine.
25. Diaz and Potter, "Social Life," 162.
26. Foster, "Peasant Character," 297.
27. Diaz and Potter, "Social Life," 162.

his shamelessness he will rise up and give to him whatever he needs.

The parable Who Has a Friend? (Luke 11:5–8) exploits the tensions of peasant village life. There are no shops, and the baking is done by families; the house is a one-room dwelling, where father, wife, and children sleep together. Supporting the village exchange is hospitality, part of the basic exchange structure of village life. The parable envisions a situation in which a guest has arrived and hospitality demands a meal be placed before him. The host goes about the village gathering the ingredients for the meal. Hospitality is an important virtue in peasant and Jewish life. "Hospitality to wayfarers is as great as early attendance at the *Beth Hamidrash*. . . . Hospitality is greater than the reception of the Shechinah."[28] Hospitality is an appropriate metaphorical vehicle for the kingdom.

To meet the needs of hospitality is so unexceptional that this parable begins with an idiom—"Which one of you?"—that demands the answer "No one!"[29] It is inconceivable that a neighbor would not meet the needs of hospitality. The formula is probably not part of the originating structure but the result of performance. The formulaic question creates an awkward grammar that loses the question by the sentence's end. The future tense verbs "drift"[30] into subjunctive verbs. Indeed, a conditional form would have been more appropriate for the sense.[31] But the strong paratactic structure indicates a Semitic or oral source. A written source would have preferred subordination.[32] The grammar indicates a strong paratactic structure that the formulaic question has modified by performance.

The formulaic question is part of an arrangement that holds together the larger self-contained unit of Luke 11:1–13.[33] Verse 1 marks the introduction of both a new theme, prayer, and a new place, which is unspecified; v. 14 shifts again both theme and place. Furthermore, the section is held together by a series of key words, typical of oral tradition. Talbert

28. *b. Sabb.* 127a (Soncino 2:632); see chap. 4 below, where there is quoted the story from the *Midrash on Psalms* that makes this same point in connection with Abraham's reception of the three visitors.

29. The phrase occurs only in Lukan material or in material common with Matthew. It does not occur in Mark, nor in Matthew without parallel material in Luke. See Jeremias, *Die Sprache*, 197.

30. Plummer, *Gospel according to St. Luke*, 298.

31. BDF, 336 (1).

32. BDF, 442 (3).

33. Catchpole ("Q and 'The Friend at Midnight'") argues that Luke 11:1–13 is a Q construction that Matthew has broken up.

notes the following:[34] (*a*) "And he said to them" (vv. 2, 5);[35] (*b*) "Father" (vv. 2, 11, 13); (*c*) "bread" (v. 3), "loaves" (v. 5);[36] (*d*) "I tell you" (vv. 8, 9). Talbert overlooked the "which of you" formula in vv. 5 and 11. Whether this unit was bound together by Luke or the oral tradition, the question "Which of you?" is part of the performance, not of the parabolic structure.

Finally the parable's curious ending challenges the place of the formulaic question in the parabolic structure. The conclusion shows a careful construction, arranged in three balancing phrases:

A	B	C
1. he does not give to him /	getting up /	because he is a friend
2. because of his *anaideia* /	rising up /	he will give to him whatever he needs

The B term is the pivot; the A and C terms are set in chiasmus. The A1 and C2 phrases both revolve around "giving," but the A phrase is negative whereas C is positive. In Greek even their construction is reversed

A1: *ou dōsei* (not he-does-give)
C2: *dōsei autō hosōn chrēzei* (he-gives to-him whatever he-needs)

The "not" of A becomes "whatever he needs" in C. Likewise C1 and A2 are set in balancing parallel. The parallel words are "friend" and *anaideia*.

Anaideia means "shamelessness,"[37] and this is its meaning in Greek from the classical period[38] through the patristic.[39] Two examples will suffice. Sirach 40:28–30, in warning against a beggar's life, says, "It is better to die than to beg. When a man looks to the table of another, his existence cannot be considered as life." The warning concludes, "In the mouth of the shameless begging is sweet, but in his stomach a fire is kindled." The beggar is one who has no life, no honor, and is shameless. In *The Jewish War*, Josephus tells of a famine in which a mother eats her son. "Why tell of the shameless resort to inanimate articles of food induced by the famine, seeing that I am here about to describe an act unparalleled in the history whether of Greeks or barbarians?"[40] There is

34. Talbert, *Reading Luke,* 127.
35. Verse 5 is in the Lukan form *pros autous* instead of the dative *autois* (v. 2). The accusative construction is used only by Luke; see Zerwick, *Biblical Greek,* no. 80, 27.
36. In v. 11, the father asks for a fish, whereas in the Matthean parallel the son asks for bread. If Luke was responsible for the collection of this material by key words, why did he make the change to fish?
37. *Aidos* means "shame," and *an* is a privative: one has no shame, i.e., is shameless.
38. LSJ, 105.
39. Lampe, *Patristic Greek Lexicon,* 103.
40. Josephus, *Jewish War,* 6.199 (LCL 3:433–35).

no evidence of *anaideia* meaning anything other than "shamelessness."[41]

If the linguistic evidence is so overwhelming, why do translations and interpreters continue to understand the word as "importunity" (RSV), "inopportuneness,"[42] or "shameless persistence"?[43] Because the parable in Luke's context exemplifies persistent request in prayer, even though the connection with prayer is secondary.[44] The Lukan interpretation employs a "how much more" argument. If a friend will fulfill a request in the middle of the night, how much more will God.[45] Thus shamelessness makes no sense in the context.[46]

But there are clear indications that even Luke's performance did understand *anaideia* to mean "shamelessness." The unit's conclusion, v. 13, where the "how much more" argument is expressed, reads, "If you then, who are evil, know how to give good gifts to your children, how much more . . ." Here the "who are evil" corresponds exactly to the description of *anaideia*. Actually the parable's application to prayer does not demand the interpretation "persistence," but the implied "Christians who are praying" has blocked the normal understanding of *anaideia*.

Finally, then, who is shameless in the parable? When *anaideia* is translated "persistence" or "inopportunity" it is the man outside beseeching his neighbor. But the parable's triadic arrangement argues against this. Part 1 sets the scene, the middle of the night, and contains the speech of the requester (vv. 5–6). Part 2 is the sleeper's response from inside, which is negative: "I am not able to get up and give to you" (v. 7). Part 3 concludes the parable. Using "requester" and "sleeper" to designate the two characters clarifies the confusing antecedents of the pronouns.

> if the sleeper does not give to the requester
> > getting up
> > > because being the sleeper's friend
> > > yet because of the sleeper's shame
> > rising up
> the sleeper will give to the requester all the requester's needs

41. For thorough surveys of the evidence, see Catchpole, "Q and 'The Friend at Midnight,'" 409–11; Bailey, *Poet and Peasant*, 125–27.

42. Jeremias (*Parables*, 158) admits the possibility of "shameless" but dismisses it.

43. Jülicher, *Die Gleichnisreden* 2:273; B. T. D. Smith, *Parables*, 147.

44. E.g., Bultmann, *History of the Synoptic Tradition*, 175. Bultmann titles the parable "The Inopportune Friend" and says it has no application, but then later (p. 199) argues that it is correctly interpreted as an "exhortation to prayer."

45. Jeremias, *Parables*, 159.

46. Even Catchpole ("Q and 'The Friend at Midnight'") and Bailey (*Poet and Peasant*), who know the evidence, ignore it. Catchpole (pp. 411–12) eliminates the offending line as a Lukan creation with logic I cannot follow, and Bailey (p. 131) believes it must be a mistranslation from the Aramaic!

Although the antecedents are admittedly awkward, the subject of the verbs of giving is the sleeper, and the causal phrase explains his activity; therefore both the friendship and the shamelessness are his attributes.[47]

If *anaideia* must be translated "shamelessness," because of both external and internal evidence, and if it applies to the sleeper, what does it mean in the parable? The parable broaches as a theme hospitality, yet accepting a request to help "is scarcely riveting or revolutionary."[48] As part of the ongoing exchange in village life the request must be met. Furthermore, since the parable ends with the sleeper's responding out of shamelessness, it is implied that its opposite, his honor, is somehow at stake. Finally, "friend" is mentioned four times in the parable: in the introduction, in the requester's greeting to the sleeper, in the requester's description of his guest, and in the parable's conclusion. Friendship would appear to be a central value in the parable.

First-century C.E. Judaism did not have the highly developed understanding of friendship so prominent in Greek thought. Friendship in the Greek sense is alien to the Hebrew Bible,[49] but in the LXX, *philos* is frequently introduced and alternates with *plesion*, "neighbor," as a translation of *rea'*, "friend," "companion."[50] The assimilation of friend and neighbor is typical of Hellenistic and Jewish society.

Aristotle in the *Nicomachean Ethics* contrasts the good and bad man in terms of how each behaves toward a neighbor:

> A bad man considers himself in all he does, and the more so the worse he is
> . . .; a good man acts from a sense of what is noble, and the better he is the
> more he so acts, and he considers his friend's interest, disregarding his
> own.[51]

Acting for the friend is the honorable thing; to act in one's own self-interest is shameless. Later in the same argument, Aristotle refers to four proverbs that demonstrate that true friendship is to act for the other's sake: "All the proverbs agree with this; for example 'Friends have one soul between them,' 'Friends' goods are common property,' 'Amity is equality,' 'The knee is nearer than the shin.'"[52] These common proverbs

---

47. Bailey, *Poet and Peasant*, 128.
48. Catchpole, "Q and 'The Friend at Midnight,'" 413.
49. Stählin, "*philos*," 156.
50. For statistics, see ibid., 154.
51. Aristotle, *Nicomachean Ethics*, 9.8.1168a (LCL 549).
52. Ibid., 1168b (LCL 549–51). The last proverb is frequently equated with "Charity begins at home." See Apostle, *Nicomachean Ethics*, 336: "It may mean that friends are closer than the knee is to the shin." For further references to these common proverbs, see Stählin, "*philos*," 152. Acts 4:32 combines these first two proverbs in the description of the ideal Christian: "Now the company of those who believed were of one heart and soul, and no one said that any of the things which he possessed was his own, but they had everything in common."

describe true friendship, and sentiments like these obviously are assumed by the hearers of the parable. The request will be met not only because of the demands of hospitality but also because of friendship.

In Sir. 6:5–17 is a short treatise on true and false friends: "A faithful friend is a sturdy shelter: he that has found one has found a treasure" (v. 14). "Whoever fears the Lord directs his friendship aright, for so he is, so is his neighbor also" (v. 17).[53] Here again friend is assimilated to neighbor. The principle of sharing with a neighbor/friend is also found in Prov. 3:28–29: "Do not say to your neighbor, 'Go and come again, tomorrow I will give it'—when you have it with you. Do not plan evil against your neighbor who dwells trustingly beside you." This teaches the appropriate behavior when neighbor calls on a neighbor.

In the parable Who Has a Friend? hospitality demands a response from the sleeper. To reinforce this the parable appeals to the interlocking web of friendship. The two neighbors are friends, and the requester has a friend at home as guest. So tight are these bonds that refusal is inconceivable. And yet that is what the man asleep inside proposes: "Do not make trouble for me. Already the door is shut, and my children are with me in bed. I am not able to help you." Nevertheless, the request for aid will be granted, though not because of friendship but because of shamelessness. The man acts not out of honor (friendship, mutual obligation) but out of shamelessness, because he will be dishonored if the villagers discover his friend standing outside begging for what ought to be freely given. He is afraid he will be disgraced in the village. He has done out of shamelessness what he ought to have done out of honor.

Village life can replicate a metaphorical system for the kingdom, because various aspects of that system can furnish a model for the kingdom. For these parables the kingdom is a village, and each parable works out different aspects of that implied metaphorical system derived from village life. The four parables of this group share a similar model evident in Who Has a Friend? The end is always achieved, whether it be caring for a guest as in this parable, the banquet as in the parable A Man Gave a Banquet, the harvest as in The Land of a Rich Man, or Lazarus's well-being as in A Rich Man Clothed in Purple. Although the end is accomplished, it is not accomplished by the approved means that form the expected metaphor for the kingdom. In Who Has a Friend? the end is achieved through an appeal not to friendship but to shamelessness. So in each of the other parables of this group, the approved way of attaining the end is subverted. The village as kingdom furnishes unexpected

53. Sirach frequently warns against false friendship. See Stählin, "*philos*," 157. Sirach evidences the inroads of Greek models on Jewish thought. For a balanced approach, see Nickelsburg, *Jewish Literature*, 64.

metaphorical shifts: not the gracious friend but the shameless one furnishes the loaves.

City and Beyond

On the peasant's map, beyond the family and village lay the outside world. The first outside circle is the city, for peasant and urban society are interdependent. Peasants create the surplus that makes possible the social life of an urban elite, the specialized life of political and religious rulers.[54] As a result there is a tension with the urban society that rules the countryside.[55] Urban elites are frequently large landowners, and peasant societies are afflicted by the ills of absentee landlords.[56] A situation of this nature was common in Palestine.

The glitter and excesses of the city both attract and repel peasants. They hate city dwellers who lord it over them.[57] The attraction and repulsion between peasant and urban elite form part of the point of view that is important in the interpretation of parables told from and to a peasant point of view. For example, in the parable From Jerusalem to Jericho a peasant would have mistrusted the priest and Levite and would have snickered at their passing by. So also in A Man Entrusts Property, when the third servant attacks the master with the charge "I knew you to be a hard man, reaping where you did not sow, and gathering where you did not winnow" (Matt. 25:24), he is repeating and summing up a peasant's belief about an urban elite. Further, the urban elite belong to the "correct" families, they enjoy power and property. Often their position is legitimated by the interpretation of the sacred writings.[58]

Although the peasant's anti–urban-elite point of view is important in a number of Jesus' parables, three of his parables use that part of the social map that draws the line between religious and nonreligious as a metaphor for the kingdom. The religious are often represented by the urban elite. The parables Two Men Went Up to the Temple (Luke 18:10–14a), In a City There Was a Judge (chap. 6), and From Jerusalem to Jericho (chap. 7) employ that map to replicate those inside and outside the kingdom.

---

54. Foster, "What Is a Peasant?" 6.
55. Redfield (*Little Community*) distinguishes between the great tradition of the urban elite and the little tradition that is embodied in peasant culture. It is usually the great tradition that survives and that scholars study.
56. Foster, "What Is a Peasant?" 5.
57. Ibid., 10.
58. Sjoberg, "Preindustrial City," 19.

Two Men Went Up to the Temple

Two men went up to the temple to pray, one a Pharisee and the other a tax collector. The Pharisee standing by himself prayed thus, "O God, I give thanks to you that I am not like the rest of men, robbers, swindlers, adulterers, or even like this tax collector. I fast twice a week, I give tithes of everything I get." And the tax collector standing a way off did not wish to raise his eyes to heaven, but he beat his breast saying, "O God, be merciful to me a sinner." I say to you, this one went up to his house having been made righteous rather than the other.

Luke's framing of the parable Two Men Went Up to the Temple and its subsequent rupture from its context in first-century Judaism have turned it into an anti-Pharisaic and anti-Semitic story.[59] In Luke's frame the parable was told "to some who trusted upon themselves that they were righteous and thought nothing of the rest" (Luke 18:9).[60] This introduction sets up the character to be rejected as false, untrue to his religiosity. Thus a reader judges the Pharisee before the parable begins. Luke concludes the parable with the floating logion: "For everyone who exalts himself will be humbled, but he who humbles himself will be exalted" (v. 14). Even before this conclusion, Jesus' "I say to you" (v. 14) authoritatively demarks the Pharisee as not righteous and therefore the one who is self-righteous, a despiser of others, haughty, and to be humbled—literally, in the history of Christianity, in pogrom after pogrom.[61]

Interpreters frequently either ignore or direct attention away from this harsh history bequeathed by the parable. Jeremias argues that the parable's point is God's mercy for the sinner,[62] but he is aware that this Lukan frame is not without problems. He asks but does not answer, "What fault had the Pharisee committed and what had the publican done by way of reparation?"[63] Jeremias has raised an interesting point, which unfortunately he neglects to pursue. In pursuing his question we must keep distinct Luke's frame (which passes negative judgment on the Pharisee), the parable's picture of the Pharisee, and the parable's con-

---

59. Linnemann (*Jesus of the Parables*, 58) makes this point strongly.

60. This is a Lukan construction; see Bultmann, *History of the Synoptic Tradition*, 193; Plummer, *Gospel according to St. Luke*, 416.

61. For the place of this parable in the overall construction of Luke 18, see chap. 6 below.

62. Jeremias, *Parables*, 139.

63. Ibid., 144. Manson (*Sayings*, 310) argues that the Pharisee is not hypocritical. Schottroff ("Die Erzählung," 448–52) maintains that the picture that emerges of the Pharisee is a caricature.

cluding judgment in favor of the tax collector. Without Luke's introduction a hearer would not automatically and initially think of the
Pharisee as a negative caricature.[64] Crossan has suggested an intriguing
modern equivalent to the parable: "A Pope and a pimp went into St.
Peter's to pray."[65] Just as we would not automatically assume that the
pope was self-righteous, so also we should not assume that the Pharisee
was.

The parable begins with two men going up to the temple to pray, and
it concludes with the same two going down to their respective houses.
The motion to temple and back to house constitutes an inclusio that
rounds off the parable. The symbolic distance between secular space
(home) and sacred space (temple) replicates the distance between characters, but more fundamentally the temple "determines from the outset
the rules of the game."[66] The temple conjures up a religious standard that
gives value to both the characters. The Pharisee is good and the tax
collector bad, because of the religious standard represented by the
temple. If they had gone to a Roman law court, their values and the
parable's point of view would have been different. Even more, the
temple could not exist without Pharisees (insiders) and tax collectors
(outsiders). The temple is the map, the metaphor, that stands for the
insiders and outsiders. Since this is a parable of contrast, the temple will
map out the contrast. The contrast form does not decide in advance
whether the first or second one will be favored,[67] although the temple
map surely favors the Pharisee.

"The Pharisee stands by himself" to pray. Standing is the normal
posture for prayer.[68] The outcome of a grammatical decision affects the
picture of Pharisee. Does *pros heauton*, "by/to himself," modify "standing"[69] or "praying"?[70] The senses of the two phrases are strikingly different. Two issues favor taking the prepositional phrase to modify "standing": (1) Standing slightly apart is normal practice.[71] The occasion is most
likely not a time of private prayer but one of the regular twice-daily
services.[72] (2) The tax collector's introduction parallels the Pharisee's
with the phrase "by himself" replaced by "at a distance":

---

64. Linnemann, *Jesus of the Parables*, 59.
65. Crossan, *Raid on the Articulate*, 108.
66. Mottu, "The Pharisee and the Tax Collector," 200.
67. See chap. 1 above, on A Man Had Two Children.
68. *b. Ber.* 31a (Soncino 1:188–89).
69. Jülicher, *Die Gleichnisreden* 2:603. Grundmann (*Das Evangelium nach Lukas*, 350)
suggests that he prayed to himself instead of God. This reading should be rejected.
70. Jeremias (*Parables*, 140) sees it as Semitic idiom. Cf. Klostermann, *Das Lukasevangelium*, 179.
71. Jeremias, *Parables*, 140.
72. So Bailey, *Through Peasant Eyes*, 145; Safrai, "The Temple," *JPFC* 2:885–87.

the Pharisee   / was standing / by himself
the tax collector / at-a-distance / standing

The two phrases form a chiasmus.

The charge against the Pharisee's prayer is that it is self-righteous. The question is whether its original hearers, especially without the prejudice of the Lukan introduction, would have so judged it. We will examine first the prayer's form and then its content.

In form it is a prayer of thanksgiving. Many commentators[73] have noted the following prayer. It occurs in the Gemara as an example of the Mishnah command to pray on entering and leaving the house of study. The Mishnah only says that on leaving, the rabbi must give thanks;[74] the Talmud gives the prayer:

> I give thanks to Thee, O Lord my God, that Thou has set my portion with those who sit in the Beth ha-Midrash [the house of study] and Thou hast not set my portion with those who sit in [street] corners[75] for I rise early and they rise early, but I rise early for words of Torah and they rise early for frivolous talk; I labour and they labour, but I labour and receive a reward and they labour and do not receive a reward; I run and they run, but I run to the life of the future world and they run to the pit of destruction.[76]

The structure of this prayer is similar to that of the Pharisee. The Talmud does not view the prayer as self-righteous or boasting. The rabbi is giving God thanks that he has been so blessed by God as to be able to study the Torah. Eta Linnemann quotes a similar thanksgiving from Tosephta.

> R. Judah said: One must utter three praises everyday: Praised (be the Lord) that He did not make me a heathen, for all the heathen are as nothing before Him (Is 40:17); praised be He, that He did not make me a woman, for woman is not under obligation to fulfill the law; praised be He that He did not make me . . . an uneducated man, for the uneducated man is not cautious to avoid sins.[77]

Here the map is at work, deciding who is on the inside and who is on the outside.

The content of the Pharisee's prayer conforms to its form. He gives thanks that he is not like "the rest," whom the map places outside: robbers,[78] swindlers,[79] adulterers, "or even like this tax collector." Ad-

73. Following Str-B 2:240.
74. *m. Ber.* 4.2 (Danby, 5).
75. "Rashi explains this to mean shopkeepers or ignorant people" (Soncino 1:172).
76. *b. Ber.* 28b (Soncino 1: 172).
77. *t. Ber.* 7.18; see Linnemann, *Jesus of the Parables,* 59.
78. BAGD, 108.
79. Jeremias, *Parables,* 140.

verting to the tax collector creates dramatic tension by recalling a character whom the temple map has defined as outside. Turning to his own
deeds the Pharisee notes two, fasting and tithing. In both cases he goes
beyond the requirement of Torah.[80] To suggest that the Pharisee is
arrogant or morally superior[81] misses the point that he has only done
what the temple map requires of those on the inside.

All peoples have such maps, and the mere having of one of them does
not constitute self-righteousness. The Christian map in its arrogance
decides that the Pharisee's map is self-righteous;[82] we even have to paint
him in negative colors so that he earns our condemnation. Our inherited
Christian map blocks us from seeing that in the Pharisee's own context
his prayer depicts him as the ideal pious man.[83] Likewise, both the
prayer's form and its content indicate that he is living up to the map
drawn by the temple: he is the model of the pious man.

The temple map also determines the tax collector's place, and so he
stands at a distance, not even daring to lift his eyes to heaven.[84] He
belongs to one of the groups that the temple map positions outside the
bounds.[85]

In contrast to the Pharisee, the tax collector prays in a way betokening
mourning: he beats his breast, a sign of mourning and even despair.[86] So
the picture is that of the tax collector standing off from those gathered
for prayer, his eyes lowered, and beating his breast in the despair of
mourning. He knows his place according to the temple map.

His prayer in form is a plea: "O God, have mercy on[87] me a sinner." He
acknowledges his standing within the temple; he is a sinner. Nothing

80. On fasting, see Safrai, "Religion in Everyday Life," *JPFC* 2:816; Str-B 2:241–44.

81. Marshall, *Commentary on Luke*, 679; Grundmann, *Das Evangelium nach Lukas*, 350.

82. The Pharisees were aware of the problem of self-righteousness as exemplified in
the famous saying of Hillel: "Keep not aloof from the congregation and trust not in
thyself until the day of thy death, and judge not thy fellow until thou art come to his
place, and say not of a thing which cannot be understood that it will be understood in
the end; and say not, When I have leisure I will study; perchance thou wilt never have
leisure" (*m. Aboth* 2.5 [Danby, 448]).

83. Jülicher, *Die Gleichnisreden* 2:603; Linnemann, *Jesus of the Parables*, 59.

84. For evidence that lifting one's eyes in prayer is normal, see Marshall, *Commentary on Luke*; 680; Str-B 2:246.

85. Michel, "*telōnēs*," 88–105. See also *b. San.* 25b (Soncino 12:148–49), which is a
discussion of those who are ineligible to be witnesses or judges; included in the list are
herdsmen, tax collectors, and publicans. All three are classed as robbers because they
take what does not belong to them. So also in the Pharisee's list.

86. See Luke 23:48, at the death of Jesus: ". . . when they saw what had taken place,
returned home beating their breasts." A characteristic of mourning was the wailing of
women who also beat their breasts (Stählin, "*kopetos*," 842–43). For a refutation of
Jeremias's remark that striking the breast is rare, see Stählin, "*typtō*," 262 n. 18.

87. In the sense of "propitiate or reconcile"; see BAGD, 375; Büchsel, "*hilaskomai*,"
315.

about the parable to this point would have struck the original hearers as out of the ordinary. It conforms to expectations. The Pharisee's prayer marks him as the ideal of the pious, and the tax collector's acknowledgment that he is a sinner acknowledges what all know to be true.

Both leave the temple space and return to their homes. They leave sacred space for secular space, and the teller of the parable remarks that the tax collector went down righteous.[88] The audience winces in disbelief. How can the storyteller reverse the temple map? What has gone wrong? What sign of repentance has the tax collector shown? Has he made any reparation like the tax collector Zacchaeus (Luke 19:1–9)? The importance of reparation is underlined in a story about a good tax collector. When the district chief came for the taxes, this village tax collector hid the villagers so that there would be no one to tax. But on his death bed, he said, "Take thirteen *ma'ahs* that are tied in my sheets and return them to so and so, for I took them from him and have no need of them."[89] Even a good tax collector is in need of making reparation.

How does the parable make its judgment? It may be that the tax collector experiences God as the truly other, "out of sight and grasp, hidden, and lost,"[90] and the Pharisee overvalues the presence of God, rejoicing in it. But we cannot find in the tax collector merit or fix blame on the Pharisee. This only creates a new map and misses the radicalness of the parable. Despite Luke's use of the parable as an example story, it is not.[91] There is no lesson to learn! The hearer cannot imitate the behavior of one or the other. The parable's message is simpler. The map has been abandoned, it can no longer predict who will be an insider or outsider. This parable subverts the metaphorical structure that sees the kingdom of God as temple. Given this metaphorical system, things associated with the temple are holy and in the kingdom, and things not associated with the temple are unholy and outside the kingdom. In the parable the holy is outside the kingdom and the unholy is inside the kingdom.

The other parables that belong to the "City, and Beyond" grouping invoke this same metaphorical structure. In From Jerusalem to Jericho, once again the temple and those who belong to it define expectations. But likewise in that parable, an outsider—a Samaritan—saves the man in the ditch. In In a City There Was a Judge, the judge who derives his value from religion carries out judgment for decidedly unreligious motives.

88. Linnemann (*Jesus of the Parables*, 62) suggests this translation because it avoids the Pauline associations with "justification."

89. *b. San.* 26a (Soncino 12:149).

90. Mottu, "The Pharisee and the Tax Collector," 209.

91. Manson (*Sayings*, 312), who rejects the conclusion about humbling and exalting as secondary, maintains that it weakens the parable.

Throughout all these parables of "Family, Village, City, and Beyond," the social landscape has furnished a map that is expected to replicate the kingdom of God. Understanding that map is a key to understanding the parables.

I
Remember Mama

A Man Had Two Sons

A certain man had two sons. And the younger of them said to the father, "Father, give me the portion of your substance that falls to my share." And he divided among them his life. And after many days, gathering together everything, the younger son departed into a far country and there he squandered his substance in wild living. When he had spent everything, there happened a great famine throughout that country and that one began to fall short. And going, he attached himself to one of the citizens of that country, and he sent him into his fields to feed his pigs and he longed to feed his belly from the carob beans which the pigs were eating, and no one gave them to him. Coming to himself, he said, "How many of my father's hired hands abound in bread, but I in famine here perish. Rising up, I will go to my father and I will say to him, 'Father, I have sinned to heaven and before you, no longer am I worthy to be called your son; make me as one of your hired hands.'" And rising up, he came to his father. While he was way far off, his father saw him and had pity and running he fell upon his neck and kissed him affectionately. Said the son to him, "Father, I have sinned to heaven and before you, no longer am I worthy to be called your son . . ." Said the father to his slaves, "Quickly, bring out the best robe and clothe him, and put a ring on his hand and sandals on his feet, and bring the fatted calf, kill, and eating let us make merry, because this my son was dead and lives again, was lost and is found." And they began to make merry.

There was his son, the elder one, in the field. And as he was coming, he drew near to the house, he heard music and dancing, and calling to one of the boys, he inquired what it might mean. He said to him, "Your brother has come, and your father has killed the fatted calf, because he has got him back in good health." He was angry and did not wish to go in; his father coming pleaded with him. Answering he said to his father, "See, how many years I have slaved for you and never went against your commandment, and never did you give me a goat so that I might make merry with my friends. When this son of yours who ate up your life with harlots came, you killed for him the fatted calf." He said to him, "Child, you always are with me, and everything that is mine is yours. [To make merry and to rejoice was necessary because this your brother was dead and lives, and being lost is found.]"

The parable A Man Had Two Sons (Luke 15:11–32) is among the most famous of Jesus' parables. The image of the downtrodden and repentant prodigal, the loving embrace of the forgiving father, and the churlish rejection by the self-righteous elder son have inspired many artists and preachers. Despite the power of the parable's images, its exegesis is beset with problems. Some have challenged the authenticity of the scene with the elder brother or the realistic depiction of the legal situation. Perhaps even more ironic, readers of Luke's Gospel have identified with the younger son, while insisting with Luke that an audience of scribes and Pharisees would have identified with the elder son. To follow this trail we must first follow the path of Luke, for he is the first available reader/performer.

Losers Keepers, Finders Weepers

Since most scholars agree that the parable was originally addressed to the scribes and Pharisees, it is critical to ascertain the influence of Lukan redaction.

Although chapter 15 was fabricated from traditional pieces, techniques characteristic of Lukan style indicate that he formed it into a literary unit. The threefold pattern of action of Jesus (v. 1), assault on him (v. 2), and response (vv. 3–32) is common in Luke.[1] Luke 13:1–9, a section also dealing with repentance, has two short sayings connected by "or" and concluded by a longer parable.[2] Similarly, the introductory vv. 1–2 are parallel to 5:29–30.[3]

Luke 5:29–30	*Luke 15:1–2*
v. 29: a great crowd	v. 1: all
v. 30: tax collectors and others[4]	tax collectors and sinners
murmured	v. 2: murmured
the Pharisees and scribes	the Pharisees and scribes
saying	saying
sinners	sinners
you eat	eats[5]

There is strong verbal and thematic similarity between these two sections. The conclusion of 5:32 could stand also for chapter 15: "I have not come to call the righteous, but sinners to repentance." Finally, the characterization of the Pharisee as self-righteous is characteristic of Luke.[6]

The key words/concepts of joy (Luke 15:6–7, 9–10, 23–24, 32), the lost being found (vv. 6, 9, 24, 32), and repentance (vv. 7, 10, 18) hold chapter 15 together. But Luke has done more than use key words[7] to organize a thematic unit. He has created a fictional point of view so powerfully subtle that few have been aware of it.

Luke 15 operates on several interrelated levels. We can imagine the chapter as operating on three distinct narrative levels. The first or primary narrative level is a subpart of the larger Gospel narrative and announces in vv. 1–2 its cast of characters: Jesus, sinners, and scribes and Pharisees. Jesus and the sinners form one set, and the scribes and Pharisees who murmur against Jesus, the story's hero, are the antisubject or opponents. This first-level story has as its purpose the vindication of Jesus' association with sinners. At the third level are the three parables of chapter 15 (A Man with a Hundred Sheep, A Woman with Ten

---

1. Talbert, *Reading Luke,* 147.
2. According to Talbert's chiastic arrangement of the Lukan travel narrative, chap. 15 is parallel to 13:1–5 (*Literary Patterns,* 51–52).
3. Luke 5:29–32 follows the action-assault-response pattern frequent in Luke.
4. The preferred reading is "others," but many manuscripts adopt "sinners."
5. This arrangement is from Jeremias's *Die Sprache,* 243.
6. In connection with 7:29–30, cf. Luke 10:29; 16:15; 18:9; 20:20.
7. Key-word organization is characteristic of oral style, but the argument here is that Luke has created the present organization of this chapter, not inherited it. The existence of A Man with a Hundred Sheep in Matthew and *Thomas* indicates that the parables did circulate separately from this context. See Ramaroson, "Le coeur," 348–60.

Drachmas, and A Man Had Two Sons) which have their own separate characters and plots. The second-level story, or, perhaps better, the intermediate story intertwines the primary-level story with the third-level stories to make a completed narrative unit out of chapter 15. In this second-level story the interpretive act takes place.[8]

The first two parables (A Man with a Hundred Sheep, A Woman with Ten Drachmas) have a similar structure and are bound together by "or," creating a close unity. Jesus directly addresses his opponents. In both stories an object is lost and then found, and there ensues a request for rejoicing and then an interpretation by the teller (Jesus) that ties the third level story directly to the first one. The intermediate story also works a transformation on the thing of value. In the two parables the thing lost has little intrinsic value and is only one of a larger number of things. Its value is in its being found, in the joy of its recovery; in the intermediate story, on the other hand, the value and joy are in the repentance of a person.[9] Likewise, nothing in these two parables corresponds to the opponents of the primary story. The fictional audience (the scribes and Pharisees) imagine themselves as people who have lost a sheep or coin and so are drawn into rejoicing (i.e., into eating with sinners). The themes of the lost and the found, and of rejoicing belong to the third-level stories, not the primary one. The implied feast of rejoicing that forms the intermediate story leads the Gospel's reader to an interpretive act that joins the primary story with the two parables.

The third parable of chapter 15, A Man Had Two Sons, functions somewhat differently. Introduced not by "or" but by "and he said," the story is narrated in the third person. Instead of beginning, "What man of you," it begins, "A certain man had two sons." This blocks the fictional audience's immediate identification with the man. The pattern of lost/found/rejoice appears in the narrative, and the banquet is no longer implied but real; the father kills the fatted calf and throws a party. Thus a key element from the intermediate story becomes part of the secondary story. Furthermore, instead of the storyteller's (Jesus') providing the interpretation (15:7, 10), the father does so in v. 24. What is missing is the direct reference to repentance; that is implied in the narrative action and the son's reference to his being a sinner (v. 18).

The second part of A Man Had Two Sons introduces an opponent to the father's plan. The elder brother is a character in the third-level story, but the intermediate story relates him to the primary story: he murmurs against the father's feast exactly as the scribes and Pharisees of the

8. The Entrevernes Group (*Signs and Parables,* 120) uses this distinction between three levels of narration.
9. Ibid., 138.

primary story do against Jesus' feast with sinners. The fictional audience (the scribes and Pharisees) see themselves in this role, and the father requests them to rejoice over what is lost (v. 32).

Luke's artifice so weaves the primary story together with the third-level stories that the fictional audience is forced to admit to the legitimacy, even the necessity (*edei*, v. 32), of rejoicing at the feast. The fictional audience constructs an intermediate story from the clues provided by the authoritative teller, Jesus. Thus the audience creates the bridges that bind the primary story of scribes and Pharisees who contest Jesus' eating with sinners with the third level of three parables. Moreover Luke's fictional audience makes the same set of identifications as his implied audience, those for whom the Gospel is intended. Thus the fictional audience stands for the implied audience: Jesus' hearers stand for Luke's readers, but with one important caveat. Since they are not Jesus' opponents but themselves repentant "sons," they identify even more powerfully with the call to rejoice at the repentance of those lost and they condemn those who do not so rejoice.

The effect of a double audience, the fictional audience of the primary narrative and the implied readers of Luke's Gospel, has gone unnoticed. So powerful is Luke's fictional web that most have assumed that the parable A Man Had Two Sons was originally addressed to scribes and Pharisees.[10] But the fictional audience and the original historical audience need not be identical. In addition, most commentators also assume that the original, historical audience would have identified with the elder son, even though Luke's readers have identified with the younger son.[11] Although it is true that Luke's construction of the chapter forces the fictional audience to identify with the elder son, Luke's readers and subsequent readers have identified with the younger son.[12] Not only have critics failed to distinguish between various levels of audience but they frequently fail to take cognizance of Luke's literary skill. Since the intermediate narrative identifies the elder son with the rejected Pharisees of the primary narrative, there is an implied rejection of the elder son. But in the parable narrative itself there is no rejection: he inherits all (v. 31).[13] The elder son's rejection results not from the parable itself but from its association in the intermediate narrative with the primary

---

10. Jeremias, *Parables*, 124; Dodd, *Parables*, 93. Plummer, *Gospel according to St. Luke*, 371: "Even if it was delivered on some other occasion unknown to Luke, he could not have given it a more happy position than this."

11. In addition to the works in the previous n., see Bailey, *Poet and Peasant*, 204.

12. E.g., Creed, *Gospel according to St. Luke*, 197. Creed argues that it is a natural extension that the younger son equals the pagans and the elder son the Jews.

13. Carlston, "Reminiscence and Redaction," 387. See also Hauck, *Das Evangelium des Lukas*, 210–12.

narrative, where the elder son/Pharisees are rejected. The original audience for the parable, like subsequent real readers and hearers, would have identified with the younger son.

So close has been the fit between the parable A Man Had Two Sons and chapter 15 that some commentators have argued that the last part of the parable is a Lukan creation. Two issues have governed the debate: the parable's language and its place in Luke's theology.

The linguistic arguments bear on the presence or absence of Semitisms and Lukanisms in the parable.[14] Charles Carlston seems to be the most methodologically sound, since he does not prejudice the case.[15] He arranges his evidence under three headings: those words or expressions characteristic of Lukan style; those which may or may not be Lukan; and those uncharacteristic of Luke. Since characteristically Lukan vocabulary occurs throughout the parable, Carlston rejects Jeremias's contention that Luke has left the parable almost untouched.[16] Either Luke has edited the parable "to the degree one would expect from Luke" or he has composed the whole parable.[17] Carlston argues, however, that there are too many non-Lukan phrases to argue that either the whole parable or the last part is a free Lukan composition.[18] His conclusions cohere with our analysis of the careful construction of Luke 15.

Because the parable seems to fit so well with Luke's understanding of repentance, L. Schottroff has maintained that it was a creation of Lukan soteriology.[19] Although on the basis of the linguistic evidence, Schottroff's argument can be dismissed, it does help focus another important aspect of Luke's performance. Luke separates repentance and forgiveness of sins into two movements, the former on our part, the latter on God's.[20] In this schema, salvation history relies on the rejection of the Jews in favor of the Gentiles.[21] Within the context of chapter 15, both the parables A Man with a Hundred Sheep and A Woman with Ten Drachmas exemplify rejoicing over one who repents (vv. 7, 10). In A Man Had Two Sons, the third parable, repentance emerges when the son ac-

---

14. Schweizer rejects the elder-brother episode, in "Zur Frage," 469–71; Jeremias defends the integrity of the parable, in "Zum Gleichnis," 228–31; Schweizer responds in "Antwort an Joachim Jeremias," 231–33. Sanders summarizes Schweizer and Jeremias, agreeing with Schweizer, in "Tradition and Redaction," 433–38; O'Rourke rejects Sanders's arguments, in "Some Notes," 431–33. See also my rejection of Sanders in "The Prodigal Son," 186– 89.

15. For a detailed argument, see Carlston, "Reminiscence and Redaction."

16. Jeremias, "Tradition und Redaktion," 181.

17. Carlston, "Reminiscence and Redaction," 373.

18. Ibid., 383.

19. Schottroff, "Das Gleichnis," 27–52.

20. Ibid., 29–30; Conzelmann, *Theology of St. Luke,* 100– 101.

21. Michelis, "La conception lucanienne," 49.

knowledges his sin against heaven and before his father (v. 18), and the joy for repentance surfaces in the reception the father affords the younger son (vv. 20–24). The elder son's refusal to repent places him outside the kingdom. For Schottroff, the parable's emphasis falls on the first part as an example of 15:7 and 15:10.

Even though Schottroff's understanding of the parable within the context of Lukan soteriology is mostly on target,[22] the parable is a less than perfect example of Lukan soteriology.[23] The elder brother, the surrogate Pharisee, is offered no opportunity for repentance, and even more, there is no hint that he is to be rejected: he is after all the heir. Although he is rebuked by the father, his fate does not correspond to the eventual rejection of Judaism envisioned by Lukan ideology.[24] The rejection comes not from the parable itself but from the implied reader's identification through the intermediate story with the primary narrative and with the larger fate of Israel. Schottroff's argument draws our attention, nevertheless, to an important point. Luke's interest is in the parable's first part, the repentance and forgiveness of the younger son. Second, in performing the inherited story, he must draw attention away from the nonrejection of the elder son. I would argue that Luke does this by repeating the conclusion of the episode of the younger as the conclusion for the episode of the elder son. This would agree with his redactional strategy.

This emphasis explains why so many have viewed the first part of the parable as complete in itself.[25] The traditional title, "The Prodigal Son," points to the primacy of the first part. Even Jeremias, whose theory of double-edged parables leads him to posit an emphasis on the second part, sees the first part as the gospel itself and the second as added by Jesus because "the parable was addressed to men who were like the elder brother, men who were offended at the gospel."[26] In the parable's second part, Jesus hopes to move the Pharisees to accept the gospel. But why should they if they indeed are always with the father and have inherited all? Now we see the power of Luke's fiction and likewise its ultimate inability to account for the parable itself. The identification of Pharisees with the elder brother, suggested not by the parable but by the primary Gospel narrative, has miscued the parable.

---

22. Bovon, (*Luc le théologien*, 302–5) positively evaluates Schottroff's understanding of Lukan redaction while rejecting her claim of Lukan authorship.

23. Carlston, "Reminiscence and Redaction, 386–87.

24. Sanders ("Tradition and Redaction," 438) says that the rejection of the elder brother is a "broadside" against the Pharisees. But how is the conclusion that all that is mine is yours and that you are always with me a "broadside" attack?

25. E.g., ibid., 434.

26. Jeremias, *Parables*, 131.

Surface Structure

The parable's power and beauty are evident in its careful construction and organization. It has two acts,[27] one about a younger son and the other about an elder son.

The first act's paratactic structure drives a hearer/reader through its narrative at record speed. Only the vaguest references record the passage of time. The accent is on action. The narrator is in control until the son comes to himself and the speeches of the son and the father slow the motion until the climax. As we will show below, at precisely this point an important identification process occurs.

Besides parataxis, the parable also uses subordinate clauses with a string of main verbs:

Section	Participle	Finite Verb
1	gathering together	he departed
		he squandered
2	having spent	it happened
		he began
3	going	he [son] was attached
		he [citizen] sent
		he [son] longed
		no one gave

With a few simple verbs, the narrator paints a story of disaster. The first participle is negated by the second, which also reinforces the final finite verb of the first clause, "he squandered." The motion of departing is continued with the third participle so that this set defines the tragic motion of the plot. The four verbs of the third section introduce a rapid shifting of subject, which shows the son no longer in control of his own story. In the second set, the finite verb is "it happened," and the son falls into passive action: "he began," "he was attached," "he longed." After the first set, he falls into passivity.

The son's and father's speeches show the same type of arrangement. The son's speech takes the following pattern:

Section	Participle	Finite Verb
4	coming	he said
5	"rising up"	"I will go"
		"I will say"
6	rising up	he came

27. Funk ("Structure," 63) proposes a threefold division consisting of the crisis of the younger son, the response of the father, and the response of the elder son. This breaks the natural rhythm of the story and places the emphasis on the younger son and not the man who had two sons.

The fourth and sixth sets are the narrator's; the fifth is the son's speech. Both speakers use virtually the same vocabulary, and that serves to identify the level of the narrator with that of the son. This is a strategy for identification. The participle of the fourth set, "coming," is the opposite of that of the third, "going," thus stopping the plot's tragic downward spiral and reversing its motion upwards toward comedy. The twice repeated "rising up," once spoken in direct speech, once in narration, metaphorically symbolizes the plot's direction.

Section	Participle	Finite Verb
7	being away	his father saw
		[he] had compassion
8	running	he fell
		he kissed

Now comes the denouement of the first act. The seventh participle indicates that the distance between father and son is not sufficient really to separate them, and in the eighth set the father overcomes that distance. The remaining part of the first act simply carries out that implication. The paratactic structure remains.

Section	Participle	Finite Verb
9	[quickly]	bring and clothe
		put
		bring and kill
10	eating	let us make merry

It, of course, would be perfect if the ninth set began with a participle, but it does not. It begins with an adverb, but the adverb belongs to the string of participles because the participles have all served to indicate orientation and this adverb orientates the father to his son.

The parable's second act, which involves the elder brother, has a somewhat similar pattern of organization, but not nearly so pronounced. This is so for several reasons. First, the narrator is less conspicuous, surfacing only in the introduction. The rest of the act is direct speech. Second, the act's tone is different because it is a confrontation, whereas the first act descends to tragedy and rises to forgiveness.

The second act begins with the same pattern around which the first act was built.

Section	Participle	Finite Verb
11	coming	he drew near
		he heard
12	calling	he inquired

This pattern, so prominent in the first act, is submerged in favor of verbs of coming. The elder son is away from the house in the field when action starts. "Coming, he drew near to the house," but he is not in the house. When the servant responds to the elder brother's question, he first notes, "Your brother has come," and then that the father has killed the fatted calf, which symbolizes the father's forgiveness.

Since the parable has used parataxis and a participle/finite-verb pattern throughout, the departure from the pattern in the response of the elder son stands out harshly: "He was angry and did not wish to come in [*eiselthein*]." As we shall see, precisely at this point the audience sides against the elder son, so that the surface structure advances the narrative's strategy.

The father's response reverts to the participle/finite-verb pattern, using a participle of coming (*ekselthon*):

Section	Participle	Finite Verb
13	coming out	he pleaded
14	answering	he said

The son's response to his father's pleading reverts to the familiar pattern, and in his grievance against his father he identifies the younger's coming (*elthen*) as the occasion of the father's killing the fatted calf.

The father's final response to the son is a pair of phrases whose balance is evident only in Greek:

	su	*pantote*	*met'emou*	*ei*	
	you	always	with me	are	
kai panta		*ta*	*ema*	*sa*	*estin*
and everything		that	[is] mine	yours	is

This rhythmic speech contrasts with the harshness of the son's protest.

The surface structure exhibits careful construction and artistry. In the first part, the participles and parataxis drive the action along its path downward toward tragedy and then upward toward the father. In the second part, the pattern continues but builds more around verbs of coming which distance the elder son from the father and the younger son. Why this strategy is necessary will become evident only when we analyze the parable's strategy to engage the hearer/reader.

A Reading

Keeping hold of the various strands interwoven throughout the parable A Man Had Two Sons exceeds the grasp of any interpretation. The parable is divided into two acts, but they are unequal. The younger brother's story (the first act) is a complete narrative with beginning, middle, and end; the elder brother's episode (the second act) responds to the first act. But it is not a mere appendage, because it transforms the overall story into something that the first act is not.

> *Line 1:* A certain man had two sons. And the younger of them said to the father, "Father, give me the portion of your substance that falls to my share." And he divided among them his life.

The first line indicates the story's possible directions.[28] Its characterizations begin to form a picture. The man has two sons, and they are specified as younger and, by implication, elder. Furthermore since the father has property, he is obviously a man of some wealth, although of how much does not become evident until later. The story also invokes two diverse elements of the repertoire: that of the legal code[29] associated with the family, and the mytheme of two-sons stories, common and frequent in the Hebrew Bible.

In this line and the next, the son receives his portion of the inheritance, sells if off, and departs. His actions are reasonably clear, but whether this conforms to normal Jewish family practice is debated. The legal distinction between the right of possession and the right of disposition are important. The younger son apparently requests and receives both. Jeremias assumes that the two go together and that the situation depicted is common. Palestine, being a place of little opportunity, younger sons would cash in their inheritance and go forth to make their fortunes.[30] The supporting evidence for Jeremias's benevolent interpretation is not nearly so clear as he would suppose.[31]

Sirach 33:19–23 seems particularly appropriate to our narrative:

> To son or wife, to brother or friend, do not give power over yourself, as long as you live; and do not give your property to another, lest you change your mind and must ask for it. While you are still alive and have breath in you, do not let any one take your place. For it is better that your children should ask from you than that you should look to the hands of your sons. Excel in all that you do; bring no stain upon your honor. At the time when you end the days of your life, in the hour of death, distribute your inheritance.

Sirach's strong warning distills the bitter experience of common wisdom

---

28. Against Linnemann (*Jesus of the Parables*, 74), who states that the first line does not reveal the story's direction.

29. Entrevernes Group, *Signs and Parables*, 148.

30. Jeremias, *Parables*, 129; following Str-B 3:550. So also, with reservations, Daube in "Inheritance," 334.

31. Derrett (*Law in the New Testament*, 106) mischievously but correctly says, "He was not the younger son of an English landed family of the pre-1925 period, to whom the virtue of adventurousness was a necessity."

against an early division and disposition of the property.[32] The father who gives the right of disposition to a son is a fool, for he may end up losing his livelihood. A traditional rabbinic saying makes this point forcefully:

> Our Rabbis taught: Three cry out and are not answered. Viz., he who has money and lends it without witnesses; . . . he who transfers his property to his children in his lifetime.[33]

Sirach clearly ties its warning about giving one's property to another with the father's honor. By surrendering his property, the father chances the loss of his honor, his position, his support, his control. His honor depends on his being embedded in the family, being himself the family's support and representative. The family and his honor are at stake with a division of the property.

Sirach places the division of property within the familial honor system. But related to this is the legal situation. *Mishnah Baba Bathra* 8 contains an extended discussion of case law relevant to our parable. Consider several pertinent cases:

> This is the order of inheritance: If a man die and have no son, then ye shall cause his inheritance to pass unto his daughter (Num 27:8)—the son precedes the daughter, and all the son's offspring precede the daughter. . . . The son and the daughter are alike concerning inheritance, save that the [firstborn] son takes a double portion of the father's property . . . and the daughters receive maintenance from the father's property. . . . If a man assign his goods to his sons he must write, "From to-day and after my death." . . . If a man assign his goods to his son to be his after his death, the father cannot sell them since they are assigned to his son, and the son cannot sell them since they are in the father's possession; . . . if the son sold them, the buyer has no claim on them until the father dies. The father may pluck up [the crop of a field which he has so assigned] and give to eat to whom he will. . . . If he left elder sons and younger sons, the elder sons may not care for themselves [out of the common inheritance] at the cost of the younger sons, nor may the younger sons claim maintenance at the cost of the elder son, but they all share alike.[34]

This case law makes several points relevant to our parable, but it is significant that it does not envision the situation described in our parable. It apparently has taken the experience described in Sirach seriously and chosen to avoid that case. Once a father gives the right of disposition, there is no effective legal case law. What case law does envision is

32. Against Bailey (*Poet and Peasant*, 163), who argues that Sirach is warning against something that seldom happened.
33. *b. B. Mes.* 75b (Soncino 10:436).
34. *m. B. Bat.* 8 (Danby, 376–78).

the possibility of a father's dividing his property before his death. But this seems closer to what we would call a will. Even more, the assumption of case law is that the property belongs to the family. The law is concerned with maintaining the property intact and with possible claims for maintenance. Even though the father in our parable has surrendered disposition, he cannot surrender his claim to maintenance. "If the son sold them, the buyer has no claim upon them until the father dies." Apparently, this was not the case in our parable. The case law of the Mishnah was apparently worked out to avoid the bad experience underlying Sirach and our parable.[35]

Finally this case law reminds us that our parable construes the family in a very narrow vein. The family consists of a father and younger and elder sons; missing are the mother and daughters. Since the claim of daughters and mother for maintenance from the property precede the sons' right of inheritance,[36] their omission from the story indicates how limited the focus is.

The evidence seems reasonably clear. The situation described in the parable, though not unknown, is surely not the norm. Nor does the situation reflect well on either the father or the younger son. The father has put his family honor in jeopardy; he has behaved in a foolhardy way. And the son, in requesting the right of disposition, has in effect pronounced his father dead,[37] because disposition of the property assumes his death.[38] This is clearly reflected in the Greek text. The son requests his portion of the substance (*ousia*), and the narrator remarks that the father "divided his life [*bios*] among them."[39] Life and death is a major thematic in this parable. The son's division of the property kills the father.

While the legal repertoire is a major element in understanding this parable, a second and extremely important repertoire of narrative possi-

---

35. Yaron (*Gifts*, 2) discusses dimission, an arrangement under which a son receives a portion of the father's property while the father is alive and thereby forfeits all claims to the inheritance. But this is extremely rare, and Yaron's evidence deals with cases of temporary title. Normally the gift becomes effective at the death of the father (see p. 79).

36. *m. B. Bat.* 9.1 (Danby, 378): "If a man died and left sons and daughters, and the property was great, the sons inherit and the daughters receive maintenance; but if the property was small the daughters receive maintenance and the sons go a-begging."

37. Derrett, *Law in the New Testament*, 105; Via, *Parables*, 169; Bailey, *Poet and Peasant*, 161.

38. Derrett (*Law in the New Testament*, 106) also says that a son requesting such an early division of the property cannot get along at home.

39. Pöhlmann notices this wordplay, in "Die Abschichtung," 209– 10. *Bios*, in the sense of "livelihood," is found only in this parable and in Luke 24:4//Mark 12:44. Luke normally uses *ta hyparchonta*; see Jeremias, *Die Sprache*, 249; Carlston, "Reminiscence and Redaction," 373 n. 47.

bilities has gone mostly unnoticed.[40] From one perspective the Hebrew Bible history of the patriarchs is a narrative of elder and younger sons, and despite the law of Deut. 21:15–17, designed to protect the elder from the favoritism frequently shown the younger,[41] the line of Israel's inheritance is through the younger. One need only call to mind the stories of Cain and Abel, Ishmael and Isaac, Esau and Jacob, Jacob's favorite son Joseph and, after his supposed death at the hands of his brothers, Benjamin. Many of the stories of these younger brothers follow a stereotype. Younger sons frequently leave the house of their father to find their wealth; there is something slightly scandalous or off-color in their stories; and they are the favorites. The story of Benjamin illustrates this final point. When the brothers come before Pharaoh's steward Joseph, whom they do not know, he finds the golden cup in Benjamin's bag and threatens to have him executed. Judah replies, "We have a father, an old man, and a young brother, the child of his old age; and his brother is dead, and he alone is left of his mother's children; and his father loves him" (Gen. 44:20). Beyond the patriarchs this type of story persists. Aaron and Moses are elder and younger brothers, and David and Solomon are younger sons. Two of David's elder sons, Absalom and Adonijah, seek to seize David's throne, but Solomon, the youngest, the son of a wife whose husband David has murdered, becomes God's anointed king. "She bore a son, and he called his name Solomon. And the Lord loved him" (2 Sam. 12:24).[42]

This tradition even persists in the folklore of Israel. A good example is from the *Midrash on Psalms*, commenting on Ps. 9:1:

> R. Berechiah said in the name of R. Jonathan: . . . The verse means therefore that God has set love of little children in their fathers' hearts. For example, there was a king who had two sons, one grown up, the other a little one. The grown-up one was scrubbed clean, and the little one was covered with dirt, but the king loved the little one more than he loved the grown-up one.[43]

Although this parable is clearly late, being ascribed to an Amoraim, it shows the consistency and persistence of the folklore motif of elder and younger sons in which each play stereotyped roles. The elder is "scrubbed clean," the younger is "dirty," but the father loves the younger more.

---

40. Abrahams (*Studies* 1:11) notices a connection with the Jacob-Esau cycle. Derrett makes extensive but misguided use of the same cycle in *Law in the New Testament*, 116–19.

41. Vaux, *Ancient Israel*, 42.

42. One could also add to this list Gideon and Judas Maccabaeus.

43. *Midrash on Psalms* 9 (Braude 1:131).

The parable's beginning is more complex than has been thought. The intersection of the various repertoires invoked by the parable places a hearer in a complex situation. On the one hand, the younger son's request for his share of the property, especially the right of disposition, effectively announces his father's death. The father, by giving in, exposes his own and his family's honor and shows himself to be foolish. On the other hand, the mytheme of elder-and-younger-brother stories encourages an audience to expect the younger to be something of a rogue and the favorite. This tension within the setting up of the story is precisely what makes it so magnificent and so difficult to interpret.

Line 2: And after many days, gathering together everything, the younger son departed into a far country and there he squandered his substance in wild living.

"After many days" intimates a sequence and delay between the father's division and the son's activity. The delay installs the son as subject of this subplot to the main story. Like a Chinese box, we have a story within a story. Line 1 introduces a man, part of his family, and the situation, as well as invoking the repertoire on which the story draws. Line 2 launches a new subject, the son, whose narrative falls immediately into tragedy.

The narrator does not directly report what the son did with his inheritance except that he gathered it in—he harvested it.[44] The metaphor pictures, rather than literally describing. A hearer must fill in the gap. "Gathering together" and "departing" complete the son's relation to his father. By taking the property with him he has refused to maintain his father from the property.[45] His disposal of the inheritance jeopardizes the family.

The departure, as in the servant parables, indicates a test.[46] A hearer expects him to make good, at least if the stories of Isaac, Jacob, and Joseph are taken into account. Without any details, the narrator reports that the son squandered his inheritance in "wild living" (*asōtōs* = "incurable"; it comes to mean living a life that will destroy one, i.e., a life of dissipation).[47] Again there is no literal description but only the implica-

---

44. For an indication that perhaps it means to convert it to cash, see BAGD, 782.

45. Derrett, *Law in the New Testament*, 109. Daube ('Inheritance,' 327) notes that the elder brother would have expected the son to dwell on the property with him.

46. See chap. 8 below. "A far country" is also used in the parable of a young nobleman (Luke 19:12). Carlston ('Reminiscence and Redaction,' 370) argues that the phrase is therefore Lukan. This is not necessarily so. Luke may have borrowed the phrase from this parable for his gloss on the parable A Man Entrusts Property. Str-B 2:212–13 indicates the phrase has Mishnaic parallels. Even if it is a Lukan addition it is implied in "departed"; see chap. 10 below.

47. Förster, "*asōtōs*," 506; Manson, *Sayings*, 287.

tion that the son's squandering was self-destructive. For a hearer, the son has certainly turned out to be a rogue. He has failed the test implied in his departure.

Line 3: When he had spent everything, there happened a great famine throughout that country and that one began to fall short. And going, he attached himself to one of the citizens of that country, and he sent him into his fields to feed his pigs and he longed to feed his belly[48] from the carob beans which the pigs were eating, and no one gave them to him.

As the story progresses the son's situation deteriorates. The narrative paints a picture of deep degradation and desperation. A famine, a feared scourge of the ancient world,[49] draws the audience's sympathy toward the son, for though he is responsible for his fate, he is not responsible for this downward turn. Now he moves to alleviate his situation. By joining a citizen of that country he attempts to reestablish his well-being and at the same time acknowledges that the break with his family is complete. He moves outside his own family, his own tribe, for help.

Motion away from the father leads the son into a precarious situation. Not only is he joined with a foreigner but he is also reduced to feeding pigs. The abhorrence of such an activity for Jews is well known, for it is a forbidden occupation: "None may rear swine anywhere."[50] A talmudic curse well summarizes the position: "Cursed be the man who would breed swine, and cursed be the man who would teach his son Grecian Wisdom."[51] In this aphorism, swine are equivalent to Gentiles—the same equation that is operative in this parable.[52]

The son's act of betrayal does not relieve his predicament. Hunger persists, as does his passivity. He does not eat the pigs' food—the carob

---

48. I have adopoted the reading "to feed his belly," *gemisai tēn koilian,* against the 26th ed. of Nestle-Aland, which reads, "to satisfy himself," *chortasthēnai,* because it is more likely that the vulgar expression would have been shifted to the euphemism. So Grundmann, *Das Evangelium nach Lukas,* 312 n. 23. The editors of the United Bible Society (Metzger, *Textual Commentary,* 164) give the reading "C," indicating about equal doubt whether the text or the apparatus contains the correct reading. For a thorough discussion, see Marshall, *Commentary on Luke,* 608–9.

49. Wettstein, *Novum Testamentum Graecum* 1:759; Creed, *Gospel according to St. Luke,* 199.

50. *m. B. Qam.* 7.7 (Danby, 342).

51. *b. B. Qam.* 82b (Soncino 10:470). The curse is part of the talmudic comment on the above section of Mishnah. It explains a story about a person who knows Greek wisdom and during the siege of Jerusalem substitutes a pig for cattle that were being smuggled into the city for sacrifices. When the pig is raised up the city wall in a basket, it causes an earthquake.

52. So also in the cure of the Gerasene demoniac (Mark 5:9–13). See Winter, *On the Trial,* 129.

beans—because no one would give them to him. He has will and desire but is without action.

The story mounts an important contrast between the son's inheritance and his present state. The inheritance is specified as "substance," and he squanders it. The metaphors underscore property and capital. Yet his lack is pictured in terms of food: a great famine besets him, he feeds swine and would eat the carob beans. There are many other possibilities for describing his poverty besides speaking of food. Why this accent? Nourishment is associated with female, maternal metaphors, and the family-system repertoire has cast the family in the especially male terms of property, inheritance, and the legal code. The mother, the unspoken binary of the father, is here implied in the son's starvation.[53]

In the final movement of this line, the son is reduced to wanting to eat the pigs' food. This makes him like an animal, so that he abandons even his humanity.[54] His degradation must now be at an end. All downward options are exhausted. He is without money and food, in a foreign land, without family, tribe, or even humanity. As a rabbinic maxim has it, Israel needs carob to be forced to repentance.[55]

An audience that according to the mytheme of the two sons views the younger as a favorite and anticipates roguish behavior has had its patience tested. The extreme action of the son calls their sympathy into question. Will he break the mode of all those other favorite sons? Regardless, a hearer now expects the son or someone else to restore him, or else the parable will end in tragedy.

Line 4: Coming to himself, he said, "How many of my father's hired hands abound in bread, but I in famine here perish. Rising up, I will go to my father and I will say to him, 'Father, I have sinned to heaven and before you, no longer am I worthy to be called your son; make me as one of your hired hands.'" And rising up, he came to his father.

If the aphorism of the carob bean's reducing Israel to repentance represents a widespread sentiment, a hearer expects some turn on the son's behalf. "Coming to himself" is the first clue that the awaited restoration is beginning. Whether it represents an Aramaic idiom is unimportant.[56] By coming to himself he begins to overcome his self-

53. Entrevernes Group, *Signs and Parables*, 151.
54. Ibid., 152–53. Dalman (*Jesus-Jeshua*, 230–31) quotes several examples in rabbinic literature in which the carob bean stands for wretchedness.
55. Feldmann (*Parables and Similes*, 124) interprets the maxim to mean that only when Israel is reduced to such a state of poverty that they must eat carob do they repent of their evil ways. See also Manson, *Sayings*, 288.
56. See Jeremias, "Zum Gleichnis," 229; following Str-B 2:215. Jeremias construes it as

destructive pattern of behavior.[57] To term this development repentance
is to turn the narrative into a theologoumenon. After all, his stomach
induced his return.[58]

The son sets out to plot his course of action. The good is still symbolized by food. The hired hands have bread, but he perishes in famine.
This contrast suggests a course of action. The son will become a hired
hand, and therefore one entitled to bread. He can no longer be a son,
because he has forfeited those rights. His sin is twofold. On the one
hand, by attaching himself to a foreigner and feeding pigs he has abrogated Judaism—his religion. On the other hand, the loss of his inheritance is a sin before his father, for he will be unable to carry out his
responsibility to take care of the old man, his familial responsibility.[59]
That which belongs to the family now belongs to foreigners.

The son views his situation in legal terms.[60] He has lost his sonship
and does not expect it to be restored. He expects things to be earned;
therefore he will earn his bread as a hired hand. As indicated above, in
describing the father-son relation, the story borrows heavily from the
legal repertoire. That the son should view his possibilities legally is not
surprising. The father represents the demands of law.[61] As a hierarchical
figure in a patron-client society,[62] not only can he divide his property but
he stands in judgment on the son's activity. In the son's speech, the
father replicates the demands of heaven, and in this way the narrative
metaphorically suggests that he stands in for God. But the parable has
also suggested an undertow, the maternal theme, associated with nourishment. Paradoxically, the son will request from the father nourishment to be earned.

The son's coming to himself and his rising up—both in speech and
narration—suggest to a hearer a fundamental change in the story's

---

an idiom meaning "to turn," i.e., "to repent." Creed (*Gospel according to St. Luke*, 199;
following Wettstein, *Novum Testamentum Graecum*, 760) argues that it is a common
Hellenistic idiom meaning "to have second thoughts." Although Luke does have a
proclivity for interior monologues in the parables, the introductory formula is usually
"he said in himself"; see Carlston, "Reminiscence and Redaction," 371.

57. Via (*Parables*, 168) says that the son can recall his past.

58. Derrett, *Law in the New Testament*, 103.

59. Jülicher, *Die Gleichnisreden* 2:348; Plummer, *Gospel according to St. Luke*, 372;
Derrett, *Law in the New Testament*, 111. Danker (*Jesus and the New Age*, 170) quotes a
Hellenistic letter that indicates the realism of the son's prepared speech: "Greetings, . . .
I was ashamed to go to Kanaris because I am so shabby. I am writing to tell you that I
am naked. I plead with you, forgive me. I know well I made a mistake. I have heard
from Postumus who met you in the area of Arisnoe. Unfortunately he told you
everything. Don't you know that I would rather be a cripple than owe so much as a
cent to any man? I plead, I plead with you . . . Antonios Longus, your son."

60. Via, "Prodigal Son," 220.

61. Entrevernes Group, *Signs and Parables*, 161.

62. See chap. 8 below.

direction. The downward spiral into tragedy is reversed. Motion toward the father rescues the son from foreign domination. The humility and proper respect shown by the son convince an audience that this son will be restored to favorite status.

Line 5: While he was way far off, his father saw him and had pity and running he fell upon his neck and kissed him affectionately.

So far, spatial metaphors have indicated failure and degradation. Being away from the father has represented failure. This line provides abundant proof that the son's return is welcomed and that he will be forgiven. The father bridges the gap between himself and his son. A rabbinic parallel makes clear the father's intention:

> A king had a son who had gone astray from his father a journey of a hundred days; his friends said to him, "Return to your father;" he said, "I cannot." Then his father sent to say, "Return as far as you can, and I will come to you the rest of the way." So God says, "Return to me, and I will return to you."[63]

While the intent of the line is clear, this line and the next one have the quality of burlesque. The father goes overboard, and his behavior is out of character for an eastern master/patron, for it violates his honor. The line even implies that the father has been watching for his son. Embracing and kissing are signs of forgiveness,[64] but to kiss affectionately hints at the maternal theme.[65] Even more surprisingly, there is no test of the son's sincerity. The father's initial response indicates that he will not follow legal or paternal roles; he will play the nourishing role.

Line 6: Said the son to him, "Father, I have sinned to heaven and before you, no longer am I worthy to be called your son . . ."

Now the son proposes terms for his restoration as a hired hand. But he is cut off in midsentence, the conclusion of which the hearer knows. The story in which the son is the subject is now effectively at an end. The father becomes the controlling subject, and the son the object of his affection.

---

63. C. Montefiore and Loewe, *Rabbinic Anthology*, 321; quoting from *Pes. R.* 184b–185a.

64. Stählin, "*phileō*," 139.

65. Entrevernes Group, *Signs and Parables*, 167. Bailey (*Poet and Peasant*, 183) argues that the feminine overtone is quite inappropriate and so wants to translate the phrase as "kiss again and again." The formulaic phrase, however, is "to weep, to fall upon the neck, and to kiss"; see Acts 20:37. The formula occurs three times in Genesis, with *kataphileō* used only in the reconciliation of Joseph and his brothers (Gen. 45:15); on the other two occasions it is *phileō* (Gen. 33:4; 50:1). The evidence from usage would seem to vindicate Manson's conclusion (*Sayings*, 288) that for a father to kiss his son affectionately would be inappropriate.

Line 7: Said the father to his slaves, "Quickly, bring out the best robe and clothe him, and put a ring on his hand and sandals on his feet, and bring the fatted calf, kill, and eating let us make merry, because this my son was dead and lives again, was lost and is found." And they began to make merry.

Befitting his control of the story, the father commands his slaves to carry out orders that have the appearance of restoring the son to the status of son, not to the requested status of a hired servant. According to Jeremias, the father's orders show forgiveness and reinstatement,[66] but this again is to reduce the text to a theologoumenon. The specific objects mentioned in the orders are also cultural clues designed to alert the audience to the son's restoration within the father's honor. The best robe must surely be that of the father himself,[67] the son and the father are thus placed in the same place. The ring, probably a signet ring, gives the son power and status. For servants to place sandals on the son's feet indicates his superiority over them.[68] The first set of orders moves in the direction of the father as patriarchal head restoring his son to his proper place of honor in a hierarchical system. The father's gifts are not simply necessities, do not simply clothe the naked. The father is making his son an object of honor. The son's place, which has been abrogated by his loss of the property, is now restored.[69]

The killing of the fatted calf and the feast correlate with the theme of nourishment. The son has been starving, now he will be feasted. The two sets of symbols are not contrasted but woven together into the full theme of restoration. This is completed when the father remarks that his dead son is alive, that the once lost is now found. Within the context of the story this makes perfect sense. The son has been dead since he requested the division of the property, insinuating a death wish for his father, and in famine faced death. In a foreign country, attached to a foreigner, he was lost.

The narrator concludes this line with the remark that "they began to make merry." The celebration and joy encompass also the hearer. The father's restoration of the son to honor restores the son in a hearer's estimation. He is indeed the favorite who has found his way back to his father's home. The hearer rejoices with the father in the return of the prodigal. The mytheme of the younger son story prepares the audience

---

66. Jeremias, *Parables,* 130.
67. So Plummer in *Gospel according to St. Luke,* 376.
68. Derrett, *Law in the New Testament,* 114. Cf. Mark 1:7.
69. The extravagance of the orders has led Rengstorf (*Die Re-Investitur*) to see this as originally a king parable. For his thorough discussion of the symbolism involved in this line, see pp. 18–51.

for his roguish behavior, for his being welcomed back, for his favorite status. In the actual telling, an audience can identify with both the father's joy and the son's relief. Father, son, and audience go into the feast together.

Line 8: There was his son, the elder one, in the field. And as he was coming, he drew near to the house, he heard music and dancing, and calling to one of the boys, he inquired what it might mean.

The contrived beginning of the elder-brother sequence is a frequent argument against its originality. How is it possible that the elder would be uninformed of the younger's return, the father's welcome, and the feast? Such a question ignores the art of fiction. The line is contrived, stage-managed,[70] but in order to locate this character in his proper place in the story.

The explicit reference to the son as "elder" recalls the mytheme of elder-and-younger-brother stories in which the elder brother is uptight ("scrubbed clean") and the least favorite. This elder brother will live up to a hearer's expectations. The prominent use of spatial metaphors continues. The son is "in the field," away from the father and yet still home. The metaphor signals objection and, given the use of similar metaphors in the first part, failure. The son draws near but does not enter. Music[71] and dancing stand for celebration. In the first part of the parable, food and nourishment stand for the positive values. Here, music and dancing stand for celebration, since the object of this sequence is for the elder son to accept the feast's necessity.

Line 9: He said to him, "Your brother has come, and your father has killed the fatted calf, because he has got him back in good health."

In this line a servant summarizes the previous narrative. Ostensibly this is done to bring the elder son up to date. But the narrator need not resort to this summary in direct discourse for such a purpose. The text could have read, "And he told him." Instead this line cements a hearer's ratification of the father's action and the identification with father and younger son. In addition, the line makes an adjustment in point of view. The narrative's terminology has derived from the father's perspective. It begins with "two sons," not "two brothers." In v. 13, the narrator refers to the younger son, the marker "son" being superfluous. Again in v. 21 the narrator says, "and the son said to him." "He said" would have sufficed. And in the introduction to the parable's second act in line 8, the narrator

---

70. Linnemann, *Jesus of the Parables*, 10.
71. For a discussion about whether it means "music" or an "instrument," see BAGD, 781. The debate is irrelevant for understanding the story.

refers to "his son, the elder one." Now there is a shift to brothers. The perspective is no longer that of the father. This is appropriate, for the elder son is going to challenge the father's acceptance of the younger son; he is going to challenge the father's control of the story.

Line 10: He was angry and did not wish to go in; his father coming pleaded with him.

Major movement in the story occurs in this line, yet it is as thin as the previous line is rich. It leaves a great deal unspoken; it is indeterminate. The refusal to go in stands for rejection of the father's activity, but precisely why the elder son is angry is left unstated. Because the father has received back the younger son and is still in control of the property, the welcome means that he can be supported from the property as long as the father lives.[72] The elder son may even fear that the younger will get more than simply maintenance. Perhaps he is angry because he resents those years of doing his duty if "scrapegraces are to receive more consideration than upright and conscientious folk."[73] In a limited-goods society, receiving the younger son back must be at the detriment of the elder.[74]

Whatever the reasons for the elder son's refusal, his anger confirms a hearer's preconceived negative image. The father comes out of the house, just as he did at the approach of the younger son. But this son comes not as a humble prospective hired hand but as an arrogant elder brother whose refusal to eat with his father and brother shames them.[75] Just as the younger son cut himself off from the father in the first act, so now the elder's anger and refusal violate the Fourth Commandment and so cut him off just as surely from the father.[76]

Line 11: Answering he said to his father, "See, how many years I slaved for you and never went against your commandment, and never did you give me a goat so that I might make merry with my friends. When this son of yours who ate up your life with harlots came, you killed for him the fatted calf."

The son's response verifies that the younger son received the right of both possession and disposition while the elder has only the right of possession. He sees himself completely dependent on the father ("I

72. Derrett, *Law in the New Testament*, 114. See the quotes from the Mishnah in line 1.

73. Manson, *Sayings*, 289.
74. C. Montefiore, *Synoptic Gospels* 2:524.
75. Bailey, *Poet and Peasant*, 195.
76. Derrett, *Law in the New Testament*, 110.

slaved"). The younger son "ate up your life"; that is, the younger is no longer able to carry out his responsibility to provide for the father. An important aspect of the son's complaint is that the father has failed to live up to the demands of honor. The younger has brought shame on the family by destroying the family life. This is the great insult that, according to the elder, the younger has compounded by consorting with prostitutes, violating the family's bloodline.[77]

If the elder's case against the younger is clear, so also is the contrast between himself and the younger. The contrast is between his view and that of the father. For the elder son, the younger is a *profiteer* who is *depraved*, while he is a *slave* to the father and *faithful*, never breaking a commandment. So sharp is the contrast that the elder refers to the younger as "that son of yours."[78] From the father's viewpoint, the younger son was lost and now is found.[79] They both view the same actions but interpret them differently. The audience sees the elder son not as a slave but as selfish, and not as faithful but as self-righteous. What is missing is the father's view of the elder son.

> *Line 12:* He said to him, "Child, you always are with me, and everything that is mine is yours. [To make merry and to rejoice was necessary because this your brother was dead and lives, and being lost is found.]"

The final line unfolds the father's view of his elder son. Where the son saw himself as a faithful slave, the father views him as a *companion* ("always with me") and *co-owner* of the farm ("all that is mine is yours").[80] Thus the elder fails to recognize that the father is always on his side and he need not earn his father's approval. He has made himself a slave for something that was already his.

The father's response goes beyond a simple legal affirmation that the elder son is the one true heir. He addresses him as "child," not son. *Teknon* in the vocative denotes affection.[81] The greeting punctures the proper titles that have characterized this parable and moves the dis-

---

77. Creed, *Gospel according to St. Luke,* 201. Prostitution was widespread in Palestine, but Hellenism took a much more lenient view. See Hauck and Schulz, "*pornē,*" 582–83, 585.

78. According to BDF, 209 (6), it appears to be used contemptuously. Manson (*Sayings,* 290) and Jeremias (*Parables,* 131) leave no doubt about its contemptuous use here.

79. The Entrevernes Group (*Signs and Parables,* 174) works out a series of logical squares demonstrating these contrasts.

80. The fact that the father asserts that the elder son has everything affirms his right of possession but not yet his right of disposition.

81. BAGD, 808; Oepke, "*pais,*" 683. Manson (*Sayings,* 290) suggests a translation of "my dear boy."

course to an entirely different level. The parable began with two sons (*hyios*), one identified as younger (*neōteros*) and the other, later, as elder (*presbyteros*),[82] and the narrator maintains the father's perspective by referring to sons. When the younger son has forfeited his sonship, he proposes to be a hired hand, a day laborer (*misthios*). By earning wages he will not be dependent like a slave, and given the importance of honor in this parable, such a proposal protects his honor. The father gives his three commands to slaves, and when the elder son asks what is going on, he addresses a boy (*pais*). There is a delicious irony between "elder" and "boy," not missed by the audience. The boy attempts to insert the perspective of "brother" into the story, but the elder rejects it with "this son of yours." Finally, the father responds with an affectionate "dear child." Except for the boyservant who tried to introduce the perspective of brothers (family), the parable has maintained a careful legal view. One might even better translate *hyios* as "heir," for it is the idea of the sons as heirs that dominates. But a subterranean movement in the story has associated nourishment with a maternal theme. That theme resurfaces in the final address, for the father dismisses the legal title and deals with his sons as children. The kissing and embracing of the younger son signals the same function as addressing the elder as child. The father combines in himself the maternal and paternal roles. As a father he is a failure, but as a mother he is a success. It is his forgiving, nourishing character that has entranced generations of hearers and readers.

As we noted above in dealing with Luke's performance of the parable, the note about the necessity for making merry and rejoicing may be Luke's way of directing interest to that part of the parable where he sees the emphasis. But the ending is not opposed to the originating parabolic structure, since it affirms this maternal, nourishing aspect of the father. It is the finding of his children that concerns him, not his honor as represented by the inheritance. If, on the other hand, one understands this remark to confirm a supposed rejection of the elder son, then the parable has suffered violence.

From Story to Parable: The Brothers

The parable's ending leaves the hearer without an ending,[83] and frequently and ending is supplied. Does the elder son go in or stay out? What is the younger son's status? Adorned with the signs of restoration and feasting on the fatted calf, the elder possesses all the property. At

---

82. Bornkamm, "*presbys*," 652: *neōteros* alone means "young"; *presbyteros* alone means "old." The comparative sense comes into play only with the expression of the other term.

83. Jones (*Art and Truth*, 169) sees the lack of ending as a sign of the parable as high art.

the father's death, will the younger become the elder's slave?

The mytheme of the two sons, found in a variety of stories, is an important constituent in the parable's repertoire. How does the parable relate to the mytheme? Does it support or subvert the mytheme? Before answering this question, we must elaborate in more detail the basic pattern of the mytheme.

The mytheme functions at a variety of levels. At its most basic level it belongs to those traditional family stories explaining in narrative why some children are more favored than others. This forms the basic pattern used at other levels. Both brothers play sterotyped roles: the younger is something of a rogue and the elder is dutiful, but in the end it is the younger who is favored. The rabbinic parable, quoted above, is typical, and its images of the younger, "dirty," son and the elder, "scrubbed clean," can metaphorically represent the sons' divergent fates. This mytheme resolves the tension of sibling rivalry experienced in all large families. The younger is the favorite because he is chosen, spoiled, favored.

The patriarchal narratives have incorporated this mytheme, where it serves a similar function. It explains why God has continually chosen his people even when they have apparently wandered from his way. There is not something here that they do, but simply their being chosen, favored.[84] In this form of the mytheme, Jacob's birthright becomes an important element in the story, since Jacob's portion becomes Israel's.[85] For example, in Mal. 1:2–3 the mytheme appears:

> "I have loved you," says the Lord. But you say, "How hast thou loved us?" "Is not Esau Jacob's brother?" says the Lord. "Yet I have loved Jacob but I have hated Esau; I have laid waste his hill country and left his heritage to jackals of the desert."

Here the narrative of the two sons is implied, and at the surface is the mytheme whose components are clearly exhibited. The story of Jacob and Esau is called on to indicate that God loves (chooses) freely. It demonstrates why Israel is given a place of privilege. Another example comes from a later period. In *Midrash on Psalms,* interpreting Jer. 3:18–19, a parable explains why Israel receives "a land of desire, a heritage of beauty desired by the nations":

> Can sibe'ot goyim [desired by the nations] mean anything else except that the Land of Israel was desired and coveted by all the nations? Consider the parable of a king who was seated at his royal table. He had many children,

---

84. Derrett (*Law in the New Testament,* 117) makes this point.
85. See also the parable A Man Planted a Vineyard, in chap. 10 below. See Alter, *Art,* 42–46.

but he loved the youngest one the most. He was about to apportion their inheritances. Among the parcels of land there was one of great beauty, which all the children coveted, and so the king said: "Let this parcel of land remain as my own portion." As Scripture says, "The Most High apportioned to the nations their inheritance" (Deut. 32:8), but to whom did He finally give His own portion? To His youngest child, for the next verse says, "The Lord's portion to His people, to Jacob the lot of His inheritance" (ibid. 32:9).[86]

In this exegesis we can see the mytheme and narrative both finding expression; the only element missing from the full pattern is a note about the youngest's being "dirty," although the Jeremiah passage goes on to compare faithless Israel to a faithless wife. But the mytheme still functions to explain why, of all the nations, God has chosen Israel. The story of Jacob and Esau provides the basis for resolving this tension. For the purposes of our analysis, it is important to see that the two-sons mytheme can tell in narrative and myth the fate of Israel.[87]

Paul turns the two-sons mytheme against Israel of the flesh to argue that the Gentiles, the sons of promise, the younger sons, are part of God's grace. In Romans 9, he uses both the Isaac and Jacob narratives to prove his point. It is through Isaac that Abraham's promise comes (Gen. 21:12; Rom. 9:7), and Rebecca was told "the elder will serve the younger" (Gen. 25:23; Rom 9:12). Again in Gal. 4:21–31, Paul uses the two sons of Abraham for an elaborate allegory. Hagar is the mother of slavery, and Sarah is the mother of freedom. "Now we, brethren, like Isaac, are children of promise" (Gal. 4:28).[88] Paul's use of this mytheme bears on the parable in three important ways. It shows that (*a*) the mytheme was a strong and powerful interpreter of existence at the time of Jesus; (*b*) the identification is with the younger son, the favored line; and (*c*) early Christians used this mytheme to understand their own chosen status against those who had been previously chosen. The Christian community used the parable A Man Had Two Sons to reflect on its self-understanding. Naturally they identified themselves with the younger son, and faithless Israel with the elder.[89]

This Christian adoption of the mytheme, however, is inappropriate to Jesus' context, to his hearers. As we have seen, the hearer of the parable would have identified with the younger son. As Claude Montefiore remarks, the first part of the parable "teaches that whenever the sinner

86. *Midrash on Psalms* 5.1 (Braude 1:82).
87. Ironically, in Christian exegesis of A Man Had Two Sons, the elder son, Esau, is the Jews, whereas in rabbinic exegesis, Esau is a set piece for the Gentiles.
88. Betz (*Galatians,* 245) works out the underlying structure of the allegory or typology employed by Paul. Doeve (*Jewish Hermeneutics,* 109) sees an elaborate Hebrew wordplay based on Hagar, *hgr,* and "mountain," *hhr.* Betz's analysis is more convincing.
89. Derrett (*Law in the New Testament,* 125) see this point.

repents, God receives him gladly. Nothing, by the way, can be more Jewish and Rabbinic than this."[90] This point of view should warn those who would claim that in the first part is the good news of the gospel.[91] Only a Christian arrogance prevents one from seeing this as Jewish.

The parable's scandal derives from its subversion of the mytheme's power to resolve between the chosen and the rejected. The purpose of this mytheme, whether used to identify favoritism within the family or between Israel and the nations, is to decide who is the favorite, the chosen. But in the parable the elder son's fate is not like Esau's: he is not hated, nor does the younger receive Jacob's portion. Actually, the elder is the heir: "All that is mine is yours." Nor is he banished: "I am always with you." The mytheme anticipates the elder's rejection and banishment. As J. D. Derrett remarks, "Is the father's estate really the elder brother's when the returning prodigal, who has eaten his cake, shows every sign of proceeding to have it?"[92] The answer, of course, is yes, much to the dismay of the audience. This parable subverts a mytheme by which the kingdom decides between the chosen and rejected. Here the father rejects no one; both are chosen.

Even more is at stake. The younger son violates the moral code and gets a feast; the elder rejects the father but gets all. The father is interested neither in morality nor in inheritance. He is concerned with the unity of his sons. If the sons play the roles laid out for them in the two-sons mytheme, the father's play seems to be Ps. 133:1: "How good and pleasant it is for brothers to dwell in unity."

In the parable the kingdom is not something that decides between but something that unifies. The father does not reject. The metaphor for the kingdom is the father's coming out, both for the younger son and for the elder. Apart from him is division and failure. In the parable, Jesus rejects any apocalyptic notion of some group's being rejected at the expense of another. The parable radically rejects Israel's self-understanding of itself as the favored, younger son. The kingdom is universal, not particularist. The universalism, however, is not based on the rejection of some. All people are called, regardless of the script the mytheme requires of them. Universalism is not a banner to parade under, but its image is the welcoming of a child. Just as the Samaritan saves the Jew in the ditch, so the elder son inherits all. The audience must come to terms with one who in myth was rejected and in parable inherits all.

90. C. Montefiore, *Synoptic Gospels* 2:524.
91. E.g., Jeremias, *Parables*, 131.
92. Derrett, *Law in the New Testament*, 104. Although Derrett sees many important aspects of this parable, he is unable to follow up his clues because he remains bound to Luke's context.

3

*How to
Mismanage
a Miracle*

The Land of a Rich Man

A certain rich man's lands brought forth bountiful crops. And he deliberated within himself, saying, "What shall I do since I do not have a place where I may gather my fruit?" And he said, "I will do this: I will tear down my granaries and larger ones I will build and I will gather there all my grain and goods and I will say to my self, 'Self, you have many good things stored up for many a year. Rest, eat, drink, enjoy.'" God said to him, "Fool, on this night they will demand your self from you. And the things which you have prepared, whose will they be?"

The parable of The Land of a Rich Man (Luke 12:16–20; *Gos. Thom.* 63) has not been of major interest in the history of parable interpretation, nor has it been at the center of controversy. Its interpretation has been stable, predictable, and unafflicted by the obscurities that so torment other parables. Its meaning is apparent. And that meaning is the meaning found in Luke's Gospel.[1]

---

1. See pp. 29–30 above for the problem, with example story as a form-critical classification.

The Fool in Luke

Understanding this parable in Luke's Gospel will lead us, first, to a grasp of the parable's place in the Lukan narrative and, second, to an investigation of the adaptations the author of Luke-Acts may have made in the parable proper.

The parable provides a negative example of the well-established Lukan theme of the necessity of poverty for following Jesus.[2] In comparison with Mark and Matthew, Luke consistently sharpens Jesus' words on poverty.[3] In the Gospel's narrative development, the parable occurs in the travel narrative (9:52—19:10). In analyzing the literary interrelation of the various themes and sections of the travel narrative, Talbert sees Luke 12:1–48 as parallel to Luke 16.[4] Luke 12:1–48 contains three themes: the threat of hell (vv. 1–12), riches (vv. 13–34), and stewardship (vv. 35–48). These themes also appear in chapter 16, but in inverse order. Thus the two chapters form a chiasmus.[5] A majority of the material in Luke 12:1–48 is also in Matthew and therefore presumably derives from a common source (Q). The only material with no parallel in Matthew is vv. 13–21. According to Talbert, Q alone could not provide a parallel to chapter 16, which is unique to Luke. Thus he concludes that the parable was essential for constructing a parallel to chapter 16.

In the section built around the theme of riches, there are two episodes: one addressed to the public, the other to the disciples. Both conclude with sayings dealing with treasure (vv. 21, 34). Verses 21 and 34 underline the point Luke is making in this section. The heart is where the treasure is: for the rich, away from God; for the poor, in heaven.

If the parable holds such a central place in the triptych of chapter 12, and alone contains material not common to Matthew, is the hand of the redactor evident in its formulation? Talbert has remarked that in the parable's introduction one could see Luke at work, although he has given no specific evidence.[6] But the handiwork is readily evident. Because of Luke's use of apothegms to introduce parables, Bultmann has maintained that the connection between vv. 13–15 and the parable is secondary.[7] Confirming evidence comes from the *Gospel of Thomas*, where the inheritance question appears in logion 72 and the parable in

2. On the theme of poverty in the travel narrative, see L. Johnson, *Literary Function*, 103–15. Pilgrim deals with the thematic of wealth and poverty in Luke-Acts; for analysis of this specific parable, see his *Good News*, 109–13.

3. Luke 14:12//Matt 22:9. See also Luke 1:53; 3:11; 4:18; 6:24–25; 12:13–21; 14:12–14, 33; 16:1–13, 19–31.

4. Talbert, *Literary Patterns*, 55.

5. Ibid.

6. Ibid.

7. Bultmann, *History of the Synoptic Tradition*, 61.

logion 63, indicating that apothegm and parable were probably joined by Luke. At any rate, the question about inheritance has little to do with the parable.[8] Similarly, as Martin Dibelius[9] and others have pointed out, v. 31 provides a generalizing, moral conclusion, the addition of which was a tendency of early preachers, thereby converting the parable to the task of exhortation. Thus either Luke or the early tradition provided the parable with an introductory apothegm on inheritance and a concluding exhortatory saying.

Luke has contributed more than simple arrangement. The vocabulary of the parable's beginning shows considerable Lukan adaptation. Verse 16a ("He said a parable to them, saying,") is clearly a Lukan construction (e.g., 14:7; 15:3; 18:1). Furthermore, the use of *tis* is a well-attested Lukan trademark. The parables From Jerusalem to Jericho (10:30), A Man Gave a Banquet (14:16), A Man Had Two Sons (15:11), A Rich Man Had a Steward (16:1), A Rich Man Clothed in Purple (16:19), In a City There Was a Judge (18:2), and A Man Entrusts Property (19:12) all employ some form of *tis* in the introduction.

According to Jeremias's detailed word study, Luke's hand can be seen in the "and he debated in himself saying . . . 'What shall I do because . . . I shall do.'" This formulation is strikingly similar to the soliloquy of the unjust steward (16:3): "He said in himself . . . 'What shall I do . . . I will do.'" For other parallels, Jeremias points to Luke 5:21; 7:49; and 20:13.[10] His evidence requires differentiation. Luke 5:21; 7:49; and 20:13 are all instances where Luke modifies material for which there are Synoptic parallels, but Luke 12:17 and 16:3 are parables that occur only in Luke. Luke has a strong preference for the stylistic arrangement of verb–participle of saying–question. In the three passages common to the Synoptics, only Luke has this formula. But he does not create the dialogue. Rather, as the examples from the Synoptic parallels show, the formulation appears to be Luke's characteristic way of introducing an interior questioning. There is no reason to believe that *dialogizomai* is Lukan.[11] Although in the parables of A Rich Man Had a Steward and

8. Derrett ("Rich Fool," 131–51) makes a number of interesting points concerning the parable but unfortunately assumes the original unity of apothegm and parable.

9. Dibelius, *From Tradition to Gospel*, 258. Jeremias (*Parables*, 106) maintains that v. 21 gives the parable a moralizing tone consistent with Luke. Cadoux (*Parables*, 205) agrees.

10. Jeremias, *Die Sprache*, 15.

11. The evidence from usage: Mark uses *dialogizomai* seven times, Matthew three times in passages parallel to Mark. Luke also uses the verb seven times: three times in passages parallel to Mark (in one parallel passage, Luke uses the adjective); three times in material unique to Luke; and once in a passage parallel to Mark and Matthew where they do not use the verb. Thus no clear pattern emerges. Luke does show a clear preference for the adjective *dialogismos*.

The Land of a Rich Man, Luke conforms the introduction of the interior monologue to his style, there can be no question of his creating the content, as distinct from the form, of the monologue.

The Thomas Parable

The *Gospel of Thomas* preserves a parable strikingly similar to that in Luke.

> Jesus said, "There was a rich man who had much money. He said, 'I shall put my money to use so that I may sow, reap, plant, and fill my storehouse with produce, with the result that I shall lack nothing.' Such were his intentions, but that same night he died. Let him who has ears hear." (*Gos. Thom.* 63)[12]

Early commentators on the *Gospel of Thomas* advanced a number of opinions about the relation of the *Thomas* parable to the Lukan one. Crossan, though not addressing the problem in detail, does seem to consider the *Thomas* version closer to original because it lacks the moral overtones associated with the Lukan version. The simple story in *Thomas* paints a stark tragedy of a man who spends his last day planning his future.[13] But Crossan is in the minority. The majority can be represented by Montefiore, who sees the *Thomas* version as a simplification with consequent loss of vividness.[14]

Jacques-E. Ménard is closer to the point yet overstates the case when he remarks that Luke and *Thomas* do not really present two versions of the same story.[15] The Lukan story is about a man who must decide what to do with a bountiful harvest; the *Thomas* story concerns a man who wants to increase his wealth to avoid suffering. This is no small point of difference. Both parables belong to the wisdom trajectory dealing with riches, but they belong to different subsets. The *Thomas* story represents the more common motif of an admonition against greed, whereas the

---

12. See Birdsall, "Luke XII, 16ff. and the Gospel of Thomas," 332–36. Birdsall deals with the fact that some manuscripts have as a conclusion to the Lukan parable the saying about those who have ears which concludes *Thomas*. According to Birdsall, there is no relation to *Thomas*, for the reading is late, from the lectionaries. There is no attestation from the Western text or the Diatesseron.

13. Crossan, *In Parables*, 85. In "Parable and Example," 78–79, Crossan is much more certain that the *Thomas* parable is original. It is the moralizing aspect of the Lukan version that Crossan finds incompatible with Jesus' style.

14. H. Montefiore and Turner, *Thomas and the Evangelists*, 50. Summers (*Secret Sayings*, 46) makes the same point. But Gärtner (*Theology*, 46) gives no opinion, remarking that it is difficult to decide. H. Schürmann (*Traditionsgeschichte Untersuchungen*, 232) sees dependence upon Luke.

15. Ménard, *L'évangile selon Thomas*, 163. Ménard provides a gnostic reading of the parable in the context of the *Gospel of Thomas*.

Lukan story belongs to a less common subset on the use of wealth.[16] Because of the evident proclivity of the Jesus parables to play in the minor keys of the tradition,[17] the *Thomas* performance is a reversion of the originating structure to the major type, while the Lukan performance preserves the originating structure more clearly.

Surface Structure

Although the parable's surface structure is not as complex as that of the more elaborate parables, it is tightly constructed. It has three main parts: introduction, soliloquy, and response. A unifying thread running through the parable is the use of verbs of saying.

> INTRODUCTION: and he **debated** [*dielogizeto*] in himself
> SOLILOQUY: and he **said** [*eipen*] "I will tear
> and I will **say** [*erō*]
> RESPONSE: **said** [*eipen de*] to him God

Other elements contribute to the parable's rapid pace. The soliloquy begins with a question, *ti poiesō*, "What shall I do?" Similarly, the response concludes with a question, *tini estai*, "Whose shall it be?" A number of chiasmatic structures tie the subsections together.

$$A \qquad\qquad B$$
I may gather together / fruit   / my [*mou*]
$$B \qquad\qquad A$$
I will tear down   / my [*mou*] / storehouses

Although the odd use of *mou* in connection with storehouses has elicited comment, no commentator has noticed the resulting chiasmus that creates an ironic relation between gathering in the harvest's results and tearing down the barns. Another chiasmus revolves around the use of *synaxō*.

$$A \qquad\qquad B$$
I do not have where (*pou*) / I may gather
$$B \qquad\qquad A$$
I will gather   / there (*ekei*)

In the first line the form is adverb (*pou*)/verb (*sunaxō*); in the second it is verb (*sunaxō*)/abverb (*ekei*). A third chiasmus in the soliloquy involves the "tearing down and building up":

---

16. On the question of repertoire, see the reading of line 1 below.
17. See pp. 66–67 above.

```
        A              B
I will tear down  /  my barns
        B              A
and greater ones  /  I will build up
```

A final chiasmus occurs in the rich man's soliloquy.

```
        A              B
you have many   /  goods
        B              A
stored up for years  /  many
```

This chiasmus revolves around "many goods" and "years many." These four chiasmi serve to tie the soliloquy tightly together, producing several interplays within the speech. The four imperatives, "rest," "eat," "drink," "enjoy," produce a nice finality to the soliloquy.

When examining the reader-response function of the text we will draw out the structure of God's speech. Suffice it to say that each of its points provides a contrary to man's soliloquy.

This careful structuring or ordering of the parable catches one's attention, moving one along through the story.

A Reading

Line 1: A certain rich man's lands brought forth bountiful crops. And he deliberated within himself, saying . . .

Stating that the man was rich and had lands, although redundant, accents his wealth. This note is reinforced when *chōra* is used for land, not *agros*. *Chōra* indicates extensive holdings, normally a district or region.[18] The richness theme continues with the hint of the harvest's size; the verb *euphoreō* indicates a good harvest.[19]

Accenting elements of richness indicates to the audience the story's intended direction; it hints what type of story this is. All stories invoke a repertoire of narrative possibilities drawn from the cultural stock. Line 1 implies that the story deals with wealth, its use and accumulation. This rich man's problem is the disposal of his wealth;[20] his lands have already brought forth a good harvest at the story's beginning.

Sirach is a treasury of information about common attitudes toward

18. BAGD, 889. Derrett ("Rich Fool," 143) maintains that *chōra* represents a whole district, a region separate from cities. Marshall (*Commentary on Luke*, 523) offers a helpful balance to Derrett's overstatement.

19. *Euphoreō* occurs only here in the New Testament. In Josepus, it is used in reference to crops and oil; see Plummer, *Gospel according to St. Luke*, 324.

20. Klostermann, *Das Lukasevangelium*, 356.

wealth. Sirach 31:5–11 can serve as a model for the repertoire's possibilities:

> He who loves gold will not be justified and he who pursues money will be led astray by it. Many have come to ruin because of gold. . . . It is a stumbling block to those who are devoted to it, and every fool will be taken captive by it. Blessed is the rich man who is found blameless, and who does not go after gold. Who is he? We will call him blessed for he has done wonderful things among his people. Who has been tested by it and been found perfect? . . . His prosperity will be established and the assembly will relate his acts of charity.

Riches pose their own problem, and a rich man has a difficult but not impossible task. The purpose of wealth is acts of charity, almsgiving (Sir. 31:5–11). The hoarding of wealth is condemned;[21] wealth must serve a public need.[22]

At the conclusion of line 1 the man becomes the subject both in grammar and in story. Although the story's beginning leads to an expectation that its subject is the use of the land's produce, the harvest turns out to be only an occasion for the real subject, the man. Further, the rich man carries on his dialogue with himself. He excludes others from his story.

Line 2: "What shall I do since I do not have a place where I may gather my fruit?"

If line 1 outlines the general possibilities open to the story, then line 2 specifies the rich man's immediate problem. Where will he store the produce of his fields? It is significant that the harvest is larger than usual, since he does not have sufficient storage space. The sensitive hearer

---

21. 1 *Enoch* 97.8–10 has a story similar to the *Thomas* parable that demonstrates how the Lukan parable plays in a minor key:

"We have grown rich and accumulated goods,
we have acquired everything that we have desired.
So now let us do whatever we like;
for we have gathered silver,
we have filled our treasuries (with money) like water.
And many are the laborers in our houses."
Your lies flow like water.
For your wealth shall not endure
but it shall take off from you quickly
for you have acquired it all unjustly,
and you shall be given over to a great curse.
                                    (Charlesworth 1:78)

22. For the evidence, see Derrett, "Rich Fool," 142. Pilgrim deals with the poor in the Hebrew Bible (*Good News,* chap. 1). Our interest is the rich, and Pilgrim presents an oblique analysis of the rich, since one cannot discuss the poor without discussing the rich.

would be alerted that something out of the ordinary is happening. If the man lacks sufficient storage space for his harvest, how large is it? A rich man ordinarily would have sufficient storage space.

Line 3: And he said, "I will do this: I will tear down my granaries and larger ones I will build and I will gather there all my grain and goods. . . .

The man responds to his dilemma with drastic action. He does not simply build more granaries or add on to his existing complex. Rather, he tears down the old barns and builds new, greater ones. Such all-or-nothing activity characterizes Jesus' parables (e.g., the selling of all to buy the land with buried treasure). It burlesques the everyday.

The line echoes through Israel's traditions, with a number of resonances. The contrast "tear down/build up" occurs in the Hebrew Bible in reference to both acts of folly and God's protection,[23] but this potential resonance remains undeveloped. The resonances draw a hearer in other directions. If all the barns are torn down and new ones built, the size of the harvest is well beyond average expectation. Such a harvest implies the miracle of God's blessing and suggests two prominent aspects of Israel's heritage. First, when Joseph was steward in Egypt, he stored up a surplus from bountiful harvests in preparation for the coming seven lean years (Gen. 41:35–36). A surplus implies a barren future. This same notion is reinforced by Sabbath preparations. While the people were in the desert, on the sixth day they gathered twice as much manna, for on the Sabbath, a day of rest, they would find nothing in the field (Exod. 16:22–27). The seventh year sabbath for the land follows this same pattern:

> The land will yield its fruit, and you will eat your fill, and dwell in it securely. And if you say, "What shall we eat in the seventh year, if we may not sow or gather in our crop?" I will command my blessing upon you in the sixth year, so that it will bring forth fruit for three years. (Lev. 25:19–21)

The parallels with the Joseph story and Sabbath preparations bring into focus a repertoire upon which the audience can draw to make sense of or fit together the story's actions. What kind of harvest demands such a drastic action? A harvest that is God's miracle. At the same time the harvest's very size leads a hearer to anticipate that certain things will happen. The miraculous character of the harvest places demands on the rich man. To tear down his granaries and build new, larger ones implies that he, like Joseph, will care for his people in the coming lean years. As

---

23. Lagrange (*Evangile selon Saint Luc,* 359) notices this contrast, as does Schneider ("*kathaireō*"), 411.

we have seen in connection with line 1, wealth implies social responsibility. At the conclusion of line 3, an audience judges the rich man prudent and wise, preparing for the lean years ahead for both himself and his people.

Line 4: ". . . and I will say to my self, 'Self, you have many good things stored up for many a year.

The evidence that *psychē* here means the whole existing person and not the soul as a spiritual entity inhabiting a body is overwhelming (cf. Pss. 41:6, 12; 42:5; *Ps. Sol.* 3.1).[24] In our translation, I have used "self" as a better English equivalent.

The scholarly literature has for the most part concerned itself with the translation and meaning of *psychē*, but that is not the most important feature from a literary perspective. After line 1, the parable has evolved as a soliloquy, a self-dialogue. Now the man addresses himself formally as "Self." The parable's literary technique mimics its actions. The anonymous narrator whose "he said", occurs in line 3 introduces the parable, but by line 4 he has disappeared. The text does not say, ". . . and he said to himself, 'Self,'" but ". . . and I will say to my self, 'Self.'" The rich man usurps the narrator's control of the story, replacing him in the story. The rich man now fully controls his own narrative. He not only is the subject of narration but is also the narrator.

His domination of the story, even at the level of literary technique, replicates the actions implied in line 4. The harvest is a miracle, and the storage of the surplus likewise assumes its use for the community. Yet by line 4, clues appear suggesting that he may have no such intention. He describes the harvest as "his" goods which will keep "him" for many seasons. Just as he takes over the story, usurps it from the narrator, so he usurps the harvest for his own well-being. This rich man is surely no Joseph in Egypt preparing to protect his people from the hard days ahead by storing up the present plenty.

Line 5: "'Rest, eat, drink, enjoy.'"

Alfred Plummer has remarked that the asyndeton marks the man's confidence,[25] climaxing the soliloquy. What began as a problem—what to do with the harvest—reaches its conclusion in the man's well-being. The line has a clear Epicurean tone, recalling the famous inscription reported to be on the tomb of Sardinapalus. "Eat, drink, and sport with

24. Ellis, "La fonction de l'eschatologie," 146; Bultmann, *Theology of the New Testament* 1:168, 202.
25. Plummer, *Gospel according to St. Luke*, 324.

love; all else is naught."[26] A legendary figure of seventh century Assyria, Sardinapalus was widely known in the Hellenistic world as an example of the Epicurean profligate life.[27] This caricature of Epicurean philosophy was well known within Judaism,[28] as well as throughout the Hellenistic world.[29] The "anti-Epicurean" attitude of Judaism is indicated by Isa. 22:12–14: "In that day the Lord God of Hosts called to weeping and mourning, to baldness and girding with sackcloth; and behold, . . . eating flesh and drinking wine. 'Let us eat and drink, for tomorrow we die.'"[30] Likewise when Tobias proposes to marry Sarah, her father, Raguel, explains, "Eat, drink, and be merry; for it is your right to take my child. But let me explain the true situation to you. I have given my daughter to seven husbands, and when each came to her he died in the night. But for the present be merry" (Tobit 7:9–11). The reference in 1 Cor. 15:32 again evidences a common form of the Epicurean saying: "If the dead are not raised, 'Let us eat and drink, for tomorrow we die.'"[31] These sayings demonstrate the widespread currency of the Epicurean sayings. Even more, the form of the saying involves a reference to death. It is the inevitable fate of death that prompts the Epicurean response.

Line 5 paints the rich man as hoarding the miracle of a fantastic harvest for his own pleasure. He refuses to share it with his community:

26. Plutarch, *Moralia*, "On the Fortune of Alexander" (LCL, 336). Plutarch relates the fate of two monarchs who both received the same power. One, the woman Semiramis, equipped great armies and defeated her enemies. The other, Sardanapalus, "spent his days at home carding purple wool, sitting with his knees drawn up in front of him among his concubines; and when he died, they made a stone statue of him dancing in a barbaric fashion and apparently snapping its fingers above its head." Then Plutarch relates the grave inscription.

27. Weissbach ("Sardinapal," 2436–37) and Wettstein (*Novum Testamentum Graecum* 2:169) give several parallel sayings. Malherbe ("Beasts of Ephesus," 76) discusses the Epicurean evidence while dealing with the passage in 1 Corinthians. He does not relate his discussion to the parable.

28. Fischel ("Epicureanism," 817) gives evidence for stereotyped rejection of Epicureanism by the rabbis. One who denied the rabbinic tradition was referred to as *apikoros*, which is derived from the Greek *epikuros*, although the rabbis did not appear to know this derivation.

29. The largest collection of references to the widespread Epicurean sayings are in Mayor's ed. of Juvenal (*Thirteen Satires of Juvenal*, 178–79).

30. When referring to the Isaiah text as anti-Epicurean, I mean that what comes to be identified as Epicurean has in fact much older currency throughout the Near East. Kaiser (*Isaiah 1—39*, 143) says that the passage may be a quotation from a song like those from Egyptian tombs. Clements (*Isaiah 1—39*, 186) identifies it as a proverbial saying. Penna (*Isaia*, 555) sees it as parallel to Gilgamesh OB x, 3, 4–9: "They allotted death to mankind, life they retained in their keeping. Thou, O Gilgamesh, let thy belly be full; Day and night be thou merry; Make every day (a day of) rejoicing. Day and night do thou dance and play" (*Ancient Near Eastern Texts*, 90). What this indicates is that the so-called Epicurean position is more ancient than Epicurus and that it is very widespread.

31. Besides Malherbe's "Beasts at Ephesus," see Robertson and Plummer, *First Epistle*, 362–63; Conzelmann, *First Corinthians*, 278.

he mismanages the miracle. In the ancient Mediterranean world he sins against two interlocking principles. The first holds that wealth should be used for the community's good. This theme is amply evidenced in wisdom literature (see line 1 above). Second, he offends against the perception of limited goods.[32] This ordering of reality sees the goods of the world as limited, not infinite, as they are so often imagined today. The perception of limited goods underlies the wisdom tradition's demand to share wealth. If one person hoards wealth, there will be none left to go around. If there is surplus today, there must be shortage tomorrow, so the rich man's saving up of his harvest to provide only for his own comfort offends against the community's possibilities, wastes God's gifts, and ensures the impoverishment of others.

The Epicurean character of the man's response also hints at his folly, for in all the Epicurean sayings one eats and drinks because of the inescapable fate of death. But this rich man believes he has fortified himself against the odds for many years to come.

Line 6: God said to him, "Fool, on this night they will demand your self from you. And the things which you have prepared, whose will they be?"

Even though only in this parable does God enter as a direct character, this does not destroy the parable's realism, for the harvest, the man's offense against the community, and his Epicurean response have assumed a divine presence offstage. A harvest of such proportions that it requires destroying all the man's barns to build new ones can only be God's work. And death lurks behind the Epicurean advice to eat and drink. Now God intervenes to restore the balance. God's question "Whose will they be?" leads the audience to the appropriate response: "Those for whom they were originally intended."

Until now the man has been in control. Beginning in line 4 he eclipsed the narrator to narrate his own story ("and I will say," rather than the narrator's "he said"). The beginning of line 6 is constructed in a suspenseful fashion. Literally the Greek reads, "He-said to him God" (grammatically, "God" is subject, but it comes last in the Greek word order). A hearer at first suspects that the narrator ("he-said," *eipen*) has again emerged to direct the story. Only at the line's end does the subject of "he-said" appear. God takes control.

God addresses the man as "Fool"—a powerful epithet signifying that the man's actions have denied God's existence.[33] The epithet confirms

32. Malina, *New Testament World,* 75–90.
33. E.g., Ps. 14:1: "The fool says in his heart, 'There is no God.'" See Mandry, *There Is No God!* esp. 49–54.

the way the audience has been putting the story together. A consistent way of viewing the story's parts emerges in which the man has mismanaged his possibilities to the point that he has committed idolatry. The epithet confirms this. Further, various elements from the man's speech are echoed in God's response:

1A	2A	3A	4A
Soul	/ you have many things	/ laid up	/ for many years
1B	2B	3B	4B
Fool	/ this night	/ your soul	/ they take away from you

There are four items in each line. Items 1A and 1B set up a contrast. The man addresses his own self in a kind of self-possession, and God labels this idolatry for usurpation of both story and harvest and calls the man a fool. Given the story's logic, God is the only character who can address the rich man, because he has eliminated all other competitors. Item 2B, "this night," contrasts with 4A, "for many years." What the man believes will last forever will not make it through the night. Item 3B contrasts with 3A. Believing that he laid up many things, he will lose the only thing that counts. Finally, 4B, "they take away from you," contrasts with 2A, "you have many things."

At one level the parable illustrates the evils that lie in the path of a wealthy man as he attempts to preserve his wealth. He did not acquire his wealth by evil means, but it is God's miracle, like the surplus of Joseph's time in Egypt or that of the land's before a sabbath. An audience soon expects this wealth to be stored up for the community's benefit. The man, however, intends to store up wealth not for community charity but for his own comfort and pleasure, to stave off death for many years to come. He mismanages. His proposal remains unfulfilled, for God promises that before the night is over, "they" will carry him away to death. The story concludes with God's question, the implication of which is that the wealth will now be used for those for whom it was originally intended.

The story seems to be an illustration of the point made in Sirach, although more cleverly told. But the cleverness raises three points that go beyond the simple illustration of Sirach. What do we make of the harvest and its size, the Epicurean saying, and God's intervention? Do these open on larger realities, or are they parts representing a whole?

From Story to Kingdom

The parable implicitly invokes the kingdom of God in the harvest figure, for the miraculous harvest stands for (i.e., it is a metaphor for) the kingdom, representing God's blessing—a miracle. Its very size hints at both the tradition of a sabbatical year and Joseph's overseeing of Pharaoh's surplus and lean years. Ominously its bountifulness suggests a lean future, as both the literary parallels and the notion of limited goods indicate. While the harvest is an established metaphor for the kingdom, its very size implies the kingdom's intervention or coming.

The parable's dramatic tension results from the relation of the narrative to the metaphorical structure that represents the kingdom as a village. The part of the village system that governs the use of wealth and bounty for the community's good is the implied metaphor for the kingdom. The man's predicament is how to manage a miracle. Yet his actions run directly contrary to the injunctions of the wisdom tradition. The morality of the wisdom traditon is assumed as a guide to the way of the kingdom. The man takes the fruit of the harvest for his own benefit and attempts thereby to ward off the threat of death. But God interrupts the man's plans by announcing that on that very night he will die. This intervention confirms the moral direction of the wisdom tradition. The literary technique of the parable, with the disappearing narrator, replicates the rich man's taking over the story. His idolatry, his usurpation of story and harvest, and his crowding out all around him can only be remedied by God's intervention. All other characters have been eliminated.

The manner of God's intervention requires careful observation. First, God does not carry out the death: "They will demand your life." That those powers are ultimately divine is not contested; it may be a reference to the angel-of-death mythology.[34] Indirection is part of the parable's strategy. The kingdom's coming is not an apocalyptic intervention; God does not seek to right the kingdom's misuse by an apocalyptic destruction of evil. Rather the man will die in his sleep! To those villagers who observe his death, it will be completely normal, carrying no special portent. They will probably give him an honorable burial as befitting a patron of the community. Only the hearer knows what really happened—what the man really planned to do. As in Luke 17:20, there will be no signs to be observed. The parable affirms the kingdom's presence in the metaphor of harvest, but it refuses to make it an apocalyptic kingdom. The man will die. Reality will continue. The fruit of the harvest is there. God's gift still must be managed! The parable's metaphor for the kingdom is not simply the harvest but the good life it is intended to produce for the community.

The parable A Man Casts Seed (Mark 4:26–29) raises a number of

---

34. Grundmann, *Das Evangelium nach Lukas*, 257. Grundmann argues that "they" refers to the angels of death. See Str-B 1:144–49.

interesting correlations to this parable. Both parables invoke the theme of harvest and implicitly relate the harvest to the sabbatical motif.[35] In A Man Casts Seed, the sabbatical presents the harvest as grace; in this parable it is bountiful grace. Further, both parables reject an apocalyptic intervention as the solution for evil. But because the Markan parable is metaphoric, the reader must interpret the quotation from Joel 4:13 that concludes the parable. In its context in Joel, the quotation indicates apocalyptic destruction; in its parabolic context it indicates peace. The hearer must decide which it is. Because this parable is metonymic, God is a direct character: the intervention is a normal death. Its point is more direct.

The story of The Land of a Rich Man reveals the deep indebtedness of parables to the wisdom tradition. We commonly associate Jesus with a radicalization of the wisdom tradition, but this parable indicates that on the theme of wealth, Jesus is in agreement with the wisdom tradition. It is already sufficiently radical. But characteristically, Jesus' tale does not belong to a major key of the tradition, that is, the warnings against greed. The *Thomas* version of this parable has transformed the originating structure into the major key. Rather, this parable is variation in a minor key: wealth's correct usage.

The parable cleverly equates the mismanagement of the miraculous harvest with idolatry. The parable parallels the sayings about the gift at the altar (Matt. 5:23–24) and the widow's mite (Mark 12:41–44). (The saying about the camel passing through the eye of a needle [Mark 10:35] is in the major key.) The gift offering must be abandoned because the offerer is out of communion with his brother, and so is out of communion with God. The widow out of her need provides for the poor. Both of these sayings and the parable The Land of a Rich Man focus the radical identification of God's kingdom with community and the demand to provide for the needs of others. "If a brother or sister is ill-clad and in lack of daily food, and one of you says to them, 'Go in peace, be warmed and filled,' without giving them the things needed for the body, what does it profit?" (James 2:15–16). Or as another saying has it, "What does it profit a man, to gain the whole world and forfeit his life?" (Mark 8:36). Yet this caring for neighbor is not based upon a moralizing or sentimentalizing principle. Not to place community first violates the First Commandment, is idolatry. No apocalyptic explosion will rid the world of evil; the parabolic kingdom exists only in the deeds of a loving community. The miracle must be managed.

35. See my *Jesus, Symbol-Maker*, 86. See also chap. 18 below.

4

*G*ood Fences *Make Good Neighbors*

A Rich Man Clothed in Purple

A certain man was rich and he put on purple and fine linen, making merry every day sumptuously. A certain poor man by the name of Lazarus had been prostrated at his gate, being full of sores and desiring to be fed from the things that fell from the table of the rich man. And even dogs coming licked his sores. And it happened that the poor man died and was carried by the angels into the bosom of Abraham. The rich man also died and was buried. And in Hades raising up his eyes, being in torment, he saw Abraham from afar and Lazarus in his bosom. And that one calling out said, "Father Abraham, have mercy on me and send Lazarus to dip the tip of his finger in water and cool my tongue, because I am in torment in this fire." Said Abraham, "Child, remember that you received your good things in your life, and Lazarus likewise evil things. Now this one is conforted, and you are in torment. And moreover, between us and you a great chasm has been fixed, so that one who wishes to cross over from here to you would not be able, nor can they cross from there to us."

In only one parable does a character have a proper name, and in only one parable is a scene from the afterlife depicted. Both these anomalies occur in A Rich Man Clothed in Purple (Luke 16:19–31), and both anomalies bear significantly on the parable's interpretation.

The Ending

The question of where the parable ends has been a matter of some debate. Does it end with Abraham's pronouncing a chasm between the rich man and Lazarus or with his refusal to send Lazarus to warn the rich man's brothers? To resolve this problem we will examine the conclusion from three angles: the angle of a possible life situation, that of internal stylistic questions, and that of the story's narrative development.

Bultmann[1] argued that the parable's conclusion was from a Jewish tradition forbidding one to ask God for a miracle (cf. Deut. 30:11–14). Employing the negative criterion, he argued that the conclusion could come neither from Jesus nor from the early church, so the parable was a piece of Jewish tradition attracted to the Jesus tradition. But Crossan has attacked one aspect of Bultmann's argument by suggesting a plausible situation in the life of the early church.[2] Though brief and lacking widespread support,[3] his argument contains, I believe, the seeds of the problem's solution. The parable's conclusion "alludes to the Jewish refusal to accept either Moses or the prophets as witnesses to the resurrection of Jesus or even to accept the risen Jesus himself."[4] It comes from the same Jewish Christianity represented by Matt. 5:18–19[5] and the proof texting of Ps. 118:22–23 (cf. Mark 12:10; Acts 4:11). Those Jews who refuse belief in Jesus as raised from the dead stand convicted by Moses and the prophets. Crossan concludes his suggestion of a possible life situation by remarking that in reading v. 31 one thinks naturally of Jesus.

Crossan's argument establishes, against Bultmann, a conceivable life situation in the early church for the parable's conclusion. By itself that does not settle whether the conclusion belongs to the parable's original form. To shed light on that issue we will turn first to Lukan style and then to the story's narrative logic.

Having suggested a plausible life situation in the early church, Crossan tries to show how the conclusion fits the style and program of Luke-Acts. There is a clear parallel between the parable's conclusion and the

1. Bultmann, *History of the Synoptic Tradition*, 203. Special thanks are due Colman Grabert, whose initial suggestions about this parable were quite formative for my own thought, even if I resisted his pleas for the originality of the conclusion.

2. Crossan, *In Parables*, 67.

3. Marshall, *Commentary on Luke*, 632; Pilgrim, *Good News*, 144.

4. Crossan, *In Parables*, 67.

5. Grobel, "'. . . Whose Name Was Neves,'" 380. Grobel deals with the names used in the parable and the history of its transmission.

resurrection account in Luke 24. Crossan advances four interlocking arguments. First, there is the recurring theme of disbelief. Abraham responds that the brothers will not "be convinced if some one should rise from the dead." In Luke 24, when the women report to the apostles the events at the tomb the narrator reports that "these words seemed to them an idle tale, and they did not believe them" (v. 12). In the story of the men on the road to Emmaus, Jesus responds, "O foolish men, and slow of heart to believe all that the prophets have spoken" (v. 25). When Jesus appears among the disciples, the narrator adds, "And while they still disbelieved" (v. 41).[6]

The second element Crossan points to is use of Moses and the prophets in Luke 16:29, 31; 24:27, 44. As Jesus and the two disciples traverse to Emmaus, the narrator reports, "And beginning with Moses and all the prophets, he interpreted to them in all the scriptures the things concerning himself" (24:27). Again, when Jesus appears among the apostles in Jerusalem after eating the broiled fish, he says, "These are my words which I spoke to you, while I was still with you, that everything written about me in the law of Moses and the prophets and the psalms must be fulfilled" (v. 44).[7] The theme of the fulfillment of Scripture, which is prominent in the early kerygmatic statements, is noticeably absent in the resurrection narratives. Thus there is a strong similarity between the conclusion of A Rich Man Clothed in Purple and Luke's account of the resurrection.

The third piece of stylistic evidence concerns the use of raising (*anistēmi*) from the dead in both 16:31 and 24:46. Only in these two places in Luke is the verb *anistēmi*, "to rise up," used with "from the dead." Taken together with the other two pieces of evidence adduced above, the usage in our parable is more than coincidental. Crossan's final piece of evidence bears on the occurrence of "they will repent" (16:30) and the frequency of the repentance theme in the kerygmatic speeches of Acts (i.e., 2:38; 3:19; 8:22; 17:30; 26:20).[8]

---

6. The theme of disbelief is not so obvious in the other Gospel accounts of the resurrection. In Mark, the women leave fearful and silent, but their belief or lack thereof is not commented on. In Matthew, the only element of disbelief occurs at the ascension, when the narrator states that the eleven had assembled and they worshiped, but some doubted. John's Gospel states explicitly that the beloved disciple upon seeing the empty tomb believed, and Thomas is clearly the butt of the story for his lack of belief and demand for extravagant proof.

7. Crossan might also have noticed the parallel usage in the narrator's summary of Paul's final speech in Acts 28:23. This will become especially important in reference to the usage of *diapartyromai* and *peithō*. The phrase "Moses and the prophets" is used only one other time in the New Testament: at John 1:45. Matthew uses "the law and the prophets" four times, Luke once, and Acts twice.

8. He might have added 5:31; 11:18; and 20:21, where the noun is used in a similar

At first glance such a lean presentation of the evidence seems less than convincing, but pursuit of the evidence provides a stronger case than Crossan originally indicated. Luke omits Mark's two uses of the verb "to repent,"[9] but he adopts Mark's one use of the noun "repentance," although the noun refers to John's preaching a baptism of repentance.[10] The very prominence of the repentance theme in Acts makes its omission in the Gospel for both Jesus and the Twelve conspicuous. Moreover, several uniquely Lukan uses suggest editorial addition. In the sign of Jonah, Luke's version concludes with "for they repented at the preaching of Jonah, and behold something greater than Jonah is here" (Luke 11:32).[11] In chapter 13, the story of the Galileans murdered by Pilate and that of the eighteen men on whom the tower of Siloam fell both conclude with "Unless you repent, you will likewise perish" (13:3, 5). In Luke, both the parables A Man with a Hundred Sheep and A Woman with Ten Drachmas conclude with a saying about the joy in heaven over sinners who repent. (This theme is missing in the Matthean parallel.) Finally, Luke 17:3–4 refers to repentance, whereas its parallels (Matt. 18:15, 21–22) do not. "If your brother sins, rebuke him, and if he repents, forgive him; and if he sins against you seven times in the day, and turns to you seven times, and says, 'I repent,' you must forgive him."[12] The proximity of this clearly Lukan saying to the present parable clearly suggests Luke's interest in the parable's conclusion.

Finally, to refocus Crossan's argument concerning the relation between Luke 24 and the ending of the parable, the final speech in the Gospel echoes the parable's conclusion:

> "These are my words which I spoke to you, while I was still with you, that everything written about me in the law of *Moses and the prophets* and the psalms must be fulfilled." Then, he opened their minds to understand the scriptures, and said to them, "Thus it is written, that the Christ should suffer and on the third day *rise from the dead*, and *repentance* and forgiveness of sins should be preached in his name to all nations." (Luke 24:44–47)

This concluding speech of Jesus in Luke contains three of the key words found in the parable's conclusion. Similarly, one theme is represented by its contrary. "He opened their minds to understand the scriptures" is the contrary of disbelief.

---

fashion. Behm ("*metanoeō*," 1003) points out that "repent and turn [*epistrephō*]" is a recurring formula in Acts and the center of the apostolic kerygma.

9. Mark 1:15 is a summary announcement of Jesus' mission to Galilee, and Mark 6:12 concerns the sending out of the Twelve where they are to preach for repentance.

10. Luke also has the parallel to Matthew concerning John's preaching of repentance (Luke 3:8//Matt 3:8).

11. Matthew concludes with a reference to Solomon.

12. Notice the use of *epistrephō* with "repent."

Besides the stylistic issues advanced but undeveloped by Crossan, one should note the use of *diamartyromai* "to bear witness" (v. 28), and *peithō*, "to convince" (v. 31), in the parable's conclusion, both words frequent in Acts.[13] In introducing Paul's preaching in the Corinthian synagogue, the narrator notes, ". . . and he persuaded [*epeithen*] Jews and Greeks . . . testifying [*diamartyromenos*] to the Jews that the Christ was Jesus" (Acts 18:4–5). Jewish lack of faith leads Paul to turn to the Gentiles. Again at the conclusion of Acts, when Paul comes to Rome and explains matters to the Jewish elders, "he expounded the matter to them from morning till evening, testifying [*diamartyromenos*] to the kingdom of God and trying to convince [*peithōn*] them about Jesus both from the law of Moses and from the prophets" (28:23). This final usage is especially striking because it brings together three themes prominent in the parable's conclusion: Jewish disbelief, the phrase "Moses and the prophets," and the combination of *diamartyromai* and *peithō*.

The inclusio of bearing witness (*diamartyretai*, v. 28) and convincing (*peisthēsontai*, v. 31), the phrase "Moses and the prophets," the references to repentance and rising from the dead, along with Jewish disbelief, indicate that Luke has at least rewritten or reshaped the conclusion of the parable to fit his apologetic needs.

Whether Luke 16:19–31 implements the narrative logic of the story has been a matter of considerable debate. Jeremias has classified the parable as one of four "double-edged" parables in which the emphasis falls on the second edge.[14] The parable of A Man Gave a Banquet (Matt. 22:1–14) is a less than helpful example, since, as Jeremias admits, the so-called second edge (concerning the wedding guest without a garment) is a Matthean addition.[15] His other two examples are A Man Had Two Sons (Luke 15:11–32) and A Householder Went Out Early (Matt. 20:1–16). In the latter the two parts are (*a*) the hiring and instructions for liberal payment, and (*b*) the indignant response of those supposedly underpaid.[16] There is no need to see two parts to this parable; it is a coherent whole. The initial agreements with the laborers set up the condition that provokes a reader's identification with the laborers' anger. At any rate, in any interpretation of this parable there is no radical break, no change of direction. The same is true of the parable A Man Had Two Sons. Though it has two acts, to borrow a dramatic metaphor, those two acts are clearly connected. The introduction of the characters in the first act demands the second. The man had two sons, and the

13. *Diamartyromai* occurs nine times in Luke-Acts and only in this parable in the Synoptics. See Jeremias, *Die Sprache*, 261. *Peithō* is used twenty-one times in Luke-Acts, thirty-two times in the rest of the New Testament.

14. Jeremias, *Parables*, 186, 37–38.

15. Ibid., 65.

16. Ibid., 38.

younger wanted his share of the property. Such specification of two sons demands or at least implies the existence of the elder brother's story.

While Jeremias's classification "double-edged" is not convincing, it does clarify and enlighten our problem. In comparing the three parables, the break at v. 19 more closely resembles the situation in Matthew's version of A Man Gave a Banquet than it does the situation one finds in the other two parables. As Raymond Brown has pointed out, there is no preparation in the story's first part for its conclusion. The five brothers appear from nowhere.[17] Unlike the first part of A Man Had Two Sons, in which the younger son implies an elder, nothing in the first part of this parable implies the supposed conclusion. Indeed the opposite is the case. Once Abraham pronounces the chasm, the great dividing line, the story has reached its conclusion, for as we shall see in an analysis of the narrative proper, the story is about boundaries and connections. After death, when the rich man and Lazarus have both crossed through the last gate, the boundary that divided them in life divides them in death, but their status is reversed. When Abraham acknowledges the great chasm, formally the narrative comes to a conclusion, for it has exhausted its possibilities.

The evidence appears compelling that the present conclusion to the parable was appended to relate the parable to Jewish disbelief in Jesus' messiahship.[18] Further, Luke reworked the parable to fit his apologetic needs, which were highly congruent with both the parable proper (wealth and poverty) and belief in the resurrection.

Surface Structure

The parable divides itself into two parts. In the first part (16:19–23) there is narration; in the second (16:24–26) the rich man beseeches Abraham in direct speech. At no point is Lazarus an active figure in the narrative.

The first part has three sections, with the *alla kai*, "but even," marking the division between sections 1 and 2, and the death of the rich man dividing sections 2 and 3. A series of verbs, dependent participles, and infinitives provides an interlocking grid.

---

17. Brown, *Gospel according to John* 1:429. Brown suggests that perhaps at some stage of development, the Lukan tradition borrowed the Lazarus reference from John's Gospel to construct the parable's conclusion. Brown is following the suggestion of Dunkerley ("Lazarus," 321–27). This seems to be a suggestion without any proof.

18. The use of the historic present *legei* indicates pre-Lukan tradition. Of the ninety parallel passages in which Mark uses the historic present, Luke has retained only one (Luke 8:49). The five historic presents in Lukan parables (13:8; 16:7, 23, 29; 19:22) probably indicate pre-Lukan material. See Jeremias, *Parables*, 182–83.

Section 1:	he put on . . .	making merry
	[he] lay . . .	being filled with sores
		desiring
Section 2:	*alla kai*	
	coming	[they] licked
	it happened	to die
		to be borne up
Section 3:	[he] died the rich man [he] was buried	
	lifting up	
	being . . .	he saw

This verbal pattern provides the skeleton on which the narration of the first part is built. The last part of the pattern contains a parallelism.

in Hades   / lifting up his eyes
being in torment / he saw

The introductions of the rich man and the poor man are parallel.

A a certain man was rich
B a certain poor man by the name of Lazarus
  A he put on purple
  B he was thrown at his gate
    A making merry
    B being covered with sores

The A lines belong to the rich man's narrative, and the B lines belong to the poor man's. In the next section, dealing with reader response, we will uncover the full significance of this parallelism. Suffice it at this point to notice how the parallelism sets up opposing pictures of the two characters.

Like the narration of the first part, the dialogue of the second part is carefully constructed in twos. It has two parts, a request by the tormented rich man and a response by Abraham:

A   B

and that one calling out said, "Father, Abraham . . ."

B   A

and said Abraham, "Child . . ."

The beginnings of the two speeches are both chiastic and clearly indicative of the relation—that of father and child.

The rich man's speech begins with two imperatives followed by two subjunctives:

have mercy on me and send Lazarus . . .
in order that he might dip his finger . . . cool my tongue

Abraham's response is built around a series of twos related chiastically:

A you received your good things in your life
B and Lazarus likewise evil things
   now
B this man is encouraged
A you are tormented

Not only are their fates reversed, but in past time—in life—the rich man came first and Lazarus last; now Lazarus comes first and the rich man last. Just as the plot reverses the relation of the rich man and Lazarus, so also the surface structure reverses their order.

A Reading

Line 1: A certain man was rich, and he put on purple and fine linen, making merry every day sumptuously.

Because the introduction (16:19–21)[19] is so long, we have divided it into three lines better to observe its effect on the hearer.

The man's richness is exemplified in his clothing and eating habits. Not only do purple and fine Egyptian linen imply wealth but purple also signals royalty or official power.[20] In Rev. 18:12, both purple and linen are mentioned among the cargoes of merchants, and according to Prov. 31:22, a good wife brings wealth to her husband by making "coverlets for herself—her clothing is linen and purple."[21] Purple as a sign of royalty is also well attested. In Judges 8:26, the Midian kings wear purple robes, and in Esth. 8:15, when Mordecai leaves the presence of the king as his envoy, he wears a purple robe and linen.[22] These same values persisted in rabbinic stories. An example makes the point:

> It can be compared to a prince whose tutor wanted to go in before the king to plead on behalf of his son, but was afraid of those who stood by lest one of them should attack him. What did the king do? He clothed him in his royal purple cloak, so that all who saw him might be afraid of him.[23]

Purple and fine linen place the man among the elite, possibly an urban elite.

19. The use of *tis* for a Lukan introduction is quite frequent and characteristic. See Jeremias, *Die Sprache*, 15.
20. Manson, *Sayings*, 296. Manson also suggests that the man could be a Sadducee, which given the parable's development, would be ironical. Whether he is a Sadducee seems beyond proof. He is, however, among the urban elite, a group to which the Sadducees belong.
21. In Ezek. 27:7, fine linen from Egypt and purple are signs of Tyre's wealth.
22. In the LXX, "purple linen clothes," *byssinon porphyroun*.
23. *Midrash Rabbah* on Exodus 38.8 (Freedman 3:456); Hadas, "Rabbinic Parallels," 46.

"To make merry," used in two other parables, means "to make a feast."[24] It entails a feast well beyond those occasional celebrations that enlivened the otherwise boring and monotonous existence of Mediterranean peasants.[25] Not only is the feasting "sumptuous"[26] but it takes place every day.

This first line serves to place the rich man at the very top of the social scale and thus to distance him from those who would normally be among Jesus' audience. There may even be a hint of urban-versus-rural snobbishness. Such a wealthy man is potentially a patron; with such wealth he is bound to be one of those on whom the society at large is dependent.

Line 2: A certain poor man by the name of Lazarus had been prostrated[27] at his gate, being full of sores and desiring to be fed from the things that fell from the table of the rich man.

The introductions of the two men are closely parallel. The first man has his richness; the poor man has only his name, Lazarus. The introductions set in parallel rich and Lazarus. Literally, the Greek text reads,

a man / certain / was / rich
a poor [man] / certain / by the name / of Lazarus

The introductory clauses are nicely balanced: the first man's introduction ends with "rich," and the second man's begins with "poor." Likewise, the first man's introduction begins with the anonymous "man," and the second ends with a proper name, Lazarus. Perhaps this may also indicate the purpose of naming the poor man, for the name means "he whom God helps."[28] The name Lazarus contrasts the two characters: one is full of possessions, and the other is empty except for a name, but the meaning of the name may well hold out a promise.[29]

---

24. BAGD, 327. Cf. Luke 12:19; 15:23, 24, 32.

25. Str-B 1:972.

26. BAGD, 465. The root sense of the term is "bright, shining, radiant." Perhaps "ostentatious" is a more accurate translation.

27. BDF, 347.1.

28. Str-B 2:223. Lazarus is a rabbinic abbreviation for Eliezar. Vermes (*Jesus the Jew,* 53) argues that Lazarus is a Galilean corruption, representative of Jesus' distinctive dialect. Eliezar was Abraham's loyal servant. For a summary of folk tales about Eliezar, see Rabinowitz, "Study of Midrash," 143–61. Derrett ("Fresh Light on St. Luke XVI:11," 364–80) and Cave ("Lazarus and the Lukan Deuteronomy," 319–25) both see the parable as a midrash upon the Eliezar and Abraham story. It is possible that the name was suggested because of the close connection to Abraham, but the state of this Lazarus is quite different from that of Eliezar.

29. Even though Lazarus is the only proper name used in a Jesus parable, I believe it is original, not the least because of Luke's proclivity not to use Semitic names. See Cadbury, "Proper Name," 399.

The designation of the story's second man as poor and the accom-
panying description indicate that he is a beggar.[30] According to Jeremias,
beggars of the time were viewed as sinners receiving their just deserts
from God.[31] There is ample evidence that poverty was viewed as a
divine chastisement.[32] Regardless of whether the society viewed the
beggar's condition as the result of sin, the description of him contrasts
sharply with that of the rich man.

The parable's beginning revolves around the two men's activity. The
rich man puts on purple and fine linen—a sign of his upper-class
status—while the poor man is laid down at his gate. The contrast
between the two men continues with a new pattern of inside-outside,
pervasive throughout the story. The rich man is inside; the poor man is
at the gate. They are in proximity, yet separated by an invisible boundary, the gate.[33] The gate can function in either of two ways: it can let in or
keep out.[34] The story sets up a contrast between the states of the two
men and simultaneously implies a relationship of patron to client. Will
the rich man use the gate to come to Lazarus's aid?

Finally, "being full of sores" contrasts with and parallels "clothed in
purple and fine linen." The poor man's desire to eat his fill[35] of what falls
from the table is parallel and in contrast to the rich man's daily feasts.
This provides a tie between the two introductions:

put on purple	making merry sumptuously
full of sores	desiring to be fed with the things that
	fall from the rich man's table

This final parallel sets out the stark differences between the two men.

The two introductions paint for the audience contrasting images
drawn from society's extremes: a wealthy man and a poor man. They are
related, for the poor man's place in life is beside the rich man's gate, but

30. Manson (*Sayings*, 298) suggests that Lazarus was a leper, but Marshall (*Commentary on Luke*, 635) rightly objects. A leper would not beg daily in public as implied in the parable.

31. Jeremias, *Parables*, 184. For a discussion of beggars, see Jeremias, *Jerusalem*, 116–18.

32. Str-B 1:819–22; Bammel, "*ptōchos*," 899–902. Pilgrim summarizes the inter-testamental evidence (*Good News*, 32–38).

33. Plummer, *The Gospel according to St. Luke*, 391. Plummer provides architectural evidence. *Pylōna* indicates a large gate of some grandeur.

34. For a suggestive analysis, see Schnider and Stenger, "Die offene Tür," 273–83.

35. *Chortazō* denotes completion. Cf. the beatitude in Matt. 5:6//Luke 6:21 and the conclusion of the feeding of the five thousand in Mark 6:42. Plummer (*The Gospel according to St. Luke*, 392) argues that if Lazarus had not been successful, he would not have persisted. But B. T. D. Smith (*Parables*) notes, against Plummer, that the contrasts between the two in Hades indicate that Lazarus never fulfilled his desire.

their relation is one of division, for the rich man is inside while the poor man is outside. Divided, they only approach each other in the wish of the poor man to eat the scraps that fall from the rich man's table. In approaching this description we must be careful not to read into it our own sentimentality or liberalism. In a limited-goods society,[36] the places of rich and poor are fixed. But there remains an expectation that the rich man will become the poor man's patron.

Line 3: And even[37] dogs coming licked his sores.

This line intensifies the poor man's extreme deprivation. The dog's licking is not an act of sympathy; these are not pets. Rather they are wild street dogs, a plague in the ancient world.[38] In the Hebrew Bible, dogs eat the bodies of the cursed dead (1 Kings 14:11; 16:4; 21:23, 24; 22:38). When the Lord sends Elijah to warn Ahab he says, "Thus says the Lord: 'In the place where dogs licked up the blood of Naboth shall dogs lick your blood" (1 Kings 21:19). Their licking continues Lazarus's passivity. At no point is he described as active: he simply lies before the rich man's gate. He possesses not even the honor of a beggar, since he does not beg. This perhaps leads the audience not to sympathize with his fate, for in a sense he has broken society's unspoken code. A beggar at least has a function in society: he provides an occasion for almsgiving.

From a literary perspective, line 3 continues the description of poverty and creates anticipation on the audience's part. Because the line relates and yet distances the rich and the poor, the audience expects a story that somehow details how the rich man will become the patron of the poor man. The gate metaphor suggests such a possibility.

Line 4: And it happened that the poor man died and was carried by the angels into the bosom of Abraham.

Having created an expectation that the rich man will somehow reach through the gate to the poor man, the story sets another course. With the poor man's death, any patron-client relation is aborted. Even in death the poor man remains passive; he is carried away by the angels.

"And it happened" denotes the beginning of a new segment, for until now the narrator has introduced the characters and set up potential interaction.

---

36. On the responsibilities of the rich to provide to the community of less fortunate, see my treatment of The Land of a Rich Man, in chap. 3 above.

37. Easton, *Gospel according to St. Luke,* 252. Easton indicates that this intensive should be translated "and worst of all."

38. Michel, "*kyōn,* 1103; Str-B 1:722.

The description of the poor man's transport and his final resting place has been the cause of debate. There is no evidence for a phrase parallel to "was carried by angels" until 150 c.e.[39] The metaphor "Abraham's bosom" suggests a child at a mother's bosom (place of protection) or a place of honor at a banquet or the place of the patriarchs (Gen. 15:15).[40]

The story makes no mention of Lazarus's burial. There is no direct indication in the parable that he remained unburied, but it may be implied. If so, it would only increase the parable's scandal, for a lack of a decent burial was a scandal and curse in Judaism.[41]

Line 5: The rich man also died and was buried.

The fates of the two remain intertwined. They both die. But the descriptions of their deaths are conspicuously different, replicating and reversing their status. The poor man's fate is lavishly described ("carried away by angels into the bosom of Abraham"), while the rich man's is marked by poverty and starkness of language ("he was buried"). The audience is given no clue to his fate after death. He is simply buried. But the inside-outside pattern persists. The poor man is lifted out of this world into the bosom of Abraham, and the rich man is buried in the ground (in this world).

The parallelism between lines 4 and 5 involves a curious omission.

the poor man	the rich man
died	died
	was buried
carried away	

Both the poor man's burial[42] and the rich man's fate are left unstated. The hearer is left with two gaps in the narrative and no way to fill them.

Line 6: And in Hades raising up his eyes, being in torment, he saw Abraham from afar and Lazarus in his bosom.

This line reestablishes the relation between the rich man and the poor man. "In Hades" contrasts with "in his bosom." The separation in life

39. Marshall, *Commentary on Luke,* 636; Str-B 2:223–25. Grobel (". . . Whose Name Was Neves,'" 378) suggests that angels are a Jewish substitute for some bearer of the dead in an Egyptian version of the story.

40. Marshall, *Commentary on Luke,* 636; Meyer, *"kolpos,"* 825–26. Str-B 2:226 quotes two clear cases that refer to martyrs.

41. Lieberman ("After Life," 405–22) argues that the rabbis resisted the popular belief that those who remain unburied could not attain the resurrection of the dead.

42. Plummer, *Gospel according to St. Luke,* 393. Plummer maintains that Jesus could not have intended to imply that Lazarus remained unburied, because that would have scandalized his Jewish audience. But in a parable where the contrasts are drawn so sharply, I remain unsure.

continues in afterlife. The rich man sees Abraham from afar. The name of the poor man is reintroduced. After his initial introduction he has been called a "poor man." The significance of the name is now manifest. The promise of his name as "one whom God helps" has been fulfilled.

The visualization of the afterlife does not conform to any contemporary schema, but this should not alarm us since there was no general consensus on the matter.[43] Hades is the place of torment. It is some distance (afar) from that of Lazarus, although within sight. The chief characteristic of Lazarus's abode is that he is in the bosom of Abraham: it is the fulfillment of the promises made to the people of God.

Why the two men are in different places is not immediately evident. One should not be too quick to assume a moralizing point about rich and poor (although Luke may well have seen such a point). As Plummer has pointed out, simply being rich cannot be the issue, for after all Abraham was rich.[44]

Line 7: And that one calling out said, "Father Abraham, have mercy on me and send Lazarus to dip the tip of his finger in water and cool my tongue, because I am in torment in this fire."

For the first time in the story the rich man seeks to bridge the gulf separating him and Lazarus. Having lost his place of honor, he begs to have Lazarus relieve, if only for a moment, his wretched condition. Once again, the poor man remains passive. The request is made not to Lazarus but to Abraham, because he is the model of hospitality. At the Oaks of Mamre (Gen. 18:1–15) Abraham received three strangers, one of whom was the Lord. This occasion fueled later speculations on the virtue of hospitality.[45] In one story Abraham's virtue exceeds that of Job, because Job fed only those accustomed to eat.

But Abraham did not act in this way. Instead he would go forth and make the rounds everywhere, and when he found wayfarers he brought them in to his house. To him who was unaccustomed to eat wheat bread, he gave wheat bread to eat. . . . Moreover he arose and built stately mansions on the

---

43. Marshall (*Commentary on Luke,* 636–37) reviews the various discussions about where the rich man and Lazarus are envisioned as being. Lieberman ("After Life," 388–89) states that the early rabbinic tradition does not contain any elaborate picture of Gehenna or Hades. Some rabbis even denied its objective existence.

44. Plummer, *Gospel according to St. Luke,* 394.

45. See chap. 1 for other references to hospitality. Quoted there is the saying that places hospitality above welcoming the presence of the Shekinah, because Abraham had left the presence of God to attend to the wants of strangers. This is a frequent theme in the Midrash. See the *Midrash on Psalms* 18.29 (Braude 1:259–8): "The verse [Ps. 18:36] . . . alludes to Abraham. For while the Lord stood, waiting for the guests to finish eating, Abraham sat [with them]. So it follows that giving hospitality is greater than doing honor to the Lord's presence."

highways and left there food and drink, and every passerby ate and drank and blessed Heaven. That is why the delight of the spirit was vouchsafed to him."[46]

From this story the Midrash draws a conclusion:

Teach the members of thy household humility. For when one is humble and the members of his household are humble, if a poor man comes and stands in the doorway of the master of the house and inquires of them, "Is your father within?" they answer, "Ay, come in, enter." Even before he has entered, a table is set for him. When he enters and eats and drinks and offers a blessing up to Heaven, great delight of spirit is vouchsafed to the master of the house.[47]

Thus Abraham indicates by contrast what was expected of the rich man. Will Abraham respond?

Line 7 introduces several details about the landscape of the after-world. In the abode of Lazarus there is running water (cf. *Enoch* 22.9), though not in that of the rich man. The water is cool, but the rich man is in fire. The narrative does not intend a literal image of the afterlife but rather the contrasts between the two. Similarly, the rich man's request for Lazarus to dip the very tip of his finger in water draws a contrast between the drop of water he so earnestly desires and his sumptuous banquets during his life. The contrast between his former life and his present life is characterized by extremes: extravagance and indigence.

Line 8: Said Abraham, "Child, remember that you received your good things in your life, and Lazarus likewise evil things. Now this one is comforted, and you are in torment."

This line maintains the contrast set at the parable's beginning; only here the contrast is between then and now. The status of "now" is the reverse of "then" (in your life). This reversal is not based on explicit morality, for nowhere does the parable imply a lack of morality by the rich man or goodness on the poor man's part.

Line 9: "And moreover, between us and you [plural] a great chasm has been fixed, so that one who wishes to cross over from here to you [plural] would not be able, nor can they cross from there to us."

The parable's final line installs a great divide, fixed for all time. The inside-outside, then-now dichotomy that has existed throughout the parable now comes to have a divine sanction ("has been fixed," a passive

---

46. *Fathers according to Rabbi Nathan* 7 (Goldin, 47).
47. *Fathers according to Rabbi Nathan* 7 (Goldin, 48).

circumlocution to avoid the name of God). But there is a great difference: the gate has been closed, and now there exists only a chasm.[48]

Two elements of this parable would have provoked a Jewish audience. First, the rich man is condemned without evidence of evident wrongdoing. His sin is only implied. He does not establish a relation with Lazarus, does not pass through the gate to his rescue. Furthermore, he is given no chance of atonement, no way to work off the guilt of his former life.[49] Second, the parable maintains that the divisions in the afterlife replicate those on earth: those divisions are the result not of divine will but of human insensitivity. Had the rich man walked through the gate, his fate in the afterlife would have been much different.

Although we have argued that the request to send Lazarus to the five brothers was added later in the tradition, it does provide an important clue to a reader's response which sanctions our reading. A Jewish audience would have felt that the rich man's punishment was unjust since he was given no warning of the critical importance of passing through the gate. The addition (vv. 27–31) is a reflection of this response and argues that it would have made no difference. For the parable, places in the kingdom are determined not by differences but by solidarity. In the first part of the story the rich man fails to come through the gate; in the second he asks Lazarus to come through. He never makes the motion himself even in desire. So the chasm he created remains fixed.

From Story to Kingdom: Tales from the Past

Customarily a study of this parable begins with a reference to Hugo Gressmann's collection of parallel Egyptian and Jewish stories.[50] Since our entrance to the story was through its conclusion, perhaps it is fitting to conclude with the mandatory beginning.

Gressmann's collection embodies a thesis concerning the relation between the parable and a series of parallel Egyptian and Jewish stories. Caught up in a genetic view of the interrelation of texts, Gressmann has posited that the parable A Rich Man Clothed in Purple was a descendant of an Egyptian tale now preserved in a second-century demotic

48. There is no evidence in Jewish literature for a chasm between the just and the unjust. See Bruyne, "Chasma," 400–405.

49. Lieberman, "After Life," 387–98. Lieberman gives representative theories for purification of the souls of the unjust. Usually apostates are the one group not able to ascend to heaven.

50. Gressmann, *Von reichen Mann.*

translation. He traces seven extant Jewish stories belonging to the same family tree. [51]

The narrator of the Egyptian story is Si-Osiris,[52] a long-dead Egyptian who was raised up by Osiris as the miraculous child of a childless couple. Eventually he was to face and defeat a mighty sorcerer from Ethiopia who threatened Egypt. The part of the story that parallels the Lukan parable is initiated by a remark the boy's father makes as he observes the loud wailing and magnificent decorations of a rich man's funeral procession and, by contrast, the humble burial of a poor man. Says the father, "How much better it shall be in Amenti [land of the dead] for great men for whom they make glory with the voice of wailing than for poor men whom they take to the desert-necropolis without the glory of funeral." [53] The son, a former dweller in Amenti, then takes his father on a trip through the twelve halls of Amenti. In the final hall, Si-Osiris reveals the standard of judgment:

> For he of whom it shall be found that his evil deeds are more numerous than his good deeds is delivered to Ama[54] of the Lord of Amenti; his soul and his body are destroyed and she does not permit him to live again for ever. But as for him of whom it shall be found that his good deeds are more numerous than his evil deeds, he is taken among the gods of the council of the Lord of Amenti, his soul going to heaven with the noble spirits.[55]

Soon after, the father sees a richly clothed man sitting next to Osiris, in a place of highest honor. The son explains to his father,

> Dost thou see this great man who is clothed in raiment of royal linen, standing near to the place where Osiris is? He is that poor man whom thou sawest being carried out from Memphis; . . . his evil deeds were weighed against his good deeds . . . and it was found that his good deeds were more numerous than his evil deeds. . . . And it was commanded before Osiris that the burial outfit of that rich man, whom thou sawest carried forth from Memphis with great laudation, should be given to this same poor man.[56]

The obverse was, of course, the fate of the rich man.

51. Ibid., 46–58. Of the seven Jewish stories, one is from the Palestinian Talmud, five from various medieval commentaries, and one from Peter of Cluny (Peter the Venerable) quoting Joshua ben Levi.

52. Griffith, *Stories*, 43. Griffith translates this as "Son of Osiris," but Grobel (". . . Whose Name Was Neves,'" 376) argues that it could just as well mean "Man of Osiris," i.e.., "Servant of Osiris."

53. Griffith, *Stories*, 45. Griffith includes a complete translation of the demotic manuscript. Creed (*Gospel according to St. Luke*, 210) presents an extensive summary of the demotic story.

54. A multiheaded monster of the underworld.

55. Griffith, *Stories*, 47.

56. Ibid., 49.

Before commenting on the Egyptian story, it is important to consider at least one Jewish story that Gressmann points to as a parallel. This story is from the Palestinian Talmud and, according to Gressmann, is the earliest Jewish version of the story.

> There were two holy men in Ashqelon, who would eat together, drink together, and study Torah together. One of them died, and he was not properly mourned. But when Bar Maayan, the village tax collector, died, the whole town took time off to mourn him. The surviving holy man began to weep saying, "Woe, for the enemies of Israel [a euphemism for Israel itself] will have no merit." [The deceased holy man] appeared to him in a dream, and said to him, "Do not despise the sons of your Lord. This one did one sin, and the other one did one good deed, and it went well for [the latter on earth, so while on earth I was punished for my one sin, he was rewarded for his one good deed]." Now what was the culpable act that the holy man had done? Heaven forfend! He committed no culpable act in his entire life. But one time he put on the phylactery of the head before that of the hand [which was an error]. Now what was the meritorious deed that Bar Maayan, the village tax collector, had done? Heaven forfend! He never did a meritorious deed in his life. But one time he made a banquet for the councillors of his town, but they did not come. He said, "Let the poor come and eat the food, so that it not go to waste." There are those who say that he was traveling along the road with a loaf of bread under his arm, and it fell. A poor man went and took it, and the tax collector sad nothing to him so as not to embarrass him. After a few days the holy man saw his fellow [in a dream] walking among gardens, orchards, and fountains of water. He saw Bar Maayan the village tax collector with his tongue hanging out, by a river. He wanted to reach the river but could not reach it.[57]

Although one does not have to accept Gressmann's genetic thesis concerning the interrelation of the several versions of the tale, obviously tales about an afterlife involving a reversal of the status of rich and poor furnished a common folklore motif. Further, this motif has found a place in the Jesus parable about Lazarus. These tales confront the problem of theodicy, explaining how God or gods can allow evil to be exalted on earth. The answer is that in death evil will be punished and the righteous will be exalted. Perhaps, to state the issue more precisely, these stories explain how those falsely exalted in this life (or vice versa) will receive their just deserts in the afterlife. In all the examples given by Gressmann, this common mytheme is present. The examples allow us to determine the common mythical structure to which the parable belongs. The kingdom of God is the manifestation of God's righteousness in the face of injustice.

---

57. *j. Hag.* 2.2 (Neusner 20:57). For an alternate translation, see Manson, *Sayings*, 297.

Poverty is a well-established motif in Luke's two-volume work, and chapter 16 of the Gospel is a major moment in the motif's development. According to Talbert,[58] the parable of the rich man and Lazarus is Luke's comment on vv. 14–18. The first part of the parable, referring to vv. 14–15, demonstrates the ambiguity of wealth as a sign of God's blessing. It fulfills v. 15b: "For what is exalted among men is an abomination in the sight of God." The parable's second part exemplifies vv. 16–18. The law is still in force. Just as v. 18 is an example of not one dot of the law passing away, so the condemnation of the rich man demonstrates that the command to take care of the poor (Deut. 15:7–11) is in force. The reference to Moses and the prophets indicates that the witness of the law is still valid. If people will not believe them, why would they believe one rising from the dead?

Luke understands the parable within the mythical, metaphorical framework of the kingdom as the manifestation of God's righteousness in the face of injustice. Luke 16:15b expresses the same metaphorical structure found in the stories of Si-Osiris and the scholar and the publican. Those falsely exalted in this world will be humbled when God's justice comes.

A close look at the examples Gressmann has presented will illuminate how our parable relates to the mytheme. In those stories where theodicy is the issue, the problematic arises because a third person (e.g., the father or the scholar) confronts a situation that appears to deny God's justice. That third-person perspective allows the story to deal with a reader's problem of how God's justice is related to the here and now. Within this format, the story provides a mythical resolution of the tension between God's justice and the apparent flouting of it. In the afterlife, God's justice will triumph.

But the parable's structure is different. The third person who asks the question is missing. Lazarus is passive in the story, and only the rich man and Abraham engage in dialogue. Because there is no objective third person for the reader to identify with, the hearer is forced to confront both Lazarus and the rich man as images of the hearer. Moreover, the parable does not deal with the ethical actions of the two participants as separated from or unrelated to each other. In the theodicy mytheme the stories of the rich and poor are not related in life. The rich man's evil is not at the expense of the poor man. But in the parable the gate metaphor implies a connection. In this parable the kingdom almost literally replicates the village, but in reverse. The rich man's fault is that he does not pass through the gate to help Lazarus. It is not simply

---

58. Talbert, *Reading Luke*, 156–59.

that at the end there will be a reversal or that God will help the poor. Even more "so long as there is time, the gate/door to the neighbor lies open to be entered and passed through while one day the chasm between those distanced from each other will not be able to be bridged."[59] In the parable, the kingdom provides a gate to the neighbor; if God must help ("Lazarus"), then the gate disappears. Grace is the gate. The parable subverts the complacency that categorizes reality into rich and poor or any other division. The standard is not moral behavior as individual, isolated acts but the ability to go through the gate, metaphorically, to the other side, solidarity.

This parable is like From Jerusalem to Jericho. In that parable the Jewish reader instituted as the man in the ditch was forced to accept aid from his enemy, the Samaritan. In this parable the rich man fails by not making contact. Just as one must lose one's life to gain it, so also one must love one's neighbor as oneself. But these paradoxes receive concrete embodiment in the parable, for it attacks the blindness that does not see the gate's purpose. The gate is not just an entrance to the house but the passageway to the other. The story is a metaphor for the unnoticed menace that Jesus' announcement of the kingdom of God places on ordinary life. In any given interpersonal or social relationship there is a gate that discloses the ultimate depths of human existence. Those who miss that gate may, like the rich man, find themselves crying in vain for a drop of cooling water. Or as Robert Frost has put it, "Something there is that doesn't love a wall."[60]

59. Schnider and Stenger, "Die offene Tür," 281.
60. Both the title and the concluding quotation of this chap. are from Robert Frost's "Mending Wall" in *Complete Poems of Robert Frost*, 47–48.

5

What If No One Came?

A Man Gave a Banquet

A man gave a banquet and invited many and at the time of the banquet sent his servant to say to those who had been invited, "Come, for all is now ready." The first said to him, "I have bought a field, and I must go out and see it; I pray you, have me excused." And another said, "I have bought five yoke of oxen, and I go to examine them; I pray you, have me excused." And another said, "I have married a wife and therefore I cannot come." So the servant reported this to his master. And the master said: "Go outside to the streets and bring back those whom you happen to meet, so that they may dine."

A dinner for friends, a great banquet, a king's feast for his son's wedding, or the messianic banquet hiding in the background—all of these are the occasions for A Man Gave a Banquet as it appears in Matt. 22:2–14, Luke 14:16–24, and *Gos. Thom.* 64. Moreover, none of the invited guests came. This parable opens a fascinating window onto both village and early Christian imagery. To follow the various performances of this parable is to experience in miniature their different visions.

Matthew: Where's your Wedding Garment?

Nearly every commentator agrees on the secondary character of the Matthean performance of this parable. Matthew's own concerns are evident throughout.[1] The kingdom motif shifts a banquet into the messianic banquet, destroying verisimilitude: the king sacks a city for not coming to his feast, then gives the banquet in that same city[2] and, on entering the feast, attacks a guest for not having a wedding garment although it is not at all evident where such a poor guest would acquire a wedding garment. The destruction of the verisimilitude forces attention away from the story's story (from what happens) to its discourse (to what it means).[3]

In Matthew, this parable is related during the temple debates in the last days of Jesus' life. The three parables A Man Had Two Children, A Man Planted a Vineyard, and A Man Gave a Banquet display the church as the true Israel—a major theme in Matthew's theology.[4] The ideology of salvation history concludes, on the one hand, that Israel has rejected God's messengers and, on the other, that the church's good fruits show forth that it is the true Israel.[5] The three parables exhibit a progression from John the Baptist, to the death of Jesus, to the Parousia and judgment. Following on questions about the authority of John the Baptist, Jesus tells the parable A Man Had Two Children, from which he draws the conclusion that tax collectors and harlots will go into the kingdom of God before the temple authorities because they have repented at the preaching of John the Baptist. In the next parable, A Man Planted a Vineyard, when the son (Jesus) is murdered, "the kingdom of God will be taken away from you and given to a nation producing the fruits of it" (Matt. 21:43).[6]

The parable A Man Gave a Banquet brings salvation history up to date. The introduction comparing the kingdom to a king continues the motif of the kingdom introduced in the concluding application of A Man Planted a Vineyard.[7] The shameful treatment and even killing of the king's servants conform to the pattern of A Man Planted a Vineyard,

---

1. E.g., Gundry, *Matthew*, 433.

2. Manson (*Sayings*, 129) asks what happened to the meal during the war.

3. See Via, "Relation of Form to Content," 171–85. Via develops this line of interpretation.

4. See chap. 10 below; Dillon, "Towards a Tradition-History," 8–12; Strecker, *Der Weg*, 110–13; Trilling, *Das Wahre Israel*, 84–87.

5. Trilling, *Das Wahre Israel*, 219.

6. Only Matthew explicitly identifies the vineyard with the kingdom. See chap. 10 below.

7. The introduction is clearly from Matthew's hand. See Matt. 18:33; chap. 12 below. So also Gundry, *Matthew*, 433; Bultmann, *History of the Synoptic Tradition*, 195.

and so both the introduction and the treatment of the servants bind together these two parables. The destruction of the city, Jerusalem,[8] signifies the final turning away from Israel and toward the Gentiles. But this turning is not without its threat, for the hall is filled with both the good and the bad—a favorite ecclesiological metaphor for Matthew.[9] The threat implied in the invitation is carried out when the king as judge excludes the one without a wedding garment, the one without the fruits of the kingdom. He is then cast out into the outer darkness, where there will be weeping and gnashing of teeth—a frequent ending to Matthew's judgment parables.[10] Salvation history has reached its completion.[11]

Even some of those who maintain that the salvation-history allegory is imposed on the parable[12] fail to see that it is only in the progression of all three parables that Matthew sketches out his vision of the kingdom and its coming.[13] When the progression within the three parables becomes apparent, the offense taken at the rejection of the man having no wedding garment disappears. That offense is the result of demanding verisimilitude—which Matthew in all three parables has undercut—and failing to see that Matthew correlates grace and its fruit. If grace calls, the threat of no fruits remains for judgment, as is most evident in his Great Judgment scene (Matt 25:31–46).

Luke: A Banquet for the Poor

If the Matthean performance is low in verisimilitude, Luke's is so realistic, its context so true, that commentators have simply assumed that Luke has correctly preserved the parable, with only a slight allegory separating him from Jesus.[14] Luke normally circumscribes the meaning for his performance by contextualization, as in chapter 15.[15] The themes

8. Rengstorf ("Die Stadt der Mörder," 106–29) argues unconvincingly against this identification.

9. Bornkamm, "End-Expectation," 19. See The Wheat and Tares (Matt. 13:24–30, 36–43, 47–50).

10. See chap. 9 below.

11. Some maintain that the passage about the wedding garment was originally a separate parable, but it so closely fits Matthew's intention that it seems more likely to be a composition on his part. So Schweizer, *Good News*, 419; Beare, *Gospel according to Matthew*, 436.

12. See Jülicher, *Die Gleichnisreden*, 2:401ff.; Funk, *Language*, 168–72. See esp. Dillon's helpful treatment of the individual parables, in "Towards a Tradition-History."

13. Schniewind (*Das Evangelium nach Matthäus*, 220) argues that the three parables as a single unit threaten Israel.

14. Manson (*Sayings*, 129), Hahn ("Das Gleichnis," 74), Marshall (*Commentary on Luke*, 587), and Haenchen ("Das Gleichnis," 144,) all argue against the introduction.

15. See pp. 100–104 above and the careful structuring of context in A Man Had Two Sons (chap. 2 above).

of the poor and the delay of the Parousia coalesce in the parable and in context. Both are enunciated in the setting of the scene that involves a conflict between Jesus and the Pharisees at meal, symbolically a time of brotherhood and cohesion, but in actuality a time of entrapment (14:1). The Pharisees are the antiheroes. In the healing of the man with dropsy, they cannot decide between the sabbath law and the need of a neighbor. Moreover, Jesus turns their scrambling for places of honor at the banquet into a parable about how the exalted will be humbled and the humble exalted. This provokes the "law of no return." "When you give a feast, invite the poor, the maimed, the lame, the blind, and you will be blessed. . . . You will be repaid at the resurrection of the just" (Luke 14:13–14). Luke brings together the two themes of the care for the poor and the delay of the Parousia.

A guest exclaims, "Blessed is he who shall eat bread in the kingdom of God" (Luke 14:16). This beatitude discloses the issue of the delay of the Parousia.[16] When will that time come? The parable provides an answer. Luke's interest is not primarily in those making excuses,[17] because he has already set up criteria for excluding them, in the preceding conflict over the Sabbath and the places at table. So as not to draw attention to those making excuses, he summarizes their action before it is reported: "And they all alike[18] began to make excuses" (14:18a). For him the parable marks out who is to be in the kingdom, who is blessed. Thus the servant makes two forays to gather guests after those first invited have rejected the invitation. The master's first injunction repeats Jesus' command as to whom to invite: "Bring in the poor and maimed and blind and lame" (v. 21, see 14:13). The preaching of the gospel to the poor is a central part of Luke's program (Luke 4:22; 1:18–19; 7:22–23). When this is not enough to fill up the banquet hall, the master orders the servant to go outside the city and gather those who dwell among the highways and hedges. This group of homeless is the same as the group described in the first injunction. For some, the command to gather those in the city refers to the Jewish mission, and the highway and hedges in the second command refers to the gentile mission.[19] This coheres with the Lukan schema of salvation history. Much like the circular and ever-expanding pattern in Acts, the double invitation, first to the city and then to those outside, creates the impression of a delay.

16. Grässer, Das Problem, 196–97.
17. Via, "Relation of Form to Content," 177.
18. The phrase apo mias is unique in Greek, and there is some question about how to supply the ellipsis. According to BDF, 241(6), the sense is "unanimously, with one accord."
19. See Martin, "Salvation and Discipleship," 366–80; Plummer, Gospel according to St. Luke, 363; Jeremias, Parables, 64.

Since the emphasis now falls on who is finally to be invited to the kingdom/banquet, Luke concludes the parable by excluding forever those first invited (v. 24).[20] This forms an inclusio with the introductory beatitude, cementing the implied reference to the banquet as the messianic banquet.[21] Further, Luke creates an ironic play on the guests' scrambling for the "places of honor" (v. 7). Those originally invited, because of their honor, have forfeited any claim to change their minds and come later. Now, ironically, the honor of the banquet demands that they not be present.[22]

Given Luke's interests in the parable, especially the context in which he has set it, it is probable that he is responsible for both the double invitation and the wording of the first invitation to those newly invited, which recalls his command about whom to invite (cf. 14:13; 14:21).[23]

Thomas: Businessmen and Merchants Need Not Apply

The third extant performance of the parable is in *Gos. Thom.* 64:

> Jesus said: "A man had received visitors. And when he had prepared the dinner, he sent his servant to invite the guests. He went to the first one and said to him, 'My master invites you.' He said, 'I have claims against some merchants. They are coming to me this evening. I must go and give them my orders. I ask to be excused from the dinner.' He went to another and said to him, 'My master has invited you.' He said to him, 'I have just bought a house and am required for the day. I shall not have any spare time.' He went to another and said to him, 'My master invites you.' He said to him, 'My friend is going to get married, and I am to prepare the banquet. I shall not be able to come. I ask to be excused from the dinner.' He went to another and said to him, 'My master invites you.' He said to him, 'I have just bought a farm, and I am on my way to collect the rent. I shall not be able to come. I ask to be excused.' The servant returned and said to his master, 'Those whom you invited to the dinner have asked to be excused.' The master said to his servant, 'Go outside to the streets and bring back those whom you happen to meet so that they may dine.' Businessmen and merchants will not enter the places of My Father."

As the concluding logion makes evident, *Thomas* also understands the banquet to be the messianic banquet.[24] But in contrast to the Synoptics,

20. For *legō hymin* as a Lukan formula, see chap. 11, n. 11, below.
21. Funk, *Language*, 173.
22. Derrett, *Law in the New Testament*, 140.
23. See Breech, *Silence of Jesus*, 119; Plummer, *Gospel according to St. Luke*, 362; Pilgrim, *Good News*, 74. Others see the second invitation as an addition: Jeremias, *Parables*, 64; Funk, *Language*, 184.
24. The places of My Father is the resting place for the gnostic soul. See Ménard, *L'évangile selon Thomas*, 165.

here the structural emphasis falls on those who reject the invitation. First, there are four examples of those who have made excuses. Then, in another difference from Luke, the reader does not learn that all have rejected the invitation until the servant reports to the master in direct discourse. Finally, within the structure of the excuses, the servant repeats the invitation formula before each guest,[25] drawing attention to the excuses. Three of the four excuses show businessmen conducting their commerce. The point is not just that these are more urban in comparison with Luke but that these are businessmen and merchants, not farmers. At first glance the third excuse about preparing a marriage banquet does not fit *Thomas*'s theme, but as Ménard points out, it does fit the antifemale theme of the Gospel.[26]

The parable in *Thomas* becomes an exhortation against the affairs of business and a life of gain. This fits well with the cluster of material in this portion of the Gospel. *Gospel of Thomas* 62 appears to be a title for this cluster, and the three parables of The Land of a Rich Man, A Man Gave a Banquet, and A Man Planted a Vineyard present stories about those who are unworthy of the mysteries. Thus they are parables of gnostic failure. The point of all three parables is that those who do not practice poverty will not participate in the heavenly meal, the mystery.

Reconstruction: Originating Structure

Although most commentators agree that a common parable underlies the three extant versions, there is debate about the original parable. Older commentators assumed the superiority of Luke's version.[27] Recently some have argued for the superiority of *Thomas*.[28] Still others, following the classic two-source theory, have argued for a Q parable underlying the synoptics.[29] Still others are skeptical about the original words and *Sitz im Leben*.[30] Although there can be little confidence about reconstructing the words of the original parable,[31] we can construct a

25. Kim ("Papyrus Invitation," 397) shows that *Thomas* reflects Egyptian custom as known from the papryri.

26. Ménard, *L'évangile selon Thomas*, 165; *Gos. Thom.* 15, 22, 46, 79, 114.

27. Manson, *Sayings*, 129.

28. Crossan, *In Parables*, 72.

29. See Schulz, *Q: Die Spruchquelle*, 391–98. Schulz argues that the Q parable closely resembles Luke.

30. Beare (*Gospel according to Matthew*, 432) speaks of the parable's being "mangled." Plummer (*Gospel according to St. Luke*, 359–60) notes the totally different contexts in Matthew and Luke and the small amount of shared vocabulary.

31. See Breech, *Silence of Jesus*, 114–15. Despite disavowing the effort to reconstruct the words, Breech proceeds to make such an effort. In honesty, one does have to work with some words, and not pure model.

model of the originating structure of the parable by carefully observing the formal characteristics of extant performances of the parable in Matthew, Luke, and *Thomas*.

In the originating structure the main character was an anonymous man, the standard character in Jesus' parables. The king derives from Matthew's performance. *Thomas* has a "dinner," Luke a "great banquet," and Matthew a "wedding feast." It is obvious that Matthew's wedding feast fits his allegory. Luke's adjective "great" for the banquet may be developing a possible reference to the messianic banquet, and therefore *Thomas*'s "dinner" may be more original, although it is not necessary to interpret "great banquet" in an allegorical sense.

In Matthew and Luke the servant announces the meal's readiness to those previously invited, whereas the situation in *Thomas* is not so obvious. Crossan interprets the *Thomas* parable so that a man prepares a dinner on the spur of the moment and then invites friends, who refuse.[32] Ménard argues that *Thomas* presupposes the same situation as the Synoptics.[33] Both oriental custom (see line 1 below) and the introduction to *Thomas* ("A man received visitors") imply, like the Synoptics, a previous invitation and now the courtesy reminder.[34]

Matthew and Luke have three excuses; *Thomas* has four. Since in *Thomas* the accent falls on the excuses, the number of excuses in *Thomas* is secondary. Further, orality prefers a triadic pattern. So most likely there were originally three excuses. In Matthew, the field and business excuses probably are abbreviations similar to what is in Luke, while the third excuse is derived from the parable A Man Planted a Vineyard. Since Matthew's feast is a wedding feast, a third excuse of attending a wedding feast would seem redundant. Because the man is a king, Matthew creates in the excuses the semblance of a large group refusing, of a rebellion in the making. In *Thomas*, the four excuses have a distinctive business cast to fit the concluding logion. But a friend's getting married and buying a farm are similar to two of the excuses in Luke, although with a distinctive *Thomas* twist: to prepare the banquet requires purchases, and the one who bought the farm is going to collect the rent. These similarities suggest that Luke's performance is closer to the parable's originating structure. It may be that in the excuses a performer had some freedom of experimentation. But the formal characteristics of each of the extant versions is the same: all make excuses, and the reasons are less than convincing.

Both Matthew and Luke report that the master was angry, but *Thomas*

32. Crossan, *In Parables*, 72–73.
33. Ménard, *L'évangile selon Thomas*, 164.
34. So Kim ("Papyrus Invitation," 397) on the basis of the papyrus evidence.

is silent on this point. Since both Matthew and Luke are concerned about the rejection of those who have refused the feast (allegorically the Jews), anger tallies with their performance. The absence of anger in *Thomas*, whose main point is the rejection of those who do not accept, is odd if it were part of the originating structure. Furthermore, the note of anger is expected by a hearer since the man's honor has been insulted, and therefore it is likely to be added in subsequent performances.[35]

In the man's command to the servant to invite new guests there are two problems: (1) How many sets of invitations are there? (2) Does the man command the room to be filled? Since all three extant performances of our parable begin with a note about "going out to the streets" and from there diverge, the originating structure probably contained such a command. This would create an ironical balance with those who live in houses—a description of those originally invited. Second, from a formal perspective, all three performances agree that the new guests are from the outcast, the lower classes. Each has elaborated this in its own way. Matthew has added a characteristic note of "good and bad" (22:10). Luke has a double invitation, the first one of which echoes 14:13: "Invite the poor, the maimed, the lame, and the blind." The double invitation is Luke's construction. The desire in the Synoptics for a full banquet hall results from the identification of the banquet with the messianic banquet. In any case, the desire to fill the hall belongs with the exclusion of those first invited, preventing them from reentering. As such it is implicit in the originating structure.

The originating structure concluded with an invitation,[36] but all three versions have constructed conclusions fitting to their performance. Matthew's "wedding garment" aligns the parable with his plan of salvation history. *Thomas* excludes the businessmen and merchants. Luke's conclusion recalls the judgment passed on the original invitees. In his concluding line the householder avenges his honor by himself rebuffing those who rebuffed him. As such, his conclusion to the parable may mark an early attempt by the oral tradition to restore the man's honor, to control the damage of the snub by those of high place.

---

35. Breech (*Silence of Jesus*, 119) argues that since both Matthew and Luke have the note about anger, it must have been in Q and Q would have had no reason to add it; therefore, he concludes, it was original. But as Schulz (*Q: Die Spruchquelle*, 402) points out, the Q parable would have also been used to justify the church's position in relation to Judaism and so Q could have had reason to add such a note.

36. Bultmann (*History of the Synoptic Tradition*, 175) points to Matthew 22:10 as probably closer to the original ending.

A Reading

Line 1: A man gave a banquet and invited many and at the time of the banquet he sent his servant to say to those who had been invited, "Come, for all is now ready."

The first line sets the coordinates by which a hearer navigates through the story. A hearer quickly learns that the man has wealth, since he can afford to entertain his friends with a banquet and has a servant. Furthermore, the so-called double invitation is a special sign of courtesy practiced by the wealthy.[37] Chan-Hie Kim has noted the relative infrequency of papyrus letters of invitation, because normally the invitation was delivered by a servant who read the invitation or, if illiterate, recited it. The invitation followed a standard form: "Chaeremon invites you to dine at a banquet of the Lord Serapis in the Serapeum tomorrow, that is, the 15th, from the 9th hour."[38] The servant would repeat the form to each of those invited. The parable's first line sets the man up as an individual of wealth and power. A banquet will redound to his honor in the village. A banquet increases the social indebtedness of others to the host.

Feasting is one sign of God's triumph over his enemies,[39] and all three extant versions of the parable have developed the metaphorical possibilities of the banquet as a sign of the final blessing. They have seen in the banquet/dinner a metaphor for salvation.[40] But in the originating structure it is a possibility that might be developed.

Line 2: The first said to him, "I have bought a field, and I must go out and see it; I pray you, have me excused." And another said, "I have bought five yoke of oxen, and I go to examine them; I pray you, have me excused." And another said, "I have married a wife and therefore I cannot come."

In analyzing the originating structure we saw that the three types of excuses as represented by Luke had the best claim to be original. Moreover, all three performances judge the excuses to be a charade, without

37. See the story of Esther's banquet for the king, which seems to imply such a double invitation (Est. 6:14). Str-B 1:880 offers rabbinic evidence, as does Jeremias in *Parables*, 176. Plummer (*Gospel according to St. Luke*, 360) recalls the Latin practice of a "vocator."

38. Kim, "Papyrus Invitation," 393.

39. Isa. 25:6; *1 Enoch* 62.13–16; and *2 Bar.* 29.4. See Jeremias, *Eucharistic Words*, 233–34; Bailey, *Through Peasant Eyes*, 89–91. It should be noted that the banquet is *one* sign, not the only sign of the messianic age. Its greatest elaboration is in Christian thought, because of its association with the Eucharist. See Behm, *"deipon, deipneō,"* 34–5.

40. Hahn, "Das Gleichnis," 68.

merit. Finally, all those invited refuse to come. It almost appears to be a conspiracy[41] or a case of social snobbery.

Since the three extant versions agree that all those invited rejected the invitation, this is surely part of the parable's originating structure. But since the excuses form a triad, a hearer would expect the third invitation to be accepted.[42] For example, in From Jerusalem to Jericho, the first two characters pass by but the third comes to the man's aid. In the parable of the talents, the first two succeed while the third fails. Since the first two reject the invitation, a hearer anticipates that the third will accept. This violation of the triadic expectation underscores the totality of the rejection.

A number of scholars have pointed to the similarity between the excuses in Luke and the excuses for refusing conscription for war in Deut. 20:5–7:

> Then the officers shall speak to the people, saying, "What man is there that has built a new house and has not dedicated it? Let him go back to his house, lest he die in the battle and another man dedicate it. And what man is there that has planted a vineyard and has not enjoyed its fruit? Let him go back to his house, lest he die in the battle and another man enjoy its fruit. And what man is there that has betrothed a wife and has not taken her? Let him go back to his house, lest he die in the battle and another man take her."

The similarity is most striking in the case of the third excuse, since the theme of a marriage is present in all three extant versions of the parable. Derrett argues that this allusion to Deuteronomy is the key to the parable,[43] so that the banquet is the meal before the final holy war. But the excuses, which are valid for a normal war, are not valid for the holy war. As the Mishnah says, "What has been said applies to a battle waged of free choice; but in a battle waged in a religious cause all go forth, even the bridegroom out of his chamber and the bride out of her bridechamber."[44] The problem with Derrett's argument is that he needs Matthew's parable with Luke's excuses![45] But the quotation from the Mish-

41. See ibid, 54–56; Plummer, *Gospel according to St. Luke,* 361.

42. Breech, *Silence of Jesus,* 132. Since Matthew and Luke both inform the reader before the action that all will refuse, we no longer see the expectation, their stories having no suspense.

43. Derrett, *Law in the New Testament,* 126–55.

44. *m. Sota* 8.7 (Danby, 303).

45. Palmer ("Just Married," 242), Gundry, (*Matthew,* 433), Ballard ("Reasons for Refusing," 341–50), and Sanders ("Ethic of Election," 245–71) are all similiar to Derrett. Derrett assumes that the full form of the parable is some combination of Matthew and Luke as a midrash on Zeph. 1:7–9, i.e., a king setting up the conditions for battle. Perhaps if Derrett had invoked Lévi-Strauss's understanding of mythemes it would have been an interesting attempt.

nah with its reference to the bridegroom, underscores that the marriage excuse can stand for the others enumerated in Deuteronomy and is the most important in an effort to introduce compassion into conscription for war. Thus it is highly likely that at least the last excuse in the originating structure did allude to Deuteronomy.[46] The allusion creates for a hearer a hint of incongruity; unlike battles, where people are killed, dinner parties are usually survived.[47] But it is important to observe at what level the allusion operates. The character giving the excuse is unaware of the allusion, so the irony is between the narrator and narratee. At the story level, it is only a banquet; at the discourse level, it is a banquet before the holy war.

At face value the excuses lack merit. A shrewd landowner would first inspect and then buy a field, and so also with oxen and the other commercial activities described in Matthew and *Thomas*.[48] Similarly with the marriage excuse. Since the servant is only bringing the courtesy reminder, the guests have previously accepted the invitation. How could the bridegroom have forgotten when he first accepted the invitation that he was going to be married on the day of the feast? Or who in a small village would give a party for his friends on the day of a marriage? A marriage feast is a major occasion in village life. So the excuses are without foundation, and they have the appearance of a concerted effort on the part of those invited. It is always possible that at the last minute one or two guests would be unable to attend, but all the guests? The hearer is left to speculate about the reason for such an insult. The man, of course, has been shamed. Honor is not something one has in isolation but is always a grant from those significant others in one's orbit. The significant others in the banquet giver's orbit have rejected him.

Line 3: So the servant reported this to his master.

The servant's report allows the master time to formulate a response. How is he to maintain his honor? Since this is a social insult, he should respond with a social insult.[49]

Jeremias[50] sees this parable as dependent on the Bar Maayan parable, so that we are to imagine the anonymous man of the parable as the publican Bar Maayan. This surely goes well beyond the evidence. But

46. Marshall (*Commentary on Luke,* 588–59) is appropriately cautious about the allusion.

47. Palmer, "Just Married," 248.

48. Bailey (*Through Peasant Eyes,* 95–99) against Derrett (*Law in the New Testament,* 136–37, 139), who sees the excuses as legitimate but the invited as united in their despising the master.

49. Derrett, *Law in the New Testament,* 140.

50. Jeremias, *Parables,* 178–79.

the parallel is instructive. The Bar Maayan parable is told to illustrate the one good deed the man did during his life so as to account for his good burial:[51]

> He never did a meritorious deed in his life. But one time he made a banquet for the councillors of his town but they did not come. He said, "Let the poor come and eat the food, so that it not go to waste."[52]

In this story the councilors were justified in dishonoring the host because he was a publican and therefore a sinner. But his response—his vengeance on those who dishonored him—points to the appropriate social response, a snub.

Line 4: And the master said: "Go outside to the streets and bring back those whom you happen to meet, so that they may dine."

The response of the man is similar to that of Bar Maayan: he sends his servant to collect the poor. Yet there are two important differences. In the Bar Maayan story the action is an example of a good deed: Bar Maayan feeds the poor. No such purpose is at stake here. Second, Bar Maayan is a publican, a sinner. In terms of honor, his proper place is with the poor. The point of the Bar Maayan story is to show how such a wicked one could ever receive the honor of a good burial in the first place. Here no honor redounds to the man. Since he is anonymous we do not know whether he had sufficient honor to issue the invitations. Now his fate rests with those he has invited. He belongs with the poor, with those who dwell along the streets. In order to insult those originally invited, he loses his place of honor.

From Story to Kingdom: A Meal without War

All three extant performances of our parable see the meal as a thing of value and identify admittance to the meal with salvation. The meal becomes the reward: the marriage feast in Matthew, the great banquet in Luke, the places of My Father in *Thomas*. This unanimity on the part of the various performances is a clue to the operative mytheme. The meal stands for the kingdom, and admittance to the meal defines those who are saved.

For those who see the parable as referring to the messianic banquet, the classic text is that of Isa. 25:6–9:

---

51. See chap. 4 above for a full quotation of the Bar Maayan parable.
52. *j. San.* 6.6 (Neusner 31:182).

On this mountain the Lord of hosts will make for all peoples a feast of fat things, a feast of wine on the lees, of fat things full of marrow, of wine on the lees well refined. And he will destroy on this mountain the covering that is cast over all peoples, the veil that is spread over all nations. He will swallow up death forever, and the Lord God will wipe away tears from all faces, and the reproach of his people he will take away from all the earth; for the Lord has spoken. It will be said on that day, "Lo, this is our God; we have waited for him, that he might save us. This is the Lord; we have waited for him; let us be glad and rejoice in his salvation."

There is no evidence that the Jesus parable directly refers to the Isaiah text, but the structure of this text exposes the mytheme at stake. The feast is a celebration of victory over the Lord's enemies. He has vanquished the "ruthless nations" (v. 3) and "has been a stronghold to the poor" (v. 4). The oppressed are restored to honor by an all-powerful God.

Allusion to Deuteronomy, with its reasons for avoiding war in the excuses of those who refuse, tips the audience off to the expected mytheme. Both the banquet and the excuses suggest that God's final vengeance is about to happen, yet the dinner never escalates to the expected messianic banquet, because the master is powerless to attack those who have snubbed him. In this village there is no upward mobility, for the master loses his upper-class status and must join those who live in the streets. In a dyadic culture, self-worth or -value is determined by significant others. In the passage from Isaiah, the poor and distressed receive new value from being associated with God: God raises such people to his status by destroying their enemies. In the parable, the householder cannot raise the poor up but must himself join them.

As the parable was transmitted, the mytheme reasserted itself. In Luke, at the story's end the master excludes those who have rejected his invitation from *ever* tasting the banquet. This is a threat only if the master is the Lord, which is the case in Luke's allegory. In Jesus' parable, the first invited would only reply, "We didn't want to come anyway." In *Thomas*, those who fail are deprived of the ultimate benefit of wisdom, a place with My Father. In Matthew, the mytheme fully reasserts itself and a king gives a wedding feast and does indeed take his vengeance on those who have insulted his honor. The king remains the significant other who defines value.

The Jesus parable, like the parable A Grain of Mustard Seed, works by misdirection. One expects a messianic banquet to parallel the cedar of Lebanon, but one ends up with a householder's feast filled with the uninvited, with those who will give him no honor. The parable reverses and subverts the system of honor. The man who gives a banquet loses his honor and joins the shameless poor. An audience expects the messianic banquet to signal that those who have suffered at the hands of Israel's enemies will be restored to honor by the power of God. Here the opposite happens. Paradoxically, in the Jesus parable the guest without the wedding garment would have remained.

6

You Can't Keep a Good Woman Down

In a City There was a Judge

A certain judge was in a certain city who neither feared God nor had respect for man. And a widow was in that city and she was coming to him saying: "Vindicate me from my opponent." And he did not wish to for a long time. After this he said to himself, "Even if I do not fear God and do not respect man, yet because this widow is causing me trouble, I will vindicate her, so that her continual coming may not batter me down."

A judge and a widow draw part of their value from the religious map, like the Pharisee and the tax collector. Widows, with orphans and foreigners, make up a special class in need of protection. The psalmist refers to God as defender of widows (Ps. 68:5). Judges carry out God's purpose, execute his torah. But if the interaction of a judge and widow is part of a metaphorical system that structures the understanding and experience of God, then the parable In a City There Was a Judge (Luke 18:2–5) is an anti-metaphor, for its judge is hardly a metaphor for God. To discover the parable's place in the metaphorical system we will first investigate Luke's and the oral tradition's understanding and use of the parable and then turn to the parable itself.

Pray Always

This parable is woven into the context of an eschatological discourse that begins in Luke 17:20 with the pharisees' question on the coming of the kingdom.[1] The question about the coming kingdom generates a warning concerning the days of the Son of man's Parousia, a time of danger and stress. In introducing the parable the narrator informs a reader that Jesus' purpose in telling the parable was to encourage the disciples "always to pray and not to lose heart" (18:1). The coming days of the Son of man demand prayer and perseverance.[2] The parable itself functions as an example based on "how much more": if an unjust judge grants a widow her petition because of constant intercession, how much more will God . . . In v. 8, Luke ties the parable to the immediate context of the Son of man's Parousia by asking whether he will find faith (i.e., prayer and persistence) on his return.

The next parable, Two Men Went Up to the Temple (18:9–14), belongs to this same nexus and is meant to indicate the correct attitude during prayer. There is even an ironic relation between the two parables. In the parable In a City There Was a Judge, the negative character is a negative metaphor for God; in Two Men Went Up to the Temple, the negative figure (the publican) is a positive example to imitate. The ironic juxtaposition of the two parables creates dramatic interest in this section of Luke.

It is clear, then, that Luke has arranged this section of the Gospel to meet his own needs and interests. The introduction in 18:1 parallels the style of introduction of 18:9, creating an ironic backloop, with the second parable dealing with prayer explicitly. The introduction to the parable is not traditional but a clear Lukan construction.[3]

The issues surrounding vv. 6–8 are not nearly so clear. Opinion divides between those who see these verses as Jesus' own interpretation and those who see them as the interpretation of the early church. Jülicher saw vv. 6–8a as the product of a Christian community facing persecution,[4] whereas Jeremias and Werner Kümmel have argued strongly for the authenticity and originality of the verses with Jesus himself. Jeremias has argued that the verses betray Aramaic idiom and that "Jesus' choice of this brutal judge to illustrate God's helpfulness

---

1. This unit is part of the larger unit of Luke 17:11—19:44. See Talbert, *Reading Luke*, 169; Ernst, *Das Evangelium nach Lukas*, 482.
2. See Spicq, "La parabole," 71. Spicq stresses this point.
3. See Bultmann, *History of the Synoptic Tradition*, 199; Jeremias, *Parables*, 156; Marshall, *Commentary on Luke*, 671.
4. See Jülicher, *Die Gleichnisreden* 2:284. See also, among many others, Bultmann, *History of the Synoptic Tradition*, 175; B. T. D. Smith, *Parables*, 152.

must have shocked his audience to a degree which simply made an interpretation indispensable."[5] The first argument concerning Aramaicism is dealt with easily. It is no proof of authenticity but proof only of Aramaic provenience.[6] But Jeremias's second argument, concerning the need for interpretation, has convinced many, including Kümmel and Linnemann. For Kümmel, the judge's decision to avenge the woman is a metaphor for God's activity in behalf of the elect, and thus there is "no necessity to detach the verses from the parable."[7] Linnemann stands this argument on its head and argues that since there is a necessary relation between the parable and its interpretation, the parable and interpretation are secondary.[8] She argues so because (a) applications to parables in the Synoptic tradition are normally secondary; (b) the notion of the "elect" is unattested in the Jesus tradition; and (c) the exhortation to general prayer is not characteristic of Jesus' teaching.

The key argument here is that the parable demands an interpretation. This is, of course, true. All metaphors demand interpretation, because connotative language is always about something else. Bridging the gap between literal and figurative requires interpretation. But that the parable demands this particular interpretation is not obvious, nor that the metaphor maker must be the one to provide an interpretation, nor again that a metaphor can have only one interpretation. On the basis of the argument of Jeremias, Kümmel, and Linnemann, every parable should have its appended interpretation. In the end, Jülicher's original argument that the interpretation results from the church under persecution seems more likely.[9]

Surface Structure

The following translation makes visually evident the recurring patterns which mark the parable's structure:

A a certain judge was in a certain city
   B *who neither God feared nor for man had respect*
A and a widow was in that city
     C and she was **coming** to him saying:
       D **Vindicate** me from my opponent

5. Jeremias, *Parables*, 156. In earlier eds. of his book, Jeremias accepted Jülicher's position.
6. See Linnemann, *Jesus of the Parables*, 187; Grässer, *Das Problem*, 36–37.
7. Kümmel, *Promise and Fulfillment*, 59.
8. Linnemann, *Jesus of the Parables*, 187–88.
9. So B. T. D. Smith (*Parables*, 152) and many others. In an effort to prove the authenticity of the interpretation, Catchpole ("Son of Man's Search," 104) actually makes a good case for a Q sequence of Luke 17:24, 26–30; 18:2–5, 7–8.

> B *Even if God I do not fear and man I do not respect* because this widow is providing me trouble
>> D I will **vindicate** her,
>> C so that her **coming** continually may not batter me down

The parable contains a clear set of parallels based on phrases A and B. The A phrases tie together the introduction, while the B phrases mark out the two movements of the story line. The C and D phrases form a chiasm based on "coming" and "vindicate." The B phrase is formulaic, creating a recurring pattern that holds the narrative together.

There is the repetition of various words and phrases, part of the backlooping of oral speech.[10] Although the parable does engage in backlooping, redundancy, the available language is sparse. "Judge," "widow," "city" (unnamed), "coming," and "vindicate" make up the principal vocabulary.

A Reading

Line 1: A certain judge was in a certain city who neither feared God nor had respect for man.

"Certain," *tis*, is part of an expected Lukan adaptation of the introduction.[11] In the pre-Lukan version the judge and city remained anonymous, as they are here.

In the first line, the narrator characterizes the judge for an audience. A positive set of features has drawn little attention, but the negative set, much. Both are connected with the honor-shame pattern so prominent in this parable.

The man has two marks of honor. He has a judge's ascribed honor, and the narrator places him in a city—which is a redundancy, since judges are found only in cities.[12] This note of location is part of the parable's economy and situates the judge among the urban elite.[13] These two initial marks of honor raise him above that of the majority of the parable's hearers. He is a judge, and he belongs to an urban elite.

Immediately after these two short markers of honor, the narrator provides a formulaic description of the judge as shameless—"who neither feared God nor had respect for man." Both aspects of this characterization are charged with overtones in a shame-honor society.

The fear of God is a well-established motif in the Hebrew Bible and

10. Ong, *Orality and Literacy*, 39–40.
11. Jeremias, *Die Sprache*, 271.
12. Str-B 1:257–70. The Mishnah in its idealized perspective sees every village of 120 with a tribunal of seven, but this was not the actual case.
13. Malina (*New Testament World*, 71–75) describes how such elites fit into an honor-shame society.

on occasion is associated with judges. When Jehoshaphat set up judges in the cities of Judah he addressed them,

> Consider what you do, for you judge not for man but for the Lord; he is with you in giving judgment. Now then, let the fear of the Lord be upon you; take heed what you do, for there is no perversion of justice with the Lord our God, or partiality, or taking bribes. (2 Chron. 19:6–7)[14]

This exhibits the God-man antipodes characteristic of formulaic statements. A God-fearer keeps God's commands and hears his word,[15] and thus is reliable. A God-fearer is established in the highest honor. For a judge who is supposed to fear God, not to fear God brands him as shameless.

Entrepō, "respect," belongs to the vocabulary of shame. In the active voice it means "to make ashamed."[16] In 1 Corinthians 4, Paul, in establishing the apostle's true marks of respect—which paradoxically turn out to be the opposite of the expected marks of honor—concludes, "I do not write this to make you ashamed, but to admonish you as my beloved children." The point of Paul's listing the marks is not to reduce the Corinthians' honor (i.e., to make them shameless) but to restore them to true honor. In the passive voice, *entrepō* means "to be put to shame" or "to be ashamed." In 2 Thessalonians, the author, in attempting to gain authority for the letter, writes, "If anyone does not obey our word through this letter, mark this one, do not mix with him so that he may be put to shame" (2 Thess. 3:14). One is put to shame by separation from the group that grants the individual honor. Without the group's solidarity, the individual in a shame-honor society is shameless. In the middle voice, which is the voice used in our parable, *entrepō* means "to turn toward something or someone," "to have regard for or to respect." The turning metaphor indicates that respect or regard has to do with one's relation to another. In the parable A Man Planted a Vineyard, the father says as he sends his son off, "They will respect my son" (Mark 12:6). Respect derives from the son's relation to the father, given his place of honor in a patriarchal society. That honor the husbandmen are supposed to recognize. C. Spicq, after an extensive review of the evidence, translates *entrepō* as "failing in a sense of honor."[17]

The phrase "fear of God and respect of man" is formulaic or prover-

---

14. Similarly, in Exod. 18:21, Moses, in commanding the choosing of judges for the people, describes them as "able men . . . bribe."
15. For a summary of the Hebrew Bible evidence, see Wanke, "*phobeō*," 201. Delling (Das Gleichnis," 7 n. 26) also surveys evidence of judge and fear. Luke more than any other New Testament writer shows a fondness for formulas dealing with the fear of God. Cf. Balz, "*phobeō*," 212–13.
16. The definitions that follow are from BAGD, 269.
17. Spicq, "La parabole," 63.

bial.[18] A close parallel occurs in the *History of Rome* by the first-century B.C.E. Greek historian and rhetorician Dionysius of Halicarnassus. In a speech to the Roman senate concerning a conspiracy by some aristocrats to take away the rights of plebeians, a tribune refers to the plans of the conspirators as concocted "without either fearing the anger of the gods or heeding the indignation of men."[19] The phrase declares the utter lack of honor of these conspirators: they have acted outside the bounds of society.[20]

For the judge neither to fear God nor to have respect for man makes him without honor, shameless. In a dyadic society this is a severe description, for in essence it describes a person outside the bounds of society, who is determined by no significant other, whether God or man. He is an outlaw judge.

Line 2: And a widow was in that city and she was coming to him saying: "Vindicate me from my opponent."

The narrator introduces the widow in a fashion reminiscent of the judge's introduction: she is a widow in a city, just as he is a judge in a city. Here the city serves to bring her into the judge's narrative space. His implied honor was denied by the narrator's description, whereas "widow" in Israel's heritage is a value term demanding response.

According to the customs of the day, a marriage contract (*ketubbah*) stated a husband's obligations to his wife, and on his death she had a right to be supported out of his estate as specified in the contract. The wife did not inherit.[21] Normally a husband's estate would take care of a widow's needs. But the normal condition was by no means universal. Many widows and their children were left destitute. So common was this state of affairs that "widow" came to mean not simply a woman whose husband was dead but also one who had no means of financial support and thus needed special protection.[22]

18. Marshall, *Commentary on Luke*, 67. See the many parallels of Wettstein in *Novum Testamentum Graecum* 2:778–79.

19. Dionysius of Halicarnassus, *Roman Antiquities*, 10.10.7 (LCL 6:197).

20. Among Wettstein's other examples, two are significant. Josephus describes Jehoiachin as "unjust and wicked by nature" and says that he "was neither reverent toward God nor kind to man" (*Jewish Antiquities*, 10.83 [LCL 6:203]). Livy wrote that the consul Flaminius "lacked all proper reverence, not only for the laws and for the senate's majesty, but even for the gods" (Livy, *Ab urbe condita*, 22.3.5 [LCL 5:209]).

21. Safrai, "Home and Family," 787. The wife could choose to remain in the house of her husband, although normally she would return to her father's or brother's house because of kinship patterns. Safrai shows strong evidence that widows were encouraged to remarry.

22. Cohen, "Widows," 488. This identification of widows and the needy is so strong that in the LXX text of Jer. 5:28, *chēra*, "widow," is substituted for '*bywnym*, "needy." Both BDB and BAGD note this connection of the needy and widows. Concern for the

The triadic formula "widows, orphans, and foreigners" summarizes in the Hebrew Bible the need of special protection. Even more, the Hebrew Bible often draws a relation between Israel's having been a slave in Egypt (i.e., being in need) and the demand to care for the widow, orphan, and foreigner.

> You shall not pervert the justice due to the sojourner or to the fatherless, or take a widow's garment in pledge; but you shall remember that you were a slave in Egypt and the Lord your God redeemed you from there. (Deut. 24:17–18)[23]

Not only is the Israelite to protect this class but God himself is their protector.

> You shall not wrong a stranger or oppress him for you were strangers in the land of Egypt. You shall not afflict any widow or orphan. If you do afflict them and they cry out to me, I will surely hear their cry, and my wrath will burn, and I will kill you with the sword, and your wives shall become widows and your children fatherless. (Exod. 22:21–24)

The psalmist says, "Father of the fatherless and protector of widows is God in his holy habitation" (Pss. 68:5; 146:9; cf. Deut. 10:18). Conversely, it is a sign of wickedness—that a people have abandoned God—when the widow, orphan, and foreigner are abused. "The sojourner suffers extortion in your midst, the fatherless and the widow are wronged in you" (Ezek 22:7; cf., Zech 7:10; Ps 94:6; Isa 1:23; 10:1–2).

In the heritage of Israel a powerful interconnection is forged between Israel's having been a slave in Egypt and the special protection to be afforded those without protection. Even as God protected the Israelites in Egypt, so will he be the ultimate protector of the widow, the orphan, and the foreigner. This idea of God as protector of last resort leads to stories about how God intervenes in behalf of the widow and orphan. Elisha's miracle for the widow is well known. A creditor had come to make slaves of her two children. As she gathered her neighbors' jars, she kept pouring from her one jar a continuous flow of oil, so that all the jars were full, enough to pay her debts and provide something for her to live on (2 Kings 4:1–7). There is a similar story but with a tragic ending in *The Fathers according to Rabbi Nathan:*

widow was not unique to Israel. Stählin ("*chēra,*" 441–44) quotes evidence that the surrounding cultures were also concerned about the welfare of widows.

23. The passage repeats this formula with harvest, olive trees, and vineyard. Cf. Deut. 14:28–29; 26:12–13. See also 27:19, at the ceremony of the covenant renewal: "Cursed be he who perverts the justice due to the sojourner, the fatherless, and the widow. And all the people shall say, Amen."

> There was once a poor woman who dwelt in the neighborhood of a land-owner. Her two sons went out to gather gleanings, but the landowner did not let them take any. Their mother kept saying: "When will my sons come back from the field; perhaps I shall find that they have brought something to eat." And they kept saying: "When shall we go back to our mother; perhaps we shall discover that she has found something to eat." She found that they had nothing and they found that she had nothing to eat. So they laid their heads on their mother's lap and the three of them died in one day. Said the Holy One, blessed be He: "Their very existence you take away from them! By your life! I shall make you, too, pay for it with your very existence!" And so indeed it says, Rob not the weak, because he is weak, neither crush the poor in the gate; for the Lord will plead their cause, and despoil of life those that despoil them (Prov. 22:22–3).[24]

Even though this parable comes from a much later period, it demonstrates a consistent theme over a long stretch of history. Even more, it illustrates the potentially tragic undertow of the theme. Behind the pleadings of a widow lie potentially tragic results. There is no welfare system, no safety net, to fall back on if the judge fails to provide the special protection needed. In a subsistence world like Palestine, death is not an unknown answer to a plea.

Terms belonging to a shame-honor schema stand out in line 2. By coming, the widow attempts to penetrate the judge's social space. As widow she has a claim on him, but as woman she is an object of shame that threatens his honor. Since she is not his equal, he does not have to respond to her request, although if he should respond it would redound to his honor, for she would then become his client. A widow is a member of the lowest social structure, one without protection and honor. Her "coming" is described in this line as constant and repetitive.[25] "Vindicate," *ekdikēson*, is used in Greek papyri to mean "settle a case," but in the LXX it means to avenge or punish, especially in issues dealing with purity of blood.[26] The usage in the parable resembles the papyri usage. But since the word is used with the preposition "from," *apo*, the LXX notion of avenging should not be discounted. The widow is making a direct and continuous plea to the judge to defend her honor. *Antidikos*, "opponent," is a litigant in a lawsuit.[27]

So while we have the appropriate technical language for a lawsuit, set

---

24. *Fathers according to Rabbi Nathan* 38 (Goldin, 158).

25. Jülicher (*Die Gleichnisreden* 2:279) refers to *ercheto* as an iterative imperfect. Cf. BDF, 325.

26. Schrenk, "*ekikeō*," 442–43.

27. Schrenk ("*antidikos*," 374) thinks it means only a general opponent, since no case is described. But the concern of the parable is not with the case but with the interaction between judge and widow.

in a situation of shame-honor, the woman's speech is particularly inappropriate for her situation. She does not begin with a respectful address. There is no "Sir, I request" nor "There is no other possibility for me because my husband is dead . . . thus, I have had to turn to you, O King, to obtain justice."[28]

Thus we see in these first two lines the curious ambivalence of the narration toward the shame-honor schema. A judge with ascribed honor is described as shameless; a widow pleading for him to become her patron addresses one above her without an appropriate honorific title.

Line 3:   And he did not wish to for a long time.

The parable's narrative structure is straightforward (see fig. 3).

$$
\text{request} \quad \left\{ \begin{array}{l} \text{judgment} \\ \\ \text{refusal} \end{array} \right. \quad \left\{ \begin{array}{l} \text{vindication} \\ \\ \text{nonvindication} \end{array} \right.
$$

The widow's request initially produces a refusal on the judge's part. Her continued requesting, however, creates a narrative loop, a vicious circle that eventually he will break by rendering judgment. What is not realized in the actual narrative is either any hint of a trial itself or what the issue for litigation might be. The narrative simply skips from request to vindication. This tight, abbreviated narration focuses attention on the interaction and confrontation between judge and widow, making the judge her opponent and not the litigant.

This gap, this lack of a trial scene, has led to considerable discussion about why the judge refused the widow and about the legal situation. The described scene is a clear violation of Jewish legal practice in several ways. A judge is required to give precedence to a widow's or orphan's case.[29] The frequent warning against judges' taking bribes indicates that offering a bribe was not unusual. Howard Marshall assumes that the woman's wealthy opponent has bribed the judge, and T. W. Manson assumes the woman is too poor to bribe the judge.[30] Actually, though either may be possible, the parable demands no such assumption. It is unconcerned about the reason for the judge's failure.

Others have grappled with the depiction of a single judge. According

---

28. Spicq, "La parabole," 74. See, e.g., the address to the master in the parable A Man Entrusts Property (chap. 9), where each of the servants begins his report with "Lord."

29. Stählin, "*chēra*," 450 n. 86.

30. Marshall, *Commentary on Luke*, 669; Manson, *Sayings*, 306.

to the Mishnah, standard practice required three judges,[31] although there were exceptions. In some civil cases an expert in the law (*mumheh la-rabbim*) could function as a single judge, if both parties agreed.[32] Actually the legal situation in Palestine at the time of Jesus was vague and complex. The Mishnah assumed that every village of at least 120 people would have a tribunal of seven judges, but this was an ideal, not an actuality. C. Chajes has found little evidence that tribunals were ever in place. Most cases were heard by one judge.[33] An additional complication is that Palestine was a conquered and occupied territory. Although the governor was the supreme judicial authority, Roman practice left civil jurisdiction under local control. In Judea, civil jurisdiction was in the hands of autonomous Jewish authorities.[34] Derrett has suggested that there were two court systems, one religious and the other secular. This would be especially true in those cases where Jews and Gentiles were involved in litigation. The Gentile would not want to submit to Jewish practice. One also could press a case in a secular court, where the standards of evidence were not as severe.[35] But there is no apparent reason to suggest that this parable envisions a situation demanding a secular court, although the description of the judge indicates that he is not a pious Pharisee.[36]

Although it is important to keep in mind the complex legal situation of Palestine and the less than full realization of the ideal of Mishnaic law in this parable, the parable turns not on the legal situation but on the confrontation between judge and widow.

Line 4: After this he said to himself, "Even if I do not fear God and do not respect man, yet because this widow is causing me trouble, I will vindicate her, so that her continual coming may not batter me down."

As the narrative structure makes evident, unless the judge resolves

31. *m. Sanh.* 3.1 (Danby, 385).

32. *b. Sanh.* 5a (Soncino 12:16). For an extensive review of the situation, see Cohen, "Bet Din," 721–23. The rabbis objected to a single judge because there is no judge but God alone (*Avot* 4.8). Jeremias (*Parables,* 153) believes that because it is a single judge it is a money matter.

33. Chajes, "Les juges juifs," 52. Chajes's study deals mostly with the situation after 70 C.E., and the study needs badly to be updated.

34. M. Stern, "Province of Judaea," 336.

35. Derrett, "Law in the New Testament: The Parable," 180. Most of Derrett's evidence comes from Egypt. Shalit (*König Herodes,* 223–32) indicates that there were two legal systems and sets of courts.

36. Sherwin-White (*Roman Society and Roman Law,* 133–34) argues that the notion of the judge represented in this parable is peculiarly Jewish and does not correspond to a Roman understanding.

the woman's case, the story will continue in an endless loop. She will keep coming forever and ever. So a hearer expects a confrontation between judge and widow at the conclusion of which he will come to her aid. The confrontation will serve as a turning point in which the judge will behave in an honorable way.

Line 4 begins with introspection (an interior monologue) that may heighten this expectation of a coming confrontation and a return to honor on the judge's part. But the soliloquy initially repeats the narrator's characterization from line 1. The grammatical construction *ei kai*, "even if," "although," indicates actual fact.[37] The judge agrees with the narrator's description. There will be no turning (i.e., denouement) in this parable. The judge will remain dishonorable, shameless.

His reasoning for coming to the widow's aid remains true to his characterization. He acts out of convenience. This is emphasized in the Greek text with the use of *ge*, "yet." The meaning of *hypōpiazō* has been a matter of some debate. I have chosen to translate it "batter down." It is derived from the language of boxing, meaning "to strike under the eye," "to give a black eye." There are several possibilities.[38] It can be taken literally, in which case the judge will be afraid of physical abuse.[39] But this does not really seem feasible. Since a chief characteristic of a widow is her defenselessness, why should a judge fear physical attack from her? They are an uneven match. Most have taken the word in a metaphorical sense, meaning "to wear down" or "to greatly annoy."[40] Derrett[41] has proposed a translation of "to black my face," or nonmetaphorically, "to slander or destroy one's good name." There is some evidence to support this, but the judge is unconcerned about his honor, so such a threat would lack credibility. It seems better to understand *hypōpiazō* as "to wear down" or "to batter down."

An audience expects the judge to come to the widow's aid for three reasons: (1) The narrative structure demands it. (2) Widows are to receive special protection. (3) His honor as judge demands that he function as patron. When he does act, it is for none of these reasons but for his own convenience. The great irony of this story is that a judge who

37. Plummer, *Gospel according to St. Luke*, 412.
38. Marshall (*Commentary on Luke*, 673) and Creed (*Gospel according to St. Luke*, 223) offer extensive summaries of positions that commentators have taken.
39. So Jülicher, *Die Gleichnisreden* 2:282; Spicq, "La parabole," 75 n. 6; Delling, "Das Gleichnis," 12. Zerwick (*Biblical Greek*, 81) indicates that the present tenses of the verbs cannot support this understanding.
40. BAGD, 848. See also Marshall, *Commentary on Luke*, 673; Linnemann, *Jesus of the Parables*, 185; Jeremias, *Parables*, 154.
41. Derrett, "Law in the New Testament: The Parable," 190.

neither fears God nor respects man comes to fear a widow, the weakest member of society.[42] The expected denouement in which the judge turns to honor is missing! This, of course, leads to a hearer's frustration, the so-called defamiliarization, a strategy by which fiction refuses to mediate.

Here Comes the Widow

An important metaphorical network in the kingdom's symbolic structure represents God as a just judge. It finds clear expression as a my-theme in Eccles. 35:12–18:[43]

> For the Lord is one who repays,
> and he will repay you seven times over.
> Do not try to bribe him, for he will not accept it,
> And do not rely on an ill-gotten sacrifice;
> For the Lord is a judge,
> And there is no partiality with him.
> But He will listen to the prayer of the man who is wronged,
> Or the widow, if she pours out her story.
> Do not the widow's tears run down her cheeks,
> While she utters her complaint against the man who has caused them to
> fall? . . .
> The prayer of the humble pierces the clouds,
> And until it reaches God, he will not be consoled.
> And he will not leave off until the Most High consider him,
> And does justice to the upright, and passes judgment.
> And the Lord will not delay,
> Or be slow about them,
> Until he crushes the lions of the unmerciful.
>
> (Chicago Bible)

Here the metaphorical structure of God as a just judge finds full expression. Those who do not receive justice now, the widow and the orphan, have an ultimate judge who will right their cause. As we have seen before, Israel's enslavement in Egypt and the recognition of foreigner, widow, and orphan as those in need now provide a powerful symbolic nexus. The protection of a widow is an example of God's caring for his people. The judge is expected to stand in the place of God. In this parable the judge is neither a metaphor nor a metonymy for God. As a metaphor, he fails to stand in God's place, for he does not act from justice. As a metonymy, he is not a part standing for the whole (i.e., some aspect of God). The metaphorical structure creates an expectation

---

42. Spicq, "La parabole," 75.
43. Manson (*Sayings*, 305) notes the similarity of this passage to the parable.

that the parable will focus on the justice associated with the kingdom, but it is ignored. The outcome of the judge's vindication of the widow may have been just (although the parable does not state that), but his intentions were not motivated by honor or justice.

The parable focuses on the widow's continual coming (cf. the imperfect tense "was coming"; "for a long time"; "trouble"; "continual coming"). Her widow's shamelessness, her intrusion into the judge's social space, her continual coming bring about vindication—not the justice of her cause or the judge's honor. Actually Luke's interpretation has seized on this point but has narrowed it to an example of prayer, using a "how much more" argument. Confirming our interpretation, for Luke the underlying metaphorical structure states that God is a just judge. But Luke's way of applying the parable has weakened, not eliminated, the parable's scandal. But the parable bypasses the implied metaphor of God as a just judge in favor of the widow's action, her continued wearing down of him, as a more viable metaphor for the kingdom. The kingdom keeps coming, keeps battering down regardless of honor or justice. It may even come under the guise of shamelessness (lack of honor).

The three parables that cluster around the theme of the city and beyond—Two Men Went Up to the Temple, From Jerusalem to Jericho, and In a City There Was a Judge—test that part of the social religious map where boundaries indicate who is inside and who outside. The judge, the priest and Levite, and the Pharisee are inside. The widow, the Samaritan, and the tax collector are outside. In this parable the outsider functions differently from the way it does in the other two parables. In those parables the outsider is a sinner; here the widow is one in need. Her being outside results from her social status. Yet as in the other two parables, here too the outsider is the bearer for the kingdom. A hearer of the parable discovers the kingdom under the guise not of a just judge but of a pestering widow who exposes her own shamelessness in continually pressing her cause on a dishonorable judge.

7

Who's That Masked Man?

From Jerusalem to Jericho

A certain man was going down from Jerusalem to Jericho and he fell among bandits, who stripping him laying on blows went away, leaving [him] half-dead. By chance a certain priest was going down on that way and seeing him passed by opposite. Likewise so too a Levite coming up to the place and seeing passed by opposite. A certain Samaritan, being on the way, came up to him and seeing had pity. And approaching him he bound up his wounds, pouring on olive oil and wine: mounting him upon his own beast he brought him to the inn and attended him. On the next day taking out he gave two denarii to the innkeeper and said: "Take care of him and whatever you may spend in addition, I when I come back will give back to you."

All cultures, modern and ancient, draw boundaries between themselves and others, whether it is a matter of defending their turf or building iron curtains. Greeks called everyone who did not speak Greek a barbarian, and Jews divided the world between themselves and the Gentiles. The temptation to draw the line, to dare someone to step across it, seems to be a universal human phenomenon. The appealing and frightening aspect of the parable From Jerusalem to Jericho (Luke 10:30–35) is the recognition that on this journey from Jerusalem to Jericho the recurring effort of humans to divide themselves from others is severely challenged and called into question. But the parable challenges more than xenophobia; in the parable a hearer's own identity is at stake. The all-important question in this parable is that of point of view: from where do I hear the parable?

Who Is My Neighbor?

Luke situates this parable in a debate between a lawyer and Jesus over inheriting eternal life. The lawyer's question by paralleling that of the ruler in Luke 18:18 causes retrospection on a reader's part.[1] When the question recurs, the answer will be read in light of the first story. In that story, Jesus challenges the man to "sell all and distribute to the poor" (18:22), just as the Samaritan gives of his resources to care for the man in the ditch. Both the Samaritan and the rich young man are called upon to do the unimaginable. The rich young man must become poor, and the Jewish fictional audience has to imagine the Samaritan as neighbor. What is impossible for human beings is possible for God (18:27).[2]

More specifically, within the immediate context, the Lukan travel narrative begins with Jesus sending messengers into a Samaritan village. That village rejects the messengers. Jesus' refusal to call down fire upon the village (9:51–54)[3] prepares the Gospel reader for Samaritan antagonism and Jesus' forbearance.

A strong internal consistency links together the lawyer's question and the parable. The section is divided into two parallel parts, vv. 25–28 and vv. 29–37:

	Part 1	*Part 2*
Lawyer's question	eternal life	my neighbor
Jesus' counter-question	what is written	who proved neighbor
Lawyer's answer	Deut. 6:4/Lev. 19:18	the one who showed mercy on him.
Jesus' command	do this and you shall live	go and do likewise

1. Talbert, (*Reading Luke,* 111–12) sees the two passages as parallel in the chiasmic arrangement of the travel narrative.

2. The lawyer's question forms a title for both the parable of the Good Samaritan and the story of Mary and Martha. The parable is a comment on loving your neighbor; the story of Mary and Martha comments on the injunction to love God as oneself. So Talbert, *Reading Luke,* 120.

3. Lambrecht (*Once More Astonished,* 78) remarks that the proximity cannot be an accident.

This structure shows how carefully the parable has been integrated into the lawyer's question "What shall I do?" His question "What shall I do?" is picked up in the final command, "Go and do likewise." This connects with the parable when the half-dead man is restored to life by the Samaritan, so that to have mercy is to give life and thus to live eternally.[4]

This internal linking of parable and question has provoked debate about how the parable relates to the question about one's neighbor. Adding to the convolution of the debate is a parallel to the lawyer's question in Mark and Matthew. Though it is outside our purview whether Luke has modified Mark[5] or Q[6] or whether there is some other source-critical solution,[7] clearly in comparison with Mark and Matthew, the Lukan setting for the lawyer's question is strikingly different. No longer is it set in the controversy of Jesus' last days in the temple;[8] no longer is the question a provocation by the Sadducees.[9] Now it is a lawyer's quiz. Only in Luke does the question concerning eternal life appear, and only in Luke does a counterquestion force the lawyer to answer. The structure of the lawyer's question is especially important because the parallel structure surrounding the parable exemplifies neighborliness. The existence of the lawyer's question in Mark and Matthew, in addition to the evidence of heavy Lukan editing, indicates that the parable and the question of eternal life were separate in the oral tradition and were very probably joined editorially by Luke.[10]

Yet unresolved is whether the parable was originally an example of neighborliness.[11] Many see the question at the parable's conclusion as original.[12] But the parallels between the first part (on the question of eternal life) and the second part (asking who my neighbor is) indicate that the question is part of the Lukan formulation.[13] Confirming this structural observation about the double controversy is Jülicher's argument that "neighbor" is used in a twofold sense between the question

4. Crespy, "Parable of the Good Samaritan," 37.
5. Klostermann, *Das Lukasevangelium*, 188.
6. So Crossan, "Parable and Example," 67; Sellin, "Lukas als Gleichniserzähler," 20–23; Hultgren, *Jesus and His Adversaries*, 48.
7. Lambrecht (*Once More Astonished*, 62–68) concludes that Luke has used both Mark and Q.
8. See chap. 10 below.
9. Mattill, "Good Samaritan," 360.
10. Against Jeremias, *Parables*, 202; in agreement with Michaelis, *Die Gleichnisse*, 205. Linnemann (*Jesus of the Parables*, 138) sees vv. 29 and 36 as part of the original parable.
11. As suggested by Bultmann in *History of the Synoptic Tradition*, 192, and Marshall in *Commentary on Luke*, 440.
12. Lambrecht, *Once More Astonished*, 68. Crossan (*In Parables*, 61) sees the double-controversy form as pre-Lukan, and Matthew as responsible for breaking it apart because of his distaste for Samaritans.
13. Jülicher, *Die Gleichnisreden* 2:196; Talbert, *Reading Luke*, 121.

and parable.[14] In vv. 27 and 29, a "neighbor" is someone I must love, an object, whereas in v. 36, a "neighbor" is someone who shows mercy on me, a subject. For many commentators this shift in meaning of "neighbor" indicates that the parable and Lukan context were originally separate.[15]

The shift in meaning of "neighbor" is significant form-critically and suggests that the parable originally circulated separately from the question about neighborliness. This observation does not, however, explain why Luke used the parable as an example of a good neighbor. Since Luke performs the parable, what did he see in the parable that suggested such an interpretation? As Manson has noted, all ancient civilizations drew the line between insiders and outsiders,[16] and a profound experience in early Christianity was the dissolution of such boundaries.[17] A major component of Luke's perspective is the breakdown of the division between Jew and Gentile, almost the transfer from Jew to Gentile. In Luke's narrative the fictional audience is the Jewish lawyer who responds to Jesus' leading questions. But Luke's implied audience is gentile. From the point of view of the fictional audience (i.e., the Jewish lawyer), the sense of "neighbor" shifts. From the point of view of the Gentile audience, no such shift ensues, for the Gentile can and does identify with the Samaritan as one who loves (i.e, the subject).[18]

This reading of Luke furnishes two important clues about the parable's originating structure. (1) In some profound way this parable has to do with breaking down barriers, which Luke has symbolized by the question, Who is my neighbor? (2) The question of point of view is critical for a reading of the parable. It is not the same parable from a Jewish or *goy* point of view. From the gentile/Lukan perspective, it is an example story. We do not yet know what it is from a Jewish perspective.

Surface Structure

This parable has a symmetrical division. An initial sequence creates a lack to be remedied (v. 30); there follow two missed opportunities in the priest and Levite (vv. 31–32) and a denouement in the Samaritan's compassion (v. 33). But the denouement lingers on with an elaborate

14. Jülicher, *Die Gleichnisreden* 2:596.
15. Binder, "Das Gleichnis," 176; C. Montefiore, *Synoptic Gospels* 2:465; Creed, *Gospel according to St. Luke*, 151; and Ramaroson, "Comme 'Le bon samaritain,'" 533.
16. Manson, *Sayings*, 261. Neighbors in Judaism mean cobrothers of the covenant. See Lev. 19:8. See also Ramaroson, "Comme 'Le bon samaritain,'" 534; Str-B 1:353.
17. E.g., Gal. 3:28. See the parallel passages in *Pauline Parallels*, ed. Francis and Sampley, 236.
18. Funk, "Good Samaritan," 79.

description of the Samaritan's actions on the man's behalf (vv. 34–35). The purpose of this extended denouement will become apparent when we analyze the response structure.

The parable's surface structure is built around a series of stairsteps:

1. a certain man was going down
$\quad\quad\quad\quad\quad$ they-*went*-away
2. a certain priest was going down
$\quad\quad$ on that way
$\quad\quad\quad$ and **seeing**
$\quad\quad\quad\quad\quad\quad$ he-*went*-by-on-the-opposite-side
3. a $\quad\quad$ Levite
$\quad\quad$ upon that place coming
$\quad\quad\quad$ and **seeing**
$\quad\quad\quad\quad\quad$ *went*-by-on-the-opposite-side
4. a certain Samaritan
$\quad$ being-on-the-way
$\quad\quad\quad\quad$ *went* up to him
$\quad\quad$ and **seeing**
$\quad\quad\quad$ had pity

This literal translation images the structure of the underlying Greek text. The introductions for the man and the priest are parallel, tying together lines 1 and 2, but their fates are wholly different. The verb for the bandits is "went-away," *apēlthon*. Lines 1, 2, and 3 end with compounds of *ēlthon*, all negative. When the Samaritan went up (*ēlthon kat'*), the hearer expects a negative reaction. The negative use of *ēlthon* is a consistent pattern in the first three lines, leading to a negative expectation in the fourth. "On that way" in line 2 is paralleled by "upon that place" in line 3 and echoed in the participle "being-on-the-way" in line 4. "Seeing" holds the same place in the last three lines.

The stairstep pattern of the first four lines makes more apparent the asymmetry of the concluding description of the Samaritan's aid. The surface structure creates a tight pattern leading to the denouement, "had pity." The extended conclusion accents this point.

A Reading

Line 1: A certain man was going down from Jerusalem to Jericho and he fell among bandits, who stripping him laying on blows went away, leaving [him] half-dead.

The initial scene presents a hearer with a tragic situation that the story will somehow seek to rectify. The man's restoration is the narrative's goal.[19] The details in the first line tease an audience about its actual flow.

The distance between Jerusalem and Jericho is about seventeen miles, and the route runs through desert and rocky hill country. Josephus describes it as wild and barren,[20] and the road between the two cities was a notorious hideout for bandits. So the robbery of a lone stranger going down the road does not pose a surprise to the hearer.[21]

The man is unnamed and remains anonymous throughout the story, although he must be Jewish,[22] for a Jewish audience would naturally assume that an anonymous person was Jewish unless other clues were given. The bandits are probably just highwaymen,[23] although it is not inconceivable that some hearers would have identified them with Zealots, for "bandits," lēstai, is used in Josephus as the term for Zealots.[24] Two other notes about the robbery deserve notice. The man is stripped and left half-dead. Robbers do not always strip their victims,[25] but since the man is left naked beside the road, he now lacks identifying clothes and those passing on the road will be unable to tell to what class, village, or nation he belongs.[26] He is truly anonymous. "Half-dead" implies that he is only barely among the living and could be taken for dead. This element will become important later.

Finally, the position of the audience is critical. We have already seen what a difference it makes in Luke where the implied reader is gentile. In Jesus' parable, the implied hearer is Jewish. Such a hearer sees the victim as also Jewish but is not drawn to identify with his fate.[27] Instead, the hearer will await a hero's arrival.

19. Patte, "Analysis of Narrative Structure," 14–15.

20. Josephus, Jewish War, 4.474 (LCL 3:141). See Bearvery, "La route romaine," 72–114, with maps, drawings, and pictures.

21. So realistic is the setting that Jeremias (Parables, 203) supposes that it must be based on an actual event. He has mistaken fictional verisimilitude for reality.

22. So Plummer, Gospel according to St. Luke, 286; Marshall, Commentary on Luke, 447; Derrett, Law and the New Testament, 209; Ramaroson, "Comme 'Le bon samaritain,'" 535; Bailey, Through Peasant Eyes, 42. Binder ("Das Gleichnis," 176–94) argues that Jesus is the unnamed man of the parable who was accepted by the Sarmaritan and rejected by the Jewish priesthood.

23. Wettstein (Novum Testamentum Graecum 1:722) offers classical parallels to the phrase "fall among bandits."

24. Daniels, "Les esseniens," 87–88. His argument is strong enough to warrant the suspicion that some in the audience would have made such an identification, esp. since the other characters in the parable receive specific identifications. But Daniels goes too far in arguing that the man is an Essene because Zealots normally attack their political enemies and the Talmud sometimes refers to the Essenes as men from Jericho.

25. Plummer, Gospel according to St. Luke, 287. In the conclusion the Samaritan binds up.

26. Bailey, Through Peasant Eyes, 42.

27. Against Funk, Language, 212; idem, "Good Samaritan," 77. Funk correctly sees the importance of the Gentile-versus-Jewish point of view but assumes that the hearer must immediately identify with the victim.

Line 2: By chance a certain priest was going down on that way and seeing him passed by opposite. Likewise so too a Levite coming up to the place and seeing passed by opposite.

The anonymous half-dead man is now joined by two characters, denoted by class as priest and Levite, who are making the same journey. As part of the religious and cultural codes of first-century Palestine, these characters conjure up specific values for the audience.

The parable is remarkably restrained in what it says about the priest and Levite, especially in light of the many suggestions scholars have made. They are on the road by coincidence.[28] They are in this space not by some plan but by accident. They may be returning from their temple duties at Jerusalem, for Jericho was a well-known habitat for priests and Levites.[29] Approaching the half-dead man, they see and pass by on the opposite side, moving to the other side of the road.[30] The parable does not speculate about their motives—a huge gap that tempts a hearer.

Some idea of how to deal with this gap about motivation enables us to grasp how an audience would respond to the story. An obvious reason for passing by is fear of robbers; they may still be lingering around to attack yet once more.[31] Concerns for ritual purity are possibly involved. According to Lev 21:1–2, a priest may not "defile himself for the dead among his people, except for his nearest of kin, his mother, his father, his son, his daughter, his brother, or his virgin sister."[32] Moreover, a high priest "shall not go in to any dead body, nor defile himself, even for his father or for his mother" (Lev. 21:11).

Although this prohibition appears absolute, the Mishnah and Talmud have extended discussions about these verses in Leviticus. The Mishnah comments,

> A high priest or a Nazarite may not contact uncleanness because of their [dead] kindred, but they may contact uncleanness because of a neglected corpse. If they were on a journey and found a neglected corpse, R. Eliezer says: The high priest may contact uncleanness but the Nazarite may not contact uncleanness.[33]

28. For classical examples, see Plummer, *Gospel according to St. Luke*, 287.
29. Str-B 2:180–81; M. Stern, "Aspects," 584. With exaggeration, *b. Taan.* 27a (Soncino 5:143) says, "Twenty-four divisions of priests were in the Land of Israel and twelve of them were in Jericho."
30. Some manuscripts have *genomenos* before "to that place." If accepted it would mean that the Levite came to the place, went up, and looked, making him even more heartless. See Metzger, *Textual Commentary*, 287.
31. So Str-B 2:183; Marshall, *Commentary on Luke*, 448.
32. See also Num. 19:11, where the touching of a dead body brings seven days' uncleanliness.
33. *m. Nazir* 7.1 (Danby, 289).

In this text the holiness of the high priest and of the Nazarite are equated, so that they both are bound not to touch their own dead. But they are enjoined to bury, without threat of uncleanness, a neglected corpse (*meth mitzwah*). A neglected corpse is defined as one "with none to bury him. Were he able to call and others answer him, he is not a *meth mitzwah*."[34] This command is then worked out in the case law of a high priest and Nazarite on a journey who come on a neglected corpse. The high priest must care for the corpse. The Mishnah is balancing the command to bury a neglected corpse and the defilement of the two most prominent religious figures. It is significant that the corpse takes priority over religious purity.

In the Talmud where this section of the Mishnah is discussed, even finer gradations of case law are elaborated. Given different levels of holiness, who is responsible to care for a neglected corpse? Someone is always charged. Consider this extreme case. A Nazarite is on his way to slaughter a paschal lamb or circumcise his son and hears that a near kinsman has died. May he defile himself to care for a dead member of his family? The answer is no, even though some think he should. But even though he may not defile himself for a family member, this does not mean that he may not defile himself for a neglected corpse. The Talmud invokes a subtle argument. "The text [Leviticus] adds 'for his sister', [implying that] for his sister he is forbidden to defile himself, but he may defile himself for a *meth mitzwah*."[35] The argument is that since Leviticus does not explicitly rule out a neglected corpse, he may defile himself to care for it.

A significant portion of the case-law examples involve those on a journey. Another example makes this clear. While a high priest and his father are traveling, the father is decapitated. May the high priest defile himself? The answer is yes, not because the dead man is his father but because he is a *meth mitzwah*: "Because they are travelling on the road, it is as though he had none to bury him."[36]

These examples make it evident that the priest and the Levite cannot invoke defilement as a reason not to stop and offer aid. To object that the man is not dead and therefore that the command of the neglected corpse does not apply[37] misses the point. That is why he is described as half-

34. *b. Nazir* 43b (Soncino 8:158). For a discussion of the importance of the *meth mitzwah*, see Moore, *Judaism* 1:71. "As between the study of the Torah and attending to a *meth mitzwah*, attending to a *meth mitzwah* takes precedence. . . . As between the temple service and attending to a *meth mitzwah*, attending to a *meth mitzwah* takes precedence" (*b. Meg.* 3b [Soncino 5:13]).
35. *b. Nazir* 48b (Soncino 8:182).
36. *b. Nazir* 43b (Soncino 8:158).
37. So Str-B 2:183. Jeremias is skeptical (*Parables*, 203).

dead, stripped, and abandoned. The priest and the Levite must stop and offer aid. Perhaps there is an even more subtle point being made. The exception of the neglected corpse is not in the Torah but in the tradition, in the Mishnah and Talmud. Maybe the priest and Levite as Sadducees follow the Torah strictly and are seeking to avoid any defilement.[38] But from the point of view of a Jewish peasant, this passing-by would play on their dislike and disapproval of priests. And for Pharisees it would show how their tradition was superior.[39] . Since the priesthood belonged to the upper stratum of Jewish society,[40] the rural prejudice against an urban elite and the anticlerical sentiment of the day[41] would have reinforced the negative image of the priest and the Levite.

In the end there is no final resolution for the priest and Levite's motivation, because the parable offers no clues. But some knowledge of an audience's guess indicates how they would judge the characters' actions.[42] If the audience were made up of priests and Levites, they might approve of the action, but ultimately the parable will not. If the audience were lay, *am haeretz*, or Pharisee, they would not approve. Given the upper-class status of the priest and Levite, the anticlericalism of the audience, and the importance of tradition as an interpreter of the Torah, an audience would look askance at the scandalous, merciless act of the priest and the Levite.

Line 3: A certain Samaritan, being on the way, came up to him and seeing had pity.

This line has a very subtle construction, forming as it does the surprising denouement. The subject, "Samaritan," is placed in a position of emphasis,[43] and the line echoes the vocabulary of the previous lines. What does a hearer expect at the initial sound "Samaritan"? The enmity between Jew and Samaritan was proverbial. "He that eats the bread of the Samaritans is like to one what eats the flesh of swine."[44] The hearer, interpreting the Samaritan as a negative figure, expects him to com-

---

38. So Derrett, *Law in the New Testament*, 212–14. Derrett argues that they were justified in passing by the man.

39. So Mann, "Jesus and the Sadducean Priests," 417–19.

40. M. Stern, "Aspects," 580. Str-B 2:182 sees this as the primary reason that they are in the parable.

41. See *T. Levi* 17:11 (Charlesworth 1:794): "In the seventh week there will come priests: idolaters, adulterers, money lovers, arrogant, lawless, voluptuaries, pederasts, those who practice bestiality."

42. Linnemann (*Jesus of the Parables*, 53) sees all such speculation as useless.

43. Marshall, *Commentary on Luke*, 449.

44. *m. Sheb.* 8.10 (Danby, 49). "For murder, whether of a Cuthean [i.e., Samaritan] by a Cuthean, or of an Israelite by a Cuthean, punishment is incurred; but of a Cuthean by an Israelite, there is no death penalty" (*b. San.* 57a [Soncino 12:388]).

pound the dastardly deed of the robbers. Not until the last part of the line does the hearer discover what the Samaritan will actually do.

The Samaritan's appearance in the story is indeed surprising, for the expected triad is priest, Levite, and Israelite,[45] in which triad the Israelite equals the layman. An English equivalent would be priest, deacon, and layman. As Montefiore has remarked, the triad in this parable "is no less queer and impossible than 'Priest, Deacon, and Frenchman' would be to us to-day."[46] Abraham offers an example of the formula from *Sifra* on Leviticus. When "the Scripture says: 'This is the law'—it does not say 'This is the law of Priests, Levites, and Israel,' but 'This is the law of *man*, O Lord God.'"[47] This formula is repeated on three other occasions where the biblical text has "man." The formula "priest, Levite, and Israelite" represents a threefold division of the Jewish people. Another example from the Mishnah evidences the hierarchical character of the formula:

> A priest precedes a levite, a levite an Israelite, an Israelite a bastard, a bastard a *Nathin*, a *Nathin* a proselyte, and a proselyte a freed slave. This applies when all are [otherwise] equal; but if a bastard is learned in the Law and a High Priest is ignorant of the Law, the bastard that is learned in the Law precedes the High Priest that is ignorant of the Law.[48]

In this example the threefold formula provides the main divisions of respectable Jewish society. Somewhat in the way of our parable, a scandalous comparison is introduced. An ignorant high priest is less than a learned bastard. The comparison is illuminating because it highlights the importance of point of view. From the point of view of the writers of the Mishnah who belong to the rabbinic tradition, the comparison is at the expense of their enemies the priests. They themselves are the Israelites.

The introduction of the Samaritan presents the hearer with a conflict in expectation. The triad is priest, Levite, and Israelite. How does the Samaritan fit in? Metaphorically, the Samaritan is diaphoric; he fits on the basis not of similarity but of dissimilarity.[49] The Samaritan's insertion into the story as its hero, the one who helps, shatters the hearer's expectation. Having expected an Israelite to be the hero, a hearer is now confronted with a problem. With whom does the hearer identify? Op-

---

45. Abrahams, *Studies*, 2:35; Mattill, "Good Samaritan," 367.
46. C. Montefiore, *Synoptic Gospels* 2:467.
47. Referring to 2 Sam. 7:19. See Abraham, *Studies* 2:35–36.
48. *m. Hor.* 3.8 (Danby, 466).
49. The failure to see the diaphoric character of the triad has led to confusion about the significance of the Samaritan. Is "Samaritan" a religious, political, or cultic term? What is the basis of the comparison between Jew and Samaritan? Some argue religion (Jülicher, *Die Gleichnisreden* 2:595); others, politics and charity (Ramaroson, "Comme 'Le bon samaritain,'" 535–36); still others, anticlericalism (Crossan, "Parable and Example," 75).

tions are limited. To identify with the Samaritan is almost impossible because of the great enmity between Jew and Samaritan. If the hearer identifies with the priest or Levite, then the story will abort with their passing. There are only two options: to identify with the half-dead man and suffer the compassion of a Samaritan, or to reply that the story is false, that the world is not like this. The true triad is priest, Levite, and Israelite.[50]

> *Line 4:* And approaching him he bound up his wounds, pouring on olive oil and wine; mounting him upon his own beast he brought him to the inn and attended him. On the next day taking out he gave two denarii to the innkeeper and said: "Take care of him and whatever you may spend in addition, I when I come back will give back to you."

This last, long line is detailed in its description of the Samaritan's ministrations to the half-dead man. The first three lines are staccatolike and work with an economy of vocabulary. Why does the scene continue beyond the denouement "He had compassion"? From a literary perspective it allows an audience a longer narration to absorb and put together the unexpected appearance and action of the Samaritan. A hearer receives a chance to reorder the world in light of this change in order. As Derrett remarks, the hearer may have preferred to say, "Begone, Cuthean, I will have none of your oil or your wine."[51]

The use of oil and wine for medicinal purposes is well attested.[52] After

50. Because of the extreme unexpectedness of the Samaritan's appearance, a number of commentators have argued that the original character was an Israelite and not a Samaritan. The classic statement of this position is that of Halévy ("Sens et origine," 249–55). His arguments can be summarized: (1) Jesus commanded his disciples to avoid contact with Samaritans (Matt. 10:5). (2) A Samaritan would not have been on the road between Jerusalem and Jericho nor been friends with an innkeeper. (3) The expected formula is "priest, Levite, and Israelite." The original parable contrasted the priest and Levite who lived off the gifts of pilgrims and would not help, with the layman who did help. Luke's gentile audience would not have understood the distinction of the triadic formula, and so Luke changed the Israelite to a Samaritan and the parable became anti-Jewish. There are a number of problems with this proposal: (1) It is not obvious that Matt. 10:5 is authentic. (2) The unlikeliness of a Samaritan on the road to Jerusalem mistakes reality for fiction (so Manson, *Sayings,* 262). (3) The proposal to remove the Samaritan converts the story back into a traditional anticlerical story as the example from the Mishnah evidences. C. Montefiore (*Synoptic Gospels* 2:466–68) and Mattill "Good Samaritan," 359–76) are strong supporters of Halévy. Creed (*Gospel according to St. Luke,* 151) and Manson (*Sayings,* 262) are cautious in their support.

51. Derrett, *Law in the New Testament,* 221.

52. Str-B 1:428. Normally wine and oil were mixed together. See *m. Shabb* 19.2 (Danby, 116): "If wine and oil had not been mixed on the eve of the Sabbath each may be applied by itself." Derrett (*Law in the New Testament,* 219–21) gives an almost fantastic series of references to possible symbolic implications of the Samaritan's ministrations.

caring for the man's wounds, the Samaritan takes him to an inn[53] and gives the innkeeper the equivalent of two days' wages to care for the man. Finally, in the only direct discourse in the parable, the Samaritan states that he, not the man,[54] will pay any extra expenses incurred by the innkeeper.

From Story to Kingdom

Luke obviously reads the parable as an example story: "Go and do likewise" (v. 37). Most commentators have agreed.[55] If the Samaritan's significance remains on the literal level, one can easily convert the story to an example.[56] Yet the Samaritan is a mortal enemy, not the model of good comportment. Only by denying this and maintaining the perspective of a gentile reader can the story be an example.[57] Such a reading contrasts "the unloving Jews and the loving Samaritan."[58]

Not only does "Samaritan," as defined by the cultural code, argue against such a reading but so also does the failure to pay attention to the significance of the triadic formula of priest, Levite, and Israelite. When the Samaritan appears in the narrative the implied Jewish hearer expects the Samaritan to behave at least as badly as the priest and Levite, and probably worse. But since the Samaritan has compassion, the expected Israelite can never come to the half-dead man's aid. What commentators have failed to notice is that the Israelite is excluded from being the parable's hero. To remain in the story the hearer cannot play hero but must become a victim.

This story also incorporates a common mytheme in which, through a series of contrasts, one is encouraged to come to the aid of those not normally deserving of aid.[59] I. Abrahams has collected several of these stories.[60] In one a rabbi bearing all his worldly possessions in his shoulder bag is asked by a leper to carry him into the city. The rabbi is confronted with choosing between the needs of his family (as represented by his worldly goods) and those of the leper. At the story's end, the rabbi both helps the leper and recovers the shoulder bag he has left behind. In another story, a rabbi helps a Roman who has suffered

53. Innkeepers were not well noted for exemplary behavior. See *b. Taan.* 23a (Soncino 5:105).
54. For the emphatic word order, see Plummer, *Gospel according to St. Luke*, 288.
55. E.g., Lambrecht, *Once More Astonished*, 71–75. Lambrecht argues that the question is secondary but implied in the narrative.
56. Crossan, "Parable and Example," 74.
57. Funk, "Good Samaritan," 79.
58. Bultmann, *History of the Synoptic Tradition*, 178.
59. Luke employs the parable to support this mytheme.
60. Abrahams, *Studies* 1:110, 2:39–40.

shipwreck, brings him home, clothes and feeds him, provides him with two hundred denarii, and goes part of the way with him on his departure. In the end the Roman repays the rabbi with gratitude and gold. In these stories the pattern presents a hearer with a difficult choice (i.e., between family and leper; home country [implied] and Roman), and the hearer/reader is led to decide in favor of the underdog. In the end there is a reward. This mytheme can also be reversed:

> It is related of Nahum of Gamzu that he was blind in both his eyes, his two hands and legs were amputated, and his whole body was covered with boils and he was lying in a dilapidated house on a bed the feet of which were standing in bowls of water in order to prevent the ants from crawling on to him; . . . his disciples said to him, Master, since you are wholly righteous, why has all this befallen you? And he replied, I have brought it all upon myself. Once I was journeying on the road and was making for the house of my father-in-law and I had with me three asses, one laden with food, one with drink and one with all kinds of dainties, when a poor man met me and stopped me on the road and said to me, Master, give me something to eat. I replied to him, Wait until I have unloaded something from the ass; I had hardly managed to unload one thing from the ass when the man died [from hunger]. I then went and laid myself on him and exclaimed, May my eyes which had no pity upon your eyes become blind, may my hands which had no pity upon your hands be cut off, may my legs be amputated, and my mind was not at rest until I added, may my whole body be covered with boils. Thereupon his pupils exclaimed, "Alas! that we see you in such a sore plight." To this he replied, "Woe would it be to me did you not see me in such a sore plight."[61]

These stories demonstrate a clear pattern encouraging the hearer/reader who belongs to the haves to aid the have-nots. What is admirable in these stories is that they help a hearer/reader overcome primary conflicts without resorting to prejudice or xenophobia to solve the tension.

The parable From Jerusalem to Jericho clearly belongs to this mytheme, but it modifies its basic thrust. There is no Israelite with whom the implied hearer can identify. If the story had encouraged a Jew to take care of a Samaritan, then it would fulfill the mytheme.[62] But the hearer's only possible course is to identify with the half-dead and be saved by a mortal enemy or else to dismiss the narrative as not like real life. The hearer who expects an Israelite to come along and play hero finds that the Israelite is already half-dead and the only option is the Samaritan.

As parable the story subverts the effort to order reality into the known hierarchy of priest, Levite, and Israelite. Utterly rejected is any notion

61. *b. Taan.* 21a (Soncino 5:104–5).
62. Which is what Halévy and his followers do.

that the kingdom can be marked off as religious: the map no longer has boundaries. The kingdom does not separate insiders and outsiders on the basis of religious categories. In the parable the Samaritan is not the enemy but the savior, and the hearer does not play hero but victim. In the parable Two Men Went Up to the Temple it is not simply that the tax collector is righteous. Rather, the temple no longer divides the world into religious and nonreligious. So here the Samaritan is not converted. Gone is the apocalyptic vision of ultimate triumph over one's enemies. The world with its sure arrangement of insiders and outsiders is no longer an adequate model for predicting the kingdom.

Masters
& Servants

8

Patrons
and Clients

Masters and servants stand out prominently on the social landscape of the Mediterranean basin in the first century. So it is not surprising that a major group of Jesus' parables draws on this social grouping. Masters and servants, however, do not play only economic roles. They represent a major way that society organized itself. Anthropologists use the patron-client model to describe societies characterized by such relations. Such a model delineates the regulation of crucial aspects of a social order: allocating resources, exchanging power and wealth, and legitimating the societal structure.[1]

Understanding the dynamic of the patron-client relationship throws light on the social matrix, an aspect of the repertoire, in which Jesus' master-servant parables originate. In a sense, the patron-client model represents a primary mode by which Mediterranean people organized, thought about, and envisioned the world. Patron-client relations are not part of the capitalist model of employer-laborer. The relationship is more familial than contractual. It is voluntary and requires a long-term relation in which roles and responsibilities are carefully defined. Solidarity is strong, and bonds extend beyond legal to even extralegal requirements. In A Rich Man Had a Steward, the steward, when threatened with dismissal, relies on his solidarity with those whose patron he had formerly been while managing his master's finances. A violation of

1. Einstadt and Roniger, "Patron-Client Relations," 49. This study is a comprehensive survey of the patron-client model.

the bonds of solidarity is evident in A King Wished to Settle Accounts. The servant violates solidarity not only with his fellow servant but also with the king who in his behalf went beyond the law and forgave him. So should he have gone beyond the law and forgiven his fellow servant's debt.

Ambiguity haunts patron-client relationships because they are based on elements of inequality and differences in power.[2] Inherent contradiction threatens this form of social organization because it combines solidarity and voluntary association with social coercion. Interactions can erupt into social chaos,[3] particularly in violable settings such as first-century Palestine. Many Gospel parables play on this ambiguity. An extreme example is A Man Planted a Vineyard: here the social system breaks down and the clients kill the patron's son. Client-patron societies are inherently unstable, not simply because they are unequal but also because they are legitimated by custom more than by law. Those servants who feel themselves aggrieved (e.g., the one-talent man, the all-day laborers, the unjust steward) have no appeal within the legal system. They can act only outside it.

Patron-client relations provide for a society's order and stability. They grant an element of security and insurance against the risks of open and undefined exchanges of power.[4] Since relations are unequal, a client accepts the patron's protection in exchange for submitting to control. For example, in A Householder Went Out Early the servants are outraged when the owner pays all the same wage, because he has made all equal. Through an arbitrary use of his power, the owner has broken the insurance that labor will be rewarded on the basis of its productivity. Or in A Man Entrusts Property, the one-talent man's rejection angers an audience because he has fulfilled his part of the bargain: the master lost nothing, and therefore the servant deserves protection. These masters violate solidarity by placing their clients at risk. Conversely, when the steward in A Rich Man Had a Steward is forced out of the security of his master's patronage, he seeks to establish close bonds with his clients by reducing their indebtedness.

Drawing on the inequality and instability of the society, Jesus' parables often take advantage of the antagonism between master and servant to draw a hearer into sympathy with the aggrieved servant. In A Householder Went Out Early, even though the master claims to be generous there is obvious tension with the servants. In A King Wished to Settle Accounts, although the master initially forgives, in the end he

2. Ibid., 50, 60.
3. Ibid., 61.
4. Ibid., 52.

revokes his forgiveness. In the former parable a hearer identifies with those who have worked the whole day, and in the latter with those servants who complain to the king. Likewise, in A Man Entrusts Property the one-talent servant voices the peasant's fear: "Master, I knew you to be a hard man, reaping where you did not sow, and gathering where you did not winnow; so I was afraid" (Matt. 25:24).

Patron-client societies must place a high stress on hierarchical relations in order to maintain control.[5] They frequently organize the sources of power and wealth so that the ruling elites control them, thus isolating patrons from clients. In imperial societies, this leads to absentee ownership and even ownership by foreign elites.[6] Galilee was characterized by absentee landlords and a mixed population in which the indigenous people were at the bottom of the social hierarchy. Absentee landlords figure prominently in Jesus' parables and frequently play the role of antagonist.

Because of the importance of the patron-client structure in the social organization of first-century Palestine, the structure was widely used as a metaphor for God's relation to Israel, for God is the ultimate patron for client Israel. One of the most common parable forms in rabbinic literature is that of the king, in which God is the king.[7] This is not surprising since the people lived in an imperial society. Such replication between different spheres is common in the sociology of knowledge and is a basis for the possibility of metaphorical transference. In rabbinic parables when the fit between the secular patron-client model and the divine one is poor, the rabbis resort to the *val vachomer* argument ("how much more").[8] In contrast, Jesus' parables seldom employ a king as patron.[9] Also the *val vachomer* argument seldom occurs, but the scandal stands as an implied subversion of the structure. Where the rabbis see replication, Jesus sees subversion!

The possibility of hierarchical replication made Jesus' parables adaptable to the early community's changing situation. When Jesus becomes the church's Lord (*kyrios* is both master and lord) or returning Son of man, he becomes their patron. The gospel interpretation of most of the master-servant parables aligns them with an expectation of the Par-

5. Ibid., 57.

6. Ibid., 62–63.

7. Of the 324 parables in Johnston's "Parabolic Traditions," the largest number involve kings. There are only a few master-servant parables. See further pp. 17 above.

8. Johnston, "Parabolic Traditions," 519.

9. The direction of the trajectory is toward making masters kings in both the rabbinic and Synoptic traditions. See Jeremias, *Parables*, 28. This substitute of king for master only shows that the basic patron-client model underlies the parables regardless of the players involved.

ousia, when the patron will create a final solidarity with his faithful clients. Since Jesus exploited the instability in the patron-client model, the early church resorted to an implied *val vachomer* argument or employed other strategies to distract attention.

Jesus' master-servant (patron-client) parables can be divided formally into two groups.[10] In the first group a master's departure and return initiate the action; in the second an extended accounting is the focus. These formal differences implement different metaphorical structures.

Parables of Departure and Return

Four parables in the Jesus tradition belong to a group in which the plot revolves around a master's departure and return. Two of these parables are so condensed that they can serve as models for the others. In this chapter we will examine The Faithful and Wise Servant (Matt. 24:45–51; Luke 12:42–46) and A Man Going on a Journey (Mark 13:34–36; Luke 12:36–38). The two other parables will receive a more elaborate treatment: A Man Entrusts Property (Matt. 25:14–30; Luke 19:12–27; see chap. 9 below) and A Man Planted a Vineyard (Mark 12:1–12; Matt. 21:33–46; Luke 20:9–19; *Gos. Thom.* 65; see chap. 10 below).

The Faithful and Wise Servant

Who then is the faithful and wise servant whom his master has set over his household to give them food at the proper time? Blessed is that servant whom his master when he comes will find so doing. Amen, I say to you, he will set him over all his possessions. But that servant says to himself, "My master is delayed," and begins to beat the menservants and the womenservants and to eat and to drink and to get drunk and the master of that servant will come on a day which he is not expecting and on an hour which he does not know and cut him in two.

A good example of the first group is the parable of The Faithful and Wise Servant. According to the classic two-source theory, this is clearly a Q

10. Crossan ("Servant Parables," 17–62) divides them into two groups between which he sees a structural interplay. In one group, the parables of normality, the good servants are rewarded and the evil punished. The second group subverts this mythical structure. Although I am in agreement with much of Crossan's argument, I have chosen to use a formal model for differentiation. Weiser (*Die Knechtsgleichnisse*) categorizes servant parables on the occurrence of *doulos*, but this is too narrow. See Crossan, "Servant Parables," 18. Bouttier ("Les paraboles du maître," 176–95) goes to the other extreme and uses *kyrios*, again too narrow. The actual terms used are irrelevant. It could be king as well as master; a servant, a slave, or steward. What is important is the invocation of the patron-client model.

parable,[11] but regardless of source theory the two texts are so similar that they demand a common source. Both Matthew and Luke have used the parable to illustrate the Parousia's delay. Luke's introduction has accented the address to the disciples (v. 41), so the parable becomes a warning to church leaders.[12] At its conclusion he introduces the gradations of punishment characteristic of Jewish piety (vv. 47–48). Matthew, who frequently stresses the theme of judgment in master-servant parables, concludes the parable with both a reference to the hypocrites and a recurring phrase of his Gospel, "there will be weeping and gnashing of teeth" (v. 51b).[13]

Besides these adjustments to fit the evangelical context, even more minute shifts are observable. Luke refers to a "steward," *oikomenos*, while Matthew has a "servant," *doulos*. Luke has a clear preference for "steward."[14] Since "servant" occurs throughout the rest of Luke's parable, the less specific designation is probably more original. Both Matthew and Luke are performing an originating structure, regardless of whether the performance is based on an oral or a literary exemplar. The direction of Luke's performance is toward specificity in context. Matthew speaks of "household servants," *oikeiteia* (Matt. 24:45) and Luke of the "household service," *therapeia* (Luke 12:42). In Luke the steward passes out a "ration of wheat," while in Matthew he gives food, in what may be an allusion to Ps. 104:27 (LXX, 103:27).

In the description of the servant's negative action, Matthew explicitly refers to him as "evil" (24:48), again a favorite word.[15] For the Lukan narrator the master delays "in coming," an obvious reference to the Parousia.[16] In Matthew, the servant beats "fellow servants,"[17] whereas in Luke it is "menservants and womenservants." In describing the servant's behavior, Matthew uses definite verbs "he eats and drinks with drunkards" (v. 49). Luke maintains the parallel infinitives: "and he began to beat . . . to eat and to drink and to be drunk."

In the parable's actual performance both Matthew and Luke have

---

11. So Weiser, *Die Knechtsgleichnisse*, 179ff.

12. Talbert, *Reading Luke*, 143.

13. *Hypocritēs* is a strongly Matthean word (Mark, once; Luke, three times; Matthew, nine times), and "weeping and gnashing" occurs six times in Matthew with only one parallel (Matt. 8:12//Luke 13:28). In Matt. 8:12, it refers to Israel, but in all the other cases (13:42, 50; 22:13; 24:51; 25:30) it refers to members of the church. Also, except for the first usage it is always used with parables, usually as a conclusion. Since in chap. 23 the Pharisees were condemned as hypocrites, Matthew here uses these two phrases to connect the fate of faithless disciples with that of faithless Israel.

14. Luke uses *oikomenos* four times. See Gundry, *Matthew*, 495.

15. Gundry, *Matthew*, 496.

16. Grässer, *Das Problem*, 92.

17. *Syndoulos* is another Matthean word: Matt. 18:28, 29, 31, 33.

increased specificity in certain respects. Not all differences are due to theological (i.e., redactional) perspectives, although some are. Many are due to the evangelists' stylistic proclivities.

Although it is obvious that Matthew and Luke have inherited a common parable, there remains a persistent doubt about the authenticity of this parable: it so closely fits the early church's situation of awaiting the return of its master (*kyrios*) that it is hard to imagine that Jesus could have invented a parable so ideally suited to the situation of the church after his resurrection. There have been primarily three approaches to this problem. The cleanest way supposes that the parable is indeed the creation of the early church.[18] Others have assumed the authenticity of the parable—that it stems from Jesus—because they assume Jesus expected his own Parousia.[19] Still others have argued that the parable originally had no reference to the Parousia. According to Jeremias, representing the last group, the parable warns Jesus' opponents, the scribes,[20] of impending judgment. But it is not obvious why the scribes should be concerned with the spiritual welfare of the people. That was the responsibility of the priests.[21] Jeremias's reconstruction reflects a post-70 C.E. situation. Against those who see the parable as reflecting Jesus' own teaching of the delay of the Parousia, Grässer contends that this was a concern of the post-Easter church.[22] His evidence for this position is overwhelming.

Apparently, only those who argue against the parable's authenticity are left by default, but that is not so. Three arguments are critical. First there is the parable's ending. Even though the RSV translates *dichoto-mēsei* as "to punish," the word actually means "to cut in two."[23] There have been several attempts to weaken the meaning,[24] beginning with Luke, who introduces as the parable's conclusion a threefold gradation in punishment,[25] and Matthew, who sees the word as referring to hell.[26] The severity of the punishment—its cruelty—is shocking in light of the servant's actual misdeeds. If the early church created an allegory, why introduce at its conclusion such a jarring note? This shocking disjunction is characteristic of Jesus' parabolic style. It is true that Jesus' parables do partake of the everyday. Yet we ought not be blinded from observing

18. E.g., Grässer, *Das Problem*, 84–95; Schulz, *Q: Die Spruchquelle*, 268–77.
19. E.g., Marshall, *Commentary on Luke*, 534.
20. Jeremias, *Parables*, 48.
21. Beare, *Gospel according to Matthew*, 477.
22. Grässer, *Das Problem*, 3–75.
23. BAGD, 200.
24. For examples, see Beare, *Gospel according to Matthew*, 479.
25. Grundmann, *Das Evangelium nach Lukas*, 266.
26. Bultmann, *History of the Synoptic Tradition*, 176.

those occasions in almost every parable which explode the everyday. This is one of them.

The second piece of evidence is the parable's style and surface structure. In the first part, a third-person narrator describes the wise servant's action. The language is exhortatory with the beatitude and amen saying. In the second part, where the emphasis falls, the structure shifts. The narrator constructs an interior monologue ("in his heart") that provides the hearer/reader a privileged position from which to observe the servant's decision. Finally the conclusion develops in a parallel series:

to beat men-servants and women-servants
  and to eat
    and to drink
      and to get drunk
will come the master of that slave
    on a day which he is not expecting
    and on a hour which he does not know
and cut him in two

This careful structuring generates tension precisely at the master's return. As Crossan has pointed out, it is the master's delay that tempts the servant.[27] This observation indicates why the departure-return pattern is essential for this first group of servant parables. All the parables that invoke the patron-client model operate with the elementary metaphorical network that the kingdom is like a master and his servant(s). Then various aspects that belong to this system can be used metaphorically for the kingdom. The parables of departure and return employ a specific part of the patron-client network. The master's departure is the occasion of a test for the servant. Usually the test involves something of the master's with which the servant is entrusted. Finally, the master's return is the accounting, the inevitable denouement. This metaphorical network involves a double motion: the departure is a test, the return is an accounting.

The third and final piece of evidence in favor of the parable's authenticity is that its investment of the metaphorical structure—"the master's departure is an occasion for a test"— coheres with Jesus' other parables. Jeremias relies too much on a specific *Sitz im Leben*, the debate with the

---

27. Crossan, "Servant Parables," 22. In discussing the parable A Man Entrusts Property, Marshall (*Commentary on Luke*, 703) sees clearly the significance of the departure-return pattern. Didier ("La parabole," 264) sees such a close formal relation between the Markan parable and the parable A Man Entrusts Property that he thinks the Markan parable a reduction to its barest elements of an oral version of A Man Entrusts Property. Bultmann (*History of the Synoptic Tradition*, 176), however, correctly sees that the journeying householder does not harmonize with dividing up property.

scribes. This parable makes the simple point that a servant who can be trusted only when his master is present is a worthless servant. As a metaphor for the kingdom, it unmasks the uselessness of an apocalyptic expectation that needs God's presence to right wrongs or to extract moral behavior. God's intervention is surely decisive,[28] but it does not change the basic situation. As in A Man Entrusts Property, the servants are responsible and the master's presence or absence makes no difference: some will double the entrusted property and pass the test, others will bury it. Or as in A Man Planted a Vineyard, some will attempt to usurp the master's vineyard and fail the test because they do not see that the vineyard has only been entrusted to them. Like the servant in this parable, they will attempt to lord it over those entrusted to their care. The servant fails in the parable by failing to realize that the kingdom is now—something with which he is entrusted.

A Man Going on a Journey

It is like a man going on a journey, when he leaves home and puts his servants in charge, each with his work, and commands the doorkeeper to be on watch. Watch therefore, for you do not know when the master of the house will come, in the evening, or at midnight, or at cockcrow, or in the morning. (Mark 13:34–35)

And be like men who are waiting for their master to come home from the marriage feast, so that they may open to him at once when he comes and knocks. Blessed are those servants whom the master finds awake when he comes; Amen, I say to you, he will gird himself and have them sit at table and he will come and serve them. If he comes in the second watch, or in the third, and finds them so, blessed are those servants. (Luke 12:36–38)

Crossan and Alfons Weiser see underlying Mark 13:34–37 and Luke 12:36–38 a common parable, now preserved in two independent versions.[29] Both versions are third-person narration that is embedded in second-person admonition. In Mark, the admonition is his eschatological discourse, and in Luke, it is his warning to the disciples on faithfulness and watchfulness. The returning master is clearly the Son of man, Jesus. According to the reconstruction of Crossan and Weiser, the original parable consisted of a master departing for a nighttime feast, the command to watch, and the master's return later at night, probably at Luke's third watch rather than Mark's sunset.

28. See chap. 4 above.
29. Crossan, "Servant Parables," 20–21; Weiser, *Die Knechtsgleichnisse*, 174–75.

Even though the reconstruction is plausible, it is perhaps unnecessary. What Crossan and Weiser have isolated is an originating parabolic structure that has been performed or implemented in strikingly different ways. This structure belongs to the departure-return pattern and exhibits the basic metaphorical structure of the first group. The master's departure/delay provides a test for the servant. The servant is entrusted with the household, and the departure is a test, with the return the denouement. That Jesus would use such a basic structure as a metaphorical framework for building parables of the kingdom is not strange. Since he proclaimed the kingdom as both present and absent, the departing and returning master is a fitting metaphorical structure with sufficient ambiguity and possibilities to be exploited. That the early church should also find this structure applicable to understanding the loss of its Lord is likewise not strange. But in contrast to The Faithful and Wise Servant, here there is nothing that one would designate as distinctive of the Jesus parables. We do not hear the voice associated with the parables. So we must conclude that this is a parable of the early church.

Parables of Accounting

A second group of patron-client parables build on an accounting scene.[30] We will use two of these parables as a paradigm: A Creditor Had Two Debtors (Luke 7:41–42); and Who Has a Servant Plowing (Luke 17:7–9). Three parables will receive a more elaborate treatment: A Rich Man Had a Steward (Luke 16:1–8; see chap. 11 below), A King Wished to Settle Accounts (Matt. 18:23–34; see chap. 12 below), and A Householder Went Out Early (Matt. 20:1–15; see chap. 13 below).

A Creditor Had Two Debtors

A certain creditor had two debtors; one owed five hundred denarii, and the other fifty. When they could not pay, he forgave them both.

A Creditor Had Two Debtors is a good example of this group of parables. As we have the parable, it is an integral part of the narrative of the woman who anoints Jesus in the house of Simon the Pharisee, and it illustrates that the one who is forgiven more will love more. This type of parable could be used on numerous occasions to illustrate many different points. This particular application tugs the parable's perception in a particular direction by accenting the love and the solidarity character-

---

30. The parable A Man Entrusts Property might well be considered to belong to this group since an accounting is prominent in the story. But there the accounting serves as a denouement for the test that has already occurred in the master's absence.

istic in patron-client relations, but it also hides the astonishment and joy of the clients when the patron forgives a sizable debt.[31] So the parable has several metaphorical possibilities, only one of which Luke and his tradition have exploited.

Parables whose plot builds upon an accounting depend on the solidarity and hierarchical pattern characteristic of patron-client relations. They implement an aspect of the undergirding metaphorical network that the kingdom is an accounting. The purpose of the accounting is to set things aright. The master, representing society's hierarchical power, establishes in his accounting the correct order. In A Man Had Two Debtors, he establishes that order as one of grace and forgiveness, thus somewhat subverting the inequality and hierarchy characteristic of patron-client societies. If all masters forgave all debts, all would be in the same situation, and order would be chaotic.[32] This is exactly what is at stake in A Householder Went Out Early: the master makes every one equal, and they murmur against him. A variation occurs in A King Wished to Settle Accounts because the servant's solidarity with his master is not strong enough to enable him to act the same way toward his fellow servant. Or in the accounting of A Rich Man Had a Steward, the master rearranges the expected order and the servant responds by trying to cancel that new order by maintaining his previous status.

Who Has a Servant Plowing

Will any one of you who has a servant plowing or keeping sheep say to him when he has come in from the field, "Come at once and sit down at table"? Will he not rather say to him, "Prepare supper for me, and gird yourself and serve me, till I eat and drink; and afterward you shall eat and drink"? Does he thank the servant because he did what was commanded?

The final parable in the accounting group, Who Has a Servant Plowing, indicates some of the variations possible in this thematic. It occurs in a Lukan discourse made up of four independent sayings addressed to the disciples. The first two deal with what the disciples are to do: not to offend the little ones, and to forgive over and over again. The last two sayings deal with how the disciples are able to do this: first, with faith

---

31. For details on the value of a denarius, see chap. 13 below.

32. Capitalism views equality as a similar threat to order. A famous joke makes this evident. Everything was to be divided anew so that each person would receive an equal share. Two men were standing in line waiting their new allotments. The capitalist turned and said to the other fellow, "I'll flip you for your share."

even as little as a mustard seed, and second, like the servant, doing all that is commanded.[33]

The parable begins with a question expecting a negative answer. Of course no one would tell a servant to come and sit at table after doing the day's chores in the field. The parable displays the correct social interaction between patron and client, the correct hierarchical order. The servant must do not only field chores but also household chores.[34] Furthermore, he receives no thanks for what he has done because it is expected (Luke 17:9). Luke applies this parable to the disciples with the application in v. 10.[35] It may be that Crossan is correct in his argument that vv. 8, 9, and 10 are a Lukan addition and that the original parable was actually a proverb, v. 7, in which Jesus questions the world of normality. The culture implies a hierarchy between master and servant; the proverb questions that hierarchy. Such a proverb would easily cohere with Jesus' other proverbs and parables. The problem remains in the question beginning the parable: "Will any one of you . . . ?" It expects a negative answer.

The parable does, however, exhibit clearly the assumptions of the hierarchical world of patrons and clients. It is a world of dependency and inequality, of clearly worked out relations. It is a world of order in which the patron-client model spells out one's ordained place in that world. For many in the Hellenistic world the patron-client world was replicated in the divine world. Yet Jesus' patron-client parables subvert the assumptions of that world.

33. Talbert, *Reading Luke*, 160–63.
34. Weiser (*Die Knechtsgleichnisse*, 108–9) sees v. 8 as an addition because of the strong Lukan vocabulary; Crossan agrees ("Servant Parables," 28–31).
35. So Weiser, *Die Knechtsgleichnisse*, 112–14; Minear, "A Note," 82–87.

9

*H*ard-Hearted *Man*

A Man Entrusts Property

It is like a man going on a journey and he entrusted to his servants his property. To one he gave five talents, to another two, to another one. Then he went away. He who had received the five talents went at once and traded with them; and he made five talents more. So also, he who had the two talents made two talents more. He who had received one talent went and dug in the ground and hid his master's silver. And the master of those servants came and settled accounts with them. And coming forward he who had received five talents brought five talents more saying, "Master, you delivered to me five talents; here! I have made a profit of five talents more." And his master said to him, "Great! good and faithful servant." And coming forward the two-talent one said, "Master, you delivered to me two talents; here! I have made a profit of two talents more." His master said to him, "Great! good and faithful servant." And coming forward the one who had received the one talent said, "Master, I know that you are a hard man, reaping where you did not sow, gathering when you did not scatter. And being afraid, going out, I hid your talent in the earth. Here! you have yours." But his master said to him, "Evil servant, you knew that I reap what I do not sow and gather where I do not scatter? You therefore should have placed my silver with the bankers and coming I could have recovered what was mine with interest. Take therefore from him the talent and give it to the one who has ten talents."

Matthew 25:14–28 and Luke 19:12–27 offer different performances of the parable A Man Entrusts Property, yet the reconstruction of an original parable does not easily emerge from the blueprint of a source theory. Although the parables are similar at the level of formal structure, there is surprisingly little verbal agreement. Such a lack makes impossible a detailed reconstruction of *ipsissima verba Jesu* (the very words of Jesus), because such a reconstruction would be hypothetical beyond verification.[1] Nevertheless, the extensive agreement between the two stories has led some to confident conclusions about their underlying structure or pattern.[2]

There is another way to look at the problem of reconstruction. The parable has been handed down in oral transmission. Oral storytellers, even when they believe they are handing on an exact reproduction, actually make changes and shifts to suit the situation, context, and their style.[3] Only a printing-press culture can have an ideal of exact verbal reproduction. Both Matthew and Luke, although written texts, still employ techniques characteristic of orality. Thus we can examine the extant versions of a given parable as performances of an implied oral structure. A basic pattern or structure undergirds each performance of the parable, and we can view that structure as an originating structure. An actual performance fills in gaps[4] as response to a structure. Matthew and Luke are not only performers but also hearers/readers, since they are responding to previous performances. When we examine any extant version of a parable we should pay close attention to (*a*) those aspects dictated by the theological and/or narrative context and (*b*) those aspects that result from a response to an underlying structure. This will allow us to grasp the parable's dynamic as performance. Our goal is not the words of some original parable but the structure that gives birth to the various performances we meet in the Gospels. We will first examine the

---

1. Tolbert, *Perspectives*, 72.
2. I am indebted to the detailed studies of Didier ("La parabole," 248–71), Weiser (*Die Knechtsgleichnisse*, 226– 72), and McGaughy ("Fear of Yahweh," 235–45).
3. Ong, *Orality and Literacy*, 57–68, esp. 67.
4. "Gaps" is a technical term from Iser (*Act of Reading*, chap. 7). It represents an indeterminacy in a text which creates asymmetry between reader and text demanding interpretation.

performances of Matthew and Luke, and then offer a reconstruction of the parable's underlying structure or pattern.

What to Do While Waiting

Matthew uses a clumsy construction to couple this parable to Ten Virgins, which concludes with Jesus' command "Watch, therefore, because you do not know the day or the hour" (25:13). "For," *gar*, ties A Man Entrusts Property to this concluding command, and "as," *hōsper*, indicates that it is a comparison, an anecdote that will illuminate the preceding conclusion.[5] But since the correlative is left unspecified,[6] there is no main verb.[7]

Despite the clumsy grammar, Matthew's intent is clear. The parable stands as the middle panel of the triptych of Jesus' eschatological sermon or discourse and underscores the discourse's theme of exhortation to vigilance until the end.[8] The discourse begins at 24:4 in response to the disciples' question "Tell us when will these things be and what will be the signs of your coming and of the end of the age?" (24:3). The sermon has three main divisions: 24:4–35 deals with the phases of the future; 24:36—25:30 concerns an exhortation to vigilance; and 25:31–46 presents the last-judgment scene. More specifically, the midsection displays a careful interweaving.

A concerning that day, no one knows the hour, neither the angels of heaven nor the son, except the father alone (24:36)
for as [*hōsper gar*] it was in the days of Noah (v. 36)

Parable of two men and two women (vv. 40–41)
B Watch for you do not know on what day the your lord will come (v. 42)

Parable of the householder and the thief (v. 43)
A therefore even you must be ready, for you do not expect the hour when the son of man will come (v. 44)

Parable of the faithful and wise servant/the evil [*kakos*] servant (vv. 45–50)
C there men will weep and gnash their teeth (v. 51)

---

5. Schweizer (*Good News*, 470), among many others, notices the effect of *gar*.
6. *BDF*, 453 (4).
7. Beare (*Gospel according to Matthew*, 488) refers to this phenomenon as an anacolouthon.
8. Lambrecht, "Parousia Discourse," 308–42, esp. 312–13.

Parable of five wise and five foolish virgins (25:1–12)
B watch, therefore, because you do not know the day or the hour (v. 13)

for as [*hōsper gar*] story of the two good and faithful servants and the third
evil [*ponēros*] and slothful servant (vv. 14–29)
C there men will weep and gnash their teeth (v. 30)[9]

"For as," *hōsper gar*, begins both the midsection (24:36) and the final
story. A series of parables all based on contrasting behavior provides the
backbone. The stories' conclusions form a pattern ABA, CBC, (i.e., two
sets of chiasms built on the B member). There is even internal consistency within this arrangement. In The Faithful and Wise Servant (24:45–
51), one is faithful (*pistis*) and wise (*phronimos*), the other evil (*kakos*). In
Ten Virgins, one group is called wise (*phronimos*), and in A Man Entrusts
Property the servants whose talents increase are called good (*agathos*)
and faithful (*pistos*) but the one-talent man is evil (*ponēros*). Set in series,
the stories promote a stark either-or situation that prepares for the
sermon's concluding judgment scene with its final either-or. In context,
A Man Entrusts Property drives home not only the necessity to watch
for an unknown hour but also the stringent demand on faith to produce
an increase or to face a tragic judgment.[10]

Given the context that Matthew has constructed for the parable, it
should be obvious that the man going on a journey is understood as
Jesus and that his return anticipates in narrative the judgment scene.
This interpretation has led Matthew to make adaptations in the parable's performance.

Several adaptations are obvious and have been widely acknowledged. The casting into the darkness and gnashing of teeth (v. 30) is a
Matthean addition[11] that allegorizes the narrative in preparation for the
impending judgment scene. The converse of condemnation is the reward of the two successful servants, with "Enter into the joy of your
master [*kyrios*]" (vv. 21b, 23b) almost certainly a Matthean addition.[12]
The reference to the "long time" the master is away reflects the delay of
the Parousia.[13]

9. I am indebted to McGaughy, Didier, and Lambrecht for suggestions on the
arrangement of this section of the sermon, although none has noticed the chiastic
arrangement of the conclusions.

10. Meier, *Vision of Matthew*, 176.

11. This is a Matthean phrase. See chap. 8 above, n. 13. See also B. T. D. Smith,
Parables, 166; Jeremias, *Parables*, 60.

12. McGaughy, "Fear of Yahweh," 237; Jeremias, *Parables*, 60 n. 42; McNeile, *Gospel
according to Matthew*, 365; Manson, *Sayings*, 247; B. T. D. Smith, *Parables*, 166; Didier,
"La parabole," 254; Weiser, *Die Knechtsgleichnisse*, 242–43.

13. Weiser, *Die Knechtsgleichnisse*, 238; McGaughy, "Fear of Yahweh," 237; Bultmann, *History of the Synoptic Tradition*, 176. Besides these items dealing with adaptation

Return of One Wellborn

The most obvious difference between Luke's parable and that of Matthew is the interweaving into the narrative of a story of a nobleman's effort to reclaim his throne. This has provoked debate: Were two originally separate parables combined, or was the original story elaborated with details about a throne claimant? A closer examination of the alternatives will lead to a clearer understanding of the originating structure of the parable.

A Man Entrusts Property (Luke 19:22–27) occurs near the conclusion of the journey to Jerusalem. The immediate unit is framed by a notice of impending suffering in Jerusalem (18:31) and the preparations for the arrival in Jerusalem (19:28). The scene is near and in Jericho. First there is the healing of the blind man with its climactic "glorifying God" (18:43)[14] and then the conversion of Zacchaeus. Sharing of goods with the poor and repentance are important Lukan themes. Just as the blind man glorified God, so at the conclusion of Zacchaeus's story, Jesus proclaims "Today salvation has come to this house" (19:9). The chief publican, an outcast, upon repenting is proclaimed to be in the realm of salvation.

The Lukan introduction ties the parable closely to the conversion of Zacchaeus.[15] "As they heard these things, he proceeded to tell a parable, because he was near to Jerusalem, and because they supposed that the kingdom of God was to appear immediately" (19:11). Having proclaimed salvation's immanence, Luke now warns against mistaking salvation for the kingdom's coming. The parable provides an allegorical timetable for the coming of the kingdom, for those things that are "not yet."

In observing Luke's performance of the parable we must differentiate between his use of the parable to address the delay of the Parousia and his response as a reader who has filled in some of the gaps of the originating structure. In comparison with Matthew, Luke's version is shorter. There is no presentation of the three servants trading, and the command to trade (v. 13b) weakens dramatic tension.[16] Narrative development is reported after the fact, and the servants' reports to the master

---

to context, there are undoubtedly items that result from Matthean style. In my judgment these are much harder. E.g., *eutheōs*, "immediately" (v. 15b), is clearly Matthean (BDF, 102 [3]), but it is not nearly so clear with "to settle accounts" (v. 19b). The phrase also occurs in 18:23, A King Wished to Settle Accounts. But does this prove it to be a Matthean addition or simply Matthew's way of phrasing the originating structure? Didier ("La parabole," 254) thinks it is a Matthean addition; Weiser (*Die Knechtgleichnisse*, 239) is uncertain.

14. Talbert, *Reading Luke*, 175.
15. Klostermann, *Das Lukasevangelium*, 185.
16. Didier, "La parabole," 260.

are shorter.[17] Moreover, because of the throne-claimant theme, there are ten servants instead of three and their reward is cities over which they are to rule. Luke also underscores the third servant's guilt by condemning him out of his own mouth and having him keep the entrusted money in a napkin, the significance of which will become clear later. Luke does not condemn the servant's failure. Rather punishment is bestowed on those who opposed the king's claim.[18]

Some changes are due to the throne-claimant theme, but some are just as likely performance responses to the originating structure. Although Luke omits the description of the servants' trading because his interest is in those challenging the legitimacy of Jesus' kingship, still the command to trade is implicit in the original story, because the failure to trade is what brings about tension in the plot. It is the failure whose lack must be overcome. "I will condemn you out of your own mouth" (v. 22) is again a development of the implied narrative, drawing the reader's attention to what actually happens in the parable. It represents an important clue to the tension present in the originating parable.

Two issues concern us about the throne claimant. First, how does the throne claimant theme fit into Lukan redaction? Second, was it an independent parable of Jesus that has been combined with A Man Entrusts Property? The theme of one of noble birth's claiming his throne fits nicely into the Lukan scheme. The notion of Jesus' kingship is prominent in Luke,[19] and the rejection of the Jews is also an important theme.[20] The throne claimant advances Luke's purpose by distinguishing salvation, which is here today, and the kingdom, which allegorically has a timetable of three parts: investiture by ascension, time between investiture and Parousia, and triumphant return at the Parousia. The successful servants are those like the blind man and Zacchaeus who in the interim bring forth fruits of repentance, while those who contest the king's claim are those unfaithful Jews.[21]

Those who defend the authenticity of the story of the throne claimant[22] do so because it is easily separated from A Man Entrusts Property and stands alone when so separated:

> A nobleman went into a far country to receive a kingdom and then returned. But his citizens hated him and sent an embassy after him, saying,

17. McGaughy, "Fear of Yahweh," 238.
18. Talbert, *Reading Luke*, 177.
19. See Luke 1:33; 19:38; 22:39–40; 23:3, 11, 37–38. See Weinart, "Parable of the Throne Claimant," 506; Ellis, *Gospel of Luke*, 222.
20. Acts 13:46; 18:6; 28:8. See Jervell, *Luke and the People*, 41–74. For the dark side of this theme, see Sanders, "Parable of the Pounds," 660–81.
21. Didier, "La parabole," 263.
22. Zerwick ("Die Parabel," 654–74) provides an extensive survey of positions. Weinart ("Parable of the Throne Claimant," 505) brings the survey up to date.

"We do not want this man to reign over us." When he returned having received the kingdom, he said, "But as for these enemies of mine, who did not want me to reign over them, bring them here and slay them before me."

The story supposedly refers to the episode of Archelaus's claiming his throne,[23] and the parable is Jesus' warning to the Jews. Though older interpreters (e.g., Maximilian Zerwick) see Jesus as the returning nobleman,[24] more recent critics (e..g, Frank Weinart) unsuccessfully try to avoid this allegorical identification. Weinart suggests that because of the specific reference to the Archelaus incident, the parable must fit a specific incident in Jesus' ministry, and he suggests the approach to Jerusalem.[25]

More recently others have questioned an independent existence for the throne claimant. The close fit with Luke's royal theology, as well as the rejection of the citizens and the Jews,[26] is primary evidence. Furthermore, the identification of Archelaus is both distant and unnecessary. The theme of a throne claimant is frequent in oriental literature.[27] The use of "citizen," *politai*, and "embassy," *presbeias*, are Lukan.[28] Lambrecht also calls attention to the trading language specific to the Lukan parable, the journey to a "far country" (a parallel phrase occurs in A Man Had Two Sons), and the parable's introduction, which clearly announces the kingship theme. [29] Finally, it would be the only example of Jesus' drawing a parable from a specific historical situation. If none of these arguments by itself is compelling, together they make a strong case for Lukan composition. Luke apparently drew on the common repertoire of the throne claimant to recast a parable about a man going on a journey into an allegory for the enthronement and return of Jesus as king.

Reconstruction and Oral Tradition

If these arguments are correct, then we may conclude that the two versions we now have are an implementation or performance of a common originating parable. Luke has more expansively elaborated the originating structure; Matthew's efforts were more modest. Both were able to use the narrative as an allegory of the Parousia because it had

23. For references, see Weinart, "Parable of the Throne Claimant," 508.
24. Zerwick, "Die Parabel," 674.
25. Weinart, "Parable of the Throne Claimant," 513.
26. Didier, "La parabole," 261; Lambrecht, *Once More Astonished*, 177.
27. For the evidence, see Förster, "Das Gleichnis," 43.
28. *Politēs*, "citizen": Luke 15:4; 19:14; Acts 21:39; only other occurrence, Heb. 8:11. *Presbeia*, "embassy": Luke 14:32. See Didier, "La parabole," 261. In *Parables*, 59, Jeremias argues that the story of the throne claimant is a separate parable, but in *Die Sprache*, 278, he argues that *politai* is redactional. This only shows that word studies are not as reliable a guide as one might like, since an author has freedom in style.
29. Lambrecht, *Once More Astonished*, 177.

already received such a tendency in the oral tradition.[30] This can be seen clearly in the master's commendation and the parable's conclusion (Matt. 25:29; Luke 19:26). We must, therefore, examine the performance of the originating structure in the oral tradition. This will involve an analysis of (*a*) the master's commendation and the story's conclusion and (*b*) the amount of money.

Matthew 25:29//Luke 19:26 has long been recognized as a free-floating logion.[31] Since it appears in both Matthew and Luke, one can conclude that it was added to the parable during its oral transmission. This conclusion gives the narrative a parenetic point, underscoring the servant's action. But this added conclusion points to what was a problem for the original hearers: taking away the third servant's money and giving it to the first servant. It softens a hearer's predicament. The third servant is punished in the parable for his failure to produce, whereas in the concluding logion it is only his "little" that is the problem.[32]

The amount of money entrusted to the servants is linked to the master's reward. In both Matthew and Luke the master remarks that because the servant has been faithful in a very little, he will be placed over much. A talent was one of the largest values of money in the Hellenistic world. A silver coinage, it weighed between fifty-seven and seventy-four pounds. One talent was equal to six thousand denarii.[33] It was, then, a large sum of money. Sixty minas equal one talent, or one hundred denarii. A mina is considerably less than a talent, but it is still a large sum of money from a peasant's viewpoint.

Most scholars consider the mina the more original sum[34] —because giving minas to someone who has cities at his control makes no sense, so Luke carelessly has preserved the original amount. But how, they ask, can Matthew argue that the servant has been faithful over a little, when he has had so much capital with which to work? Since both stories have the remark about being faithful over a little, the little amount (the mina),

30. See McGaughy, "Fear of Yahweh," 238. Schulz (*Q: Die Spruchquelle,* 293) finds this so dominating that he concludes that the parable originates in Q.

31. Cf. Matt. 13:12; Mark 4:25; Luke 8:18. See Jülicher, *Die Gleichnisreden* 2:479; Bultmann, *History of the Synoptic Tradition,* 176; Jeremias, *Parables,* 60; Michaelis, *Die Gleichnisse,* 111; Didier, "La parabole," 255; Weiser, *Die Knechtsgleichnisse,* 253; Manson, *Sayings,* 248.

32. Lambrecht, *Once More Astonished,* 182.

33. One denarius was an average subsistence wage for a day's labor, i.e., a wage insufficient to generate a surplus. See chap. 13 below. I have not given modern equivalents because the economic basis of our two societies is so different that comparisons would be very misleading. We operate in a surplus economy; they in a subsistence one.

34. Crossan, *In Parables,* 101; Jeremias, *Parables,* 60 n. 41; Didier, "La parabole," 264; Lambrecht, *Once More Astonished,* 176; Beare, *Gospel according to Matthew,* 487; Marshall, *Commentary on Luke,* 701; Michaelis, *Die Gleichnisse,* 111.

must, they conclude, be the more authentic. This argument seems contrived. What is actually being argued is that the minas would fit better in Matthew's story and the talents in Luke's story!

Since both authors have extensively edited their stories, why did they both use amounts of money that are apparently so inconsistent with the thrust of their narrative logic? Why did Luke not make the money appropriate for a king? The resolution lies in the action of the third servant, who hid the money entrusted to him in a napkin. By burying the money he is no longer responsible for it. In Luke, the ultimate blame falls on those who oppose the new king, while the penultimate falls on the third servant. By wrapping the money in a napkin the third servant has behaved responsibly. If he had been entrusted with talents (fifty to seventy pounds of silver), wrapping it in a napkin would have been foolish. Thus the minas may be Lukan. Why does Matthew use talents when the master states that the servant has been faithful over a little? For Matthew the parable is an allegory of faithfulness for the kingdom. The little over which the servant is faithful is money, while the much more is the kingdom. Talents are not at all incongruous with the saying. It is a "how much more," or *val vakomer*, argument.[35]

This leads us to examine the master's speech of commendation. Matthew had already understood the reward to be heaven, with the specification "Enter into the joy of your master" (v. 21b, 23b). Faithfulness over a little and a reward of greater responsibility look forward to the conclusion: "For to everyone who has will more be given" (Matt. 25:29). This concluding logion is simply a restatement of the common piece of wisdom that "the rich get richer and the poor get poorer," applied to a spiritual level. The main problem is not the amount of money, the talent, but the master's reward, which appears to cohere with the allegorical adaptation as an eschatological warning.[36]

A Reading

The interest in offering a reconstructed parable for analysis is not to reconstruct a primal, pristine parable or the original words but to uncover an originating structure or pattern that gave birth to the extant versions.

> *Line 1:* It is like a man going on a journey and he entrusted to his servants his property.

35. Cf. Who Has a Friend? Cf. also lilies of the field, salt of the earth. See Edwards, *Theology of Q,* 144.
36. McGaughy ("Fear of Yahweh," 242) argues that the parable should not be interpreted as from little to great.

The opening line announces the story's theme, intimating the implied metaphorical structure. Departure is an essential element in the departure-return parables.[37] A hearer knows from the beginning that this will be a test, and so the opening line invokes a repertoire dealing with stewardship.

Line 2: To one he gave five talents, to another two, to another one. Then he went away.

It is difficult to know whether the division into five, two, and one is part of the originating structure or a traditional elaboration. In its favor is the Lukan report to the master of ten and five minas gained (Luke 19:16–17) and the so-called law of threes. In the long run it makes little difference to the story's development how much each servant received. As we saw above, Matthew's note about "each [receiving] according to his ability" is redactional, reflecting both his interest in the servants' bearing fruit and the need of an actual performer to fill in a gap in the originating structure created by the story's conclusion. Since the third servant will eventually be condemned, the note in Matthew represents a rereading of the story in which an implied hearer's potential objection is cut off in advance. Similarly, Luke's command to trade makes explicit what is implied in the story.[38]

Line 3: He who had received the five talents went at once and traded with them; and he made five talents more. So also, he who had the two talents made two talents more.

The situation depicted is realistic. These servants are not slaves but stewards[39] acting in the master's stead. From the profit they make for their master they will be able to enrich themselves, for they expect to share in his good fortune.[40] The amount of profit made by the servants in Matthew is not unusual by the standards of the day.[41] The line allows a hearer to observe the two servants' activity, to know in advance what is happening.

Line 4: He who had received one talent went and dug in the ground and hid his master's silver.

---

37. See chap. 8 above.

38. Michaelis, *Die Gleichnisse,* 107; Manson, *Sayings,* 315. The first line sets the story up as dealing with a test of stewardship, and the way that test is to be conducted is by trading.

39. Derrett, *Law in the New Testament,* 19–24.

40. Cf. A Rich Man Had a Steward, at the conclusion of which the steward claims his share of the profits. Str-B 1:970 presents relevant evidence.

41. Derrett, *Law in the New Testament,* 24. On the other hand, Luke's return of ten to one in the case of the first servant is very high.

The hearer already knows what the first two servants have done; now the third servant's activity is narrated. In the Matthean version he has received only one talent (still a large amount of money) and goes out to bury it. This activity shows him prudent and trustworthy. In commenting on the Mishnah,[42] "If he guarded it [money] in the manner of guardians [and it was lost] he is not liable," the Gemara quotes Rabbi Samuel: "Money can only be guarded [by placing it] in the earth."[43] In the ancient world, underground was the only safe place, and the finding of buried treasure was not unusual. Josephus remarks how people buried their treasure against the ill fortunes of war.[44] By burying the silver the third servant ensures a verdict of responsible behavior, at the time of accounting.[45]

Line 5:   And the master of those servants came and settled accounts with them.

Although Matthew and Luke phrase this line differently, they make essentially the same point: the master returns and wants to know what has happened in his absence. His return is an essential formal part of this first group of patron-client parables. Without it there can be no accounting, no denouement.

Line 6:   And coming forward
he who had received five talents brought five talents more saying, "Master,
    you delivered to me five talents;
        here! I have made a profit of five talents more."
And his master said to him,
    "Great! good and faithful servant."
And coming forward the two-talent one said, "Master,
    you delivered to me two talents;
        here! I have made a profit of two talents more."
His master said to him,
    "Great! good and faithful servant."

As indicated above, the structure of the originating parable at this point is obvious even if the details are difficult to decide. Matthew, Luke,

---

42. *m. B. Mes.* 3.10 (Danby, 352).
43. *b. B. Mes.* 42a (Soncino 10:250–51).
44. Josephus, *Jewish War*, 6.5.2 (LCL 3:539). See chap. 20 below.
45. Derrett (*Law in the New Testament*, 22) suggests that he took this action because he did not have a sufficient amount with which to make a profit. But this seems unlikely in view of the value of a talent, or even a mina, should that be the original amount.

and the oral tradition were interested in this section because it represents the moment of judgment. Two servants report an increase that has occurred during their stewardship, and the master commends them. Some scholars believe that Luke's more modest "Master, your mina has made ten minas" may be the more original formula.[46] Probably "good and faithful" was part of the original commendation. "Faithful," *pistis*, characterizes an expected virtue of a steward,[47] and the presence of "faithful" in the originating structure would explain the attraction in the oral tradition of the saying concerning being faithful over a little.[48]

> *Line 7:* And coming forward
> the one who had received the one talent said,
> "Master,
> I know that you are a hard man,
>> reaping where you did not sow,
>> gathering when you did not scatter.
> And being afraid, going out, I hid your talent in the earth.
>> Here! you have yours."

Both the underlying mytheme and the aesthetic response the parable seeks to effect now converge, raising up a host of complex issues. Besides, Luke's aims are somewhat contrary to those of the originating parable at precisely this juncture.

The first clue is the third servant's action. In Matthew, he hides the money in the ground. Burying absolves him from further responsibility. In Luke, the servant hides the money in a napkin, not a responsible action, thus leaving him liable. Luke thereby makes the servant more responsible at the accounting. Lukan context does not necessitate this change, for Luke's narrative concentrates the real blame on those who resisted the nobleman's claim to the throne. Rather, this change comes from an audience's response. A hearer identifies and sympathizes with the third servant; he has acted prudently. Luke's change to a napkin takes away the servant's claim to prudent action.[49] This shows how arbitrary audiences have found the master's eventual condemnation of his servant.

Luke—or his tradition—has also shifted the servant's charge from

---

46. Didier, "La parabole," 292.

47. See chap. 11 below.

48. If this saying is part of the originating structure, then it would only mark out a reward, a passing of the test.

49. Just as Matthew notes that each was allotted according to his ability and Luke gives the command to trade, this detail about the napkin attempts to make the servant somewhat more blameful.

farming metaphors to, in one instance, a banking metaphor: "You take up what you did not lay down." Plummer has remarked that this was probably a proverbial saying for a grasping person.[50] Actually, evidence indicates that the proverbial saying is normally framed in the negative. Diogenes Laertius attributes a similar saying to Solon: "What has been put down shall not be taken up except by the one who put it down on the pain of death."[51] Plato refers to a divine command, "Take not up what you laid not down,"[52] and Philo, in a series of maxims, quotes, "What he has not laid down, he must not take up."[53] Regardless of whether Matthew's farming metaphors or Luke's farming and banking metaphors are preferred, the master's characterization by the third servant remains consistent: he is a hardhearted man.

Lane McGaughy has noted that the closest verbal similarity between Matthew and Luke occurs in the response of the third servant. In both books there is the same combination of elements, only in reverse order:[54]

Description of the master
Two aphorisms describing the master's hardness
Therefore the servant was afraid
Return of the money intact

The similarity of vocabulary and elements between Matthew and Luke indicates that not only is the originating parable close to the surface text but also this is the story's most important element. This line accomplishes two functions: (1) It establishes sympathy for the third servant by drawing the audience to his side. (2) It invokes an important mytheme from Israel's heritage.

A comparison of the reporting scene of the first and second servants with that of the third brings out important differences. Via has remarked that the scenes are essentially the same,[55] but the differences are important. The repetition of the scene for both servants reinforces the contrasts. The first two servants (*a*) come forward, (*b*) address the master, (*c*) report on what has happened, and (*d*) are commended by him. In the third servant's scene the third element (the reporting on what happened) is greatly expanded.[56] The third servant describes the master as

50. Plummer, *Gospel according to St. Luke*, 441.
51. Diogenes Laertius, *Solon*, 1.57 (LCL 2:57), au. trans.
52. Plato, *Laws*, 11.C (LCL 2:391).
53. Philo, *Hypothetica*, 7.7 (LCL 9:427). The preceding maxim in Philo is a negative formulation of the Golden Rule. See the extensive list of such parallels in Brightman's "Six Notes," 158.
54. McGaughy, "Fear of Yahweh," 235.
55. Via, *Parables*, 115.
56. For a more detailed arrangement, see my *Jesus, Symbol-Maker*, 41.

hard or severe,[57] invokes two aphorisms, reports what he has done, and attempts to return the money. The additional features present to a hearer an image of the master as a "rapacious man, heedlessly intent on his own profit."[58] This image appeals to an audience's conventional, fixed[59] image of an absentee landlord who bleeds the land dry. In his report, the third servant shows himself to be cautious and blameless. In burying the money, he no longer has any responsibility for its possible loss. As Dodd notes, the servant expects to be commended for his caution and honesty,[60] and the audience expects him to be. Finally, the return of the money indicates that the master, having lost nothing, has no claim on the servant. The servant has fulfilled his obligations. From a literary perspective, his speech draws an audience to his side, creating a firm identification and solidarity with him.

The identification is reinforced because the servant's speech recalls one aspect of Israel's response to the Torah. The Torah is Israel's joy, that which sets it apart from the nations. As the first saying in *Aboth* proposes, "Be deliberate in judgment, raise up many disciples, and make a fence around the law."[61] One of Israel's important responses to the law is its preservation, its protection. A rabbinic parable, sometimes noted as parallel to A Man Entrusts Property,[62] makes this point graphically. A son of Rabbi Johanan ben Zakkai has died, and various rabbis attempt to console him by recalling examples of biblical personages who lost their sons and allowed themselves to be comforted. But these stories only increase Zakkai's grief, because they remind him of the biblical personages' grief. Rabbi Eleazar tells this parable:

> I shall tell thee a parable: to what may this be likened? To a man with whom the king deposited some object. Every single day the man would weep and cry out, saying: "Woe unto me! When shall I be quit of this trust in peace?" Thou too, master, thou hast a son: he studied Torah, the Prophets, the Holy Writings, he studied Mishnah, Halakha, Agada, and he departed from the world without sin. And thou shouldst be comforted when thou hast returned thy trust unimpaired.[63]

57. According to Beare (*Gospel according to Matthew*, 490) *sklēros*, in Matthew, means "hardfisted" and is used of a person merciless in his dealings with others, whereas *austēros*, in Luke, is used of government officials who are strict in their examination of accounts.

58. Jeremias, *Parables*, 60.

59. The use of an aphorism to appeal to a conventional or fixed image is appropriate, for aphorisms are a depository for a community's conventional wisdom and experience.

60. Dodd, *Parables*, 117.

61. *m. Aboth* 1.1 (Danby, 446).

62. Str-B 1:971; B. T. D. Smith, *Parables*, 164; McGaughy, "Fear of Yahweh," 243.

63. *Fathers according to Rabbi Nathan* 14 (Goldin, 77).

The parable consoled Rabbi ben Zakkai. It underscores two important aspects related to our parable. The Torah is something to be protected, a trust, but also a burden. Having kept the Torah throughout life, one should rejoice at returning it "unimpaired." As McGaughy has pointed out, this leads at times in the postexilic period to a bitterness against God. He quotes as examples Ps. 119:120, Job 4:14; and especially Job 23:13–17:[64]

> But he is unchangeable and who can trust him?
>   What he desires, that he does.
> For he will complete what he appoints for me;
>   and many such things are in his mind.
> Therefore I am terrified at his presence;
>   when I consider, I am in dread of him.
> God has made my heart faint;
>   the Almighty has terrified me;
> For I am hemmed in by darkness,
>   and thick darkness covers my face.

The third servant's speech not only moves an audience toward identification with his plight but also recalls an important mytheme used in Israel to deal with the people's responsibility toward the Torah.

Line 8: But his master said to him, "Evil servant, you knew that I reap what I do not sow and gather where I do not scatter? You therefore should have placed my silver with the bankers and coming I could have recovered what was mine with interest. Take therefore from him the talent and give it to the one who has ten talents."

This last line creates a dilemma for a hearer: Who is telling the truth? Whom do I trust to tell the story? The Lukan version makes evident this contest over truth with the master's "I will condemn you out of your own mouth" (19:22). Some later hearer/reader is filling in the gap indicating the direction of the action.

The master's response formally parallels the scenes of the first two servants. But instead of commending the servant as good and faithful, he attacks him, calling him evil. The audience, whose sympathy is with the servant, hears this response as confirming the servant's aphoristic description of the master. Has the servant done the master evil? Yet the master calls the servant evil. He repeats the servant's characterization of him, not indicating its truth or falsity. The servant, and the audience, argue implicitly that the master has coming only what is his and that the

---

64. McGaughy, "Fear of Yahweh," 244.

servant has taken every legal precaution to make sure that the master will on his return receive what is his. The master argues that the servant's characterization does not account for his action. If he were such a rapacious man, should the servant not at least have ensured some gain?

Finally, the master instructs those standing around to take the talent from the servant and give it to the one who has ten talents. In Luke, the audience objects. Whether this verse belongs to the original text of Luke or is a scribal addition is beside the point,[65] for it indicates how actual readers have heard the text. The taking-away of the talent and the giving of it to the first servant only compound the master's apparent injustice. At the same time, they force an audience into retrospection, to ask how the master dealt with the first two servants. Nothing in the narration indicates that the master was hard and ruthless with them or that they were in fear of him. At the story's end, a hearer is left with a dilemma: Whom do I trust? Where does the truth lie?

From Story to Kingdom: Whose Story Is This?

Our reading indicates that an audience identifies and sympathizes with the third servant. The various performances represented in the Synoptic tradition try to explain the servant's guilt so that his condemnation does not appear so arbitrary. Matthew remarks that the property was divided among the servants according to their ability; Luke has the command to trade, the keeping of the money in a napkin, as well as the remark that the servant is condemned out of his own mouth. The Synoptic tradition attempts to explain the third servant's guilt, but another version of this story in the *Gospel of the Hebrews* completely avoids the problem. In that version there are again three servants.[66] The first trades, the second hides the money, and the third squanders it with harlots and flute players. The third servant is condemned, but now there is evident reason. This extracanonical reading of the parable confirms our analysis. The parable manipulates a hearer/reader into identifying with the third servant, who is then roundly condemned, leading to an experience of

---

65. Metzger, *Textual Commentary*, 169.

66. The quotation from the *Gospel of the Hebrews*, with appropriate context from Eusebius:

> But since the Gospel (written) in Hebrew characters which has come into our hands enters the threat not against the man who had hid (the talent), but against him who had lived dissolutely— "for he (the master) had three servants: one who squandered his master's substance with harlots and flute-girls, one who multiplied the gain, and one who hid the talent; and accordingly one was accepted (with joy), another merely rebuked, and another cast into prison. (Quoted by Eusebius in *Theophania*, 22; in *Sayings Parallels*, ed. Crossan, 11).

unjust action. Why would a parable want to lead to such an aesthetic experience?

McGaughy, with his identification of the parable's underlying my-theme, has indicated one important element in this puzzle. As a steward story, it deals with a steward's management of the master's property. Steward stories belong to the metaphorical network in which the master's departure is the occasion of a test. Therefore, knowing the rules of success is important. For McGaughy, the third servant's complaint against the master echoes the postexilic complaints against Yahweh's "hardness": "Jesus's parable . . . is leveled against the rabbinic response to the spiritual crisis alluded to in the saying, viz., that Israel's mission is to guard the traditions of the fathers during Yahweh's absence."[67] But Israel saw the Torah not as an overwhelming burden but as God's gift that made it stand out from among the nations. And yet there is a hidden side to this great gift, the burden of its preservation. The Torah is the "yoke of the commandments." The yoke metaphor indicates the double possibility of being the law's guardian.

A Jew would not immediately recognize himself in the character-ization of the third servant. For the yoke of the commandments is not borne out of fear of God (read "master"). A Jew would see the parable as a caricature and not a realistic description. Although McGaughy quotes passages that show a negative feeling about God and his demands, these certainly do not represent the majority. The yoke of the commandments is a cause for rejoicing.

McGaughy is on the correct trail, but he has misread the parable. In the narrative a hearer is allowed a glimpse of the price for protecting and preserving the Torah. In the narrative that price is loss of a future! By burying the property the servant forfeits any future. The cases of the first two servants show what the future is. But the yoke was to be borne in order to have a future.[68] Another rabbinic parable makes this point. A king was betrothed, and in the marriage contract he specified all the wealth that would be the bride's. Then he went into a far country and stayed there a long time. This parable has the same structure as ours, with the journey denoting a test. While the king was away, the bride-to-be was tempted by many suitors, but each time she took out the mar-riage contract and its promises would comfort her. When the king came back he marveled that she had waited for him. "My lord, if it had not been for the large marriage contract you wrote for me, my companions

67. McGaughy, "Fear of Yahweh," 245.
68. See Rabbi Eleazar's parable of comfort for Rabbi ben Zakkai, quoted on p. 230 above.

would long ago have made me give you up." The parable is then applied to Israel. The nations taunt Israel,

"How long will you die for your God, and give your lives for Him, and be slaughtered for Him? How much pain does He not bring upon you, how much contempt and suffering? . . ." Then the Israelites go into their synagogues and houses of study, and they take up the book of the Law, and they read in it, "And I will turn unto you, and make you fruitful and multiply you, and will establish my covenant with you" (Lev 26:9), and they are comforted. When the end shall have come, God will say to the Israelites, "My sons, I marvel that you have waited for me all these years," and Israel will say, "Lord, if it had not been for the book of the Law which thou didst write for us, the nations would long ago have caused us to abandon thee."[69]

Here the hardness theme is placed on the lips of the nations that taunt Israel, but the parable shows how the law comforts and how the future is the reward at stake.

In our parable's narrative the third servant's image of the master deprives him of a future,[70] for it freezes the servant in fear. But this constitutes the story's ambiguity. The master never accepts the description of the third servant's aphorism but points back to the first two servants. His refusal to take back the talent implies his rejection of that image. A hearer is asked to choose between two competing images of the master: the explicit image put forward in aphorism by the third servant, and the image implied in the actions of the first two servants. Is the master the hardhearted man of the third servant's attack, or is he gracious and generous, as he was toward the first two servants? How do we know which of these two views is correct?

If this reading of the story as parable is correct, then it marks out a fundamental disagreement between Jesus and the Pharisees. To mark out the difference, one need not castigate the Pharisees as burdened under the Torah, raging against God's hardness. The evidence of their own writings indicates that this is not the case. Rather, in the parable it emerges how one goes about claiming the future. Is it claimed by preserving the precious gift? Or is it claimed in the present as freedom of action, liberating the servant from an aphoristic, conventional vision that paralyzes him? The parable as a window onto the kingdom demands that the servant act neither as preserver nor as one afraid; but act boldly he must. If one is to act boldly, then the rules have been changed. They are no longer predictable.

69. *Pesiq. Rab Kah.* 19, 139b; quoted by C. Montefiore and Loewe, *Rabbinic Anthology*, 119–20.
70. Via, *Parables*, 119.

This parable, like Jesus' parody of legal sayings in the Sermon on the Mount,[71] forces a hearer to choose a future in which to live. Jesus parodies legal form for the same reason he parodies the rabbinic trusting in the yoke of the law—for freedom.

71. See Tannehill, *Sword of His Mouth*, 67ff.; Crossan, *Raid on the Articulate*, 63–69,

10

Reading of the Will

A Man Planted a Vineyard

A man planted a vineyard and gave it out to farmers and left home. When the time came, he sent a servant to the farmers to get from them some fruit of the vineyard. And they took him and beat him and sent him away empty. He sent another servant and they beat him. Then the master sent his son, saying, "They will respect my son." But those farmers said to one another, "This is the heir; come, let us kill him, and the inheritance will be ours." And they took him and killed him.

A thicket of problems confronts the interpreter of the parable A Man Planted a Vineyard. Some critics believe the master is a fool; others that Jesus foreshadows his own death. Most agree that strong verbal agreement between the Synoptic versions points to a literary relationship,[1] but J. A. T. Robinson ends his recent study with a question about source analysis.[2] Still others argue that the story was always an allegory—a conclusion with strong proponents since the turn of the century.[3] Even

---

1. Farmer, *Synoptic Problem*, 208.
2. Robinson, "Parable of the Wicked Husbandmen," 443–61.
3. Loisy, *Les évangiles synoptiques* 2:312. Jülicher (*Die Gleichnisreden* 2:406) argues also for inauthenticity but allows a little doubt.

more remarkably, the close resemblance between Dodd's 1933 hypothetical reconstruction of an original parable and the version later found
in the newly discovered *Gospel of Thomas* (1945) seems to confirm the
reconstruction. This confusing history of interpretation leads one to
have little confidence about jumping into the thicket again. Yet a patient,
careful study of the tradition and the history of scholarship may prove
rewarding. We begin by examining each of the extant versions of the
story, assuming no source theory.

Mark: A Day in the Temple

How the parable sounded or read when Mark received it, we will never
know. Since Mark himself performed the parable, however, in his performance we encounter clues about the originating structure.

A Man Planted a Vineyard belongs to a complex of material surrounding Jesus' last days in Jerusalem and his controversy with Judaism's
official leaders. Antagonism runs high. The temporal context is a fiction
of three days: on the first day, Jesus enters Jerusalem (10:46—11:11); on
the second, he cleanses the temple (11:12–19); on the third, he engages in
public debates and a private discussion about the future (11:20—13:37).
Within the three-day schema, the second and third days form a unity.
Action and discourse center on the temple. At the conclusion of the first
day, Jesus enters the temple, looks around, and departs, "for the hour
was already late" (11:11). This verse forms a frame with 13:1, when on
coming out of the temple, Jesus' disciples marvel at the building's
beauty.[4] The late hour may refer not just to the time but to the temple
and Judaism as well. Given the debates that follow, a reader might well
see such a double meaning. Furthermore, within this section a reader
twice is warned of the Jewish leaders' desire to destroy Jesus (11:18;
12:12).[5]

The overall construction of this section is clear:[6]

Cursing of the fig tree (vv. 11–14)
  Cleansing of the temple (vv. 15–19)

4. Dewey, *Markan Public Debate*, 153. I am dependent on Dewey's analysis of the
rhetorical structure of this debate section.

5. Dewey (ibid., 55) points to the similarity of the other debate material in 3:6ff.,
where twice there are warnings of attempts to kill Jesus. Lambrecht (*Once More
Astonished*, 128) sees these two attempts to kill Jesus as frustrated by the crowd; the
third attempt, with the help of Judas, is successful.

6. Dewey (*Markan Public Debate*, 58) does not arrange this unit in this chiasmic
structure. Rather she sees it organized by an action-objection-vindication pattern: action
is the cleansing of the temple; objection is the authorities' question about his authority;
vindication is the parable.

Explanation of the cursing of the fig tree (vv. 20–25)
Conundrum about authority (vv. 27–33)
   The parable A Man Planted a Vineyard (vv. 1–9)
New cornerstone (vv. 10–12)

Jesus' entrance into Jerusalem places the destiny of the temple and its leadership at risk. The cursing of the fig tree and its explanation frame the cleansing of the temple, providing a bracket for its interpretation. The temple is to be a house of prayer for the nations, but the authorities have made it a den of robbers. When Jesus explains the cursing of the fig tree, he interprets it as an example of true prayer. Similarly, when the authorities question his authority, he poses a conundrum that shows them to be as barren as the fig tree. A Man Planted a Vineyard, like the cleansing of the temple, displays those in charge of the vineyard to be murderers and thieves, keeping out the lawful owners; and the quotation about the cornerstone states the authority by which he does these things. The controversy is fundamental and sharp: Who speaks for God? Jesus or the temple authorities? So sharp is the antagonism that each seeks to destroy the other: "What will the owner of the vineyard do? He will come and destroy the tenants, and give the vineyard to others" (12:9). This response by Jesus to his own parable parallels not only the authorities seeking to destroy Jesus (11:18) but the promise that the temple should be a house of prayer for all the *nations* (11:17)—for others. Consequently, the parable has received a strong salvation-history reading.

If the organization of this section through the parable's end is clear, do the sayings following the parable (vv. 13–44) to the frame's conclusion (13:1) relate to the parable? Most commentators see these as only loosely connected by catchwords and a sequential introduction of opponents.[7] But Joanna Dewey sees a complex structuring process in chapters 11—12 in which the parable both concludes 11:1—12:12 and introduces the next complex of debate material.[8]

    A The parable A Man Planted a Vineyard; threat of God's judgment (vv. 1–9).
     B Public teaching; psalm citation; audience reaction (vv. 10–12).
      C The things of God are to be given to God; audience reaction (vv. 13–17).
       D The hope in resurrection is real (vv. 18–27).
      C' The things of God are the commands to love God and neighbor; audience reaction (vv. 28–34).

7. Donahue, *Are You the Christ?* 116.
8. Dewey, *Markan Public Debate*, 162.

B' Psalm citation; audience reaction (vv. 35–37).
A' Warning against the scribes; threat of God's judgment (vv. 30–40).

What is intriguing about this rhetorical schema is that once again the parable and the psalm ciataion are separated. In the rhetorical structure of 11:1—12:12, the parable condemns the Jewish leadership and the psalm citation makes a christological point about the son's centrality in the new Israel. In the rhetorical structure of chapter 12, the extremely negative view of Israel presented in the parable/psalm is muted in the next debates. In questions about taxation, resurrection, and the chief commandment, Jesus agrees with the "Pharisaic scribal position."[9] But in B' and A' he attacks the scribal understanding of Christology and prophesies their condemnation (12:35–40). Thus the intensity of the parable grows: it begins to rise with the entrance into Jerusalem, subsides in the following debates, and rises again in the final section. By contextual and rhetorical arrangement, Mark has stressed the christological issue (the son's identity) and the rejection of temple leadership.

The parable itself exhibits specific changes that Mark has introduced to relate it to the context. The introduction, "to speak in parables," is a Markan phrase.[10] But whereas in Mark 4 the parables harden and are mysterious, now Jesus' opponents understand immediately the parable's significance and seek to destroy him.[11]

Though many interpreters point to the vineyard's description as reminiscent of the LXX version[12] of Isa. 5:1–2, it is not clear that Mark introduced the allusion. He clearly accents the vineyard as Israel, but he usually does not quote Scripture in this style.[13] The sending of the servant is confusing. Wounding the second servant in the head may be a reference to John the Baptist,[14] and the multiple sendings, beatings, and killings probably recall Israel's rejections of the prophets.[15] The reference to the "beloved" son refers to the baptism and transfiguration (Mark 1:11; 9:7). Since in Mark's version, the son is Jesus, a reference to him as beloved may be almost a reflex, the preference of oral performance for heroic, formulaic titles.[16] At the parable's conclusion, the

9. Ibid.
10. Mark 3:23; 4:2, 11. See Dodd, *Parables*, 101.
11. Lambrecht (*Once More Astonished*, 132) uses this passage to point out correctly that there is no consistent Markan parable theory. Here the parable provokes the leaders to seek to kill Jesus. In 3:6, the Pharisees seek to kill him after he heals on the Sabbath, and the parables of chap. 4 obfuscate.
12. For details, see Taylor, *Gospel according to Saint Mark*, 473.
13. Pesch, *Das Markusevangelium* 2:215.
14. So Crossan, *In Parables*, 87.
15. Carlston, *Parables*, 78; Pesch, *Das Markusevangelium*, 216.
16. Ong, *Orality and Literacy*, 70.

narrator (Jesus) asks what the master will do to those tenants and answers his own question. "He will come and destroy the tenants, and give the vineyard to others." As we shall see, this response is a natural one, but the theme of destruction is repeated several times in this section of Mark, so either he has accented this point or he has provided his own conclusion to the parable.

Matthew: The Fruits of the Vineyard

The Matthean version of the parable is similar to the version in Mark, and even if the context is also similar there are some striking differences. Mark divides the teaching in the temple into three days; Matthew depicts one day of teaching. Beginning with his entrance into Jerusalem (21:23) until he pronounces it desolate (23:38), Jesus, the legitimate teacher of God's will, challenges the Jewish leaders within the temple's sacred precincts.[17] The material consists of a controversy story about Jesus' authority, three parables of judgment on Israel, four controversy stories, and the woes on the scribes and Pharisees. Parables surround A Man Planted a Vineyard; first, the parable A Man Had Two Children and then A Man Gave a Banquet, with its addendum, The Wedding Garment. These three parables with their either-or structure support Matthew's ideology[18] of the true Israel, pitting the Christian church against Judaism.[19] His ideology leads him to read these three parables in a two-sided fashion. Negatively, they deprive Judaism of its claim to be the true Israel, and positively, they commend the church's claim.[20]

In the parable A Man Planted a Vineyard a salvation-history reading advances the negative aim. There are two sendings of servants. The first follows a triad: one they beat, one they killed, one they stoned;[21] the second simply repeats that "they did the same to them." Many see in the two sendings a reference to the former and latter prophets.[22] The reference in 23:24 to Jerusalem's killing and stoning of the prophets may confirm this. The killing of the son outside the vineyard[23] verifies the tenants' (i.e., Judaism's) evident unfitness to the claim to be the true Israel.

17. Meier, *Vision of Matthew*, 148.
18. Ideology is used in the sense of Uspensky (*Poetics of Composition*, 8).
19. Dillon, "Towards a Tradition-History," 14; Strecker, *Der Weg*, 111; Trilling, *Das wahre Israel*, 85; Schniewind, *Das Evangelium nach Matthäus*, 220.
20. Trilling, *Das wahre Israel*, 219.
21. Gundry, (*Matthew*, 426) notes that the *men . . . de . . . de* construction is a favorite of Matthew.
22. So Carlston, *Parables*, 41, with many references.
23. A change from Mark perhaps to conform to the known story of Jesus' death (i.e., that he was killed outside the walls of the city).

On the other hand, Matthew must demonstrate the Christian community's fitness to be the new Israel. One aspect of this is Matthew's eschatologically motivated ethics, the concern for "good fruits."[24] Servants are sent out first at the time of fruits (21:34), and the owner refers to his fruit. After the murder of the owner's son, the audience responds, "He will let out the vineyard to other tenants, who will give back to him the fruits in their times" (v. 41). In turn the concluding prophecy echoes that the vineyard will be given to other nations "doing its fruits" (v. 43).[25]

The Matthean performance of the parable climaxes in vv. 41–43, which denote Israel's guilt.[26] We have already noted the references to "fruit." The tenants are described as "evilly evil," *kakous kakōs*,[27] and in interpreting the Scripture quotation, Jesus identifies the vineyard with the kingdom so that the true Israel is the kingdom. Furthermore, the kingdom is to be taken away from "you," that is, Jesus' audience in the temple, and given to a nation (*ethnos*) producing fruits. The use of *ethnos* is significant. *Laos* is the normal word for "nation," meaning Israel, whereas *ethnos* refers to the Gentiles.[28] Finally, the audience for the parable is the chief priests and Pharisees, whereas in Mark it is the chief priests, scribes, and elders (Mark 11:27).

Matthew performs the parable similarly to Mark but with unique traits due to his theological position. Interestingly, he does not radically alter Mark's understanding but agrees on the parable's basic direction.

Luke: A Warning to Bureaucracy

Luke's presentation of this parable is again remarkably similar to Mark's but with distinctive accents and puzzling problems. The Lukan version poses a threat to Markan priority, because it is more restrained than Mark's. Is Luke dependent on Mark, or does he have a different version of the story? Although we are not able to answer these questions in any definitive fashion, we can show how Luke has understood or performed the underlying parabolic structure.

24. See Dillon, "Towards a Tradition-History," 9–10; Strecker, *Der Weg*, 185; Trilling, *Das wahre Israel*, 150. Gundry (*Matthew*, 425) has the statistical evidence on the use of *karpos* in Matthew.

25. Dillon ("Towards a Tradition-History," esp. 37) stresses this use of fruits by Matthew to highlight an ethical understanding of the parable, but he goes on to argue that its *Sitz im Leben* is the Matthean baptismal catechesis.

26. Trilling, *Das wahre Israel*, 55–56.

27. According to BDF, 488 (1) (a), this is a classical figure and an example of paronomasia.

28. So Schweizer, *Good News*, 414; Meier, *Vision of Matthew*, 150. But Dillon ("Towards a Tradition-History," 20) objects to the meaning "Gentiles" and rather sees the reference as being parallel to 1 Peter 2:9, where it means a holy nation. But minimally it certainly distinguishes what it refers to from Israel.

In Luke's Gospel, Jesus' ministry in Jerusalem is not segmented into days. Luke gives the impression that it took place over a longer period of time.[29] Though Jesus is obviously active in Jerusalem, Luke does not state so explicitly. At the entry, Jesus approaches Jerusalem (19:28), but the actual entrance is at Mount Olivet. Furthermore, Jesus' activity is in the temple, which is surely in Jerusalem, although Luke never calls this to his reader's attention (19:45, 47; 20:1).

After the entrance, Jesus draws near, sees the city, and weeps over it: "For the days shall come upon you, when your enemies will cast up a bank about you and surround you, and hem you in on every side, and dash you to the ground, you and your children within you, and they will not leave one stone upon another in you" (19:43–44). Luke also has no cursing of the fig tree, probably because he has begun Jesus' ministry in Jerusalem with its explicit condemnation.[30] Moreover, the trial before the high priest lacks an accusation about his destroying the temple.[31]

Hans Conzelmann has argued that this reluctance about Jerusalem relates to Luke's program of the delay of the Parousia. A Man Entrusts Property (19:11) opens with the distinction between the coming of the kingdom and Jesus' arrival in Jerusalem. In its allegory the king will return to destroy his enemies. The introduction warns a reader to dissociate Jerusalem from the king's final return. So also in A Man Planted a Vineyard, the Isaianic allusion identifying the vineyard with Israel is omitted because the owner's final punishment refers not to the destruction of Jerusalem but rather to the Parousia. For a reader, this final set of clues is completed in Luke 21, when after the prophecy of the destruction of Jerusalem, Jesus warns, "Take heed that you are not led astray, . . . and when you hear of wars and tumults, do not be terrified for this must first take place, but the end will not be at once" (Luke 21:8–9).

Not only would the Isaiah quotation conflict with Luke's agenda but the three sendings of a single servant avoid an identification with the prophets.[32] The reference to the owner's going into another country for a long time (v. 9b)[33] refers a reader to A Man Entrusts Property (19:12). Retrospection points to that previous parable as an example of how to read this parable.

The fictional auditors, when warned that the owner will come and destroy the vineyard, exclaim, "God forbid." The people's alarm sepa-

---

29. Conzelmann, *Theology of St. Luke*, 74. See, e.g., 19:47 ("teaching daily in the temple"); 21:1 (One day, as he was teaching . . .").

30. In Luke, the leaders of Judaism seek to destroy Jesus because of his teaching (19:47), not because of the cleansing of the temple (Mark 11:18).

31. Talbert, *Reading Luke*, 185.

32. Hauck (*Das Evangelium des Lukas*, 242) sees the Lukan simplification as the result of dramatic sensitivity. So also Crossan, *In Parables*, 88; Carlston, *Parables*, 78.

33. Grässer (*Das Problem*, 113) sees a clear reference to the delay of the Parousia.

rates them from their leaders, who at the parable's conclusion try "to lay hands on him at that very hour but they feared the people [*laos*]." Verse 18, peculiar to Luke, warns the religious establishment that it is doomed.[34]

The Lukan performance can ignore the vineyard as Israel, suppress the salvation-history reading, and use the parable as a selective condemnation of Israel's leaders, not the people.

Thomas: Lost Wisdom

In *Thomas* the allegorical references are less obvious and do not dominate the story line:

> He said, "There was a good man who owned a vineyard. He leased it to tenant farmers so that they might work it and he might collect produce [*karpos*] from them. He sent his servant so that the tenants might give him the produce [*karpos*] of the vineyard. They seized his servant and beat him, all but killing him. The servant went back and told his master. The master said, 'Perhaps [they] did not recognize [him].' He sent another servant. The tenants beat this one as well. Then the owner sent his son and said, 'Perhaps they will show respect to my son.' Because the tenants knew that it was he who was the heir [*kleronomos*] to the vineyard, they seized him and killed him. Let him who has ears hear." Jesus said, "Show me the stone which the builders have rejected. That one is the cornerstone" (*Gos. Thom.* 65–66).

Thomas's version has received attention primarily as an alternative to the Synoptic parable. Crossan has defended its originality, but others have argued against it.[35] What concerns us is how the parable functions in the *Gospel of Thomas*. Since *Thomas* has no narrative context, we must discern how to read the parable in its ideological context, and that context is a matter of debate.

Perhaps *Thomas* did not give the parable a salvation-history reading, since in Gnosticism a savior is not a suffering redeemer but a revealer.[36] At any rate, in *Thomas*, wisdom is the goal achieved apart from Jesus' death. The saying about the stone (*Gos. Thom.* 66) is separated from the parable by the saying "Let him who has ears hear," thereby severely muting the salvation-history reading. This does not prove dependence on the Synoptic Gospels but shows only that the interpretation evident therein predates both Thomas and the Synoptics.

34. Talbert (*Reading Luke*, 189) and Carlston (*Parables*, 80) both deal with the issue of the free quotation in v. 18.

35. Schoedel, "Parables in the Gospel of Thomas," 557–60; Snodgrass, "Wicked Husbandmen," 142–44.

36. Ménard, *L'évangile selon Thomas*, 167.

The master of the vineyard is called a "good man." Schoedel suggests that this underscores the master as a good God,[37] but Crossan sees it as a realistic description of a person who does not reckon with the tenants' "lethal intent."[38] It seems more probable that the man is "good" in order to block a reader's automatic identification of him as evil, especially given the conclusion of the preceding logion: "Businessmen and merchants will not enter the Places of My Father" (*Gos. Thom.* 64). The marker "good" alerts a reader to the character's true value. Moreover, since the man is not the vineyard's planter, as in the Synoptics, but its owner, a businessman who collects the profits, such a marker is doubly important.

At the conclusion of the sending of the first servant, he reports what has happened and the owner responds that "perhaps they did not recognize him." Likewise when the son is sent, the narrator reports that the tenants "knew" he was the heir. The parable's structure stresses the servant's report and the owner's reply,[39] with its theme of recognition and knowledge.[40] The story is a parable of failure to grasp wisdom.

Reconstruction: Originating Structure

In isolating the parable's originating structure we face several clear problems. First, among the Synoptic versions there is an evident literary relation. Those who adhere to the two-source theory assume Markan priority and go about their business.[41] But Robinson in a thorough review of the matter has concluded that the real problem is that no one version can be regarded throughout as the prototype, and so he has proposed a proto-Mark source.[42] When the *Gospel of Thomas* is considered, the issue becomes more complex. Even if the *Thomas* tradition is independent, it is not obvious that it is superior.[43] Its so-called simplicity could result from its wisdom ideology.

A second problem concerns the parable's consistent salvation-history interpretation, dominant in the Synoptics and evident even in *Thomas* with the quotation from Psalm 118. Dodd and then Jeremias have attempted to rid the parable of its allegorical taint, but their insistence on

37. Schoedel, "Parables in the Gospel of Thomas," 560. Ménard (*L'évangile selon Thomas,* 167) doubts this.
38. Crossan, *In Parables,* 94.
39. Ibid., 33–34.
40. Ménard interprets this in a gnostic direction (*L'évangile selon Thomas,* 166).
41. E.g., Crossan, *In Parables,* 86; Carlston, *Parables,* 178–79.
42. J. A. T. Robinson, "Parable of the Wicked Husbandmen," 455.
43. The problem with Crossan's argument for the priority of *Thomas* is that he does not attempt to understand the parable in the context of the Gospel. He assumes what he sets out to prove.

seeing Mark as having correctly situated the parable and on seeing the son as Jesus' reference to himself only reinforces the allegory. Jeremias admits that an audience would not grasp the reference to the son as Jesus. Why then tell the parable? Its meaning would be obvious to no one except the teller, in which case it would be only after the resurrection that the early church could understand it.[44]

In response to this situation, some interpreters have maintained that the parable/allegory is a product of the early church. Kümmel argues that no Jew on hearing of the son's murder would have applied it to the sending of the messiah.[45] The salvation-history understanding is so great, so strong, that these critics can understand the parable only as the early church's invention.

Crossan has mounted a strong argument for the authenticity of the *Thomas* version. Although his arguments are not compelling (since he did not sufficiently account for the possibility of a wisdom/gnostic reading), he has segregated those elements from the originating structure that have irritated and disturbed the allegorical telling. More important, he has developed a convincing history of the allegory's development. We will now examine the originating structure.

The Vineyard

In both Matthew and Mark the vineyard's description alludes to Isa. 5:2–3. The vineyard metaphor is frequent in the Hebrew Bible but usually in the context of judgment,[46] and the contest is not over the vineyard, as in this story, but over the fruit of the vineyard, as in the Isaiah passage.[47] Though the identification of Israel fits the salvation-history allegory, the quotation is formulaic and allusive and so could be naturally attracted as a result of the church's use of the parable to interpret what happened to Jesus.[48] Crossan prefers the *Thomas* version, with its good man who owns a vineyard, but as we indicated above, that could well be due to ideology and the context in *Thomas*. It seems more likely that the originating parable involved a man who planted a vineyard and let it out to tenants and then left. "Planting" would suggest eventually the Isaiah

---

44. Newell and Newell ("Parable of the Wicked Tenants," 231) gives a list of those who follow Dodd's and Jeremias's semiallegorical understanding. Add to their list now Lambrecht, *Once More Astonished*, 130; Hengel, "Das Gleichnis," 1–39.

45. Kümmel, "Das Gleichnis," 130; idem, *Promise and Fulfillment*, 83. See also Bultmann, *History of the Synoptic Tradition*, 177; Carlston, *Parables*, 187; Beare, *Gospel according to Matthew*, 428.

46. Ps. 80:8; Jer. 2:21; 12:10; Ezek. 15:1, 6; 19:10; Hosea 10:1.

47. Crossan, *In Parables*, 87.

48. So Jeremias, *Parables*, 71.

allusion, given the salvation-history ideology. The departure theme is part of the form associated with steward-master parables.

The Sendings

The simple sending of a single servant, twice, argues for the originality of *Thomas*. With the sending of the son, there are three sendings. The single servant is more realistic, and the three sendings follow the law of three common to parables.[49] According to Robinson, the Markan text can be explained from *Thomas*, but not vice versa.[50] Before concluding that *Thomas* is superior, it should be noted (against Crossan) that the strong parallel between the sendings of the first servant and of the son may be due to ideology. Furthermore, it is precisely in the sending that the reteller of the tale probably has the most freedom of expression. This is the point in the structure for elaboration (cf. the excuses of those invited to the feast in A Man Gave a Banquet). One should be cautious in overreconstructing the sendings.[51] There were probably two sendings of single servants, and the servants were at least beaten. This much is certain and is necessary for the tale's narrative structure. In the Synoptics, the alignment of the sendings with the fate of the prophets has produced a riot of violence that leaves the owner's behavior not only foolish but incomprehensible.

The sending of the son and the response of the tenants are clearly the climax. Given the allegory, Jesus becomes a clear model for the son. Referring to the son as beloved is probably part of the formulaic tendency of oral tradition. Whether the casting-out of the son from the vineyard belongs to the originating structure is unclear. The lack of burial could be the final insult, or it could be a reference to the last act of the crime, a theme associated with Jesus' death in the early kerygmatic speeches of Acts.[52]

The notes about respect and inheritance are problematic for an allegorical reading. Although Jesus can be viewed as an heir (cf. Heb. 1:2), what, as Crossan asks, can respect for the son and inheritance for the tenants mean in the allegory?[53] The real issue is the tenants' motivation: how can they possibly hope to inherit? Crossan pointedly notes that if the story is a created allegory, why create one that fits so poorly?

In the originating structure a father sent his son because they would

49. Crossan, *In Parables*, 94; J. A. T. Robinson, "Parable of the Wicked Husbandmen," 446; Jeremias, *Parables*, 71.

50. J. A. T. Robinson, "Parable of the Wicked Husbandmen," 446.

51. Via, *Parables*, 134.

52. Fuller, *Formation*, 54–55—referring to Acts 13:29.

53. Crossan, *In Parables*, 88.

respect him, and tenants killed the heir because they sought his inheritance. As Crossan argues, the motivation involved is the crux of interpretation.

The Ending

For most commentators who hold that there is an original parable supporting the Synoptic versions, the ending is the question and answer about the master's response to the murder of his son.[54] But normally Jesus does not answer the questions provoked by his parables.[55] Even more telling is Crossan's question: How can an impotent master suddenly become powerful? He sees the question coming from the mission to the Gentiles and the failure of the Jewish mission (i.e., as part of the salvation-history ideology). The lack of such a question in *Thomas* confirms Crossan's observation.[56] It is also a normal response by a reader/performer to expect a master to punish, given the expectations of a patron-client culture. Once the master is identified as God, his response is demanded. One must, therefore, agree with Crossan. The originating structure did not have the question and answer. It lacked such final closure. Even though subsequent performances have given it closure, closure jars with the parable's characterization of the master while conforming to the ideology's.

There is wide and general consensus that the quotation from Psalm 118 is not part of the originating structure.[57] But it is worth noting the effect of the quotation, for it provides for the resurrection of Jesus outside the story. The use of this proof text about the rejected stone's becoming the cornerstone—popular in the repertoire of the early church—turns a story of defeat into one of triumph! The restoration of the son outside the story allows the allegorization within the story to take place.[58]

A Reading

Line 1:   A man planted a vineyard and gave it out to farmers and left home.

The first line sets conditions for the parable's encounter, alerting a

---

54. E.g., Dodd, *Parables*, 97.
55. So admits Dodd.
56. Crossan, *In Parables*, 90.
57. Carlston, *Parables*, 180 n. 14. Carlston gives a long list of those rejecting the Psalm quotation. This quotation also betrays the influence of the LXX. See Jeremias, *Parables*, 74; B. T. D. Smith, *Parables*, 224.
58. Crossan, *In Parables*, 90–91.

hearer to its repertoire. The owner's leaving the vineyard in the care of others and his departure warn a hearer to expect a future accounting. *Thomas* has no departure but makes explicit the expectation of an accounting: the tenants are to work the land, and the owner is to receive the proper fruit. The man is an absentee landlord.[59] After setting up the vineyard, he leaves it in the hands of others.[60] As such he is potentially a negative character. *Thomas* counters this with the note that he was "good."

In all steward parables the basic metaphorical structure is a test of stewardship. Both Matthew and Mark have interpreted the vineyard (the thing entrusted to stewardship) with a midrash on Isa. 5:1–2. Interpreting the vineyard as Israel is certainly one way to fill in the gap, but originally it was left blank.

> *Line 2:* When the time came, he sent a servant to the farmers to get from them some fruit of the vineyard. And they took him and beat him and sent him away empty.

The sending of the servant has occasioned extensive elaboration. The point of the originating structure was the servant's rejection and mistreatment. A storyteller had a good deal of freedom to ad-lib in the actual telling.

The parable leaves a large gap between the master's departure and the first sending. We are not told any details of the contract between master and tenants, although *Thomas* implies one. The time between planting the vineyard and the first payment was probably about five years,[61] so there is a considerable lapse.

The shocking aspect of this line is first that the tenants refuse to pay rent, breaking the implied contract. Then they mistreat the servant. Since he is a stand-in for the master, it is the same as mistreating the master himself. The master has the acquired honor consistent with his economic and social power. In a shame-honor culture like that of the first-century Mediterranean basin, it is expected that the tenants will challenge his honor.[62] Frequently the bargaining associated with a contract is really part of a shame-honor challenge. Or as in A Rich Man Had

---

59. Matthew calls him an *oikodespotēs*, employing a favorite term of his. See also Gundry, *Matthew*, 424.

60. *Apedēmēsein* means "to leave home," "to take a trip abroad." So Hengel, "Das Gleichnis," 21. But see Leon-Dufour, "La parabole des vignerons homicides," 318. Contrary to Jeremias (*Parables*, 75) and Dodd (*Parables*, 97), there is no reason for him to be a foreigner. See also Michaelis, *Die Gleichnisse*, 117.

61. Derrett, *Law in the New Testament*, 290.

62. For the challenge-response model, see Malina, *New Testament World*, 30–39; Pitt-Rivers, *Fate of Shechem*, chap. 1.

a Steward, a rogue's activity is a challenge to the master's honor. But here tenants challenge the master's honor with a physical insult. He must judge an appropriate response to maintain his honor. In the *Thomas* version this is explicit when the master says, "They did not recognize him [the servant]," implying that had they recognized him they would have accorded him the appropriate honor.

An audience awaits the master's response. The provocation has been extreme. A response is expected at two levels. At the level of shame and honor the master must calculate an appropriate response to maintain his honor. In narrative logic, the beating of the servant invalidates the implied contract of producing fruit and demands that the master reinstate the contact.

Line 3: He sent another servant and they beat him.

A second sending reiterates the first with another rejection. Storytellers are free to develop this sending as they see fit.

The master has miscalculated. His response to the challenge is insufficient to maintain his honor, and in the audience's eyes the tenants have shamed him. Mark makes this plain when he remarks that the tenants have "dishonored" the servant. Not only has the master miscalculated but now his honor, doubly scorned and insulted, demands vengeance. The audience's calculation at this point is that the master is probably a fool.

Line 4: Then the master sent his son, saying, "They will respect my son."

The master realizes the shame-honor challenge when he hopes that the tenants will "respect my son."[63] His strategy is that his honor as represented by his son will bring the tenants to their senses. Given their response in lines 2 and 3, an audience cannot be sure. Is the owner a fool, as lines 2 and 3 imply, or will his strategy work?

Line 5: But those farmers said to one another, "This is the heir; come, let us kill him, and the inheritance will be ours." And they took him and killed him.

Again the master miscalculates and with tragic results, for he loses his honor, his vineyard, and his son. The parable leaves unspoken whether this is the story's end, although it is the end of the narrative. The man could reclaim his vineyard through some ultimate act of vengeance,

---

63. See the parallel phrase in the parable In a City There Was a Judge (chap. 6 above).

though not his full honor nor his dead son. The tenants' legal claim to the vineyard is shaky, to say the least.[64] In this final line they change the narrative thrust. Until now they have refused only to pay the rent; now they claim the inheritance by murdering the son. His murder marks an escalation in the plot.

The allegorical interpretation has opted to end the story with the owner's wreaking his vengeance on the tenants. The quotation from Ps. 118:22 restores the son to life, so as fully to restore the father to honor.

But the critical question is why the tenants believed the inheritance could be theirs. Here the parable's verisimilitude breaks down. For a hearer the story ends with a foolish master, devoid of vineyard, honor, and son. The vineyard is in the hands of the shameless.

From Story to Kingdom: The Inheritance

The story invokes from the repertoire several metaphorical possibilities that have given it rich performances within the tradition. The planting of the vineyard, renting to tenants, and departure of the master all denote a form of master-servant parable which invokes the metaphorical network of the master's departure as the occasion of a test. But the tenants subvert the story into a test of the master. His failure in the story to regain his vineyard ultimately sets the narrative on a tragic trajectory. Ironically, the tenants maintain control of the thing with which they were entrusted, the vineyard, at the master's expense. Given the political situation and the audience's tendency to identify with the tenants, this parable creates for its hearer extreme frustration. In contrast to A Rich Man Had a Steward, in which the steward's action is sanctioned by the audience as that of a rogue getting even with an absentee landlord, here the tenants behave outrageously, escalating violence at every point. The violence culminates with the ill-conceived plot to become heirs by killing the son.

An item for potential development in the story is the vineyard as metaphor for Israel. But this remains undeveloped, for the story does not deal with the fruits of the vineyard, a normal move in this form of the repertoire. The vineyard is suggestive since it raises the expectation on the hearer's part that the narrative will develop metaphorical interrelations between the characters of the story as they deal with the vineyard, the thing entrusted. The narrative, however, consistently blocks identification, disorientating any metaphorical transfer. The

64. See Bammel, "Das Gleichnis," 14; Hengel, "Das Gleichnis," 30. Even given the unstable political situation in Galilee at the time, no law of inheritance would ever substantiate the claim of the tenants. So also Carlston, *Parables*, 184.

story's primary characters are the owner and tenants.[65] There are two possible references for the owner, God and Israel, and likewise two for the tenants, Rome and Israel. The parable's narrative frustrates any combination of identification. If God is the owner, then God fails to reclaim the vineyard. Or if Israel is the owner, then that nation fails in its restoration. Likewise, if the Romans are the tenants (i.e., occupiers), then they remain in possession, and if Israel is the tenants, then it is in opposition to the true owner. All these elaborations of the potential and implied metaphorical structure involve unacceptable conclusions. There is no way to work it out, to produce a convincing configuration of the story's fragments. The parable frustrates not only allegory but also any effort to make sense of it!

The story frustrates metaphorical referencing and consistency building, thus creating an alienating and defamiliarizing experience that blocks closure and resolution, forcing upon a hearer the one item that stands out: the tenants' recognition of the son as *heir* and their proposal to gain the *inheritance*. This makes no sense at the level of narrative structure, because it is impossible. The prominence of "inheritance" at the parable's end suggests its importance. This theme operates at the level not of narrative structure but of symbolic discourse, calling on another element of the repertoire.

Many commentators have noticed the similarity between the tenants' statement "Come, let us kill him" and that of the brothers of Joseph, "Come, now, let us kill him" (Gen. 37:20), but they have been unable to make sense of it.[66] This is a form of intertextuality, echoing a well-known story. The theme of inheritance and a contest over inheritance is prominent in the Hebrew Bible. The classic story is that of Esau and Jacob, in which Jacob tricks his father into giving him Esau's portion of the inheritance.[67] In Jeremiah the portion of Jacob becomes God:

> Not like these is he who is the portion of Jacob,
> For he is the one who formed all things,
> And Israel is the tribe of his inheritance;
> The Lord of hosts is his name.
> (Jer. 10:16)

By alluding to the patriarchal story the parable questions whether the kingdom will surely go to the promised heirs. Since the parable provides

---

65. The servants and the son are extensions of the owner.
66. E.g., Taylor, *Gospel according to Saint Mark*, 475.
67. See C. Montefiore and Loewe, *Rabbinic Anthology*, 686. Esau is generally wicked and identified with Rome in rabbinic allegories, because Herod, a friend of Rome, was an Idumean, (esau = edom, Gen. 36:43). See also A Man Had Two Sons (chap. 2 above) for an elaboration of the two-sons tradition.

no ready identification models, no clear metaphorical referencing, an audience is left in a precarious position: *In the plot the kingdom fails and the inheritance is in doubt.* Thwarted is the mytheme's power to draw a sure map, to identify to whom comes the inheritance. To whom does the inheritance belong? Who has the power to claim it?

The parable's frustrated closure shifts the focus from the kingdom's predictable apocalyptic victory, to the kingdom as an object of tragedy. A parallel to this parable is Matt. 11:12: "From the days of John the Baptist the kingdom of heaven is breaking out by violence and violent men are raping it."[68] The Matthean saying reminds us that violence is an element of the kingdom, but the parable highlights the kingdom as an object of violence. The owner is a fool, the tenants are bandits, and the messengers are beaten or murdered. In this way this parable resembles another parable: From Jerusalem to Jericho. The man in the ditch is beaten and left for dead. His only salvation comes from a Samaritan, his mortal enemy. Like Jesus' association with the outcast, this parable challenges the predictability of the kingdom's heirs as good and the apocalyptic assumption that the kingdom's true heirs will in the end triumph. In the parable, the final fate of the vineyard is unresolved because the owner is still alive, but no evidence is given for its eventual liberation. The owner's fate may be that of his son.

The Church's Allegory

At one level the early church's performance of the parable within the context of salvation history seizes on the inheritance motif and interprets it as confirming the illegitimacy of the tenants. As such, it follows out one element of the parable's trajectory in a different context. But the attempt to overcome the death of the son and to use the allegory apocalyptically to predict the destruction of the tenants falls victim to the reemergence of the mytheme with which Jesus is at odds. From the vantage point of the parable, Jesus' resurrection does not overcome death but confirms God's willingness to pay the price.

68. See my *Jesus, Symbol-Maker*, 145–48.

11

*M*aster's Praise

A Rich Man Had a Steward

A certain man was rich who had a steward. And this one was hostilely accused to him as squandering his goods. And calling he said to him, "Give in the account of your stewardship for you are no longer able to be steward." The steward said to himself, "What shall I do because my master is separating the stewardship from me? To dig I am not strong enough; to beg I am ashamed. I know what I shall do in order that when I am removed from the stewardship they will receive me into their houses." And calling together each one of the debtors of his master, he said to the first, "How much do you owe my master?" And he said, "A hundred measures of oil." And he said to him, "Take your bill and sit down quickly and write fifty." Then to another he said, "How much do you owe?" He said, "A hundred measures of wheat." He said to him, "Take your bill and write eighty." And the master praised the unjust steward for he acted prudently.

The master's praise for his unjust steward has created confusion, controversy, and embarrassment[1] in the interpretation of the parable A Rich

---

1. See Derrett, "Fresh Light on St. Luke XVI. I. The Parable of the Unjust Steward," 199 n. 2 (= *Law in the New Testament*, 48–77). Derrett lists several authors who remark

Man Had a Steward.[2] How could the master praise the servant? What is the master praising? What in the steward's behavior is unjust? Finally, is the master's praise the parable's conclusion or its penultimate conclusion, or is it even part of the originating parabolic structure?[3] Verse 8a is a key to understanding the parable, so we will begin by examining, under three aspects, how it relates to the parable: we will look at the ending from a stylistic perspective, the economic background presupposed by the story, and the structural narrative model.

How Does It End?

There is no unanimity about the parable's conclusion, although several commentators have maintained that v. 8a is the conclusion.[4] The argument turns on the referent of *ho kyrios*, "lord" or "master"—is it Jesus or the master in the story? Jeremias's argument typifies those which see Jesus as the referent.[5] For him the original parable ended at v. 7. Jeremias's argument is twofold: (1) It is not believable that a master would have praised the servant, therefore *ho kyrios* must refer to someone other than the master. (2) On analogy with Luke 18:6, *ho kyrios* is Luke's way of referring to Jesus.[6] In Jeremias's reconstruction, v. 8 was originally

on the parable's puzzling or embarrassing character. Topel ("On the Injustice of the Unjust Steward," 216 nn. 1, 2) provides a classification of significant literature on the parable. Unfortunately, owing to homoeoteleuton, in the references Derrett's article was confused with Fletcher's "Riddle of the Unjust Steward." Via's discussion (*Parables*, 155–62) and the exchange between Crossan and Via (*Semeia* 1:31–33, 124, 206–8) should be added to Topel's list.

2. See Dodd's often quoted remark in *Parables*, 17: "We can almost see here notes for three separate sermons on the parable as text."

3. We are concerned not with the parable's redactional usage but with its functioning in the corpus of Jesus' language. Most recent literature has been concerned with its redactional use.

4. See Via, *Parables*, 156; Topel, "On the Injustice," 218; Fitzmyer, "Story of the Dishonest Manager," 27–28; Fuchs, "L'évangile et l'argent," 4–5. Crossan (*In Parables*, 109) argues that the parable ends at v. 7. Merkelback ("Über das Gleichnis," 180–87) maintains that vv. 8–9 are part of the parable and should be read as questions demanding a negative answer. Barth ("Dishonest Steward," 64–65) sees vv. 9–13 as Jesus' comment on the parable, which in turn is a commentary on Matt. 10:16b.

5. Jeremias, *Parables*, 45–47. See also Fitzmyer, "Story of the Dishonest Manager," 27; Topel, "On the Injustice," 218 n. 10. Both Fitzmyer and Topel provide summaries of various positions.

6. The statistical evidence: Luke uses *kyrios* eighty times (Mark, fifteen times; Matthew, seventy-six times). The word refers to God eighteen times, of which ten are quotations from the Old Testament. It refers to "master" (but not Jesus) twenty-one times, of which sixteen are in parables. It refers to Jesus forty-one times, twenty-five times in material only to be found in Luke, eight in material common to the Synoptics, and eight where the parallel text does not have *kyrios*. The evidence for Matthew is somewhat similar; see Förster, "*kyrios*," 1093. Actually, the more significant question is Mark's restraint.

Jesus' own interpretation of the parable but Luke later inserted *ho kyrios* into the verse as a reference to Jesus. Jeremias must argue that Jesus is responsible for all of v. 8, because if the conclusion is only the first half of the verse, Jesus praises an unjust steward. In v. 8b, Jesus, commenting on his own parable, points to the commendation's correct understanding: it is the prudence of the children of this world in their affairs with others, not their relations with God, that is the point of comparison.[7]

Jeremias's arguments are forced and strained. Joseph Fitzmyer has pointed out that it is more natural to understand *ho kyrios* in v. 8a as referring to the master of the story, because without it the story has no ending. From the story's beginning one expects the master to respond.[8] A natural reading would understand the final *kyrios* as the same *kyrios* of vv. 3 and 5. Only after the change of subject in v. 9 ("But I say") might one identify the *kyrios* of v. 8 with Jesus. Finally, Fitzmyer believes that v. 8b is not part of the original story, because "it actually reads like a generalizing commentary on the parable,"[9] common in the oral tradition.

Fitzmyer bases his rejection of Jeremias's position implicitly on the parable's narrative possibilities. He refuses to accept as a valid argument what Jesus could or could not have said. Even more, he calls attention to the natural need for narrative closure, even if the closure is not what one expects.

Jeremias's proposed parallel with Luke 18:6 is also not so clear as he supposes. In that parable the judge's response to the widow's persistence creates narrative closure. In v. 6, the Lord calls attention to what the judge has said to draw a correspondence with the application in v. 7. The next verse begins, "I tell you [*legō hymin*],"[10] which indicates the story's actual point. A similar pattern occurs in both the parable A Man Entrusts Property (Luke 19:12–28) and the saying on watchful servants (Luke 12:35–37).[11] At the conclusion of A Man Entrusts Property, the

---

7. Jeremias, *Parables*, 46. Via (*Parables*, 156) also understands Jeremias in this fashion.

8. Fitzmyer, "Story of the Dishonest Manager," 27; in support, Topel, "On the Injustice, 218. By maintaining that the master could not praise the servant, Jeremias assumes what needs to be proved and eliminates the unexpected from the art of storytelling.

9. Fitzmyer, "Story of the Dishonest Manager," 28.

10. *Legō hymin* is a Lukan formula. The normal formula in Matthew and Mark is *amēn legō hymin*, but that occurs in Luke only five times, of which three are parallel to occurrences in other Synoptics. In other parallel passages, Luke drops the *amēn* (fifteen times). The *legō hymin* formula occurs in fourteen passages found only in Luke. Five times it appears in passages parallel to Matthew.

11. The *legō hymin* formula is also used to draw attention to the application in the parables Who Has a Friend? (11:8), A Man Gave a Banquet (14:24), A Man with a Hundred Sheep (15:7), A Woman with Ten Drachmas (15:10), and Two Men Went Up to the Temple (18:14). In both the parables A Grain of Mustard Seed (13:18) and The Leaven (13:20), Luke uses the comparative verb in the first person (*homoiosō*).

disciples ask the Lord about its ending.[12] He responds, "I say to you [*legō hymin*]" and then provides a generalizing application. Similarly, in the saying on watchful servants: "Blessed are those servants whom the master [*ho kyrios*] finds awake when he comes; truly I say to you [*amēn legō hymin*], he will gird himself and have them sit at table, and he will come and serve them." In all three cases where there is a *kyrios* in the story, Luke provides clear clues to the reader for a change of subject.[13] In Luke 16:8–9 a clear change in subject does not occur until v. 9, from third-person narration to first- and second-person address. Thus Luke probably understood the narrative as ending at v. 8, with *kyrios* referring to the master and the application beginning in v. 9. The application is really to v. 8b.[14]

The stylistic argument clearly indicates that Luke received the parable with v. 8 as the conclusion. Since v. 8b was added during oral transmission, is it likely that v. 8a was also a hearer's response to the parable? Via's observation on this matter is on target. Why would the oral tradition have appended a statement that Jesus praised the steward?[15] Via sees v. 8b as trying to relieve the parable's tension by pointing the reader somewhere else. Thus we can conclude on the basis of internal stylistic evidence that the parable originally concluded with the master praising an unjust steward.

Others have tried to resolve the story's provocation by viewing it against its economic background.[16] In Palestine, a steward acted for his master as an agent capable of making binding agreements. What is more, a steward customarily made a profit by adding a share for himself to any debt owed his master. Since loans were frequently usurious and

12. The textual witnesses for v. 25 are problematic. Nestle and Aland (*Novum Testamentum Graece*) include the verse. Metzger (*Textual Commentary*, 169) gives the reading a "C," indicating considerable doubt. The United Bible Socieities' committee includes the verse because its omission from some manuscripts has seemed to result from a tendency to assimilate toward Matthew and an "attempt to provide a closer connection between vv. 24 and 26."

13. Luke may intend a double meaning or a play on words. At the level of Luke's fictional narrative in which Jesus is addressing an audience, *kyrios* refers to the master. This the stylistic evidence about Lukan usage clearly indicates. But at a second level, at which the implied author and the implied reader share an omniscient viewpoint, the referent could be Jesus.

14. Topel ("On the Injustice," 219) sees v. 8b as an explicit application by the oral tradition and v. 9 as the beginning of Luke's application. I essentially agree with this, only I may case on stylistic grounds.

15. Via, *Parables*, 156. Jeremias's argument that Luke inserted *kyrios* (which we disproved on stylistic grounds above) also cannot meet Via's argument. Why would Luke have drawn attention to v. 8a?

16. Fitzmyer ("Story of the Dishonest Manager," 34–35) makes the best argument for this position. He in turn is highly dependent on the work of Derrett in "Fresh Light on the Unjust Steward."

therefore against Jewish law, it was common practice to state the debt in terms of some commodity (e.g., wheat or oil).[17] Accordingly, when the steward is dismissed from his master's employ, he is not cheating the master by reducing the debts but forgoing his own profit in return for future upkeep. The master praises the steward for his decisive action in a time of emergency, and the accusation of being unjust refers to some prior action.[18]

This line of argument is ultimately unconvincing. In vv. 5 and 7, the debt is clearly owed to the master.[19] Even more, the steward is not called unjust until the parable's final line. The master praises the steward for his prudence (*phronimōs*) while calling him unjust (*adikia*),[20] indicating a relation between the two. This serves once again to call attention back to the parable's narrative.

Crossan has put forward a structural-narrative argument.[21] Crossan accepts Derrett's economic reconstruction in part but sees the narrative developing as follows. The steward fails to gain for his master sufficient profits and so is threatened with the loss of his stewardship. In response he cancels his part of the agreed-on return (here following Derrett) in hopes of being taken in by the debtors after his dismissal. Crossan concludes that when vv. 2 and 5–7 "are read together . . . one has a picture of laziness organizing itself under crisis."[22] For him there is no need for v. 8a. The parable ends "adequately" without it.

If this were all there were to Crossan's argument, the positions advanced above in support of v. 8a would be telling. But he has introduced a new element. He sees this story (in dependence on Via; see below) as belonging to a cycle of trickster-dupe stories. He follows Heda Jason's model for such stories:[23]

1. (*a*) A situation evolves which enables a rascal to play a trick on a dupe.
   (*b*) The dupe reveals his foolishness so that the rascal can exploit it.
2. The rascal plans a trick.
3. The rascal plays a trick.
4. The dupe reacts as the rascal wishes him to do.
5. The dupe loses, and the rascal wins.

The parable is a trickster tale, with steps 4 and 5 unused. The master/

17. Derrett, "Fresh Light on the Unjust Steward," 212.
18. Fitzmyer, "Story of the Dishonest Manager," 31–33.
19. So Maas, "Das Gleichnis," 179.
20. Topel, "On the Injustice," 218.
21. Crossan, "Servant Parables," 17–62; idem, "Structuralist Analysis," 192–221.
22. Crossan "Servant Parables," 33.
23. I have modified the diagram from Crossan's "Structural Analysis," 202. For a full listing of the model's functions, see Jason, *Narrative Structure*, 7.

dupe reveals his foolishness by allowing a steward/rascal to carry out his own dismissal.

Crossan has oversimplified the narrative in two ways. (1) The parable is not simply a trickster-dupe narrative. The trickster narrative is a subplot (or subnarrative) in what is initiated as an accounting story. The master's accounting is complete only in v. 8a. The trickster subplot is a response to the master's negative judgment in v. 2. Without v. 8a there is no closure of the main plot.[24] (2) Crossan has confused the demands of a formal model with the actual story (the formal model's investment). A formal model (like Jason's) indicates how most stories of this type operate. But a chief characteristic of art is to vary or play on the model, to juxtapose the familiar against the unfamiliar.[25]

The parable surface structure builds around an initial accounting, the servant's response, and then the master's response. The servant's response is itself a subplot drawn from the repertoire of trickster-dupe stories in which the servant attempts to overturn the master's accounting. The final response of the master completes the original accounting.

A Reading

Line 1:   A certain man was rich who had a steward.

All stories draw on a repertoire[26] of genres, literary techniques, social expectations, cultural conventions, and so forth, that make a narrative lifelike. Line 1 invokes elements from the social repertoire of the patron-client model in which a rich man and a steward represent values for a hearer. Since the master is rich—a redundant marker if he has a steward to look after his property—he may well play the role of antagonist. In the world of Galilean peasants, rich masters play the expected role of despots, and the master in this story may be an absentee landlord, a common phenomenon in Galilee.[27] Jesus' parables frequently exploit the inequality existing in a patron-client society with a stereotyped animosity between masters and servants. Luke 7:25 can stand for a summary of the attitude of the *'am ha 'arets* (the people of the land) toward the rich: "What then did you go out to see? A man clothed in soft raiment?

---

24. Via, "Parable and Example Story," 124.
25. Ibid.
26. See p. 36 above.
27. So Jeremias, *Parables*, 181. For a discussion of absentee landlords in Galilee, see pp. 74–75, esp. n. 97. Jeremias quotes an aphorism from the Mishnah which indicates how extensive the phenomenon was. The saying deals with the assignment of property to princes: "The people of Galilee need not assign their share, since their fathers have done so for them already" (*m. Ned.* 5.5 [Danby, 271]). Hengel (*Die Zeloten*, 89) indicates that the pervasiveness of absentee landlords drew the people to the side of the zealots.

Behold, those who are gorgeously appareled and live in luxury are in kings' courts" (RSV). Line 1, drawing from a repertoire of social expectation, casts the man in a predetermined role: being rich distances and alienates him from a hearer who expects him to behave in a stereotyped manner.

Line 2:   And this one [the steward] was hostilely accused to him as squandering his goods.

The Greek word for "was accused"—*dieblēthē*—is a morpheme of *diabolos*, "devil." Johannes Bauer says it signifies "to bring charges with hostile intent."[28] W. Förster gives numerous examples of the word's negative sense, indicating that it is difficult "to distinguish between *diabellein* and 'to calumniate.'"[29] Then, like most commentators, he rejects the negative sense in the Lukan parable.[30] Yet there are several good arguments in support of the negative sense. First, it is the normal meaning of *diabellein*. Second, Derrett has noticed that a master would dismiss a steward by "the heaping up of reproaches, and blackening of his character."[31] That is what *diabellein* describes. These two reasons warrant a strong argument against abandoning the negative sense.

The hostile intent of the accusation causes both retrospection and anticipation.[32] It confirms the previous negative impression of the rich man and highlights the steward's precarious position. His fate evokes sympathy, a motive for identification. Similarly, one anticipates that the steward will respond to the accusation by laying out a defense. A hearer's ability to anticipate action is important. One must know a story (repertoire) to understand it. The accusation against the steward offers many narrative possibilities (see fig. 4).[33]

28. BAGD, 181. LSJ, 389–90, summarizes the section heading for *diabellō* as "*attack a man's character, calumniate.*"

29. Förster, "*diabellō*, 71.

30. "There is no necessary thought of calumniation" (Förster, "*diabellō*," 71). In rejecting the negative sense, Fitzmyer ("Story of the Dishonest Manager," 31 n. 19) says, "But this meaning does not suit the context. The manager did not try to defend himself, and his subsequent conduct would be illogical if he had not been guilty." I will argue that this is not necessarily the case. The problem here is similar to that of v. 8a, the presumption of what can be. The real reason for rejecting the pejorative sense is the allegorical identification of the master with God.

31. Derrett, "Fresh Light on the Unjust Steward," 203.

32. See Iser, *Implied Reader*, 290–91.

33. For the theory, see Bremond, "Logic of Narrative Possibilities," 387–411. Several of Jesus' parables follow this narrative logic. In A King Wished to Settle Accounts, trial leads to nonpunishmnent and concludes in punishment. In the parable In a City There Was a Judge, the widow requests a trial, the judge responds with a nontrial but eventually moves to success. The accounting scenes of A Man Entrusts Property present a binary on this pattern. In the two scenes of the successful servants, the test leads to trial, which leads to success, and thus the binary of punishment and reward. In the

Figure 4

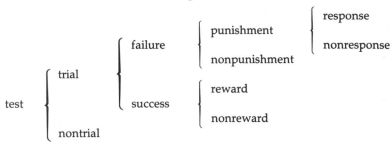

These narrative possibilities are part of the repertoire of conventions that inform a hearer about what to expect in narrative action. How a model of narrative expectations is implemented involves the storyteller's skill and artistry.

Line 3: And calling he said to him, "Give in the account of your stewardship for you are no longer able to be steward."

The rich man's response aligns him with the accusers, and he lives up to the repertoire's expectation. Such is what rich men do; fiction imitates reality. The rich man's action confirms that the story reflects the world of the lower classes. In terms of narrative expectation (see fig. 4), there is no trial; instead the story jumps immediately to failure and punishment. The steward gains sympathy and identification since he has no opportunity to explain his actions, to respond to his accusers, or even to know what the accusations are, except that he has supposedly scattered the master's property abroad.[34] The apparently arbitrary and summary judgment by the rich man only confirms a hearer's expectations.

Line 4: The steward said to himself, "What shall I do because my master is separating the stewardship from me?

By entering into the steward's mind, an audience takes up his perspective and begins to identify with him.[35] The steward's reference to the rich man as "my master," a term accentuating social distance ("master") and dependency ("my"), continues the process. Stewardship is not simply "taken away." The Greek *aphairetai* uses the metaphor to cut off, to tear away—a matter of violence.

one-talent man's scene he seeks nontrial when he attempts to return the talent to the master. The master responds with trial, failure, and punishment.

34. Topel, "On the Injustice," 217 n. 7. His accusation hardly squares with Derrett's suggestion that he is making an excessive (usurious) profit.

35. The issue of Luke's fondness for interior monologues is dealt with in chap. 3 above.

Line 5: "To dig I am not strong enough; to beg I am ashamed.

As the steward plots a course of action, his own character emerges. Identification with him to this point has depended on the rich master's negative image. Expectations about his character result from rejecting the rich man. But now expectations are frustrated. By admitting that he lacks the strength to dig and is ashamed to beg, he distances himself from the hearer. In his stewardship he has taken on the airs of the rich, forcing a hearer to reflect on the estimation of the steward.

Line 6: "I know[36] what I shall do in order that when I am removed from the stewardship they will receive me into their houses." And calling together each one of the debtors of his master, he said to the first, "How much do you owe my master?" And he said, "A hundred measures of oil." And he said to him, "Take your bill and sit down quickly and write fifty." Then to another he said, "How much do you owe?" He said, "A hundred measures of wheat." He said to him, "Take your bill and write eighty."

The servant's remark that he can neither dig nor beg leads to the expectation of a counterplot (see fig. 4, "response"). But how does a hearer respond to the steward's actions? Via has argued that the actions of the steward belong to a "picaresque comedy . . . the story of a successful rogue."[37] The steward can play the rogue because previously his master has been painted in villainous terms. To use Via's phrase, the hearer can go on a moral holiday at the master's expense. A rogue is getting even. The rogue pattern, drawn from the repertoire of literary conventions, provides a hearer with a way of making sense (forming a consistency) of the steward's actions. The one who refuses to beg or dig is a rogue, and the rich man is getting what he deserves. Now it is apparent why the steward's interior monologue is important. Drawing a hearer into the steward's subjectivity makes identification possible. With the rogue the audience experiences getting even.

We can now observe the effect of the servant's remark about digging and begging. That remark was the audience's first opportunity to consider the steward directly. Until then the only direct portrayal had been the master's. The refusal to dig or to beg not only sets up the rogue subplot as response to the steward's dismissal but paradoxically heightens the hearer's identification with the steward. The initial distancing caused by the remark is overcome in the rogue's activity, and the audi-

---

36. Burton, (*Syntax*, 22) refers to this as a dramatic aorist with the sense of "I have it." I have been unable to confirm this in any other grammar.
37. Via, *Parables*, 159. See Crossan, "Structural Analysis," 202.

ence's moral holiday at the master's expense cements identification with the steward.

Line 7: And the master praised the unjust steward for he acted prudently.

The parable's last line creates tension within the narrative.[38] That the steward acted prudently (i.e., shrewdly and successfully)[39] confirms the rogue image, but the master's commendation frustrates a hearer's anticipation that he would respond in anger. The repertoire casts the master in a negative role and the plot's logic demands punishment (see fig. 4), not evasion. The unexpectedness and oxymoronic tension of the last line jolts the repertoire's use of familiar and expected patterns. The three unexpected ideas are those of the master's praise and the steward's unjustness and shrewdness. In noting the steward's shrewdness or prudence, which is the typical virtue of a steward, the master ironically recognizes that the steward has finally done his job, although in an inappropriate circumstance. Praise runs directly contrary to expectations of punishment. The reminder that the steward, however, is unjust is threatening to the hearer. Although forewarned that the steward would neither dig nor beg, the hearer accepted his actions as a rogue. The hearer sanctioned the picaresque comedy, poking light fun at the master's expense. Now the comedy has a barbed end: the action was unjust. The story ends by leaving the hearer in an uncomfortable position. The hearer has supported immorality by sanctioning the rogue's deceiving the master.

A hearer tries to make sense of a story by putting its various parts together to form a consistency,[40] a consistent way of viewing narrative events. The first consistency to emerge in this short story is the one that suggests the rich man is bad and the steward by implication is good. The opening sequence portrays the rich man as antagonist; he is rich, and his judgment is arbitrary and summary. The steward disturbs part of the first consistency by refusing to dig or to beg. A second consistency forms with the description of the steward's actions in response to the master.

38. Maas ("Das Gleichnis," 173–84) points out the tension but sees the redactional point of the parable in the apparently "unjust forgiveness."
39. BAGD, 866, indicates a translation of "wisely, shrewdly." Preisker ("Lukas 16, 1–7," 85–92) argues that normally the adjective in the New Testament refers to one's grasping the eschatological situation. Jeremias (*Parables,* 46) extends this to the adverb used in this parable. But *pistos* and *phronimos* are normal adjectives describing a steward's expected activity (Luke 12:42), loyalty and shrewdness in his master's behalf. Fletcher, ("Riddle," 28) argues for a secular understanding of *phronimos* but sees the irony in v. 9, which he takes to be authentic.
40. Iser, *Act of Reading,* 16–18.

The hearer applies from the repertoire a pattern of picaresque comedy. In the first consistency the steward was a victim of the rich man's arbitrariness; in the second the rich man is the deserved victim of a rogue's schemes. The story's conclusion shatters the latter consistency when the antagonist does not respond as expected (he offers praise instead of showing anger) and reminds the hearer that the steward is unjust. What is a hearer to make of this?

From Story to Kingdom

The allegorical interpretation of this parable has sensed the inappropriateness of the conjunction of picaresque comedy and the kingdom of God. The two summary conclusions (vv. 8a–9) attempt to impose sense (consistency) on the parable by diverting attention from the story's roguish character. But the oddness of the allegories only demonstrates the parable's deeply disturbing effect. On the one hand, its off-color cast results from the steward's behavior. On the other hand, the master's praise of his dishonest action clashes with the sense of justice normally implied in the symbol of the kingdom of God. How are these reconciled?

When the master's praise and the steward's behavior clash with the justice implied in the kingdom (i.e., when story and kingdom expectations collide), the hearer must reconsider what justice in the kingdom can mean. The parable does not redefine justice, so it can offer no new definition (law) of justice in the kingdom. It does suggest, however, that justice is somehow to be seen or heard in the parable's contours. Because this parable belongs to the accounting group, it implements the metaphorical network of the kingdom as an accounting. The purpose of the accounting is justice, and the rogue misdirects an audience's attention when he attempts to subvert the setting of matters aright. The accounting metaphor leads a hearer to expect the master to intervene and restore order. Thus the parable's ending deconstructs its own metaphorical structure, while the allegories try to reinstate it.

At the parable's conclusion a hearer discovers that the price for going on a moral holiday was the sanctioning of a rogue's behavior. As the master reminds, the hearer has witnessed and condoned injustice. His praise compels a hearer into retrospection, into looking back and reconsidering the characterizations in the parable. Was the master being arbitrary in his judgment? Was the accusation of wasting goods true or false? Was the steward's behavior simply harmless fun at the master's expense? The parable offers no answers to these questions, it only provokes them! The way in which the hearer has made sense of the story collapses as the retrospection caused by the last line takes hold. Now the parable challenges the hearer's implicit world by challenging the way justice operates in that world.

The parable presents a counterworld to the hearer's normal, implicit world. In that normal world of patron and clients, power and justice are coordinates. The rich man possesses power, and his initial judgment, arbitrary and summary, can be carried out because he is powerful. The steward also possesses the power of a victim: he draws the hearer to his side by sympathy, allowing one and all to enjoy his getting even. The victim's power as a rogue is clearly greater than the supposed power of the rich man as a dupe. But the story is not a simple trickster story in which a hearer is allowed to go on a moral holiday with no penalty exacted. The master in the end demands from a hearer a price—the admission that the action was unjust—and at the same time forfeits his power of tyranny by praising the steward. This act of praise forces a hearer to reconsider the rich man's stereotypical image that is operative in the parable. The hearer now has no way to navigate in the world; its solid moorings have been lost. Are masters cruel or not? Are victims right in striking back? By a powerful questioning and juxtaposition of images, the parable breaks the bond between power and justice. Instead it equates justice and vulnerability.[41] The hearer in the world of the kingdom must establish new coordinates for power, justice, and vulnerability. The kingdom is for the vulnerable, for masters and stewards who do not get even.

41. This coheres with Jesus' association with the outcast, as well as, e.g., his use of leaven in the parable The Leaven. See Funk, *Jesus as Precursor*, 62–63.

12

The King's Accounting

A King Wished to Settle Accounts

A king wished to settle accounts with his servants. When he began the accounting there was brought to him one of the debtors who owed ten thousand talents. As he could not pay back, the master ordered him to be sold and his wife and children, and everything which he had and to be repaid. Then falling down, the servant worshiped him, saying, "Have patience with me and I will repay you everything." But having pity, the master of that servant set him free and canceled for him the loan. And coming out, that servant found one of his fellow servants who owed him a hundred denarii and seizing him he nearly choked him, saying, "Pay back what you owe." Falling down, his fellow servant begged him saying, "Have patience with me and I will repay you." He did not wish, but going out he cast him into prison until he should pay what he owed. Then the fellow servants, seeing what had happened, were deeply grieved and coming they made clear to their master everything that had happened. Then summoning him, his master said to him, "Evil servant, all that debt I forgave you since you begged me. And was it not necessary that even you have mercy on your fellow servant as I had mercy on you?" And being angry his master handed him over to the torturers until he should pay back all that he owed.

A major problem in the interpretation of Jesus' parables is the preservation of them in contexts created by others. The parable A King Wished to Settle Accounts (Matt. 18:23–34) concludes Matthew's ecclesiastical discourse. Jülicher and many since have noted the parable's inappropriateness in its present context,[1] but what has gone unnoticed is the subtle effect that Matthew's allegory has had on the parable's subsequent interpretation.

Matthew as Interpreter

The discourse in which the parable appears is that of "Matthew's advice to a divided community," to borrow the title of William Thompson's book.[2] The first verse, "Who is the greatest in the kingdom of heaven?" sets out the theme of chapter 18. Throughout, Matthew pleads for humility, forgiveness, and mercy. In this context he locates a story of a king and his servants.

The immediate context is Peter's question about how often he should forgive and Jesus' answer of seventy-seven times[3] (i.e., forever and ever). The parable furnishes an example of forgiveness, although a poor one, for it contains no repeated forgiveness.[4] Since in the parallel passage (Luke 17:4) the challenge to forgive appears without the narrative of the unforgiving servant, we are able to conclude that Matthew probably joined them together.

Besides a redactional context, Matthew has provided the parable with an introduction and a conclusion. The introductory formula ("Therefore the kingdom of heaven may be compared") fits well with the theme of the chapter, "Who is the greatest in the kingdom of heaven?" (v. 1). The formula also occurs more frequently in Matthew than in any other Gospel.[5] But Matthew's more significant contribution is "So my heav-

---

1. Jülicher (*Die Gleichnisreden* 1:313) argues that the parable and Peter's question are joined by Matthew. Modern commentators have tended to follow his lead.
2. Thompson, *Matthew's Advice*. This is the most detailed redactional study of the chap. available.
3. See BAGD, 213; Goodspeed, *Problems*, 29–31.
4. Jeremias, *Parables*, 97. Among recent important studies supporting Jeremias's position, see Deidun, "Parable of the Unmerciful Servant," 203; Deitzelbinger, "Das Gleichnis," 438; Linnemann, *Jesus of the Parables*, 107; Via, *Parables*, 138; Weiser, *Die Knechtsgleichnisse*, 99.
5. Whether the introductory formula is redactional is a very difficult case. Matthew definitely has a preference for the introductory formula (cf. Jeremias, *Parables*, 102). Dodd (*Parables*, 19) sees no reason to connect the parable with the kingdom. For the formula as secondary, see Deidun, "Parable of the Unmerciful Servant," 206; Linnemann, *Jesus of the Parables*, 108; Thompson, *Matthew's Advice*, 208; Weiser, *Die Knechtsgleichnisse*, 75. In defense of the authenticity of the formula, see Jeremias, 210; Spicq, *Dieu et l'homme*, 54. Kingsbury (*Parables of Jesus*, 19–20) states no opinion on the

enly Father[6] will do to every one of you, if you do not forgive your brother from your heart" (v. 35). The line causes retrospection on the part of a reader, who looks back on the story to understand, making it a negative example: Don't do likewise. More important, in contrasting the king's forgiveness with the servant's lack thereof, it identifies the king as a stand-in for "my heavenly Father." He is no longer a king but God. The last line (v. 35), with its identification of the king as God, transposes the narrative into the key of allegory, a "twice-told tale."[7] At one level it is a story of a king and his servants, but at another level it details how God deals with those who do not forgive. For Matthew, the allegory conditions the narrative's primary mode of meaning.[8]

Matthew's allegorical transposition of the story is his most subtle contribution, because it draws attention to the king's mercy, in the story's beginning, at the expense of his revenge, in the end. As a result, subsequent exegesis has accented themes of judgment, mercy, and forgiveness.[9] The parable's "point" is "Was it not necessary [*dei*] to have mercy on your fellow servant?" (v. 33).[10] Actually, only the creation of a God-king perspective prevents a revolt against a God who demands multiple forgiveness but lashes out at the first failure[11] or who, having once forgiven, then withdraws that forgiveness.

While it is easy to separate the parable from its redactional context, Matthew's allegorical interpretation is less easy to screen out of our point of view. And without another context into which to set the story, how can we interpret it?[12] To deal with this question we will focus on the narrative itself to see what clues it provides for its interpretation.

authenticity of the formula. There are only two kingdom parables in Mark and Luke, whereas Matthew has eleven.

6. This phrase occurs fifteen times in Matthew, once in Mark (11:25), and not at all in Luke. See Kümmel, *Introduction to the New Testament*, 113.

7. Via, *Parables*, 5. Cf. Honig, *Dark Conceit*, 12. The narrative in Matthew is not itself an allegory but has been given an allegorical framework through Matthew's redaction. Thus the characterization of the king is determined from *outside* the story.

8. The term is from the helpful distinction of Boucher in *Mysterious Parable*, 17.

9. E.g., a parable of the last judgment (Jeremias), unlimited mercy (Linnemann), forgiveness as God's gift (Via), or existence as gratuitously given (Deitzelbinger). Fuchs ("Parable of the Unmerciful Servant," 487–94) deals with similar themes but within the context of Matthew's redaction.

10. Linnemann, *Jesus of the Parables*, 110. While Via (*Parables*, 140) rejects seeking after a parable's point, he admits "that 18:33 does come close to summing up the thematic side of the parable."

11. Derrett ("The Parable of the Unmerciful Servant," in *Law in the New Testament*, 34–35) stresses this point. He quotes evidence demanding the trustworthiness of a Hellenistic king. For a king or God to remove his forgiveness violates the canons of justice.

12. Deidun, "Parable of the Unmerciful Servant," 206–7. Although admitting that Matthew has created the context, Deidun attackes Deitzelbinger for abandoning

Affairs of State

The story partakes of an undergirding phenomenal world that constitutes the horizon of author, text, and receiver. A part of that horizon is the story's repertoire, which includes the familiar expectations of literary, social, and cultural conventions that author and receiver share.[13] Without a repertoire a text cannot communicate. Therefore, to identify a text's repertoire is an important step toward its interpretation.

Among those shared conventions of importance for this story are its implied economic conventions.[14] Derrett has made several helpful suggestions in this regard.[15] We need not agree with his analysis of the parable to find some of his clues valuable. For Derrett, the story revolves around the transactions of gentile tax farmers. A king would normally farm out tax collections at an auction to the highest bidder. The contract was lucrative because, after adding on his percentage, a contractor subcontracted the actual collection to others, creating a chain of collectors, each adding his percentage to the tax due. The present story deals with an exceedingly large collection, since Herod's total collection was only nine hundred talents.[16]

On the day of accounting, when the tax farmer must turn over to the king the amount bid, he comes up short. As Derrett notes, one need not imagine that the man is penniless but must simply suppose that he is unable to produce the amount bid. The narrative offers no explanation: it may be due to famine, bad harvests, or the like. There is no reason to suspect inefficiency, since an inefficient servant would hardly have received so huge a contract.

Derrett interprets the king's threat to throw the man into prison not as a way of recovering the funds but as normal punishment for failure to

---

Matthew's context a priori. My thesis is that the parable must generate its own perspective. See Tolbert, *Perspectives*, 67–71.

13. "Repertoire" refers to all those conventions necessary for the establishment of the situation of the text—the extratextual reality of the text. See Iser, *Act of Reading*, 69–85.

14. By beginning with an economic code, I am not suggesting that the text does not invoke other elements of repertoire. But at first glance, a knowledge of the economic situation implied in the narrative would be a primary (foundational) element shared by author and hearer.

15. Derrett, *Law in the New Testament*, 35–40. Derrett deals with the economic situation. Unless otherwise noted, the following references to Derrett come from these pages.

16. Linnemann, *Jesus of the Parables*, 108. Josephus (*Antiquities* [trans. W. Whiston], 17.11.4) reports that the yearly taxation for Judea during the Roman period was six hundred talents. Spicq (*Dieu et l'homme*, 57–58) provides comparative references for the amount involved. For taxation during the ministry of Jesus, see Jeremias, *Jerusalem*, 124–26.

live up to a contract.[17] The servant's request for patience to repay all is not as ridiculous as it first appears. He is asking for the amount due to be added to next year's collection. The linchpin in Derrett's argument is his explanation of the king's forgiving *to daneion*, a word that means "loan" but in the parable is usually translated "debt."[18] Derrett argues that "loan" is indeed the proper translation, since by forgoing the amount due until next year the king is actually making a loan.

Derrett has sketched a possible, even probable, economic and cultural repertoire for the story's actions and characterizations. It is a thoroughly gentile world. Yet his analysis is ultimately unconvincing and insufficient for two reasons. (1) He identifies knowing the repertoire with understanding. That is, he believes that having located a historical context or set of conventions for the story, he understands it. Repertoire, however, is a vehicle for understanding, not understanding itself. It is simply the shared conventions of a culture which are prerequisites for understanding. (2) Derrett also confuses fiction and reality by attempting to construct for the parable a one-to-one correspondence with the referential world. The ways of fiction are more subtle. Fiction creates its own world by narrative. Though it attempts verisimilitude, exact reproduction of the outside world is not the story's point. For this reason, Derrett does not see that the ten thousand talents represent not an actual amount but an exaggerated, imaginary amount common in folk tales. For Derrett, the characters and the numbers in the parable are literal, not fictional, and thus he misses the truly important clues presented in the parable's narrative.

Although Derrett's analysis is unconvincing, he does provide a strong indication that the story's setting is gentile. This is so for three reasons: (1) The king is most likely a Gentile. (2) The vast amount of money involved conjures up the high finances of the empire. (3) *To daneion*, a loan, suggests the conditions of tax farming. The repertoire presupposes a gentile situation, although not necessarily the specific one identified by Derrett.

17. For the evidence, see Derrett, *Law in the New Testament*, 37. Derrett summarizes the evidence as, "Pay what you owe or you and your family will be sold as slaves!" E.g., the father of Bion of Borysthenes, a tax farmer, failed to meet his obligations and was sold into slavery with his whole family (*Diogenes Laertius*, "Bion," 4.46–47 [LCL 1:425]). Derrett correctly points out that those like Jeremias who attempt to show that the story does not follow rabbinic practice—which is true—simply miss the point. Jewish law is not applicable to the characters' performance. That does not mean that it is unrelated to the reader's expectations.

18. BAGD, 171, translates the phrase, "to cancel a loan." Jeremias (*Parables*, 211) argues that this does not make sense and follows the early Syriac translation of "debt." For him the mistake was made in the supposed translation of the parable from an Aramaic original.

Surface Structure

The story exhibits a clear organization by threes. There are three scenes: the king's accounting, the servant's accounting, and the king's response. Crossan has divided the three scenes into three parts corresponding to introduction (vv. 23–25, 28, 31), words (vv. 26, 29, 32–33), and action (vv. 27, 30, 34).[19] F. H. Breukelmann has proposed a more ambitious and satisfactory division. Each of the three scenes is organized around master and servant. Breukelmann divides each scene in a way (see table 3)[20] that leads him to organize the story around its characters:

Table 3

DIVISION OF SCENES

	Scene 1	*Scene 2*	*Scene 3*
Introduction	v. 24	v. 28a	v. 31
A	v. 25	v. 28b	v. 32
B	v. 26	v. 29	v. 33
C	v. 27	v. 30	v. 34

Scene 1

Master
- (A) Master
- (B) Servant
- (C) Master

Scene 2

Servant
- (A) Servant
- (B) Fellowservant
- (C) Servant

Scene 3

Master
- (A) Master
- (B) Servant
- (C) Master

Breukelmann's analysis of the surface structure clearly indicates the rapid shifting that characterizes the story. The surface organization, of triads around the two central characters, concentrates attention on their activity, weaving a tight web that circumscribes the narrative world.[21]

---

19. Crossan, *In Parables*, 106. Thompson (*Matthew's Advice*, 211) has an identical scheme except that he does not include v. 23 in the introduction.

20. Breukelmann, "Eine Erklärung," 262–63. The schema is my own.

21. Although I find Breukelmann's analysis of the organization of the surface convincing, I do not share his conviction that the narrative is a composition by Matthew (ibid., 287). This is true for the simple reason that if it is a Matthean composition to serve as an example for Peter's question, it is a poor example. Thompson (*Matthew's Advice*, 211–12) notes the use of participles and main verbs to organize the sentence structure of the parable. He indicates that this is more typical of written than of oral composition. He concludes that "it is difficult to say whether Matthew was

A Reading

Line 1: A king[22] wished to settle accounts with his servants.

The first line evokes several expectations. The depicted scene transcends the everyday experience of an average Palestinian, because affairs of kings, despite affecting peasants, are not part of their everyday life. Yet this does not mean that the narrative is a fantasy, or even that it verges on one. Rather, it has more the character of a tale. Second, the line alerts a hearer to the story's expected development, namely as an accounting story in which the king (and audience) will sit in judgment on those who must give an account. In a patron-client culture an accounting invokes the hierarchical structure through which the patron sets things in their right order.

A narrative line (logic) creates anticipation, leading a hearer ahead. If a hearer did not know what to expect, the story would make no sense. There must be an underlying framework. The model in figure 5 represents the potential narrative logic.[23]

Figure 5

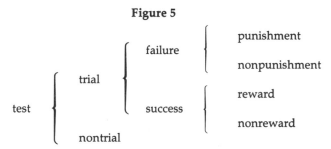

responsible for such a deliberate composition. The subordinating style throughout the parable suggests a literary composition, but more characteristic signs of Matthean redaction are absent" (p. 221). Black (*Aramaic Approach*, 63) points to the same participle style in the parable A Man Had Two Sons. Though the parable shows clear signs of literacy, that does not mean that it is not performance of the originating structure, but it is a written performance.

22. Schlatter (*Der Evangelist Matthäus*, 559) suggests that *anthrōpos basileus* is used to distinguish an earthly king from a heavenly king. It represents an Aramaic circumlocution equivalent to "king of flesh and blood." Spicq (*Dieu et l'homme*, 54) accepts this. On the "king of flesh and blood" as a type of rabbinic parable, see Johnston, "Parabolic Traditions, 519.

23. For the theory, see Bremond, "Logic of Narrative Possibilities," 387–411. A number of Jesus' parables follow this narrative logic. In A Rich Man Had a Steward, trial leads to failure and punishment, with the steward trying to avoid punishment; in In a City There Was a Judge, the widow requests a trial, the judge responds with no trial but eventually moves to success. The accounting scenes of A Man Entrusts Property present a variation on this pattern. In the scenes of the successful servants a test leads to a trial, which leads to success and thus reward. In the one-talent man's scene he seeks nontrial when he attempts to return the talent to the master. The master responds with trial, failure, and punishment.

In narrative logic, the accounting is a test and the hearer awaits an outcome based on results determined prior to story time. The accent falls on failure and success, and punishment and reward, not on the test itself as is the case in the steward (departure-return) parables.

Line 2:   When he began the accounting there was brought to him one of the debtors who owed ten thousand talents.

The trial begins. "Was brought" implies a scene with actors besides the principals. Even though Jeremias's suggestion that the man was brought from prison does not necessarily follow,[24] the passive does indicate an element of coercion, the involvement of others. The amount, ten thousand talents, signals the affairs of the high and mighty. The almost fantastic[25] amount distances servant and king from a hearer and may also cast the servant in a negative light, since such rich and powerful people must be greedy and responsible for the audience's woes.[26] The passive voice ("was brought") objectifies the action, and the amount of debt alienates servant from hearer, who shares the narrator's viewpoint and observes with interest these happenings of the rich and mighty.

Line 3:   As he could not pay back, the master ordered him to be sold and his wife and children, and everything which he had and to be repaid.

Since the man is unable to make good on what he owes, narrative logic implies failure and punishment. The form of punishment is not unusual among Gentiles.[27] Furthermore, from a Jewish perspective, such punishment only accentuates gentile cruelty, since Jewish law forbade the sale of wife and children to settle a husband's debts.[28] A hearer's viewpoint remains that of the narrator: See how these Gentiles go about their business with such cruelty. The story draws on two elements of the repertoire: the economic situation of tax farming and, now, the Jewish

24. Jeremias (*Parables*, 211) reads *prosēnechtē* and indicates, without evidence, that it means "was brought from prison." BAGD, 719, gives no such meaning for Matt. 18:24. See Thompson (*Matthew's Advice*, 212 n. 41) for the text-critical question.

25. See n. 16 above. One should not take the amount as literal, in spite of Derrett. Rather, the amount is the highest conceivable number—exaggeration common to folk tales.

26. The oppressive character of Roman taxation hardly needs to be pointed out. See Jeremias, *Jerusalem*, 124–26. Hengel (*Judaism and Hellenism* 1:180–81) describes both the process and the problems of Ptolemaic taxation policies. The Romans carried many of these same features over into their own system.

27. See n. 17 above.

28. Jeremias, *Parables*, 211. See *m. Sota* 3.8 (Danby, 297) for a listing of how men and women are different: "A man may be sold [to make restitution] for what he has stolen, but a woman cannot be sold [to make restitution] for what she has stolen."

stereotyped propaganda[29] against Gentiles. A hearer fills in the gaps in the story, builds a consistency[30] in which the story illustrates gentile degradation and, by implication, Jewish superiority.

Line 4:   Then falling down, the servant worshiped him, saying, "Have patience with me and I will repay you everything."

The servant's "worshiping" confirms not only that the characters are gentile but also an emerging consistency that enables a Jewish hearer to assert superiority. Groveling before a master, "worshiping him," is something no Jew would ever do.[31]

Line 5:   But having pity, the master of that servant set him free and cancelled for him the loan.

The master's pity is unexpected. Normally, narrative logic (see fig. 5) would warrant punishment for failure. By not following the expected pattern, the king's action disturbs the effort to hold the story together, to build a consistency. The consistency to this point has been Jewish superiority, but the king's pity calls that consistency into question and a hearer begins to doubt the way in which the story is going together. This turn of events results solely from the king's action. The servant is called "that servant," maintaining his distance from a hearer. The nonpunishment of failure (or maybe even reward for failure) ends the king's accounting. Thus, narrative logic demands a new story or new sequence.

Line 6:   And coming out, that servant found one of his fellow servants who owed him a hundred denarii and seizing him he nearly choked him, saying, "Pay back what you owe."

This line initiates a new scene that follows the servant's actions. It parallels the initial sequence of the king's test but with two differences: (1) Having seen the first plot (failure leads to nonpunishment and forgiveness), a hearer does not know precisely what to expect. (2) In the first line, the servant "was brought in," but here the fellow servant is seized by the throat. A hearer foresees the worst. Even though in the previous scene the king's forgiveness disturbed the consistency of Jewish superiority, the servant's seizing his fellow servant confirms that way of holding the story together. The relative smallness of the fellow ser-

---

29. E.g., Wisd. of Sol. 13—14; Rom. 1:18–32. Although primarily concerned with the influence of Hellenism upon Judaism, Hengel does deal with Jewish negative reaction; see *Judaism and Hellenism* 1:131–53, 303–9.

30. See Iser, *Act of Reading,* 16–18. Consistency building takes place at the discourse level and is the way a hearer puts the elements of a text together.

31. Lohse, *New Testament Environment,* 216–21.

vant's debt only reinforces the negative view of the servant. Hearer stands against the servant.

Line 7: Falling down, his fellow servant begged him saying, "Have patience with me and I will repay you."

The fellow servant's response parallels the first servant's own response to the king, except that the fellow servant does not worship, which would be inappropriate. He is called a fellow or co-servant (*syndoulos autou*). The *syn* and *autou* bond the two servants together. The small amount of debt[32] and the cry for pity draw one to sympathize with the fellow servant. The story sets up a double and contradictory expectation. On the one hand it structures a positive expectation for the fellow servant. The king's previous forgiveness, the smallness of the debt, and the common bond between fellow servants lead one to expect forgiveness. On the other hand, the negative terms associated with the servant suggest he will not forgive. The narrative deliberately creates tension that prevents a hearer from adopting a single viewpoint.

Line 8: He did not wish, but going out he cast him into prison until he should pay what he owed.

The servant plays out his role, thereby confirming the negative expectation. The parallel to the king's sequence leads a hearer to expect forgiveness. The injustice of the servant's action has outraged many actual readers,[33] including Matthew, and verifies our analysis of how the narrative structures consistency building. It leads a hearer to pass judgment on the servant: See how these pagans treat one another!

Line 9: Then the fellow servants, seeing what had happened, were deeply grieved and coming they made clear to their master everything that had happened.

Offstage, other fellow servants have witnessed the injustice, and their view corresponds exactly with that of a hearer: they are outraged at the servant's behavior. In this they are the first characters in the story who have shared a hearer's viewpoint. (Previously the omniscient narrator has structured viewpoint.) Now a hearer is drawn into the story and begins to identify with the fellow servants.

32. Derrett, *Law in the New Testament*, 41. The debt is small relative to ten thousand talents but large for a peasant. In A Householder Went Out Early, the laborers bargain for a denarius a day.

33. E.g., Schweizer, *Good News*, 378. Schweizer refers to the servant's activity as vicious and grostesque. Crossan (*In Parables*, 107) says, "The ordinary human reaction to such a story would be that the first servant got what he deserved and should certainly have known better in such a situation."

Line 10: Then summoning him, his master said to him, "Evil servant, all that debt I forgave you since you begged me.

Now a third test begins which a hearer expects to turn out differently from the first. The servant's failure to forgive his fellow servant demands punishment. This is clear when the king greets him as "evil servant." Judgment has already been passed. A hearer, along with the fellow servants, witnesses the king's wrath.

Line 11: "And was it not necessary that even you have mercy on your fellow servant as I had mercy on you?"

A subtle change has taken place in a hearer's consistency building. In the first part of the story the dominating consistency was Jewish superiority. This has now been supplanted by a new consistency clearly stated in line 11. The king's charge states a hearer's position: the servant must (*dei*) behave as the king did. Such an explicit statement of the consistency implicates a hearer further in structuring the narrative. Now hearer, fellow servants, and king share an identical viewpoint. Identification and entrance into the story are complete.

Line 12: And being angry his master handed him over to the torturers until he should pay back all that he owed.

The expectation is punishment; that much is clear from the narrative logic. But this punishment differs from that proposed in the first test (line 3). The servant will suffer forever the torments of his torturers.[34] The punishment's harshness creates a disturbance for consistency building. It corresponds to the extremeness of the debt. Both the punishment and the size of the debt shatter the everyday and are parts of the literary pattern of defamiliarization.[35] But the excessiveness is compounded because an oriental king has gone back on his word: *he has taken back his forgiveness* and reinstated the original debt. In the Hellenistic world such an act threatens to destroy the ordered world. With the solidarity of the patron and client violated, the king moves outside the law and all are at risk.

A chaotic situation entraps the audience. The king's brutal action forces a hearer to reconsider the consistency building that has held the

34. Jeremias (*Parables*, 213) sees the extreme nature of the penalty, but because God is the king he misses its profoundly disturbing character. Derrett (*Law in the New Testament*) accentuates the extreme nature when attacking Jeremias (p. 34) but explains away the problem in his own interpretation (p. 47).

35. This term, derived from Russian formalism, is used to describe the strategy of art whereby the anesthetic power of the everyday is destroyed so as to allow the new to break through. See Jameson, *Prison-House*, 50–59, 75–79; Culler, *Structuralist Poetics*, chap. 7.

story together. By identifying with the fellow servants in reporting the servant, a hearer bears with them responsibility for unleashing the king's wrath. By bringing vengeance on the servant, the fellow servants (and the hearer) have left their own situation in jeopardy. The demand for "like for like," for apparent justice, has left them exposed. If a king can take back his forgiveness, who is safe? But the disturbance goes deeper. The fellow servants' reporting is like the first servant's own activity. In the end the fellow servants have behaved the same way he did; they failed to forgive and demanded punishment. A hearer must go deeper yet. The initial consistency that held the story together involved the superiority of Jew over Gentile. By joining forces with the fellow servants, a hearer has entered the gentile world and forfeited superiority.

The narrative presents a complex structured and structuring process. It leads a hearer to structure its sequences in a certain way in order to build a consistency and at the conclusion proceeds to dismantle that structuring process. We can summarize the motion of the implied hearer:

Consistency Building
    1. Superiority of Jew over Gentile (vv. 24–28).
    2. Do likewise (vv. 29–33).
Principal Disturbances
    1. The king's revocation of forgiveness (v. 34).
    2. Reporting leads to chaos (vv. 31b–34).
       (*a*) Hearer behaves as first servant, negating consistency 2.
       (*b*) Hearer behaves like Gentile, negating consistency 1.

From Story to Kingdom

This story of a king and his servants is more than a narrative; it is a parable. In some way it stands for the kingdom of God. Whether Matthew is responsible for the introductory formula is beside the point; the king as a main character suggests the formula. That the king turns out in the end to be an inappropriate cipher for God only adds to the parable's tease[36] and demonstrates the inadequacy of Matthew's allegorical mode of interpretation.

One of the most common characters in rabbinic parables is the king. These parables imply a correspondence between the king's rule and God's dealing with Israel. This parable subverts the metaphorical structure of God as a king by demonstrating that the standards of this world

---

36. See Dodd's definition of a parable: "a metaphor . . . leaving the mind in sufficient doubt about its precise application to tease it into active thought" (*Parables*, 5).

are totally inadequate for the kingdom. God's is a kingdom based not on justice—like for like—but, by implication, on mercy. When the king, at the fellow servants' request, holds an accounting to set matters aright, it brings chaos, just as in A Rich Man Clothed in Purple, when God helps Lazarus, there appears a great chasm between the rich man and Lazarus.

Part of the story's scandal derives from associations implied in the received symbol of the kingdom of God. A hearer's expectations for the kingdom conflict with those of the story. The conflict between expectations and story blocks the normal transference of metaphor, because in this parable the transference is on the basis not of similarity but of dissimilarity or juxtaposition.[37] There is then a gap[38] between story and kingdom. A hearer is left to draw the lines bridging story and kingdom. A hearer must complete the parable, the laying-beside of narrative and symbol.

A hearer can fill in the gap in some of the following ways. The threat created by the parable's end, when the king goes back on his word, conflicts with the expectation of peace in the kingdom.[39] But much more is at stake. The outcome is of a hearer's own doing, for by joining forces with the fellow servants in calling on a higher authority, a hearer is enticed into a threatening world whose boundaries and guidelines begin to dissolve. The fellow servants and a hearer seek to make the story follow its narrative logic; failure leads to punishment. Instead of order and logic, chaos comes. A profound irony in this parable is that the accounting is supposed to set things aright. By appealing to the hierarchical structure to bring right order, the servants have instead brought chaos. The story is a narrative imitation of the final petition of the Lord's Prayer, "Let us not succumb to the test."[40] Or it is like A Rich Man Had a Steward, where a hearer sanctions the activity of the rogue steward only to be reminded by the master that he is unjust. Swept into a vortex of chaos, a hearer fails, at least in the story.[41]

A second gap between the story and the kingdom derives from the

37. Wheelwright (*Metaphor and Reality*, chap. 4) develops the distinction between two ways of metaphor: epiphor (transference by similarity) and diaphor (transference by dissimilarity or juxtaposition).

38. Gaps or indeterminacy creates the suspense that forces a hearer/reader to engage a text. Gaps are blanks to be filled in. See Iser, *Act of Reading*, 165–69.

39. Jesus' language frequently contains violent images: e.g., Matt. 5:39b–42, 10:34–36. See Tannehill, *Sword of His Mouth*, 67–78, 140–47.

40. For a justification of this translation of the final petition, see Jeremias, *Prayers*, 104–6.

41. A number of Jesus' parables have potentially chaotic endings: e.g., From Jerusalem to Jericho, in which the Jewish victim in the ditch is left at the mercy of the Samaritan enemy, and A Man Gave a Banquet, which contains at its ending not the social elite but the socially disgraced.

ending's second move. A hearer is entrapped in a web of evil that results from the attempt to bring justice, or what the hearer and fellow servants judge to be justice. This dimension of the parable is similar to the saying about turning the other cheek (Matt. 5:39).[42] Both demand unlimited mercy as the counterworld to justice. This leads to the recognition that the fellow servants and a hearer have behaved just like the first servant. They too have failed to forgive. The narrative leads to a parabolic experience of evil, not intentional evil but implicit, unanticipated, systemic evil. The ability to acknowledge one's entanglement in evil is part of the experience of the kingdom.[43] Like Paul's argument in Romans that all have sinned and fallen short of the glory of God (Rom. 3:23), the kingdom makes no distinctions. All are sinners—all are called but only on the condition of the recognition that they are sinners.[44] In Synoptic Gospel language, the parable leads to the point where the only option left is repentance.

A final gap emerges from the initial consistency based on the contrast between Jew and Gentile. The implied Jewish hearer must finally surrender the implication of Jewish moral superiority. This implies both a rejection of elites in and the universality of the kingdom. So also in A Householder Went Out Early, the master makes all his workers equal by paying them the same wage.

The latter remarks are attempts to fill in some of the gaps between story and kingdom. Such an effort entails risk because one may mistake the implicit for the reality itself. A. R. Ammons once wrote that with every literary work "a world [comes] into being about which any statement, however revelatory, is a lessening."[45] The parable suggests, but it leaves to its hearer the responsibility for meaning.

42. Tannehill, *Sword of His Mouth*, 67–77.

43. For this reason, Jesus' ministry is among the outcast. See Two Men Went Up to the Temple. See also the use of leaven, a sign of moral corruption, in the parable The Leaven.

44. Käsemann (*Commentary*, 102) remarks that in Paul's understanding, justification "attacks the religious person and only in so doing preserves the sense of the justification of the ungodly. . . . Grace is simultaneously judgment because it fundamentally sets even a religious person in the place of the godless."

45. Ammons, "A Poem Is a Walk," 115.

13

Am I Not Doing You Right?

A Householder Went Out Early

The kingdom of heaven is like a man, a householder, who came out early in the morning to hire laborers for his vineyard. On agreeing with the laborers for a denarius a day, he sent them into his vineyard. And going out about the third hour, he saw others standing in the marketplace idle and to those he said, "Go down into the vineyard and whatever is right I will give you." And they went. And again going out about the sixth and ninth hour he did the same. And about the eleventh hour going out, he found others standing, and he said to them, "Why are you standing here the whole day idle?" They said to him, "Because no one has hired us." He said to them, "Go into the vineyard." When evening came, the master of the vineyard said to his steward, "Call the workers and give them their wages [beginning with the first until the last]." And coming, those of the eleventh hour received one denarius. And coming, the first thought that they would receive more, and they received one denarius, even they. And on receiving, they grumbled against the householder, saying, "These last have worked only one hour, and you have made them equal to us who have borne the burden of the day and the scorching heat." And replying to one of them, he said,

"Friend, am I not doing you right? Did you not agree with me for a denarius? Take yours and go!"

How often hearers and readers of the parable A Householder Went Out Early (Matt. 20:1–15) have wondered why it was right for the owner to pay those who worked only one hour the same as those who worked the whole day. This crux of interpretation is built into the parable, for the laborers themselves grumble aloud the audience's dissatisfaction. Why does the parable do this? Three steps will lead us toward a solution of this dilemma: first, an examination of what has emerged as a standard interpretation of the parable; then, an unfolding of the more subtle influences of Matthew's narrative redaction; and finally, a reading of the parable that accounts for the feelings of anger toward the householder.

The Generous Employer

Since Jülicher, a consistent pattern for interpreting the parable has emerged.[1] Most see v. 16 as a Matthean addition linking together the parable and chapter 19. The result is artificial because the parable does not furnish a good example of the last as first or the first as last. Most commentators see the accent of the original telling falling on the householder's graciousness, goodness, or generosity. Such a reading involves curious interpretive gymnastics.

The parable comes to a head in the confrontation between the householder and those first-hired servants. The master may appear unjust in paying all the same wage,[2] but the injustice is only apparent, because, as his reply notes, no injustice has occurred: "Did you not agree with me for a denarius?" (v. 13). Now the gymnastics begin, for not only is he just but most agree that he has acted with generosity toward those hired last. What is apparent injustice is actually justice with generosity. For some, the householder is motivated by his concern for the poor.[3] If he had not hired them, their families would have starved. So overwhelming is the impression of generosity and goodness on the master's part that Linnemann says, "One cannot grumble against generosity.[4] . . . What appeared as a break in the ordered system of justice was in truth the appearance of

---

1. Jülicher, *Die Gleichnisreden* 42:459–71. Among the most important studies in the Jülicher mode, note Jeremias, *Parables*, 136–39; Michaelis, *Die Gleichnisse*, 171–78; Linnemann, *Jesus of the Parables*, 81–88; Dupont, "Les ouvriers," 28–51; Ru, "Conception of Reward," 202–22; Via, *Parables*, 147–55.
2. Jeremias, *Parables*, 27; Mitton, "Expounding the Parables," 307.
3. Jeremias, *Parables*, 37; Ru, "Conception of Reward," 208.
4. Linnemann, *Jesus of the Parables*, 84.

goodness."[5] The parable finds its *Sitz im Leben* in Jesus' debate with the scribes and Pharisees,[6] and thus justifies his association with the outcast and represents the free gift of grace associated with the kingdom's coming.

There are several problems with this reading. It assumes an identification of the story's characters. The first-hired are the Pharisees, the householder is God, and the last-hired are the outcast.[7] The fatal flaw in this assumption is that the Pharisees would have seen themselves in the characterization of those first hired. They surely would not have seen themselves as rejecting God's generosity to sinners.[8] Moreover, the interpretation demands Christendom as an ideological support and assumes the Christian myth of Judaism as the elder son and Christianity as the younger son. Only Christians as recipients of God's grace see generosity in the story.[9] Second, as Manson has pointed out, "The parable cannot be made to support the thoroughgoing Pauline and Lutheran doctrine of salvation by grace alone. There is not a shadow of suggestion that those who have worked in the vineyard all day have not earned their wages."[10] Manson's point is well taken, for the parable is too often turned into a defense of free grace.[11] The command to depart does not mean that they lose their wages.[12]

A third problem concerns the master's generosity. A denarius for an hour's work is generous in comparison with a denarius for a full day's labor. But in and of itself it is not generous. It represents the average peasant's wage, no more. A peasant earning a denarius a day will live in the shadow of poverty (see below). Moreover, such an interpretation requires a hearer to take up a highly legalistic perspective. Although it is true that in a narrow legal sense the householder is just, in that he pays what he bargains, the appearance of foul play is evident. To see the

5. Ibid., 86.

6. See Jülicher, *Die Gleichnisreden* 2:466; Dodd, *Parables*, 95; Jeremias, *Parables*, 38; Ru, "Conception of Reward," 209; Via, *Parables*, 149. Linnemann (*Jesus of the Parables*, 156–58 n. 15) provides an extensive footnote surveying the various options.

7. In Christian interpretation the last-hired become those favored to enter the kingdom: e.g., in Origen's famous allegory the different hours represent the different stages of life at which people become Christians. See *Commentaris secundum Matthaeum* 13:1342–46.

8. I contend that almost all readers would identify with the complaint of the first-hired, but the point here is that the Pharisees would not have recognized themselves in the allegorical characterization.

9. This same Christian myth, with the same resulting misinterpretation, is at work in the traditional reading of the parable A Man Had Two Sons.

10. Manson, *Sayings*, 218.

11. See Jülicher, *Die Gleichnisreden* 2:467; Jeremias, *Parables*, 139; Michaelis, *Die Gleichnisse*, 177–78; Mitton, "Expounding the Parables," 309.

12. Jeremias (*Parables*, 34) argues this point against Raucourt ("Les ouvriers," 492).

householder as generous, a hearer must switch sympathy from the apparently wronged first-hired to the householder, on the basis of a technicality. That is possible only if one has decided in advance that the householder is God and that therefore one must switch allegiance.

Finally, the standard reading fails because it does not ask why the parable deliberately antagonizes a hearer. Why create such a strong impression of injustice? Any successful reading of the parable must answer that question.

Matthew as Interpreter

As noted above, commentators usually understand Matt. 19:31 (Mark 13:31) as an introduction to the parable, with a version of the logion repeated as its conclusion (v. 16). With the parable so easily excised from its redactional context, attention quickly turns to Jesus' intention.

Matthew's interpretation exerts a subtle and unnoticed influence. Although Matthew 19 largely parallels Mark 10, there are several important differences that affect the parable. Matthew 19:1—20:28 constitutes a unit in the larger narrative of Jesus' trip to Jerusalem and his eventual death and resurrection.[13] The formula of 19:1–2 marks a beginning of a new unit, with a departure from Galilee and entrance into the region of Judea.[14] Throughout the unit, Jesus prepares his disciples for the coming judgment. The narrative indicates the disciples' place in the kingdom to come before judgment is passed on others (cf. chap. 25 below). Matthew 19:1—20:28 unfolds a series of tests that affirm the disciples' position.

The first characters offering a test are the Pharisees. They challenge Jesus on a point of law concerning divorce. In comparison with Mark, Matthew arranges the argument so that Jesus first presents God's command (vv. 4–6) and then the Pharisees take Moses' position, which Jesus rejects in favor of the position of God. In the test's final part (vv. 10–12), Jesus implies to the disciples that his command cannot be met by all, but he implicitly assures them of support. The initial test serves to align the Pharisees with Moses, Jesus with God, and the disciples with Jesus. After the test the Pharisees retire from the narrative until the unit's completion.

In the blessing of the children, Matthew mutes the saying so that only "such" enter the kingdom (v. 14), and there is no command about becoming like a child.[15] In the story of the rich young man[16] the question

---

13. So Kümmel, *Introduction to the New Testament*, 104; Kingsbury, *Matthew*, 23–24.

14. Motion often denotes the beginning of a new narrative unit. See Patte, *What Is Structural Exegesis?* 39–40.

15. Cf. Mark 10:15. Matthew has a form of the saying at 18:3.

16. Matt. 19:16 does not start a new journey as Mark 10:17 does, thus indicating that it is part of one continuous unit in Matthew.

about who is good differs from the version found in both Mark and Luke. Jesus is not addressed as the good teacher, nor is it remarked that only God is good. Instead the young man asks what good deed (*agathon*) he must do to have eternal life. Jesus responds, "Why do you ask me concerning the good? One is good [*heis estin ho agathos*]" (v. 17). The young man's test about eternal life orients the answer toward what the good is. The response concerns not only the following of the commandments but also the love of neighbor (v. 19), perfection (*teleios*, v. 20), and the giving of all to the poor.

The immediately preceding scene begins with a saying comparing a rich man's difficulties in entering the kingdom to those of a camel in passing through the eye of a needle (19:24). The implied impossibility of entering the kingdom leads the disciples to ask whether they who have left all will be included. Here Matthew's text differs significantly from both Mark and Luke: "Amen, I say to you who have followed me, at the rebirth [*paliggenesia*] when the son of man shall sit upon his throne of glory, you will be the ones sitting on the twelve thrones judging the twelve tribes of Israel" (19:28). The verse defines and assures the future place of the disciples in the kingdom. The saying "Many that are first will be last, and the last first" (v. 30) is not a generalized saying in Matthew but has specific reference in the narrative. The first who will be last are the Pharisees, those who have tested the Lord and failed (in the divorce question), and those last who will be first are the disciples, who are promised to sit on the thrones of Israel.[17] The parable of the laborers in the vineyard confirms this position. The latecomers are the disciples, and those first hired are the Pharisees. Furthermore, the lord of the parable is Jesus as judge—a frequent theme in Matthew's parables.[18]

Several observations indicating the parable's relation to the preceding chapter reinforce the analysis. Matthew's phrasing of the question of the good in 19:17 keeps the good from lying exclusively with God. Instead it promises that there is one who is good (i.e., Jesus, the Son of man as judge). Too, in the parable the owner is introduced as *oikodespotēs*, but at the time of payment in the evening (i.e., the time of judgment) he is called master (*kyrios*).

For Crossan, Matthew's reworking of the parable extends beyond the addition of v. 16, so that vv. 14 and 15 are a Matthean creation. He maintains that Matthew prefers a good-evil (*agathos-ponēros*) contrast.[19] The evidence is stronger than Crossan has indicated. A good-evil con-

---

17. Meier (*Vision of Matthew*, 141) maintains that the apostles are the first-hired. It is hard to understand how this can be so. See Schweizer, *Good News according to Matthew*, 394–95.

18. Cf. Matt. 22:1–14; 25:1–31.

19. Crossan, "Servant Parables," 35.

trast has eight occurrences in Matthew, of which two have true parallels (Matt. 12:34–35//Luke 6:44–45; Matt. 25:14–30//Luke 19:11–27).[20] Two are without any parallel (Matt. 20:15; 12:34), but it is significant that in the four remaining instances there are parallel contexts in Luke but without Matthew's accent on the good-evil contrast. The context surrounding Matt. 5:45 is parallel to Luke, but the verse is missing. In Matt. 7:17–18, the fruit is contrasted as "good" and "evil," whereas in Luke the negative term is "bad," *sapron* (6:43). At Matt. 7:11 the Father gives "good things," whereas in Luke 11:13 he gives the Holy Spirit. In A Man Gave a Banquet, the servant in Matthew's story goes out and gathers both the bad and the good (Matt. 22:10); such a description of those gathered is missing in Luke. Matthew furthermore has a clear preference for the use of "evil," *ponēros*.[21] The stylistic evidence supports Crossan's contention of the secondary nature of v. 15. Matthew introduced the moralizing tone into the parable[22] and into subsequent interpretation as well.

Crossan also employs an aesthetic argument.[23] He sees a chiasm between vv. 2, 4 and 13:

agreeing . . . for denarius . . . what is just
symphōnesas . . . ex denariou . . . dikaiou

I am not unjust to you; did you not for a denarius agree with me
ouk adikō se,   ouchi   denariou synephōnesas moi

This ties the opening and closing of the parable together.

A majority of Crossan's arguments apply to v. 15, but he also maintains that v. 14 is Matthean. Via, who accepts Crossan's position on v. 15, rejects it on v. 14a, since without v. 14a the parable has no ending. Crossan has argued that v. 14 makes no conceptual difference to the parable, but Via responds that it makes a formal difference, because in Jesus' parables "actions have consequences which come to expression."[24] The debate is difficult but important to adjudicate. Crossan's best evi-

---

20. Matthew emphasizes the evil of the third servant in A Man Entrusts Property.

21. *Ponēros* is used only twice in Mark and is absent in the Matthean parallel Mark 7:21–23//Matt 15:18–20. Once in a passage parallel with Mark, Matt. 15:9 uses *ponēros* where Mark does not. Seven times Matthew uses *ponēros* in common with Luke, but in three parallels with Mark and Luke, Matthew uses *ponēros* where they do not, and likewise in three passages parallel to Luke. Luke uses *ponēros* eleven times, of which eight are parallel; three are unique.

22. Crossan, "Servant Parables," 34.

23. Ibid., 36.

24. Via, "Parable and Example Story," 125. Via continues with the standard interpretation: "Then the theme becomes the estrangement from the source of unexpected generosity of those who believe that they can justify themselves in the order of justice."

dence applies to v. 15, and as indicated above, his original evidence can be strengthened.

Verse 14b is suspect for two reasons: (1) The "I wish," *thelō*, construction is repeated in vv. 14b and 15.[25] Again the evidence is perhaps stronger than Crossan originally indicated. In 19:17 and 19:21 Matthew adds to the story of the young man the phrases "if you wish eternal life" and "if you wish to be perfect." These phrases are absent in the parallel passages in Mark and Luke. (2) We have already shown that Matthew intends in retelling the parable to accent the acceptance of those who come last. Verse 14b drives that point home. The preponderance of evidence indicates that v. 14b is secondary.

The evidence, however, would seem to support the view that v. 14a is part of the originating structure. I remain uneasy with Via's argument from formal necessity, since this may be the one case where formal necessity does not apply. What if the parable teller decided to do something different? Nevertheless, I think Via is correct in resisting the rejection of v. 14a. Without compelling evidence indicating its secondary nature, the assumption should be that it belongs to the parable. Furthermore, the pattern of coming and going is a primary element in the parable's construction (cf. "Surface Structure" below). In vv. 4 and 7 the householder commands the workers to go (*hypagete*) into the vineyard. It is only fitting that he command their representative to depart (*hypage*). Thus v. 14a is clearly tied to the parable's narrative structure.

Once Matthew's subtle but profound influence becomes evident, it is only natural to ask whether he is responsible for the note that the steward was to pay the wages "beginning with the last until the first" (v. 8c). Jülicher has already noted that the order of payment is not important, since all would quickly discover the outcome.[26] Moreover, the theme of reversal of first and last is a clear Matthean addition. Is it not possible that Matthew has added this note to strengthen the parable's tie to its redactional context? Or it may be that the order of payment was what made the parable attractive from his perspective. In any case, the evidence is not compelling. Nevertheless, the verse is suspect, and I will treat it as doubtful.

The analysis of Matthew's literary and redactional intention has led us to conclude that he has read the parable as an example of the theme that the first shall be last and of the moral contrast between good and evil. To advance his aim, he has cast the householder as Jesus and added not only v. 16 but also vv. 14b–15 and maybe v. 8c.

---

25. Crossan, "Servant Parables," 34.
26. Jülicher, *Die Gleichnisreden* 2:462.

Surface Structure

The organization of the parable's surface structure is careful and consistent. The narrative consists of five scenes based on the hours of the day—from sunup to sundown. The time pattern furnishes the overall divisions. Within this pattern one can distinguish two major sections: first, the hiring, and second, the payment. The hiring scenes are organized as follows:

1. he came out / time   / narration   vv. 1–2
2. coming out / time   / direct discourse   vv. 3–5a
         saw others standing
              go you also into the vineyard
3. coming out / time   / narration   v. 5b
4. time   / coming out / direct discourse   vv. 6–7
         found others standing
              go you also into the vineyard

The construction is clear and straightforward. In the first three scenes the opening involves an aorist of *exerchomai*, "he came"—a time marker. In scene 4, these two elements are reversed, forming a chiasm. Scenes 1 and 3 contain narration, and scenes 2 and 4 direct discourse. Also scenes 2 and 4 contain repetitive parallel lines. The first four scenes form a pleasing symmetry.

The fifth and final scene begins with a notice of time—"when it was evening"—and exhibits patterns similar to those employed previously:

1.   time   / direct discourse   v. 8
2. (a) coming / eleventh hour / narration   v. 9
                        received one denarius
   (b) coming / the first   / narration   vv. 10–11
                        received one denarius
3. (a) first-hired's direct discourse   v. 12
   (b) householder's direct discourse   vv. 13–14a

A time indicator and "coming" continue to form an organizing frame, but whereas in the first four scenes the householder came out, now the workers come. An alternating between direct discourse and narration continues, with direct discourse becoming more dominant. Again, two parallel lines are used in the centerpiece to tie together the eleventh hour and first laborers. Finally, in the third part the first laborers and then the householder speak, nicely matching the direct discourses in the first four scenes. The following pattern emerges.

Section I   Section II
2. Householder speaks.   1. Householder speaks.

4. Householder speaks.	3. (a) Laborers speak.
Laborers respond.	(b) Householder responds.

As should be evident, the parable is carefully organized and struc-tured.[27] The symmetry balances the scenes providing a repetitive pattern characteristic of oral language.[28] Within the parable are several even more closely coordinated stylistic and rhetorical devices that we will comment on below.

A Reading

If the standard interpretation has failed and has been under Matthew's influence more than was previously suspected, how are we to proceed? The place to begin is with the common observation that the parable provokes a feeling that the first-hired laborers have somehow been cheated. The question, then, is how and why it provokes this response. How does the parable structure a response, and likewise, how does a hearer structure the story?

Line 1: The kingdom of heaven is like a man, a householder, who came out early in the morning to hire laborers for his vineyard.

The first line presents a hearer with only vague clues about the story's direction. The man clearly is identified as a property owner, a house-holder. This is the consistent identification throughout the parable, ex-cept in v. 8, where he is addressing his steward. The stress is not on master-slave but on patron-client. The text draws from the repertoire of labor for hire, and the story will turn on the interaction. It invokes a temporary relationship between someone with a need—in this case, to have work done—and someone who can fulfill that need.

The time of day is specified, but the time of year is not. The time of day is the normal time for hiring.[29] It may be harvest,[30] but the parable does not state this. A hearer is left with a gap,[31] one of many in the parable.

27. As noted above, Crossan ("Servant Parables," 36) had already pointed out the chiasm between the parable's beginning and end.

28. Ong, *Interfaces*, esp. 102–17.

29. Str-B 1:830.

30. See Curtis, "Parable of the Labourers," 8; Jeremias, *Parables*, 136; Michaelis, *Die Gleichnisse*, 172–73. But against this, see Bultmann, *History of the Synoptic Tradition*, 190; Linnemann, *Jesus of the Parables*, 82. Gryglewicz ("Gospel of the Overworked," 191–92) deals with various issues about the length of the day and the hiring practices in Palestine. Derrett ("Workers in the Vineyard," 79–80) corrects the problems created by Bauer ("Gnadelohn oder Tageslohn?" 224–28) when he confused Roman and Palestinian hiring practices.

31. See chap. 12, n. 38.

Finally, this is not simply any farm work but labor in a vineyard. The vineyard implies a metaphor, for vines and vineyards have a rich symbolic heritage in Israel's language stock. One need only recall Isaiah's Song of the Vineyard (5:1–7) or God's mournful complaint in Jer. 12:10 that "many shepherds have destroyed my vineyard," the vineyard being Israel. Vineyards have a strong metaphorical potential.[32]

In sum, the parable's opening unit is full of possibilities, of gaps to be bridged. There are an owner and laborers: is the accent on wages? The time of year is left open: is it a story of harvest or planting or pruning? The place is a vineyard: is it a tale of Israel's fate? All are temptations to the hearer, gaps suggesting the story's possible course.

Line 2: On agreeing with the laborers for a denarius a day, he sent them into his vineyard.

Lines 1 and 2 are tied together by a chiasm, with time marking the two poles.

> early in the morning . . . laborers/laborers . . . a day
> *hama proi . . . ergatas/ergaton . . . hemeran*

The terms within the chiasm are "to hire" and "denarius." The stylistic accent of the first two lines falls on hiring and the exact wages to be paid. To tie the two lines together more closely, they both end in the phrase "into his vineyard."

The wages are now no longer a gap, for the workers will be paid a denarius a day. The amount is not irrelevant, since it connotes a value, a worth, relative to other values. If, for example, this were a contemporary tale, then the audience would respond differently if the wage were twenty dollars or a hundred dollars. The relative value of a denarius is not as clear as some commentators would have it. W. Michaelis, for example, maintains that the householder is being extremely generous.[33] Others maintain that a denarius was an average wage for a day laborer. Frequently the proof for such an assertion is this parable.[34]

F. Heichelheim's study of the economic situation in Syria[35] provides evidence about the relative worth of a denarius. He calculates that a second-century C.E. adult in Palestine would need about half a denarius a day for basic survival.[36] He collects evidence for daily wages which indicates that the householder was probably on target. The angel in

---

32. For an expanded treatment, see Feldman, *Parables and Similes*, 125–49.
33. *Die Gleichnisse*, 172.
34. BAGD, 179.
35. Heichelheim, "Syria."
36. Ibid., 179–80.

Tobit 5:15 receives one drachma (a denarius) to accompany Tobias, besides traveling expenses. But given Tobit's literary genre as a pseudo-archaic work, is it correct to conclude that the angel's wage is an ordinary wage? Heichelheim's second piece of evidence is an Aramaic graffito found on an ossuary at Bethpage, dated around the first century C.E. The graffito consists of a listing of names followed by numbers. The list gives no indication of its purpose. Its publisher conjectures that it represents wages.[37] He uses Matt. 20:2 to argue that the sums were the days the laborers worked for a wage of a denarius a day. This may be true, but it is conjecture and does not advance a calculation of the value of a denarius. Heichelheim's third piece of evidence is the report that Rabbi Hillel (ca. 20 B.C.E.) earned half a denarius a day while in Jerusalem and was considered impoverished.[38] Rabbi Meir (ca. 150 C.E.), an accomplished scribe, earned two denarii a day.[39]

Because of a lack of hard evidence, inflation, and the variation in local conditions, a precise value for a denarius cannot be determined. The evidence suggests that a wage of a denarius a day would be sufficient to support a worker and his family at a *subsistence* level, that is, at the level of a peasant. In no way can it be viewed as a wage generating a surplus. Of itself the wage is not generous.

> *Line 3:* And going out about the third hour, he saw others standing in the marketplace idle and to those he said, "Go you also into the vineyard and whatever is right I will give you." And they went.

As we noted above, the line's opening continues the parallelism, "going out," *exēlthōn*, and the specification of time. A carefully crafted wordplay appears between lines 2 and 3. "Others" are described as standing in the marketplace *argous* (idle), which sets them in contrast with the *ergatas* (workers) in the vineyard.

The householder remains on the initiative and engages in direct discourse; no longer is the story content with a narrator's summary. But the action is different from that of the first laborers. The first *bargained* an agreement, whereas the idlers are told to go into the vineyard and they will receive what is *right*.

Another contrast emerges between the first group and the new workers. The former's wage was specified at a denarius whereas the latter's is blank. They will receive what is right (*dikaios*). The word *dikaios* has a

---

37. Dussaud, "Comptes d'ouvriers," esp. 244–45. Heichelheim apparently does not recognize that Dussaud reconstructed graffiti on the basis of Matt. 20:2, thus making the argument circular.

38. Jeremias, *Jerusalem*, 116. The reference is to *b. Yom.* 35b (Soncino 4:136).

39. Str-B 1:831.

distinctive religious heritage in Judaism, for it characterizes the man who under the law has the correct orientation toward God, God who is Himself *dikaios*. To be unrighteous is to be a sinner or impious. A "right" person is virtuous, a person who fulfills his duties toward God and society.[40] "Right" involves not simply strict, legalistic justice but also liberality and charity.[41]

The description of the wage as "what is right" creates a blank. What will the right wage turn out to be? A hearer expects some portion of a denarius.[42] The story now has a direction, a lack to be fulfilled. The remaining elements of the story play out the options for fulfilling that lack. A hearer begins to anticipate the options. Will the laborers fail to deliver sufficient labor for a just wage? Or will the householder fail to deliver what is right? Given the conditions of the day, the latter is a real possibility.[43]

The time-of-the-year and vineyard motifs are left undeveloped. While the master's action is urgent and therefore suggests harvest, the idle laborers do not. The audience has no way to know the time of year. Similarly with the vineyard; it is not explicitly developed as a theme. The question of wages dominates the narrative line. The story creates its own suspense: What are right wages?

Line 4: And again going out about the sixth and ninth hour he did the same.

This short line has two functions in the narrative. First, it reinforces the dynamic of the previous line: the same thing has happened again. A hearer still does not know what time of year it is or why the householder needs laborers so urgently. But more workers have hired on without bargaining. The purpose of the householder's action and the amount he will pay remain unspoken.

Second, the line furnishes a transition to the dialogue that follows. By repeating "going out" and indicating the time, the story moves through the daytime hours. The repetition indicates more of the same until the climax.

The parable's literary technique exemplifies the folklore law of three. Usually three characters provide the best balance, but this story implies a large cast of characters: all those hired at each of the hours. Line 4 collapses the different groups into one, so that they eventually drop

---

40. Schrenk, "*dikaios*," 185.
41. Rosenthal, "*Sedaka*, Charity," 411–30.
42. Jeremias, *Parables*, 136; Linnemann, *Jesus of the Parables*, 83.
43. Gryglewicz ("Gospel of the Overworked," 191) indicates that owners frequently tried to underpay their laborers. Katz (*Protection of the Weak*, 30) indicates that this was the reason that the "laws of labor" in rabbinic writings are actually the rights of laborers.

from sight in favor of those hired at the eleventh hour. The storyteller has no desire for a direct correspondence to the world outside the narrative. If he had, he would be at pains to inform a hearer about what happened to each of the groups, and the story would soon dissolve into disorder.

> *Line 5:* And about the eleventh hour going out, he found others standing, and he said to them, "Why are you standing here the whole day idle?" They said to him, "Because no one has hired us." He said to them, "Go into the vineyard."

The beginning reverses the introductory formula of the three previous lines; the time indicator comes first, then "going out," creating a chiasm with the other scenes. The line exhibits an economy of vocabulary. "He found others standing" parallels "he saw others standing" (v. 3b). His question marks the third time we have been told that others are standing. "The whole day" recalls the "day" of v. 2, in which an agreement for a denarius a day was struck, and "idle" recalls the idleness of v. 3. Finally, his command to go into the vineyard repeats the command of v. 4. The repeated vocabulary recalls, implies, and summarizes the householder's previous dealings with "the others."

At a stylistic level the discussion between householder and laborers echoes that of previous workers, and the story's strategy remains the same. The householder's urgency becomes more obvious; he is now hiring laborers at the very last hour. But a hearer is given no real information on why the urgency. If it is harvest, why have the laborers been idle the whole day? Or is their excuse even believable? If these have been "standing" in the marketplace all day, why did the householder not hire them sooner? In v. 3, it says that "he saw others," whereas in the present unit it says that "he found others." Does finding indicate surprise on his part? The narrative furnishes no evidence. It creates a series of gaps or blanks that invite a hearer to offer a solution.

> *Line 6:* When evening came, the master of the vineyard said to his steward, "Call the workers and give them their wages [beginning with the first until the last."] And coming, those of the eleventh hour received one denarius.

This line initiates the second and final section. Its vocabulary signals a new beginning. The time is evening,[44] and the householder is addressed as master (*kyrios*), either because he is speaking to his steward or because of Matthew's redactional need for a judge figure. The workers are

---

44. The payment of wages at evening was required by Deut. 24:14–15 and Lev. 19:13.

referred to again as *ergatas* instead of "them" or "others." The formal terms of a patron-client relationship are reintroduced.

A denouement begins that will erase significant gaps. The first important gap is the wage to be paid those laborers who have worked less than a full day. They will receive a denarius. It is important to recall how this particular gap was created. In hiring the laborers of the third hour, the householder promised to pay what was right but left the amount unspecified. As other workers were hired throughout the day, this same implicit contract remained in effect, even though not mentioned again. The repetitive patterns and economy of vocabulary suggest that the same thing occurred with each group. A hearer has expected that this important gap will be filled in. What is "right" turns out to be the amount agreed on with those workers who labored the whole day.[45] At this point a hearer may entertain consideration of the householder's generosity. If a denarius is for a peasant an average day's wage, the householder is generous to the last-hired in comparison with what he is proposing to pay the first-hired. But even to those last-hired he is not generous in absolute terms. Similarly, if the theme of generosity is to be maintained, then a hearer expects those who have labored the whole day to receive more.

If the note about the order of payment is authentic, then its purpose is not to affront those hired first, but to serve as a literary device to allow the earlier-hired to witness the events.[46]

Line 7: And coming, the first thought that they would receive more, and they received one denarius, even they. And on receiving, they grumbled against the householder, saying, "These last have worked only one hour, and you have made them equal to us who have borne the burden of the day and the scorching heat."

The householder's comings and goings have provided the story's shape. A hearer has observed without explanation the householder's

45. Derrett ("Workers in the Vineyard," 76–77) argues that the key to the parable is the custom of *po el batel* (literally, "unemployed or idle laborer"). Because leisure was a value in the East, *po el batel* represented the amount required to induce a laborer to work. Therefore Derrett argues, the householder would have expected to pay those hired at the last hour proportionally more per hour than those who worked the whole day. Knowing that the first-hired had eaten from the harvest, he decided that there would be such little difference between the amounts due to the various laborers that, to avoid hassle, he would pay all the same. There are a number of problems with Derrett's suggestion: (1) It is not certain whether the time is that of harvest. (2) Why do the first-hired complain? Under Derrett's proposal, Jesus is teaching a complicated rabbinic lesson. (3) Derrett reads the story not as fiction but as an actual occurrence. He tries to create an actual correspondence to something out there, outside the story. He fills in all the gaps in such a way as to destroy the parable as creator of aesthetic experience.

46. Jülicher, *Die Gleichnisreden* 2:462.

frequent forays into the marketplace to hire more workers. One may have guessed at his purpose, but no reason is given. Some of the story's gaps turn out to be forever blank. The comings and goings serve only to move the narrative forward. The final climax deals with wages. Two expectations concerning wages have arisen. The original bargain was for a denarius a day, with the later laborers receiving a promise of "what is right." The conclusion is that the householder is an upright, honest, and even charitable man on urgent business. When he pays those of the eleventh hour a denarius, a hearer expects not only honesty (what is right) for all but also generosity. Such is also the expectation of the first workers. *In the place of the bargained-for denarius has been substituted "what is right."* The hearer identifies with the first-hired's expectation. Their complaint contrasts one hour's labor with the burden of a whole day, implying even laziness by the eleventh hour workers—an implication one might draw from their idleness. Thus the householder's injustice results from a comparison with what he paid those who worked only one hour, just as generosity emerges only in comparison with what he bargained for the whole day's wage.

Line 8: And replying to one of them, he said, "Friend, am I not doing you right? Did you not agree with me for a denarius? Take yours and go!"

The irony of the address "friend" stands out especially since the workers had omitted a title of respect for the householder.[47] He also addresses one of them, not the group. To single out one is at odds with the rest of the parable's style, since previously the householder has always addressed workers in groups.[48] Why now address one of them in the second-person singular? The parable's overall strategy provides the answer. In line 1, the parable employed formal relations based on wages. A bargain joined householder to workers. As the story progressed, an implied hierarchy emerged among workers based on the time of day at which they were hired.[49] When the master agreed to pay what was right to those who would work less than a whole day, the bargained-for wage

47. Rengstorf, *"hetairos,"* 701. Only Matthew uses the noun and then always in the vocative (Matt. 22:12; 26:50). While warning against making too much of the usage, Rengstorf says that in Matthew "it always denotes a mutually binding relation between the speaker and the hearer which the latter has disregarded and scorned." But the evidence Rengstorf adduces from normal Greek usage does not support this reading of Matthew. I would suggest that he has violated his own warning.

48. Jeremias (*Parables,* 137) and Michaelis (*Die Gleichnisse,* 176) argue that the one singled out is the chief objector, the ringleader. Linnemann (*Jesus of the Parables,* 154) correctly objects to this.

49. The hierarchy is abetted by the contrasts of vineyard-marketplace and laborers-idle (the others).

and the amount to be paid the later workers became ingredients in a hierarchy of labor. How much would be paid was blank, and even though the hearer did not fill in that blank, one had expectations about the hierarchial relations implied at the time of hiring. The hierarchical pattern of the parable replicates the hierarchical pattern of a patron-client society.

Line 6, in which those hired at the eleventh hour are paid, relativizes wages as a basis of relationships. What is right is amplified by a suggestion of generosity. Even "generosity" becomes part of the hierarchical expectation. It is all right to be generous to those who have labored only an hour, but justice requires even more generosity for those who have labored the whole day.

We can now see the significance of the householder's address to only one worker. He recognizes no distinctions. Every laborer is needed at every hour in his vineyard. He offers to treat all alike. The address "friend" bridges the householder-them relationship. He operates on an I-thou pattern.

From Story to Kingdom

The crux of interpretation is that the parable deliberately provokes its audience to an accusation of injustice about the payment to the first laborers. The provocation sets in sharp juxtaposition the expected values of the kingdom and the values the parable associates with the kingdom.

In the master's accounting the hierarchy of wages represents how things should be. The relative value of wages determines one's place. It is a matter of justice. A rabbinic parable illustrates the close relation between wages and a hierarchy of value. In the rabbinic parable the issue is the rewards for fulfilling the various commandments. God has not revealed which commandments would receive a rich reward and which less. Rabbi Abba bar Kahana tells the parable to illustrate the lesson:

> The matter is like a king who hired labourers, and brought them into his garden; he hid, and did not reveal, what was the reward of [working in] the garden, so that they might not neglect that part of the work for which the reward was small, and go and do that part for which the reward was great. In the evening he summoned them all, and said, "Under which tree did you work?" The first answered, "Under this one." The king said, "That is a pepper tree; its reward is one gold piece." He said to the next, "Under which tree did you work?" He said, "Under that one." The king said, "It is a white flower tree; its reward is half a gold piece." He asked a third, "Under which tree did you work?" He said, "Under this one." The king replied, "That is an

olive tree; its reward is 200 zuzim." The labourers said to him, "Ought you not to have told us the tree under which the reward was greatest?" The king replied, "If I had done that, how could all of my garden have been tilled?"[50]

This parable is quite similar to A Householder Went Out Early. It even supports the same mytheme. In the rabbinic parable, the king pays different wages for different work, only he conceals the scale from the workers. In our parable the wages for different work are the same. Thus our parable subverts the mytheme equating wages with worth.

The parable A Householder Went Out Early demonstrates how relative are notions of justice. The householder promises to pay those hired from the third hour on what is right; and he responds to the first-hired when they complain that he has paid them what was right. In identifying with the complaint of the first-hired, a hearer opts for a world in which justice is defined by a hierarchical relation between individuals (i.e., for a world in which the accounting should set matters aright). To treat all the same is not just, because all are not alike, all have not earned the same. As the first-hired reply, the householder makes all equal (*isoys*). According to one vision of the kingdom the function of justice is not to make all equal but to ensure all their appropriate places. The parable relativizes justice to show that it is incapable of organizing the world of the kingdom. The householder has paid what was just, yet the parable's clever strategy still maneuvers him into the appearance of injustice.

The lack in the parable of any absolute standard of justice undermines any human standard for the kingdom. For the parable, value or worth (i.e., a place in the kingdom) is determined not by what is right but by acceptance. The householder's urgent though unexplained need for laborers is the parable's metaphor for grace.[51] It is not wages or hierarchy that counts but the call to go into the vineyard. The householder's generosity lies not in the wage but in the need. Those commentators who have seen in the parable a justification for Jesus' association with the outcast are correct, insofar as the parable provokes a response in which all are invited to the kingdom not on just deserts but by invitation. The parable's strategy is not unlike Paul's argument that with God there is no distinction, that justification (making right) is through gift (Rom. 3:22–24).

50. C. Montefiore and Loewe, *Rabbinic Anthology,* 126. The quotation is from *Midrash Rabbah* on Deut. 6.2, a ninth-century compilation. Abba bar Kahana is a third-century rabbi.

51. Those commentators who see grace as the major theme of the parable are correct. The denarius, however, is not the metaphor of grace; rather, the need for workers, the call, is the metaphor.

To insist, as the parable does, that invitation, not justice, is the way of the kingdom radically subverts the kingdom of God as a reward for a faithful and just life. In A King Wished to Settle Accounts the fellow servants demand justice from the king only to realize that the kingdom is mercy. When the king carries out justice, chaos ensues. Our parable's conclusion insists on this. The householder tells the first-hired, "Take what is yours and go." The problem with justice as a standard is that it misses the invitation. All along they have been in the kingdom, "in your midst" (Luke 17:21); now in justice they must depart.

4

Home
& Farm

$\mathcal{A}$rtifacts

Tool-making aided our move up the evolutionary ladder, and the so-called neolithic revolution—the mastery of pottery, weaving, agriculture, and the domestication of animals—set the pattern on which civilizations rested until the rise of the scientific method. When tools received names, those newly named artifacts could symbolize other realities that folks experience but that lack obvious physical presence. The archaeological evidence of early humans uncovers their art and symbol in everyday life.

In "Family, Village, City, and Beyond" and "Masters and Servants," the horizontal and vertical aspects of society provided models for and were replicated in the parables' narrative and metaphorical network. The parables of this group, "Home and Farm," explicitly use the semiotic sign itself. Language is metaphorically structured, understanding concepts in terms of other concepts. Even more, "we conceptualize the less clearly delineated in terms of the more clearly delineated."[1] The more abstract a phenomenon is, the more it depends on concrete metaphors to symbolize and even to structure it.

Since we cannot directly apprehend or experience many abstract realities, a variety and range of experiential metaphors give them structure. For example, love, something real that we experience, is nevertheless abstract. Its definition and our experience of it are determined by the metaphors used to describe it. Similarly, the kingdom of God is a sym-

---

1. Lakoff and M. Johnson, *Metaphors We Live By*, 59.

bol, but the symbol is made up of two lexi, "kingdom" and "God." The metaphorical structure of the kingdom is derived from the experience of those who are ruled by a king, and the various aspects of kingdoms and kings can be applied to God, so that God rules, saves, defeats his enemies, conquers, and so forth. Metaphors both structure abstract phenomena by their own structure and highlight our experience of the phenomena. Without metaphors, such abstractions could not be experienced, since they would not be recognized.

These metaphors, derived from experience, form complex systems of metaphors, or gestalts. Such systems of metaphors both allow an understanding and experience of abstract phenomena and promote the emergence of other aspects of the metaphorical system to stand for the phenomena. If God is a king, then winning is an aspect of God. So a metaphorical network allows the development of an extended narrative about divine war, as for example in the Qumran War Scroll. The system operates by congruency: what is congruent with the system, the gestalt, is metaphorically true. On the other hand, those things that are incongruent are not true. For God to be defeated, to lose, is incongruent with God as king, although not because of the lexi "king," for kings do lose battles and wars, but because the lexi "God" signifies something powerful, indeed, omnipotent. Thus the two metaphorical networks interact.

When a metaphorical network must change to expose a new experience of an abstract phenomenon, the user of metaphor can either attack the metaphorical system or offer new metaphors. When we begin to understand our experience in terms of new metaphors, or new metaphorical alignments, we comprehend a new reality.[2]

The ability to use those things that surround us, the everyday, to symbolize and give structure to our experience of the sacred, is what Lévi-Strauss refers to as the reciprocity of perspectives.[3] Humanity and the world mirror each other. Natural phenomena are assimilated to human actions, but also simultaneously the power and efficacy of nature are attributed to humans. For example, in the storytelling and dancing that take place prior to a hunt, the hunters are not just imitating the animals but also trying to take on their powers. This reciprocity is the basis of mythical thinking, a vision of the essential oneness of reality.

The parables of this unit, "Home and Farm," focus on the artifacts of everyday life. In these parables the artifact is the metaphorical vehicle, not a social dynamic, as in the previous two units. Allegorical interpretation correctly sensed this when, as in the interpretation of A Sower

2. Ibid., 145.
3. Lévi-Strauss, *Savage Mind*, 222.

Went Out, it tried to explain what the various seeds mean: the allegory realized that these seeds, these artifacts, are metaphors for, stand in the place of, something else. Yet it failed to comprehend how that metaphorical process operates.

The recognition that these parables highlight a metaphor has led to a confusion of classification. Jülicher has distinguished between parable proper and similitude. Similitude is for him a picture, whereas the parable is a narrative.[4] Most of the texts Jülicher classifies as similitude have not been dealt with in this book and would more properly be classified as aphorisms or proverbs. Most commentators admit that the boundary between similitude and parable is blurred.[5] The ground for the distinction is not clear, because narrative (the classification for parable) and word picture (the classification for similitude) belong to different species. Dodd has suggested a grammatical distinction,[6] and Bultmann has tried to distinguish between typical condition or event, for similitude, and interesting particular situation, for parable.[7] Similitude and parable mark efforts to make distinctions within a form, *mashal*, that the ancients viewed as one.

Jülicher's original distinction based on narrative is correct. In my definition of parable, I have insisted on narrative as an essential element. All the parables in this unit are narratives. The narrative may be minimal, but it is there; when it is only implied, there is no longer a parable but something else, probably a proverb. The Leaven has minimal narrative: the woman hides leaven in bread until it is all leaven. It has a sequence of events. But in comparison with A Man Had Two Sons or From Jerusalem to Jericho, its narrative is not fully developed. What is missing is plot, a contest between characters. The suspense evolves at the discourse level, where the implied hearer makes sense of the sequence of events and the juxtaposition of images.[8]

These mininarratives sit on the borderline between parable and proverb, both *meshalim*. In another place,[9] I have developed this difference under the heading of the one-liner. These parables share with the other parables narrativity, whereas in proverbs the narrative is implied. A proverb is a summary of a community's wisdom and as such sum-

4. For a definition of similitude, see Jülicher, *Die Gleichnisreden* 1:80; for a definition of parable, see 1:90. See pp. 29–30 above for a discussion of Jülicher's third form, the example story.

5. So Bultmann, *History of the Synoptic Tradition*, 174; Dodd, *Parables*, 7; B. T. D. Smith, *Parables*, 17.

6. Dodd, *Parables*, 7.

7. Bultmann, *History of the Synoptic Tradition*, 174.

8. This distinction between story and discourse is from Chatman's *Story and Discourse*, 19.

9. Scott, *Jesus, Symbol-Maker*, 66–67.

marizes a common story. It presupposes a story of common human experience of which it is the distillation. It "is a statement about a particular kind of occurrence or situation, an orderly tract of experience which can be repeated."[10] The presupposed story is that tract of experience from which a "cluster of insights" is drawn.[11] The function of the proverbial insight is, in William Beardslee's words, to create a "continuous whole out of one's existence." In this sense, proverb belongs to language's mythological dimension, since it seeks to totalize in summary our experience. Like myths, proverbs seek to "think for us," to relieve us of the responsibility for thought.

I have called these parables one-liners, on the analogy of one-line jokes. They share with proverbs the intensification and concentration of language but are parables because they are narratives. Unlike the other parables, they lack explicit plot development at the level of story, yet at the level of discourse the implied hearer must work out the insight proposed by the parable. Like the one-line joke, the hearer has to "catch on." Unlike proverbs, which summarize community insight, these seek to transform a hearer's insight into a metaphor for the kingdom.

The strategy of these parables is to juxtapose a proposed metaphor for the kingdom within a narrative development in such a way that a hearer must construct a discourse for the parabolic transference. In general these parables accomplish this by a process of demythologization. They attack myth. If the fundamental task of myth is to resolve conflict, the myth of God the king resolves the conflict between religious expectation and actual human experience. God as king can right those realities that come into conflict with the expectations of Israel. The parables in this group operate in a similar way but begin at different metaphorical points. All but two of the parables make use of appropriate metaphors. The Leaven and A Grain of Mustard Seed contain in the signified of their primary metaphors associations that conflict with associations in the signified of "kingdom of God." The smallness of the mustard seed is inappropriate for the greatness of the kingdom, and the leaven signifies moral corruption whereas the kingdom of God signifies moral goodness. This conflict is unresolved at the level of story but left to the hearer to resolve, if possible, at the level of discourse.

The remaining parables in this unit employ appropriate metaphors in inappropriate ways. In Treasure, the initial image is a very appropriate, well-established metaphor for the kingdom. But in its narrative development, the finder of the treasure engages in immoral action by deceiving

10. Beardslee, "Uses of Proverbs," 65.
11. Ibid., 66.

the original owner. The narrative offers no resolution for this conflict, but a hearer must deal with it at the level of discourse. The parable From the Fig Tree offers a variation on this pattern. It begins with an appropriate metaphor, a fig tree, a sign of blessing for the kingdom, but fails to develop the metaphor in a religious sense. Instead, the metaphor maintains its strictly secular tone, forcing a hearer to question how the kingdom is manifested in the metaphor.

One way of dealing with the mythological conflict inherent in this group of parables has been to classify many of them as parables of growth.[12] In his classic article on the topic, Nils Dahl has summarized the state of scholarship at the time of the article and presented a mature paradigm, for which reason it has gone almost unchallenged.[13]

Dahl's contribution is really a subtle reworking of Dodd and Jeremias. He borrows Dodd's classification of the parables of growth, but employs Jeremias's understanding of Jesus' eschatology. It is a two-stage eschatology in which the kingdom is both present and yet to come. Thus the phenomenon of growth is the perfect metaphorical vehicle for this two-stage kingdom. The context for the parables involves the debate between Jesus and his opponents concerning eschatological expectations, and the metaphor of growth is the vehicle of resolution. "To the growth which God in accordance with his own established order gives in the sphere of organic life, corresponds the series of events by which God in accordance with his plan of salvation leads history towards the end of the world and the beginning of the new aeon."[14]

Many problems beset Dahl's proposal, beginning with his idea of parable as a one-point debating technique.[15] But more critically, his echatological model for understanding the parable is derived from outside the parable and reduces a parable to the general idea of growth without any investigation of how each parable is operative—of what symbols and metaphors it invokes. By ignoring the specificity of each parable's metaphorical reference, the classification "parables of growth" submerges the scandal.

The initial discriminating factor for the taxonomy of these parables is their focus on a metaphorical network as the parabolic vehicle. Furthermore, the strategy they employ to exploit the metaphorical network is clear. But micro divisions are less so. We have rejected the notion of

12. I have been unable to discover who first used this classification, although Dodd (*Parables,* chap. 6) is the first to give these parables a separate and extended treatment.

13. Dahl, "Parables of Growth." See my analysis and critique in "Parables of Growth Revisited," 3–9.

14. Dahl, "Parables of Growth," 146.

15. See pp. 43–45 above.

parables of growth because it is built on an ideology foreign to the corpus, yet what is helpful about this classification is its recognition that the agricultural process is prominent in this group.[16] I propose two divisions within this unit. The first group operates with the metaphorical network of the kingdom as a home; the second assumes that the kingdom is a farm. These parables select from their metaphorical network (either home or farm) a specific set of metaphors and develop them within a narrative framework.[17] Though it might be possible to make further subdivisions between farm and commerce, as in The Net, basically these parables employ the metaphorical networks connected with the home and agriculture and their associated activities.

Parables of the Home

Three parables exploit metaphors of the home: A Woman with a Jar, A Woman with Ten Drachmas, and The Leaven (see chap. 15 below). These parables accent the woman in the home, and this suggests shame and uncleanliness, themes not normally associated with the kingdom.

A Woman with a Jar

The parable A Woman with a Jar appears only in the *Gospel of Thomas*. This short, quixotic parable has been proposed by several as an authentic parable of Jesus,[18] but few have ventured an interpretation.

> *A Woman with a Jar*
>
> Jesus said, "The kingdom of the [Father] is like a certain woman who was carrying a jar full of meal. While she was walking [on] the road, still some distance from home, the handle of the jar broke and the meal emptied out behind her on the road. She did not realize it; she had noticed no accident. When she reached her house, she set the jar down and found it empty." (*Gos. Thom.* 97)

The parable occurs in the Gospel as the middle panel of a triptych built around a series of contrasts: little leaven and large loaves; full jar and empty jar; powerful man and weak man. Within these contrasts the middle one of the woman and her jar is an example of failure. Ménard in his gnostic reading of the parable sees it as exhibiting the remoteness of the redeemer from the foreign earth and points to a passage in the

---

16. Feldman (*Parables and Similes*) deals with agricultural and pastoral similes.

17. This is to insist on the correctness of Jeremias's insight in *Parables*, 146, that the kingdom is compared to situations, not a specific object. Cf. Breech, "Kingdom of God," 21.

18. H. Montefiore and Turner, *Thomas and the Evangelists*, 71.

Gospel of Truth where spoiled jars are broken "and the master of the house does not suffer loss. Rather [he] is glad because in place of the bad jars there are full ones which are made perfect."[19] But this analysis seems far-fetched. More to the point is the comment of H. Montefiore, who notes that the point in *Thomas* is the imperceptible loss of the meal,[20] and that the woman is an example of those who do not know wisdom. Since the parable in *Thomas* exemplifies unknowing, the repetitive "she did not realize it, she had noticed no accident" is probably an addition to fit *Thomas*'s performance.

Montefiore notes further that the parable "is as homely as the parable of the Leaven" and then provides an eschatological interpretation. The parable refers to the imperceptible coming of the kingdom until it is suddenly revealed, referring to the parable A Man Casts Seed. Montefiore is correct in pointing to The Leaven, for both parables employ the metaphorical network of the kingdom as a home, and, in a way he does not suspect, the parable is like A Man Casts Seed because both make a scriptural allusion.

The parable operates on two levels, or to be more precise, requires of its hearer two deliberate operations at the discourse level. Initially one observes that the woman arrives home empty-handed. How is that like the kingdom? The kingdom is identified with loss, with accident, with emptiness, with barrenness. If the kingdom is a home, this parable highlights the female aspects of the home, the system of shame as opposed to male honor. Thus Montefiore is right: the parable is much like The Leaven, for it identifies the kingdom with the unclean.

The next operation does not relieve this tension but increases it. The parable echoes the story of the widow of Zarephath (1 Kings 17:8–16).[21] There is a famine, and Elijah is told to go to Zarephath and there "I have commanded a widow to feed you" (v. 9). He spies a widow at the city gate and asks for a piece of bread. She replies, "As the Lord your God lives, I have nothing baked, only a handful of meal in a jar, and a little oil in a cruse" (v. 12). She has been gathering sticks in order to bake some cakes for her child and herself. Elijah commands her to bake but bring him the first cake. "For thus says the Lord the God of Israel, 'The jar of meal shall not be spent . . . until the day that the Lord sends rain upon the earth'" (v. 14). She does as Elijah commands, and the prophet, she,

---

19. *Gospel of Truth* 25, in *Naq Hammadi Library*, ed. Robinson, 41. The text is quite confused, according to Grobel (*Gospel of Truth*, 103).

20. H. Montefiore and Turner, *Thomas and the Evangelists*, 71. Montefiore, who argues for the authenticity of the parable, notes that Gnostics would hardly have created a parable about a woman; but this is not necessarily true, since it is here a negative example.

21. Waller ("Parable of Leaven," 103) notices this similarity.

and her child eat for many days. "The meal was not spent . . . according to the word of the Lord which he spoke by Elijah" (v. 16).[22]

The parable of A Woman with a Jar reverses the 1 Kings story. Given the significance of Elijah in eschatological speculation and the prominent protection promised widows,[23] this parable's referencing of the Elijah story creates a real scandal. There is no prophet to come to the woman's aid, nor will her jar be filled. The kingdom is identified not with divine intervention but with divine emptiness. Like The Leaven, this parable attacks and subverts the myth of the appearance of God. God is identified with the unclean, and the kingdom as home is unclean. This not only coheres with Jesus' association with the outcast but parallels Mark's climax to Jesus' death: "My God, my God, why have you forsaken me?" (Mark 15:34) At the moment of emptiness and despair the centurion confesses that Jesus was truly the Son of God (Mark 15:39). Whoever can see the kingdom of God in this parable which runs counter to the story of the widow of Zarephath stands with the centurion.

A Woman with Ten Drachmas

A Woman with Ten Drachma

What woman having ten drachmas, if she loses one drachma, does not light a lamp and sweep the house and seek carefully until she finds it?

This parable, coupled in Luke 15 with A Man with a Hundred Sheep, is often seen as making the same point as that parable. The two are frequently referred to as twin parables. And no doubt Luke so views the two parables, but they do have their differences.

The first two verses of chapter 15 establish the redactional context for the three parables of A Man with a Hundred Sheep, A Woman with Ten Drachmas, and A Man Had Two Sons. "Now tax collectors and sinners were all drawing near to hear him. And the Pharisees and the scribes murmured, saying, 'This man receives sinners and eats with them.'"[24] This superscription indicates the double motion that reappears throughout the chapter: first a motion of sinners toward God, which involves hearing and repentance, and then their reception, signaled by eating. The classic example of the double motion is the parable A Man Had Two Sons, in which the younger son moves toward the father and the father

---

22. In the next story, the woman's child dies and Elijah raises him to life: "See, your son lives (1 Kings 17:23).

23. See chap. 6 above.

24. For an extensive analysis of Luke's construction of the chap., see chap. 2 above.

receives him with a banquet of rejoicing. The other side of this repentance-and-eating theme is the rejection of those who do not join in the banquet (i.e., the Pharisees), which occurs in the second part of the final parable. In the two short parables A Man with a Hundred Sheep and A Woman with Ten Drachmas, the repentance does not occur in the parables but occurs in their applications (vv. 7, 10: "There will be more joy in heaven over one sinner who repents") and the meal is implied in "Rejoice with me." In the narrative the lost object moves away, and the finder moves toward the lost object.

Not only has Luke provided a narrative perspective from which to view the parables but the extensive verbal similarities between the two parables suggest extensive reworking on Luke's part. Does this mean that one or the other parable is a Lukan composition?[25] It is important to examine where the two parables are parallel to decide this question. First we compare the similarity of language.

having a hundred sheep (v. 4)	drachma having ten (v. 8)
having-lost	if she-loses
until he-finds it	until when she-finds
finding he-lays on his (v. 5) shoulders	finding (v. 9)

he-calls-together   (v. 6)
    friends and neighbors
	she-calls-together
	    friends and neighbors

saying to-them	saying

rejoice with-me because
    I-have-found my sheep
    which was-lost
	rejoice with-me because
	    I-have-found the drachma
	    which was-lost

In A Woman with Ten Drachmas, "finding, she-calls-together" forms a single phrase, whereas in A Man with a Hundred Sheep a description of the shepherd placing the found sheep on his shoulders intervenes. The similarity of vocabulary makes it evident that Luke has performed both parables so that they are similar. His joining them with "or" (v. 8) indicates their close relation in his scheme. But the diagram indicates where the conformity occurs. First, the introduction and conclusion accent the lost-found theme to fit the interpretation of the rejoicing over one sinner who repents, thereby justifying at the narrative level the table fellowship with sinners. Both parables end with the finding of the lost object, but the theme of rejoicing is due to the Lukan performance.[26]

Similarly, there is tension between the parables and their application. In both parables the lost object must be sought after, whereas Luke is

25. Bultmann, *History of the Synoptic Tradition*, 185.
26. So also Jeremias, *Die Sprache*, 247.

interested in the penitent's return.[27] In the parable A Man with a Hundred Sheep a hearer may well decide that the shepherd was a fool for abandoning the ninety-nine in the wilderness and risking their loss. The rejoicing man may have only one sheep. This disturbing element eventually subverts Luke's usage. In A Woman with Ten Drachmas, the woman loses the coin; it has not separated itself from her as would be the case of a sinner. Since there is no risk or implied rejection of the other coins, they cannot be compared to the righteous (the Pharisees). Thus we can see traces of an originating structure in both stories whose verbal skin has been rearranged.

Still Luke's reading of the parable is helpful because he indicates a response to the originating structure. Identifying the lost object with the sinner indicates that it is a thing of little value.[28] The parable depends in Luke on the ironic observation that what is of little value is of high value to God. If the coin were very valuable, it would be ineffective. Further, he sees the motion of both stories as parallel, from deprivation to restoration:

man with one hundred sheep	man with one hundred sheep
woman with ten coins	woman with ten coins
loses one	I have found sheep/coin
searches	calls friends
finds sheep/coin	

In A Man with a Hundred Sheep the deprivation-restoration model will not account for the parable since the final restoration is left unspoken and may be in jeopardy, the flock having been left in the wilderness. But this jeopardy is lacking in A Woman with Ten Drachmas since the narrative implies no threat to the other nine coins. The deprivation-restoration motif results from Luke's performance. It shows how he made sense out of the story, formed it into a consistency. For Luke, both parables illustrate the joy over finding the thing lost.

The parable has a simple and predicable narrative structure (see fig. 6).

Figure 6

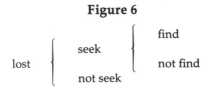

27. This is why Luke uses *apollymi*, "lost," "unsaved," to describe the lost sheep rather than *planaō*, "wander away," as in Matthew. See chap. 21 below.

28. Against Jeremias, *Parables*, 134; Perrin, *Rediscovering the Teaching*, 101.

This narrative structure is implemented in a straightforward, paratactic form built around the verbs "having," "losing," "lighting," "sweeping," and "seeking."

> what woman who *has* ten drachmas
> if she *loses* one drachma
> does not *light* a lamp
> and *sweep* the house
> and *seek* carefully

Outside of the initial deprivation, the narrative moves in positive steps toward resolution and restoration. Because of this positive progression the hearer/reader is led quickly along to identify with the woman's plight. The paratactic structure, typical of oral speech patterns, creates a sense of both realism and verisimilitude by directing a hearer's attention to the physical activities involved in finding. Jeremias vividly fills out the details: "'She lights a candle,' not because it is night, but because the low door lets very little light into the miserable, windowless dwelling, and she 'sweeps the house' with a palm-twig because in the dark the broom may make the coin tinkle on the floor."[29]

The parable's realism and structure sweep the hearer up in the woman's seeking, which is where the verbs center attention. By concentrating on the physical act of seeking, a hearer has little time to reflect on what the search is about. The parable is one that concludes with fullness: the woman has at the parable's end what she began with, ten coins. As in the parables A Man Had Two Sons and A Man Gave a Banquet, the kingdom must be full. The father has at the end the same two sons he had at the beginning. Even in A Man Gave a Banquet the hall is full even if the meal is no longer a banquet of the upper classes but of those who dwell in the byways.

What the woman seeks, a lost drachma, is one of ten. A drachma was a Greek silver coin equal in value to a denarius,[30] which is equivalent to a peasant's subsistence wage for a day's work. Thus its intrinsic value is not great, certainly not that of a kingdom, but it is worth searching for if one is a peasant. It may be that the coin has sentimental value, although the parable does not say this. That there are ten coins may suggest that it belonged to a headdress or dowry,[31] although again the parable pro-

29. Jeremias, *Parables*, 135.
30. For the value of the denarius, see chap. 13 above.
31. So Jeremias, *Parables*, 134. In *m. Kel.* 12.7 (Danby, 622) there is a description of a denarius made for a necklace for a young girl, although when so fashioned the coin is unclean, i.e., not usable for coinage.

vides no such evidence.[32] A rabbinic parable that has the same structure as this parable provides an illuminating parallel.

> If a man loses a *sela* or an *obol* in his house, he lights lamp after lamp, wick after wick, till he finds it. Now does it stand to reason: if for these things which are only ephemeral and of this world a man will light so many lamps and lights till he finds where they are hidden, for the words of Torah which after the life both of this world and the next world, ought you not to search as for hidden treasures?[33]

The value of the thing sought in the rabbinic parable is established, whereas in A Woman with Ten Drachmas its value is not commented on except in the woman's searching: her searching gives it value and draws a hearer into the story. Even more, a *woman* searches, not a man. Luke has set both A Man with a Hundred Sheep and A Woman with Ten Drachmas in the form of a question, but he does not repeat the question of the first parable, "Which one of you?" To address males so would be an insult.[34] The position of women in this period is well known as is made evident by the frequently quoted prayer "Blessed be God that he has not made me a woman."[35] The Mishnah forbids a man to teach his son a woman's trade,[36] and the Gemara comments, "Our Rabbis taught: He whose business is with women has a bad character. . . . The world cannot exist without males and females—happy is he whose children are males, and woe to him whose children are females."[37]

A hearer is caught up in the search, the search of a woman, the search of a woman for a thing of little intrinsic value. Thus is the kingdom. This parable is a burlesque, similar to the mustard seed (instead of the cedar of Lebanon), or a father's embarrassing greeting of his prodigal son and his tolerance of the elder son, or the recruiting of only the outcast to fill up the banquet hall. The burlesque may even dampen a hearer's enthusiasm for the search. And it is a woman's search, not that of a mighty warrior or even an eminent rabbi. On reflection, a hearer begins to understand that the parable's proposed metaphorical network for the kingdom is less than anticipated and may even be a burlesque of the

---

32. Klostermann, *Das Lukasevangelium*, 157.

33. *Midrash Rabbah* on the Song of Songs 1.1.9 (Freedman 9:11). The *sela* and *obol* are small coins.

34. Bailey (*Poet and Peasant*, 158) notes that the woman in an illustration would be scandalous but fails to see why Luke shifted the question form.

35. *t. Ber.* 7.18.16. For a survey of studies on women in the ancient world, see Kraemer, "Women," 127–39.

36. *m. Kid.* 4.14 (Danby, 329).

37. *b. Kid.* 82b (Soncino 9:424–25).

traditional expectations. Yet more serious is the scandal of identifying God's ruling, kingly activity with the unclean.

Parables of the Farm

Seven of Jesus' parables employ the metaphorical network associated with the farm. These assume that the kingdom is a farm, and various aspects of agriculture are used as a metaphor for the kingdom. The parables are The Net, The Merchant, A Man Had a Fig Tree (see chap. 16 below), From the Fig Tree (chap. 16), A Sower Went Out (chap. 17), A Man Casts Seed (chap. 18), A Grain of Mustard Seed (chap. 19), Treasure (chap. 20), and A Man with a Hundred Sheep (chap. 21). These parables use planting as well as specific agricultural products for their metaphorical vehicle. The Net and Treasure employ auxiliary models in their metaphorical structures.

The Net

There are two versions of the parable of The Net extant in the tradition: Matt. 13:47–48 and *Gos. Thom.* 8. Because the differences between the two are so significant, some have argued that they are two different parables.[38] This is clearly possible, since the two parables of Treasure are also separate parables.[39] We must leave this option open, remembering that the tradition is fluid and creative.

The Net

Again the kingdom of heaven is like a net which was thrown into the sea and gathered fish of every kind; when it was full, men drew it ashore and sat down and sorted the good into vessels but threw away the bad.

The parable of The Net is the last parable in Matthew's parable/kingdom discourse. Along with A Sower Went Out and The Wheat and Tares, it receives an explicit interpretation and climaxes the chapter's judgment motif.[40] Consequently we would expect Matthew's hand to be evident. As Jack Kingsbury has observed, the situation envisioned by The Wheat and Tares differs from that of The Net. In the parable The Wheat and Tares, the mixed seeds are left together until the end of the

38. E.g., Jeremias, *Parables*, 24; Hunzinger, "Unbekannte Gleichnisse," 217; Perrin, *Rediscovering the Teaching*, 90.
39. See chap. 20 below.
40. See chap. 17 below.

age. The field is the world. But the situation in The Net is different. "It is the righteous as opposed to the evil within the framework of the Church."[41] As the interpretation makes explicit, "so it will be at the close of the age."

Verses 48–49 appear to be a "Matthean embroidery,"[42] and v. 50 is a frequent Matthean addition.[43] Furthermore the contrast between *kalos*, "good," and *sapros*, "rotten," is one Matthew has used before in connection with fruit (Matt. 7:18; 12:33). Even more, *sapros* is somewhat inappropriate for freshly caught fish since the word normally means "rotten."[44] Confirming the observation that v. 48 is composed by Matthew is the shift from the singular "net" to "the angels who will separate."

The evidence indicates that Matthew has inherited a saying about a net which he has then conformed to the format of the parables in this section[45] and interpreted by means of his judgment motif to create a conclusion for the discourse.

The Parable in the *Gospel of Thomas* reads,

> And He said to them: "The man is like a wise fisherman who has cast his net into the sea and drew it up from the sea full of small fish. Among them the wise fisherman found a fine large fish. He threw all the small fish back into the sea and chose the large fish without difficulty. Whoever has ears to hear, let him hear." (*Gos. Thom.* 8).

Following close upon the announcement of the Gospel's main theme, "Whoever finds the interpretation of these sayings will not taste death" (*Gos. Thom.* 2), the narrative of the wise fisherman exemplifies the enlightened person who discovers the true value of Jesus' words among all the competing distractions of "little fish."[46] This explains why it begins, "The man is like . . . ," for the individual is the chief concern. Probably "the man" has replaced the kingdom, since those other parallel parables that are kingdom parables in the Synoptics are also kingdom parables in *Thomas*. The Net is the only exception.[47]

The parable proper introduces as the first item of comparison a wise fisherman. Even though *Thomas* has a proclivity to begin parables with a person, it does not necessarily make a great difference whether a parable

41. Kingsbury, *Parables of Jesus*, 118. See his elaborate analysis of the parable as developing the judgment theme.

42. Manson, *Sayings*, 198.

43. See chap. 9 above.

44. BAGD, 742. Bauernfeind ("*sapros*," 97) tries to explain this away.

45. For my schema of these parables, see chap. 20 below.

46. This basic interpretive stance is true whether one adopts wisdom or Gnosticism as the basic mode of interpretation. For a gnostic reading, see Ménard, *L' évangile selon Thomas*, 88–91; Quispel, "Gnosis and the New Sayings," 190.

47. See p. 34 above.

begins with a net or a fisherman, since the whole narrative unit is the object of comparison. The marker "wise" results from *Thomas*'s redaction. This parable, which is the first one to appear in *Thomas*, is an example of a "wise man," and so the marker makes the point explicit. Similarly, *Thomas* has a tendency, where there is any doubt about the value of a character, to provide an explicit marker.[48] Finally, in the *Thomas* parables the theme of large or largest is often editorial,[49] although in this case it does not seem to be so,[50] since it is hard to understand what the point would be without some note of separation.

Both Matthew and *Thomas* have given the parable The Net a place of prominence; for the former it concludes the kingdom discourse, and for the latter it is the first parable in the Gospel and exhibits the seeking of true wisdom and the interpretation of Jesus' words. Both Gospels have performed the parable in distinct ways. This returns us to the original question: What were they performing—two separate parables, as some have suggested, or an originating parabolic structure? Neither case is likely.

Several commentators have pointed to a parallel saying in Clement of Alexandria that does not seem dependent on either the Matthean or *Thomas* version:[51] "The kingdom of heaven is like a man who cast a net into the sea and from the multitude of fish that were caught chose the better."[52] At a different place in the same work, Clement refers to the pearl and the fish: "Among a great number of small pearls there is the one, and in a great catch of fish there is the fine fish."[53] Clement reflects the proverbial insight that from a great catch one selects out the better. This insight is also the basis of two Hellenistic stories, one from the Aesopic tradition:

> A fisherman drew in the net which he had cast a short time before and, as luck would have it, it was full of all kinds of delectable fish. But the little ones fled to the bottom of the net and slipped out through its many meshes, whereas the big ones were caught and lay stretched out in the boat.[54]

The proverbial insight forms the basis of both the Matthean and *Thomas*

---

48. See chap. 10 above. Cameron ("Parable and Interpretation," 26) is in agreement.

49. See p. 34 above; *Gos. Thom.* 63 (The Land of a Rich Man); *Gos. Thom.* 20 (A Grain of Mustard Seed); *Gos. Thom.* 96 (The Leaven).

50. Against Quispel, "Some Remarks," 290.

51. See Bauer, "Synoptic Tradition," 315–16; Ménard, *L' évangile selon Thomas*, 89; Morrice, "Parable of the Dragnet," 269.

52. Clement, *Stromata*, 6.95.3 (*Clemens Alexandrinus*, ed. Stählin, 2:479).

53. Clement, *Stromata*, 1.16.3 (*Clemens Alexandrinus*, ed. Stählin, 2:12).

54. *Babrius and Phaedrus*, 4 (LCL 9). Cameron ("Parable and Interpretation") also quotes another version of the proverb from Herodotus's *History*, 1.141 (LCL 1:181).

parables.[55] It seems impossible to reconstruct an originating structure for a Jesus parable from this history of the tradition, because the source of both stories is a proverbial insight from common wisdom which does not exhibit the distinctive voice of the implied speaker of the corpus.[56] But what these two parables indicate is the close connection between proverbs and one-liners. Both parables were probably built on the basis of a proverb and given the form of a one-liner.

The Merchant

The Merchant (Matt. 13:45; *Gos. Thom.* 76) represents several anomalies within the corpus of Jesus parables. It alone deals exclusively with a member of the upper classes, a merchant. In other parables in which an upper-class character appears, he interacts with another character who is from the peasant class (e.g., in A Man Entrusts Property and A Rich Man Had a Steward). Here he stands alone. Similarly, what he seeks or finds, a pearl, comes from faraway seas, the Red Sea, the Persian Gulf, or the Indian Ocean. Finding a pearl conjures up the exotic.

In the ancient world, pearls were regarded as precious stones, and the phrase "jewels and pearls" denotes great wealth, as in the listing in Revelation 18 of Babylon's wealth: "The merchants of the earth weep and mourn for her, since no one buys their cargo any more, cargo of gold, silver, jewels and pearls, fine linen, purple, silk and scarlet, all kinds of scented wood" (vv. 11–12). By extension it is a metaphor for something of supreme value.[57] Again the New Testament provides a typical example: "Do not give dogs what is holy; and do not throw your pearls before swine" (Matt. 7:6). In a parallel rabbinic usage, the pearl is frequently a metaphor for a beautiful saying: "The mouth that uttered pearls licks the dust."[58] Because of its great value, in eschatological scenes it depicts the wealth of the new age. "J. Jochanan [explained] when he [once] sat and gave an exposition: The Holy One, blessed be He, will in time bring precious stones and pearls which are 30 [cubits] by thirty and will cut out from them [openings] ten [cubits] by twenty, and will set them up in the gates of Jerusalem."[59] A parallel image occurs in Revelation: "And the twelve gates were twelve pearls, each of the gates made of a single pearl, and the street of the city was pure gold, trans-

---

55. So also Bauer, "Synoptic Tradition," 316.
56. See pp. 66–68 above.
57. Hauck, "*margarítēs*," 472.
58. *b. Qid.* 39b (Soncino 9:195); Str-B 1:447, 3:325.
59. *b. B. Bat.* 75a (Soncino 11:300). The story continues with a student who doubts the word of the rabbi. The student then takes a sea journey, during which he sees angels carving the huge pearls. When he confesses his new-found faith to the rabbi, the rabbi condemns him for not believing the word and needing proof.

parent as glass" (21:21). Finally, in Gnosticism the pearl is a symbol of Christ or the soul.[60] The most famous example is *The Hymn of the Pearl:*

> And he promised me that to the gate
> Of the king of kings I should journey with him again
> And with my gift and my pearl
> With him appear before our king.[61]

This use of the pearl in the hymn has made it difficult to see the *Thomas* parable as independent of the hymn, assuming that the *Gospel of Thomas* is gnostic.[62]

Despite the pearl's widespread use as a symbol of wealth and value, *margarités* does not appear in the LXX.[63] It clearly enters the Jewish repertoire in the Hellenistic age.

The parable of The Merchant occurs in Matthew in the concluding section of the kingdom discourse, between Treasure and The Net:

The Merchant

Again the kingdom of heaven is like a merchant in search of fine pearls, who on finding one pearl of great value, went and sold all that he had and bought it.

For Matthew, the significance of the first two parables lies in the value of the thing found and "in the sphere of sacrifice, or total investment" required to seek the kingdom.[64] The parable is obviously cast in the format of the other one-liners of this discourse.[65] Mentioning that the merchant was in search of fine pearls destroys the story's tension and narrative suspense,[66] and selling everything is probably dependent on Treasure.[67] But while the phrasing "sold all" is dependent on Matthew, it may have been present formally in the originating structure as "eliminating capital," which could be expressed in a variety of ways. "In search

---

60. Hauck (*"margarités,"* 473 n. 13) argues that the pearl is a symbol of Christ or the soul.

61. *Acts of Thomas* 113.105 (*New Testament Apocrypha,* ed. Hennecke and Schneemelcher, 2:504; see pp. 433–37 for a discussion of the hymn).

62. E.g., Dupont, "Les paraboles," 409. This puzzles me since Matthew's "one pearl of great value" fits a gnostic ideology at least as well as and probably better than *Thomas's* "a pearl."

63. The Hebrew *pnynym,* sometimes translated "pearl," really means "coral." See Baumgartner, *Lexicon in Veteris Testamenti Libros,* 768.

64. See Kingsbury, *The Parables of Jesus,* 115. Kingsbury also argues against other suggestions: hiddenness, finding, searching, joy.

65. See chap. 20 below.

66. Jeremias, *Parables,* 199; Hunzinger, "Unbekannte Gleichnisse," 218.

67. Jeremias, *Parables,* 198; Hunzinger, "Unbekannte Gleichnisse," 220.

of fine pearls" probably resulted from anticipating the story, something that happens in retelling.

The parable of The Merchant is similar in *Thomas*, but more realistic.

> Jesus said, "The kingdom of the Father is like a merchant who had a consignment of merchandise and who discovered a pearl. That merchant was shrewd. He sold the merchandise and bought the pearl alone for himself. You too, seek this unfailing and enduring treasure where no moth comes near to devour and no worm destroys."(*Gos. Thom.* 76)[68]

The appended saying plays on the common metaphor of the pearl as a thing of great value, and so the treasure is the kingdom, knowledge of oneself.[69] Finding a rich thing is a theme frequent in the *Gospel of Thomas*: "Let him who seeks continue seeking until he finds. When he finds he will become troubled. When he becomes troubled, he will be astonished, and he will rule over the All" (*Gos. Thom.* 2).[70] The rich thing is important to find, but it must not be possessed as a thing of power; so one must be troubled, or it must be a treasure where no mouth consumes, that is, spiritual treasure. In order to block against false riches, which lead to power, the merchant is described as shrewd.[71] With this phrase exempted, the *Thomas* version most clearly represents the originating structure. The selling of the merchandise parallels Matthew's remark that "he sold all" and fits better with the narrative's structure, which is about a merchant and his merchandise.[72]

The Merchant is frequently presented as a twin to Treasure, even though some who see the two parables as twins admit that they could have been spoken in different situations.[73] Even Ménard, in his analysis of the *Thomas* parable, reads it in light of Treasure, from which it is separated in *Thomas*. But the differences are important to notice. Otto Glombitza lists five differences.[74] (For convenience I will use his conven-

---

68. The Coptic text reads literally, "a man a merchant" (a redundancy eliminated in the Eng. trans.), and "a consignment of merchandise" is "some merchandise." These differences are not significant.

69. Against Dehandshutter, "La parabole," 248. This does not mean that *Thomas* knew of the association of the parables of Treasure and The Merchant. So also Hedrick, "Treasure Parable," 42 n. 5.

70. See Davies, *Gospel of Thomas*, 142.

71. Seen also as secondary by Cameron ("Parable and Interpretation," 26).

72. Hunzinger ("Unbekannte Gleichnisse," 219–21) presents the strongest argument for the more primitive character of *Thomas*'s version of the parable.

73. E.g., Jeremias, *Parables*, 198. I would add that they were spoken (performed) on many different occasions in differing situations. Jeremias (pp. 90–94) deals with the so-called twin parables. He sees the double parables as original and thinks that in the course of transmission many were separated. To me the evidence seems to point in the opposite direction. There is no necessary relation between any of the so-called twin parables.

74. Otto Glombitza, "Der Perlenkaufmann," 157.

tion of referring to the parable Treasure as *A* and The Merchant as *B*.) (1) *A* speaks of the kingdom's being like treasure; *B* speaks of a merchant. The parallel is not treasure and pearl. The specific metaphorical networks are the kingdom as finding hidden treasure and the kingdom as commerce. (2) In *A* the treasure is concealed; *B* involves the merchant's effort. (3) The treasure is accidentally found; the finding of the pearl is the result of extended effort. (4) The verbs used in *A* are generally in the present tense; those in *B* are generally in the past. (5) The character of the selling is different, in that the peasant dayworker sells those small things he has but the merchant is accustomed to buying and selling as part of his normal activity and has capital for the activity. Of these five differences, the fourth is the least convincing, because it may represent only performance differences. But the other four substantiate the strong differences between the two parables and lead to the conclusion that The Merchant neither is dependent on Treasure nor should be interpreted under its aegis.[75]

The parable does exhibit the distinctive voice of the implied speaker of the parables, but unfortunately that voice is sometimes muffled. Dodd notes the merchant's rashness in selling all his assets to buy the single pearl yet concludes that "to know when to take the plunge makes the successful financier."[76] More to the point, Manson indicates why it might be rash. The merchant "deems it good business to sell everything he has in order to obtain it. The fact that he would presumably have to sell it again in order to live is also not relevant to the parable."[77] But it is relevant, for it relativizes, demythologizes, the value of the pearl. If to buy the pearl he has sold off his capital, whether all he owns or his merchandise, he will again have to sell the pearl, or else he will be broke, because the pearl only generates in being sold. Thus the thing of value, the pearl, has no ultimate value. It turns out to be like the leaven, corrupting. This conclusion can be avoided only if the whole narrative is not taken seriously—if one takes part of it to be irrelevant to the parable, as Manson does. The kingdom cannot be possessed as a value in itself, "alone for himself," as *Thomas* says, for the merchant will sooner or later have to sell his pearl. And that is the kingdom's corrupting power—the desire to possess it.

75. Jeremias (*Parables,* 200) is not alone in reading the notion of joy into The Merchant from Treasure.
76. Dodd, *Parables,* 86.
77. Manson, *Sayings,* 196.

15

One Rotten Apple

The Leaven

It is like leaven which a women took and hid in three measures of flour until it was all leavened.

In modern English, "to leaven" means figuratively "to mingle or permeate with some modifying, alleviating, or vivifying element," as one dictionary example makes clear: "a large fund of shrewd ability leavened by charm."[1] The entry in the *Oxford English Dictionary* discloses a subtle shift in language. The entry notes the references to both Matt. 13:33 and 16:6: "Take heed and beware of the leaven of the Pharisees and Sadducees." Surprisingly, most of the entries prior to 1800 are dependent on Matt. 16:6 and so are negative.[2] Only a few have a positive sense, which is the only figurative sense noted by Webster's.

Under the parable's influence, modern English remembers only the positive sense and does not know the negative. But as many scholars have remarked, only the negative sense is evidenced in ancient literature. The parable The Leaven exposes a capital problem in parable exegesis: In which direction is the transference, from kingdom to parable or from parable to kingdom? What determines the symbolic value of "leaven," its cultural matrix or the kingdom of God?

1. *Webster's Third New International Dictionary*, col. 1287.
2. *Oxford English Dictionary*, 166.

One way actual readers have dealt with the problem is to ignore its implications. While noting leaven's negative aspects, Dodd argues that the emphasis falls on the process of leavening. Thus the initial action of the leaven is hidden, "but soon the whole mass swells and bubbles, as fermentation rapidly advances."[3] Such a picture, he argues, is true to the ministry of Jesus.

Others see the parable as a twin to A Grain of Mustard Seed, and so see the contrast as between the small beginning and the great growth at the end.[4] Both are parables of growth. But the problem with all these interpretations is that they ignore the metaphorical structure to which the words belong; they abstract the language from its cultural, historical context.

The Parable in the Gospels

The parable is almost identical in Matthew and Luke, and for adherents of the two-source theory it as a Q parable. Matthew has created his introduction with the characteristic phrase "kingdom of heaven" and has probably employed *egkruptō* instead of the more common *kruptō*.[5] Both Matthew and Luke situate The Leaven as a companion to A Grain of Mustard Seed,[6] yet they have performed A Grain of Mustard Seed differently. Matthew's parable conflates both Mark and Luke; Luke's version appears as a performance independent of Mark.[7] Neither Matthew nor Luke offers an interpretation of The Leaven, and so the development of a discourse is left to the reader. By tying the parable to A Grain of Mustard Seed both evangelists (or Q) are probably accenting the growth of the kingdom, and so are using the parables to offer encouragement.

The *Thomas* parable differs from the Synoptic versions:

> Jesus [said], "The Kingdom of the Father is like a certain woman. She took a little leaven, [concealed] it in some dough, and made it into large loaves. Let him who has ears hear". (*Gos. Thom.* 96)

Even though A Grain of Mustard Seed (*Gos. Thom.* 20) appears much earlier in *Thomas*, it and The Leaven share a similar structure. In *Thomas*, the mustard seed is the smallest of all seeds and produces a great plant. The attraction of the marker "smallest" is probably due to the proverbial

---

3. Dodd, *Parables*, 155.
4. So Jeremias, *Parables*, 148; Dahl, "Parables of Growth," 148–49.
5. Schulz, *Q: Die Spruchquelle*, 307.
6. For the arrangement of parables in chap. 13 of Matthew, see chap. 17 below.
7. See chap. 19 below. Schulz (*Q: Die Spruchquelle*, 302) sees the Q version in Luke.

character of the mustard seed. Once that attraction is made, the metaphorical structure of the kingdom as the greatest thing subverts the structure of both stories, relieving their original tension.

Were the parables always coupled?[8] In favor of this view is the grouping in the oral tradition inherited by Matthew and Luke (Q) and the possible attraction of the small-great motif in *Thomas*. On that basis one might argue that the *Thomas* tradition at one point held the two parables together. On the contrary, since Mark does not contain the parable The Leaven, his tradition obviously does not see them connected. Nor does the present form of the *Thomas* tradition. So the two parables could and did circulate separately. Performers of the parables did not see their connection to be necessary.

The smallest-greatest theme is also problematic. Jeremias, who treats the parables as a doublet, sees the contrast in The Leaven between the tiny morsel of leaven and the "great mass of more than a bushel of meal."[9] Both the mustard seed and the leaven are proverbially small,[10] yet in Q, which is the only extant version in which the two parables are coupled, the smallest-greatest theme is absent. It is present in Matthew's version of A Grain of Mustard Seed, but that is clearly the result of his accommodation to Mark. The note about the smallest of seeds in Mark's version is the result of his performance.[11] In *Thomas*, the smallness more likely results from an oral attraction because of the proverbial character of the mustard seed. Because other aspects of Markan redaction are missing in *Thomas*'s version, we can discount accommodation to Mark, thus maintaining our general position of *Thomas*'s independence. Similarly, in the parable The Leaven, the "little" leaven and the "large" loaves are better explained by a double motion. The leaven is proverbially small, and "large" represents in the performance of the parable a generalization of the more specific three measures (about fifty pounds).[12] It is easier to explain three measures and the obscure reference to Gen. 18:6 as part of the originating structure than *Thomas*'s great loaves as original and the Q version as specifying that reference.

Therefore the parables A Grain of Mustard Seed and The Leaven were separate and The Leaven's originating structure was closer to that of Matthew and Luke, with *Thomas* in this case representing a generalization or loss of specificity.

8. Among many who argue that they were originally told together is Lambrecht (*Once More Astonished*, 100). He even sees Mark replacing the original twins with the substitute A Grain of Mustard Seed and A Man Casts Seed.
9. Jeremias, *Parables*, 148.
10. See the proverb quoted by Paul in Gal. 5:9 and 1 Cor. 5:7.
11. See chap. 19 below.
12. *Thomas* makes a similar move in A Man with a Hundred Sheep (*Gos. Thom.* 107).

A Reading

Line 1: It is like leaven . . .[13]

Repertoire is a critical problem in this parable, for the parable's significance lies in the metaphorical structure to which its individual words
belong. Leaven belongs to conventional language, to an established
metaphorical network. That leaven in the ancient world was a symbol
for moral corruption has long been recognized. "In the view of all
antiquity, Semitic and non-Semitic, panary fermentation represented a
process of corruption and putrefaction in the mass of dough."[14] The
usage of the Hebrew Bible and the New Testament furnishes a complete
survey of usage.

The physical characteristics of leaven support the metaphor for corrupting. Leaven is made by taking a piece of bread and storing it in a
damp, dark place until mold forms. The bread rots and decays, unlike
modern yeast, which is domesticated.[15]

In the commands for the feast of unleavened bread, leavened bread
must not be eaten and must even be cleansed out of the house. "For
seven days no leaven shall be found in your houses; for if any one eats
what is leavened, that person shall be cut off from the congregation of
Israel" (Exod. 12:19).[16] Not only does leaven symbolize unholy Israel but
unleavened bread also symbolizes holy Israel. "Seven days you shall eat
unleavened bread; on the first day you shall put away leaven out of your
houses. . . . On the first day you shall hold a holy assembly" (Exod.
12:15–16). During the seven days of the feast, a feast of the Lord to be
observed forever, unleavened bread replaces leavened bread to symbolize the people's holiness. In Israel there is an equation that leaven is the
unholy everyday, and unleaven the holy, the sacred, the feast.

This negative association with leaven persists in the New Testament.
Twice Paul quotes the otherwise unattested proverb "A little leaven
leavens the whole lump." In Gal. 5:9, he uses the proverb to warn that
someone is leading the Galatians from the true path by demanding
circumcision.[17] The proverb implies that this one is corrupting them, is
destroying the good of the group. This analogy of the leaven exactly
parallels the proverb "One rotten apple spoils the whole barrel." In 1

13. *Thomas* begins, "is like a certain woman." It makes no difference whether leaven
or woman is first.
14. Kennedy, "Leaven," 2754.
15. The NAB translation completely domesticates the parable by equating leaven
with yeast and hiding with kneading.
16. See also Exod. 13:3, 6–7; Deut. 16:3–4.
17. See Betz, *Galatians,* 266–67.

Cor. 5:7, Paul interweaves the proverb into a more complex rhetorical structure. Boasting, like a little leaven, can corrupt all the good one does. But then leaven suggests the feast of unleavened bread: "Cleanse out the old leaven that you may be a new lump, as you really are unleavened." The distinction between leaven as evil and the unleavened as holy is implied. The metaphor is somewhat mixed because old leaven suggests new leaven, based on the metaphorical structure of old-new, but Paul switches to leaven-unleavened as the contrast. This leads naturally then to "For Christ, our paschal lamb, has been sacrificed." Finally Paul concludes by contrasting the symbols of leaven and unleavened as representing moral states: "Let us, therefore, celebrate the festival, not with the old leaven, the leaven of malice and evil, but with the unleavened bread of sincerity and truth."[18]

The Pauline proverb, like all proverbs, summarizes a piece of common wisdom: that the involvement with even a little evil can corrupt the whole. This same proverbial understanding of leaven underlies Jesus' warning to the disciples: "Beware of the leaven of the Pharisees." In Mark, the warning is combined with a warning against the "leaven of Herod" (8:15). It follows immediately on the feeding of the four thousand and the Pharisees' request for a sign. In Mark, the warning is enigmatic, its specific reference unclear, but in Matthew and Luke the reference is made clear. Matthew interprets the leaven to be the "teaching of the Pharisees and Sadducees" (16:12),[19] and Luke appends the explanation that the leaven is hypocrisy (12:1), for which he has just condemned them (11:37–52). Regardless of application, all three understand leaven to be negative and corrupting. Furthermore, as both Paul and the Synoptics prove, not only is leaven itself a negative metaphor but the action of leavening is likewise viewed negatively, as corrupting.

Given the conventionally negative proverbial character of leaven, a hearer initially responds with shock and wonder. How can the kingdom be like leaven? Surely the appropriate conventional metaphor is unleaven? Does the parable repudiate Passover and the exodus? So a hearer is confronted with frustration and disorientation.

Line 2: ... which a woman took and hid ...

---

18. Ignatius (*Epistle to the Magnesians* 10.1 [Loeb 1:207]) in an apparent reference to 1 Corinthians contrasts the "old evil leaven" with the new leaven, Jesus Christ: "Set aside, then, the evil leaven, old and sour, and turn to the new leaven, which is Jesus Christ" (Schoedel, *Ignatius of Antioch*, 126).

19. Abrahams, *Studies* 1:53. Abrahams points to a rabbinic parallel similar to Matthew where leaven is equated with the evil inclination—a familiar identification in rabbinic literature. See Str-B 1:728–29.

If the parable teller means to overturn the conventional, proverbial metaphorical structure of leaven, as commentators assert, then hints must be provided. Yet the next two terms both imply negativity.

Woman as a symbolic structure was associated in Judaism, as in other Mediterranean cultures, with the unclean, the religiously impure. The male was the symbol for purity. This is so well established that it needs no comment. Albrecht Oepke summarizes the issue well: "Characteristic of the traditional position and estimation of woman is a saying current in different forms among the Persians, Greeks and Jews in which man gives thanks that he is not an unbeliever or uncivilized, that he is not a woman and that he is not a slave."[20] Normally baking bread was a family activity, done once a week before the Sabbath. Jeremiah's picture seems to have held true for later times as well: "The children gather wood, the fathers kindle the fire, and the women knead dough" (Jer. 7:18).[21] In the parable, the narrator blocks out the family scene and concentrates on the woman.

As the passage from Jeremiah makes evident, the woman's function is kneading dough, and at this point, as Funk has observed, the parable is dissonant: instead of kneading (*phyraō*), the woman hides (*kryptō*) the leaven in the mass of dough. The figurative use of hiding to describe the mixing of leaven and flour is otherwise unattested in either Greek or Hebrew. Even more, *kryptō* implies a more negative sense than the more neutral *kalyptō*, "to cover." It emphasizes the subjective element, that "the concealment is often for selfish reasons, e.g., to prevent others from using the object, to keep it for one self."[22] The verb *kryptō* also occurs in two other parables. It describes both the hiding action in Treasure (Matt. 13:14) after the plowing but before the purchase of the field (Matt. 13:44) and the action of the third servant in burying his capital in A Man Entrusts Property (Matt. 28:18).

The woman's hiding confirms, not overturns, the leaven's negative connotation. Frustration is now intensified: how can the kingdom be like leaven, a woman, and hiding? Surely the proper terms are unleaven, a man, and open (or revealed)!

Line 3: . . .in three measures of flour. . .

As is so often the case in this parable, our ears are deceived, for we do

---

20. Oepke, "*gynē*," 777; with evidence. See chap. 14, esp. the sec. on the parable A Woman with Ten Drachmas and nn. 33–35. "Praise be He that He did not make me a woman" (*t. Ber.* 7.18) is often quoted as a summary of the place of women.
21. Safrai, "Home and Family," 740.
22. Oepke, "*kryptō*," 958.

not know the parable's repertoire. "Measure" is meaningless to us. How much is it? Jeremias estimates that three measures equal about fifty pounds of flour; in other words, the cakes from this baking would feed more than a hundred persons.[23] Jeremias has pointed to Gen. 18:6 as a possible background for the amount. That story deals with Abraham's reception of three visitors, one of them the Lord, at the Oaks of Mamre. Abraham instructs Sarah to make cakes from three measures of fine flour.[24] Funk also notices two other occasions where there are references to three measures.[25] When the angel of the Lord appears to Gideon, Gideon prepares "a kid, and unleavened flour from an ephah of flour" (Judges 6:19). An ephah of flour is three measures. Likewise, when Hannah dedicates Samuel to the temple, among her offerings is an ephah of flour (1 Sam. 1:24). These examples suggest that not only are three measures much more than normal but that the amount is connected with an epiphany.

Finally, in "three measures" the parable presents a term that coheres with the announced referent, the kingdom of God. Yet how is a hearer to combine three measures with the preceding negative terms?

Line 4: ... until it was all leavened.

Until this point the parable has focused on the woman's activity, her kneading of the leaven into the dough. Now it flashes forward to the end of the process, when the dough is leavened. In the metaphorical structure of leaven, the conclusion of the process is not baking but the rising of the dough, which represents corruption. The prophet Hosea, in a neglected parallel to our parable exemplifies this metaphorical structure:

> They are all adulterers;
> > they are like a heated oven,
> whose baker ceases to stir the fire,
> > from the kneading of the dough
> > until it is leavened.
>
> > > (Hosea 7:4)

In Hosea, as in the parable, "until it is leavened" denotes the inevitability of the process's end. All will be corrupted.

---

23. Jeremias, *Parables*, 147.
24. Waller, "Parable of the Leaven," 102–3. Waller argues that the Sarah story is the immediate background for the parable, but he ignores the negative aspect of both leaven and women.
25. Funk, *Jesus as Precursor*, 50.

From Story to Kingdom

Traditional interpretations have ignored the negative aspects not only of leaven but also of "woman," "hid," and "until all was leaven." Why? Because the metaphorical structure of the kingdom of God implies "holy and good," and so conflicts with leaven's metaphorical structure, which implies "moral corruption." I. Abrahams, who surveys rabbinic usage thoroughly and shows leaven to be a negative, exempts the Jesus parable from the universal negative connotation. "It is probable, however, that the parable also takes account of the result; the leavened mass of humanity, through intrusion of the leaven, attains a superior moral condition, just as the leavened bread is a more perfect food than unleavened."[26] Yet precisely the process of leavening is seen as moral corruption in the ancient world. Only the repeated though subtle Christian insistence that leaven is good can explain how a Jew could envision leavened bread as "more perfect food than unleavened."

The radical disjunction between the metaphorical structures of the kingdom of God and the parable drive a hearer beyond the literal meaning of the words, even beyond the metaphorical sense. That is why their metaphorical sense has so often been overlooked. This parable exemplifies what Wheelwright has identified as the second way of metaphor (diaphor). Most metaphors operate by means of epiphor, similarity between the A and B terms, whereas diaphor operates by means of dissimilarity, disjunction.[27] But because diaphor relies on disjunction, it seeks to expose the new, the not before conjoined. It demands that a hearer construct the parable's discourse[28] from a minimum of elements.

The effort to construct a discourse can turn in several directions, but since diaphor conjoins the disjunctive, creating something new, the discourse will be without precedents. The parable's radical nature coheres with those parables of Jesus that attack the boundaries—for example, the parable From Jerusalem to Jericho, in which the boundary between Jew and non-Jew is destroyed, where Samaritan is hero/savior and Jew victim. Here a boundary at least as deep and perhaps deeper is attacked. The kingdom (the holy and good) is pictured in terms of an epiphany of corruption. How radical is the parable's intention? Does it mean to state that good is evil in an ethics of absurdity? Or is its function to subvert a hearer's ready dependency on the rules of the sacred, the predicability of what is good, and warn that instead the expected evil

26. Abrahams, *Studies* 1:51.
27. Wheelwright, *Metaphor and Reality*, 78–86.
28. Chatman, *Story and Discourse*, 146. The discourse belongs to the plane of expression, the story to the plane of content.

that corrupts may indeed turn out to be the kingdom. On the analogy of *From Jerusalem to Jericho*, such would be the case.

Such a discourse is corroborated by Jesus' association with the outcast or even those accusations that he has a demon or the beatitude "Blessed are the poor." The kingdom is present among the marginal. "Let the children come to me, do not hinder them; for to such belongs the kingdom of God" (Mark 10:14). In the end, the parable, because it is diaphor, can have no closure, because it seeks to join what cannot be joined. The parable calls into question ready attempts to predict on the basis of our knowledge of the holy and good where the kingdom is active. Instead it insists on the kingdom's freedom to appear under its own guise, even if it be the guise of corruption.

G A arden of Delights

A Man Had a Fig Tree

A fig tree a certain man had which was planted in his vineyard, and he came seeking fruit on it and he did not find any. He said to the vinedresser, "For three years I have been coming, seeking fruit on this fig tree and I did not find any. Cut it down! Why should it render the ground useless?" He answered and said to him, "Master, let it alone even this year until I dig around it and throw dung and if it makes fruit in the coming . . . otherwise if not you can cut it down."

From the Fig Tree

It is like a fig tree, when its branches become tender and it puts forth leaves, the summer is near.

Two parables in the Jesus corpus make use of the fig tree and also delineate the extremes of narrative structure represented in this group. A Man Had a Fig Tree (Luke 13:6–9) has a full narrative with an initial tension, a middle proposal to resolve the tension, and an ending that leaves open what the owner will do and whether the tree will bear fruit. The parable From the Fig Tree (Mark 13:28; Matt. 24:32; Luke 21:29–30) executes the minimalist creed that less is more. Its minimal narrative structure is its beauty and difficulty. We shall begin by examining the repertoire assumed by both parables, for the fig tree has strong metaphorical and symbolic possibilities.

Under a Fig Tree

The fig tree was and is among the more prominent trees of Palestine[1] and is often a figure in the Hebrew Bible for the blessings of the land. In Moses' speech in Deut. 8:7–8, the fig tree appears among the promised land's characteristics. "For the Lord your God is bringing you into a good land, a land of brooks of water, of fountains and springs, flowing forth in valleys and hills, a land of wheat and barley, of vines and fig trees and pomegranates. . . ." In time the list is narrowed down so that vine and fig tree[2] are signs of blessing: "Judah and Israel dwelt in safety, from Dan even to Beersheba, every man under his vine and under his fig tree, all the days of Solomon" (1 Kings 4:25).[3] The fig tree is the only tree mentioned by name in the garden of paradise, where Adam and Eve make covering from fig leaves (Gen. 3:7).[4] Moreover, the fig tree's destruction stands for a curse on the land: "'I smote you with blight and mildew; I laid waste your gardens and your vineyard; your fig trees and your olive trees the locust devoured; yet you did not return to me,' says the Lord" (Amos 4:9).

The fig tree's literal presence as a blessing or its literal absence as a curse allows it to function as a metaphor for blessings and curses. For example, in Hosea 9:10 the fig tree is used as an image of God's love for Israel's fathers: "Like grapes in the wilderness, I found Israel. Like the first fruit on the fig tree, in its first season, I saw your fathers." Or in Micah 4:4, the fig tree is part of the vision of Israel's future blessing associated with the restoration of the Davidic kingdom: "But they shall sit every man under his vine and under his fig tree, and none shall make them afraid; for the mouth of the Lord of hosts has spoken." Similarly, in Joel the prophet sees the devastation of the land by a swarm of locusts as God's judgment. He compares the locusts to a "nation . . . powerful without number; its teeth are lion's teeth." And he says, "It has laid

1. Josephus (*Jewish Wars*, 3.519 [LCL 2:723]), in describing the area around Genesareth as especially fertile, refers to "those kings of fruits, the grape and the fig."
2. For an extensive listing of the combination, see Tilford, *Barren Fig Tree*, 165 n. 19. Tilford's analysis of Hebrew Bible and the rabbinic usage is extensive. I have reviewed this material before in *Jesus, Symbol-Maker*, 77–78.
3. The fig tree's broad leafage and spreading bough make it a prominent shade tree. See Hunzinger, "*sukē*," 753.
4. For further speculation on the fig tree in rabbinic literature in connection with Eden, see ibid., 752 n. 19. See also Tilford, *Barren Fig Tree*, 189–91.

waste my vines, and splintered my fig trees; it has stripped off their bark and thrown it down; and their branches are made white" (Joel 1:6–7).[5]

The fig tree is as prominent in rabbinic literature as it is in the Hebrew Bible, and its basic symbolic and metaphorical possibilities remain.[6] For example, in commenting on Jer. 24:2, where bad figs and good figs are presented to the king, the Talmud quotes the exegesis of Mari b. Mar: "'Good figs' are an allusion to those who are righteous in every respect; 'bad figs' are an allusion to those who are wicked in every respect." But then the text concludes with a comment that is significant for our first parable, A Man Had a Fig Tree: "But in case you should imagine that their hope is lost and their prospect is frustrated it was explicitly stated, 'The baskets give forth fragrance' [Cant 7:14], both will in the time to come give forth fragrance."[7]

Picking the fig in season, exactly when it was ripe, was important in the fig's viticulture. Thus the in-season fig is used to denote the appropriate time for death. In commenting on Gen. 30:8 and the fact that Abraham died in old age, the Midrash relates a variety of sayings and parables about the death of old and young people:

> What is the difference between the death of young men and that of old men? R. Judah said: When a lamp goes out of itself, it is good for it and good for the wick; but if it does not go out of itself, it is bad for itself and bad for the wick. R. Abbahu said: When a fig is gathered at the proper time, it is good for itself and good for the tree; but if it is gathered prematurely, it is bad for itself and bad for the tree.[8]

To illustrate these two sayings the Midrash quotes two versions of the same parable. The parable itself is quite humorous:

> R. Hiyya and his disciples . . . were accustomed to rise early and sit under a certain fig tree, the owner of which used to rise early to gather its fruit. Said they: "Perhaps he suspects us [of taking his fruit]; let us change our place." Accordingly they changed their place. He then went to them and said: "My masters! This one merit that ye had conferred upon me by sitting and studying under my fig tree—ye have now deprived me of it." "We thought perhaps you suspected us," they replied. But he reassured them, and they returned to their original place. What did he do? He did not gather its fruit in the morning, whereupon the figs became wormy. Said they: "The owner

---

5. Tilford (*Barren Fig Tree*, 134) summarizes his findings concerning the Hebrew Bible: "The fig is *an emblem of peace, prosperity and security* and is prominent when descriptions of *the Golden Ages of Israel's history,* past, present and future are given."

6. So Tilford, *Barren Fig Tree*, 176.

7. *b. Erub.* 21a (Soncino 3:148). Tilford does not quote this last line and thus misses the significance of the quotation.

8. *Midrash Rabbah* on Genesis 62.2 (Freedman 2:550–51).

of the fig tree knows when their fruit is ripe for plucking, and he plucks it."
In the same way, the Holy One, blessed be He, knows when the time of the
righteous has come, whereupon He removed them. What is the proof? "My
beloved is gone down to his garden." (Can 6:2).[9]

The core story concerns the owner's charity and honor and has little to
do with its illustrand, which depends on the situation of sitting under a
fig tree and the picking at the proper time. The conclusion was probably
added to the story to adjust it to the illustrand.

Just as the absence of figs can be a metaphor for evil times, so also the
out-of-time fig can be a curse:

> Once R. Jose had day-labourers [working] in the field; night set in and no
> food was brought to them and they said to his son, "We are hungry." Now
> they were resting under a fig tree and he exclaimed: Fig tree, fig tree, bring
> forth thy fruit that my father's labourers may eat. It brought forth fruit and
> they ate. Meanwhile the father came and said to them, Do not bear a
> grievance against me; the reason for my delay is because I have been
> occupied up till now on an errand of charity. The labourers replied, May
> God satisfy you even as your son has satisfied us. Whereupon he asked:
> Whence? And they told him what had happened. Thereupon he said to his
> son: "My son, you have troubled our Creator to cause the fig tree to bring
> forth its fruit before its time, may you too be taken hence before your
> time."[10]

The father curses his son, shocking though it may be, because the son
has presumed to call for disturbing the natural order and also because in
disturbing it he may be unwittingly advancing the conditions of the
messianic age.[11]

Even though the fig tree receives widespead metaphorical use in
rabbinic literature, the repertoire remains within the bounds of the
Hebrew Bible, associated with the blessings of God, with the messianic
age. Its prominence in the land, its association with the garden of paradise, its tender fruit, are all metaphorical possibilities that are exploited
in a wide variety of usages. In contrast, a bad fig stands for a curse.

Three Years Awaiting

The first of the two Jesus fig parables, A Man Had A Fig Tree, occurs in
Luke as part of his travel narrative. The basic unit is Luke 13:1–9. The
apothegm, about the Galileans killed by Pilate and those killed by the

9. *Midrash Rabbah* on Genesis 62.2 (Freedman 2:551); the second parable is almost
identical. It poses an interesting "Synoptic problem."
10. *b. Taan.* 24a (Soncino 5:122).
11. For a detailed discussion of this passage, see Tilford, *Barren Fig Tree*, 188–89.

falling tower of Siloam, is built on the common assumption that punishment and sin are related.[12] But Jesus denies this linkage and instead requires repentance of all: "Unless you repent all likewise you will perish." The placement of *pantes*, "all," between the two verbs emphasizes it, since it can be the subject of both verbs. But the lesson of the parable is different: "The parable indicates that mercy is available for those who repent in time."[13] The transition from apothegm to parable becomes clear when it is seen from the perspective of the larger rhetorical argument it supports. Talbert marks out this larger unit as 12:49—13:9.[14] It has five blocks in its argument. Verses 49–53 set up the theme of apocalyptic trial and judgment, and vv. 54–56 call on the fictional audience to correctly interpret the signs of the times, which are then listed in the following three episodes. First, from the sign of being taken before a magistrate one is to learn that if the case is not settled, "you will never get out till you have paid the very last copper" (v. 59). From the tragedy of the Galileans and those on whom the tower of Siloam fell, one should not draw the conclusion that they were greater sinners, "but unless you repent you will all likewise perish" (13:3, 5). From the parable one learns how to interpret the present. Though the apocalyptic trial is real and final, now is the time of mercy—when the fig tree has one more chance to bring forth fruit. Despite the imperfect fit between parable and apothegm which Marshall observes to arise from the fact that they do not make the same point, they execute a progressive logic within the Lukan context which is powerful, for it has convinced most interpreters that the parable is about repentance and mercy. That is undoubtedly Luke's intention, but it misses many of the more subtle clues of this well-developed narrative.

The parable divides into two clear acts. The initial act deals with the owner of the vineyard and reports the situation.

> *Line 1:* A fig tree a certain man had which was planted in his vineyard, and he came seeking fruit on it and he did not find any. He said to the vinedresser, "For[15] three years I have been coming, seeking fruit on this fig tree and I did not find any. Cut it down! Why should it render the ground useless?"

This first scene is a complete narrative. It has a problem, the barren fig tree, and a solution, to cut it down, and could stand by itself as a *mashal* warning against failing to produce. The passage, like all the parable, has

---

12. Job 4:7; 8:20; 22:4–5; John 9:1–2; Str-B 2:193–97.
13. So Marshall, *Commentary on Luke*, 552.
14. Talbert, *Literary Patterns*, 52. Talbert sees it as parallel to 14:25—15:32.
15. For the grammar of the construction, see BDF, 144.

a strong paratactic structure,[16] indicating its oral roots. The pattern of coming, seeking, and not finding is repeated twice, once by the narrator and once in direct speech. A strong drumbeat builds up to the imperative "Cut it down!"

Not only does the triadic formula of coming, seeking, and not finding lead to a sense of doom and barrenness but so also does a specific detail in the parable. The owner has been coming for three years. Normally fig trees bear annually, usually from early spring until late fall. Three years was the normal time for maturation of a fig tree.[17] But according to Lev. 19:23, during the first three years of bearing, the fruit is unclean. Jeremias interprets the master's statement to mean that the plant is now six years old and thus hopelessly barren. Kenneth Bailey accepts Jeremias's suggestion but argues that since the owner would not come during the first three unclean years, the plant is now nine years old.[18] Regardless of the computation, the point is clear: the passage of three years indicates that the fig tree is hopelessly infertile. So, as the master says, why should it continue to waste good ground?

The parable's second act presents a counterresponse to the owner's proposal.

> *Line 2:* He answered and said to him, "Master, let it alone even this year until I dig around it and throw dung and if it makes fruit in the coming . . . otherwise if not you can cut it down."

This second section is carefully and intriguingly constructed. The style is again paratactic. The vinedresser wants to care for the tree one more year, to fertilize it with dung—a word that Bailey notes is irreverent in religious address. It gives the parable an earthy, off-color tone.[19] But the more intriguing aspect is in the double conditional proposition of the vinedresser. In the first condition, the protasis ("if") is not followed by an apodosis (a consequence), but it is implied.[20] Futhermore, there is no explicit statement about how long he should wait, although one year is surely implied since the master has been coming each year.

The critical issue is the elliptical apodosis of the first condition. It draws a hearer into supplying the missing details, the hoped future bearing of fruit. In the second condition, nothing is implied. The apo-

---

16. Jeremias, *Die Sprache,* 227.

17. For evidence that three years is the normal time for maturation and that after that the tree is not likely to bear fruit, see Wettstein, *Novum Testamentum Graecum* 1:744–75.

18. Bailey, *Through Peasant Eyes,* 82.

19. Ibid., 84.

20. The RSV supplies "well and good." See BDF, 454.4. Creed (*Gospel according to St. Luke,* 340–41) has an extensive treatment of the conditional statement.

dosis repeats the command of the owner, although in the owner's speech it had been a command to the vinedresser but now it is an address by the vinedresser to the owner: "You [meaning the owner, not I] can cut it down."

Yet the ellipsis remains. It creates hope on a hearer's part. In the exegesis of Jeremiah 24, where the allusion to good and bad figs is explained, the final comment is added, "But in case you should imagine that their hope is lost and their prospect is frustrated it was explicitly stated, 'The baskets give forth fragrance' [Cant 7:14], both will in the time to come give forth fragrance."[21] In the time to come, even the unrighteous will have a chance, and that same hope is implied in the ellipsis of the first condition. But how realistic is such a hope? The passage of three years indicates that the fig tree is hopelessly barren. A story frequently noted as parallel to this parable makes the point nicely:

> My son, thou hast been like that palm-tree that stood by a river, and cast all its fruit into the river, and when its lord came to cut it down, it said to him, "Let me alone this year, and I will bring thee forth carobs." And its lord said unto it, "Thou hast not been industrious in what is thine own, and how wilt thou be industrious in what is not thine own?"[22]

In this story the father (master) rejects the offer, although it is an offer that involves an element of fantasy, not associated with the parable. This story reminds us of the impossibility of filling in the ellipsis.

What is missing is a third act. What was the master's response? What happened in future years? Did some miracle occur that saved the tree? A rabbinic parable makes a similar point. In a discussion of the evil inclination, a parable is quoted to indicate why, even with the evil inclination, all is not hopeless:

> To a king of flesh and blood who had an inferior field. Some men came along and rented it at ten kor of wheat per year. They fertilized it, tilled it, watered it, cleared it—and harvested from it no more than one kor of wheat for the year.

Much as in the situation of A King Wished to Settle Accounts, the tenants will come up short on their contract of ten kor, for they have only one kor.

> "What is this?" the king demanded. "Our lord, the king!" they cried, "thou

21. *b. Erub.* 21a (Soncino 3:148).
22. *Story of Ahikar* 8.35 (*Apocrypha and Pseudepigrapha of the Old Testament*, ed. Charles, 2:775). Charles presents in parallel columns translations from the Syriac (which is the quotation given), Arabic, and Armenian. All three have slightly different versions of this story. But the story is missing from the Aramaic version, which is the earliest form of the text; see *Ahiquar*, in Charlesworth 2:480.

knowest that from the field which thou didst give us, thou didst harvest naught at first. And now that we have fertilized it and cleared it and watered it, we harvested from it at least one kor of wheat!" So shall Israel plead before the Holy One, blessed be He: Master of the Universe, Thou knowest that the evil impulse stirs us up.[23]

Even though ten kor is due, they plead that before he had got nothing from the field. The implication is, of course, that God will accept even a little bit. Still there is no miracle of a great harvest to meet the master's demand of ten kor.

Pleading in the face of a hopeless cause is the basis of hope. The ellipsis of the present is the possibility for the future. But it is more complicated than this. Why is it a fig tree? The fig tree, as the tree of blessing, is a promise of the future: it stands for Israel's golden past and future. But the tree is barren, fruitless, whereas the expectation is that it will be fruitful—as the Akibar and Rabbi Nathan quotations indicate. The fruitful fig tree is a blessing; a barren fig tree is a curse. Usually barren images and curses are associated with female symbols. Barren women are shamed, cursed. Yet divine intervention in the case of barrenness is a frequent theme in the Hebrew Bible. Both Sarah and Rachel experienced barrenness until God intervened. Leviticus 25:19 identifies keeping the statutes and fruitfulness: "Therefore you shall do my statutes and keep my ordinances and perform them; so you will dwell in the land securely. The land will yield its fruit, and you will eat your fill, and dwell in it securely." Barrenness is also a sign of lawlessness.

The ellipsis creates tension for a hearer. Is the hope possible, or is this tree barren? Can the miracle of birth come from a barren fig tree? This parable has no final act. On the one hand is realism, and on the other the apocalyptic fantasy of future boundless fruitfulness. But in the parable the ellipsis is the kingdom. We keep on manuring. What else is there to do?

The Fig's Parable

The parable From the Fig Tree (Mark 13:28; Matt. 24:32; Luke 21:29) occurs in the context of Jesus' final eschatological discourse. This final discourse of Jesus overlooking Jerusalem brings together in Mark a number of interlocking themes. It parallels the only other extended discourse in Mark, the parable discourse of chapter 4, in which the mystery of the kingdom is revealed. Here the mystery of the last days is almost revealed. The discourse's point is summed up in its last verse:

23. *Fathers according to Rabbi Nathan* 16 (Goldin, 86).

"What I say to you I say to all, watch!" (13:37). It ties together the themes of Jerusalem, the destruction of the temple, the persecution of the community, and the final days, and relates them all to the revelation of the mystery of Jesus' identity. The discourse encourages the community to be faithful, reassures them that Jesus will in the end make clear his lordship over history, and affirms that that climax is near although it is not to be confused with the destruction of Jerusalem.

The parable of the fig tree occurs in the discourse's concluding section.[24] Preceding the parable is the promised return of the Son of man at the conclusion of history (Mark 13:24–27). The parable is the opening transition to the final section on watchfulness.[25] It is balanced with the *mashal* fragment in 13:34. The parable of the fig tree provides a hermeneutical example. Just as when the fig tree buds you know that summer is near, so also when you see "these things" then "he is near the doors." But what is the referent for "these things"? It cannot be the coming of the Son of man, because this event constitutes the end of history. Rather, "these things" must refer to the initial question of the discourse: "Tell us when these things are to be, and what is the sign when all these things will be accomplished" (13:4). *Tauta* must refer, then, to those premonitory signs listed throughout the chapter.[26]

When we look at the Matthean and Lukan parallels we notice a striking difference in the way Matthew and Luke have handled the same passage. The two agree almost word for word, but Luke records some significant variations. The vagueness of "these things" is replaced by "the kingdom of God is near" (21:31), which means that he sees the discourse as clearly eschatological. No longer an example of only a fig tree, it now is a parable of fig "and all the trees" (21:29). Luke obviously sees the example as applying to all trees, there being nothing specific in the significance of the fig tree. Julius Wellhausen has also noted that the rising of the sap is really a sign not of summer or harvest but of spring, and thus somewhat inappropriate as a reference to the end.[27] Luke's generalizing indicates that the fig tree as the example is problematic. As Jeremias notes, the fig tree is normally a sign of the blessing associated with the messianic age, whereas here it points to tribulations.[28] Finally, Luke uses his normal parable introduction: "And he told them a parable." The Lukan clues are important because they not only indicate

24. Lambrecht offers a helpful outline of the discourse (*Once More Astonished*, 133).
25. Taylor, *Gospel according to Saint Mark*, 500.
26. So Tilford, *Barren Fig Tree*, 217; McNicol, "Lesson of the Fig Tree," 201.
27. Wellhausen, *Das Evangelium Marci*, 106. Wellhausen thinks the reference is to a specific fig tree which Jesus cursed and prophesied would bear again before his Parousia. For a thorough discussion of this position, see Tilford, *Barren Fig Tree*, 215.
28. Jeremias, *Parables*, 119.

how an early reader read and performed Mark but also indicate the misuse of the metaphor.

Since there is a wide agreement among scholars that Mark 13 is a compilation of eschatological sayings, given its final form by Mark,[29] did he rework the parable to fit the demands of performance? There are several indications that he did. Luke is not the only interpreter to notice the strange use of parable in Mark's introduction, which is without parallel. The use of the imperative appears to be Markan, for imperatives are used throughout the discourse as markers. "Learn," *mathete* (v.28), is parallel to "see," *blepete* (v. 33), which in turn is used in vv. 5, 9, and 23. Finally, the imperative is used strongly throughout this last section of the discourse:

> learn the parable (v. 28)
> know that summer is near (v. 28)
> know that he is near the doors (v. 29)
> see, watch [*agrypneite*],
>   you do not know when will be (v. 33)
> watch [*grēgoreite*], therefore, for you know not when the
>   master [*kyrios*] what I say to you to all I say, watch [*grēgoreite*]

Verse 28 indicates the hand of Mark,[30] and following these clues Klauck has suggested a reconstruction:

> It is like a fig tree, when its branches become tender and it puts forth leaves, the summer is near.[31]

Klauck's reconstruction conforms to the expected one-liner format and removes those elements that clearly result from Markan performance. It has a high claim to represent the originating structure.

Since the repertoire suggests powerful symbolic and metaphorical possibilities for the fig tree, when the parable announces the metaphor of the fig tree a hearer awaits the development of the metaphorical network. The parable, however, moves immediately to the tree's budding with two graphic images, the rising of the sap and the spreading of the leaves. Since the fig tree is not an evergreen, it loses its leaves, and when it comes back alive the sap is clearly visible. This aspect of the fig tree's botany is exploited by a rabbinic saying:

> Just as the leaves fade from off the vine and the fig tree, and the latter remain standing as a dry tree, and again they blossom afresh and bear buds

29. Pesch, *Naherwartungen*; Marxsen, *Mark the Evangelist*, 151–206; Kelber, *Kingdom in Mark*, chap. 6; and Grässer, *Das Problem*, 152–70.

30. So also Lambrecht, *Once More Astonished*, 137.

31. Klauck, *Allegorie und Allegorese*, 319.

and produce new leaves and fresh leaves. Likewise in the future will all the host of heaven fade away like a vine and a fig tree, and they will again be renewed before Him to make known that there is passing away [which] does not [really] pass away.[32]

This passage shows how the double motion of falling leaves and rising sap can function as a metaphor for the new age. Our parable exploits only the budding process. Nor is there any mention of the harvest or even of the first fruits, an aspect frequently employed in reference to Hosea 9:10: "Like grapes in the wilderness, I found Israel. Like the first fruit on the fig tree, in its first season, I saw your fathers." The Midrash comments,

> R. Judan said: At first the fruit of the fig-tree is gathered one by one, then two by two, then three by three, until eventually they are gathered in baskets with shovels. Even so, at the beginning, Abraham was one (Ezek 33:24); then there were Abraham and Isaac; then Abraham, Isaac, and Jacob. Until eventually, and the children of Israel were fruitful, and increased abundantly, and multiplied (Exod 7:1).[33]

Neither of these possibilities is exploited; instead the parable concludes that summer is near. But this is puzzling, for summer is not quite correct. A very similar phrase occurs in the Song of Solomon 2:11–13:

> For lo, the winter is past,
> the rain is over and gone.
> The flowers appear on the earth,
> the time of singing has come,
> and the voice of the turtledove
> is heard in our land.
> The fig tree puts forth its figs,
> and the vines are in blossom;
> they bring forth fragrance.

As this passage indicates, the correct time is spring, not summer. The Greek word *theros* means "summer," "summer fruits," "harvest," or "crop,"[34] and its cognates, *therizo*, "to harvest," and *therismos*, "harvest," indicate what aspect of summer it signals. As Telford points out, the Hebrew word that the LXX translates by *theros* is *qyts*, which means "summer," "summer fruits," "fig harvest," or "dried figs." This word is involved in a significant wordplay in Amos. The Lord shows the prophet a basket of ripe fruit (*qyst*), and then God says, "The end [*qst*] has come

---

32. *Pirke de Rabbi Eliezer* 51 (trans. Friedlander, 411). The allusion is to Isa. 34:4; see Tilford, *Barren Fig Tree*, 185.
33. *Midrash Rabbah* on Genesis 46.1 (Freedman 1:389).
34. LSJ, 794. See the thorough treatment of Tilford in *Barren Fig Tree*, 242 n. 33.

upon my people Israel" (Amos 8:2). Summer belongs to the metaphorical network for the end time.

Yet with all the metaphorical and symbolic possibilities suggested by the fig tree, none are explored in our parable. In modern terms, this parable is an experiment in minimalism. The narrative line is reduced to the minimal: rising sap, spreading leaves, the nearness of summer. It collapses time. The time span from planting to harvest is elongated both in A Sower Went Out, through the various fortunes of the seeds, and in A Man Casts Seed, through the notion of a man's rising day and night and of the seed's growing "first the blade, then the ear, then the full grain in the ear" (Mark 4:28). In both parables the time process is on display. Here time disappears. The parable jumps from budding to summer harvest. All is collapsed into the present. The end is now. Thus the growth metaphor, first Abraham and finally all, is undercut so that all that is left is not the harvest to come but the now. Now is the age of the fig tree; there is no golden future, no apocalyptic future. This is like the parable The Leaven, where the leaven (moral corruption) is not to be replaced by the unleavened (the good). Or like A Woman with a Jar, where no prophet comes to fill up her jar. There is no future over-abundant fig tree, but in its very ordinariness there is only this tree. We are left with leaven, an empty jar, a budding fig tree, as the metaphorical network for the kingdom.

17

*W*hat Did
the Farmer
Sow?

A Sower Went Out

Now a sower went out, took a handful of seeds, and scattered them.
Some fell upon the path and the birds came and devoured them.
Some fell on rock, did not take root in soil, and they did not
produce. Other seeds fell among thorns and the thorns grew up and
choked them. And other seeds fell into good soil and brought forth
fruit, coming up and growing and bearing one thirtyfold, and one
sixtyfold, and one a hundredfold.

This parable has occasioned a longstanding debate about the allegorical
character of Jesus' parables, because in the Synoptics it appears with
appended allegory. Is that interpretation Jesus' or the early community's?

Even though Jülicher[1] has demonstrated that the interpretations proposed for the parable in the Synoptics are internally inconsistent with
the parable, the internal contradictions are not the most interesting
factor, for there is always a distance between an interpretation and the
thing it interprets. By far the more interesting feature, as Dodd observes,[2] is how the various interpretations meet the preoccupations of

1. Jülicher, *Die Gliechnisreden* 2:514–38.
2. Dodd, *Parables*, 145.

the early church, both in encouraging the hearing of the word and in accounting for lack of belief in it.[3]

The parable exhibits some distinctively Christian vocabulary—for example, the use of "word," *logos,* for gospel, and "sowing," *speirein,* as a metaphor for preaching.[4] Although not persuasive to all, the existence in the *Gospel of Thomas* of a version without any interpretation or elaboration (*Gos. Thom.* 9) indicates that the parable circulated in the oral tradition without the specific allegorical interpretation of the Synoptics. Even more interesting is the version or the allusion to the parable in *1 Clem.* 24.5:

> The Sower went forth and cast each of the seeds into the ground, and they fall on to the ground, parched and bare, and suffer decay; then from their decay the greatness of the providence of the Master raises them up, and from one grain more grow and bring forth fruit.

Since *1 Clement* probably does not draw directly on the Synoptics,[5] the allusion to the sower is an oral performance of the parable's originating structure. It is significant that the author interprets it as a reference to resurrection, a not impossible reading given the usage of sowing as a metaphor for resurrection (1 Cor. 15:36–44).[6] *Clement,* like *Thomas,* indicates that the Synoptic interpretation is not demanded.

For those defending Jesus' parables as allegory, this becomes the test case. Frequently they link the parable, its interpretation, and the connecting Isaiah quotation.[7] For reasons given in the Prolegomena, I have argued that the connection is from Mark. But C. Moule makes the important point that Isaiah 6 does not have to be understood as a literal description of Jesus' ministry but can be understood as hyperbole.[8] Yet the language of who is inside and who outside conforms more to the ideology of the early church, and specifically to the vocabulary of Mark. It represents a period of community formation, a concern of the church and not of Jesus.[9]

3. Among many who note this, see Didier ("La parabole," 29).

4. For an extensive listing of Christian vocabulary found in the interpretation, see Jeremias, *Parables,* 77–78; Didier, "La parabole," 29.

5. Koester (*Synoptische Überlieferung,* 20) says that it is an allusion to the beginning of Mark 4:3 (which has wording that is very similar in all three Synoptics). For Koester, *1 Clement* is drawing on oral tradition. See R. Grant and Graham (*Apostolic Fathers* 2:50), who are apparently in agreement. Actually "cast into the ground," *epi tēn gēn,* is similar to A Man Casts Seed.

6. Koester (*Synoptische Überlieferung,* 20) suggests that *Clement* is drawing upon a common Jewish stock.

7. The classic article is that of Moule: "Mark 4:1–20 Yet Once More," 95–113. See Boucher, *Mysterious Parable,* 43–44; Evans, "A Note," 234–35; idem, "On the Isaianic Background," 464–68.

8. Moule, "Mark 4:1–20 Yet Once More," 100.

9. Drury (*Parables in the Gospels,* 54–55) goes so far as to argue that Mark composed

Defenders of the allegory's authenticity have correctly sensed that parables which employ agricultural activity for their metaphorical vehicle draw attention to the metaphor with an insistency unlike that of parables dealing with the interaction of characters. The parable's traditional title, "The Sower," misses the point by implying that the parable conforms to those where a character dominates the action. The sower immediately disappears from the parable and is present only by implication. Since it is easier to identify with a character than a process, such parables pose insistently, "What does it stand for?"

The Secret of the Kingdom

Source critics have argued about whether there exists a pre-Markan parable collection.[10] Nonetheless, there is wide agreement that Mark did inherit the parable's interpretation. Regardless of the reconstruction of a possible pre-Markan parable cycle, Mark certainly has placed his own stamp on the parables of chapter 4 by ordering the discourse, his emphasis on themes, and finally, the discourse's place in the overall structure of the Gospel.

Lambrecht has proposed a cyclic organization of chapter 4 that has merit:[11]

A Introduction (vv. 1–4)
  Teaching in parables
B Sower
  (a) A Sower Went Out (vv. 3–9)
  (b) Perceiving and not hearing
  (c) Interpretation
C Sayings (vv. 21–25)
  (a) Lamp and explanation
  (b) Summons to hear
  (a1) Measure and its explanation
B1 Seed similitudes (vv. 26–32)
  (a) A Man Casts Seed
  (a1) A Grain of Mustard Seed
A1 Conclusion
  He taught them in parables

---

not only the interpretation and Isaiah quotation but also the parable. But this fails to account for *Thomas* and *1 Clement*, which are independent witnesses to the parable.

10. See Kuhn, *Ältere Sammlungen*, 99–146. Kuhn's observations are often forceful, but in the end his methodology assumes a literate model and so he sometimes is too confident about his ability to separate redaction from tradition.

11. Lambrecht, *Once More Astonished*, 86–87; idem, "Redaction and Theology," 303. I have elaborated upon Lambrecht's proposal.

What is attractive about Lambrecht's suggestion is that it illuminates both an internal and an external consistency of Mark 4.

The discourse of Mark 4 disrupts the Gospel's narrative flow. Chapters 4 and 13 are the Gospel's only two extended discourses. Conflict scenes dominate the narrative until chapter 4, and then after chapter 13 they resume.[12] The conflict theme is incorporated into chapter 4, with the Markan insertion between the parable A Sower Went Out and its interpretation. This insertion (4:10–20) on the purpose of parables is transmuted into the secrecy motif: for those outside all is in parables, for those inside the mystery of the kingdom of God is revealed.

The introduction (vv. 1–2) to Mark 4 stamps what follows as teaching. Three times in the introduction, words with the root *didas*, "teach," are employed.[13] The size of the crowd necessitates moving to a boat and sitting in the sea. This may recall Ps. 29:10. The various elements of the introduction earmark the beginning of a solemn discourse.

John Drury has suggested that the parable's interpretation foreshadows the development of Mark's story.[14] Thus parable and interpretation organize a reader's perspective on upcoming events and set in motion a series of retrospections. In Mark 8:27, while Jesus and the disciples are "on the way," Peter rebukes Jesus for his teaching about the Son of man and in turn Jesus accuses him of being on the side of Satan. In the first planting, in which the seed falls "beside the way," the birds are interpreted as Satan, who snatches the word after it is first heard. The third interpretation looks forward to the story of the man who questions Jesus about inheriting eternal life (10:17) and fails to respond to the call, for he had many possessions (10:22). The second planting, on rocky ground, Drury suggests, parallels Jesus' arrest (14:43–50), which concludes with the narrator's remarking that they all fled. Although there are no verbal parallels between this scene and the second planting with its interpretation, the thematic parallel is strong. Yet the parallel is even stronger, I would suggest, with Mark 13, the only other long discourse in Mark. The discourse begins with the warning against being led astray (v. 5). The disciples will be persecuted before councils and synagogue (vv. 9–11), but the Gospel must be preached to all the nations (v. 10). Twice the great tribulation is mentioned (vv. 17, 24), and in the final instance a reader is told that "the sun will be darkened," an inversion of the third planting. A form-critical analysis of the parable confirms this connection

---

12. For an analysis of the relation of Mark 12 to the earlier controversy stories in Mark, see chap. 10 above.

13. For a short summary of the issue, see Achtemeier, *Mark*, 60–70. For a detailed study, see Robbins, *Jesus the Teacher*.

14. Drury, *Parables in the Gospels*, 51–52.

with chapter 13, for precisely in the second planting is Mark's hand most evident. The double mention of no depth, no root indicates a Markan insertion, so that the intervening clause about the sun is additional. Thus, this second planting looks forward to the climactic chapter 13.

By instructing the disciples secretly, Mark makes the parable's interpretation part of his secret teaching, which is a prominent literary motif in the Gospel (7:17–22; 9:28–29; 13:3–37). The parable's interpretation is fulfilled in the Gospel's narrative. It also warns the reader of the fate of those preaching the gospel.

The Word of the Kingdom

A Sower Went Out inaugurates the third major discourse in the Gospel of Matthew. We will examine, first, the structure of the discourse and, then, Matthew's specific performance of the parable.

The chapter is ordered in a complex arrangement built around a series of doublets. Three parables, A Sower Went Out, The Wheat and Tares, and The Net, receive interpretation and form the primary grid for the chapter.

> *A* A Sower Went Out
>   *B* Interpretation
> *A* The Wheat and Tares
>   *B* A Grain of Mustard Seed
>   *B* The Leaven
> *A* Interpretation
>   *B* Treasure
>   *B* A Merchant
> *A* The Net

The Wheat and Tares is clearly the central section of Matthew's discourse. Furthermore, the three organizing parables all deal with separation—the major metaphorical theme of the chapter.

Though Matthew has no standard introduction to his major discourses, there are striking similarities between the beginning of this third discourse and the first, the Sermon on the Mount. In both discourses, Jesus is seated in a specific place (on a mountain, in a boat) and there are crowds around. The parable discourse is not teaching or preaching for Matthew. Rather, Jesus tells or speaks parables.[15] The formulaic conclusion of the first two discourses mentions teaching (see 7:28; 11:1), but the conclusion to this one does not (13:53).

Why does Matthew begin a discourse about parables and the king-

15. Kingsbury, *Parables of Jesus*, 28–30.

dom with a parable that does not deal explicitly with the kingdom?[16]
Since he has no interest in Mark's so-called hardening theory, the language about inside and outside is missing. For Matthew, Jesus speaks in parables "because seeing they do not see, and hearing they do not hear nor understand" (v. 13).[17] The theme of seeing and hearing is picked up in the concluding beatitude (vv. 16–17), which begins with an emphatic *hymin*, literally, "Your blessed are the eyes that . . ."[18] The primary place of "your" highlights those who are blessed and not those who are excluded.

Similarly, in the interpretation of the parable the accent falls on hearing,[19] and the seed is the "word of the kingdom" (v. 19), which ties the parable to the chapter's major theme.

> you then hear the parable (v. 18)
> everyone who hears the word of the kingdom and does not understand it (v. 19)
> this is the one who hears the word (v. 22)
> this is the one who hears the word and understands (v. 23)

The repetition of the same phrase throughout the interpretation focuses a reader's attention on hearing, while both the introductory phrase and the final phrase conclude with notices about understanding. The parable then instructs a reader that all hear the word of the kingdom but only those who are blessed understand. The separation is on the basis not of hearing but of understanding. The discourse concludes on this note: "Have you understood all this?" (v. 51).

Hearing the Gospel

Unlike both Matthew and Mark, who use the parable of A Sower Went Out to introduce an extended discourse, Luke uses the parable in a fashion quite different from his normal usage.[20] It does not introduce a generalized teaching about parables, but the interest falls on this single parable. Jesus speaks a parable (8:4), and the disciples ask about this parable (v. 9). The parable and its explanation are combined with the proverb of the lamp. An inclusio is formed around the parable which

16. Cope (*Matthew*, 15) poses this problem.

17. Stendahl (*School*, 129) and Gnilka (*Die Verstockung Israels*, 103–5) argue that the quotation from Isa. 6:14–15 is not part of Matthew's original text, because it is the only formula quotation on the lips of Jesus and it conforms to the LXX.

18. The parallel to the beatitude in Luke is the conclusion of Jesus' thanksgiving to the Father (Luke 10:21–24).

19. Cope, *Matthew*, 20.

20. See p. 28 above.

exhibits a response to the preaching of the gospel of the kingdom of God (v. 1). The parable is introduced with the Twelve and the women who follow Jesus; the second concludes with Jesus proclaiming, "My mother and my brothers are those who hear the word of God and do it" (8:21). For Luke, the parable is an example of hearing the gospel.

The key words "hear" (vv. 8, 10, 12, 13, 14, 15, 18, 21) and "word" (vv. 11, 13, 15, 21) hold the passage together like glue.[21] This distinctive Lukan feature occurs in the interpretation of the good soil: "And as for the good soil, they are those who, hearing the word, hold it fast in an honest and good heart, and bring forth fruit with patience" (v. 15).

Finding the Kingdom

Thomas's version of A Sower Went Out has impressed many scholars.[22] This is especially evident in the description of the seed that fell among the rock, which is direct and to the point in *Thomas* but convoluted in Mark. Even more, *Thomas* does not have the extended allegory found in the Synoptics.[23]

> Jesus said, "Now the sower went out, took a handful [of seeds] and scattered them. Some fell on the road; the birds came and gathered them up. Others fell on rock, did not take root in the soil, and did not produce ears. And others fell on thorns; they choked the seed[s] and worms ate them. And others fell on the good soil and produced good fruit: it bore sixty per measure and a hundred and twenty per measure." (*Gos. Thom.* 9)

The parable occurs in the first section of the *Gospel of Thomas*, where the theme of seeking and finding is established. What is to be found is the kingdom, which is "inside you and outside you" (*Gos. Thom.* 3). Immediately prior to this parable is that of The Net (*Gos. Thom.* 8), in which the wise fisherman is the one who finds a large fish and throws back the smaller ones. The pattern of finding and keeping is probably the rhetorical context in which the parable A Sower Went Out is to be read. The seeds that do not produce are those "little fishes," and the good seed is the "big fish," the kingdom. For that reason the conclusion was probably shifted in performance so that it moves in the correct geometrical progression: sixty to one hundred twenty. *Gospel of Thomas* 10 reinforces this reading: "Jesus said 'I have cast fire upon the world and see, I am

---

21. Talbert, *Reading Luke*, 90.
22. Crossan, *In Parables*, 42–43; idem, *Cliffs of Fall*, 45; Horman, "Source," 326–43.
23. As Davies (*Gospel of Thomas*, 7–8) points out, every saying from Mark 3:35—4:34 occurs in *Thomas* except the interpretation of A Sower Went Out and the reason for speaking in parables.

guarding it until it blazes.'" This would indicate that the fire is being guarded until it is found.

The context in *Thomas* leads to a different reading of the parable from the one in the Synoptics. There, owing probably to the influence of Mark, the emphasis falls on the seeds that fail to produce, and so the parable is given an ethical slant: it serves as a warning to the community of the failure to hear the word, although Luke has muted this point. This dimension is missing in *Thomas*. Since the parable does not accord particularly well with the theme of finding, it is subordinated to the parable of The Net, which has the appended saying "Whoever has ears to hear, let him hear." *Thomas* thus draws attention away from A Sower Went Out and toward The Net.

Reconstruction: Originating Structure

We now have excellent studies of the interrelation of the four extant versions of the parable.[24] Crossan makes a compelling argument for Matthew's dependence on Mark, since Matthew repeats the Markan expansion of 4:5–6.[25] His arguments for Luke's dependence on Mark are less convincing.[26] In order to be on the safe side, we will assume that Luke has an independent tradition and that he knows Mark.[27] We may have, then, three independent performances of the same originating structure: Mark, Luke, and *Thomas*.[28]

Since we are concerned with the originating structure and are not pursuing the illusion of an original wording, the obvious triadic structure underlying all three versions will guide our reconstruction. Where there is deviation from the triadic structure, we will investigate for variations in performance.

The parable is constructed in such a way that it has an initial scene of sowing and a concluding scene of produce, forming an inclusio for three scenes of failure and one of triple growth. The initial scene is virtually identical in all three versions.[29] It is impossible to decide between

24. See Wenham, "Interpretation," 299–319; Weeden, "Recovering the Parabolic Intent," 97–120; Crossan, *Cliffs of Fall*, 25–64; Lambrecht, "Redaction and Theology," 269–307. For a summary of prior positions, see Kuhn, *Ältere Sammlungen*, 24–27.

25. Crossan, *Cliffs of Fall*, 35.

26. Ibid., 35–37. By Crossan's own admission it is a close call.

27. With Wenham, "Interpretation," 318. See the similar situation with A Grain of Mustard Seed. Carlston (*Parables*, 70) argues that Luke is simplifying Mark.

28. I operate with a hypothesis that *Thomas* represents independent tradition. See pp. 32–33 above.

29. Lambrecht ("Redaction and Theology," 299) has argued that *exēlthen . . . speirai* was possibly Markan, but this shows the excessively literate presuppositions of redaction criticism. It may be a characteristic of Markan style reflected in his performance of the structure, but that does not mean he created it.

Thomas's "took a handful [of seeds]"[30] and "to sow"; both implement the same structure.

All three extant versions of A Sower Went Out agree that the initial verb in the four scenes is "fell," a repetitive patterning characteristic of oral tradition. The first scene dealing with the path is again virtually the same. Luke's variation, "trodden under foot" (8:5), is probably less original.[31] The convincing agreement between Mark and *Thomas*'s performances points to the originating structure. Luke still retained the three-fold structure.

The scene dealing with the rock is less firm in its adherence to the triadic structure. *Thomas* maintains it, but Luke has the obvious addition of "because it had no moisture" (v. 6). Mark's version betrays his special interests and style. Vincent Taylor has noted the redundancy of "where it had not much soil,"[32] and Crossan has also drawn attention to the presence of the Markan insertion technique,[33] which consists of a repetition of a phrase on either side of an insertion. In this case the double phrases are "since it had no depth of soil" (v. 5) and "since it had no root" (v. 6); the insertion deals with the sun's scorching the seed. This corresponds in the parable's interpretation with "When tribulation or persecution arises on account of the word, immediately they fall away" (4:17), which expresses a strong motif in Mark.[34] So reconstructed, the Markan text is remarkably close to *Thomas* and Luke and so confirms the preservation of the originating structure in *Thomas*.

The scene of the seed among the thorns exhibits only minor variations. Both Luke and *Thomas* have preserved the triad; Mark has a fourth element, "and it yielded no grain." Both Theodore Weeden and Carlston[35] maintain that this was added in anticipation of the interpretation in 4:19, where the unfruitfulness properly belongs. It may be that *Thomas*'s note about the worms eating the seed is secondary,[36] but I find no compelling reason for this. It represents variation in the performance of the structure.

After three scenes of misadventure, the seed finally finds fertile soil. Only Mark has "growing up and increasing." Weeden has argued that these words were added in the oral tradition,[37] and Lambrecht has

30. Ménard (*L'évangile selon Thomas*, 92) argues without explanation that it is from *Thomas*.
31. So Carlston, *Parables*, 73.
32. Taylor, *Gospel according to Saint Mark*, 252–60. So also Gnilka, *Die Verstockung Israels*, 61; Lambrecht, "Redaction and Theology," 299.
33. See Donahue, *Are You the Christ?* 77–84; Kee, *Community of the New Age*, 54–56.
34. Crossan, *Cliffs of Fall*, 32–34.
35. Weeden "Rediscovering the Parabolic Intent," 103; Carlston, *Parables*, 70.
36. So Crossan, *Cliffs of Fall*, 39–40.
37. Weeden, "Rediscovering the Parabolic Intent," 104. Crossan (*Cliffs of Fall*, 40) is in agreement.

pointed to the duality of the phrase as a characteristic of Markan style.[38] Whatever the situation, the double phrase obviously breaks the rhythm and so should not be considered part of the originating structure. Finally, the amount of the harvest varies in each version. Luke simply has a hundredfold, *Thomas* has a doublet (sixty and one hundred twenty), and Mark has a triplet (thirtyfold, sixtyfold, and a hundredfold). Given the triadic structure of the parable, the Markan version is to be preferred. But there is more to be said. Luke's single number imparts finality, closure, to the parable, while *Thomas*'s sixty and one hundred twenty have a nice mathematical symmetry. Mark's thirty, sixty, and a hundredfold lack both symmetry and logical closure, and thus probably represent the originating structure.

A Reading

Line 1: Now a sower went out, took a handful of seeds, and scattered them.

Both *Thomas* and Mark implement in slightly different ways the triadic form of originating structure. *Thomas*'s performance is preferable because he has the stronger triad: "went out"/"took"/"scattered." The Synoptics have used the third member of the triad as a bridge to the second line.

The first line initiates a planting scene and implies a narrative logic of planting → growth → harvest at a minimum. This metaphorical structure is readily available to be exploited in a variety of ways. The simplicity of the narrative structure requires a hearer to listen for the clues indicating direction. Initially the parable does not disclose where it is heading.

Line 2: Some fell upon the path and the birds came and devoured them.

Jeremias has defended the farmer's action of sowing the seed on the path as expressing normal Palestinian farming conditions.[39] One first sows and then plows, so that later the farmer was to come back and plow up the path. Jeremias is, of course, trying to defend the farmer against bad or absurd farming practices. He has adduced as his primary evidence *m. Shab.* 7.2, where there is a discussion of the tasks to be

---

38. Lambrecht, "Redaction and Theology," 300. For a list of double participles used in Mark, see Neirynck, *Duality in Mark*, 82– 84.

39. Jeremias, *Parables*, 11–12. For Jeremias, this is a primary example of the everydayness, the particularity of Palestinian custom, exhibited by the parables.

avoided on the Sabbath: "The primary labors are forty less one, sowing, ploughing, reaping, binding sheaves, etc."[40] Jeremias takes this order to indicate that in Palestine it was customary to sow and then plow. Thus the parable is describing normal conditions.

K. D. White[41] has responded to Jeremias by quoting extensive evidence from the ancient world, especially Columella's *De re rustica,* that the normal practice was to plow first, then to sow. Actually, one plowed several times in order to break up the soil. Against Jeremias, who argues that the sower deliberately sows on the path to await later plowing, White argues that broadcast sowing inevitably means that some seed will be lost. Furthermore, he points out that even if the path were plowed, it would not be suitable for planting, because the ground would not work up well but would remain too lumpy.

Payne[42] has reviewed the evidence once again and argued that White was wrong when he insisted that plowing always preceded sowing. That was certainly normal, but sometimes at the second planting, of autumn, there was no first plowing, because the ground was already broken and the autumn rains would weaken the soil. There was also at times a second plowing, which buried the seed. Against Jeremias, Payne agrees with White that the sower would not deliberately sow on the path, since it would be unsuitable.[43] In the end, Payne concludes that from the parable one cannot deduce what particular farming situation is in mind. Is it spring, in which case there should have been a plowing before sowing, or is it autumn, in which case there might not have been a plowing? Payne contends that the debate about the order of the plowing and sowing is irrelevant to the parable.

Payne's conclusion, I think, is correct. Regardless of normal farming technique, the parable's narration shifts the hearer's point of view to the seeds and their fate; it does not focus upon the sower and his practices. The focus on the seeds remains constant throughout the narration. This is unlike A Man Casts Seed, where the farmer always remains in the background of the parable, fading in and out of the action.

The path is no suitable place for germination. In broadcast sowing it is inevitable that a certain amount of seed will be lost. In this case the birds devour the seed even before it can germinate. This first planting is one of total failure. Line 1 had provided the hearer with a temporal perspective, namely, the time of sowing, although whether spring or autumn is left unstated. Line 2 maintains that perspective, only concentrated: this line

40. *m. Shab.* 7.2 (Danby, 106).
41. White, "Parable of the Sower," 301–2.
42. Payne, "Order of Sowing and Ploughing," 123–29.
43. Ibid., 128.

takes place on the day of sowing. A hearer is provided with two perspectives: a temporal one and a paradigm of failure.

Line 3: Some fell on rock, did not take root in soil, and they did not produce.

Mark has elaborated this scene to fit his interests, and Matthew has followed suit. Luke and *Thomas*, on the other hand, have maintained a simple triadic structure. The differences between them are due to variations in performance. Luke and *Thomas*, therefore, represent the same originating structure.

Jeremias states that the rocky ground is underlying, thinly covered limestone,[44] which may be true. Yet more important, like the path it is unsuitable ground. The rock denotes barrenness, something that cannot give birth, as Mark's elaboration of the metaphor makes plain. Sirach 40:15 also employs the same metaphor: "The children of the ungodly will not put forth many branches; they are unhealthy roots upon sheer rock."

Still, in comparison with the seeds on the path, the narrative has moved forward. The seed falls on poor, rocky ground. It germinates, but it does not grow. Temporally this line begins on the day of sowing but presumes a time span of at least several days, that is, the time needed for germination. Nevertheless, the fate of this seed is essentially the same as that in line 2. But the failure is not so total; the seed at least germinates.

Line 4: Other seeds fell among thorns and the thorns grew up and choked them.

The devouring of the growth by worms in *Thomas* is not necessarily secondary but may be an alternate performance of the originating structure. Thorns are a common metaphor for the wicked in both the Hebrew Bible and rabbinic literature.[45] Jeremiah 4:3 is a good example of the metaphor:

Break up your fallow ground, and sow not among thorns.

Thorns would destroy the young growth of wheat. In commenting on Exod. 27:8, the Midrash says, "When at Sinai they were like lilies and roses, now [i.e., after the incident of the golden calf] they have become like rubble, like thorn-bushes."[46]

The mention at the beginning of the line that the seed fell among thorns reveals its inevitable fate. Temporally, the seed in this line does

---

44. Jeremias, *Parables*, 11.
45. Feldman, *Parables and Similes*, 186–87.
46. Ibid., 187; quoting *Rab. Exod.* 42.7.

better than the previous seed. It germinates and grows, but it fails to make it to harvest, although, ironically, in *Thomas* it is harvested by the worms and in the Synoptics by thorns. Likewise, the temporal perspective is now implicitly elongated. Time is past the days of sowing and nearing the days of harvest. The failure in this case is also less total than in lines 2 and 3. There has been a progression both temporally and in terms of failure. This progression leads a hearer to expect now the harvest, and by implication a successful one.

Line 5: And other seeds fell into good soil and brought forth fruit, coming up and growing and bearing one thirtyfold and one sixty-fold and one a hundredfold.

This is a double line, both parts of which maintain the triadic structure. Given the strong paratactic structure of the parable, this line moves quickly to success and climax. Even though this is the climax, we need to look carefully at its structure. It presents a hearer with a completed narrative and encompasses temporally the entire story time from sowing to harvest. Obviously the temporal sequence replicates the demarcation between success and failure. As the time span has lengthened, the failure decreases until at last there is success. Thus the triadic patterns of the parable lead a hearer inevitably toward an expectation of success, actually of overwhelming success, so as to triumph over the three scenes of failure.[47] Jeremias argues that "the tripling ... of the harvest's yield ... symbolizes the eschatological overflowing of the divine fullness, surpassing all human measure."[48] Two issues are at stake: Is the tripling a tripling of individual seeds or of the harvest itself? Does the yield surpass all human measure?

There are three compelling reasons to reject Jeremias's contention that the tripling refers to the harvest of the field. The plain sense of the Greek demands that the yield refer to individual seeds.[49] Second, the structure of the parable attends to the seeds, not to the sower or the harvest. Since Jeremias construes this parable as one of contrast, he sees the contrast between the three scenes of failure and the harvest of success. But that motif is imposed. The actual structure leads a hearer to view the seed. Finally, how can one field or harvest have three different yields?[50]

47. Wilder, *Jesus' Parables*, 93. Wilder makes the point that the rhetoric of the parable leads to this expectation of triumphant harvest, and he sees the parable as exemplifying the metaphor of extravagant harvest.
48. Jeremias, *Parables*, 150.
49. See BDF, 207 (2); Zerwick, *Biblical Greek*, no. 158. In agreement: Linnemann, *Jesus of the Parables*, 117; Payne, "Order of Sowing and Ploughing," 181; White, "Parable of the Sower," 302.
50. See Crossan, *Cliffs of Fall*, 44. White ("Parable of the Sower," 301) shows that referring to the yield of individual seeds is normal in ancient texts.

Jeremias also contends that the harvest surpasses human measure. He asserts this only in *The Parables of Jesus*. But in an article he points to Gen. 26:12, where Isaac reaps a harvest of a hundredfold, as an example of an eschatological text promising an overabundant harvest.[51] But neither is this text eschatological nor is it interpreted eschatologically. Both the *Targum Onkelos*[52] and the *Targum Neophyti*[53] fail to develop the passage. The comments on the verse in *Midrash Rabbah* on Genesis are quite interesting. First the Midrash notes that the land was infertile and the year poor ("How much more then had they been favourable!"),[54] and in another comment it remarks that "this means a hundred kor." A kor is the largest unit of measure, so this interpretation greatly expands the amount in the Genesis text. The Midrashist obviously does not think a yield of a hundredfold is very significant and so devises two strategies to make it more significant.

There certainly existed the eschatological expectation that in the day of the Lord the land would give forth fantastic crops. A typical example is Isa. 27:6: "In days to come Jacob shall take root, Israel shall blossom and put forth shoots, and fill the whole world with fruit."[55] But seldom are figures given. One example of a figure comes from the Babylonian Talmud:

> The world to come is not like this world. In this world there is the trouble of harvesting and treading [of the grapes], but in the world to come a man will bring one grape on a wagon or a ship, put it in a corner of his house and use its contents as [if it had been] a large wine cask, while its timber [branches] would be used to make fires for cooking. There will be no grape that will not contain thirty kegs of wine.[56]

A similar tradition may underlie the Jesus saying reported by Papias:

> The day shall come wherein vines shall grow, each having ten thousand shoots and on one shoot ten thousand branches, and on one branch ten thousand tendrils, and on every tendril ten thousand clusters, in every cluster ten thousand grapes, and every grape when it is pressed shall yield five and twenty measure of wine.[57]

Clearly there is an expectation of a superabundance associated with the day of the Lord.

---

51. Jeremias, "Palästinakundliches," 53.
52. *Targums of Onkelos and Jonathan ben Uzziel*, ed. Etherdidge, 243.
53. *Neophyti 1, Genesis*, ed. Machjo, 564.
54. *Midrash Rabbah* on Genesis 64.6 (Feldman 1:577).
55. For additional examples, see Payne, "Order of Sowing and Ploughing," 202 n. 68.
56. *b. Ketub.* 111b (Soncino 7:721–22).
57. Irenaeus, *Adversus Haereses*, 5.33.3–4.

But is this harvest of thirtyfold, sixtyfold, and a hundredfold super-abundant? The contemporary evidence indicates that it is within the range of the normal. Pliny in his *Natural History* reports,

> The deputy governor of that region [Byzacium in Africa] sent to his late Majesty Augustus—almost incredible as it seems—a parcel of very nearly 400 shoots obtained from a single grain as seed, and there are still in existence dispatches relating to the matter. He likewise sent to Nero also 360 stalks obtained from one grain. At all events the plains of Lentini and other districts in Sicily, and the whole of Andalusia, and particularly Egypt reproduce at the rate of a hundredfold.[58]

Pliny has probably mistaken *germina*, "shoots," for *grana*, "grains."[59] Pliny indicates a scale from incredible (superabundant), four hundred-fold, to what is very good, one hundredfold. The talmudic numbers quoted above are much larger than four hundredfold.

Varro reports on plantings of beans, wheat, barley, and spelt, so his figures are harder to interpret. He notes that yields vary from region to region depending on fertility. But then he remarks, "Around Sybaris in Italy the normal yield is said to be even a hundred to one, and a like yield is reported near Gadara in Syria, and for the district of Byzacium in Africa."[60] Thus one hundredfold is a good harvest.

Herodotus in his description of the fertility of Babylonia reports,

> Its corn is so abundant that it yields for the most part two hundred fold, and even three hundred fold when the harvest is best. The blades of the wheat and barley there are easily four fingers broad; and for millet and sesame, I will not say, though it is known to me, to what a height they grow; for I am well aware that even what I have said respecting corn is wholly disbelieved by those who have never visited Babylonia.[61]

Again Herodotus's report for the high figures are, he thinks, almost unbelievable—much as we have seen in Pliny.

Assuredly this review of ancient texts undermines Jeremias's conclusion about the harvest's superabundance. Given the rabbinic texts with their wild numbers, and the Greek and Latin texts with four hundred-fold as the incredible number, the thirty-, sixty-, and a hundredfold are well within the bounds of the believable. They are an average-to-good harvest.[62]

58. Pliny, *Natural History*, 18.21.95 (LCL 5:249).
59. So White, "Parable of the Sower," 302.
60. Varro, *On Agriculture*, 1.44.2 (LCL, 275).
61. *Herodotus*, 1.193 (LCL 1:243–44).
62. Payne ("Order of Sowing and Ploughing," 181–86) reaches the same conclusion. See also Linnemann, *Jesus of the Parables*, 117; Crossan (*Cliffs of Fall*, 44), who does not survey the evidence.

How then does a hearer respond? Matthew responded by reversing the numbers, and Luke reported only the hundredfold. Both sought to emphasize the big number. *Thomas* doubled the numbers, sixty to a hundred twenty, for a similar reason. These responses seek to avoid the quandary created by the underlying structure—the disjunction between form and content. As Amos Wilder remarks, the form of three failures and the threefold numbers of growth lead to an expectation of hyperbolic growth. The ascending serial enumeration intensifies expectation.[63] Yet the content is not hyperbolic. Jeremias, Dodd, Wilder, and others have been tricked by the form. The content is quite normal. Thirty-, sixty-, and one hundredfold represent a modest success, a good harvest, quite within everyday expectations. It is neither hyperbolic nor superabundant. Even the serialization warns the hearer. The last number is out of order. It should be as in *Thomas*—sixty and one hundred twenty. The final oddness points to the disjunction between form and content. Thus a hearer is left in a quandary: What has happened?

From Story to Kingdom

W. O. E. Oesterley once remarked that the parable "must have sounded pointless to those who heard it without any explanation."[64] He, of course, said this in order to argue for the authenticity of the allegorical interpretation. Yet Oesterley's observation is not without merit, for as we have seen, the very disjunction of form and content in the parable makes it difficult to make a consistency out of the parabolic narrative. How does the hearer put it together so as to make sense of it?

At first glance the repertoire does not alleviate the problem. Sowing and reaping constitute a common process that supports a wide-ranging metaphorical network. The process engenders the common proverb "What you sow is what you reap" (e.g., Gal. 6:7). In both Hellenistic and Jewish wisdom this proverb is exploited in a variety of directions.

In Hellenistic wisdom, the proverb is frequently elaborated in the interests of *paideia*. An example from a letter of Seneca makes the point:

> Words should be scattered like seed; no matter how small the seed may be, if it has once found favourable ground, it unfolds its strength and from an insignificant thing spreads to its greatest growth. Reason grows in the same; it is not large to the outward view, but increases as it does its work. Few words are spoken; but if the mind has truly caught them, they come into their strength and spring up. Yes, precepts and seeds have the same

63. Didier, "La parabole," 25.
64. Oesterley, *Gospel Parables*, 32.

quality; they produce much, and yet they are slight things. Only, as I said, let a favourable mind receive and assimilate them.[65]

The same proverbial structure is found in Jewish wisdom, although with a distinctive moralizing tone:

> Sow good things in your souls
> and you will find them in your lives.
> If you sow evil,
> you will reap every trouble and tribulation.[66]

Paul uses the same proverbial structure to encourage giving to his Jerusalem collection: "Whoever sows sparingly will also reap sparingly and whoever sows bountifully will also reap bountifully" (2 Cor. 9:6). Metaphorically one can mix good sowing with bad sowing and draw the appropriate conclusions. Paul in Gal. 6:7–8 preserves such a usage:

> Whatever a man sows, he will also reap. For he who sows to his own flesh will from the flesh reap corruption; but he who sows to the spirit will from the spirit reap eternal life. And let us not grow weary in well-doing for in due season we shall reap, if we do not lose heart.

The proverbial structure is clearly stated, then moralized in the direction of both good and bad.

The proverb likewise can encompass an apocalyptic or eschatological sense, as evidenced by *2 Baruch*:

> Behold the days are coming and it will happen when the time of the world has ripened and the harvest of the seed of the evil ones and the good ones has come that the Mighty One will cause to come over the earth and its inhabitants and its rulers confusion of the spirit and amazement of the heart.[67]

This latter development is possible because miracle belongs to the metaphorical structure of sowing. Common wisdom employs the germination process as a sign of miracle: the giving of life and even, by extension, resurrection. Paul in 1 Cor. 15:35–38 clearly employs this metaphor to elaborate his understanding of the resurrection of the body. The same point is made in a story about Rabbi Meir (ca. 200 c.e.). When asked by

---

65. Seneca, *Ad Lucilium Epistulae Morales*, 38.2 (LCL 1:257– 59). Cameron ("Parable and Interpretation," 19–24) notes a number of Hellenistic uses and draws the conclusion that the parable must be a product of a later Christian community interested in its own *paideia*. That the allegory explicates the parable as an example of Christian *paideia* is true, but the metaphorical structure of sowing and reaping can be elaborated in a variety of directions. Hence, Cameron's conclusion is not necessary.

66. *Testament of Levi* 13.6 (Charlesworth 1:793). See also Prov. 22:8; Job 4:8; Sir. 7:3.

67. *2 Baruch* 70.2 (Charlesworth 1:645).

Queen Cleopatra if the dead will rise again in bodies, he responds, "Thou mayest deduce by an *a fortiori* argument [the answer] from a wheat grain: if a grain of wheat, which is buried naked, sprouteth forth in many robes, how much more so the righteous, who are buried in their raiment!"[68]

The author of 1 *Clement* interprets the parable of the sower by use of this metaphorical structure. In discussing the resurrection he first draws on the metaphor of day and night: "The night sleeps, the day rises." Then he turns his attention to sowing:

> "The sower went forth" and cast each of the seeds into the ground, and they fall on to the ground, parched and bare, and suffer decay; then from their decay the greatness of the providence of the Master raises them up, and from one grain more grow and bring forth fruit.[69]

First Clement makes sense of part of the parable by fusing it with an aspect of its metaphorical structure.

Finally the proverbial structure is expanded by 2 Esdras in a direction that recalls our parable. Initially God is speaking to his prophet:

> For indeed I will not concern myself about the fashioning of those who have sinned, or about their death, their judgment, or their destruction; but I will rejoice over the creation of the righteous, over their pilgrimage also, and their salvation, and their receiving their reward. As I have spoken, therefore, so it shall be. For just as the farmer sows many seeds upon the ground and plants a multitude of seedlings, and yet not all that have been sown will come up in due season, and not all that were planted will take root; so also those who have sown in the world will not all be saved. (2 Esd. 8:38–41)

The text confronts whether all will be saved, and God uses the extended proverb of a mixed sowing to answer that they will not. But the prophet sees a problem in this analogy:

> For if the farmer's seed does not come up, because it has not received thy rain in due season, or if it has been ruined by too much rain, it perishes. But man, who has been formed by thy hands and is called thy own image because he is made like thee, and for whose sake thou hast formed all things—hast thou also made him like the farmer's seed? (2 Esd. 8:43–44)

The prophet senses that the metaphor implies determinism, that God has willed people's destruction. But God responds, "For they also re-

---

68. *b San.* 90b (Soncino 12:607). The same answer without Cleopatra's question is attributed to Rabbi Hiyy ben Joseph in *b. Ketub.* 111b (Soncino 7:720).
69. 1 *Clement* 24.5 (LCL 1:51–53).

ceived freedom, but they despised the Most High, and were contemptuous of his law, and forsook his ways" (2 Esd. 8:56).[70]

As the repertoire makes clear, the proverbial structure of sowing and
reaping has a wide and extensive set of metaphorical possibilities. It also
has an inherent problematic when used morally, because it can imply
determinism.

As a hearer tries to form the parable into a consistency, this repertoire
is invoked to make sense of the parable. Yet the parable resists. The
elaboration of the failure, its gradual extension from the day of sowing
to almost harvest, places an emphasis on the seed's failure that is unique
among preserved examples. Furthermore, the accent on failure challenges the expectation of success associated with the kingdom.

Much in the spirit of 2 Esdras, the Synoptic allegory seizes on the
failures and makes them the result of people who fail to respond to the
kingdom's word. In this way the failure is pushed outside the kingdom
and is not part of it. Dodd and Jeremias attempt a similar move when
they symbolize the kingdom in the "abundant and miraculous har-
vest."[71] For Dodd it means that "in spite of all, the harvest is plentiful: it is
only the labourers that are lacking."[72] He has actually used his understanding of A Man Casts Seed and the proverb from John 4:35 to read
the parable. For Jeremias, "the breaking-in of the Kingdom of God is
compared as, so often, to the harvest."[73] But unlike Dodd, he draws not a
conclusion of realized eschatology but a yet–not-yet eschatology: "To
human eyes much of the labour seems futile and fruitless, resulting
apparently in repeated failure, but Jesus is full of joyful confidence: he
knows that God has made a beginning, bringing with it a harvest of
reward beyond all asking or conceiving."[74]

Yet the parable's structure does not lead to such an equation. Failure is
inevitable in sowing, but this parable draws attention to failure. There
are three scenes of what can only be described as accidents, not deliberate acts at all, and only one notice of success. The triadic balance of the
parable draws attention to the parable as a whole. This is reinforced by
the broken serial enumeration: thirty-, sixty-, and a hundredfold. The
final incomplete number points to nonclosure, not to a final climax.

A hearer is left with a kingdom in which failure, miracle, and normality are the coordinates. The parable's structure leads to the expectation

70. See also 2 Esdras 7:19.
71. See also Dahl, "Parables of Growth," 153.
72. Dodd, *Parables*, 147.
73. Jeremias, *Parables*, 150.
74. Ibid.

of abundant growth as a metaphor of God's mighty activity. But in the end the harvest is ordinary and everyday. In failure and everydayness lies the miracle of God's activity. The accidents of failure are not exploited for their possible moral overtones but are coordinated with the harvest. The hearer who navigates within this triangle can experience God's ruling activity under the most unfamiliar guises, even among prostitutes and tax collectors—in the everyday. In a Woman with Ten Drachmas, the woman searches for what is ordinary like the harvest and she as a woman is unclean corresponding to the failed seed. Both the ordinary and the unclean belong to the miracle of the kingdom. The kingdom does not need the moral perfection of Torah nor the apocalyptic solution of overwhelming harvest.

18

What If They Gave a War?

A Man Casts Seed

The kingdom of God is as if a man should scatter seed upon the earth. And should sleep and rise night and day, and the seed should sprout and grow, he knows not how. By itself the earth produces, first the blade, then the ear, then the full grain in the ear. But when the harvest is ripe, he puts in the sickle, because the harvest has come.

This parable (Mark 4:26–29) is a curiosity item. It presents a difficulty for its hearer, a conundrum that is not always evident. It occurs only in Mark, and its omission from the other Synoptic Gospels is a puzzle. *Gospel of Thomas* quotes the last line, a reference to Joel 13:3—which is itself a puzzle. Such an explicit quotation is unique in the parables. And as Bultmann notes, it is without application of any kind.[1] Its meaning in Mark is implicit and must be deduced from its contextual arrangement.

Even though the parable A Man Casts Seed is, for Dodd, the archetype for the parables of growth, it is so not because it decisively exposes the meaning of the kingdom but because it illustrates the problem of how parable relates to the kingdom. For Dodd the preunderstanding of

---

1. Bultmann, *History of the Synoptic Tradition*, 173.

the kingdom predetermines what the parable means. He asks, What is the kingdom like?

Three options have been proposed. If it is like the seed, then the kingdom is within you.[2] In this model the kingdom is a creative principle at work for centuries. Dodd is probably referring to the vision of Adolf von Harnack and Protestant liberalism. For still others, the kingdom is like the process of growth itself, and such an interpretation, Dodd notes, appeals to the evolutionary mentality of the late nineteenth century.[3] Finally, the kingdom is like the harvest. Dodd identifies this view with Schweitzer and the eschatological school. The parable becomes a code for the movement begun by John's preaching of repentance and Jesus' taking-up of that cause. Jesus himself is the harvester who is awaiting his revelation in glory at the harvest.

Dodd makes no effort to refute these various interpretations, because for him the interpreter's view of the kingdom determines the line of interpretation.[4] Although he is correct that this has been the case,[5] should it be so? Such a process reverses the function of parable and destroys its metaphorical and cognitive value. If parable is something laid beside, then parable references the kingdom, rather than the kingdom's being a code to unravel the parable's meaning.[6] We must first understand the parable's narrative structure before we can lay it beside (*parabolein*) the kingdom.

The Parable in Mark

A Man Casts Seed parallels A Grain of Mustard Seed in Mark. A reader needs to draw out the meaning of both parables by implication, probably using A Sower Went Out and its interpretation as a guide. If so, both parables are examples of the fate of the seed. Obviously, for Mark neither parable is critical, since both only furnish examples of Jesus' teaching in parables about the secret of the kingdom.

Lambrecht notes as similarities between the two parables that they both have "and he said" as a connective phrase, an introductory clause on the kingdom of God, a seed comparison, a conclusion with a Hebrew Bible quotation or allusion, and the phrase "upon the ground."[7] So strong are the similarities that Lambrecht argues that one cannot rule out

2. Following the mistranslation of *entos hymin*, "within you" (Luke 17:21).
3. Dodd, *Parables*, 142.
4. Ibid.
5. See the views of Jeremias and Kümmel surveyed and evaluated in my *Jesus, Symbol-Maker*, 80–81.
6. See pp. 41–52 above.
7. Lambrecht, "Redaction and Theology," 296.

Markan composition, but he concludes against such a possibility because of the lack of specific Markan vocabulary.[8]

Lambrecht's comments are of unequal weight, but they demand a response. Some of the common vocabulary may be due to a similarity of theme and because of common performance of the originating structure by the author of Mark's Gospel. For example, "upon the ground" is characteristic of Markan style, as is clear from its insertion in A Grain of Mustard Seed.[9] Similarity of themes may well account for why the two parables were attracted to each other, either in the oral tradition or in the composition of the Gospel. "And he said," *kai elegen*, does not affect the interpretation of the parable but indicates how hard it is to settle whether these two parables were joined in the oral tradition or were joined by Mark. Is it the pre-Markan connective formula[10] or a Markan connective?[11] It would be interesting to know if Mark or his tradition was responsible for joining these two parables, but I see no way to adjudicate this matter on the basis of a simple connecting phrase.[12]

Finally, both parables have a kingdom introduction. Bultmann doubted the originality of the kingdom introduction with A Man Casts Seed for two reasons: (1) It is not easy to relate the parable to the kingdom. (2) "It gives the impression of being one of the introductory formulae that are frequently added."[13] Relating the kingdom and parable may simply be a failure of imagination. Kelber too has challenged the kingdom introduction because of the clumsiness of the introduction.[14] But if Mark is responsible for the introduction, as Kelber maintains, he could have cleared up the clumsiness. Actually, clumsiness in introductions is common given the great flexibility in formulas of introduction.[15] Whether or not the introductory formula is part of the originating structure is irrelevant, since all parables of Jesus reference the kingdom of God as hermeneutical symbol.

8. Lambrecht, *Once More Astonished*, 101. Kuhn (*Ältere Sammlungen*, 105) overstates the case when he says that nothing specifically points to Mark.

9. For the evidence, see chap. 19 below.

10. So Weeden, *Mark*, 147; Kuhn, *Ältere Sammlungen*, 99–146.

11. So Kelber, *Kingdom in Mark*, 30. Kelber is in dependence on Zerwick (*Untersuchungen*, 8).

12. Lambrecht's argument (*Once More Astonished*, 100) that Mark replaced The Leaven (which was originally coupled with A Grain of Mustard Seed) with A Man Casts Seed depends on the notion that Mark knew Q, which seems unlikely. Furthermore, *Thomas* also has A Grain of Mustard Seed without The Leaven. The coupling of A Grain of Mustard Seed and The Leaven so that they are twin parables is a contrivance of the modern model of the parables of growth.

13. Bultmann, *History of the Synoptic Tradition*, 173.

14. Kelber, *Kingdom in Mark*, 29–30.

15. For a listing of introductory formulas, see Jeremias, *Parables*, 101; Guttmann, *Das Mashal-Gleichnis*, 3–6; Johnston, "Parabolic Traditions," 642–45.

In the parable's conclusion, "at once," *euthys*, is probably Markan. It occurs forty-two times in Mark; seven in Matthew; and once in Luke.[16] Crossan has suggested that v. 28 draws attention away from the farmer and so is secondary. He points to the *Thomas* version: "Let there be among you a man of understanding. . . . When the grain is ripened, he came quickly with his sickle in his hand and reaped it" (*Gos. Thom.* 21). For him, it maintains the focus on the farmer.[17] This suggestion is unconvincing since the *Thomas* quotation is only a fragment. Second, it is common in Jesus' parables to shift focus, especially in one-liner parables (e.g., leaven, woman, fermenting). Finally, as we shall see, it fits the parable's stair-step pattern.

Surface Structure

The parable exhibits a careful arrangement around a stair-step pattern.

1. a man / should cast / *seed* / upon the **ground**
2. — / should sleep and should rise up
3. *seed* / should sprout and grow
   (as he does not know)
4. (by itself) the **ground** / FRUIT-produces
   first grass, then an ear, then the full seed in the ear
5. and when it is ready / the FRUIT

The nouns of line 1 each in turn become the subject of the next three clauses, pointing out that there is no single unifying subject to the parable. There are two verbs in lines 2 and 3 each. Lines 3 and 4 form a chiasm, as we shall see later. The verb of line 4 is a compound word, *karpophereō*, "to bear fruit," and its nominal component *karpos*, "fruit," is the subject of the next verb, *paradoi*, "ready." Finally, the description of growth in line 4 echoes the threefold pattern of lines 1, 2, and 3.

A Reading

Line 1: The kingdom of God is as if a man should scatter seed upon the earth.

"What you sow is what your reap" is a common proverb,[18] and this common wisdom network connecting sowing and harvest sets up a pattern of expectation that governs the parable. The story's strategy will be to move from sowing to harvest.

16. Ironically, Jeremias's reading (*Parables*, 151) depends on *euthys* to justify itself. For him it contrasts the farmer's passivity with the harvest's suddenness.

17. Crossan, *In Parables*, 85.

18. For evidence, see chap. 17 above.

Line 2: And should sleep and rise night and day, and the seed should sprout and grow, he knows not how.

In the second line the farmer withdraws from his crop. Unlike the man in the parable A Sower Went Out this man is not even given the title "sower" but is only a "man" who casts seed on the ground. His action of sleeping night and day, of not knowing[19] how the seed grows, runs contrary to the injunctions of the wisdom tradition. In that tradition, "a son who gathers in summer is prudent, but a son who sleeps in harvest brings shame" (Prov. 10:5). Or again, "the sluggard does not plow in the autumn; he will seek at harvest and have nothing" (Prov. 20:5). This reciprocity between the work of sowing and the joy of harvest can also function at a spiritual level. "May those who sow in tears reap with shouts of joy" (Ps. 126:5–6). In Isa. 28:24, one encounters the regularity of the farmer's activity as an example of how the Lord instructs his people:

> Does he who plows for sowing plow continually?
>> does he continually open and harrow his ground?
> When he has leveled its surface,
>> does he not scatter dill, sow cummin,
> and put in wheat in rows
>> and barley in its proper place,
>> and spelt as the border?

This text from Isaiah illustrates the many steps between sowing and harvest. In A Man Casts Seed, the man engages in none of these but sleeps and rises night and day and knows not how the seed grows. This farmer is not patient[20] but ignorant, maybe even a sluggard who will seek in vain for a harvest. A hearer senses that the everyday has been disturbed. If his sleeping and ignorance are taken literally, the fields will be overrun with weeds. Is this to be an example of sowing in righteousness and reaping steadfast love (Hosea 10:11–12) or sowing evil and reaping evil?

Line 3: By itself the earth produces, first the blade, then the ear, then the full grain in the ear.

Even though the man's activity is nonexistent, the seed bears fruit in normal progression up to the point of harvest. How is this possible given proverbial wisdom's admonition that you reap what you sow?

The first clue appears in what the parable sets in opposition. In

---

19. Zerwick (*Grammatical Analysis* 1:113) suggests as a translation "how, he knows not" or "while he is all unknowing." In either alternative the accent is upon the man's ignorance.

20. Jeremias, *Parables*, 151.

organization of the surface structure the last phrase of line 2 is set
against the beginning of line 3:

should-sprout and grow   as not know he (*autos*)
by-itself (*automotē*)   the earth bears-fruit

In the chiastic structure the activity of the seeds is paralleled and two
words with the same root (*auto*) are used at opposing ends of the chiasm.
Thus the ignorance of *autos*, "he," is contrasted with *automatē*, "by itself."

The second clue concerns the significance of *automatos*, "by itself."
From this Greek adjective comes the English word "automatic." The
adjective is used of things that have no visible cause and therefore are
mysterious. In Acts 12:10, it is used of doors opening by themselves
when the angel is leading Peter out of prison before Herod can kill
him.[21]

The LXX underscores this mysterious sense. When the Lord tells
Joshua how Jericho is to be destroyed, the LXX reads, "And when they
shall have shouted, the walls of the city shall fall of themselves [*automata*]" (Joshua 6:5), clearly indicating a divine activity.[22] Or the Wisdom
of Solomon describes the terrible night of the plague of darkness on the
Egyptians: "Nothing was shining through to them except a dreadful,
self-kindled [*automatē*] fire, and in terror they deemed the things which
they saw to be worse than the unseen appearance" (17:6). The self-
kindled fire creates a mysterious presence, frightening the Egyptians. In
Job 24:24, the fall of the evil man is described as an ear of corn that falls
from its stalk by itself. Thus his fall is by the mysterious hand of God.

Besides this use of *automatos* as a mysterious happening, the word is
also used to translate Hebrew *sapiyah*, which is "what springs up of itself
in the second year, and served as food when no grain could be sown."[23]
The Hebrew *sapiyah* refers to the free growth of the sabbatical year:

Six years you shall sow your field . . . but in the seventh year there shall be a
sabbath of solemn rest for the land, a sabbath to the Lord, you shall not sow
your field. . . . What grows by itself [LXX: *automata*] in your harvest you
shall not reap (Lev. 25:5).

This same command is repeated later in the chapter for the celebration
of the jubilee year. In the similar sabbatical command in Exod. 23:10–11,
the land must lie fallow so that the poor may eat, whereas the purpose of
jubilee and sabbatical years is that "the land shall not be sold in perpetu-

21. BAGD, 122, gives a number of references in secular Greek to similar usage.
22. The MT has no corresponding referent.
23. BDB, 705.

ity, for the land is mine." It is a recognition of God's claim that under-girds the command.[24]

The fruit that grows of itself (*sapiyah*) is also used in 2 Kings 19:29 as a signal for God's grace, that he cares for his people:

> And this shall be the sign for you; this year eat what grows of itself [*automatos*], and in the second year what springs of the same; then in the third year sow and reap.[25]

In rabbinic literature a discussion concerning *sapiyah* arises about which of the things that grow by themselves may be harvested. In *m. Shib.* 9.1,[26] the discussion revolves around cabbage.[27] In *m. Sheq.* 4.1,[28] there is a discussion of how those who watch over the *sapiyah* are to be paid.

To the attuned hearer the contrast between the ignorance of the man, his nonaction, and the mention of *automatos* indicates that the land is on sabbatical. The allusion is meant not literally but as a metaphorical reference to the graced character of the growth event.

Line 4: But when the grain is ripe, he puts in the sickle, because the harvest has come.

The hearer has been whisked from an ignorant farmer and the land on sabbatical, producing gracefully by itself, to the harvest, in this final line with its allusion to Joel 3:13:

> Proclaim this among the nations:
> Prepare war, . . .
> Beat your plowshares into swords,
>   and your pruning forks into spears; . . .
> Let the nations . . .
>   come up to the valley of Jehoshaphat;
>   for there I will sit to judge
>   all the nations round about.
> Put in the sickle,
>   for the harvest is ripe.
> Go in, tread,
>   for the wine press is full.
> The vats overflow,
>   for their wickedness is great . . .
> For the day of the Lord is near.
>   (Joel 3:9–14)

---

24. Noth, *Leviticus*, 186.
25. See also the parallel passage in Isa. 37:30.
26. *m. Shib.* 9.1 (Danby, 49).
27. For an extended discussion of the issue, see also *b. Pesah.* 51b (Soncino 3:250).
28. *m. Sheg.* 4.1 (Danby, 155).

In the prophecy of Joel the reference is to the apocalyptic war and judgment. This is especially clear not only from the context but from the reversal in v. 10 of the famous judgment scene from Isaiah:

> He shall decide for many peoples; and they shall beat their swords into plowshares, and their spears into pruning hooks; nations shall not lift up sword against nation, neither shall they learn war any more. (Isa. 2:4; see also Micah 4:3)

The strong contrast between the Isaiah passage and Joel clearly indicates the apocalyptic tone of the quote.

Joel's metaphor of harvest remains a reference to God's final judgment and vindication. In Rev. 14:15, there is an allusion to Joel's text when one like a Son of man comes in judgment on the world. *Midrash Rabbah* on the The Song of Songs[29] compares the greatness or redemption of Israel to four things: harvest, wine gathering, spices, and a woman bearing a child. To illustrate the harvest, the quotation from Joel is used from which the *Midrash* draws the conclusion that Israel's greatness will be manifested at the proper time.

To understand the significance of the quotation and the meaning of the parable, the parable's hearer must choose its proper context. Which is determinative—the context in Joel or the context in the parable? Jeremias and others clearly see the context of Joel as the appropriate vehicle for interpreting the parable,[30] and so the kingdom/harvest concludes with the apocalyptic harvest. Yet I think the parable suggests something quite different. Just as Joel reversed the beating of plowshares into swords, so this parable reverses the quotation from Joel. In the parable the harvest is no longer the apocalyptic war but a harvest of sabbatical aftergrowth planted by an ignorant farmer.

From Story to Kingdom

The parable does not offer its hearer a definition of the kingdom nor even tell what the kingdom is. Rather it offers a hearer a chance to define the kingdom. How is a hearer to make sense of the quotation from Joel? Does its context in Joel define the parable, or does the parable redefine the quotation from Joel? To recall a rabbinic metaphor, is the parable a handle[31] for the kingdom, or does the hearer's expectations for the kingdom determine what the parable means? The description of an

---

29. *Midrash Rabbah* on the Song of Songs 8.14.1 (Freedman 9:327).
30. Jeremias, *Parables*, 152; Kümmel, *Promise and Fulfillment*, 128; Dodd, *Parables*, 143.
31. *Midrash Rabbah* on the Song of Songs 1.1.8 (Freedman 9:9–10). See also pp. 52–53 above.

ignorant farmer and the land on sabbatical, a sign of God's grace and peace, stands in sharp contrast to the apocalyptic war motif of Joel and so demands a redefinition of the harvest.

This technique of forcing a hearer to decide what is happening is found in other parables of Jesus. In A Man Entrusts Property, the third servant pictures the master as hard and rapacious, reaping where he did not sow. That draws a hearer's sympathy to the servant. Yet the first two servants do not behave as though they share the third servant's stereotype. A hearer must decide whether the master is cruel and ruthless, as the third servant says, or fair and rewarding, as the first two imply. The choice delimits the kingdom.

Similarly, in A Grain of Mustard Seed, the parable's end alludes to the great cedar of Lebanon. But is the mustard plant still a shrub or is it now a tree? To choose decides what sort of kingdom one expects and what sort one dwells within.

If the apocalyptic war is yet to come, if the mustard plant must become a great tree, if tyrannical masters must be defeated, then the kingdom is yet to come. But if we can chance that masters are trustworthy, mustard plants become shrubs, and an ignorant farmer harvests God's grace, then the kingdom is among us (Luke 17:21). But not in the sense of realized eschatology, for what is really redefined is the possibility of the manifestation of God. These narratives in their literalness are metaphors for God. The God of the everyday need only be seen in the everyday. The kingdom comes without "signs to be observed, nor will they say 'Lo here it is' or 'There.'" The apocalyptic judge is only a possibility in the future; the God of aftergrowth is here in the sabbatical of his grace.

 The Mustard Tree

A Grain of Mustard Seed

Like a grain of mustard seed which a man took and sowed in his garden and it grew and became a great shrub and puts forth large branches so that the birds of heaven make nests in its shade/ shelter.

The four extant versions of A Grain of Mustard Seed offer a fascinating look at how early performers responded to the implied mytheme that the parable itself attempts to subvert. Although there are significant variations among the four variations, for the most part the differences do not seem to derive from the performers' ideologies but from expectations that the kingdom is more appropriately mighty.

The versions of *Thomas* and Luke, which probably represents the Q tradition,[1] recommend themselves because of their brevity and simplicity. By contrast, Mark's phrasing is needlessly complex and wordy, and Matthew conflates Luke and Mark. With this in view we will be begin with Luke and *Thomas*, and then turn to Mark and Matthew.

---

1. Schulz, *Q: Die Spruchquelle*, 300–302.

Mustard in the Garden

A Grain of Mustard Seed is paired in Luke[2] with The Leaven. Both parables form the conclusion of a unit that begins at Luke 13:1. The unit has a clear bifold schema:

	Tragedy
Galileans/tower of Siloam	Healing of crippled woman
(vv. 1–4)	(vv. 10–13)
	Response
Repent	Freed from the bond of Satan
(v. 5)	(vv. 14–17)
	Parable
Barren fig tree	Mustard seed/leaven
(vv. 6–9)	(vv. 18–21)

In this unit, Luke explains why tragedy and release from it are occasions for mercy, on God's part, and repentance, on the reader's.[3] The two parables that conclude the unit do not draw his special attention, but both merely indicate the time of response before the inevitable end. Further confirming Luke's lack of redactional interest in these parables is the fact that The Leaven is almost identical in Luke and Matthew. Thus we can be reasonably assured that Luke is simply passing on tradition.

The Lukan parable has a paratactic structure and is arranged in an A/B pattern:

A a grain of mustard seed
B which taking a man threw in his garden
A grew and changed into a tree
B and the birds of heaven dwelt in its branches

The *A* lines are the main sentence; the *B* lines each have a different subject. Thus the mustard seed binds the parable together. Yet even with the parable's tight organization, there are two anomalies in it: the garden and the tree.

The mustard, a common plant in the eastern world, grew and spread quickly. Consequently, a farmer sought to control its seeds. The plant also figures prominently in the rabbinic discussions of "diverse kinds." The rules of diverse kinds had as their purpose to bring order into the disorderly world, and the creation of order in this world replicates the division between the sacred and the profane.[4] Where things could or could not be planted and what could be planted or mixed together were important for the maintenance of purity boundaries. As a number of

2. And probably Q. See chap. 15 above for details.
3. Talbert, *Reading Luke*, 140–46.
4. See Mandelbaum, *History*, 1.

commentators have noticed, a mustard seed could not be planted in a garden.[5] *Mishnah Kilayim* 3.2 is very clear on this point: "Not every kind of seed may be sown in a garden-bed, but any kind of vegetable may be sown therein. Mustard and small beans are deemed a kind of seed and large beans a kind of vegetable."[6]

Since planting in a garden is clearly forbidden, most argue that Luke's note about the garden is secondary, and that it is due to his adjustment to urban or Roman practice,[7] where mustard clearly is grown in a garden.[8] Siegfried Schulz argues that because of the rarity of word "garden" in the New Testament, Luke is not responsible for the adjustment; rather he found the word in his source.[9] How does one decide between these two options, or is it important to decide?

In the four extant versions, the place where the man plants the mustard seeds varies from the very specific to the very general. Luke has a "garden," *kēpos,* which generally designates the household garden. Both Matthew and *Thomas* have similar terms. In Matthew, the man plants in a field (*agros*), which is the "plot of ground used mainly for agriculture,"[10] and in *Thomas,* he plants in "tilled soil." Finally, Mark has the least specific term, "earth," *gēs*—soil or ground[11]—not necessarily designating ground set aside for agriculture. Why this spectrum from the most specific to the least specific?

Matthew's *en tō agrō,* "in the field," probably represents his stereotyped phrase. It occurs twice in the parable of The Wheat and Tares, which immediately precedes A Grain of Mustard Seed, and again in Treasure. Also in the interpretation of The Wheat and Tares the disciples ask about the "parable of the weeds of the field" (Matt. 13:36), and Jesus responds that "the field is the world." Finally, the man in Treasure buys "that field" (Matt. 13:44). Matthew uses the phrase twice more. Matthew 24:18 parallels Mark 13:16, but Mark uses *eis* and Matthew *en.* Matthew 24:40 parallels Luke 17:34, where Luke employs the bed metaphor rather than the field. Mark never uses *agros* with the preposition *en* but always with *eis;* Luke uses the preposition *en* four times but never with the definite article. "In the field" would appear to be a characteristic of Matthean style.

Similarly, Mark's "on the ground," *epi tēs gēs,* appears to be the direct result of his performance. In this parable it occurs twice, both times

5. Jeremias, *Parables,* 27 n. 11; Str-B 1:699.
6. *m. Kil.* 3.2 (Danby, 31).
7. See Marshall, *Commentary on Luke,* 561; McArthur, "Parable of the Mustard Seed," 201.
8. Theophrastus, *Enquiry into Plants,* 7.1.1 (LCL 2:59).
9. Schulz, *Q: Die Spruchquelle,* 299. *Kēpos* occurs four other times in John.
10. BAGD, 13. Its derived meanings are related to farming.
11. BAGD, 157.

within a Markan insertion. The seed "is sown on the ground" and is the smallest of those seeds "which are on the ground." The same phrase appears in the introduction to the preceding parable, A Man Casts Seed; and again in that parable the "ground by itself" brings forth the produce (Mark 4:26, 28). Also in the introduction to Mark 4, the narrator notes that "the crowd was next to the sea on the ground [*epi tēs gēs*]." In Matthew and Luke this clumsy phrase is missing. In the parable A Sower Went Out, *gēs* is used three times. In the description of the seed sown on rocks, which has been elaborated by means of a Markan insertion, the seed falls where it had not much ground and it had no depth of ground (Mark 4:5).[12] At the parable's end, some seed falls "into good ground [*eis tēn gēn*]" (Mark 4:8).[13] In the interpretation of the parable those who hear the word are the seeds "sown on the good earth [*epi tēs gēs*]" (Mark 4:20).[14] In chapter 4, Mark exhibits a marked proclivity for *gēs* and *epi tēs gēs* not found in the parallel texts. That proclivity, taken with the presence of the phrase twice within a Markan insertion, clearly indicates its secondary character here.

Both Matthew and Mark are most probably responsible for the particular description of where the mustard seed is planted, but Luke and *Thomas* have no special reason for their description. Moreover, "garden" is used only here in Luke and is at odds with the requirements of Palestinian custom as represented in the *Kilayim*. Though it is possible that Luke is conforming to Roman custom,[15] it is just as likely that he found "garden" in his inherited tradition[16] and that "garden" belongs to the parable's originating structure. Moreover, because planting mustard seed is proscribed in Palestinian custom as represented by the *Kilayim*, the more difficult reading should be preferred. It is easier to understand the movement to "field" and "ground" as circumventions of the proscription against planting in a garden. Most likely, the parable begins, like the parable The Leaven, with a metaphor of impurity: the planting of mustard seed in a garden.

In Luke, the mustard plant grows into a tree and the birds make nests in its shade.[17] But why describe the mustard plant as a tree, when botanically it is a shrub? Some try to justify Luke's tree as technically

12. The phrase is repeated verbatim in Matt. 13:5, but similar phrases are absent in Luke's and *Thomas*'s versions of the parable.

13. Parallel with variations in Matt. 13:23; Luke 8:15.

14. See the variations in Matt. 13:23; Luke 8:15.

15. Luke usually conforms to urban custom. E.g., in the man let down through the roof the tiles are separated in Luke 5:19, whereas in Mark 2:4 a hole is opened in the thatched roof.

16. Schulz, *Q: Die Spruchquelle*, 299.

17. The ending is from Q. So Schulz, *Q: Die Spruchquelle*, 299.

correct,[18] because even though Theophrastus distinguishes between "tree," "shrub," "under-shrub," and "herb,"[19] he admits that the distinctions apply only generally and that there are frequent cases of overlapping.[20] But nowhere among the examples that Theophrastus cites is the mustard plant mentioned. In the discussion in *Mishnah Kilayim* where trees, vegetables, and shrubs are dealt with in distinct groups, mustard is classified with shrubs.[21] So, clearly, "tree" is wrong. Why then did a shrub become a tree? Because the shrub is an inappropriate metaphor for the final state of the kingdom. A tree with birds nesting in it, perhaps the apocalyptic tree, is more fitting.[22] Thus it would appear that the tree results from a response to the underlying conflict between the metaphorical network of the kingdom and the actual performance of the originating structure.

The Great Branch

The parable in *Thomas* is comparatively straightforward:

> The disciples said to Jesus, "Tell us what the Kingdom of Heaven is like." He said to them, "It is like a mustard seed, the smallest of all seeds. But when it falls on tilled soil, it produces a great plant[23] and becomes a shelter for birds of the sky." (*Gos. Thom.* 20)

Thomas too has made its own accommodation with the originating structure and the implied metaphorical network. *Thomas* notes that the mustard seed is the "smallest of all seeds." This marker results from the fondness of oral performance for formulas. The mustard seed is proverbially small and a frequent example for smallness: "The Daughters of Israel have undertaken to be so strict with themselves that if they see a drop of blood no bigger than a mustard seed they wait seven [clean] days after it."[24] Thus, attraction of the smallness theme would almost be inevitable in the course of performance. *Thomas* has not balanced it with the biggest or greatest but simply with the "great branch,"[25] which is neither tree nor shrub.

18. E.g., Hunzinger, "*sinapi*," 289.
19. Theophrastus, *Enquiry into Plants*, 1.3.1 (LCL 1:23).
20. Ibid., 1.3.2 (LCL 1:25).
21. Trees are dealt with in *m. Kil.* 1.4 (Danby, 29).
22. Crossan (*In Parables*, 49) says Q has brought the parable into "better alignment with the figure of the great apocalyptic tree."
23. See n. 25 below.
24. *b. Ber.* 31a (Soncino 1:188–89).
25. Lambdin (*Gos. Thom.*, p. 120). Lambdin translates the Coptic *tar* as "plant," whereas the primary meaning is "branch." Cf. Crum, *Coptic Dictionary*, 423. Lambdin (*Introduction*, 280) gives "branch" as the meaning.

"Tilled soil" has neither the specificity of Luke's garden nor the generality of Mark's "ground" but seems more in line with Matthew's "field," a normal place of agriculture. There is no reason to see it as part of a gnostic allusion to the soul.[26]

Finally, in *Thomas* the plant "becomes a shelter" for the birds. In the Coptic text of *Thomas*, the word translated by "shelter" is actually a Greek word (*skepē*) that means primarily "shelter" but has the derived meaning of "shade," which would indicate a possible agreement with the Markan text.

The Smallest of Seeds

The Markan performance of the parable is somewhat garbled and repetitive. Many have argued that the note about the smallest of seeds is an intrusion.[27] But the real evidence for its secondary character is the presence of the Markan insertion technique.[28] When Mark inserts material, he frequently repeats a phrase: "which when *sown upon the ground* is the smallest of all those seeds which are *sown upon the ground*." This same pattern was exhibited in A Sower Went Out, in the description of the seed that fell on rocky ground (Mark 4:5). On the basis of this stylistic pattern, Mark inserted the note about the smallest of all seeds.[29] If so, then the reference to the greatest of all shrubs is also from Mark, making Mark responsible for the contrast between the smallest and the greatest.

If Mark is responsible for introducing the reference to the greatest, at least "shrub" is the correct botanical description of what a mustard plant grows to be, and nesting in the shade likewise coheres with the possibilities of "shrub."[30] The "large branch" is in agreement with *Thomas* and possibly "shade."

Mark's performance of the parable amplifies the mustard seed's proverbial smallness and contrasts it with the greatest shrub, introducing thereby a note of contrast. "Upon the ground," twice repeated to mark the boundary of the insertion technique, results most probably from style rather than ideology. But the agreement with *Thomas* concerning the parable's ending indicates that it belongs to the originating structure.

26. Against Ménard, *L'évangile selon Thomas*, 110–11; Crossan, *In Parables*, 49.
27. So Dodd, *Parables*, 153; Taylor, *Gospel according to Saint Mark*, 270; Funk, *Jesus as Precursor*, 21.
28. On the technique, see Donahue, *Are You the Christ?* 58–59.
29. So Crossan, *In Parables*, 46.
30. Funk, *Jesus as Precursor*, 22.

Unlike Luke, who responded to the expectation of the mighty in the metaphorical network of the kingdom by conjuring up a tree, Mark has responded to the same expectation by contrasting the smallest seed with the imaginary greatest of shrubs.

Matthew's version is clearer stylistically than Mark's and does not exhibit the paratactic structure characteristic of Luke's and Mark's versions. It contains the Markan note about the smallest and greatest but without the clumsiness of the insertion; it is edited into a separate sentence. Instead of the paratactic connection "and," *kai*, there is a subordinate temporal clause, "when it grows."

Matthew in the parable's conclusion has conflated Mark and Q[31] so that the greatest of shrubs becomes a tree. The construction of Matthew's version with subordinate clause and conflation seems to indicate a written performance and not an oral one.

Reconstruction: Originating Structure

The seed was most likely planted in a garden, because (*a*) "garden" is rare in New Testament; (*b*) it resembles *Thomas*'s "tilled ground"; (*c*) Matthew's "in the field" and Mark's "upon the ground" more likely result from their own styles; and (*d*) "garden" is the more difficult reading. Both *Thomas* and Mark have adopted the proverbial formula about the mustard seed's being the smallest of all seeds, which Mark has further elaborated with a contrast between smallest and greatest. The impressive agreement between *Thomas* and Mark on the parable's conclusion suggests an ending with a shrub in the shade and shelter of which the birds of the air make nests. So the originating structure dealt with a grain of mustard seed that a man took and planted in his garden and that grew and became a shrub putting forth large branches in the shade and shelter of which the birds of the air made nests. All four versions have responded to the conflict between the metaphorical network of the mustard seed, with its associations of smallness, and that of the kingdom, with its associations of mightiness and greatness. Luke and Matthew have responded explicitly by conforming the shrub to a tree. Crossan has identified this as the interpretive crux: "When one starts a parable with a mustard seed one cannot end it with a tree."[32] Where, then, did the tree come from if it was not part of the originating structure?

---

31. Among many others, Schulz, *Q: Die Spruchquelle*, 299–300.
32. Crossan, *In Parables*, 48.

A Reading

Line 1: Like a grain of mustard seed . . .

This first line exposes the proposed metaphor for the kingdom: the parable for the kingdom will emerge from the possibilities implied in a mustard seed's metaphorical network. Thus to understand the repertoire we must work out the metaphorical associations of the mustard seed and plant.

The mustard plant is an annual. It grows wild and comes in three varieties, of which the most common in Palestine, *sinapis nigra*, is a plant that normally grows to four feet, although at times more.[33] Pliny's description is helpful:

> It grows entirely wild, though it is improved by being transplanted: but on the other hand when it has once been sown it is scarcely possible to get the place free of it, as the seed when it falls germinates at once.[34]

Consequently, a parable about a grain of mustard seed could deal with its speed of germination or with its rapidity in spreading, along the lines of The Leaven that leavens everything.

The mustard plant has a very pungent taste and so was used as a seasoning in food and for medicinal purposes. Once again Pliny is helpful:

> Pythagoras judged [mustard] to be chief of those whose pungent properties reach a high level, since no other penetrates further into the nostrils and brain. Pounded it is applied with vinegar to the bites of serpents and scorpion stings. It counteracts the poisons of fungi. For phlegm it is kept in the mouth until it melts, or is used as a gargle with hydromel. For toothache it is chewed. . . . It is very beneficial for all stomach troubles. . . . It clears the senses, and by the sneezing caused by it, the head; it relaxes the bowels; it promotes menstruation and urine.[35]

Pliny then goes on to explain how in combination with other things it cures many other illnesses. From his description, there appears to be no illness that mustard will not cure. Again, the parable could exploit the medicinal, curative aspects of mustard and relate those to the kingdom.

The aspect best known to moderns, because of associations with the

---

33. Sproule, "Problem of the Mustard Seed," 37–42. Sproule tries to defend Jesus' inerrancy. He collects relevant data about the mustard seed, showing that the parable does refer to *sinapis nigra*, a garden seed. The mustard plant is not mentioned in the Hebrew Bible.

34. Pliny, *Natural History*, 29.54.170 (LCL, 529).

35. Ibid., 20.87.236–37 (LCL, 137–39).

parable, is the mustard seed's proverbial smallness. The mustard seed can even be a metaphor for smallness. In the only other case in which the mustard seed is used in the Gospels, it functions in just this way: "If you have faith as a mustard seed, you will say to this mountain, 'Move from here to there,' and it will move" (Matt. 17:20). The context is a discussion of little faith, and the mustard seed is contrasted in the saying with the mountain: the smallest thing can move the largest thing.[36] This use of the mustard seed as a metaphor for the smallest possible continues in rabbinic usage: "If a man was eating Heave-offering and he felt his limbs tremble, he must lay hold on the member and swallow the Heave-offering. And [the discharge] renders him unclean whatsoever its bulk, even though it be like to a grain of mustard, or less than this."[37] Above we quoted an example from the Talmud about a woman's menstruation as small as a mustard seed.[38] Thus a hearer could expect the parable to exploit the notion of smallness in the signified of mustard seed. But as the rabbinic citations intimate, the smallness at times is associated with uncleanness (e.g., blood or sexual discharge), although as the Synoptic example of little faith makes clear, it need not always be associated with unclean things. And yet it has a derogatory sense: small faith, though not unclean, is not desirable. Smallness is not particularly appropriate for the kingdom since it conflicts with the notions of greatest implied in the signified of the kingdom.

Line 2: . . .which a man took and sowed in his garden . . .

Potential associations of mustard seed heighten expectations for a hearer. But at the very first chance to exploit those possibilities the man sows the mustard seed in his garden, and an alert hearer notices something amiss, for the farmer has violated the law of diverse kinds.[39] This law evolves from the scriptural prohibition against commingling different classes of plants, animals, and fibers. Two prohibitions in the Hebrew Bible provide the scriptural basis:

> You shall keep my statutes. You shall not let your cattle breed with a different kind; you shall not sow your field with two kinds of seed; nor shall there come upon you a garment of cloth made of two kinds of stuff. (Lev. 19:19)

36. Luke 17:6 has "sycamine tree" instead of "mountain." Schulz (*Q: Die Spruchquelle*, 465–68) argues that Luke's version follows Q, and that Matthew has made the change to "mountain" on the pattern of Mark 11:23.

37. *m. Nid.* 5.2 (Danby, 750).

38. See Str-B 1:669. See also the extensive note of Michel ("*kokkos*," 810 n. 1).

39. I am indebted to Ruth Brooks, a former student, for calling this aspect of the parable to my attention.

> You shall not sow your vineyard with two kinds of seed, lest the whole yield be forfeited to the sanctuary, the crop which you have sown and the yield of vineyard. You shall not plow with an ox and ass together. You shall not wear a mingled stuff, wool and linen together. (Deut. 22:9–11)

These early prohibitions have as their purpose maintaining the order of creation (Gen. 1:11–12, 21, 24–25). Order represents holiness, and disorder uncleanliness. But the simplicity of the early statutes inevitably gives rise to greater specificity. The tractate *Kilayim* preserves the resulting arguments.[40] When the mustard seed is planted, it is important that it not be commingled, that it be in its proper place. The basic rule is simple: Maintain order and separation, keep plants in their proper place, and do not mix them. Keep like things separate. The problem arises in a field garden where different types of plants are to grow. How can they be placed? "They may not flank a field of grain with mustard seed or safflower, but they may flank a field of vegetables."[41] Normally mustard is to be sown in small patches and at the edges of a field. Mustard and safflower seed may not be sown as the border of a grain field, because the tall mustard plants with their yellow flowers would look too much like ripened stalks of grain[42] and thus not be different enough. In addition, since mustard tends to run wild when sown, it would soon move into the wheat and even more confuse what should be distinct. But since mustard and safflower do not resemble vegetables, they may be sown next to these.

Since most mustard seed is sown in patches within a field, care must be taken that there be no mixing of like things. Each patch is considered a field, and so long as each patch contains a single kind, all is well. So in a field of grain the amount of mustard is strictly limited. "If [in a field of grain] there was but one patch or two [each of a quarter-kab's space], he may sow them with mustard-seed; but if three he may not sow them with mustard-seed, since it might appear like to a field of mustard."[43] Small patches of a minimum space are considered acceptable because they can easily be distinguished, but if the patches become too large, they will be indistinguishable from the grain.

Finally, there is the situation of sowing mustard seed in a garden plot. Normally garden plots are reserved for vegetables and their layout and borders strictly regulated. "Not every kind of seed may be sown in a garden-bed, but any kind of vegetable may be sown therein. Mustard

---

40. Mandelbaum (*History*, 2–3) deals with the difference in perspective between Scripture and the Mishnah on the law of diverse kinds.
41. *m. Kil.* 2.8 (Danby, 30).
42. So Mandelbaum, *History*, 103.
43. *m. Kil.* 2.9 (Danby, 30–31); see Mandelbaum, *History*, 108.

and small beans are deemed a kind of seed and large beans a kind of vegetable."[44] "Seeds" means those plants which are grown for their dried seeds, so the mustard seed is used as the clear example of such. Such may not be sown in a garden, because this would be mixing dissimilar things. Under controlled conditions mustard seed can be planted in a field, because the space is large enough to make distinctions. But it cannot be sown in a garden, because the small space would result in mingling.

Because of the potential for uncleanliness in planting a mustard seed, a hearer would be sensitive to where and how the mustard seed was planted. The parables that deal only with "seed," not with a specific seed, do not consider this problem. But by naming the mustard seed, the potential of diverse kinds is introduced. By planting the seed in a garden, the man has risked breaking the law of diverse kinds by mixing what should not be mixed, creating the garden as an unclean space.

Line 3: . . . and it grew and became a great shrub . . .

For those who see the parable's point in the kingdom's growth, this is the key line.[45] But would the ancients, without a Darwinian perspective, have seen growth as the point? They knew about biological growth,[46] but they accentuated not natural growth but God's miracle. Paul's use of the seed analogy to explain the resurrection of the body in 1 Cor. 15:34–44 is an example.[47]

The seed's planting and its growth create a conflict for a hearer. Is this growth a divine blessing or a violation? Is it clean or unclean? How is one to decide?

Line 4: . . . and puts forth large branches so that the birds of heaven can make nests in its shade/shelter.

The parable's final line has prompted many suggestions as to the Scripture verse to which it alludes. That in Luke and Matthew the seed grows into a tree, in Mark the greatest of shrubs, and in *Thomas* a great branch has suggested the great cedar of Lebanon, the most imposing tree in the ancient world. But obviously a mustard plant does not grow into any such thing. We will now look at the suggested scriptural verses

44. *m. Kil.* 3.2 (Danby, 31). Mandelbaum explains that the commentator's interest is in the beans, not the mustard. The mustard is used as an example of the case (*History*, 119–20).

45. Dahl, "Parables of Growth," 147.

46. Ibid., 141–43.

47. Käsemann ("On Paul's Anthropology," 8–10) develops the theme of God's miracle associated with the analogy of growth. Crossan (*In Parables*, 50) correctly accents the theme of miracle over against growth in connection with these parables.

before we try to solve the puzzle of a mustard plant transmuted into a cedar of Lebanon.

Dodd in his analysis of this parable has pointed to three texts from the Hebrew Bible that bear a strong resemblance to the vocabulary of the parable's ending. In one of the dreams that Daniel interprets, King Nebuchadnezzar sees a great tree that reaches all the way to heaven. "Its leaves were fair and its fruit abundant, and in it was food for all. The beasts of the field found shade under it, and the birds of the air dwelt in its branches, and all flesh was fed from it" (Dan. 4:12). Even though this text is built on a triple reference—to beasts, birds, and flesh—and the parable employs only birds, there is similarity of language: there is the shade and there are the birds of the air that dwell in the branches. Furthermore, this text is probably meant to recall a similar passage in Ezek. 31:6 where the great tree is Pharaoh and Ezekiel in his interpretation identifies the tree with the king and prophesies his downfall. In Ezek. 31:5-6, the prophet speaks a word to Pharaoh in which he likens him to a cedar in Lebanon "of great height, its top among the clouds." And as it "grew large and its branches long, . . . [a]ll the birds of the air made their nests in its boughs; under its branches all the beasts of the field brought forth their young; and under its shadow dwelt all the nations." But because it was proud of heart it was to be destroyed (Ezek. 31:10-11). Again there is similarity of vocabulary: "grew large," "nests," "branches," and "shadow"/"shade." But this is only similarity and certainly not exactness of reference. At most the parable A Grain of Mustard Seed may allude to Ezekiel 31.

If the previous examples offer possible echoes in the parable's ending, Ezek. 17:23 offers a close parallel.[48] The Lord himself says that he will take a sprig from a giant cedar and plant it himself "on the mountain height of Israel . . . and it will produce branches and bear fruit and become as a noble cedar and the birds of every wing will nest in it; in the shade of its branches they will find shelter" (Ezek. 17:23).[49] Walther Zimmerli remarks that the mixed metaphor of producing branches and fruit is inappropriate for a cedar, which cannot bear fruit. But he contends that the author has in mind neither a real cedar nor a vine but the divine tree under which the world gathers: "The description used of the mountain of God, the paradisal place of God's presence and the 'world tree' under which all the creatures of the earth gather stems from the language of myth."[50]

48. Funk (*Jesus as Precursor*, 23) points directly to this text.
49. My own translation. The RSV is closer to the LXX, which speaks of beasts, perhaps assimilating to the Daniel text.
50. Zimmerli, *Ezekiel* 1:367.

In Daniel 4 and Ezekiel 31 the cedar represents an enemy of Israel that, because it stood proud (high as a tall cedar), was brought low by God. So also the Ezekiel 17 passage ends with such a reference: "And all the trees of the field shall know that I the Lord bring low the high tree, and make high the low tree" (17:24). Only now Israel is the low tree made high. The motif of high and low is part of the expected mytheme associated with the cedar.

Crossan in his study of this passage suggests that Ps. 104:12 is perhaps the closest parallel, although he rejects all the parallels as inappropriate.[51] Psalm 104 is a hymn to the majesty of God the creator. Verses 10–13 deal with water, especially springs feeding the valleys. "By them [springs] the birds of the air have their habitation; they sing among the branches." A similar theme is picked up later in the psalm. "The trees of the Lord are watered abundantly, the cedars of Lebanon which he planted. In them the birds build their nests; the stork has her home in the fir trees" (Ps. 104:16–17). These references seem somewhat far-fetched to me, yet they do associate the theme of birds nesting in the great cedars with the signs of God's blessings for creation and ultimately the kingdom.[52]

The hearer faces a quandary: what to make of the mixed allusion. As Funk has noted, "It is hardly speculation to say that the eschatological tree of Ezekiel and Daniel has influenced the transmission of the parable in the New Testament period."[53] As Crossan notes, however, "If one makes the mistake of actually looking up these references, one immediately senses a problem: the allusion is not very explicit and not very appropriate."[54] These two remarks define both a modern interpreter's and an ancient hearer's predicament. How can a parable about a mustard seed be concluded with allusions that more properly belong to the cedar of Lebanon? Yet the Q tradition clearly saw the reference, and so the shrub became a tree, and *Thomas* and Mark sense the dilemma and

51. Crossan, *In Parables*, 47.

52. Manson (*Teaching*, 133 n. 1) argues that "birds" is a reference to the Gentiles and points to *Midrash on Psalms* 104.2, which probably should be 104.14. But there the birds nesting in the cedars of Lebanon are clearly identified with the Levites (Braude 2:173). Manson has mistaken a *Gimel* for a *Lamed*. The Hebrew for Levite is *lwy* and for Gentile is *gwy*. He has also pointed to *Enoch* 90.30, where the seer has a vision in which all the animals and birds fall down and worship the sheep—where the sheep are clearly Israel, and so by implication the birds and animals are the Gentiles (Charlesworth 1:71). Grässer (*Das Problem*, 142), following Manson, sees the possibility of the birds' being the Gentiles as a secondary allegory. Jeremias (*Parables*, 147), accepting Manson's evidence, adds *Joseph and Aseneth* 15.70 (Charlesworth 2:226), but the reference is to God as a mighty bird who shelters the nations under his wings. Thus there is no compelling evidence that the birds are the Gentiles.

53. Funk, *Jesus as Precursor*, 21.

54. Crossan, *In Parables*, 47.

refer to the great and greatest; so the allusion and tension must be original.[55] A hearer is left to make sense, to fit together a mustard plant that has pretensions to the grandeur of a cedar of Lebanon. How that resolution takes place leads from story to kingdom.

From Story to Kingdom

As a hearer struggles to make sense of the parable, to form a consistency out of its parts, three possibilities suggest themselves. At an initial level the parable makes a light-hearted burlesque of the noble cedar as a metaphor for the kingdom of God by substituting the mustard shrub.[56] Crossan strongly rejects this possibility because there is no tree in the parable, much less the cedar of Lebanon or the great apocalyptic tree of myth. Yet Crossan misses the point; the absence of the literal tree in references that are more fitting for the tree than a shrub is precisely what creates the tension and confusion for a hearer and calls into question and burlesques the expectation of the kingdom under the symbol of the cedar or apocalyptic tree.

More is at stake, for the burlesque does not account for the mytheme associated with the tree. The cedar's height suggests an ambivalence in its metaphorical network. It can stand not only as a symbol of strength and protection but also as one of pride. When the cedar or tree is the nations, God lowers or humbles it. In Ezekiel 17, it begins as a sprig (small) and grows into a mighty tree. Israel is a sprig (small) and a descendant of the secular trees (kingdoms), but when it is raised up the other trees (nations) are humbled in its presence. A Grain of Mustard Seed extends the logic of Ezekiel. All cedars and trees, even Israel, will be brought low. It is the mustard plant that will "bear Israel's true destiny."[57]

A third step is also possible. If the parable begins with the planting of the mustard seed in the garden, in violation of the law of diverse kinds, then the planting and growth are a scandal—illegitimate, tainted, unclean. This theme is prominent in the parables of Jesus—what I call the tendency to play in minor keys. In From Jerusalem to Jericho the hero is the unclean and forbidden Samaritan, and in The Leaven the initial terms of comparision are all associated with uncleanness: leaven, woman, hiding. In A Rich Man Had a Steward, the action of the steward which is praised is that of a rogue, and in Who Has a Friend? the man acts out of shame, not neighborliness. Thus the planting of the mustard

---

55. See my *Jesus, Symbol-Maker*, 70–71. I make this argument there.
56. So Funk, *Jesus as Precursor*, 23.
57. Funk stresses this point. See ibid.

seed in the garden coheres with those other parables. The kingdom is associated with uncleanness just as Jesus himself associates with the unclean, the outcast.

Another element of playing in a minor key is the choice of the mustard seed as the vehicle for the kingdom. The mustard seed and the kingdom contain in their metaphorical networks diametrically opposed signifieds. The mustard seed is proverbially small, whereas the kingdom is mighty—raised up on high like the mighty cedar. Jesus' parable stays with the kingdom of insignificance. A mustard seed becomes a shrub. But in the parable's performance in the oral tradition, the cedar reincarnates itself so that the mustard seed grows into a tree. In the original parable, the birds nesting in the shade or shelter alluded to the cedar, but it remained a mustard plant, so that a hearer was reminded of and provoked by the contrast. The parable begins with signs of the unclean, a planting in a garden, and will not meet grandiose expectations. Yet, like the leaven, which leavens all, the birds will find shelter in the shrub's shade. Many have preferred the mustard tree, this unnatural malformity of mythical botany, to the recognition that God's mighty works are among the unclean and insignificant.

$\mathcal{T}$inders Keepers

A Man Who Had Hidden Treasure

Jesus said, "The Kingdom is like a man who had a [hidden] treasure in his field without knowing it. And [after] he died, he left it to his son. The son did not know [about the treasure]. He inherited the field and sold [it]. And the one who bought it went plowing and found the treasure. He began to lend money at interest to whomever he wished."

Treasure

The kingdom of heaven is like treasure hidden in a field which, on finding, a man hid and in his joy he goes and sells all he has and buys that field.

The parables Treasure and A Man Who Had Hidden Treasure (Matt. 13:44; *Gos. Thom.* 109)[1] evince "that fine novel note of Jesus's teaching—its passion, its enthusiasm, its glow. There is to be no compromise; no half measures will serve our turn."[2] So the Jewish scholar Montefiore succinctly sums up the standard interpretation. The joy in finding and

1. Throughout this analysis I am indebted to Crossan's *Finding*. To deal with this parable is to engage Crossan's thought. He is its precursor.
2. C. Montefiore, *Synoptic Gospels* 2:213.

the rush to sell all grab our attention, but do they draw away or cancel out what the man has done to the original owner? Derrett offers a modern version of the parable that highlights the incongruity: "A man left his family and work and all that he had, in order to follow a pretty woman. The Kingdom of Heaven is like such a case."[3] The *Thomas* parable, though ever so different, is similar in its nagging undertow, for in the end the man becomes a moneylender, a man with a forbidden occupation.

The Money Lender

The *Thomas* parable makes a fitting beginning, because even though not well known it exhibits the more common traits of Jewish treasure stories. A Man Who Had Hidden Treasure occurs in a section of *Thomas* that is seamed together by the key words "finding" and "hiding."

True Finding
   Parable: A Man with a Hundred Sheep (*Gos. Thom.* 107)
   [he] looked for that one until he **found** it . . .
   I care more for you than the ninety-nine.
   Saying (*Gos. Thom.* 108)
   I myself shall become he
   and things that are **hidden** will be revealed to him

False Finding
   Parable: A Man Who Had Hidden Treasure (*Gos. Thom.* 109)
   [he] went plowing and **found** the treasure
   he began to lend money at interest to whomever he wished
   Saying (*Gos. Thom.* 110)
   whoever **finds** the world and becomes rich, let him renounce the world
   Conclusion (*Gos. Thom.* 111)
   Whoever **finds** himself is superior to the world

This rhetorical unit is built around two parables, each with a companion saying, and a concluding saying that summarizes the point of the unit. The first parable and saying exhibit true finding, which is seeking after wisdom.[4] The second contrasts a false seeking after the world's riches. At the parable's conclusion the man lends out money, something expli-

---

3. Derrett, *Law in the New Testament*, 2.
4. For Ménard (*L'évangile selon Thomas*, 208), the parable illustrates that most men do not recognize that the treasure has been deposited in them. Gärtner (*Theology*, 237–38) offers an extensive gnostic reading of the parable, in which the kingdom is within man and is the divine light of which most men are ignorant.

citly forbidden by *Gos. Thom.* 95.[5] The companion saying demands renunciation of this false finding, and the concluding logion (*Gos. Thom.* 110) exults that the one who finds himself is superior to the world.

The analysis of the rhetorical context is important because it implies that *Thomas* inherited the parable in its present form. The Gospel distrusts merchants and businessmen, as can be seen in the concluding logion to the parable A Man Gave a Banquet: "Businessmen and merchants will not enter the Places of my Father" (*Gos. Thom.* 64). The parable A Man Planted a Vineyard immediately follows on this condemnation of businessmen, and the man is an owner of a vineyard that he leases. Since for *Thomas* this is forbidden, the man is described in the parable as "good."[6] Likewise in The Merchant (*Gos. Thom.* 76), the concluding logion guides the reader to its correct interpretation: "You too seek his unfailing and enduring treasure, where no moth comes near to devour and no worm destroys."[7] In both parables, when *Thomas* wants to draw a positive inference there are direct markers in the text. Unlike the Synoptic Gospels, *Thomas* does not automatically assume that the activity of businessmen and merchants is good but rather inserts a positive marker to counter a negative assumption.

The *Thomas* parable also exhibits important elements of the repertoire of treasure. Treasure is frequently associated with wisdom, although in the context of *Thomas* the parable is a negative example. Proverbs 8:10 offers a typical example:

> Take my instruction instead of silver,
> and knowledge rather than choice gold;
> For wisdom is better than jewels,
> and all that you may desire
> cannot compare with her.

When we turn to the examine the metaphorical structure of treasure, this connection with wisdom will become important.

The *Thomas* parable is remarkably similar to a rabbinic parable:[8]

> R. Simeon b. Yohai taught [the Egyptians were] like a man who inherited a piece of ground used as a dunghill. Being an indolent man he went and sold it for a trifling sum. The purchaser began working and digging it up and he found a treasure there out of which he built himself a fine palace. He began going about in public followed by a retinue of servants, all out of the

5. Because of the contradiction with *Gos. Thom.* 95, Davies (*Gospel of Thomas*, 10) argues that the parable's conclusion is a copying error, but this is not necessary.

6. See chap. 10 above.

7. A saying parallel to this occurs at Matt. 6:19–21, disconnected from the parable The Merchant.

8. First noticed by Cerfaux ("Les paraboles due royaume," 314).

treasure he found in it. When the seller saw it, he was ready to choke and exclaimed, "Alas what have I thrown away." So when Israel were in Egypt they were set to work at bricks and mortar, and they were despised in the eyes of the Egyptians. But when the Egyptians saw them encamped under their standards by the sea in military array, they were deeply mortified and exclaimed, "Alas, what have we sent forth from our land!"[9]

The similarities and differences between the *Thomas* and rabbinic parables are striking. Both have the same plot structure, recognized and analyzed by Crossan.[10] The treasure is hidden but not by the owner; the field is sold, then the treasure is found by a new owner. Because the treasure is not hidden by the first owner, he has no claim on the treasure when he sells. Both *Thomas* and the rabbinic parable have embroidered this plot in their own ways. In the rabbinic parable the contrast is between indolence and hard work; in *Thomas* it is between knowledge and lack thereof. Also in the rabbinic parable the first owner is called back on stage at the narrative's end to make the point, See what I have lost by not recognizing the value of the dunghill. In *Thomas*, the initial contrast is between the lack of knowledge of the first owner and the knowledge of the second. But the first owner is not called back at the parable's end to testify. Instead, the new owner becomes a businessman and turns a profit on his newly found treasure. This is possible because in *Thomas*'s rhetorical structure the new owner's action is an example of false finding.

How does the parable relate to the Matthean parable? Jeremias,[11] who calls the *Thomas* parable "utterly degenerated," sees it as being under the influence of the rabbinic parable. The popular folk story, as represented by the rabbinic parable, has corrupted the Jesus parable, as preserved by Matthew. Crossan goes even further: "*It is certain* that *Thomas* does not have a version of Jesus' but rather a gnostic variation" on the Jewish parable.[12] But James Hedrick has advanced a counterargument for the authenticity of the *Thomas* version.[13] For him the similarity of *Thomas* to the rabbinic parable speaks in its favor. Hedrick invokes the criterion of

9. *Midrash Rabbah* on the Song of Songs 4.12.1 (Freedman 9:219–20). Two other parables follow with the same format. In the second parable a man sells a field and the buyer digs wells and turns the field into an orchard. In the third parable it is a thicket of cedars and the buyer makes wooden objects. This same treasure parable occurs in *Mekilta de-Rabbi Ishmael*, Exod. 14:5 (ed. and trans. Lauterbach, 1:198). See Crossan, *Finding*, 65–66, 106.

10. Crossan has accented how similar the *Thomas* and rabbinic parables are, missing the significant differences.

11. Jeremias, *Parables*, 32.

12. Crossan, *Finding*, 106. His emphasis.

13. Hedrick, "Treasure Parable," 41–56. Hedrick's rejection of the Matthean parable (pp. 47–48) is without foundation.

dissimilarity. In the parable's conclusion the man lends out the found treasure for profit. This offends the piety of both *Thomas* and Judaism, which forbids usury.[14] This point is well taken. On the grounds of the formal demands of the criterion of dissimilarity, the *Thomas* parable has as high a claim to authenticity as the Matthean parable. It does exhibit the distinctive voice, using a major story form but playing in a minor key so typical of the Jesus parables. Instead of discovering the treasure of the kingdom, the man becomes a moneylender. What is most striking is that both treasure parables ascribed to Jesus involve the finder of the treasure in scandal, in impiety; and that may be the most important point.

The Joy in Finding

The parable Treasure occurs in Matthew's third discourse, which contains parables of the kingdom (chap. 13). In the rhetorical organization of the chapter, Treasure is paired with The Merchant, just as A Grain of Mustard Seed is paired with The Leaven. Only The Wheat and Tares and The Net receive interpretation.[15] Both the parables Treasure and The Merchant are examples of finding the kingdom, the thing of great value; The Net, the final parable of the triad, concludes with a judgment motif in the separation of the good from the bad, which is also the theme of The Wheat and Tares.

Some have suggested that Matthew composed the parable himself.[16] Robert Gundry points to the strong grammatical and verbal similarity between the six parables (see table 4). The similarity is indeed striking and may well indicate that Matthew has patterned these six parables to fit a similar form. But more probably the format is traditional. In A Grain of Mustard Seed and The Leaven, two parables for which we have Synoptic parallels, the parallel language and structures, including the introductions, are also found in Luke, and thus most probably in Q.[17] Therefore, it seems more likely that Matthew is imitating or has inherited a traditional formulation.[18] Where we can observe Matthew's use of sources in this chapter, his usage is conservative, except in the case of explicit interpretation.[19]

14. Ibid., 52. On usury, see Exod. 22:25–27; Deut. 23:19–20; *m. B. Mes.* 5.1–11 (Danby, 355–57).

15. For the redaction of Matthew 13, see chap. 15 above.

16. So Hedrick, "Treasure Parable," 47–48; Gundry, *Matthew*, 276.

17. So Schulz, *Q: Die Spruchquelle*, 299–300, 307.

18. Because of the strong patterning, Cope (*Matthew*, 26) argues that Matthew has inherited a source for the six parables.

19. See chap. 19 below. Both Hedrick "Treasure Parable," 47) and Gundry (*Matthew*, 276) see "joy" as Matthean redaction, but both Luke (eight times) and Matthew (six times) have a predilection for the word in comparison with Mark (once). The only other

Table 4

Comparison of Parables

Introduction	Subject	Predicate	Dative noun	Relative pronoun	Participle	Subject	Aorist verb
another parable he put before them	kingdom of heaven	may be likened	man		who-sowed		
another parable he put before them	kingdom of heaven	is like	mustard seed	which	taking	man	sowed
another parable he spoke to them	kingdom of heaven	is like	leaven	which	taking	woman	hid
	kingdom of heaven	is like	treasure hidden	which	finding	man	hid
again	kingdom of heaven	is like	man/merchant		finding		bought
again	kingdom of heaven	is like	net thrown	which	drawing up		sorted

A Reading

Based on the arguments advanced above, I maintain that the two treasure parables, both with high claims to authenticity, are part of the
originating structure. In this reading I will follow the Matthean parable,
not because of some canonical privilege but because I think its plot more
interesting. I will refer to *Thomas* to exploit the interrelations of their
plots.

Line 1: The kingdom of heaven is like treasure hidden in a field . . .

Hiding treasure in ancient times was not uncommon, especially in
times of distress. Josephus reports that among the ruins of Jerusalem
after its destruction the Romans recovered much of the city's wealth of
"gold and silver and other most precious articles, which the owners in
view of the uncertain fortunes of war had stored underground" [*kata
gēs*]."[20] In A Man Entrusts Property, the third servant buries his talent in
the ground.[21] Many of the ancient gold and silver coins in modern
collections come from caches buried in the ground, usually in a pot.
Modern archaeologists are not the only ones who recover the hidden
treasures of the ancients, as both the Qumran scrolls and the Nag
Hammadi library have made evident.

Both the *Thomas* and Matthean parables imply that the treasure is a
metaphor for the kingdom. Treasure, as a thing of value, can itself be a
metaphor for other things of value. The opening poem of Proverbs 2
indicates some ways in which this metaphorical structure can be exploited. When the son is advised to "treasure up my commandments"
(Prov. 2:1), treasure is a metaphor for high value, something to be kept
and guarded. But other aspects of the metaphorical structure of treasure
are also exploited in the poem, namely, those of seeking and finding:

> If you **seek** it [wisdom] like silver
>   and **search** for it as for **hidden treasures**;
> then you will understand the fear of the Lord
>   and **find** the knowledge of God.
>   (Prov. 2:4–5)

"Seek," "search," and "find" belong to the metaphorical structure of
hidden treasure and may also be applied to wisdom.[22] In Proverbs the

use of "joy" in chap. 13 is derived from Mark's interpretation of A Sower Went Out
(Mark 4:16//Matt. 13:20//Luke 8:13).

20. Josephus, *Jewish War*, 7.5.2 (Loeb 3:539).

21. For a discussion of the rabbinic rules for responsibility in burying another's
property, see chap. 9 above.

22. *Gos. Thom.* 76; Matt. 6:19–20; Luke 12:33.

treasure is hidden and actively sought: "you seek." But both the Matthean and *Thomas* parables begin with the treasure hidden and no one seeking it.

Because the parable begins with hidden treasure, we know nothing about the one who will find it. In the *Thomas* parable the one who initially owns the field is "unknowing" and therefore not worthy.[23] In the passage from Proverbs the one seeking the treasure/wisdom is worthy by implication. In the Jewish treasure tradition there must be reciprocity between the treasure, as a thing of value, and the finder of the treasure.[24] This reciprocity is clearly brought out in another well-attested treasure story:

> Now there was a certain man there, by the name of Abba Judah. He would fulfill the commandment [of supporting the sages] in a liberal spirit. One time he lost all his money, and he saw our rabbis and despaired [of helping them]. He went home, and his face was filled with suffering. His wife said to him, "Why is your face filled with suffering?" He said to her, "Our rabbis are here, and I simply do not know what I can do for them." His wife, who was even more righteous than he, said to him, "You have a single field left. Go and sell half of it and give the proceeds to them." He went and did just that. He came to our rabbis, and he gave them the proceeds.

This story begins with a sketch of the man's character. When he was rich, he was generous; now that he is poor he is ashamed that he can no longer fulfill the command. His wife too is virtuous, and though they do not sell all to give to the rabbis, they do sell half.

> Our rabbis prayed in his behalf. They said to him, "Abba Judah, may the Holy One, blessed be He, make up all the things you lack." When they went their way, he went down to plow the half-field that remained in his possession. Now while he was ploughing in the half-field that remained to him, his cow fell and broke a leg. He went down to bring her up, and the Holy One, blessed be He, opened his eyes, and he found a jewel. He said, "It was for my own good that my cow broke its leg."[25]

This unit is the actual treasure-finding story. The treasure is in land owned by the man; he was not looking for it, and it is clearly a reward for his piety.

> Now when our rabbis returned, they asked about him. They said, "How are

23. In the rabbinic parable quoted above as parallel to *Thomas*, the initial owner is indolent.

24. Crossan, *Finding*, 55: "The biblical and moral aspects of such stories must always be remembered in Jewish tradition."

25. In another version (*Midrash Rabbah* on Deuteronomy 4.8 [Freedman 6:97]) the man finds gold coins.

things with Abba Judah?" People replied, "Who can [even] gaze upon the face of Abba Judah—Abba Judah of the oxen! Abba Judah of the camels! Abba Judah of the asses!" So Abba Judah had returned to his former wealth. Now he came to our rabbis and asked after their welfare. They said to him, "How is Abba Judah doing?" He said to them, "Your prayer in my behalf has yielded fruit." They said to him, "Even though to begin with other people gave more than you did, you were the one whom we wrote down at the top of the register." They took and seated him with themselves, and they pronounced upon him the following scriptural verse: "A man's gift makes room for him and brings him before great men"(Prov. 18:16).[26]

In another version of this story,[27] when the rabbis return Abba Judah makes another generous donation to their cause, thus underlining his piety and equating almsgiving with treasure. But even in this version, the quotation from Prov. 18:16 (in all three versions the illustrand is this verse) makes it evident that Abba Judah's gift giving, almsgiving, has made him prominent.

The *Thomas* parable also informs the hearer that the new owner of the field is a hard worker, yet line 1 of this parable tells us nothing about the man; it begins with the hidden treasure. It thus breaks the form of the common Jewish treasure story. A hearer is forewarned.

Line 2: ... which, on finding, a man hid ...

Now a man is introduced but a hearer is given no explicit indication of his piety. He finds the treasure and immediately covers it up. Why? Does he cover it up to protect it from others? Or does "hid," *kryptō*, have some darker overtone? The narrative offers no indication.

Line 3: ... and in his joy he goes and sells all he has and buys that field.

This line abruptly ends the story. The story line is clear. He cashes in all his property and buys the field for his own, and so by implication the treasure is his. At the discourse level—the level at which one makes sense of the sequence of events—the story has laid traps that await the hearer after story time.

Only after the man buys the field does a hearer learn that he is not its owner.[28] This creates several simultaneous problems. It causes retrospection, since the parable has given no indication that the man was not the property's owner, and not being the owner creates complications.

---

26. *j. Hor.* 3.4 (Neusner 34:114–15). A third version of the parable occurs in *Midrash Rabbah* on Leviticus 5.4 (Freedman 4:66–67).

27. *Midrash Rabbah* on Deuteronomy 4.8 (Freedman 6:97–98).

28. Crossan, *Finding*, 77.

Thus he is a day laborer and hid the treasure not to protect it from others but to conceal it from the property's owner. A hearer must calculate the morality involved in the man's action: What is at stake? Is it legal? Can he get away with it? Finally, a hearer must project beyond the story: What happens to the man now that he has his newfound wealth? Will he, like Abba Judah, have many camels and asses, or will he build "himself a fine palace" and go "about in public followed by a retinue of servants"? Or will he, like the man in the *Thomas* parable, lend out the proceeds from the treasure at interest?

What moral calculus is operative? Since the man does not own the field and is in the employ of the owner, there are the owner's rights to consider. The debate on this issue is extensive, confusing, and critical, because it determines how a hearer judges the behavior of the man who finds the treasure. If what he did was correct and legal, then the point of the parable becomes the joy and risk in selling all. But if what he did was not correct, then at the level of discourse a hearer faces incongruity: How is ill-gotten treasure related to the kingdom? Several mistakes must be avoided. Some have confused the ownership of the land with ownership of the treasure. They argue that since the man has bought the field that contains the treasure, the treasure is his. The evidence is the Mishnaic axiom governing the selling of property: "If a man sold a courtyard, he has sold also its houses, cisterns, trenches, and vaults, but not the movable property; but if he had said, 'It and all that is in it', all these are sold also."[29] Thus the day laborer's activity is perfectly legal since he now owns the land and all that is in it.[30]

Yet in the haste to bring a verdict, this view overlooks the question of the ownership of the treasure, which takes precedence over that concerning the ownership of the land. Derrett has reviewed the talmudic case law about "lifting" (i.e., removing treasure after a find). A day-laborer may lift the treasure if he finds it while in the employ of another, depending on what instructions he was given. "That which is found by a labourer [whilst working for another] belongs to himself. When is that? If the employer had instructed him, 'Weed or dig for me to-day.' But if the employer had instructed him, 'Work for me to-day' [without specifying the nature of the work], his findings belong to the employer."[31] According to Derrett, the worker, having received explicit directions now has a claim on the treasure. But again the talmudic argument

---

29. *m. B. Bat.* 4.4 (Danby, 371). See Manson, *Sayings*, 196.
30. This argument was first advanced by Duvallier, in "La parabole du trésor," 107–15. It was accepted by Jeremias (*Parables*, 199). For refutation, see Derrett, *Law in the New Testament*, 6–9.
31. *b. B. Mes.* 118a (Soncino 10:670–71). See Crossan, *Finding*, 91.

concerns a thing that is ownerless. In other arguments, the rabbis are specific that found objects are divided into two groups, those with an owner and those without:

> What lost goods belong to the finder and what must be proclaimed? These goods belong to the finder: If man found scattered fruit, scattered money, small sheaves in the public domain, cakes of figs, bakers' loaves, strings of fig, pieces of flesh, wool-shearings [in the condition in which they have been] brought from their country [of origin], stalks of flax, and strips of purple wool; these belong to the finder.[32]

What all these things have in common is that they are in disorder, have no specific marks of identification, and are things the owner could not reasonably expect to recover. This is sometimes referred to as the law of the owner's despair: to despair "of recovering his property constitutes relinquishing rights of ownership and declaring the property to be ownerless, hence available to whoever finds it."[33] The Mishnah continues by saying, "Whatsoever has in it aught unusual must be proclaimed: thus if he found a fig-cake with a potsherd in it or a loaf with coins in it [he must proclaim it]."[34] Again the legal principle is clear: it is that things with a clear mark of ownership must be proclaimed. Both the Palestinian and Babylonian Talmuds go into long discussions of what constitutes this mark. For example, ownership of scattered coins does not have to be proclaimed but of stacked coins does. When are coins stacked rather than scattered? "If they overlap."[35]

This review of the rabbinic traditions concerning finding treasure, despite the fact that the traditions are sometimes complex and confusing, makes evident what is common sense. Treasure that can be presumed to have an owner cannot be claimed by the finder. Crossan quotes with approval the summary from George Hill's magesterial work *Treasure Trove in Law and Practice:* "But the fact that the buyer knows of the treasure before purchase implies that it has already been discovered (and with finding the landowner's right comes into existence)."[36] But the most telling point, one frequently overlooked by those who claim that the finder is doing the right, is emphasized by Crossan: *"If the treasure belongs to the finder, buying the land is unnecessary. But, if the treasure does not belong to the finder, buying the land is unjust."*[37] If the dayworker has

32. *m. B. Met.* 2.1 (Danby, 348).
33. Neusner in his comments upon *j. B. Mes.* 2.1 (Neusner 29:40).
34. *m. B. Met.* 2.1 (Danby, 349).
35. *b. B. Met.* 25a (Soncino 10:157). For a detailed discussion about various marks of identification, see *j. B. Met.* 2.3–10 (Neusner 29:43–58) and *b. B. Met.* 24b–25b (Soncino 10:155–59).
36. Hill, *Treasure Trove,* 99 n. 4; quoted also by Crossan in *Finding,* 82.
37. Crossan, *Finding,* 91. His emphasis.

claim to the treasure, he has no need to rehide the treasure and buy the land. He can simply claim the treasure. That he does rehide the treasure and buy the land indicates that he does not believe he can make such a claim. Also from the point of view of narrative structure, a hearer discovers that the finder is not the landowner only when he buys the field, thus concentrating narrative attention on the buying. The structure of the line involves finding and joy/selling and buying. But because buying signifies that he does not own, does not not owning call into question the joy of finding?

Finally, there is the normal pattern of treasure plots to consider. In plots where there is buying of the field, normally litigation ensues.[38] The following example can stand for the type. Alexander the Great is visiting the king of Qasya, and Alexander explicitly says that he has come to see how the king distributes alms and how he judges:

> While he was chatting with him, someone came with a case against his fellow. He had bought a piece of a field with its rubbish dump, and he had found a trove of money in it. The one who had bought the property said, "I bought a junk pile; a trove I didn't buy." The one who had sold the property said, "A junk pile and everything in it is what I sold you."[39] While they were arguing with one another, the king said to one of them, "Do you have a male child?" He said to him, "Yes." He said to his fellow, "Do you have a female child?" He said to him, "Yes." He said to them, "Let this one marry that one, and let the treasure-trove belong to the two of them." [Alexander] began to laugh. He said to him, "Now why are you laughing? Didn't I judge the case properly?" He said to him, "If such a case came before you, how would you have judged it?" He said to him, "We should have killed both this one and that one, and kept the treasure for the king."[40]

The narrative's interest is not in the case but the example of Jewish piety and wisdom, reminiscent of Solomon's decision concerning the true mother (1 Kings 3:16–27). But the contrast to our parable is striking. The virtue of both men is on display, and the buyer of the dunghill is ignorant of what is contained in it, so there is no need to rehide it and then buy the field.

The *Thomas* parable completely avoids the dilemma posed in the Synoptic parable by interposing two generations between the start of the story and the finding of the treasure, with neither generation knowing about the treasure, and by placing the finding of the treasure after

---

38. Ibid., 67–70.
39. The seller clearly follows Mishnaic law quoted above; see n. 29.
40. *j. B. Mes* 2.6 (Neusner 29:49–50). See Crossan, *Finding*, 68–69. Alexander's response represents the "regality system" by which the government claims all. This was not the policy of Roman law. See Crossan, *Finding*, 82. Crossan is completely dependent on Hill (*Treasure Trove*).

the field's purchase by the finder. To warn off any trouble for the finder, he is contrasted morally with the former owners, as in the parallel rabbinic parable.[41]

Both the *Thomas* and Matthean parables end with an implication of scandal. In *Thomas*, the man's knowledge is completely undone by his lending out money, and the man in Matthew has acted in a despicable fashion. Buying the field makes a claim on the treasure; he intends to possess it for himself. But the story ends without his possession. The other treasure stories we have seen all end with a report of the man's new wealthy status: "He built himself a fine palace, and he began going about in public followed by a retinue of servants."[42] Or in the *Thomas* parable we know that the man is wealthy, even if he does become a moneylender. But in the Matthean treasure parable the story line is unfinished, and a hearer must complete it in imagination, developing the logic of the plot.

Since the man's purchase of the field is for an illegal purpose, it is likely that if he reveals the treasure he will risk its loss. He can certainly not just dig it up—that is why the parable has no such conclusion. Crossan, in his survey of Jewish and world treasure stories, has noted that he could find no parallel to "selling all."[43] For example, in the parable of Abba Judah, the owner sells half his field, although not to buy a treasure but to give alms. But if a man has sold *all*, then he is impoverished, even though he possess a treasure—ill gotten and of no use.

From Story to Kingdom

Many scholars argue that whether the man's action is immoral is beside the point.[44] Jeremias says the joy is the point of the parable: "When that great joy, surpassing all measure, seizes a man, it carries him away, penetrates his inmost being, subjugates his mind."[45] The tradition is correct to draw attention to the joy, because it is in sharp contrast with the man's action. Jeremias's description of the great joy is more to the point than he may realize. What he is describing—joy seizing a man, carrying him away—is the narcissism of finding a lost object.

Treasure receives its value, its joy, because it appears outside the

---

41. Crossan (*Finding*, 87), after surveying international folklore themes of finding treasure in bought land, concludes, "Folklore culture does not approve of taking another's treasure, even treasure hidden on another's land and unknown to the land's owner, *unless* it is established in the story that the loser is not worthy of our approval."

42. *Midrash Rabbah* on the Song of Songs 4.12.1 (Freedman 9:219).

43. Crossan, *Finding*, 79.

44. E.g., Jeremias, *Parables*, 199; Manson, *Sayings*, 196; Schweizer, *Good News*, 312.

45. Jeremias, *Parables*, 200–201. Dodd (*Parables*, 86–87) is in agreement.

bounds of the everyday. It is an occurrence that breaks expectations and interrupts the everyday. Because it is not something earned or labored for but something found, it is lawless. Its joy is precisely in its lawlessness, its unearned, not worked for character.[46] Even modern treasure hunters who sell stock in their ventures are in search of super returns on their investment and are notorious scams. There is a narcissism in finding treasure, which is why it is joyful. "Finders keepers, losers weepers" is the joyful shout in defiance of order. In finding treasure we escape from the bonds of the everyday, to a lawless world where we are rewarded for not working.

The lawless, narcissistic character of treasure makes it an appropriate vehicle as a divine reward for piety. It can be a sign of God's grace working outside the laws of the everyday. This aspect is clearly at work in the Jewish treasure stories. But the two Jesus parables exploit the hidden side of treasure as a metaphor for God's reward. All metaphors both reveal and hide.[47] Although we are more accustomed to the revealing aspect, both treasure parables reveal an aspect about treasure normally kept hidden: that its lawless narcissism can corrupt those who gain it. In the *Thomas* parable the treasure tempts the man to gain more treasure, and in the Matthean parable his joy at discovery so overtakes him that he brashly sells all and buys the field. His joy has led him astray. So now the man has sold all, is impoverished, yet possesses a treasure he dare not dig up unless he wants to face the rather embarrassing question of whence it came.

This corrupting aspect of the kingdom is part of the scandalous, hidden aspect of the kingdom that Jesus' parables reveal—his distinctive voice—which we frequently overlook or ignore. In the parable In a City There Was a Judge, the judge finally vindicates the widow not because of the justice of her cause or the fear of God but because she continues to bother him. Or the rogue in A Rich Man Had a Steward has drawn the condemnation not only of his master but also of those who see only good in connection with the kingdom. The Leaven is the mirror reversal of the treasure. That parable begins with an inappropriate metaphor, leaven, but at its conclusion all is leavened. This parable begins with treasure, an appropriate metaphor, but ends with the conclusion in jeopardy, the man corrupted. But more than the activity of the man is scandalous. As Crossan has accented, the treasure in the Matthean parable is given *before* we know whether the man deserves it. To describe this, he has borrowed a line from Emily Dickinson: "Finding is the

46. See the helpful analysis of Collins ("Found Object," 43–74).
47. Lackoff and Johnson, *Metaphors We Live By*, 10–13.

First Act."[48] The treasure comes at the beginning, not the conclusion. Perhaps this finding as the first act is itself the corruption, for it tempts the man before he has been proved. Without the test of piety and virtue, how can he respond to the lawless narcissism of treasure? Like the father in A Man Had Two Sons, who spoils both his sons, always taking them back regardless of what they do, the kingdom, according to the parable Treasure, comes before our deeds. And that is not only grace but potential corruption.

48. Dickinson, *Poems of Emily Dickinson* 2:647–48.

21

Where's the Fox?

A Man with a Hundred Sheep

A man has a hundred sheep and one of them went astray and he leaves the ninety-nine on the mountain and goes out to seek the one until he has found it.

Sheep and shepherd play a prominent role in the tradition of Israel. "The Lord is my shepherd" (Ps. 23:1) recalls the importance of such images and metaphors. Doubtless this is due to Israel's nomadic heritage, when sheep and herding were central to its existence. But Israel in the first century was an agriculturally based economy, and shepherds had become part of society's marginal element, representing one of the forbidden occupations. How then does one interpret the activity of the shepherd in the parable A Man with a Hundred Sheep—against the positive images of the religious repertoire or the negative images of real shepherds?

The parable is extant in three versions: Matt. 18:12; Luke 15:4–6; and *Gos. Thom.* 107. The contexts in the Synoptic Gospels are different, although the applications are similar. As usual, in *Thomas* there is no explicit context, yet there is strong debate about whether the parable should be read against a gnostic or wisdom background.

The Little One

In Matthew, the parable occurs in the ecclesiastical discourse (18:1–35). In the Gospel's narrative the fictional audience is the disciples, and the implied reader is the church official who is to deal with the little ones. Krister Stendahl summarizes well the sense of the parable in its Matthean context: "It is God's will that you should go after your apostate brother as persistently as the shepherd of the parable seeks the lost sheep."[1] The context, then, is so completely that of the early church that Matthew's version of the parable cannot possibly be original.[2]

Verses 10 and 14 provide an inclusio for the parable. Verse 10 addresses both the fictional audience of disciples and the implied reader directly, as is appropriate in a speech. The key words "little ones" and "Father" stand out in each. A command is given ("do not despise") whose object is identified as "little ones." Underlying this first part of the discourse (18:1–14) is an ironical contrast between the audience of leaders and the metaphorical structure of child which supports the speech. A literal child is presented in v. 2, who then becomes a metaphor for those who would enter the kingdom. There follow two warnings, the first against causing one of these little ones to sin (v. 6) and the other against despising one of the little ones (v. 10). Each warning is illustrated, the first by a series of woes and the latter by the parable. The second part of the discourse switches from the child metaphor to one based on brothers (vv. 15–35).

The end of the conclusio (v. 14) repeats the key words "Father" and "little ones." With the inclusio as a guide, the implied reader must identify the figures in the parable. The shepherd is the disciple or church leader, while the sheep that wanders astray is the little one entrusted to the shepherd.[3]

When we turn to the parable itself, aspects of Matthean style are in evidence. Although the initial question "What do you think?" (v. 12) is most probably Matthean in style,[4] there is little doubt that he inherited the parable in the form of a question, because it so appears in Luke, and so, probably also in Q.[5] Most likely the conditional formula is also

1. Stendahl, *School*, 27.
2. So, among many others, Jeremias, *Parables*, 40.
3. Jülicher, *Die Gleichnisreden* 2:331. After Jülicher, many others have argued that v. 14 was composed by Matthew. See the similar ending to A King Wished to Settle Accounts.
4. *Ti dokei* occurs six times in Matthew while not occurring in either Mark or Luke. Bultmann (*History of the Synoptic Tradition*, 171) sees the question as original.
5. Schulz, *Q: Die Spruchquelle*, 387.

Matthean, since the illustrations in vv. 8–9 and vv. 15–19 are cast in a similar form.[6]

The Lost Sheep

A Man with a Hundred Sheep occurs in the Lukan travel narrative and belongs to a unit that extends to 18:14.[7] In connection with A Man Had Two Sons, I have already developed an extensive analysis of Luke 15 in which I argue that Luke has created a subtle but powerful point of view from which the implied reader interprets the parables, and that the context of chapter 15 is fictional, the creation of its author. Here I will summarize only the important points.[8]

A Man with a Hundred Sheep forms with A Woman with Ten Drachmas a pair[9] with a similar structure which are bound together by "or," indicating their interchangeability. Their almost identical conclusions and applications (vv. 6b-7; 9b-10) reinforce the bonding. The three parables of Luke 15 are addressed to Jesus' opponents, the Pharisees, who object to eating at table with sinners. Thus the narrative object is to entice the Pharisees to table fellowship or to indicate why such table fellowship is necessary (v. 32). In both parables an object is lost and found; this is followed by a request for rejoicing, and then there is an interpretation by the teller (Jesus) that ties the parable to the larger story about Pharisees and table fellowship. In the connection of the parable to its larger narrative context of Luke 15, the value of the thing lost undergoes a transformation. In the two parables the lost sheep or coin has little intrinsic value. Rather its value is in being found, in the joy of its recovery. In the transition to the larger narrative cycle of Luke 15, the value and joy are in repentance. What is more, nothing in the parable corresponds to the opponents, the Pharisees, of the primary narrative, but the themes of lost and found belong to the parable. The implied feast of rejoicing bridges the parable with the larger narrative and leads the Gospel's implied reader to make the proper associations.

The skill with which Luke has created the context of controversy with the Pharisees has fooled many of the parable's interpreters. Although

---

6. Ibid. But Perrin (*Rediscovering the Teaching*, 99) sees "if he finds" as a mark of the parable's realism. Cf. Breech (*Silence of Jesus*, 79) in support.

7. For an outline, see Fitzmyer, *Gospel according to Luke* 2:1072. For an outline, Fitzmyer quotes with approval Manson's characterization (*Sayings*, 282) of this section of Luke as the "gospel of the outcast."

8. See chap. 2 above.

9. Some think these were originally twin parables. See A Woman with Ten Drachmas for a discussion of this issue.

Jeremias's argument that Luke has preserved the original context of the parable has won few supporters,[10] a number of interpreters have followed Dodd's lead. He has maintained that, though the context is secondary, Luke has hit upon the correct context.[11] Dodd has recognized Luke's creation but is unable to shake off Luke's point of view.

Upon close examination of the parable, one can easily see shifts in Luke's performance that facilitate the parable's use as an illustration in the debate with the Pharisees over table fellowship. Verse 6 probably is the result of Lukan performance.[12] After finding the sheep he rejoices (v. 5), so that the rejoicing of v. 6 seems redundant. The calling together of neighbors hints at table fellowship, the conflict that begins the chapter. Finally, the repetition of the "lost sheep" fits the recurring pattern of what is lost (coins, sheep, son) that ties the chapter together.

The Largest Sheep

The *Thomas* parable is obviously a performance of the same parabolic structure that underlies Matthew and Luke, yet there are striking differences. The parable reads,

> Jesus said, "The Kingdom is like a shepherd who had a hundred sheep. One of them, the largest, went astray. He left the ninety-nine and looked for that one until he found it. When he had gone to such trouble, he said to the sheep, 'I care for you more than the ninety-nine.'" (*Gos. Thom.* 107)

There are similarities here to the Synoptic parable, but there are also three conspicuous differences: (1) The parable is in direct narrative and not in the form of a question. (2) The sheep is the largest. (3) At the conclusion the narrator (Jesus) speaks directly to the sheep. The contrast between large and small is a major theme in the *Thomas* parables, and the note about the sheep's being the largest has led to the charge that it represents a gnostic expansion. The "largest" is the gnostic believer who is most important to the savior (shepherd).[13]

---

10. Jeremias, *Parables*, 40; Derrett "Fresh Light on the Lost Sheep," 36. But Jeremias later argues (*Die Sprache*, 243–44) that 15:1–3 is Lukan.

11. Dodd, *Parables*, 92. Similarly, Linnemann, *Jesus of the Parables*, 69. Bultmann (*History of the Synoptic Tradition*, 184) rejects the context as secondary; so also Schottroff ("Das Gleichnis," 32–35). Schottroff sees v. 7 as a summary of Lukan theology. Waelkens ("L'analyse structurale," 160–78) demonstrates the literary unity of the chapter through a structuralist method.

12. Linnemann (*Jesus of the Parables*, 68) and C. W. F. Smith (*Jesus of the Parables*, 105) see it as an attraction to the conclusion of A Woman with Ten Drachmas.

13. See Ménard, *L'évangile selon Thomas*, 205–6; R. Grant and Freedman, *Secret Sayings*, 181. For a contrast between large and small in the *Thomas* parables, see p. 34 above.

An alternative reading suggests a Jewish background. Quispel[14] has pointed to Ezek. 34:16: "I will seek the lost, and I will bring back the strayed, and I will bind up the crippled, and I will strengthen the weak, and the fat and the strong I will watch over;[15] I will feed them in justice." He suggests that the "largest" sheep of the *Thomas* parable reflects this background. Independently of Quispel, William Petersen had extended this line of reasoning into an extensive search for a Jewish background. I present only a sample of the texts quoted by Petersen:[16]

> The Holy one blessed be He, said to Israel, "I have never loved any created being more than you. . . ." (*Num. Rab.* 1.9)

> It is Israel alone that is to be innumerable and immeasurable. (*Num. Rab.* 2.17)

> [In explanation of God's commanding Moses to count Israel . . .] R. Menahema cited R. Bebai's parable of the king who had a flock of sheep which wolves came to rend. Thereupon the king said to the shepherd: Number my flock to find out how many are gone. Even so the Holy One said to Moses: Count Israel to find out how many are gone. (*Pesiq. Rab. Kah.* 2.8)

> All these hosts that you see are not mine. They belong to Gehenna. . . . But these children of Israel whose sum I keep telling you to take, they are Mine own treasure. (*Pesiq. R.* 10.5)

From these and other texts Petersen concludes that Israel is "loved more" than other nations and that she alone has superlatives used of her. Moreover, he argues that the other nations do not belong to God. More specifically, Israel can be compared to sheep being counted. He concludes that "the final numbering of Israel is represented as an eschatological counting of sheep in the future."[17]

Petersen has clearly shown that the parable makes more consistent sense read against a Jewish background than against a gnostic one. Yet has he discovered, as he thinks, that the background indicates that the *Thomas* version of the parable is more original than the Synoptics? I think not, primarily because the parable as interpeted by *Thomas* does not cohere with other established themes in the Jesus tradition. The parables From Jerusalem to Jericho and Two Men Went Up to the Temple argue against the xenophobia[18] that Petersen sees underlying his

14. Quispel, "Gospel of Thomas Revisited," 233.
15. LXX reading. MT reads, "destroy"; Syriac agrees with LXX. Zimmerli (*Ezekiel* 2:208) explains the difference in reading as an orthographic problem, preferring the reading of the LXX.
16. Petersen, "Parable of the Lost Sheep." Quotations are from pp. 133–44.
17. Ibid., 135.
18. Petersen's word (ibid., 134).

first three conclusions. But this does not dismiss the significance of Petersen's argument, because what Quispel and he have uncovered is how the parable has reverted to its mythological structure and expectation. The expectation is that something of great value is lost and found. In the Synoptic Gospels a thing of little intrinsic value is found but its value is transformed in the application to a thing of great value, whereas in *Thomas* the transformation takes place within the parable's narrative.

Surface Structure

In most discussions of this parable the argument concerns whether Matthew or Luke has preserved the more original version of the parable. But each has performed the parable, and no extant version has preserved the original parable. Rather, by carefully comparing the three extant versions we can reconstruct the originating structure that supports all three parables.

A chart indicates the significant agreements and disagreements between the three versions:

Matthew	*Luke*	*Thomas*
man	man	shepherd
one hundred	one hundred	one hundred
one	one	the largest
astray	lost	astray
on the mountain	in the wilderness	
if he finds	until he finds	until he found
on his shoulders	such trouble	
rejoices	rejoicing	I care more

Since both Matthew and Luke preserve the parable in the form of a question, it is assumed that Q was also a question.[19] *Thomas*, on the other hand, treats the parable as a simile: "The kingdom is like . . ." It is impossible to decide whether the original structure was interrogative or in direct statement, since as Bultmann notes, Jewish similitudes are found both ways.[20] Normally Jesus' parables employ the anonymous "man" as the chief character. *Thomas*'s "shepherd" only makes specific his occupation. The note about the sheep's being the largest probably is dependent upon the Ezekiel text and signals the mytheme reasserting itself.

In Matthew and *Thomas*'s versions the sheep goes astray (*planaō*), whereas in Luke's performance the shepherd has lost one sheep and

19. So, e.g., Schulz, *Q: Die Spruchquelle*, 389.
20. Bultmann, *History of the Synoptic Tradition*, 179.

goes after the one that is lost (v. 4) and, coming home, announces that he has found the lost sheep (v. 6). In all three cases the Greek word for lost is *apollumi*, which has as a primary sense "ruin" or "destroy,"[21] and in the LXX and New Testament the religious sense of "perish."[22] Since the parable's application identifies the sheep with a sinner who repents, *apollumi* is a fitting description of the "lost" sheep. Thus the signified of *apollumi* sets up the interpretation and facilitates it.[23] *Apollumi* is also the key word in A Woman with Ten Drachmas (vv. 8–9), and in A Man Had Two Sons it concludes the scenes of the younger son (v. 24) and the elder (v. 32).[24]

Where the sheep are left while the shepherd searches differs between the versions. In Matthew the sheep are left in the mountains (v. 13), in Luke the desert (v. 4), while *Thomas* does not specify any particular place. Matthew Black suggests that mountain and desert represent the underlying Aramaic *betura*, "in the hill country."[25] Fitzmyer,[26] however, sees no reason to posit an Aramaic *Vortext* but points to 1 Sam. 17:28, where Eliab asks David, "And with whom did you leave those few sheep in the desert?" Since shepherds cared for their flocks in marginal areas, there is probably no difference between the implications of desert and mountain.

When the shepherd returns in Luke he carries the sheep on his shoulders. This has occasioned considerable controversy, with many describing it as normal[27] while still others have maintained its secondary character.[28] The representation of a shepherd carrying sheep on his shoulders is widespread in both pagan and Christian art[29] and occurs in Jewish midrash: "'That you ran away because of thirst; you must be weary.' So he placed the kid on his shoulder and walked away. Thereupon God said, 'because thou hast mercy in leading the flock of a mortal, thou wilt assuredly tend my flock Israel.'"[30] The widespread usage may account for its attraction to the Lukan performance, but it does not prove it.

The current endings of all three extant versions result from the speci-

21. BAGD, 95.

22. Oepke, "*apollumi*," 394–96.

23. In Matthew's application (18:13) the little ones are not to perish (*apollumi*).

24. Among many others, Schulz (*Q: Die Spruchquelle*, 387) argues for the secondary character of *apollumi*.

25. Black, *Aramaic Approach*, 133.

26. Fitzmyer, *Gospel according to Luke* 2:1076.

27. E.g., Jeremias, *Parables*, 134; Derrett, "Fresh Light on the Lost Sheep," 34.

28. Linnemann, *Jesus of the Parables*, 67.

29. For extensive references, see Fitzmyer, *Gospel according to Luke* 2:1077.

30. *Midrash Rabbah* on Exodus 2.2 (Str-B 2:209). Isa. 40:11 may also be in the background.

fics of each individual performance and were not part of the originating structure. In *Thomas*, there is no rejoicing, but the sheep is directly addressed and its supreme worth affirmed. The rejoicing note was introduced by Q and elaborated by Luke (Luke 15:6–7 parallels 15:9–10). Thus the originating structure ended with "until he finds it" (Luke 15:4; *Gos. Thom.*),[31] which does cohere with the ending of The Leaven (Matt. 13:33). Matthew's conditional "if he finds it" results from his conditional patterning of the discourse (Matt. 18:8–9, 13, 15–17, 19).

A Reading

Line 1: A man has a hundred sheep and one of them went astray . . .

The initial line depicts an everyday situation. The size of the flock was probably ordinary,[32] and a sheep wandering off was not extraordinary. But the hearer's quandary is to decide how the metaphorical structure is being invoked. What does it stand for?

Shepherd is surprisingly rare as a title for God,[33] although the metaphorical structure of shepherd language frequently is applied to God as one going before his flock (Ps. 68:7) and leading it to pastures (Jer. 50:19).[34] The figure is found most often in the Psalms, especially the Twenty-third Psalm, and in the prophecies of the exilic period.[35]

The shepherd metaphor is often used of military leaders and kings (e.g., 1 Sam. 21:8). Sometimes the shepherd is unworthy. The apocalyptic prophecy of Zechariah catches the tone: "Awake, O sword, against my shepherd, against the man who stands next to me," says the Lord of hosts. "Strike the shepherd, that the sheep may be scattered; I will turn my hand against the little ones" (Zech. 13:7).

Outside of Psalm 23, perhaps the most famous extended use of the shepherd-sheep metaphorical structure in the Hebrew Bible is Ezekiel 34. Much of the language from that passage finds its way into the extant versions of the parable.[36] The shepherds (kings) of Israel have betrayed the sheep, and "my sheep were scattered, they wandered over all the mountains and on every high hill" (v. 6). As the prophecy continues, God promises, "I myself will search for my sheep and will seek them out.

31. Breech (*Silence of Jesus*, 79) is in agreement.
32. So Jeremias, *Parables*, 133. See Gen. 32:14; *t. B. Qam.* 6.20.
33. See Gen. 49:24; 48:15; Pss. 23:1; 80:1. The titular usage is obscured in the RSV trans. of Gen. 48:15. Jeremias (*"poimēn,"* 487) quotes the extensive use of the title for ancient Near Eastern deities. See also Zimmerli, *Ezekiel* 2:213–14.
34. For further examples, see Jeremias, *"poimēn,"* 487.
35. Jer. 23:3; 31:10; 50:19; Ezek. 34:11–22; Isa. 40:10; 49:9; Micah 4:6–8; 7:14.
36. Derrett ("Fresh Light on the Lost Sheep," 37) does not doubt that the Ezekiel text lies behind the parable.

As a shepherd seeks out his flock when some of his sheep have been scattered abroad, so will I seek out my sheep" (vv. 11–12). When the sheep have been gathered and fed "on the mountains of Israel" (vv. 13, 14), "I myself will be the shepherd of my sheep, and I will make them lie down. . . . I will seek the lost, and I will bring back the strayed" (vv. 15–16). In the end, God will be the judge between "sheep and sheep, rams and he-goats" (v. 17), and then "I will set up over them one shepherd, my servant David, and he shall feed them" (v. 23). Ezekiel 34 and the parable share not only the sheep-shepherd metaphor but also specific elements from the metaphorical network: mountains, search/seek, lost/strayed,[37] and probably, the fat (largest) sheep of *Thomas*. So common is the vocabulary stock that we must consider Ezekiel 34 part of the my-theme invoked by the parabolic structure. But how that mytheme is invoked is the critical problem for both hearer and interpreter.[38]

The shepherd is basically a positive metaphor that denotes a leader who protects (feeds, nourishes, looks after) his flock. In this sense, God is a shepherd and Israel is his flock. Bad leaders of the nation are those who fail to live up to the expectations of a good shepherd. But by the first century, Jews were no longer a nomadic people but had adapted to a primarily agricultural and urban economy, and shepherds were disdained as marginal members of society. So negative was the evaluation that shepherds, were among the forbidden occupations and were equated with robbers: "A man should not teach his son to be an ass-driver or a camel-driver, or a barber or a sailor, or a herdsman or a shopkeeper, for their craft is the craft of robbers."[39] In the talmudic discussion concerning eligible witnesses, shepherds are classed with tax collectors and publicans. They are not to be trusted, because they cross boundaries intentionally so their sheep can graze on another's land (i.e., they steal from others).[40] Even more, in the opinion of Rab Judah, "a herdsman in general is ineligible [to testify] while a tax collector in general is eligible."[41]

---

37. *Apollumi* and *planaō* occur in parallel in LXX, v. 16. Luke uses *apollumi* for "lost," while Matthew uses *planaō* for "astray."

38. The metaphorical structure of shepherds and sheep is used in 1 *Epoch* 89–90 (Charlesworth 1:65–72) to retell allegorically the history of Israel from the flood to the establishment of the messianic kingdom. But this allegorical vision has no direct bearing on the parable.

39. *m. Qidd.* 4.14 (Danby, 329). See also the prohibition against buying produce from those whose rightful ownership cannot be established: "None may buy wool or milk from herdsmen, or wood or fruit from them that watch over fruit-trees" (*m. B. Qam.* 10.9 [Danby, 347]).

40. *b. San.* 25b (Soncino 12:148).

41. *b. San.* 25b (Soncino 12:149). Philo, *On Husbandry,* 61: "The care of literal goats and sheep . . . such pursuits are held mean and inglorious" (LCL 3:139). Philo's argument is much like that of the *Midrash on Psalms* (see following n.). He is discussing

The *Midrash on Psalms* for Ps. 23:1 catches very nicely the ambivalence about shepherds. The midrash offers two separate sets of comments. In the first comment there is elaborated a series of parallel metaphors.

> The Lord is my shepherd; I shall not want (Ps 23:1). These words are to be considered in the light of the verse *My beloved is mine, and I am His: He feedeth His flock among the lilies* (Song 2:16), by which is meant that the congregation of Israel said to the Holy One, blessed be He, "As He is God to me, so am I a people to Him."[42]

The reference to the Song of Solomon furnishes a double barbed thrust to understand the potentially offensive Ps. 23:1. First, the relation between God and God's people is that of a beloved to his loved one. Second, it is in that sense that the metaphors of shepherd and sheep are to be used. Then a series of pairs is offered with supporting Scripture quotations that follow the basic structure of beloved–his loved: God-people, father-son, shepherd-sheep, and finally, brother-sister. In this way the potentially threatening metaphor is neutralized by selecting a particular element of the signified as the point of comparison. The second comment on the verse "The Lord is my shepherd" begins,

> These words are to be considered in the light of the verse *I understand more from the ancients* (Ps. 119:100). R. Jose bar Hanina taught: In the whole world you find no occupations more despised than that of the shepherd, who all his days walks about with his staff and his pouch. Yet David presumed to call the Holy One, blessed be He, a shepherd! But David said: *I understand more from the ancients*, meaning that Jacob called God Shepherd, as it is said *The God who hath been my shepherd all my life long* (Gen. 48:15); so I, too, call God shepherd.[43]

The quotation from Rabbi Jose bar Hanina makes evident what the problem is. If a shepherd's status is that of the lowest of the low, how can a shepherd be a metaphor for God? The proof text from Psalm 119 indicates the solution, namely, that the ancients know more about these things than we do. So out of loyalty to the tradition, God is my shepherd. The rabbis both revered the shepherd of the Hebrew Bible and classed the contemporary shepherd among robbers and thieves, the outcast.[44]

The hearer has to decide what kind of shepherd this is: the divine

---

the patriarchs as shepherds but argues that they could not be literal shepherds because that is something of which they could not be proud.

42. *Midrash on Psalms* 23.1 (Braude 1:327).
43. *Midrash on Psalms* 23.2 (Braude 1:327).
44. Bailey (*Poet and Peasant*, 147) also sees this point.

shepherd in search of his flock Israel, the remnant from among the nations, or a secular shepherd, one of the outcast. The sheep going astray compounds the problem: what does it indicate of the sheep?

Line 2: ... and he leaves the ninety-nine on the mountain and goes out to seek the one until he has found it.

Does the shepherd leave the sheep alone on the mountain—or in the desert—while he goes in search of the strayed sheep? How a hearer resolves this question is the single most important factor in determining the value placed on the shepherd. Jeremias and E. F. F. Bishop[45] agree that a real shepherd would not leave the sheep alone. Jeremias suggests that the shepherd leaves them in the watch of someone else or puts them in a cave for protection. Bailey[46] assumes that the sheep would be left in the care of the extended family who own the flock. Yet the parable says nothing of this, and the sense of the text is that the sheep are left on the mountain. Both Matthew and Luke clearly imply that the ninety-nine are abandoned.[47]

On the other hand, Perrin argues that the shepherd, forgetful of normal custom, simply leaves the sheep unattended.[48] Actually the parable says nothing about caring for the ninety-nine sheep.[49] But three points argue in favor of Perrin's observation. First the allegory assumes that the ninety-nine are left alone; otherwise the effectiveness of the contrast between one and ninety-nine would lose its significance. This is true of all three extant versions.[50] The clear sense of the Greek text is that the sheep are abandoned on the mountain or in the desert, both of which are places of inherent danger. *Thomas*, while specifying no place, also implies that they are abandoned. Finally, there are the Hebrew Bible references, especially Ezekiel 34, where it is specifically mentioned that the shepherd has abandoned the sheep on the mountains: "My sheep were scattered, they wandered over all the mountains and on every high hill; my sheep were scattered over all the face of the earth, with none to search or seek for them" (Ezek. 34:6). The prophecy of Micah also announces the same theme: "I saw all Israel scattered upon the mountains, as sheep that have no shepherd" (1 Kings 22:17).

45. Jeremias, *Parables*, 133; Bishop, "Parable of the Lost or Wandering Sheep," 50.
46. Bailey, *Poet and Peasant*, 149–50.
47. *Aaphiēmi* (Matthew), "to leave" or "abandon" (BAGD, 126); *kataleipō* (Luke), "to leave behind," sometimes "to leave behind without help" (BAGD, 413). Until the RSV, in English translations the shepherd went to search out the mountain. E.g., "Doth he not leave the ninety and nine, and goeth into the mountains?" (KJ). See Bishop, "Parable of the Lost or Wandering Sheep," 46–47.
48. Perrin, *Rediscovering the Teaching*, 99–101.
49. As Linnemann (*Jesus of the Parables*, 65) accurately observes.
50. So also ibid., 64.

The texts from Ezekiel and 1 Kings call attention to both a strong similarity and a strong dissimilarity with the parable. In both passages the sheep are abandoned on the mountain. So we should assume this is the case in our parable, for it is the plain reading of the text. But dissonance arises because the shepherd seeks only one of the sheep, whereas in the mytheme Israel is the many.

From Story to Kingdom

When we consider the mytheme to which this parable belongs, especially as represented by Ezekiel 34, a number of anomalies claim our attention. The most obvious has just been mentioned, namely, that the lost sheep is only one and not many. So in comparison with the scale of Ezekiel 34, the parable is modest, everyday. But if we pay attention to the narrative structure another anomaly appears. That structure is diagramed in figure 7.

Figure 7

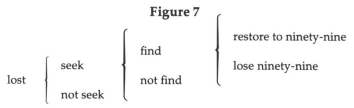

```
                                              ┌ restore to ninety-nine
                              ┌ find ─────────┤
              ┌ seek ─────────┤               └ lose ninety-nine
lost ─────────┤               └ not find
              └ not seek
```

The narrative structure makes evident the risk the shepherd runs. When one of the sheep wanders away, should he go after it and leave the ninety-nine in the mountains, where they too may scatter or be attacked by a wolf? Precisely because of the risk involved, each of the three extant versions seek to lessen the risk, the Synoptics by phrasing the parable as a question that demands an answer of yes, and *Thomas* by naming the sheep as the largest. But even if the shepherd finds the one, will he in the end be able to restore it to the flock of ninety-nine, or will he find the flock dispersed? In taking such a risk to find the one, has the shepherd been a fool?

At the end of the narrative drama described in Ezekiel 34, God vindicates his scattered sheep, gathers them together and destroys their enemies (34:22–31). In the parable the sheep is found, yet the outcome of the flock is left unanswered. There are two tracks to the parable, a surface story and a substory. The hearer knows the substory from the mytheme that challenges the surface story. Is the man foolish for abandoning the ninety-nine to search for the one? Will the ninety-nine still be intact when he returns? Why this concern for just one? The surface story answers none of these questions which it provokes.

The ambivalent notion of shepherds—the positive evaluation of shepherds in the Hebrew Bible and the negative evaluation of shepherds in the first century—sets up the text and subtext. The shepherd is not God but perhaps a fool; the scattered to be saved are not Israel but a lone sheep. This is the story of a possible fool, who may have gambled all and lost. The surety of apocalyptic eschatology is short-circuited. In its place we have a story whose conclusion is outside the story. The various allegories have tried to reassure hearers that the point is the will of the Father that the little ones not perish, or the rejoicing in heaven over the repentance of one sinner, or the love for the largest sheep. But in the parable the outcome is unknown. Creation is not a perfect inclusio, with the end replicating the paradisiacal beginning. The metaphor for the kingdom is not the mighty act but the literalness of the shepherd and his actions. In A Householder Went Out Early, all are invited to the vineyard, but those who have worked all day, who believe they deserve more, are rejected. The undeserving remain. Or in A Man Gave a Banquet, the hall is filled with the socially outcast. In this parable one must risk a story with a foolish shepherd whose ending is not ensured but remains in jeopardy. Is the kingdom the restoration of the flock or simply being one of those who are lost and then found?

Epilogue

After writing a commentary on all the parables, I am faced with a curious contradiction: much more remains to be written about the parables, and I have written too much. Each parable is a gem. At whatever angle you hold it to the light, the gem and the light will appear pristinely different, as though never before seen. The parables are always refracted anew in the angle of each new performance.

The parable as employed by Jesus is an open genre. It creates discomfort for the hearer, exposes the hearer to the new, to a kingdom not yet experienced. The parable does not seek closure, regardless of how often during its transmission various interpreters have sought closure. For precisely this reason the parabolic narrative is always primary and can never be replaced by its supposed meaning. The parable is "laid beside," is "like," and therefore its meaning is found in its being laid beside.

To write a commentary on Jesus' parables is almost a contradiction, although many have tried. A commentary or exegesis seeks explanation and perhaps at times even explains away. A commentary by its very essence seeks closure. Thus the interpreter needs to be careful not to work at cross-purposes to the parable. Both Funk and Crossan have sought to avoid this problem inherent in a commentary by laying the parable beside something else.[1] I have sought to avoid the problem by

---

1. See Funk, *Jesus as Precursor*, esp. 149–59; Crossan, *Raid on the Articulate*.

highlighting the performance character of the parable. Instead of accenting what the parable means, I have chosen to describe how it creates meaning. This has led explicitly to renunciation of the search for a *Sitz im Leben*—a specific context in the ministry of Jesus—as the primary key for interpreting a parable. Rather, the context is twofold: the cultural context is first-century Judaism, and the linguistic context is the symbol the kingdom of God. To underscore further the polyvalence of parables, I have paid close attention to how each parable functions in its extant contexts in the various Gospels. But these versions are only performances of the parable, layings-beside, in an effort to create new meaning. Canonical performances are not privileged in relation to the parable itself. The story is always primary, always available for generating new meaning, as witness several parables that are preserved in different performances in different contexts.

Jesus' parables are laid beside the kingdom of God. This laying-beside is a two-way street. The parable is about the kingdom, whether the connection is immediate or implied. The strategy of referencing the kingdom with a narrative places the parable at risk, for it may well be that expectations about the kingdom will overwhelm the parable, even silence it, in the twice-told tale of allegory. The expectations of the kingdom (good, holy, powerful, triumphant, and so forth) instruct the reader about the parable's meaning and at times reconfigure the parable. The overcoded symbol of the kingdom of God is laid upon the parable. The challenge of the parable is clear enough: "Listen"; "Whoever has ears to hear, let that one hear." How then does one hear without imposing what one already has heard?

The coordinates of the narrative world of the parable can be summarized under three headings: the everyday, the unclean, and miracle. Each coordinate is not equally prominent in each parable. But all the coordinates are there. The everydayness of the parables was a stress of modern parable exegesis beginning with Jülicher and continuing with Dodd, Jeremias, and Funk. I would underscore two aspects of the parables' everydayness. First, the repertoire from which the parables draw their stock of images is the repertoire of common folk—the peasant—of first-century Palestinian Judaism. The parables can even be divided into three groups based on this common life pattern. In the first group, "Family, Village, City, and Beyond," the parables employ the horizontal structure of society, the map of the world of social relations used to identify insiders and outsiders. A second group, "Masters and Servants," exhibit the vertical or hierarchical pattern of society in the patron-client model, a primary way of organizing social interchange in the ancient world. Finally, in the third group, "Home and Farm," the artifacts of everyday life are subsumed into the parabolic world.

There is yet a second aspect of the everyday in the parables. Jesus' parables seldom invoke aspects of the first-century world that would parallel the expectations of the kingdom. To put it more prosaically, the standard character in a Jesus parable is simply an anonymous man, or as Luke prefers, a "certain man." Absent are the vast number of king parables of rabbinic Judaism, which are surely more appropriate if the parable is to be laid beside something kingly. Only one parable has a king as a character, and in that parable the king behaves in a way that upon reflection is completely contrary to the expectations concerning a God/king. Even further, the parables do not invoke the fantasy world of the peasant. The world of the parables is one of sons who get lost and get angry, of stewards who cheat, of masters whose reputation is that they harvest where they do not sow, of widows who beat down a judge who cares not about justice, of fig trees that do not bear, of a harvest that is very average, of an absentee landlord whose tenants kill his son. Such is the world of a first-century peasant, and it is deemed an appropriate description in parable of the kingdom.

The unclean is the second coordinate of the narrative world of the parable. It has found little voice in parable criticism and for the most part has been ignored because it does not belong to the signified of the kingdom. And yet it is an important and obvious coordinate, if only we have ears. The archetype of the unclean is The Leaven. The Jewish scholar Abrahams exemplifies the problem of perceiving the unclean as a coordinate of the parable. He states that the parable The Leaven must be the one instance in the ancient world where leaven is used to signify the holy and the perfect, even though he surely knows that in the tradition of Israel unleaven is the symbol of the perfect and the holy.[2] The unclean surfaces in still other ways. A woman hides the leaven: this baking is not a family enterprise as would normally be expected. Women are hidden in other parables. In A Man Had Two Sons, the prodigal's father behaves much more like a mother in his constant forgiveness and nurture of the two sons; he refuses to defend his male honor, which both sons insult. A widow wears down the judge; a woman, not a man, searches diligently for a small coin; and the various harvest themes certainly suggest female fertility. The harvest is yet more pregnant when it bears fruit by itself (*automatē*), in contrast to the lazy farmer who sleeps and rises night and day as "the seed grows he knows

2. See chap. 15 above.

not how" (Mark 4:27). The unclean surfaces in other aspects of the parables: a dishonest steward is commended for his prudence; Lazarus, the beggar, is in the bosom of Abraham; the last-hired, those who have worked only an hour and may be the village bums, are made equal to those who have borne the heat of the day; the mustard seed is planted in a garden; the banquet is no longer for the elite but for those who dwell in the streets; the treasure corrupts its finder; the publican goes home justified; and the Samaritan comes to the rescue of the man in the ditch while the priest and Levite remain ritually clean.

Miracle, the third coordinate, is the most problematic. It is the one narrative coordinate predicted by the signified of the kingdom, and it should be a chief one. And yet its appearance in the parables is muted. Miracle threatens, on the one hand, to overcome the everyday and blot out the unclean. On the other hand, it threatens to make of the kingdom the superordinary and the holy. The archetype of miracle in the parabolic narrative is A Sower Went Out. The miracle is in the harvest—that it happens after so much failure. Miracle appears subdued in other parables. In The Leaven it is the three measures, an immense amount of bread, and a reference to the oaks of Mamre (Gen. 18:1); the Samaritan takes care of the man in the ditch; the father does take back both sons; the man does fill his hall for the banquet; the steward is commended; the widow is cared for; the man who owns the vineyard continues in the parable to give the tenants yet another chance; and the lands of a rich man create such a bounty that he must tear down his barns and build new ones.

These parables, with their three coordinates, are laid beside the symbol of the kingdom of God. This laying-beside generates tension and consternation in the parables' interpretation because the kingdom of God is a known quantity, both then and now. As a symbol its content is *nebula,* known yet waiting to be filled with content. The symbol of the kingdom of God raises certain expectations connected with kingdom, kings, and God. But of the parables' three coordinates, only one coincides with the expectations of the kingdom. The symbol of the kingdom of God invokes the myth of God's ruling over the world and restoring that world to his chosen people. The power of myth is its ability to resolve fundamental conflicts in our experience. The mythemes that make up the myth that supports the kingdom of God are all those stories that explain how God will triumph over the vicissitudes of our experience.

The myth resolves an implied disjunction between the promises of God and everyday life. The story in 2 Maccabees of a mother and her seven sons who are martyred because they refuse to violate the laws of their ancestors dramatically portrays the situation that gives rise to the apocalyptic myth. The persecution of the just for their righteousness points to a radical disjunction between the expectations of God's power in the present and its actuality. The apocalyptic myth resolves this tension with the story of a future redeemer or messiah who will restore the age of holiness or of another world to which one can escape. A less radical tension is present in the everyday world when the faithful confront the disjunctive and difficult mysteries of ordinary veniality. Why do bad things happen to good people? The wisdom myth meets this challenge, especially in proverbs, by making a whole out of life. The proverb transmits in summary form the wisdom of bygone sages on how to cope with life. Both the apocalyptic and wisdom myths seek to resolve a fundamental dilemma of Israel's life; both are inheritances of the Hebrew Bible. As a land occupied by the Romans, Israel faced Job's problem: Was the occupation divine punishment that called for a more moral life of repentance, or was it simply evil imposed from the outside awaiting divine release? The wisdom and apocalyptic myths in their various ways resolve this fundamental conflict.

These conflicts were a part of Jesus' world, and he could not escape them. Actually he faced them head-on in his parables, both negatively and positively. To put it boldly, Jesus was both antiwisdom and antiapocalyptic, although ironically the tradition confessed him as both rabbi and messiah. Both apocalyptic and wisdom seek to resolve the tension between our experience of life and our expectations of God's sovereignty. Wisdom invokes the fantasy of the perfect life, and apocalyptic dreams the fantasy of a future world or another world. The parables over and over again reject both of these options. They depict a world of everyday veniality, at times tragic and unclean, with miracle muted or hidden. The three coordinates of the parabolic world have as one of their points a denial of the wisdom and apocalyptic solutions. The Land of a Rich Man makes these points deftly. The harvest is so superabundant that the man decides to build all new barns to hold the harvest. As a wise man his task is how to manage this blessing for the good of the community. But he turns out to be a fool and dies in his sleep. There is no apocalyptic judgment that rights his error. There is no vindication. The kingdom is identified not with wise decisions or apocalyptic vindication but rather with the passing of ordinary time. God intervenes but not so as anyone would notice.

Are the parables simply anti, simply against? Do they propose a positive stance? Their positive stance is in their vision of the king who is missing from the world of the parable. The God of the parables is one who engages in a radical solidarity with folks. In A Man Entrusts Property, the two servants who double their investment do so regardless of how they imagine the master. The third servant, with his image of a hardhearted master, freezes in fear. In A King Wished to Settle Accounts, the king's initial forgiveness of a huge debt sets on course a world of forgiveness and mercy, which is wrecked by both the first servant's and his fellowservants' refusals to forgive. If the world is a place of vindication and punishment, it is because we do not forgive. In A Man Planted a Vineyard, the master continues to send his servants and his son in hope, perhaps a foolish one, that the tenants will respond. In the world of the parable the standards are askew from the standards of the everyday world. A master commends a dishonest steward, a widow is relieved by a dishonest judge, and a sluggard farmer has a harvest. Perhaps Jesus is a throwback to an older view in Israel, that of the prophets. But his God identifies with common folk, in solidarity with them.

The parables are only one aspect of the artifacts that remain of Jesus. Other aspects of the Jesus tradition need to be investigated. I have already tried tentatively to conduct this investigation in a previous work,[3] which logically should have been written after this one. But like the parable, life is not always logical. Yet there is nothing in that earlier investigation that contradicts what I have just written—only I have written at present, I hope, somewhat more clearly. The wonderworking tradition needs to be examined afresh. Perhaps the exorcisms and healings are, like the parables, the places in action where one meets solidarity with God. But much remains to be done on that point.

It has been said that a teller of parables, one who deals only in words, could not develop antagonism sufficient to warrant somebody's killing him. This completely undervalues the power of language. One need only point to the prophets or to Socrates to see that the ancient world feared the power of language. The threat of the parable is that it subverts the myths that sustain our world and force us to see a world with which God is in solidarity. The death and resurrection of Jesus are the Christian test of the parable. Do the death and resurrection invoke some new wisdom, apocalyptic, or gnostic myth? Or in Jesus' death, with Mark's centurion, do we see God's solidarity with our life and death?

It is appropriate that the parable is so identified with Jesus. The parable gives the appearance of being a simple story. The rabbis were well aware of the parable's trivial appearance, and they warned against looking down on it. For them the parable's father was Solomon, but even more important, the parable was a handle on the Torah. Referring

---

3. Scott, *Jesus, Symbol-Maker.*

to the parable as a "handle" involves in Hebrew an elaborate wordplay based upon Eccles. 12:9.[4] The same Hebrew root (*a-z-n*) for "weighing" or "pondering" also means, by extension, a "handle." So since Solomon taught the people the meaning of the Torah by weighing and studying many parables, so those parables became handles for the Torah. What in appearance is very trivial—the parable—becomes important in exposing the treasures of the Torah. It is appropriate that Jesus be remembered as a teller of parables, because their very triviality matches major coordinates of his parables—the everyday, the unclean, and the muted miracle. The parable is ironically appropriate for the kingdom; the epic would be inappropriate. Finally, the challenge of the parable is to hear, to listen. The root and primary meaning of the Hebrew word for "handle" is "ear," since the ears are the handles of the head and it is only by extension that the word means "handle." So Solomon made handles for the Torah and Jesus made handles for the kingdom. The challenge remains the same: "Hear then the parable."

4. See pp. 52–54 above for a detailed explanation of the wordplay.

Glossary

Amoraim. Those rabbis active in making commentaries on the *Mishnah* from the third to sixth century C.E. They are the rabbis active during the formation of the *Talmud*s. See also *Tannaim*.

Chiasmus. The arrangement of parallel phrases, sentences, and even larger units in such a way that they are inverted to create a X. The term is derived from the shape of the Greek letter chi (X).

Connotation. The functioning of a sign so that it has "soft focus" or "blurred edges," because the *signified* is secondary to the expected *signified*. It appeals to the imagination and belongs to the symbolic and metaphoric dimension of language. Contrasted with *Denotation*.

Consistency Building. The effort of a reader to make sense of a narrative, to form the parts of a narrative system into a consistent viewpoint. By this means the reader reconstructs a textual world, and thus consistency building is the basis for identification with the textual world.

Defamiliarization. The strategy of art forms (verbal, visual, and aural) to destroy the anesthetic power of the everyday so as to allow the new to break through. The receiver of the artistic image is presented with a deconstructing element in the everyday that will block the use of everyday paradigms to make sense (*Consistency Building*) of the message.

Denotation. The functioning of a sign so that it is clear, precise, logical, and unambiguous because its *Signified* has a clear reference to concrete things, personages, events, situations, or ideas. Contrasted with *Connotation*.

Dyadic. The dominant personality type of the first century C.E., in which one's worth, values, and so forth are determined by the significant others in one's life. There is great pressure to comform to socially held values, with strong corporate identity and clear distinctions between in-group and out-group, there being sharp boundaries separating the two. Contrasted with the individualistic style of society in the United States.

Gaps. The indeterminacies that exist in narration. This creates an asymmetry between reader and text that gives rise to the reading process. It is by filling in the gaps that a reader constructs the textual world, makes meaning of a text, and thus eventually forms a consistent textual reality.

Ideology. The most basic element in a point of view. It is the value system that supports the way of viewing the world or the conceptual system that supports the values of the text.

Implied Reader. A textual function that embodies all those functions necessary to read a text. It is implied because it is the reading function implied by the text. It is contrasted with the implied author, and is sometimes referred to as the implied audience or hearer. It should not be confused with real readers, who will implement the role of the implied reader in a variety of ways.

Inclusio. A rhetorical device in which the beginning and ending of an element (clause, sentence, paragraph, or the like) are similar.

Intertextuality. The referencing of one text by another text. Frequently this is not in the form of a direct quotation but is achieved by allusion, echoing, reversal of theme, image, and so forth.

Langue. The system of language itself. It is a theoretic construct and is social in nature, not individualistic. The basic model of the system of language is the sign. Contrasted with *Parole*.

Metaphorical Structure (Network). The systematic interconnections and implications of a metaphor.

Midrash. The rabbinic exegesis either on the Mishnah, to discover the rule, or on Scripture, to discover the theological truth.

Mishnah. The corpus of traditional rabbinic laws codified around 200 C.E. It in turn was the basis for further reflection and discussion that led to the Babylonian and Jerusalem *Talmud*s.

Mytheme. The bundles or sets of traditional narrative elements that are combined by myth tellers to form a coherent mythical story. Mythemes are part of the *Repertoire* of a cultural system.

Originating Structure. Exists at the level of *Langue*. It contains those features that would account for the subsequent performances (*Parole*) of the parable's structure. It is contrasted with *ipsissima verba*—an effort of an older methodology to discover the very words of the parable.

Parataxis. A characteristic of the *Surface Structure* in which clauses are not subordinated but strung together by simple connectives. It is typical of oral speech.

Parole. The actual performance of a speech act. Contrasted with *Langue*.

Performance. The dynamic process that produces an extant text. This involves the *Originating Structure*, the skills and *Ideology* of the performer, the concrete situation of the performance, and the real or expected interaction of the audience.

Point of view. The perspective or prism by which a text is mediated. This is frequently represented by the narrator. Other characters will support or challenge this point of view.

Repertoire. The familiar literary themes and patterns as well as the social matrix that an author uses to build up the phenomenal world of a literary text. It is the bridge to the outside, extratextual, world, and it makes the text seem real to the reader.

Semiotics. The study of the systems of signs. It views the communication act as a formal system, tracing out the basic relations between sign, *signifier*, and *signified*.

Signifier/Signified. Two main components of the sign. The *signifier* is the physical component of the sign, the soundword. The *signified* is the conceptual element. Louis Hjelmslev and others have referred to these as expression (*signifier*) and content (*signified*). It is the relation between these two that is the sign.

Surface Structure. The arrangement of *Signifier*s into sentences and larger rhetorical units.

Talmud. Commentaries on the *Mishnah* produced between 200 and 600 C.E. There are two *Talmud*s. The Jerusalem *Talmud* was redacted in Israel around 400 C.E., and the Babylonian *Talmud* was redacted around 600 C.E.

Tannaim. The group of rabbis active between the beginning of the Common Era and the formation of the *Mishnah* (ca. 220 C.E.).

Targum. Translations or paraphrases of the Hebrew Bible into Aramaic. These were the popular texts used in the synagogue.

Tosephta. A rabbinic collection of supplementary rules to the *Mishnah*. Its date and exact relation to the *Mishnah* are highly debated.

Verisimilitude. The ability of a text to convince the reader that the fictional world is a real world.

Bibliography

Short References to Translations

Braude
: *The Midrash on Psalms*. Trans. William Braude. 2 vols. Yale Judaica Series. New Haven: Yale Univ. Press, 1959.

Charlesworth
: *The Old Testament Pseudepigrapha*. Ed. James Charlesworth. 2 vols. Garden City, N.Y.: Doubleday & Co., 1983–85.

Danby
: *The Mishnah*. Trans. Herbert Danby. Oxford: At the Clarendon Press, 1933.

Freedman
: *Midrash Rabbah*. Trans. H. Freedman and Maurice Simon. 10 vols. London: Soncino Press, 1939.

Goldin
: *The Fathers according to Rabbi Nathan*. Trans. Judah Goldin. Yale Judaica Series. New Haven: Yale Univ. Press, 1955.

Gos. Thom.
: *The Gospel of Thomas*. Trans. Thomas O. Lambdin. In *The Nag Hammadi Library*, Ed. James M. Robinson, 118–30. San Francisco: Harper & Row, 1977.

LCL
: Loeb Classical Library. Cambridge: Harvard Univ. Press; London: William Heinemann.

Neusner
: *The Talmud of the Land of Israel*. Trans. Jacob Neusner. 35 vols. Chicago: Univ. of Chicago Press, 1983–.

Soncino
: *The Babylonian Talmud*. Ed. I. Epstein. 16 vols. London: Soncino Press, 1961.

Abbreviations

BAGD
: Walter Bauer, W. F. Arndt, F. W. Gingrich, and F. W. Danker. *Greek-English*

431

Lexicon of the New Testament. 2d ed., rev. and aug. Gingrich and Danker from the 5th Ger. ed. of Bauer, 1958. Chicago: Univ. of Chicago Press, 1979.

BDB

Francis Brown, S. R. Driver, and Charles A. Briggs. *Hebrew and English Lexicon of the Old Testament.* Oxford: At the Clarendon Press, 1907.

BDF

F. Blass, A. Debrunner, and Robert Funk. *A Greek Grammar of the New Testament.* Chicago: Univ. of Chicago Press, 1961.

EncJud

Encyclopaedia Judaica. 16 vols. Jerusalem: MacMillan Co., 1971.

JPFC

The Jewish People in the First Century. Ed. S. Safari and M. Stern. 2 vols. Compendia Rerum Iudaicarum ad Novum Testamentum. Philadelphia: Fortress Press; Assen: Van Gorcum, 1974.

LSJ

Henry Liddell and Robert Scott. *A Greek-English Lexicon.* Revised H. S. Jones. Oxford: At the Clarendon Press, 1925–40.

Str-B

Hermann Strack and Paul Billerbeck. *Kommentar zum Neuen Testament aus Talmud und Midrasch.* 5 vols. Munich: C. H. Beck'sche Verlagsbuchhandlung, 1956.

TDNT

Theological Dictionary of the New Testament. Ed. Gerhard Kittel. Trans. Geoffrey Bromiley. 9 vols. Grand Rapids: Wm. B. Eerdmans, 1964–74.

Translations and Texts

Ancient Near Eastern Texts. Ed. James Pritchard. Princeton: Princeton Univ. Press, 1955.

The Apocrypha and Pseudepigrapha of the Old Testament. Ed. R. H. Charles. Oxford: At the Clarendon Press, 1913.

Clemens Alexandrinus, Stromata Buch I-VI. Ed. Otto Stählin. Vol. 2. Berlin: Akademie-Verlag, 1960.

The Ethiopic Book of Enoch. Trans. Michael A. Knibb. 2 vols. Oxford: Oxford Univ. Press, 1978.

Mekilta de-Rabbi Ishmael. Ed. and trans. J. Z. Lauterbach. 3 vols. Philadelphia: Jewish Pub. Soc., 1933–35.

The Nag Hammadi Library. Ed. James M. Robinson. San Francisco: Harper & Row, 1977.

Neophyti 1, Genesis. Ed. A. P. Machjo. Madrid: Consejo superior de investigaciones scientificas, 1968.

New Testament Apocrypha. Ed. E. Hennecke and W. Schneemelcher. 2 vols. Philadelphia: Westminster Press, 1965.

Novum Testamentum Graece. Ed. Eberhard Nestle, Erwin Nestle, Kurt Aland, et al. 26th ed. Stuttgart: Deutsche Bibelstiftung, 1979.

Origen, *Commentaris secundum Matthaeum: Patrologiae cursus completus . . . series graeca* 13: cols. 1342–46. Paris: J. P. Migne, 1957.

Pauline Parallels. Ed. Fred O. Francis and J. Paul Sampley. Foundations and Facets. Philadelphia: Fortress Press, 1984.

Pirke de Rabbi Eliezer. Trans. G. Friedlander. London: Kegan, Trench, Trubner & Co., 1916.

Sayings Parallels. Ed. John Dominic Crossan. Foundations and Facets. Philadelphia: Fortress Press, 1986.

The Talmud of Babylonia, Tractate Berakhot. Ed. Jacob Neusner. Brown Judaic Studies 78. Chico, Calif.: Scholars Press, 1984.

The Targums of Onkelos and Jonathan ben Uzziel. Ed. W. Etherdidge. New York: Ktav, 1968.

Thirteen Satires of Juvenal. Ed. J. E. B. Mayor. London: Macmillan & Co., 1886.

The Works of Aristotle. Vol. 11, *Rhetorica.* Trans. W. Rhys Roberts. Oxford: At the Clarendon Press, 1927.

Secondary Works

Abrahams, I. *Studies in Pharisaism and the Gospels.* Library of Biblical Studies. New York: Ktav, 1967 (1917, 1924).

Achtemeier, Paul. *Mark.* Proclamation Commentaries. Philadelphia: Fortress Press, 1975.

Alter, Robert. *The Art of Biblical Narrative.* New York: Basic Books, 1981.

Ammons, A. R. "A Poem Is a Walk." *Epoch* 18 (1968): 115.

Anderson, Hugh. *The Gospel of Mark.* New Century Bible. Grand Rapids: Wm. B. Eerdmans, 1976.

Apostle, H. *The Nicomachean Ethics.* Boston and Dordrecht: D. Reidel Pub. Co., 1975.

Bailey, Kenneth. *Poet and Peasant.* Grand Rapids: Wm. B. Eerdmans, 1976.

———. *Through Peasant Eyes.* Grand Rapids: Wm. B. Eerdmans, 1980.

Ballard, P. "Reasons for Refusing the Great Supper." *Journal of Theological Studies* 23 (1972): 341–50.

Balz, Horst. "*phobeō.*" *TDNT* 9:205–19.

Bammel, Ernst. "Das Gleichnis von den bösen Winzern (Mk 12, 1–9)." *Revue internationale des droits de l'antiquité* 6 (1959): 11–17.

———. "*ptōchos.*" *TDNT* 6:885–915.

Barth, Markus. "The Dishonest Steward and His Lord: Reflections on Luke 16:1–13." In *From Faith to Faith: Essays in Honor of Donald G. Miller on His Seventieth Birthday*, ed. Dikran Y. Hadidian. Pittsburgh: Pickwick Press, 1979.

Bauer, Johannes. "Gnadelohn oder Tageslohn?" *Biblica* 42 (1961): 224–28.

———. "Synoptic Tradition in the Gospel of Thomas." In *Studia Evangelica* 3: 314–17. Texte und Untersuchungen 88. Berlin: Akademie-Verlag, 1964.

Bauernfeind, Otto. "*sapros.*" *TDNT* 7:94–97.

Bauman, Richard. *Verbal Art as Performance.* Rowley, Mass.: Newbury House Pubs., 1977.

Baumgartner, Walter. *Lexicon in Veteris Testamenti Libros*. Leiden: E. J. Brill, 1958.

Beardslee, William. "The Uses of Proverbs in the Synoptic Gospels." *Interpretation* 24 (1970): 61–76.

Beare, Frank. *The Gospel according to Matthew*. San Francisco: Harper & Row, 1981.

Bearvery, R. "La route romaine de Jerusalem à Jericho." *Revue biblique* 64 (1957): 72–114.

Behm, Johannes. "*deipon, deipneō*." *TDNT* 2:34–35.

————. "*metanoeō*." *TDNT* 4:975–1008.

Betz, Hans Dieter. *Galatians*. Hermeneia. Philadelphia: Fortress Press, 1979.

Binder, Hans. "Das Gleichnis vom barmherzigen Samariter." *Theologische Zeitschrift* 15 (1959): 176–94.

Birdsall, J. "Luke XII, 16ff. and the Gospel of Thomas." *Journal of Theological Studies* 13 (1962): 332–36.

Bishop, E. F. F. "The Parable of the Lost or Wandering Sheep." *Anglican Theological Review* 44 (1962): 44–57.

Black, Matthew. *Aramaic Approach to the Gospels and Acts*. 2d ed. Oxford: At the Clarendon Press, 1954.

Bornkamm, Günther. "End-Expectation and Church in Matthew." In *Tradition and Interpretation in Matthew*, 15–51. Philadelphia: Westminster Press; London: SCM Press, 1963.

————. "*presbys*." *TDNT* 6:651–83.

————. "Die Verzögerung Parusie." In *Geschichte und Glaube* 1:46–55. Munich: Chr. Kaiser, 1968.

Boucher, Madeleine. *The Mysterious Parable: A Literary Study*. Catholic Biblical Quarterly Monograph Series 6. Washington, D.C.: Catholic Biblical Assn. of America, 1977.

Bousset, Wilhelm. *Jesus*. Trans. Penrose. New York and London, 1911.

Bouttier, M. "Les paraboles du maître dans la tradition synoptique." *Etudes théologiques et religieuses* 48 (1973): 176–95.

Bovon, F. *Luc le théologien*. Paris: Delachaux & Niestlé Spes, 1978.

Breech, James. "Kingdom of God and the Parables of Jesus." *Semeia* 12 (1978): 15–40.

————. *The Silence of Jesus: The Authentic Voice of the Historical Jesus*. Philadelphia: Fortress Press, 1983.

Bremond, Claude. "The Logic of Narrative Possibilities." *New Literary History* 11 (1980): 387–411.

Breukelmann, F. H. "Eine Erklärung des Gleichnisses vom Schalksknecht (Matth. 18, 23–35)." In *Parrhesia: Karl Barth zum achtzigsten Geburtstag*, 261–87. Zurich: EVA-Verlag, 1966.

Brightman, F. E. "Six Notes." *Journal of Theological Studies* 29 (1928): 158–61.

Brown, Raymond. *The Gospel according to John*. 2 vols. Anchor Bible. Garden City, N.Y.: Doubleday & Co., 1966–70.

Bruyne, Donatien de. "Chasma (Lc. 16,26)." *Revue biblique* 30 (1921): 400–405.

Büchsel, Friedrich. "*hilaskomai*." *TDNT* 3:301–17.

Bultmann, Rudolf. *History of the Synoptic Tradition.* Trans. J. Marsh. New York: Harper & Row, 1963.

————. *Theology of the New Testament.* Trans. Kendrick Grobel. 2 vols. New York: Charles Scribner's Sons, 1955.

Burton, E. *Syntax of the Moods and Tenses in New Testament Greek.* 5th ed. Chicago: Univ. of Chicago Press, 1903.

Cadbury, Henry. "A Proper Name for Dives." *Journal of Biblical Literature* 81 (1962): 399–402.

Cadoux, A. T. *The Parables of Jesus: Their Art and Use.* London: James Clarke & Co.

Cameron, Ron. "Parable and Interpretation in the Gospel of Thomas." *Forum* 2/2 (1986): 3–40.

Carlston, Charles. *Parables of the Triple Tradition.* Philadelphia: Fortress Press, 1975.

————. "Reminiscence and Redaction in Luke 15:11–32." *Journal of Biblical Literature* 94 (1975): 368–90.

Catchpole, David. "Q and 'The Friend at Midnight.'" *Journal of Theological Studies* 34 (1983): 407–24.

————. "The Son of Man's Search for Faith (Luke XVIII 8b)." *Novum Testamentum* 19 (1977): 81–104.

Cave, C. "Lazarus and the Lukan Deuteronomy." *New Testament Studies* 15 (1969): 319–25.

Cerfaux, L. "Les paraboles du royaume dans l'évangile de Thomas." *Muséon* 70 (1957): 307–27.

Chajes, C. "Les juges juifs en Palestine." *Revue des études juives* 39 (1892): 39–52.

Chatman, Seymour. *Story and Discourse.* Ithaca, N.Y.: Cornell Univ. Press, 1978.

Chilton, Bruce. *A Galilean Rabbi and His Bible.* Wilmington, Del.: Michael Glazier, 1984.

————. *God Is Strength.* Studien zur Umwelt des Neuen Testaments B1. Freistadt: Verlag F. Plöchl, 1979.

————. "REGNUM DEI DEUS EST." *Scottish Journal of Theology* 31 (1978): 261–70.

————, ed. *The Kingdom of God.* Issues in Religion and Theology 5. Philadelphia: Fortress Press, 1984.

Clements, R. *Isaiah 1—39.* New Century Bible. Grand Rapids: Wm. B. Eerdmans, 1980.

Cohen, H. "Bet Din and Judges." *EncJud* 2:721–23.

————. "Widows." *EncJud* 16:487–96.

Collins, Douglas. "The Found Object." *The Willamette Journal* 1 (1983): 43–74.

Conley, Thomas. "The Enthymeme in Perspective." *Quarterly Journal of Speech* 70 (1984): 168–87.

Conzelmann, Hans. *First Corinthians.* Trans. James Leitch. Hermeneia. Philadelphia: Fortress Press, 1975.

————. *Jesus.* Trans. Raymond Lord. Philadelphia: Fortress Press, 1973.

———. *The Theology of St. Luke.* Trans. Geoffrey Busell. Philadelphia: Fortress Press, 1982 (1960).

Cope, Lamar. *Matthew: A Scribe Trained for the Kingdom of Heaven.* Catholic Biblical Quarterly Monograph Series 5. Washington, D.C.: Catholic Biblical Assn. of America, 1976.

Creed, John. *The Gospel according to St. Luke.* London: Macmillan & Co., 1930.

Crenshaw, James. *Samson: A Secret Betrayed, a Vow Ignored.* Atlanta: John Knox Press, 1978.

Crespy, Georges. "The Parable of the Good Samaritan: An Essay in Structural Research." *Semeia* 2 (1974): 27–50.

Crossan, John Dominic. *Cliffs of Fall.* New York: Seabury Press, 1980.

———. *Finding Is the First Act.* Semeia Supplements. Philadelphia: Fortress Press; Missoula, Mont.: Scholars Press, 1979.

———. "The Good Samaritan: Towards a Generic Definition of Parable." *Semeia* 2 (1974): 82–112

———. *In Parables: The Challenge of the Historical Jesus.* New York: Harper & Row, 1973.

———. "Literary Criticism and Biblical Hermeneutics." *Journal of Religion* 57 (1977): 76–80.

———. "Parable and Example in the Teaching of Jesus." *Semeia* 1 (1974): 63–104.

———. *Raid on the Articulate: Cosmic Eschatology in Jesus and Borges.* New York: Harper & Row, 1976.

———. "The Servant Parables of Jesus." *Semeia* 1 (1974): 17–62.

———. "Structuralist Analysis and the Parables of Jesus." *Semeia* 1 (1974): 192–221.

Crum, Walter. *Coptic Dictionary.* Oxford: At the Clarendon Press, 1939.

Culler, Jonathan. *Structuralist Poetics.* Ithaca, N.Y.: Cornell Univ. Press, 1975.

Curtis, W. "The Parable of the Labourers, Matt. XX, 1–16." *Expository Times* 38 (1926–27): 6–10.

Dahl, Nils. "The Parables of Growth." *Studia Theologica* 5 (1951): 132–66. Reprinted in Dahl's *Jesus in the Memory of the Early Church,* 141–66. Minneapolis: Augsburg Pub. House, 1976.

Dalman, Gustav. *Jesus-Jeshua: Studies in the Gospels.* Trans. Paul P. Levertoff. New York: Macmillan Co., 1929.

———. *The Words of Jesus Considered in the Light of Post-Biblical Jewish Writings and the Aramaic Language.* Trans. Kay. Edinburgh: T. & T. Clark, 1902.

Daniels, C. "Les esseniens et l'arrière-fond historique de la parabole du bon Samaritain." *Novum Testamentum* 11 (1969): 71–104.

Danker, F. W. *Jesus and the New Age.* St. Louis: Clayton Pub. House, 1972.

Daube, David. "Inheritance in Two Lukan Pericopes." *Zeitschrift der Savigny-Stiftung für Rechtsgeschichte* 72 (1955): 326–34.

Davies, Stevan. *Gospel of Thomas and Christian Wisdom.* New York: Seabury Press, 1983.

Dehandshutter, Boudewijn. "The Gospel of Thomas and the Synoptics: The Status Quaestionis." *Studia Evangelica* 7:157–60. Texte und Untersuchungen 162. Berlin: Akademie-Verlag, 1982.

_____. "La parabole de la perle (Mt 13, 45–46) et l'évangile selon Thomas." *Ephemerides theologicae lovanienses* 55 (1979): 243–65.

Deidun, Thomas. "The Parable of the Unmerciful Servant." *Biblical Theology Bulletin* 6 (1976): 203–24.

Deitzelbinger, C. "Das Gleichnis von der erlassenen Schuld: Eine theologische Untersuchung von Matthäus 18, 23–35." *Evangelische Theologie* 32 (1972): 437–51.

Delling, G. "Das Gleichnis vom gottlosen Richter." *Zeitschrift für die neutestamentliche Wissenschaft* 53 (1962): 1–25.

Derrett, J. D. "Fresh Light on St. Luke XVI:11: Dives and Lazarus and the Preceding Sayings." *New Testament Studies* 7 (1961): 364–80.

_____. "Fresh Light on the Lost Sheep and the Lost Coin." *New Testament Studies* 26 (1979): 36–60.

_____. *Law in the New Testament*. London: Darton, Longman & Todd, 1970.

_____. "Law in the New Testament: The Parable of the Unjust Judge." *New Testament Studies* 18 (1971–72): 178–91.

_____. "The Rich Fool: A Parable of Jesus concerning Inheritance." *Heythrop Journal* 18 (1977): 131–51.

_____. "Workers in the Vineyard: A Parable of Jesus." *Journal of Jewish Studies* 25 (1974): 64–91.

Dewey, Joanna. *Markan Public Debate: Literary Technique, Concentric Structure, and Theology in Mark 2:1—3:6*. Society of Biblical Literature Dissertation Series 48. Chico, Calif.: Scholars Press, 1980.

Diaz, May. "Economic Relations in Peasant Society." In *Peasant Society: A Reader*, ed. Jack Potter, May Diaz, and George Foster, 50–56. Boston: Little, Brown & Co., 1967.

Diaz, May, and Jack Potter. "The Social Life of Peasants." In *Peasant Society: A Reader*, 154–68.

Dibelius, Martin. *From Tradition to Gospel*. Trans. Bertram Woolf. New York: Charles Scribner's Sons, 1917.

Dickinson, Emily. *The Poems of Emily Dickinson*. Ed. Thomas Johnson. Cambridge: Harvard Univ. Press, Belknap Press, 1951.

Didier, M. "La parabole des talents et des mines." In *De Jesus aux évangiles* 2:248–71. Bibliotheca ephemeridum theologicarum lovaniensium 25. Gembloux: Editions J. Duculot, 1967.

_____. "La parabole du semeur." In *Au service de la parole de Dieu*, 21–41. Gembloux: Editions J. Duculot, 1969.

Dillon, Richard. "Towards a Tradition-History of the Parables of the True Israel." *Biblica* 46 (1966): 1–42.

Dodd, Charles D. *The Parables of the Kingdom*. New York: Charles Scribner's Sons, 1961.

Doeve, J. W. *Jewish Hermeneutics in the Synoptic Gospels and Acts*. Assen: Van Gorcum, 1958.

Donahue, John. *Are You the Christ? The Trial Narrative in the Gospel of Mark*. Society of Biblical Literature Dissertation Series. Missoula, Mont.: Scholars Press, 1973.

Donfried, Karl. "The Allegory of the Ten Virgins (Mt 25.1–13) as a Summary of Matthean Theology." *Journal of Biblical Literature* 93 (1974): 415–28.

Drury, John. *The Parables in the Gospels: History and Allegory.* New York: Crossroad, 1985.

Duling, Dennis. "Norman Perrin and the Kingdom of God: Review and Response." *Journal of Religion* 64 (1984): 484–500.

Dundes, Alan. "On the Structure of the Proverb." In *Analytic Essays in Folklore,* 103–18. Studies in Folklore 2. The Hague: Mouton, 1975.

Dunkerley, R. "Lazarus." *New Testament Studies* 5 (1958–59): 321–27.

Dupont, J. "Les ouvriers de la vigne." *Assemblées du Seigneur* 22 (1965): 28–51.

_____. "Les paraboles du trésor et de la perle." *New Testament Studies* 14 (1968): 408–18.

Dussaud, R. "Comptes d'ouvriers d'une entreprise funeraire juif." *Syria* 4 (1924): 230–56.

Duvallier, Jean. "La parabole du trésor et les droits orientaux." *Revue internationale des droits de l'antiquite'* 4 (1957): 107–15.

Easton. B. S. *The Gospel according to St. Luke.* Edinburgh: T. & T. Clark, 1926.

Eco, Umberto. *Semiotics and the Philosophy of Language.* Bloomington: Indiana Univ. Press, 1984.

_____. *A Theory of Semiotics.* Bloomington: Indiana Univ. Press, 1979.

Edwards, Richard. *A Theology of Q: Eschatology, Prophecy, and Wisdom.* Philadelphia: Fortress Press, 1976.

Einstadt, S., and L. Roniger. "Patron-Client Relations as a Model of Structuring Social Exchange." *Comparative Studies in Society and History* 22 (1980): 42–77.

Eissfeldt, Otto. *Der Mashal im Alten Testament.* Beihefte zur Zeitschrift für die alttestamentliche Wissenschaft 24. Giessen: Alfred Töpelmann, 1913.

Ellis, Earl. "La fonction de l'eschatologie dans Luc." In *L'évangile de Luc,* ed. Franz Neirynck, 141–55. Bibliotheca ephemeridum theologicarum lovaniensium 32. Gembloux: Editions J. Duculot, 1974.

_____. *The Gospel of Luke.* New Century Bible. Grand Rapids: Wm. B. Eerdmanns, 1981.

Entrevernes Group. *Signs and Parables.* Pittsburgh Theological Monograph Series. Pittsburgh: Pickwick Press, 1978.

Ernst, Josef. *Das Evangelium nach Lukas.* Regensburger Neues Testament. Regensburg: Friedrich Pustet, 1976.

Evans, C. A. "A Note on the Function of Isaiah, VI, 9–10 in Mark IV." *Revue biblique* 88 (1981): 234–35.

_____. "On the Isaianic Background of the Sower Parable." *Catholic Biblical Quarterly* 47 (1985): 464–68.

Farmer, William. *The Synoptic Problem.* New York: Macmillan & Co., 1964.

Feldmann, Asher. *The Parables and Similes of the Rabbis.* Cambridge: At the Univ. Press, 1927.

Fiebig, Paul. *Altjüdische Gleichnisse und die Gleichnisse Jesu.* Tübingen and Leipzig: J. C. B. Mohr (Paul Siebeck), 1904.

Fischel, Henry. "Epicureanism." *EncJud* 6:817.

Fishbane, Michael. "Torah and Tradition." In *Tradition and Theology in the Old Testament*, ed. Douglas Knight, 275–300. Philadelphia: Fortress Press, 1977.

Fitzmyer, Joseph. *The Gospel according to Luke*. 2 vols. Anchor Bible. Garden City, N.Y.: Doubleday & Co., 1981.

―――. "The Story of the Dishonest Manager (Lk 16:1–13)." *Theological Studies* 25 (1964): 23–42.

Fletcher, R. "The Riddle of the Unjust Steward: Is Irony the Key?" *Journal of Biblical Literature* 82 (1963): 15–30.

Förster. W. "*asōtōs*." *TDNT* 1:506–7.

―――. "*diabellō*." *TDNT* 2:71.

―――. "Das Gleichnis von den anvertrauten Pfunden." In *Verbi Dei Manet in Aeternum*, 37–56. Witten: Luther-Verlag, 1953.

―――. "*kyrios*." *TDNT* 3:1039–95.

Foster, George. "Peasant Character and Personality." In *Peasant Society: A Reader*, ed. Jack Potter, May Diaz, and George Foster, 296–300. Boston: Little, Brown & Co., 1967.

―――. "What Is a Peasant?" In *Peasant Society: A Reader*, 2–14.

Frost, Robert. *The Complete Poems of Robert Frost*. New York: Henry Holt & Co., 1959.

Fuchs, Ernst. "L'évangile et l'argent: La parabole de l'intendant intelligent." *Bulletin du Centre protestant d'études* 20 (1978): 1–14.

―――. "The Parable of the Unmerciful Servant (Matt. 18:23–35)." In *Studia Evangelica* 5:487–91. Texte und Untersuchungen 73. Berlin: Akademie-Verlag, 1959.

Fuller, Reginald. *Formation of the Resurrection Narratives*. Philadelphia: Fortress Press, 1980.

Funk, Robert W. "The Good Samaritan as Metaphor." *Semeia* 2 (1974): 74–81.

―――. *Jesus as Precursor*. Semeia Studies. Philadelphia: Fortress Press, 1975.

―――. *Language, Hermeneutics, and the Word of God*. New York: Harper & Row, 1966.

―――. *Parables and Presence*. Philadelphia: Fortress Press, 1982.

―――. "Structure in the Narrative Parables of Jesus." *Semeia* 2 (1974): 51–73.

Gärtner, Bertil. *The Theology of the Gospel according to Thomas*. New York: Harper & Row, 1961.

George, A. "Parabole." *Dictionnarie de Bible Supplement*. 6:1149–77. Paris: Librairie Letouzey et Ané Sàrl, 1960.

Gereboff, Joel. *Early Rabbinic Storytelling*. Atlanta: Scholars Press, forthcoming.

Glasson, T. F. "The Kingdom as Cosmic Catastrophe." In *Studia Evangelica* 3:187–200. Texte und Untersuchungen 88. Berlin: Akademie-Verlag, 1952.

Glombitza, Otto. "Der Perlenkaufmann." *New Testament Studies* 7 (1960–61): 153–61.

Gnilka, Joachim. *Die Verstockung Israels: Isaias 6, 9–10 in der Theologie der Synoptiker*. Munich: Kösel-Verlag, 1961.

Goodspeed, Edgar. *Problems of New Testament Translation*. Chicago: Univ. of Chicago Press, 1945.

Grant, Fredrick. "Mark." *Interpreter's Bible* 7:629–45. Nashville: Abingdon Press, 1951.

Grant, Robert, and David Freedman. *The Secret Sayings of Jesus according to the Gospel of Thomas.* Garden City, N.Y.: Doubleday & Co., 1960.

Grant, Robert, and Holt Graham. *The Apostolic Fathers.* Vol 2. Camden, N.J.: Thomas Nelson & Sons, 1965.

Grässer, Erich. *Das Problem der Parusieverzögerung in den synoptischen Evangelien und in der Apostelgeschichte.* Berlin: Alfred Töpelmann, 1960.

Gressmann, Hugo. *Von reichen Mann und armen Lazarus.* Berlin: Verlag der Königl. Akademie der Wissenschaften, 1918.

Griffith, F. *Stories of the High Priests of Memphis.* Oxford: At the Clarendon Press, 1900.

Grobel, Kendrick. *The Gospel of Truth.* London: A. & C. Black, 1960.

―――. "'. . . Whose Name Was Neves.'" *New Testament Studies* 10 (1963–64): 373–82.

Grundmann, Walter. *Das Evangelium nach Lukas.* Theologischer Handkommentar zum Neuen Testament. Berlin: Evangelische Verlangsanstalt, 1959.

Gryglewicz, F. "The Gospel of the Overworked Workers." *Catholic Biblical Quarterly* 19 (1957): 190–98.

Gundry, Robert. *Matthew: A Commentary on His Literary and Theological Art.* Grand Rapids: Wm. B. Eerdmans, 1982.

Guttmann, Theodor. *Das Mashal-Gleichnis in Tannaitischer Zeit.* Frankfurt am Main: Hermon Druckerei & Verlag, 1929.

Hadas, Moses. "Rabbinic Parallels to *Scriptores Historiae Augustae.*" In *Essays in Greco-Roman and Related Talmudic Literature,* ed. Henry Fischel, 43–47. New York: Ktav, 1977.

Haenchen, Ernst. "Das Gleichnis vom grossen Mahl." In *Die Bibel und wir,* 135–55. Tübingen: J. C. B. Mohr (Paul Siebeck), 1968.

Hahn, Ferdinand. "Das Gleichnis von der Einladung zum Festmahl." In *Verborum Veritas,* 51–82. Wuppertal: Theologischer Verlag Brockhaus, 1970.

Halévy, J. "Sens et origine de la parabole évangelique dité du bon samaritain." *Revue des études juives* 4 (1882): 249–55.

Hauck, F. *Das Evangelium des Lukas.* Theologischer Handkommentar zum Neuen Testament. Leipzig: Evangelische Verlagsanstalt, 1934.

―――. "*margaritēs.*" *TDNT* 4:472–73.

―――. "*parabolē.*" *TDNT* 5:744–61.

Hauck, F. and Siegfried Schulz. "*pornē.*" *TDNT* 6:579–95.

Haufe, Günter. "Erwähungen zum Ursprung der sogenannten Parabeltheorie Markus 4, 11–12." *Evangelische Theologie* 32 (1972): 413–21.

Hedrick, James. "Kingdom Sayings and Parables of Jesus in *The Apocryphon of James:* Tradition and Redaction." *New Testament Studies* 29 (1983): 1–24.

―――. "The Treasure Parable in Thomas and Matthew." *Forum* 2/2 (1986): 41–56.

Heichelheim, F. "Syria." In *An Economic Survey of Ancient Rome,* Ed. Tenney Frank, 4:121–258. Baltimore: Johns Hopkins Press, 1938.

Hengel, Martin. "Das Gleichnis von den Weingärtnern Mc. 12, 1–12 im Lichte der Zenonpapyri und der rabbinischen Gleichnisse." *Zeitschrift für die neutestamentliche Wissenschaft* 59 (1968): 1—39.

————. *Judaism and Hellenism*. Trans. John Bowden. 2 vols. Philadelphia: Fortress Press, 1974.

————. *Die Zeloten*. Arbeiten zur Geschichte des antiken Judentums und des Urchristentums 1. Leiden: E. J. Brill, 1961.

Hill, George. *Treasure Trove in Law and Practice*. Oxford: At the Clarendon Press, 1936.

Honig, Edwin. *Dark Conceit*. Evanston, Ill.: Northwestern Univ. Press, 1959.

Horman, John. "The Source of the Version of the Parable of the Sower in the Gospel of Thomas." *Novum Testamentum* 21 (1979): 326–43.

Hultgren, Arland. *Jesus and His Adversaries*. Minneapolis: Augsburg Pub. House, 1979.

Hunzinger, Claus. "*sinapi*." *TDNT* 7:287–91.

————. "*sukē*." *TDNT* 7:751–59.

————. "Unbekannte Gleichnisse Jesu aus dem Thomas-Evangelium." In *Judentum, Urchristentum, Kirche: Festschrift für Joachim Jeremias*, ed. Walther Eltester, 209–20. Beihefte zur Zeitschrift für die neutestamentliche Wissenschaft 26. Berlin: Alfred Töpelmann, 1960.

Iser, Wolfgang. *The Act of Reading*. Baltimore: Johns Hopkins Univ. Press, 1978.

————. *The Implied Reader*. Baltimore: Johns Hopkins Press, 1974.

Jakobson, Roman. "Aphasia as a Linguistic Problem." In *Fundamentals of Language*, 55–82. Janua Linguarum. The Hague: Mouton, 1956.

Jameson, Fredric. *The Prison-House of Language*. Princeton: Princeton Univ. Press, 1972.

Jason, Heda. *The Narrative Structure of Swindler Tales*. Rand paper. Santa Monica, Calif., 1968.

Jastrow, Marcus. *A Dictionary of the Targumin, the Talmud Babli and Yerushalmi, and the Midrashic Literature*. New York: Padres Pub. House, 1950 (1903).

Jeremias, Joachim. *The Eucharistic Words of Jesus*. Trans. Norman Perrin. London: SCM Press, 1966.

————. *Jerusalem in the Time of Jesus*. Trans. F. H. Cave and C. H. Cave. Philadelphia: Fortress Press, 1969.

————. "Palästinakundliches zum Gleichnis vom Säsemann, Mark IV.3–8 par." *New Testament Studies* 13 (1966–67): 53.

————. *The Parables of Jesus*. Trans. S. H. Hooke. New York: Charles Scribner's Sons, 1972.

————. "*poimēn*." *TDNT* 6:485–502.

————. *The Prayers of Jesus*. Trans. John Bowden. Studies in Biblical Theology, 2d ser. 6. Naperville, Ill.: Alec R. Allenson, 1967.

————. *Die Sprache des Lukasevangeliums*. Göttingen: Vandenhoeck & Ruprecht, 1980.

————. "Tradition und Redaktion in Lukas 15." *Zeitschrift für die neutestamentliche Wissenschaft* 62 (1971): 172–89.

————. "Zum Gleichnis vom verlorenen Sohn, Luke 15, 11–32." *Theologische Zeitschrift* 5 (1949): 228–31.

Jervell, Jacob. *Luke and the People of God*. Minneapolis: Augsburg Pub. House, 1979.

Johnson, A. R. *"Mashal."* In *Wisdom in Israel and the Ancient Near East*, ed. Martin North and Winton Thomas, 162–69. Supplements to Vetus Testamentum 3. Leiden: E. J. Brill, 1955.

Johnson, Luke. *The Literary Function of Possessions in Luke-Acts*. Society of Biblical Literature Dissertation Series 39. Missoula, Mont.: Scholars Press, 1977.

Johnston, Robert. "Parabolic Traditions Attributed to Tannaim." Diss. Hartford Sem., 1978.

———. "The Study of Rabbinic Parables: Some Preliminary Observations." In *Society of Biblical Literature 1976 Seminar Papers*, 337–57. Missoula, Mont.: Scholars Press, 1977.

Jones, Geraint. *The Art and Truth of the Parables*. London: SPCK, 1964.

Jülicher, Adolf. *Die Gleichnisreden Jesu*. 2 vols. Tübingen: J. C. B. Mohr (Paul Siebeck), 1910. Reprint. Darmstadt: Wissenschaftliche Buchgesellschaft, 1919.

Kafka, Franz. *Parables and Paradoxes*. New York: Schocken Books, 1961.

Kaiser, Otto. *Isaiah 1—39*. Old Testament Library. Philadelphia: Westminster Press, 1974.

Käsemann, Ernst. *Commentary on Romans*. Trans. Geoffrey Bromiley. Grand Rapids: Wm. B. Eerdmans, 1980.

———. "On Paul's Anthropology." In *Perspectives on Paul*, trans. Margaret Kohl, 1–31. Philadelphia: Fortress Press, 1971.

Katz, M. *Protection of the Weak in the Talmud*. Columbia Univ. Oriental Studies 24. New York: Columbia Univ. Press, 1925.

Kea, Perry A. "Perceiving the Mystery, Encountering the Reticence of Mark's Gospel." *Eastern Great Lakes and Midwest Biblical Societies Proceedings* 4 (1984): 181–94.

Keck, Leander. *A Future for the Historical Jesus*. Philadelphia: Fortress Press, 1981 (1971).

Kee, Howard. *Community of the New Age: Studies in Mark's Gospel*. Philadelphia: Westminster Press, 1977.

Kelber, Werner. *The Kingdom in Mark*. Philadelphia: Fortress Press, 1974.

———. *The Oral and the Written Gospel*. Philadelphia: Fortress Press, 1983.

Kennedy, A. *"Leaven."* *Encyclopaedia Biblica*, 2752–54. London: A. and C. Black, 1902.

Kermode, Frank. *The Genesis of Secrecy: On the Interpretation of Narrative*. Cambridge: Harvard Univ. Press, 1979.

Kertelge, K. "Die Funktion der 'Zwölft' im Markusevangelium." *Trierer theologische Zeitschrift* 68 (1969): 193–206.

Kim, Chan-Hie. "The Papyrus Invitation." *Journal of Biblical Literature* 94 (1975): 391–402.

Kingsbury, Jack. *Matthew*. Proclamation Commentaries. Philadelphia: Fortress Press, 1977.

———. *The Parables of Jesus in Matthew 13*. Richmond: John Knox Press, 1969.

Kirshenblatt-Gimblett, Barbara. "Towards a Theory of Proverb Meaning." *Proverbium* 22 (1973): 821–27.

Kissinger, Warren S. *The Parables of Jesus*. American Theological Library Assn. Bibliography Series 4. Metuchen, N.J.: Scarecrow Press, 1979.

Klauck, Hans-Josef. *Allegorie und Allegorese in synoptischen Gleichnistexten*. Neutestamentliche Abhandlungen 13. Münster: Aschendorff, 1978.

Klausner, Joseph. *Jesus of Nazareth: His Life, Times, and Teaching*. Trans. Herbert Danby. New York: Macmillan Co., 1944.

Klostermann, Erich. *Das Lukasevangelium*. Handbuch zum Neuen Testament. Tübingen: J. C. B. Mohr (Paul Siebeck), 1919.

Koester, Helmut. *Synoptische Überlieferung bei den apostolischen Vätern*. Texte und Untersuchungen 65. Berlin: Akademie-Verlag, 1957.

―――. "Three Thomas Parables." In *The New Testament and Gnosis*, ed. A. H. B. Logan and A. J. M. Wedderburn, 195–203. Edinburgh: T. & T. Clark, 1983.

Kraemer, Ross. "Women in the Religions of the Greco-Roman World." *Religious Studies Review* 9 (1983): 127–39.

Kuhn, Heinz-Wolfgang. *Ältere Sammlungen in Markusevangelium*. Göttingen: Vandenhoeck & Ruprecht, 1971.

Kümmel, Werner. "Das Gleichnis von den bösen Weingärtnern (Mark 12, 1–12)." In *Aux sources de la tradition chrétienne: Mélanges M. Goguel*, 120–31. Paris: Delachaux & Niestlé Spes, 1950.

―――. *Introduction to the New Testament*. Trans. Howard Clark Kee. Nashville: Abingdon Press, 1975.

―――. *Promise and Fulfillment*. Trans. Dorothea Barton. Studies in Biblical Theology 23. Naperville, Ill.: Alec R. Allenson, 1957.

Lagrange, M.-J. *Evangile selon Saint Luc*. 2d ed. Etudes bibliques. Paris: J. Gabalda, 1941.

Lakoff, George, and Mark Johnson. *Metaphors We Live By*. Chicago: Univ. of Chicago Press, 1980.

Lambdin, Thomas. *Introduction to Sahidic Coptic*. Macon, Ga.: Mercer Univ. Press, 1983.

Lambrecht, Jan. *Once More Astonished: The Parables of Jesus*. New York: Crossroad, 1981.

―――. "The Parousia Discourse." In *L'évangile selon Matthieu*, ed. M. Didier, 308–42. Bibliotheca ephemeridum theologicarum lovaniensium 29. Gembloux: Editions J. Duculot, 1970.

―――. "Redaction and Theology in Mk. IV." In *L'évangile selon Marc*, ed. M. Sabbe, 269–307. Bibliotheca ephemeridum theologicarum lovaniensium 24. Louvain: Louvain Univ. Press, 1971.

Lampe, G. W. H. *A Patristic Greek Lexicon*. Oxford: At the Clarendon Press, 1961.

Leon-Dufour, X. "La parabole des vignerons homicides." *Sciences ecclésiastiques* 17 (1965): 365–96.

Lévi-Strauss, Claude. *The Raw and the Cooked*. Trans. John Weightman and Doreen Weightman. New York: Harper & Row, 1969.

―――. *The Savage Mind*. Chicago: Univ. of Chicago Press, 1966.

―――. "The Structural Study of Myth." In *Structural Anthropology*, trans. Claire Jacobson and Brooke Schoepf, 202–31. New York: Harper & Row, 1963.

Lieberman, Saul. "After Life in Early Rabbinic Literature." In *Essays in Greco-Roman and Related Talmudic Literature*, ed. Henry Fischel, 405–22. Library of Biblical Studies. New York: Ktav, 1977.

Lindemann, Andreas. "Zur Gleichnisinterpretation im Thomas-Evangelium." *Zeitschrift für die neutestamentliche Wissenschaft* 71 (1980): 214–43.

Linnemann, Eta. *Jesus of the Parables*. Trans. John Sturdy. New York: Harper & Row, 1966.

Lohse, Eduard. *The New Testament Environment*. Trans. John Steely. Nashville: Abingdon Press, 1976.

Loisy, Alfred. *Les évangiles synoptiques*. 2 vols. Ceffonds: By the author, 1908.

Lord, Albert. *The Singer of Tales*. New York: Atheneum, 1978.

Maas, Fritz. "Das Gleichnis vom ungerechten Haushalter: Lucas 16, 1–8." *Theologie Viatorum* 8 (1961): 173–84.

McArthur, Harvey. "The Parable of the Mustard Seed." *Catholic Biblical Quarterly* 33 (1971): 198–210.

McCall, M. *Ancient Rhetorical Theories of Simile and Comparison*. Cambridge: Harvard Univ. Press, 1969.

McGaughy, Lane. "The Fear of Yahweh and the Mission of Judaism: A Postexilic Maxim and Its Early Christian Expansion in the Parable of the Talents." *Journal of Biblical Literature* 94 (1975): 235–45.

McKane, William. *Proverbs*. Old Testament Library. Philadelphia: Westminster Press; London: SCM Press, 1970.

McKnight, Edgar. *The Bible and the Reader*. Philadelphia: Fortress Press, 1985.

McNeile, A. *The Gospel according to Matthew*. London: Macmillan & Co., 1957.

McNicol, Allan. "The Lesson of the Fig Tree in Mark 13:28–32." *Restoration Quarterly* 27 (1984): 193–207.

Magass, W. "Zur Semiotik der Hausfrommigkeit (Lk 12, 16–31): Der Beispielerzählung vom reichen Kornbauer." *Linguistica Biblica* 4 (1971): 2–5.

Malherbe, Abraham. "The Beasts of Ephesus." *Journal of Biblical Literature* 87 (1968): 71–80.

Malina, Bruce. *The New Testament World: Insights from Cultural Anthropology*. Atlanta: John Knox Press, 1981.

Man, Paul de. "The Rhetoric of Temporality." In *Interpretation: Theory and Practice*, ed. C. S. Singleton, 173–91. Baltimore: Johns Hopkins Press, 1969.

Mandelbaum, Irving. *A History of the Mishnaic Law of Agriculture: Kilayim*. Brown Judaic Studies. Chico, Calif.: Scholars Press, 1982.

Mandry, Stephen. *There Is No God! A Study of the Fool in the Old Testament, Particularly in Proverbs and Qoheleth*. Rome: Catholic Book Agency, 1972.

Mann, J. "Jesus and the Sadducean Priests: Luke 10:25–37." *Jewish Quarterly Review* 6 (1914): 417–19.

Manson, T. W. *The Sayings of Jesus*. Grand Rapids: Wm. B. Eerdmans, 1979; London: SCM Press, 1957.

―――. *The Teaching of Jesus*. Cambridge: At the Univ. Press, 1951.

Marshall, Howard. *Commentary on Luke*. New International Greek Commentary on the New Testament. Grand Rapids: Wm. B. Eerdmans, 1978.

Martin, P. "Salvation and Discipleship in Luke's Gospel." *Interpretation* 30 (1976): 366–80.

Marxsen, Willi. *Mark the Evangelist*. Trans. James Boyce, Donald Juel, William Poehlmann, and Roy Harrisville. Nashville: Abingdon Press, 1969.

Mattill, A. "The Good Samaritan and the Purpose of Luke-Acts: Halévy Reconsidered." *Encounter* 33 (1972): 359–76.

Meagher, John. *Clumsy Construction in Mark's Gospel*. Toronto Studies in Theology 3. Lewiston, N.Y.: Edwin Mellen Press, 1979.

Meier, John. *The Vision of Matthew*. New York: Paulist Press, 1979.

Ménard, Jacques-E. *L'évangile selon Thomas*. Nag Hammadi Studies 5. Leiden: E. J. Brill, 1975.

Merkelback, R. "Über das Gleichnis vom ungerechten Haushalter (Lucas 16, 1–13)." *Vigiliae Christianae* 33 (1979): 180–87.

Metzger, Bruce. *A Textual Commentary on the Greek New Testament*. London: United Bible Societies, 1971.

Meyer, Rudolf. "*kolpos*." *TDNT* 3:824–30.

Michaelis, Wilhelm. *Die Gleichnisse Jesu*. Hamburg: Furche-Verlag, 1956.

Michaels, Ramsey. "Parable of the Regretful Son." *Harvard Theological Review* 61 (1968): 15–26.

Michel, Otto. "*kokkos*." *TDNT* 3:810–14.

———. "*kyōn*." *TDNT* 3:1101–4.

———. "*metamēlomai*." *TDNT* 4:626–29.

———. "*telōnēs*." *TDNT* 8:88–105.

Michelis, R. "La conception lucanienne de la conversion." *Ephemerides theologicae lovanienses* 41 (1965): 42–78.

Miller, J. Hillis. "The Fiction of Realism: *Sketches by Boz, Oliver Twist*, and Cruikshank's *Illustrations*." In *Charles Dickens and George Cruikshank*. Los Angeles: William Andrews Clark Memorial Library, 1971.

———. "Parable and Performative in the Gospels and in Modern Literature." In *Humanizing America's Iconic Book*, ed. Gene Tucker and Douglas Knight, 57–71. Chico, Calif.: Scholars Press, 1980.

Minear, Paul. "A Note on Luke 17, 7–10." *Journal of Biblical Literature* 93 (1974): 82–87.

Mitton, C. L. "Expounding the Parables: The Workers in the Vineyard." *Expository Times* 77 (1966): 307–11.

Montefiore, Claude. *The Synoptic Gospels*. 3 vols. London: Macmillan & Co., 1909.

Montefiore, Claude, and A. Loewe. *A Rabbinic Anthology*. London: Macmilllan & Co., 1938.

Montefiore, Hugh, and H. Turner. *Thomas and the Evangelists*. Studies in Biblical Theology 35. Naperville, Ill.: Alec R. Allenson, 1962.

Moore, George. *Judaism*. 2 vols. Cambridge: Harvard Univ. Press, 1954.

Morrice, W. "The Parable of the Dragnet and the Gospel of Thomas." *Expository Times* 95 (1984): 269–73.

Mottu, Henry. "The Pharisee and the Tax Collector: Sectarian Notions as Applied to the Reading of Scripture." *Union Seminary Quarterly Review* (1974): 195–213.

Moule. C. "Mark 4:1–20 Yet Once More." In *Neotestamentica et Semitica: Studies in Honor of Matthew Black*, ed. E. Ellis and M. Wilcox, 95–113. Edinburgh: T. & T. Clark, 1969.

Neirynck, Franz. *Duality in Mark.* Bibliotheca ephemeridum theologicarum lovaniensium 31. Louvain: Louvain Univ. Press, 1972.

Neusner, Jacob. *Rabbinic Traditions about the Pharisees before 70.* 3 vols. Leiden: E. J. Brill, 1971.

———. "Types and Forms in Ancient Jewish Literature: Some Comparisons." *History of Religions* 11 (1972): 354–90.

Newell, J., and R. Newell. "The Parable of the Wicked Tenants." *Novum Testamentum* 14 (1972): 226–37.

Nickelsburg, George. *Jewish Literature between the Bible and the Mishnah.* Philadelphia: Fortress Press, 1981.

Noth, Martin. *Leviticus.* Old Testament Library. Philadelphia: Westminster Press, 1965.

Oepke, Albrecht. "*apollumi.*" *TDNT* 1:394–96.

———. "*gynē.*" *TDNT* 1:776–89.

———. "*kryptō.*" *TDNT* 3:957–1000.

———. "*pais.*" *TDNT* 5:636–54.

Oesterley, W. O. E. *The Gospel Parables in the Light of Their Jewish Background.* London: SPCK, 1936.

Ong, Walter. *Interfaces of the Word.* Ithaca, N.Y.: Cornell Univ. Press, 1977.

———. *Orality and Literacy.* New York: Methuen, 1982.

O'Rourke, John. "Some Notes on Luke XV.11–32." *New Testament Studies* 18 (1971–72): 431–33.

Oxford English Dictionary. Oxford: At the Clarendon Press, 1933.

Palmer, Humphrey. "Just Married, Cannot Come (Matthew 22, Luke 14, Thomas 44, Dt 20)." *Novum Testamentum* 18 (1976): 241–57.

Patte, Daniel. "An Analysis of Narrative Structure and the Good Samaritan." *Semeia* 2 (1974): 1–26.

———. *What Is Structural Exegesis?* Guides to Biblical Scholarship. Philadelphia: Fortress Press, 1976.

Pautrel, Raymond. "Les canons du mashal rabbinique." *Recherches de science religieuse* 26 (1936): 6–45; 28 (1938): 264–81.

Payne, P. "The Order of Sowing and Ploughing in the Parable of the Sower." *New Testament Studies* 25 (1978–79) 123–29.

Penna, A. *Isaia.* La Sacra Bibbia. Turin and Rome: Marietti, 1964.

Perdue, Leo. "The Wisdom Sayings of Jesus." *Forum* 2/3 (1986): 3–35.

Perrin, Norman. *Jesus and the Language of the Kingdom.* Philadelphia: Fortress Press, 1976.

———. *The Kingdom of God in the Teaching of Jesus.* New Testament Library. London: SCM Press, 1963.

———. *Rediscovering the Teaching of Jesus.* New York: Harper & Row, 1967.

Pesch, Rudolf. *Das Markusevangelium.* 2 vols. Herders theologischer Kommentar zum Neuen Testament. Freiburg: Herder & Herder, 1977.

————. *Naherwartungen.* Düsseldorf: Patmos-Verlag, 1968.

Petersen, William. "The Parable of the Lost Sheep in the Gospel of Thomas and the Synoptics." *Novum Testamentum* 23 (1981): 128–47.

Petuchowski, Jakob. "The Theological Significance of the Parable in Rabbinic Literature and the New Testament." *Christian News from Israel* 23 (1972–73): 76–86.

Pilgrim, Walter. *Good News to the Poor: Wealth and Poverty in Luke-Acts.* Minneapolis: Augsburg Pub. House, 1981.

Pitt-Rivers, J. *The Fate of Shechem.* Cambridge: Cambridge Univ. Press, 1977.

Plummer, Alfred. *The Gospel according to St. Luke.* International Critical Commentary. New York: Charles Scribner's Sons, 1898.

Pöhlmann, W. "Die Abschichtung des Verlorenen Sohnes (Lk 15 12f.) und die erzählte Welt der Parabel." *Zeitschrift für die neutestamentliche Wissenschaft* 70 (1979): 209–10.

Preisker, Herbert. "Lukas 16, 1–7." *Theologische Literaturzeitung* 64 (1949): 85–92.

Quillaumont, A., et al. *The Gospel according to Thomas.* New York: Harper & Bros., 1959.

Quispel, Giles. "Gnosis and the New Sayings of Jesus." In *Gnostic Studies* 2:180–209. Uitgaven van het Nederlands Historisch-Archaeologisch Instituut te Istanbul 34/2. Istanbul: Nederlands Historisch-Archaeologisch Instituut te Istanbul, 1975.

————. "*Gospel of Thomas* Revisited." In *Colloque international sur les textes de Nag Hammadi,* ed. B. Barc, 218–66. Quebec: Presses de l'Université, 1981.

————. "Some Remarks on the Gospel of Thomas," *New Testament Studies* 5 (1958–59): 276–90.

Rabinowitz. "Study of a Midrash." *Jewish Quarterly Review* 58 (1967–68): 143–61.

Ramaroson, Leonard. "Le coeur de troisième évangile: Lc 15." *Biblica* 60 (1979): 348–60.

————. "Comme 'Le bon samaritain' ne chercher qu'à aimer (Lc 10, 29–37)." *Biblica* 56 (1975): 533–36.

Raucourt, G. de. "Les ouvriers de la onzième heure." *Recherches de science religieuse* 15 (1925): 492–95.

Redfield, Robert. *The Little Community and Peasant Society and Culture.* Chicago: Univ. of Chicago Press, 1973.

Rengstorf, K. "*hetairos.*" TDNT 2:699–701.

————. *Die Re-Investitur des verlorenen Sohnes in der Gleichniserzählung Jesu Luk. 15, 11–32.* Cologne: Westdeutscher Verlag, 1967.

————. "Die Stadt der Mörder (Mt 22:7)." In *Judentum, Urchristentum, Kirche: Festschrift für Joachim Jeremias,* ed. Walther Eltester, 106–29. Beihefte zur Zeitschrift für die neutestamentliche Wissenschaft 26. Berlin: Alfred Töpelmann, 1960.

Rhoads, David. *Israel in Revolution: 6–74 C.E.* Philadelphia: Fortress Press, 1976.

Richards, I. A. *The Philosophy of Rhetoric.* London: Oxford Univ. Press, 1936.

Ricoeur, Paul. "Biblical Hermeneutics." *Semeia* 4 (1975): 29–148.

―――. *The Rule of Metaphor*. Trans. Robert Czerny. Toronto: Univ. of Toronto Press, 1977.

Rimmon-Kenan, Shlomith. *Narrative Fiction*. New York: Methuen, 1983.

Robbins, Vernon. *Jesus the Teacher*. Philadelphia: Fortress Press, 1984.

Robertson, Archibald, and Alfred Plummer. *First Epistle of St. Paul to the Corinthians*. International Critical Commentary. Edinburgh: T. & T. Clark, 1914.

Robinson, John A. T. "The Parable of the Wicked Husbandmen: A Test of Synoptic Relationships." *New Testament Studies* 21 (1974–75): 443–61.

Rosenthal, F. "*Sedaka*, Charity." *Hebrew Union College Annual* 23/1 (1950–51): 411–30.

Ru, G. de. "Conception of Reward in the Teaching of Jesus." *Novum Testamentum* 8 (1966): 202–22.

Safrai, S. "Home and Family." *JPFC* 2:728–92.

Sanders, James. "The Ethic of Election in Luke's Great Banquet Parable." In *Essays in Old Testament Ethics (J. Philip Hyatt in Memoriam)*, ed. James Crenshaw and John Willis, 245–71. New York: Ktav, 1974.

―――. "The Parable of the Pounds and Lucan Anti-Semitism." *Theological Studies* 42 (1981): 660–81.

―――. "Tradition and Redaction in Luke xv.11–32." *New Testament Studies* 15 (1969): 433–38.

Schlatter, Adolf. *Der Evangelist Matthäus*. 5th ed. Stuttgart: Calwer Verlag, 1959.

Schneider, Johannes. "*kathaireō*." *TDNT* 3:411–13.

Schnider, F., and W. Stenger. "Die offene Tür und die unüberschreitbare Kluft: Strukturanalytische Überlegungen zur Gleichnis vom reichen Mann und armen Lazarus (Lk 16.19–31)." *New Testament Studies* 25 (1979): 273–83.

Schniewind, Julius. *Das Evangelium nach Matthäus*. Das Neue Testament Deutsch. Göttingen: Vandenhoeck & Ruprecht, 1960.

Schoedel, William. *Ignatius of Antioch*. Hermeneia. Philadelphia: Fortress Press, 1985.

―――. "Parables in the Gospel of Thomas: Oral Tradition or Gnostic Exegesis?" *Concordia Theological Monthly* 43 (1972): 548–60.

Scholes, Robert, and Robert Kellogg. *The Nature of Narrative*. London: Oxford Univ. Press, 1966.

Schottroff, L. "Die Erzählung vom Pharisäer und Zöllner als Beispiel für die theologische Kunst des Überredens." In *Neues Testament und christliche Existenz*, ed. H. D. Betz and L. Schottroff, 448–52. Tübingen: J. C. B. Mohr (Paul Siebeck), 1973.

―――. "Das Gleichnis vom verlorenen Sohn," *Zeitschrift für Theologie und Kirche* 68 (1971): 27–52.

Schrage, W. *Das Verhältnis des Thomas Evangeliums zur synoptischen Tradition und zu den koptischen Evangelienübersetzungen*. Beihefte zur Zeitschrift für die neutestamentliche Wissenschaft 29. Berlin: Alfred Töpelmann, 1964.

Schrenk, Gustav. "*antidikos*." *TDNT* 1:374–75.

―――. "*dikaios*." *TDNT* 2:182–91.

———. *"ekikeō." TDNT* 2:442–44.

Schulz, Siegfried. *Q: Die Spruchquelle der Evangelisten.* Zurich: Theologischer Verlag Zürich, 1972.

Schürer, Emil. *The History of the Jewish People in the Age of Jesus.* Rev. Geza Vermes and Fergus Millar. 2 vols. Edinburgh: T. & T. Clark, 1973.

Schürmann, H. *Traditionsgeschichte Untersuchungen zu den synoptischen Evangelien.* Düsseldorf: Patmos-Verlag, 1968.

Schweizer, Eduard. "Antwort an Joachim Jeremias, S. 228–231." *Theologische Zeitschrift* 5 (1949): 231–33.

———. *The Good News according to Matthew.* Trans. David Green. Atlanta: John Knox Press, 1975.

———. "Zur Frage der Lukasquellen, Analyse von Luke 15, 11–32." *Theologische Zeitschrift* 4 (1948): 469–71.

Scott, Bernard. *Jesus, Symbol-Maker for the Kingdom.* Philadelphia: Fortress Press, 1981.

———. "Parables of Growth Revisited." *Biblical Theology Bulletin* 11 (1981): 3–9.

———. "The Prodigal Son: A Structuralist Interpretation." In *Seminar Papers, 1975, Society of Biblical Literature* 2:185–205. Missoula, Mont.: Scholars Press, 1975.

Scott, R. B. Y. *The Way of Wisdom in the Old Testament.* New York: Macmillan Co., 1971.

Sellin, G. "Lukas als Gleichniserzähler: Die Erzahlung vom barmherzigen Samariter, Lk. 10:25–37." *Zeitschrift für die neutestamentliche Wissenschaft* 66 (1975): 19–60.

Shalit, A. *König Herodes: Der Mann und sein Werk.* Berlin: Walter de Gruyter, 1969.

Sherwin-White, A. N. *Roman Society and Roman Law in the New Testament.* Oxford: At the Clarendon Press, 1963.

Sider, J. W. "The Meaning of *Parabolē* in the Usage of the Synoptic Evangelists." *Biblica* 62 (1981): 453–70.

Sjoberg, Gideon. "The Preindustrial City." In *Peasant Society: A Reader,* ed. Jack Potter, May Diaz, and George Foster, 19–24. Boston: Little, Brown & Co., 1967.

Smith, B. T. D. *Parables of the Synoptic Gospels.* Cambridge: At the Univ. Press, 1937.

Smith, C. W. F. *The Jesus of the Parables.* Philadelphia: Pilgrim Press, 1975.

Snodgrass, Klyne. "The Parable of the Wicked Husbandmen: Is the Gospel of Thomas Version the Original?" *New Testament Studies* 20 (1974): 142–44.

———. *The Parable of the Wicked Tenants.* Wissenschaftliche Untersuchungen zum Neuen Testament 27. Tübingen: J. C. B. Mohr (Paul Siebeck), 1983.

Snoy, T. "La rédaction marcienne de la marche sur les eaux (Mc., VI, 45–52)." *Ephemerides theologicae louvanienses* 44 (1968): 205–41, 433–81.

Solages, B. "L'évangile de Thomas et les évangiles canoniques: L'ordre des pericopes." *Bulletin de littérature ecclésiastique* 80 (1979): 102–8.

Sperber, D. "Claude Lévi-Strauss." In *Structuralism and Since,* ed. J. Sturrock, 19–51. Oxford: Oxford Univ. Press, 1979.

Spicq, C. *Dieu et l'homme selon Nouveau Testament.* Lectio divina 29. Paris: Editions du Cerf, 1961.

———. "La parabole de la veuve obstinée et du judge inerté aux decisions impromptues (Lc xviii, 1–8)." *Revue biblique* 68 (1961): 68–90.

Sproule, John. "The Problem of the Mustard Seed." *Grace Theological Journal* 1 (1980): 37–42.

Stählin, Gustav. "*chēra.*" *TDNT* 9:441–44,

———. "*kopetos.*" *TDNT* 3:842–43.

———. "*phileō.*" *TDNT* 9:114–46.

———. "*philos.*" *TDNT* 9:146–71.

———. "*typtō.*" *TDNT* 8:260–69.

Stendahl, Krister. *The School of St. Matthew.* Philadelphia: Fortress Press, 1968 (1954).

Stern, David. "Rhetoric and Midrash: The Case of Mashal." *Prooftexts* 1 (1981): 261–91.

Stern, M. "Aspects of Jewish Society: The Priesthood and Other Classes." *JPFC* 2:561–630.

———. "The Province of Judaea." *JPFC* 1:308–76.

Strecker, Georg. *Der Weg der Gerechtigkeit.* Forschungen zur Religion und Literatur des Alten und Neuen Testaments. Göttingen: Vandenhoeck & Ruprecht, 1966.

Stroker, William. *Extra-Canonical Sayings of Jesus.* Atlanta: Scholars Press, 1988.

Summers, Ray. *The Secret Sayings of the Living Jesus.* Waco, Tex.: Word, 1968.

Talbert, Charles. *Literary Patterns, Theological Themes, and the Genre of Luke-Acts.* Society of Biblical Literature Monograph Series 20. Missoula, Mont.: Scholars Press, 1974.

———. *Reading Luke.* New York: Crossroad, 1982.

———. "Shifting Sands: The Recent Study of the Gospel of Luke." *Interpretation* 30 (1976): 381–95.

Tannehill, Robert. *The Sword of His Mouth.* Semeia Supplements 1. Missoula, Mont.: Scholars Press; Philadelphia: Fortress Press, 1975.

Tarrech, Armand. *La parabole des dix vierges.* Analecta biblica 28. Rome: Biblical Institute Press, 1983.

Taylor, Vincent. *The Gospel according to Saint Mark.* London: Macmillan & Co., 1952.

Telford, William. *The Barren Temple and the Withered Tree.* Journal for the Study of the New Testamnet sup. ser. 1. Sheffield: JSOT Press, 1980.

Thompson, William. *Matthew's Advice to a Divided Community. Mt. 17,22—18,35.* Analecta biblica 44. Rome: Biblical Institute Press, 1970.

Tolbert, Mary Ann. *Perspectives on the Parables.* Philadelphia: Fortress Press, 1979.

Tompkins, Jane. *Reader-Response Criticism.* Baltimore: Johns Hopkins Univ. Press, 1980.

Topel, L. "On the Injustice of the Unjust Steward: Lk 16:1–13." *Catholic Biblical Quarterly* 37 (1975): 216–27.

Trilling, Wolfgang. *Das wahre Israel*. Studien zum Alten und Neuen Testament. Munich: Kösel-Verlag, 1964.

Uspensky, Boris. *A Poetics of Composition*. Berkeley and Los Angeles: Univ. of California Press, 1973.

Vaux, Roland de. *Ancient Israel*. New York: McGraw-Hill, 1961.

Vermes, Geza. *Jesus the Jew*. London: Fontana, 1976.

Via, Dan O., Jr. *The Ethics of Mark's Gospel*. Philadelphia: Fortress Press, 1985.

————. "Kingdom and Parable: The Search for a New Grasp of Symbol, Metaphor, and Myth." *Interpretation* 31 (1971): 181–83.

————. "Parable and Example Story: A Literary Structuralist Approach." *Semeia* 1 (1974): 105–33.

————. *The Parables: Their Literary and Existential Dimension*. Philadelphia: Fortress Press, 1967.

————. "The Prodigal Son: A Jungian Reading." *Semeia* 9 (1977): 21–43.

————. "The Relation of Form to Content in the Parables of the Wedding Feast." *Interpretation* 25 (1971): 171–85.

Waelkens, Robert. "L'analyse structurale des paraboles." *Revue theologique de Louvain* 8 (1977): 160–78.

Waller, Elizabeth. "The Parable of the Leaven: A Sectarian Teaching and the Inclusion of Women." *Union Seminary Quarterly Review* 35 (1979–80): 99–109.

Wanke, Günther. "*phobeō*." *TDNT* 9:197–205.

Weeden, Theodore. *Mark—Traditions in Conflict*. Philadelphia: Fortress Press, 1971.

————. "Recovering the Parabolic Intent in the Parable of the Sower." *Journal of the American Academy of Religion* 47 (1979): 97–120.

Weinart, Frank. "The Parable of the Throne Claimant (Luke 19:12, 14–15a, 27) Reconsidered." *Catholic Biblical Quarterly* 39 (1977): 505–14.

Weiser, Alfons. *Die Knechtsgleichnisse der synoptischen Evangelien*. Studien zum Alten und Neuen Testament 29. Munich: Kösel-Verlag, 1971.

Weissbach, Franz. "Sardinapal." *Paulys Real-Encyclopädie der classischen Altertumswissenschaft*, ed. Georg Wissowa, 1/A:2436–37.

Wellhausen, Julius. *Das Evangelium Marci*. Berlin: Georg Reimer, 1909.

Wenham, David. "The Interpretation of the Parable of the Sower." *New Testament Studies* 20 (1973–74): 299–319.

Wettstein, Jakob. *Novum Testamentum Graecum* 2 vols. Graz: Akademische Druck-U. Verlagsanstalt, 1962 (1752).

Wheelwright, Philip. *Metaphor and Reality*. Bloomington: Indiana Univ. Press, 1962; Midland Book, 1968.

White, K. D. "The Parable of the Sower." *Journal of Theological Studies* 15 (1964): 301–2.

Wilder, Amos. *Jesus' Parables and the War of Myths*. Philadelphia: Fortress Press, 1982.

Williams, James. *Those Who Ponder Proverbs*. Bible and Literature. Sheffield: Almond Press, 1981.

Wilson, R. McL. "'Thomas' and the Growth of the Gospels." *Harvard Theological Review* 53 (1960): 231–50.

Wink, Walter. *John the Baptist in the Gospel Tradition.* Society for New Testament Studies Monograph Series 7. Cambridge: At the Univ. Press, 1968.

Winter, Paul. *On the Trial of Jesus.* Studia Judaica, Forschung zur Wissenschaft des Judentums 1. Berlin: Walter de Gruyter, 1961.

Wolf, Eric. *Peasants.* Englewood Cliffs, N.J.: Prentice-Hall, 1966.

Yaron, A. *Gifts in Contemplation of Death.* Oxford: At the Clarendon Press, 1960.

Zerwick, Maximilian. *Biblical Greek.* Rome: Pontifical Biblical Institute, 1963.

_____. *A Grammatical Analysis of the Greek New Testament.* Rome: Pontifical Biblical Institute, 1963.

_____. "Die Parabel von Thronanwärter." *Biblica* 40 (1959): 654–74.

_____. *Untersuchungen zum Markus-Stil: Ein Beitrag zur stilistischen Durcharbeitung des Neuen Testaments.* Rome: Pontifical Biblical Institute, 1937.

Ziegler, Ignace. *Die Königsgleichnisse des Midrasch.* Breslau: Schlesische Verlags-Anstalt v. S. Schottlaender, 1903.

Zimmerli, Walther. *Ezekiel.* 2 vols. Hermeneia. Philadelphia: Fortress Press, 1979–83.

Index

Hebrew Bible

Greek and Latin Authors

New Testament

Early Christian Literature

Parables

Modern Authors

Index of Parable Titles